Society As It Is

SOCIETY

Glen Gaviglio
David E. Raye

AS IT IS

A Reader

SECOND EDITION

Macmillan Publishing Co., Inc.
NEW YORK
Collier Macmillan Publishers
LONDON

Printed in the United States of America

Macmillan Publishing Co., Inc.
866 Third Avenue, New York, New York 10022

Collier Macmillan Canada, Ltd.

Library of Congress Cataloging in Publication Data

Gaviglio, Glen, comp.
Society as it is.

Includes bibliographies.
1. United States—Social conditions—1960–
—Addresses, essays, lectures. I. Raye, David E., joint comp. II. Title.
HN65.G37 1976 309.1'73'092 74–33095
ISBN 0–02–341080–9

Printing: 2 3 4 5 6 7 8 Year: 7 8 9 0 1 2

Preface

THIS BOOK was compiled to turn students on to the educational process—everything else is secondary. The student (almost any student) can be educated if he can be motivated, and we believe student interest to be foremost in any introductory course. It is our hope that the introductions, selections, cartoons, and satires will whet the intellectual appetite of every student and initiate a lifelong educational trip for those who involve their minds beyond the black print. In order to have the student's interest in social science continue after the few years he will spend in college, he must be turned on to what's happening in society, for without intellectual involvement, education becomes a meaningless pedagogical exercise.

We have tried to be scholarly, but there are no detailed and obtuse statistically oriented analyses contained within this book. When we had to choose between a cold, carefully worded article from a sociological journal and a popularized account from the mass media, we tended to select the latter. If possible, we used the work of well-known social scientists that appeared in quality mass-circulation periodicals (for example, *The Nation*, *Harper's*, or *Atlantic*). We feel, therefore, that we have purged the book of complicated, verbose, and turgid prose. The selections are vibrant and dynamic, chosen primarily for their controversial and stimulating nature. Selections from dry, passionless tomes will not inundate the student with a sense of futility in this book. We have tried to go where the student is; therefore, we have avoided issues of sociological infighting (for example, conflict analysis versus structural functionalism). The emphasis is centered on significant contemporary issues of student relevance: political corruption, alienation, education, women's rights, social change, bureaucracy, and minority revolt. We have searched for selections that will stimulate, motivate, and involve students in examining their own position in our society.

Selections were chosen for clarity and vividness and most will be comprehensible to any reasonably intelligent adult without prior exposure to the social sciences. This is perfectly logical because most introductory students will be of just that variety. We stress that the student must be able to grasp what he reads. Because some of the essays are fairly complex, we have introduced each section of the book with a summary statement. These statements include basic concepts, reasons for the inclusion of the essays within each section, and some thought-provoking questions. Most of the essays are critically oriented, concerned with social change and the future; some of them wander into idealism and utopianism. This, we feel, is essential in any introductory analysis of society.

Because we have emphasized the broader sociological issues, we could not hope to be as scientifically exact as is possible with problems involving fewer variables and we fully realize this. It was necessary to sacrifice statistical accuracy and refined methodology in favor of interest, importance, and relevance.

Although they will certainly not agree with all the points of view expressed in this book (and no one should), we would like to acknowledge an intellectual debt to our former professors, Snell Putney, Mervyn Cadwallader, and Harold M. Hodges. We also would like to thank Randall Jiminez for preparing the introductory comments on the Chicano movement. Finally, we owe our largest debt to our students.

G. G.
D. E. R.

Contents

SEVEN *The Family, Education, and Religion: Institutions in Conflict* **253**

EIGHT *Ecology: The Community and the Spaceship Earth* **321**

ONE

Invitation to Sociology

Some men see things as they are, and say "why?"
I dream of things that never were and say "why not?"
—George Bernard Shaw

Live the questions now.
Perhaps you will then . . .
live along some distant day
into the answer.
—Rainer Maria Rilke

WE INVITE YOU to enjoy a vital intellectual experience: the study of sociology, the science of society. You could say we are prejudiced in our estimation of the excitement sociology can generate, but we hope you will agree with us after sampling this fascinating subject. Simply stated, sociology is a systematic and scientific charting and analysis of human interaction, the effects of society on man, and of man on society. But sociology is more than this. For us it is the study of "what's happening." It is contemporary, relevant, and meaningful. Sociology deals with the drama of now.

Most students recoil from much of the jargon, shop talk and statistics with which he is bombarded in many texts and anthologies. This book deals these irrelevancies out. For us sociology must relate to the issues and problems of today. Why is there racism and intolerance? Why is there inequality and poverty? Can work be meaningful? Will politicians always be beyond the control of the people? Who rules America? Is war inevitable? Is intelligence a product of genes or environment? What roles should men and women play in this society? Unless sociology confronts and examines these and other timely issues, it is doomed to a static irrelevancy, the plaything of an ivory-towered intellectual elite.

Sociology can also produce a cultural shock and wrench beginning students out of their complacency. We all feel that our society, our group, our race, our institutions, our values, and our political philosophy are better than those of others. This phenomenon is referred to as ethnocentrism. Sociology has a tendency to shatter the sacred "givens" of any society, especially its built-in ethnocentric tendencies. Sociology can strip away the cultural blinders, expose mythology, and wipe away the façade and rhetoric that are the biblical guide in any society. Everything stands naked before the glare of sociology; it is an iconoclastic trip. Every society exists with inconsistencies and imperfections; these must be analyzed logically and critically.

Any sociological perspective must also contain within it a vision of change. In essence, sociology is the study of change. No society is ever static, certainly not one experiencing our rapid rate of technological change. The essays included in this volume will introduce you, the student, to different possible approaches to "society as it is." And when you, the students, begin asking yourselves questions of real significance, we, the editors of this anthology, have succeeded. How would you improve our society? How could you arrange our social institutions so that there is a maximization of human fulfillment? Are many in our society doomed to lives of quiet desolation and boredom? You the student must develop what C. Wright Mills termed the "sociological imagination." You must be able to critically analyze society as it is and envision society as it could be.

A student, a sociologist, or any social scientist can look at society with a cold and objective sense of detachment. Knowledge can elevate us and sterilize us; it can lift us beyond involvement with the world around us. We can become safe, secure, and serene with a sophisticated understanding of society. We can, but we must not. As we become more aware of human folly, self-deception, and irrationality, we begin to realize that humanity need not endure the misery, frustration, and hatred that infest this world. We created this society and we can remake it. It is like the Odd Bodkins cartoon that introduces this section: Change comes when the sheep get together and realize that the shepherd is alone. We, the creatures of the present, bear the legacy of past miscalculations, but we must strive to model a humane future. Sociology is a vital tool in this monumental venture. —G. G.

Selected References

(All are available in paperback editions.)

Berger, Peter *Invitation to Sociology: A Humanistic Perspective* Garden City, N.Y.: Doubleday & Company, Inc., 1963.

Hinkle, Roscoe C., and J. Gisela. *The Development of Modern Sociology*. New York: Random House, Inc., 1954.

Horowitz,. Irving L. (ed.). *The New Sociology*. New York: Oxford University Press, 1964.

Mills, C. Wright. *The Sociological Imagination*. New York: Oxford University Press, 1959.

Stein, Maurice, and Arthur Vidich (eds.). *Sociology on Trial*. Englewood Cliffs, N.J.: Prentice-Hall, Inc., 1963.

Sociology as a Form of Consciousness

PETER L. BERGER

In this selection Berger examines the hidden realities that fascinate sociologists. Things are rarely what they seem to be. Beneath the smoke screen of official rhetoric, a society teems with informal and subtle activity.

The peculiarity of sociological perspective becomes clear with some reflection concerning the meaning of the term "society," a term that refers to the object *par excellence* of the discipline. Like most terms used by sociologists, this one is derived from common usage, where its meaning is imprecise. Sometimes it means a particular band of people (as in "Society for the Prevention of Cruelty to Animals"), sometimes only those people endowed with great prestige or privilege (as in "Boston society ladies"), and on other occasions it is simply used to denote company of any sort (for example, "he greatly suffered in those years for lack of society"). There are other, less frequent meanings as well. The sociologist uses the term in a more precise sense, though, of course, there are differences in usage within the discipline itself. The sociologist thinks of "society" as denoting a large complex of human relationships, or to put it in more technical language, as referring to a system of interaction. The word "large" is difficult to specify quantitatively in this context. The sociologist may speak of a "society" including millions of human beings (say, "American society"), but he may also use the term to refer to a numerically much smaller collectivity (say, "the society of sophomores on this campus"). Two people chatting on a street corner will hardly constitute a "society," but three people stranded on an island certainly will. The applicability of the concept, then, cannot be decided on quantitative grounds alone. It rather applies when a complex of relationships is sufficiently succinct to be analyzed by itself, understood as an autonomous entity, set against others of the same kind.

The adjective "social" must be similarly sharpened for sociological use. In common speech it may denote, once more, a number of different things—the informal quality of a certain gathering ("this is a social meeting—let's not discuss business"), an altruistic attitude on somebody's part ("he had a strong social concern in his job"), or, more generally, anything derived from contact with other people ("a social disease"). The sociologist will use the term more narrowly and more precisely to refer to the quality of interaction, interrelationship, mutuality. Thus two men chatting on a street corner do not constitute a "society," but what transpires between them is certainly "social." "Society" consists of a complex of such "social" events. As to the exact definition of the "social," it is difficult to improve on Max Weber's definition of a "social" situation as one in which people orient their actions towards one another. The web of meanings, expectations and conduct resulting from such mutual orientation is the stuff of sociological analysis.

Yet this refinement of terminology is not enough to show up the distinctiveness of the sociological angle of vision. We may get closer by comparing the latter with the perspective of other disciplines concerned with human actions. The economist, for example, is concerned with the analyses of processes that occur in society and that can be described as social. These processes have to do with the basic problem of economic activity—the allocation of scarce goods and services within a society. The economist will be concerned with these processes in terms of the way in which they carry out, or fail to carry out, this function. The sociologist, in looking at the same processes, will naturally have to take into consideration their economic purpose. But his distinctive interest is not necessarily related to this purpose as such. He will be interested in a variety of human relationships and interactions that may occur here and that may be quite irrelevant to the economic goals in question. Thus economic activity involves relationships of power, prestige, prejudice or even play that can be analyzed with only marginal reference to the properly economic function of the activity. . . .

To ask sociological questions, then, presupposes that one is interested in looking some distance beyond the commonly accepted or officially defined goals of human actions. It presupposes a certain awareness that human events have different levels of meaning, some of which are hidden from the consciousness of everyday life. It may even presuppose a measure of suspicion about the way in which human events are officially interpreted by the authorities, be they political, juridical or religious in character. If one is willing to go as far as that, it would seem evident that not all historical circumstances are equally favorable for the development of sociological perspective.

It would appear plausible, in consequence, that sociological thought would have the best chance to develop in historical circumstances marked by severe jolts to the self-conception, especially the official and authoritative and generally accepted self-conception, of a culture. It is only in such circumstances that perceptive men are likely to be motivated to think beyond the assertions of this self-conception and, as a result, question the authorities. Albert Salomon has argued cogently that the concept of "society," in its modern sociological sense, could emerge only as the normative structures of Christendom and later of the *ancien régime* were collapsing. We can, then, again conceive of "society" as the hidden fabric of an edifice, the outside façade of which hides that fabric from the common view. In medieval Christendom, "society" was rendered invisible by the imposing religiopolitical façade that constituted the common world of European man. As Salomon pointed out, the more secular political façade of the absolute state performed the same function after the Reformation had broken up the unity of Christendom. It was with the disintegration of the absolute state that the underlying frame of "society" came into view—that is, a world of motives and forces that could not be understood in terms of the official interpretations of social reality. Sociological perspective can then be understood in terms of such phrases as "seeing through," "looking behind," very much as such phrases would be employed in common speech—"seeing through his game," "looking behind the scenes" —in other words, "being up on all the tricks.". . .

Let us [continue with] the proposition that sociological perspective involves a process of "seeing through" the façades of social structures. We could think of this in terms of a common experience of people living in large cities. One of the fascinations of a large city is the immense variety of human activities taking place behind the seemingly anonymous and endlessly undifferentiated rows of houses. A person who lives in such a city will time and again experience surprise or even shock as he discovers the strange pursuits that some men engage in quite unobtrusively in houses that, from the outside, look like all the others on a certain street. Having had this experience once or twice, one will repeatedly find oneself walking down a street, perhaps late in the evening, and wondering what may be going on under the bright lights showing through a line of drawn curtains. An ordinary family engaged in pleasant talk with guests? A scene of desperation amid illness or death? Or a scene of debauched pleasures? Perhaps a strange cult or a dangerous conspiracy? The façades of the houses cannot tell us, proclaiming nothing but an architectural conformity to the tastes of some group or class that may not even inhabit the street any longer. The social mysteries lie behind the façades. The wish to penetrate to these mysteries is an analogon to sociological curiosity. In some cities that are suddenly struck by calamity this wish may be abruptly realized. Those who have experienced wartime bombings know of the sudden encounters with unsuspected (and sometimes unimaginable) fellow tenants in the air-raid shelter of one's apartment building. Or they can recollect the startling morning sight of a house hit by a bomb during the night, neatly sliced in half, the façade torn away and the previously hidden interior mercilessly revealed in the daylight. But in most cities that one may normally live in, the façades must be penetrated by one's own inquisitive intrusions. Similarly, there are historical situations in which the façades of society are violently torn apart and all but the most incurious are forced to see that there was a reality behind the façades all along. Usually this does not happen and the façades continue to confront us with seemingly rocklike permanence. The perception of the reality behind the façades then demands a considerable intellectual effort.

A few examples of the way in which sociology "looks behind" the façades of social structures might serve to make our argument clearer. Take, for instance, the political organization of a community. If one wants to find out how a modern American city is governed, it is very easy to get the official information about this subject. The city will have a charter, operating under the laws of the state. With some advice from informed individuals, one may look up various statutes that define the constitution of the city. Thus one may find out that this particular community has a city-manager form of administration, or that party affiliations do not appear on the ballot in municipal elections, or that the city government participates in a regional water district. In similar fashion, with the help of some newspaper reading, one may find out the officially recognized political problems of the community. One may read that the city plans to annex a certain suburban area, or that there has been a change in the zoning ordinances to facilitate industrial development in another area, or even that one of the members of the city council has been accused of using his office for personal gain. All such matters still occur on the, as it were, visible, official or public level of political life. However, it would be an exceedingly naive person who would believe that this kind of information gives him a rounded picture of the political reality of that community. The sociologist will want to know above all the constituency of the "informal power structure" (as it has been called by Floyd Hunter, an American sociologist interested in such studies), which is a configuration of men and their power that cannot be found in any statutes, and probably cannot be read about in the newspapers. The political scientist or the legal expert might find it very interesting to compare the city charter with the constitutions of other similar communities. The sociologist will be far more concerned with discovering the way in which powerful vested interests influence or even control the actions of officials elected under the charter. These vested interests will not be found in city hall, but rather in the executive suites of corporations that may not even be located in that community, in the private mansions of a handful of powerful men, perhaps in the offices of certain labor unions or even, in some instances, in the headquarters of criminal organizations. When the sociologist concerns himself with power, he will "look behind" the official mechanisms that are supposed to regulate power in the community. This does not necessarily mean that he will regard the official mechanisms as totally ineffective or their legal definition as totally illusionary. But at the very least he will insist that there is another level of reality to be investigated in the particular system of power. In some cases he might conclude that to look for real power in the publicly recognized places is quite delusional. . . .

Or take an example from economic life. The personnel manager of an industrial plant will take delight in preparing brightly colored charts that show the table of organization that is supposed to administer the production process. Every man has his place, every person in the organization knows from whom he receives his orders and to whom he must transmit them, every work team has its assigned role in the great drama of production. In reality things rarely work this way—and every good personnel manager knows this. Superimposed on the official blueprint of the organization is a much subtler, much less visible network of human groups, with their loyalties, prejudices, antipathies and (most important) codes of behavior. Industrial sociology is full of data on the operations of this informal network, which always exists in varying degrees of accommodation and conflict with the official system. Very much the same coexistence of formal and informal organization are to be found wherever large numbers of men work together or live together under a system of discipline—military organizations, prisons, hospitals, schools, going back to the mysterious leagues that children form among themselves and that their parents only rarely discern. Once more, the sociologist will seek to penetrate the smoke screen of the official versions of reality (those of the foreman, the officer, the teacher) and try to grasp the signals that come from the "underworld" (those of the worker, the enlisted man, the schoolboy).

Let us take one further example. In Western countries, and especially in America, it is assumed that men and women marry because they are in love. There is a broadly based popular mythology about the character of love as a violent, irresistible emotion that strikes where it will, a mystery that is the goal of most young people and often of the not-so-young as well. As soon as one investigates, however, which people actually marry each other, one finds that the lightning-shaft of Cupid seems to be guided rather strongly within very definite channels of class, income, education, racial and religious background. If one then investigates a little further into the behavior that is engaged in prior to marriage under the rather misleading euphemism of "courtship," one finds channels of interaction that are often rigid to the point of ritual. The suspicion begins to dawn on one that, most of the time, it is not so much the emotion of love that creates a certain kind of relationship, but that carefully predefined and often planned relationships eventually generate the desired emotion. In other words, when certain conditions are met or have been constructed, one allows oneself "to fall in love." The sociologist investigating our patterns of "courtship" and marriage soon discovers a complex web of motives related in many ways to the entire institutional structure within which an individual lives his life—class, career, economic ambition, aspirations of power and prestige. The miracle of love now begins to look somewhat synthetic. Again, this need not mean in any given instance that the sociologist will declare the romantic interpretation to be an illusion. But, once more, he will look beyond the immediately given and publicly approved interpretations. Contemplating a couple that in its turn is contemplating the moon, the sociologist need not feel constrained to deny the emotional impact of the scene thus illuminated. But he will observe the machinery that went into the construction of the scene in its nonlunar aspects—the status index of the automobile from which the contemplation occurs, the canons of taste and tactics that determine the costume of the contemplators, the many ways in which language and demeanor place them socially, thus the social location and intentionality of the entire enterprise. . . .

We would contend, then, that there is a debunking motif inherent in sociological consciousness. The sociologist will be driven time and again, by the very logic of his discipline, to debunk the social systems he is studying.

This unmasking tendency need not necessarily be due to the sociologist's temperament or inclinations. Indeed, it may happen that the sociologist, who as an individual may be of a conciliatory disposition and quite disinclined to disturb the comfortable assumptions on which he rests his own social existence, is nevertheless compelled by what he is doing to fly in the face of what those around him take for granted. In other words, we would contend that the roots of the debunking motif in sociology are not psychological but methodological. The sociological frame of reference, with its built-in procedure of looking for levels of reality other than those given in the official interpretations of society, carries with it a logical imperative to unmask the pretensions and the propaganda by which men cloak their actions with each other. This unmasking imperative is one of the characteristics of sociology particularly at home in the temper of the modern era.

The debunking tendency in sociological thought can be illustrated by a variety of developments within the field. For example, one of the major themes in Weber's sociology is that of the unintended, unforeseen consequences of human actions in society. Weber's most famous work, *The Protestant Ethic and the Spirit of Capitalism,* in which he demonstrated the relationship between certain consequences of Protestant values and the development of the capitalist ethos, has often been misunderstood by critics precisely because they missed this theme. Such critics have pointed out that the Protestant thinkers quoted by Weber never intended their teachings to be applied so as to produce the specific economic results in question. Specifically, Weber argued that the Calvinist doctrine of predestination led people to behave in what he called an "inner-worldly ascetic" way, that is, in a manner that concerns itself intensively, systematically and selflessly with the affairs of this world, especially with economic affairs. Weber's critics have then pointed out that nothing was further from the mind of Calvin and the other leaders of the Calvinist Reformation. But Weber never maintained that Calvinist thought *intended* to produce these economic action patterns. On the contrary, he knew very well that the intentions were drastically different. The consequences took place regardless of intentions. In other words, Weber's work (and not only the famous part of it just mentioned) gives us a vivid picture of the *irony* of human actions. Weber's sociology thus provides us with a radical antithesis to any views that understand history as the realization of ideas or as the fruit of the deliberate efforts of individuals or collectivities. This does not mean at all that ideas are not important. It does mean that the outcome of ideas is commonly very different from what those who had the ideas in the first place planned or hoped. Such a consciousness of the ironic aspect of history is sobering, a strong antidote to all kinds of revolutionary uptopianism.

The debunking tendency of sociology is implicit in all sociological theories that emphasize the autonomous character of social processes. For instance, Émile Durkheim, the founder of the most important school in French sociology, emphasized that society was a reality *sui generis,* that is, a reality that could not be reduced to psychological or other factors on different levels of analysis. The effect of this insistence has been a sovereign disregard for individually intended motives and meanings in Durkheim's study of various phenomena. This is perhaps most sharply revealed in his well-known study of suicide, in the work of that title, where individual intentions of those who commit or try to commit suicide are completely left out of the analysis in favor of statistics concerning various social characteristics of these individuals. In the Durkheimian perspective, to live in society means to exist under the domination of society's logic. Very often men act by this logic without knowing it. To discover this inner dynamic of society, therefore, the sociologist must frequently disregard the answers that the social actors themselves would give to his questions and look for explanations that are hidden from their own awareness. This essentially Durkheimian approach has been carried over into the theoretical approach now called functionalism. In functional analysis society is analyzed in terms of its own workings as a system, workings that are often obscure or opaque to those acting within the system. The contemporary American sociologist Robert Merton has expressed this approach well in his concepts of "manifest" and "latent" functions. The former are the conscious and deliberate functions of social processes, the latter the unconscious and unintended ones. Thus the "manifest" function of antigambling legislation may be to suppress gambling, its "latent" function to create an illegal empire for the gambling syndicates. Or Christian missions in parts of Africa "manifestly" tried to convert Africans to Christianity, "latently" helped to destroy the indigenous tribal cultures and thus provided an important impetus towards rapid social transformation. Or the control of the Communist Party over all sectors of social life in Russia "manifestly" was to assure the continued dominance of the revolutionary ethos, "latently" created a new class of comfortable bureaucrats uncannily bourgeois in its aspirations and increasingly disinclined toward the self-denial of Bolshevik dedication. Or the "manifest" function of many voluntary associations in America is sociability and public service, the "latent" function to attach status indices to those permitted to belong to such associations.

The concept of "ideology," a central one in some sociological theories, could serve as another illustration of the debunking tendency discussed. Sociologists speak of "ideology" in discussing views that serve to rationalize the vested interests of some group. Very frequently such views systematically distort social reality in much the same way that an individual may neurotically deny, deform or reinterpret aspects of his life that are inconvenient to him. The important approach of the Italian sociologist Vilfredo Pareto has a central place for this perspective and . . . the concept of "ideology" is essential for the approach called the "sociology of knowledge." In such analyses the ideas by which men explain their actions are unmasked as self-deception, sales talk, the kind of "sincerity" that David Riesman has aptly described as the state of mind of a man who habitually believes his own propaganda. In this way, we can speak of "ideology" when we analyze the belief of many

American psysicians that standards of health will decline if the fee-for-service method is abolished, or the conviction of many undertakers that expensive funerals show lack of affection for the departed, or the definition of their activity by quizmasters on television as "education." The self-image of the insurance salesman as a fatherly adviser to young families, of the burlesque stripper as an artist, of the propadandist as a communications expert, of the hangman as a public servant—all these notions are not only individual assuagements of guilt or status anxiety, but constitute the official self-interpretations of entire social groups, obligatory for their members on pain of excommunication. In uncovering the social functionality of ideological pretentions the sociologist will try not to resemble those historians of whom Marx said that every corner grocer is superior to them in knowing the difference between what a man is and what he claims to be. The debunking motif of sociology lies in this penetration of verbal smoke screens to the unadmitted and often unpleasant mainsprings of action.

Teaching as a Subversive Activity: Crap Detecting

NEIL POSTMAN AND CHARLES WEINGARTNER

How can you determine where truth lies? Are objective facts just statistical commodities that we all can agree upon? How do you categorize and analyze the world around you? Where and from whom do you seek information? Does truth flow from a wise guru? Does the voice of tradition and authority weigh heavily in your mind? Can you only really know what you personally experience? Can sensitive novelists effectively translate the experience of others?

Sociology has certain methods of examining reality. As sociologists we have our own little corner of the world that we see through our own eyes. We could expose you to some sophisticated and complex sociological methodology, but before you proceeded, the following essay would be mandatory. The point of this essay is very direct: everyone must develop the ability to detect crap. We sociologists are also included.

"In 1492, Columbus discovered America. . . ." Starting from this disputed fact, each one of us will describe the history of this country in a somewhat different way. Nonetheless, it is reasonable to assume that most of us would include something about what is called the "democratic process," and how Americans have valued it, or at least have said they valued it. Therein lies a problem: one of the tenets of a democratic society is that men be allowed to think and express themselves freely on any subject, even to the point of speaking out against the idea of a democratic society. To the extent that our schools are instruments of such a society, they must develop in the young not only an awareness of this freedom but a will to exercise it, and the intellectual power and perspective to do so effectively. This is necessary so that the society may continue to change and modify itself to meet unforeseen threats, problems, and opportunities. Thus, we can achieve what John Gardner calls an "ever-renewing society."

So goes the theory.

In practice, we mostly get a different story. In our society, as in others, we find that there are influential men at the head of important institutions who cannot afford to be found wrong, who find change inconvenient, perhaps intolerable, and who have financial or political interests they must conserve at any cost. Such men are, therefore, threatened in many respects by the theory of the democratic process and the concept of an ever-renewing society. Moreover, we find that there are obscure men who do *not* head important institutions who are similarly threatened because they have identified themselves with certain ideas and institutions which they wish to keep free from either criticism or change.

Such men as these would much prefer that the schools do little or nothing to encourage youth to question, doubt, or challenge any part of the society in which they live, especially those parts which are most vulnerable. "After all," say the practical men, "they are *our* schools, and they ought to promote *our* interests, and *that* is part of the democratic process, too." True enough; and here we have a serious point of conflict. Whose schools are they, anyway, and whose interests should they be designed to serve? We realize that these are questions about which any self-respecting professor of education could write several books, each one beginning with a reminder that the problem is not black or white, either/or, yes or no. But if you have read our introduction, you will not expect us to be either professorial or prudent. We are, after all, trying to suggest strategies for survival as they may be developed in our schools, and the situation requires emphatic responses. We believe that the schools must serve as the principal medium for developing in youth the attitudes and skills of social, political, and cultural criticism. No. That is not emphatic enough. Try this: In the early 1960s, an interviewer was trying to get Ernest Hemingway to identify the characteristics required for a person to be a "great writer." As the interviewer offered a list of various possibilities, Hemingway disparaged each in sequence. Finally, frustrated, the interviewer asked, "Isn't there any one essential ingredient that you can identify?" Hemingway replied, "Yes, there is. In order to be a great writer a person must have a built-in, shockproof crap detector."

It seems to us that, in his response, Hemingway identified an essential scrvival strategy and the essential function of the schools in today's world. One way of looking at the history of the human group is that it has been a continuing struggle against the veneration of "crap." Our intellectual history is a chronicle of the anguish and suffering of men who tried to help their contemporaries see that some part of their fondest beliefs were misconceptions, faulty assumptions, superstitions, and even outright lies. The mileposts along the road of our intellecutal development signal those points at which some person developed a new perspective, a new meaning, or a new metaphor. We have in mind a new education that would set out to cultivate just such people—experts at "crap detecting."

There are many ways of describing this function of the schools, and many men who have. David Riesman, for example, calls this the "counter-cyclical" approach to education, meaning that schools should stress values that are not stressed by other major institutions in the culture. Norbert Wiener insisted that the schools now must function as "anti-entropic feedback systems," "entropy" being the word used to denote a general and unmistakable tendency of all systems—natural and man-made—in the universe to "run down," to reduce to chaos and uselessness. This is a process that cannot be reversed but that can be slowed down and partly controlled. One way to control it is through "maintenance." This is Eric Hoffer's term, and he believes that the quality of maintenance is one of the best indices of the quality of life in a culture. But Wiener uses a different metaphor to get at the same idea. He says that in order for there to be an anti-entropic force, we must have adequate feedback. In other words, we must have instruments to tell us when we are running down, when maintenance is required. For Wiener, such instruments would be people who have been educated to recognize change, to be sensitive to problems caused by change, and who have the motivation and courage to sound alarms when entropy accelerates to a dangerous degree. This is what we mean by "crap detecting." It is also what John Gardner means by the "ever-renewing society," and what Kenneth Boulding means by "social self-consciousness." We are talking about the schools' cultivating in the young that most "subversive" intellectual instrument—the anthropological perspective. This perspective allows one to be part of his own culture and, at the same time, to be out if it. One views the activities of his own group as would an anthropologist, observing its tribal rituals, its fears, its conceits, its ethnocentrism. In this way, one is able to recognize when reality begins to drift too far away from the grasp of the tribe.

We need hardly say that achieving such a perspective is extremely difficult, requiring, among other things, considerable courage. We are, after all, talking about achieving a high degree of freedom from the intellectual and social constraints of one's tribe. For example, it is generally assumed that people of other tribes have been victimized by indoctrination from which our tribe has remained free. Our own outlook seems "natural" to us, and we wonder that other men can perversely persist in believing nonsense. Yet, it is undoubtedly true that, for most people, the acceptance of a particular doctrine is largely attributable to the accident of birth. They might be said to be "ideologically interchangeable," which means that they would have accepted any set if doctrines that happened to be valued by the tribe to which they were born. Each of us, whether from the American tribe, Russian tribe, or Hopi tribe, is born into a symbolic environment as well as a physical one. We become accustomed very early to a "natural" way of talking, and being talked to, about "truth." Quite arbitrarily, one's perception of what is "true" or real is shaped by the symbols and symbol-manipulating institutions of his tribe. Most men, in time, learn to respond with fervor and obedience to a set of verbal abstractions which they feel provides them with an ideological identity. One word for this, of course, is "prejudice." None of us is free of it, but it is the sign of a competent "crap detector" that he is not completely captivated by the arbitrary abstractions of the community in which he happened to grow up.

In our own society, if one grows up in a language environment which includes and approves such a concept as "white supremacy," one can quite "morally" engage in the process of murdering civil-rights workers. Similarly, if one is living in a language environment where the term "black power" crystalizes an ideological identity, one can engage, again quite "morally," in acts of violence against any nonblack persons or their property. An insensitivity to the unconscious effects of our "natural" metaphors condemns us to highly constricted perceptions of how things are and, therefore, to highly limited alternative modes of behavior.

Those who *are* sensitive to the verbally built-in biases of their "natural" environment seem "subversive" to those who are not. There is probably nothing more dangerous to the prejudices of the latter than a man in the process of discovering that the language of his group is limited, misleading, or one-sided. Such a man is dangerous because he is not easily enlisted on the side of one ideology or another, because he sees beyond the words to the processes which give an ideology its reality. In his *May Man Prevail?*, Erich Fromm gives us an example of a man (himself) in the process of doing just that:

> The Russians believe that they represent socialism because they talk in terms of Marxist ideology, and they do not recognize how similar their system is to the most developed form of capitalism. We in the West believe that we represent the system of individualism, private initiative, and humanistic ethics, because we hold on to *our* ideology, and we do not see that our institutions have, in fact, in many ways become more and more similar to the hated system of communism.

Religious indoctrination is still another example of this point. As Alan Watts has noted: "Irrevocable commitment to any religion is not only intellectual suicide; it is positive unfaith because it closes the mind to any new vision of the world. Faith is, above all, openness—an act of trust in the unknown." And so "crap detecting" requires a perspective on what Watts calls "the standard-brand religions." That perspective can also be applied to knowledge. If you substitute the phrase "set of facts" for the word "religion" in the quotation above, the statement is equally important and accurate.

The need for this kind of perspective has always been urgent but never so urgent as now. We will not take you again through that painful catalogue of twentieth-century problems we cited in our Introduction. There are, however, three particular problems which force us to conclude that the schools must consciously remake themselves into training center for "subversion." In one sense, they are all one problem but for purposes of focus may be distinguished from each other.

The first goes under the name of the "communications revolution," or media change. As father John Culkin of Fordham University likes to say, a lot of things have happened in this century and most of them plug into walls. To get some perspective on the electric plug, imagine that your home and all the other homes and buildings in your neighborhood have been cordoned off, and from them will be removed all the electric and electronic inventions that have appeared in the last 50 years. The media will be subtracted in reverse order, with the most recent going first. The first thing to leave your house, then, is the television set—and everybody will stand there as if they are attending the funeral of a friend, wondering, "What are we going to do tonight?" After rearranging the furniture so that it is no longer aimed at a blank space in the room, you suggest going to the movies. But there won't be any. Nor will there be LP records, tapes, radio, telephone, or telegraph. If you are thinking that the absence of the media would only affect your entertainment and information, remember that, at some point, your electric lights would be removed, and your refrigerator, and your heating system, and your air conditioner. In short, you would have to be a totally different person from what you are in order to survive for more than a day. The chances are slim that you could modify yourself and your patterns of living and believing fast enough to save yourself. As you were expiring, you would at least know something about how it was before the electric plug. Or perhaps you wouldn't. In any case, if you had energy and interest enough to hear him, any good ecologist could inform you of the logic of your problem: a change in an environment is rarely only additive or linear. You seldom, if ever, have an old environment *plus* a new element, such as a printing press or an electric plug. *What you have is a totally new environment requiring a whole new repertoire of survival strategies.* In no case is this more certain than when the new elements are technological. Then, in no case will the new environment be more radically different from the old than in political and social forms of life. When you plug something into a wall, someone is getting plugged into you. Which means you need new patterns of defense, perception, understanding, evaluation. You need a new kind of education.

It was George Counts who observed that technology repealed the Bill of

Rights. In the eighteenth century, a pamphlet could influence an entire nation. Today all the ideas of the Noam Chomskys, Paul Goodmans, Edgar Friedenbergs, I. F. Stones, and even the William Buckleys, cannot command as much attention as a 30-minute broadcast by Walter Cronkite. Unless, of course, one of them were given a prime-time network program, in which case he would most likely come out more like Walter Cronkite than himself. Even Marshall McLuhan, who is leading the field in understanding media, is having his ideas transformed and truncated by the forms of the media to fit present media functions. (One requirement, for example, is that an idea or a man must be "sensational" in order to get a hearing; thus, McLuhan comes out not as a scholar studying media but as the "Apostle of the Electronic Age.")

We trust it is clear that we are not making the typical, whimpering academic attack on the media. We are not "against" the media. Any more, incidentally, than McLuhan is "for" the media. You cannot reverse technological change. Things that plug in are here to stay. But you can study media, with a view toward discovering what they are doing to you. As McLuhan has said, there is no inevitability so long as there is a willingness to contemplate what is happening.

Very few of us have contemplated more rigorously what is happening through media change than Jacques Ellul, who has sounded some chilling alarms. Without mass media, Ellul insists, there can be no effective propaganda. With them, there is almost nothing but. "Only through concentration of a large number of media in a few hands can one attain a true orchestration, a continuity, and an application of scientific methods of influencing individuals." That such concentration is occurring daily, Ellul says, is an established fact, and its results may well be an almost total homogenization of thought among those the media reach. We cannot afford to ignore Norbert Wiener's observation of a paradox that results from our increasing technological capability in electronic communication: as the number of messages increases, the amount of information carried decreases. We have more media to communicate fewer significant ideas.

Still another way of saying this is that, while there has been a tremendous increase in media, there has been, at the same time, a decrease in available and viable "democratic" channels of communication because the mass media are entirely one-way communication. For example, as a means of affecting public policy, the town meeting is dead. Significant community action (without violence) is increasingly rare. A small printing press in one's home, as an instrument of social change, is absurd. Traditional forms of dissent and protest seem impractical, e.g., letters to the editor, street-corner speeches, etc. no one can reach many people unless he has access to the mass media. As this is written, for example, there is no operational two-way communication possible with respect to United States polices and procedures in Vietnam. The communication is virtually all one way: from the top down, via the mass media, especially TV. The pressure on everyone is to subscribe without question to policies formulated in the Pentagon. The President appears on TV and clearly makes the point that anyone who does not accept "our policy" can be viewed only as lending aid and comfort to the enemy. The position has been elaborately developed in all media that "peaceniks" are failing in the obligation to "support our boys overseas." The effect of this process on all of us is to leave no alternative but to accept policy, act on orders from above, and implement the policy without question or dialogue. This is what Edgar Friedenberg calls "creeping Eichmannism," a sort of spiritless, mechanical, abstract functioning which does not allow much room for individual thought and action.

As Paul Goodman has pointed out, there are many forms of censorship, and one of them is to deny access to "loudspeakers" to those with dissident ideas, or even *any* ideas. This is easy to do (and not necessarily conspiratorial) when the loudspeakers are owned and operated by mammoth corporations with enormous investments in the proprietorship. What we get is an entirely new politics, including the possibility that a major requirement for the holding of political office be prior success as a show-busineses personality. Goodman writes in *Like a Conquered Province:*

> The traditional American sentiment is that a decent society cannot be built by dominant official policy anyway, but only by grassroots resistance, community cooperation, individual enterprise, and citizenly vigilance to protect liberty. . . . *The question is whether or not our beautiful libertarian, pluralist, and populist experiment is viable in modern conditions.* If it's not, I don't know any other acceptable politics, and I am a man without a country.

Is it possible that there are millions becoming men without a country? Men who are increasingly removed from the sources of power? Men who have fewer and fewer ideas available to them, and fewer and fewer ways of expressing themselves meaningfully and effectively? Might the frustration thus engendered be one of the causes of the increasing use of violence as a form of statement?

We come then to a second problem which makes necessary a "subversive" role for the schools. This one may appropriately be called the "Change Revolution." In order to illustrate what this means, we will use the media again and the metaphor of a clock face. Imagine a clock face with 60 minutes on it. Let the clock stand for the time men have had access to writing systems. Our clock would thus represent something like 3,000 years, and each minute on our clock 50 years. On this scale, there were no significant media changes until about nine minutes ago. At that time, the printing press came into use in Western culture. About three minutes ago, the telegraph, photograph, and locomotive arrived. Two minutes ago, the telephone, rotary press, motion pictures, automobile, airplane, and radio. One minute ago, the talking picture. Television has appeared in the last ten seconds, the computer in the last five, and communications satellites in the last second. The laser beam—perhaps, the most potent medium of communication of all—appeared only a fraction of a second ago.

It would be possible to place almost any area of life on our clock face and get roughly the same measurements. For example, in medicine, you would have almost no significant changes until about one minute ago. In fact, until one minute ago, as Jerome Frank has said, almost the whole history of medicine is the history of the placebo effect. About a minute ago, antibiotics arrived. About ten seconds ago, open-heart surgery. In fact, within the past ten seconds there probably have been more changes in medicine than is represented by all the rest of the time on our clock. This is what some people call the "knowledge explosion." It is happening in every field of knowledge susceptible to scientific inquiry.

The standard reply to any comment about change (for example, from many educators) is that change isn't new and that it is easy to exaggerate its meaning. To such replies, Norbert Wiener had a useful answer: the difference between a fatal and a therapeutic dose of strychnine is "only a matter of degree." In other words, change isn't new; what is new is the *degree of change*. As our clock-face metaphor was intended to suggest, about three minutes ago there developed a qualitative difference in the character of change. Change changed.

This is really quite a new problem. For example, up until the last generation it was possible to be born, grow up, and spend a life in the United States without moving more than 50 miles from home, without ever confronting serious questions about one's basic values, beliefs, and patterns of behavior. Indeed, without ever confronting serious challenges to anything one knew. Stability and consequent predictability—within "natural cycles" was the characteristic mode. But now, in just the last minute, we've reached the stage where change occurs so rapidly that each of us in the course of our lives has continuously to work out a set of values, beliefs, and patterns of behavior that are viable, or *seem* viable, to each of us personally. And just when we have identified a workable system, it turns out to be irrelevant because so much has changed while we were doing it.

Of course, this frustrating state of affairs applies to our education as well. If you are over twenty-five years of age, the mathematics you were taught in school is "old"; the grammar you were taught is obsolete and in disrepute; the biology, completely out of date, and the history, open to serious question. The best that can be said of you, assuming that you *remember* most of what you were told and read, is that you are a walking encyclopedia of outdated information. As Alfred North Whitehead pointed out in *The Adventure of Ideas:*

> Our sociological theories, our political philosophy, our practical maxims of business, our political economy, and our doctrines of education are derived from an unbroken tradition of great thinkers and of practical examples from the age of Plato . . . to the end of the last century. The whole of this tradition is warped by the vicious assumption that each generation will substantially live amid the

conditions governing the lives of its fathers and will transmit those conditions to mould with equal force the lives of its children. *We are living in the first period of human history for which this assumption is false.*

All of which brings us to the third problem: the "burgeoning bureaucracy." We are brought there because bureaucracies, in spite of their seeming indispensability, are by their nature highly resistant to change. The motto of most bureaucracies is "Carry On, Regardless." There is an essential mindlessness about them which causes them, in most circumstances, to accelerate entropy rather than to impede it. Bureaucracies rarely ask themselves Why?, but only How? John Gardner, who as President of the Carnegie Corporation and (as of this writing) Secretary of Health, Education and Welfare has learned about bureaucracies at first hand, has explained them very well:

> To accomplish renewal, we need to understand what prevents it. When we talk about revitalizing a society, we tend to put exclusive emphasis on finding new ideas. But there is usually no shortage of new ideas; the problem is to get a hearing for them. And that means breaking through the crusty rigidity and stubborn complacency of the *status quo*. The aging society develops elaborate defenses against new ideas—"mind-forged manacles," in William Blake's vivid phrase. . . . As a society becomes more concerned with precedent and custom, it comes to care more about how things are done and less about *whether* they are done. The man who wins acclaim is not the one who "gets things done" but the one who has an ingrained knowledge of the rules and accepted practices. Whether he accomplishes anything is less important than whether he conducts himself in an "appropriate" manner.
>
> The body of custom, convention, and "reputable" standards exercises such an oppressive effect on creative minds that new developments in a field often originate outside the area of respectable practice.

In other words, bureaucracies are the repositories of conventional assumptions and standard practices—two of the greatest accelerators of entropy.

We could put before you a volume of other quotations—from Machiavelli to Paul Goodman—describing how bureacratic structures retard the development and application of new survival strategies. But in doing so, we would risk creating the impression that we stand with Goodman in yearning for some anarchistic Utopia in which the Army, the Police, General Motors, the U.S. Office of Education, the Post Office, et al. do not exist. We are not "against" bureaucracies, any more than we are "for" them. They are like electric plugs. They will probably not go away, but they do need to be controlled if the prerogatives of a democratic society are to remain visible and usable. This is why we ask that the schools be "subversive," that they serve as a kind of antibureaucracy bureaucracy, providing the young with a "What is it good for?" perspective on its own society. Certainly, it is unrealistic to expect those who control the media to perform that function. Nor the generals and the politicians. Nor is it reasonable to expect the "intellectuals" to do it, for they do not have access to the majority of youth. But schoolteachers do, and so the primary responsibility rests with them.

The trouble is that most teachers have the idea that they are in some other sort of business. Some believe, for example, that they are in the "information dissemination" business. This was a reasonable business up to about a minute or two ago on our clock. (But then, so was the horseshoe business and the candle-snuffer business.) The signs that their business is failing are abundant, but they keep at it all the more diligently. Santayana told us that a fanatic is someone who redoubles his efforts when he has forgotten his aim. In this case, even if the aim has not been forgotten, it is simply irrelevant. But the effort has been redoubled anyway.

There are some teachers who think they are in the "transmission of our cultural heritage" business, which is not an unreasonable business if you are concerned with the whole clock and not just its first 57 minutes. The trouble is that most teachers find the last three minutes too distressing to deal with, which is exactly why they are in the wrong business. Their students find the last three minutes distressing—and confusing—too, especially the last 30 seconds, and they neeed *help*. While they have to live with TV, film, the LP record, communication satellites, and the laser beam, their teachers are still talking as if the only medium on the scene is Gutenberg's printing press. While they have to understand psychology and psychedelics, anthropology and anthropomorphism, birth control and biochemistry, their teachers are teaching "subjects" that mostly don't exist anymore. While they need to find new roles for themselves as social, political, and religious organisms, their teachers (as Edgar Friedenberg has documented so painfully) are acting almost entirely as shills for corporate interests, shaping them up to be functionaries in one bureaucracy or another.

Unless our schools can switch to the right business, their clientele will either go elsewhere (as many are doing) or go into a severe case of "future shock," to use a relatively new phrase. Future shock occurs when you are confronted by the fact that the world you were educated to believe in doesn't exist. Your images of reality are apparitions that disappear on contact. There are several ways of responding to such a condition, one of which is to withdraw and allow oneself to be overcome by a sense of impotence. More commonly, one continues to act *as if* his apparitions were substantial, relentlessly pursuing a course of action that he knows will fail him. You may have noticed that there are scores of political, social, and religious leaders who are clearly suffering from advanced cases of future shock. They repeat over and over again the words that are supposed to represent the world about them. But nothing seems to work out. And then they repeat the words again and again. Alfred Korzybski used a somewhat different metaphor to describe what we have been calling "future shock." He likened one's language to a map. The map is intended to describe the territory that we call "reality," i.e., the world outside of our skins. When there is a close correspondence between map and territory, there tends to be a high degree of effective functioning, especially where it relates to survival. When there is little correspondence between map and territory, there is a strong tendency for entropy to make substantial gains. In this context, the terrifying question What did you learn in school today? assumes immense importance for all of us. We just may not survive another generation of inadvertent entropy helpers.

What is the necessary business of the schools? To create eager consumers? To transmit the dead ideas, values, metaphors, and information of three minutes ago? To create smoothly functioning bureaucrats? *These* aims are truly subversive since they undermine our chances of surviving as a viable, democratic society. And they do their work in the name of convention and standard practice. We would like to see the schools go into the anti-entropy business. Now, that is subversive, too. But the purpose is to subvert attitudes, beliefs, and assumptions that foster chaos and uselessness.

TWO

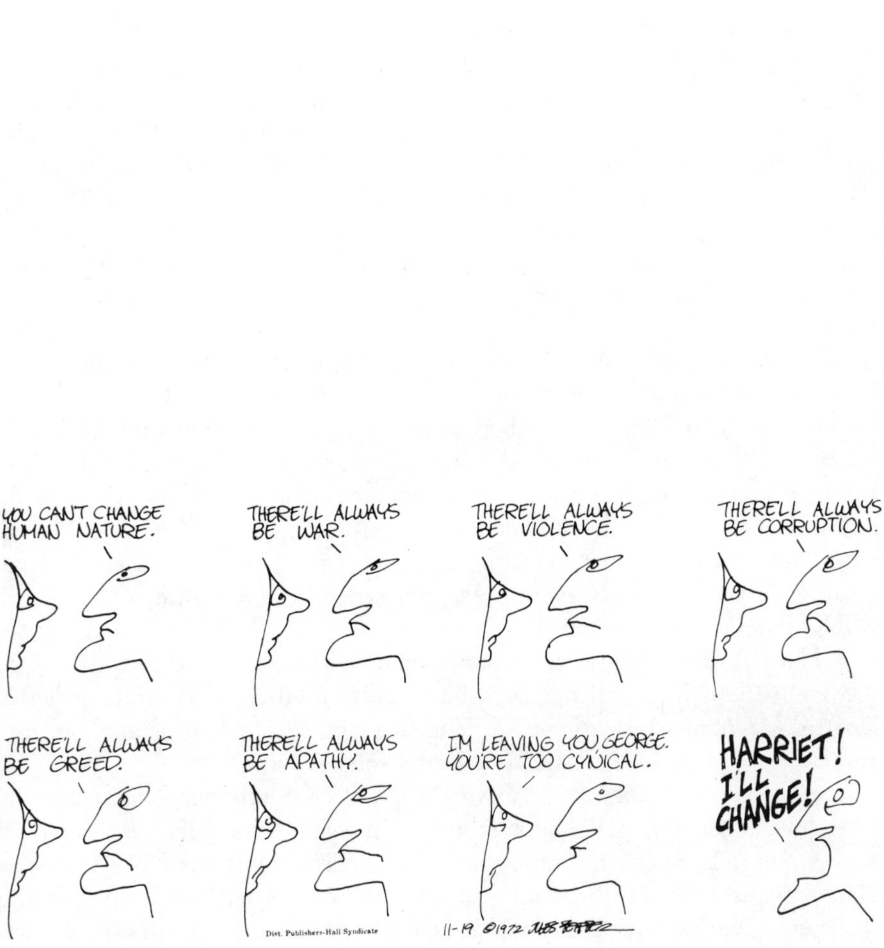

YOU CAN'T CHANGE HUMAN NATURE.
THERE'LL ALWAYS BE WAR.
THERE'LL ALWAYS BE VIOLENCE.
THERE'LL ALWAYS BE CORRUPTION.
THERE'LL ALWAYS BE GREED.
THERE'LL ALWAYS BE APATHY.
I'M LEAVING YOU GEORGE. YOU'RE TOO CYNICAL.
HARRIET! I'LL CHANGE!
Dist. Publishers-Hall Syndicate
11-19 ©1972 Jules Feiffer

Culture

All good people agree,
And all good people say,
That all nice people like Us are We,
And everyone else is They;

But if you cross over the sea,
Instead of over the way,
You may end by (think of it!) looking on We
As only a sort of They!
RUDYARD KIPLING

THE CONCEPT of culture is fundamental to the discipline of sociology, and the social sciences in general. It is essential to a real understanding of man and society, and it points directly to the key difference between man and the other animals. For although most animals within a species reveal essentially the same patterns of behavior, man does not. Human behavior is primarily regulated by culture rather than by instinct; for this reason *Homo sapiens* demonstrates a remarkable variation in patterns of behavior, whether these center around food habits, sexual mores, religious rituals, or political institutions.

Culture has been called the way of life of any society. We may define it more precisely as that complex whole consisting of everything that is socially learned and shared by the members of a society (including attitudes, values, beliefs, and behavior patterns). All *learned, shared* behavior, then, falls into the culture bag. We have learned, largely through the studies of cultural anthropologists, that the difference between cultures is staggering. Man's basic biological needs such as hunger or sex can be, and are, satisfied in a great variety of ways. For example, almost all societies think of certain edible items in their environment as being inedible, and there are immense cross-cultural differences in these food taboos. What one society regards as a tasty, nutritious food will not even be considered edible by another society. Roast dog is a perfectly acceptable food in many cultures but a non-food in the United States. In fact, we have many food taboos, certainly more than a hunting and gathering society with a subsistence economy could afford. Rats, mice, gophers, grasshoppers, ants, ant eggs, larvae of flies, lizzards, snakes, squirrels, robins and other birds, and snails are just a few of the many animal foods avialable to us and ignored, yet considered edible by certain societies. (The area of California in which I teach is fairly urbanized but could support a certain number of hunters and gatherers *if* they could change their food taboos. I have offered this as a suggestion to certain students who

Drawing (overleaf) by Jules Feiffer. Used by permission of Publishers-Hall Syndicate.

were "back-to-nature" in orientation, but they have always declined to give it a try.)

An important point to note is that these attitudes can be very deeply ingrained. The thought of swallowing another person's saliva is so repugnant to most of us that the mere suggestion produces a wince. Even one's own saliva, when it has been removed from the mouth and put, for example, into a glass is eyed with suspicion. However, in the upper Amazon area the Jivaro make an alcohol brew from manioc root which is chewed and fermented in saliva and water. Needless to say, certain Western anthropologists have had difficulty being hospitable when it involved drinking this brew. Notice that the strength of the cultural attitudes regarding these foods often bears no relationship to the nutritiousness of the food. The tomato was considered poisonous in the United States in the last century. The peoples of pre-Columbian Mexico, where the tomato was domesticated, knew better. In other words, cultural beliefs and attitudes may sometimes be irrational in terms of meeting human needs.

Culture, then, channels or directs the way in which basic biological or psychological needs are satisfied. Examine the cross-cultural variability in relation to marriage and sexual patterns. In the United States we are very much interested in this area of behavior, but often a bit uneasy about it. We have traditionally considered sexual behavior to be the measure of a person's (or a society's) "morality." Other societies have a much more casual approach to sex. Among the Trobriand Islanders of Melanesia described by Malinowski, it is expected that unmarried men and women will have a number of trial sexual liaisons before marriage. In fact, children begin to imitate the sexual acts of their parents at 4 or 5 years of age and have actual intercourse with whomever they are attracted to as soon as they are biologically able. Their imitation results from the fact that they have seen their parents engage in sexual intercourse for as long as they can remember because of a lack of privacy. Several years after puberty sexual loyalties to a particular individual tend to develop. There is a major rule that limits the behavior of two lovers about to be married which seems strange to us: they must not eat a meal together! This is as important to the Trobriand Islanders as the traditional premarital sex taboo has been in the United States. It is an immoral act which would bring disgrace to the girl and her family (they, too, have a double standard).

This kind of variability also applies to cultural definitions of marriage. The Baganda of East Africa have a system of plural wives (polygyny), whereas the Toda of South India had a system of plural husbands (polyandry). In certain societies sexual partners are not restricted to marriage partners as has been traditionally the case in the United States where monogamy, a system in which one man marries one woman (one at a time, at least), is considered the naturally correct pattern. The feeling that any other system is incorrect, or immoral, was so strong that the Mormons were finally forced to give up polygyny even though *they* felt that it was morally correct.

This tendency for each group to take for granted the superiority of its own culture is called ethnocentrism. Most people in all societies believe that their own values and behavior patterns are the best. Other societies are strange, and perhaps immoral, because they do things *differently*. We judged the Central Eskimo custom of "wife-exchange" (which occurred only in certain circumstances) to be highly immoral, and the Eskimo judged the phenomenon of organized warfare to be highly ridiculous. Which society is right? We tend to judge the way of life of other societies in terms of the norms and values prevailing in our own society, and the same act that constitutes hospitality in one society constitutes adultery in another. Each nation or society defines social and political reality for the majority of its members. Truth, in a political and cultural sense, is extremely variable. An utterance considered biblical in the United States may be considered the drivel of capitalist warmongers in China. This is, of course, a contributing factor to international tensions and war (wars were fought over the issue of Mormon polygyny). Each nation feels that its institutions are superior and should be preserved, and possibly extended.

The concept of ethnocentrism and the related concept of cultural relativity (the characteristics of a culture can be fruitfully evaluated only in the context of that culture) do not mean that values are unimportant or that they do not really exist. Values, conceptions of what is good and desirable, are created, transmitted, and can be changed by human beings. Much of our daily behavior and many of the decisions we make are based upon underlying values. For example, whether we are willing to pay the price for a clean environment depends not only on the amount we must pay but also on how much a clean environment is worth to us. The important question is whether or not our values and institutions are contributing to a society whose members are leading healthy, fulfilling, self-actualizing lives. This may be a reasonable kind of standard to apply in judging cultures. How would you apply it to our culture? Most of us would not be content with the proposition that Nazy Germany was as good as any other society or that we should not judge cultures at all. The error lies in a strictly ethnocentric appraisal of other cultures or subcultures.

Recently, several writers have popularized the notion that man has a variety of instincts which explain his behavior. An aggressive or territorial instinct is said to explain the existence of violence and war. But if we define an instinct as being a (1) relatively complex behavior pattern which is (2) biologically inherited and (3) universal for the species, then Homo sapiens has none. (The cartoon at the beginning of this section indicates that an individual may use the "you can't change evil human nature" approach when it serves as a convenient rationalization, and discard it when it does not). This is not to say that the biological characteristics of Homo sapiens are unimportant in terms of behavior. For example, our biological inheritance includes reflexes and drives, but we have seen how a drive such as hunger or sex is channeled by different cultures into a great variety of behaviors. This flexibility is precisely that trait that has allowed humanity to adapt and survive in such an assortment of environments throughout the world, and it indicates that "human nature" is extremely malleable. Will there always be war? Possibly, but it will not be due to any innate biological need in man. Are we competitive or cooperative animals? We are obviously both, and the culture and manner in which an individual is raised will usually determine which trait will predominate. Various "Western" cultural values sometimes assumed to be characteristic of "human nature" have been absent in many societies (for example, economic competition, monogamy, and our male and female sex roles). Men and women have created the cultures in which they live and they can change those cultures. If our species continues to destroy itself in violence and war then humanity, and not an "instinct," must bear the responsibility. —D. R.

Selected References

(All are available in paperback editions.)

Benedict, Ruth. *Patterns of Culture*. Boston: Houghton Mifflin Company, 1934.

Goodman, Mary Ellen. *The Individual and Culture*. Homewood, Ill.: The Dorsey Press, 1967.

Mead, Margaret. *Sex and Temperament in Three Primitive Societies*. New York: William Morrow and Company, 1935.

Ruesch, Hans. *Top of the World*. New York: Harper & Row, Publishers, 1950.

Turnbull, Colin. *The Forest People*. New York: Simon and Schuster, 1961.

Apes and Original Sin

SALLY BINFORD

Is humanity biologically programmed for aggression? Does this explain the occurrence of violent and destructive behavior? Recently, several best-selling authors have argued that humanity's evolutionary past explains its violent present. Sally Binford examines several such theories and finds them inadequate. We are not, she concludes, doomed by genetic programming to a future of violence and war. Rather, we are cultural animals with many potential futures.

. . . millionaires are a product of natural selection, acting on the whole body of men to pick those who can meet the requirements of certain work to be done.
—WILLIAM S. SUMNER

The growth of a large business is merely a survival of the fittest . . . It is merely the working-out of a law of nature and a law of God.
—JOHN D. ROCKEFELLER, SR.

The publication of Charles Darwin's *Origin of Species* in 1859 and *The Descent of Man* in 1871 profoundly influenced our view of ourselves. We were no longer the special darlings of divine creation but another vertebrate species subject to the same laws of nature as other living forms. The latter half of the last century was also the period of the settling of the American West and of the destruction of native American populations who stood in the way of our manifest destiny. The cutthroat competitiveness of the nineteenth-century robber barons and the slaughter of native American populations were rationalized by an ideoloy based on a peculiar misunderstanding of Darwin's work, an ideology that became known as Social Darwinism.

Darwin's major statements on evolution can be restated simply:

1. All living forms produce more offspring than can survive.
2. These offspring resemble (but not exactly) the parental generation.
3. Those living forms that are best suited (adapted) to the particular environment in which they find thmselves will produce more viable offspring —i.e., they will "succeed."

The differences in members of the same species that result in differential fertility and survival of offspring were described metaphorically by Darwin by the phrase "struggle for life," and he soon came to regret his use of this phrase. It was seized upon by apologists for colonial expansion, and Darwin's metaphor was taken literally as scientific justification for a *laissez-faire* economic system. "Natural selection" was for Darwin the process by which differential fertility occurred; to the Social Darwinists of the late nineteenth century it somehow became equated with intergroup rivalry, and social philosophers wrote of "nature red in tooth and claw." The metaphor of the struggle for life became the dogma justifying exploitation and the extermination of colonial peoples.

In 1899 the United States Senate was told: "God has not been preparing the English-speaking peoples for a thousand years for nothing but idle and vain self-admiration . . . He has made us adept in government that we may administer government among savages" (quoted by Dobzhansky in *Mankind Evolving*).

Social Darwinism proposed that progress demanded competitive struggles between individuals, races, classes and countries, and this peculiar philosophy produced extraordinary statements of self-congratulation among the rich and powerful who saw themselves as winners in the "struggle for life." The underpinnings of nazism in Germany were essentially the tenets of Social Darwinism, and the use of pseudo-science to determine which were the masters and which the inferior races soon fell into disrepute.

During the past 10 years, however, there has been a rebirth of Social Darwinism, one that emphasizes a kind of biologically determined original sin. The spate of authors who have turned out best-sellers along this line tell us that humans are genetically programmed, for aggression and territoriality, that our phylogenetic relationship to other forms of life cannot be denied by social science (an effort, incidentally, that social science never made), that our responses are essentially like those of stickleback fish or greylag geese.

One of the best known of these authors is Robert Ardrey, a playwright unencumbered by scientific training. In his bestseller *African Genesis,* Ardrey makes use of what he claims are the findings of anthropology, and he goes on to tell us that: "It was my [Presbyterian] Sunday-school class in Chicago, I believe, that prepared me for African anthropology." The results of Ardrey's training are clearly visible in his work. Presbyterian original sin is presented in only slightly disguised language: "Not in innocence and not in Asia was mankind born. The home of our fathers was . . . a sky-swept savannah glowing with menace."

Ardrey's language, glowing with menace, continues throughout the book to color nature of our early ancestors, and interesting verbal games are played. For example, our early manlike ancestors in Africa are referred to as "killer-apes" although they were not apes nor were they killers in the sense that Audrey's language implies. The tools made by these creatures take on a sinister tone when they are called "weapons." All evidence that these early hominids were hunters is equated with evidence for a "killer instinct." The distinction between killing other animal species for food (hunting) and killing members of one's own species (murder) is not made by Ardrey, and we are left with a vague "aggressive instinct" that accounts for hunting, economic competition and warfare. According to Ardrey, the biological nature of our aggressive instinct is demonstrated by its (asserted) presence in the social relations of closely related animals, monkeys and apes.

Ardrey asserts that the aggression displayed by our close primate cousins serves to bolster an even more basic "instinct"—the maintenance and defense of territory. This thesis is more fully developed in *The Territorial Imperative* and *The Social Contract*. We are told that warfare is simply a natural expression of our instinct to defend territory, that economic competition is "natural" in that it allows for expression of our aggressive (territorial) instincts. The rather astonishing conclusion is drawn that the "Jewish problem" is merely the result of the Jews having spent almost 2,000 years without a "turf" or homeland.

The need to acquire and defend property is, according to Ardrey, *the* basic human drive. Sexual desires appear only in the context of desire for territorial possession, and the custom of marriage is based on the desire for one's own territory. Such a view of human marriage and sexuality is wildly inaccurate. The desire of members of some Western cultures for a place of their own after marriage is in no way a cultural universal; rules of postmarital residence in other cultures more often require that a young couple live with relatives than on their own. Ardrey's linking human sexual needs with the desire for property is more an expression of this remarkable author's male chauvinism than it is a valid generalization of human behavior.

But, according to Ardrey, a man is not happy with territory alone; it is the need and desire for affluence that drives him on. This desire for affluence reaches its most perfect expression in the economic system known as capitalism, and economic competition is santified by its inherent qualifications at meeting our basic biological needs. This formulation of Ardrey's, while certainly not good biology or even reasonable anthropology, is certainly a perfect expression of latter-day Social Darwinism.

As Ardrey probably fails to realize, most of the hunting and gathering peoples of the world do not share our desire for possessions. For families who must move their households every season, possessions are a nuisance. Two or three million years elapsed between the time humans began to live as hunter-gatherers and development of the capitalist system. If we are instinctively programmed for capitalism and if it is the basically satisfying human economic arrangement, why was it not developed sooner and why is it not the most common form of human economy?

A few years after the publication of *African Genesis*, another work of amateur anthropology hit the best-seller lists: Konrad Lorenz's *On Aggression*. Drawing largely on the behavior of jackdaws, ducks and greylag geese, Lorenz argues for an aggressive instinct in man, one that is inadequately channelized by ritual or suppressed by ethical considerations. Much of

Lorenz's argument rests on the anthropomorphizing of animal behavior. Ritual behavior in geese and in humans is purportedly analogous because Lorenz tells us what the geese and the men are feeling. Love, friendship, jealousy and other complex emotions are, according to Lorenz, the result of an imperfect dialectic between instinctive aggression and culturally developed morality. Since our cultural values develop slowly, humankind is still at the mercy of innate aggressive drives that our poorly developed system of ethics cannot contain.

The specter of original sin stalks these pages also, and, as in the Old Testament, the tree of knowledge is at fault: "All the great dangers threatening humanity with extinction are direct consequences of conceptual thought and verbal speech." Man's intelligence and knowledge allowed him to develop complex technologies, and ". . . the evolution of social instincts and . . . social inhibitions could not keep pace with the rapid development [of] . . . material culture."

Lorenz tells us the Cro-Magnon man must have had hostile neighbors against whom he could discharge his "aggressive drive," and Lorenz's principal objection to push-button warfare seems to be that it does not allow for adequate discharge of aggression.

Drawing a picture of Paleolithic scarcity and hardship that is in no way supported by the archeological record, Lorenz tips his hand when he tells us: "Their life was so hard that there was no danger of healthy sensuality degenerating into debauch." The economics of scarcity so dear to the nineteenth century Social Darwinists is resurrected as the saving grace of humankind. Hunger, hard work, and a small chance of success are what keep us from debauchery.

Another "true autonomous instinct" attributed to the human species by Lorenz is that of "militant enthusiasm." (Probably a more accurate rendering into English of Lorenz's phrase would be "military enthusiasm.") The following quotation gives a clear indication of the circularity and the judgmental nature of Lorenz's arguments:

> *Like the triumph ceremony of the greylag goose, militant enthusiasm in man is a true autonomous instinct: it has its own appetitive behavior, its own releasing mechanisms, and, like the sexual urge or any other strong instinct, it engenders a specific feeling of intense satisfaction. The strength of its seductive lure explains why intelligent men may behave as irrationally and immorally in their political as in their sexual lives. Like the triumph ceremony, it has an essential influence on the social structure of the species. Humanity is not enthusiastically combative because it is split into political parties, but it is divided into opposing camps because this is the adequate stimulus situation to arouse militant enthusiasm in a satisfying manner.*

The method employed by Lorenz appears to be the observation of certain kinds of behavior in birds and barnyard fowl, drawing analogies between those and human behavior by interpreting the emotional meaning of such behavior, stating that since this behavior occurs in both birds and humans it must be instinctive, then explaining further occurrences of such behavior in terms of the postulated instinct. The circularity is perfect, and there is no means of independent testing of Lorenz's assertions. What is plausible is assumed to be true—scarcely a scientific procedure.

In 1967 Desmond Morris published *The Naked Ape*, a work that has met with even greater popular success than *African Genesis*. Morris is a zoologist by training, and he too is concerned with tracing human behavior to our animal ancestry. He is not quite so grim as Ardrey and does not saddle us quite so heavily with biologically determined original sin. But he does make some interesting statements, particularly for a trained zoologist.

Morris' basic premise is that when our ancestors left the tropical forest and began eating meat, much of our social and sexual behavior was radically modified. So far, so good: the evolution of hunting behavior and its effect on human social organization are proper fields of anthropological inquiry. However, Morris' unsupported assertions and his incorrect use of language considerably diminish his credibility. For example, he consistently refers to humans as carnivores—a strange designation for a zoologist to use for human eating habits. Humans are omnivorous, as are most of the monkeys and apes. Morris asserts that territoriality is a natural and instinctual by-product of hunting, and he states the evolutionary sequence as follows: "The forest ape became a ground ape that became a hunting ape that became a territorial ape that become a cultural ape." Those critical symbol-manipulating parts of the human behavioral repertoire that define our humanity are ignored by Morris. By definition, culture is a human product, and the term "cultural ape" violates our most basic understanding of the principal means of human adaptation.

"We are vegetarians turned carnivores . . . a major switch of this kind produces an animal with a dual personality." Perhaps this a subtler, more psychologically oriented formulation of original sin. If only our ancestors had been happy with fruits and nuts, we might have been spared our apparently inherent schizophrenia. According to Morris, smoking, drinking, eating snacks and competitive automobile driving are all attributable to displacement behavior of our "aggressive instincts" that developed when humans became "carnivores."

The evolution of human social institutions is viewed as a direct and uncomplicated result of hunting. It is in the realm of sex, however, that Morris makes some of his most colorful statements—statements that reveal more about his own sexual hangups than they do about evolution of human behavior. For example: ". . . the males had to be sure that their females were going to be faithful to them when they left them alone to go hunting. So the females had to develop a pairing instinct."

Morris views monogamy as a biologically determined norm, and statements are made that boggle the mind of anyone familiar with either the range of variation in sexual and marital patterns on a cross-cultural basis or with sexual practices in industrialized societies as revealed by Kinsey and others. Morris flatly states: "All major societies (which account for the vast majority of the world population of the species) are monogamous."

Most societies distinguish clearly between marriage as an economic arrangement and sexual behavior; even among societies like our own that make no such formal distinction, the discrepancies between monogamous ideals and sexual behavior are enormous. The strength of the sexual bond in cementing male-female relations is recognized by Morris, but he also assumes that extramarital relations must have a weakening effect on that primary bond. This tells us much more about Morris' anxieties than it does about human behavior.

Religion is, according to Morris, not the rationalization of the social order but an expression of a fixed biological need inherited from our primate ancestors and their dominance hierarchy: "From our ancient background there remained a need for an all-powerful figure . . . and this vacancy was filled by the invention of a god . . . The extreme success of religion is simply a measure of the strength of our fundamental biological tendency, inherited directly from our monkey and ape ancestors, to submit ourselves to an all powerful dominant member of the group." Facile psychologizing of this kind can sound plausible, but it hardly accounts for the known range of variability in human behavior. Jehovah, the all-powerful male god, is certainly not a cultural universal. Once again, we might ask why female gods, divine animals and non-anthropomorphic figures abound in other religions if, indeed, the omnipotent male god is the answer to a basic human biological need.

Morris is not only ignorant of cultural variability; he takes a strong stand defending his emphasis on western culture as the norm. Anthropologists have, according to Morris, misled us by their studies of "remote cultural backwaters," "bizarre mating customs" and "weird religious procedures." One of the major contributions of anthropolgy has been to demonstrate that members of the human species employ a wide range of cultural behavior to solve similar problems. Ethnocentric statements by Morris that non-western customs are weird and bizarre reveal a great deal of Morris' insularity but do nothing to support his claim that western culture is "typical."

Ardrey's insistence on our "killer-ape" ancestry and our innate drive to acquire and defend territory, Lorenz's assertions of human aggressive instincts covered by a thin and often ineffective veneer of culture and Morris' "explanation" of religion, sexual customs and economic arrangements on the basis of human "carnivorous" diets have all been embraced by the American reading public. In addition to providing easy answers to difficult and complex questions, the wide appeal of these works during a period when we have been engaged in an unpopular and apparently endless war is probably more than coincidental. If humans are the victims of biological determinism and if waging war is merely an expression of a deep-seated aggressive instinct, then responsibility for the destruction of Indo-Chinese villages and for urban unrest and violence rest not with ourselves nor with our elected officials but with our distant primate ancestors. But *is* war between human groups merely an expression of human nature? Is our behavior determined genetically, or is human nature not so inherently vicious as the new Social Darwinists would have us believe?

The study of the evolution of human behavior is a fairly recent enterprise; it is an inter-disciplinary effort that includes the findings of cultural anthropology, evolutionary biology, prehistoric archeology and field observations of our closest living relatives—monkeys and apes. It was not until the late 1950s that Sherwood L. Washburn, professor of anthropology at the University of California, Berkeley, and his student, Irven DeVore (now professor of anthropology at Harvard), undertook their pilot study of baboons in East Africa. The purpose of their study was twofold: first, to understand the kind of social adaptation made by baboons. Although baboons are monkeys and therefore not so closely related to humans as are chimpanzees and gorillas, they were selected for study since they have very successfully adapted to life in the East African savanna where the earliest man-like creatures, the australopithecines, lived more than two million years ago. Washburn and DeVore wanted to know how babaoons had succeeded in an environment that also contains many of the world's most powerful predatory carnivores, such as lion and cheetah. Presumably analogous kinds of behavioral adaptations were made by our near-human ancestors who were coping with many of the same problems of survival.

The second objective of the Washburn–DeVore study was to attempt to answer difficult questions concerning the biological basis of human behavior. Monkeys, apes and humans are all primates, and one of the questions being asked was the extent to which human behavior has been determined by our primate ancestry. Is there something we can define as a Primate Way of Life? In what way is human behavior similar to, and how does it differ from, the behavior of our close biological cousins?

Obviously broad questions like this required observations on more than one kind of primate, and in the past 10 to 12 years there have been many excellent studies of wild primates, including observations on our closest relatives—chimpanzees and gorillas. It should be stressed that these have been studies of wild animals in their native habitat, since for many years observations on captive animals were the usual thing. Men in prison do not exhibit the full range of human behavior, and monkeys and apes in zoos are at least as far from their natural range of behavior as are the inmates of San Quentin. Recent field studies of wild primates have given us a wealth of data, and from observations made on several species of monkeys and apes we can now generalize about the way primates live.

There are several features of the way of life shared by monkeys, apes and humans that set them apart from other animals, and it is this shared substratum of primate behavior that provided the evolutionary basis for behavior that is uniquely human. Monkeys, apes and humans are all intensely social animals, and the nature of their sociability differs markedly from that of many other social animals such as bees or termites. The infant higher primate is born while still very immature and helpless, and intensive maternal care is necessary for survival. Natural selection has operated to favor those individuals whose mothers knew their business. Among monkeys and apes, the closest and most consistently observed social pair is mother and child (not male–female as Morris would have us believe), and this relationship often continues into the adult life of the offspring.

The helpless state of the primate infant means also that most of the learning period occurs in a social context; the very matrix of primate learning ability is social. Studies conducted at the University of Wisconsin demonstrate that the primate reared in isolation becomes a psychopath. Positive interaction with other individuals of the same species is just as much a requirement for survival as is food or water. Monkeys reared in isolation do not even know how to copulate, and survival of the species requires the ability to produce offspring.

Primate sociality is actually quite different from that set forth in the killer-ape-ancestry school of popular writing. Washburn and DeVore's study of baboons, George Schaller's investigation of gorillas, Jane von Lawick-Goodall's observations of chimpanzees all point up the peaceful and affectionate nature of primate social relations. Open aggression is very rare, and these groups of animals have worked out rules of peaceful co-existence that minimize both within-group and between-group conflicts. Within a primate group, each young animal in the course of growing up achieves a status in his group's social hierarchy, and this status is more often a function of the mother's status or the individual's strength of personality than of physical prowess.

When two groups of baboons meet at a water-hole, one steps back and waits for the other to finish drinking. Open fights over water rights would attract predators. Among baboons, trees for sleeping appear to be an important factor limiting population growth, since animals sleeping on the ground would be easy prey for predators. Each baboon's range contains sleeping trees, yet baboons do not engage in pitched battles over available trees. Each group seems to know the limits of its territory, but it should be emphasized that defense of territory is virtually unknown since hostile incursions by other groups simply do not occur. How this kind of behavior became transmuted by Ardrey into a "territorial imperative" is mind-boggling to those familiar with the scientific findings in the field.

All animals are "territorial" to the extent that they are not distributed randomly in space. There are groups of animals in some places but not in others; this is an empirical fact. To move from this fact to postulating an "instinct" for territorial behavior and concluding that this is the basis for human nationalism is an interesting phenomenon but one that has nothing to do with the findings of anthropology.

Ardrey argues that since humans are related to many of the higher primates whose social organization is based on a hierarchy of dominant males, human egalitarianism is a romantic fallacy that runs counter to our biological heritage. Morris states that once our distant ancestors acquired a taste of meat, humans were thenceforward committed to a life of violence and bloodlust, and modern-day city dwellers are little more than advanced apes with a thin veneer of civilization—a notion expanded into a book, *The Human Zoo*. Lorenz argues that our culturally derived ethics are so weak that periodically they are overwhelmed by biologically determined forces, that humans are still in the clutches of an aggressive instinct.

Such statements are tempting, since the onus for modern violence is placed on the forces of evolution rather than on social conditions that require our immediate attention. But are such formulations consistent with what we know of the biological and cultural evolution of the human species?

The earliest man-like creatures that can be distinguished from the apes are the australopithecines who inhabited eastern and southern Africa beginning about three million years ago. The archeological remains associated with these fossils indicate that the apes lived as small migratory bands of hunter-gatherers. They made stone tools whose function was to kill and butcher the animals they hunted and to process plant foods. There is not a shred of evidence that these tools served as "weapons" in integroup rivalry.

Our best means for deducing the life-style of the australopithecines is to use the baboon troop and living hunter-gatherers as base lines and perform a kind of cultural triangulation. Admittedly the australopithecines were neither baboons nor modern humans, but methodologically we must proceed from the known to the unknown with complete awareness of the fragility of the method. The baboon troop is a peaceful, closely knit social unit in which social learning and affectionate exchanges are enormously important. Young baboons work out their place in the group over a period of years of play and exploration with firm guidance from the adults around them. Any outbreak of hostility between youngsters is quickly settled by the appearance on the scene of adults.

Hunter-gatherers with technologically simple levels of adaptation might be the Bushmen of southern Africa or the aboriginal populations of central Australia. Such human groups are small in size (generally from about 30 to 100 individuals), and population density is low (about one person per square mile). Warfare is virtually unknown among them, and within a band, power is distributed in an egalitarian fashion. A series of culturally determined rules insure that aggressive behavior that might endanger the group does not occur.

On the basis of primate studies and what is known ethnographically of hunting-gathering peoples, it is highly unlikely that our early ancestors engaged in inter-group rivalry. The archeological record supports this conclusion: the first evidence of warfare appears about 6,000 years ago—a brief span of the long millennia that humans have been in existence. If war were a genetically programmed component of all human behavior, certainly the many sites and human fossils known for this huge stretch of time would have yielded some evidence to support the proposition that from the time our ancestors came out of the trees we have been engaged in mutual slaughter (fortified sites, inflicted deaths, mass burials).

Raiding among tribal peoples is not uncommon, but the tribal level of sociocultural development is fairly recent. Warfare appears to be a luxury reserved for societies more complex than those of hunter-gatherer bands. Investment in corporate facilities (temples, granaries, irrigation systems) along with formally recognized distinctions between social groups (classes) appear to be correlates of warfare. Whether the systematic killing of our own species is the result of population density or of the kind of ownership of the means of production, or both, is a fascinating question that deserves serious research attention. To postulate that warfare is part of our biological and/or psychological heritage in spite of the evidence to the contrary is to soothe ourselves into believing that we can do nothing about war or its causes.

In order to evaluate the work of Ardrey, Lorenz and Morris, the distinction between learned and instinctive behavior must be made clear. A man making a net for fishing and a spider spinning a web are two radically different phenomena, despite the superficial similarity of purpose and of the form of the product. The spider is genetically programmed to spin her web; no one must teach her how. Humans must learn how to make nets, how to make spears and arrows and how to kill each other. Learned behavior is what anthropologists call culture, and the major finding of anthropology over the past hundred years is that virtually all of our behavior is learned. We are born with the capacity for behavior, but the form it takes depends upon what we are taught. Whether we choose to settle our differences by violence or by peaceful means is culturally determined; it is not a matter of genetics.

The new Social Darwinists would have us believe that we are automatons, carrying in our chromosomes the desire to kill that we inherited from our primate ancestors. In a recently published book, *The Human Imperative*, anthropologist Alexander Alland, Jr., presents the most comprehensive response to the work of simplistic biological determinists. The book opens with a succinct and excellent introductory chapter that summarizes evolutionary theory. Alland then moves on to his analysis of Ardrey, Lorenz and Morris; with painstaking patience and skill, he points out their major flaws in logic and in their knowledge of the relevant data. Using highly illustrative materials from his own fieldwork, Alland demonstrates the emptiness of formulations such as the territorial imperative and their lack of conformity to the facts. Alland offers no simple answers to difficult questions; instead, he points out that the relationship between biology and culture is complex. Within this complexity, however, is room for choice: we are not doomed to act out a drama whose lines were written millions of years ago. Culture is cumulative; humans can and do learn more about their environment and themselves. Unfortunately, Alland's book will probably not be the seller that *African Genesis* and *The Naked Ape* were. Complex truths too often fail to catch up with the simple, attractive lie.

Forty years ago the intellectual community in America saw the pitfalls of Social Darwinism and the consequences of their formulation into national policy in Nazi Germany. We must hope that the new Social Darwinism, slickly packaged but riddled with the same flaws, will be rejected as well.

The Sounds of Silence

EDWARD T. HALL AND MILDRED REED HALL

Speech is only one of the ways in which we communicate with other individuals. Nonverbal "body language" (slouching, frowning, type of eye contact, etc.) also communicates a great deal of information. This kind of behavior is an important part of any group's culture. The Halls describe the nonverbal communication systems of many cultures and subcultures and note the high degree of cross-cultural variability that exists.

Bob leaves his apartment at 8:15 A.M. and stops at the corner drugstore for breakfast. Before he can speak, the counterman says, "The usual?" Bob nods yes. While he savors his Danish, a fat man pushes onto the adjoining stool and overflows into his space. Bob scowls and the man pulls himself in as much as he can. Bob has sent two messages without speaking a syllable.

Henry has an appointment to meet Arthur at 11 o'clock; he arrives at 11:30. Their conversation is friendly, but Arthur retains a lingering hostility. Henry has unconsciously communicated that he doesn't think the appointment is very important or that Arthur is a person who needs to be treated with respect.

George is talking to Charley's wife at a party. Their conversation is entirely trivial, yet Charley glares at them suspiciously. Their physical proximity and the movements of their eyes reveal that they are powerfully attracted to each other.

José Ybarra and Sir Edmund Jones are at the same party and it is important for them to establish a cordial relationship for business reasons. Each is trying to be warm and friendly, yet they will part with mutual distrust and their business transaction will probably fall through. José, in Latin fashion, moved closer and closer to Sir Edmund as they spoke, and this movement was miscommunicated as pushiness to Sir Edmund, who kept backing away from this intimacy, and this was miscommunicated to José as coldness. The silent languages of Latin and English cultures are more difficult to learn than their spoken languages.

In each of these cases, we see the subtle power of nonverbal communication. The only language used throughout most of the history of humanity (in evolutionary terms, vocal communication is relatively recent), it is the first form of communication you learn. You use this preverbal language, consciously and unconsciously, every day to tell other people how you feel about yourself and them. This language includes your posture, gestures, facial expressions, costume, the way you walk, even your treatment of time and space and material things. All people communicate on several different levels at the same time but are usually aware of only the verbal dialog and don't realize that they respond to nonverbal messages. But when a person says one thing and really believes something else, the discrepancy between the two can usually be sensed. Nonverbal-communication systems are much less subject to the conscious deception that often occurs in verbal systems. When we find ourselves thinking, "I don't know what it is about him, but he doesn't seem sincere," it's usually this lack of congruity between a person's words and his behavior that makes us anxious and uncomfortable.

Few of us realize how much we all depend on body movement in our conversation or are aware of the hidden rules that govern listening behavior. But we know instantly whether or not the person we're talking to is "tuned in" and we're very sensitive to any breach in listening etiquette. In white middle-class American culture, when someone wants to show he is listening to someone else, he looks either at the other person's face or, specifically, at his eyes, shifting his gaze from one eye to the other.

If you observe a person conversing, you'll notice that he indicates he's listening by nodding his head. He also makes little "Hmm" noises. If he agrees with what's being said, he may give a vigorous nod. To show pleasure or affirmation, he smiles; if he has some reservations, he looks skeptical by raising an eyebrow or pulling down the corners of his mouth. If a participant wants to terminate the conversation, he may start shifting his body position, stretching his legs, crossing or uncrossing them, bobbing his foot or diverting his gaze from the speaker. The more he fidgets, the more the speaker becomes aware that he has lost his audience. As a last measure, the listener may look at his watch to indicate the imminent end of the conversation.

Talking and listening are so intricately intertwined that a person cannot do one without the other. Even when one is alone and talking to oneself, there is part of the brain that speaks while another part listens. In all conversations, the listener is positively or negatively reinforcing the speaker all the time. He may even guide the conversation without knowing it, by laughing or frowning or dismissing the argument with a wave of his hand.

The language of the eyes—another age-old way of exchanging feelings—

is both subtle and complex. Not only do men and women use their eyes differently but there are class, generation, regional, ethnic and national cultural differences. Americans often complain about the way foreigners stare at people or hold a glance too long. Most Americans look away from someone who is using his eyes in an unfamiliar way because it makes them self-conscious. If a man looks at another man's wife in a certain way, he's asking for trouble, as indicated earlier. But he might not be ill-mannered or seeking to challenge the husband. He might be a European in this country who hasn't learned our visual mores. Many American women visiting France or Italy are acutely embarrassed because, for the first time in their lives, men really look at them—their eyes, hair, nose, lips, breasts, hips, legs, thighs, knees, ankles, feet, clothes, hairdo, even their walk. These same women, once they have become used to being looked at, often return to the United States and are overcome with the feeling that "No one ever really looks at me anymore."

Analyzing the mass of data on the eyes, it is possible to sort out at least three ways in which the eyes are used to communicate: dominance vs. submission, involvement vs. detachment and positive vs. negative attitude. In addition, there are three levels of consciousness and control, which can be categorized as follows: (1) conscious use of the eyes to communicate, such as the flirting blink and the intimate nose-wrinkling squint; (2) the very extensive category of unconscious but learned behavior governing where the eyes are directed and when (this unwritten set of rules dictates how and under what circumstances the sexes, as well as people of all status categories, look at each other); and (3) the response of the eye itself, which is completely outside both awareness and control—changes in the cast (the sparkle) of the eye and the pupillary reflex.

The eye is unlike any other organ of the body, for it is an extension of the brain. The unconscious pupillary reflex and the cast of the eye have been known by people of Middle Eastern origin for years—although most are unaware of their knowledge. Depending on the context, Arabs and others look either directly at the eyes or deeply *into* the eyes of their interlocutor. We became aware of this in the Middle East several years ago while looking at jewelry. The merchant suddenly started to push a particular bracelet at a customer and said, "You buy this one." What interested us was that the bracelet was not the one that had been consciously selected by the purchaser. But the merchant, watching the pupils of the eyes, knew what the purchaser really wanted to buy. Whether he specifically knew *how* he knew is debatable.

A psychologist at the University of Chicago, Eckhard Hess, was the first to conduct systematic studies of the pupillary reflex. His wife remarked one evening, while watching him reading in bed, that he must be very interested in the text because his pupils were dilated. Following up on this, Hess slipped some pictures of nudes into a stack of photographs that he gave to his male assistant. Not looking at the photographs but watching his assistant's pupils, Hess was able to tell precisely when the assistant came to the nudes. In further experiments, Hess retouched the eyes in a photograph of a woman. In one print, he made the pupils small, in another, large; nothing else was changed. Subjects who were given the photographs found the woman with the dilated pupils much more attractive. Any man who has had the experience of seeing a woman look at him as her pupils widen with reflex speed knows that she's flashing him a message.

The eye-sparkle phenomenon frequently turns up in our interviews of couples in love. It's apparently one of the first reliable clues in the other person that love is genuine. To date, there is no scientific data to explain eye sparkle; no investigation of the pupil, the cornea or even the white sclera of the eye shows how the sparkle originates. Yet we all know it when we see it.

One common situation for most people involves the use of the eyes in the street and in public. Although eye behavior follows a definite set of rules, the rules vary according to the place, the needs and feelings of the people, and their ethnic background. For urban whites, once they're within definite recognition distance (16–32 feet for people with average eyesight), there is mutual avoidance of eye contact—unless they want something specific: a pickup, a handout or information of some kind. In the West and in small towns generally, however, people are much more likely to look at and greet one another, even if they're strangers.

It's permissible to look at people if they're beyond recognition distance; but once inside this sacred zone, you can only steal a glance at strangers. You *must* greet friends, however; to fail to do so is insulting. Yet, to stare too fixedly even at them is considered rude and hostile. Of course, all of these rules are variable.

A great many blacks, for example, greet each other in public even if they don't know each other. To blacks, most eye behavior of whites has the effect of giving the impression that they aren't there, but this is due to white avoidance of eye contact with *anyone* in the street.

Another very basic difference between people of different ethnic backgrounds is their sense of territoriality and how they handle space. This is the silent communication, or miscommunication, that caused friction between Mr. Ybarra and Sir Edmund Jones in our earlier example. We know from research that everyone has around himself an invisible bubble of space that contracts and expands depending on several factors: his emotional state, the activity he's performing at the time and his cultural background. This bubble is a kind of mobile territory that he will defend against intrusion. If he is accustomed to close personal distance between himself and others, his bubble will be smaller than that of someone who's accustomed to greater personal distance. People of North European heritage—English, Scandinavian, Swiss and German—tend to avoid contact. Those whose heritage is Italian, French, Spanish, Russian, Latin American or Middle Eastern like close personal contact.

People are very sensitive to any intrusion into their spatial bubble. If someone stands too close to you, your first instinct is to back up. If that's not possible, you lean away and pull yourself in, tensing your muscles. If the intruder doesn't respond to these body signals, you may then try to protect yourself, using a briefcase, umbrella or raincoat. Women—especially when traveling alone—often plant their pocketbook in such a way that no one can get very close to them. As a last resort, you may move to another spot and position yourself behind a desk or a chair that provides screening. Everyone tries to adjust the space around himself in a way that's comfortable for him; most often, he does this unconsciously.

Emotions also have a direct effect on the size of a person's territory. When you're angry or under stress, your bubble expands and you require more space. New York psychiatrist Augustus Kinzel found a difference in what he calls Body-Buffer Zones between violent and nonviolent prison inmates. Dr. Kinzel conducted experiments in which each prisoner was placed in the center of a small room and then Dr. Kinzel slowly walked toward him. Nonviolent prisoners allowed him to come quite close, while prisoners with a history of violent behavior couldn't tolerate his proximity and reacted with some vehemence.

Apparently, people under stress experience other people as looming larger and closer than they actually are. Studies of schizophrenic patients have indicated that they sometimes have a distorted perception of space, and several psychiatrists have reported patients who experience their body boundaries as filling up an entire room. For these patients, anyone who comes into the room is actually inside their body, and such an intrusion may trigger a violent outburst.

Unfortunately, there is little detailed information about normal people who live in highly congested urban areas. We do know, of course, that the noise, pollution, dirt, crowding and confusion of our cities induce feelings of stress in most of us, and stress leads to a need for greater space. The man who's packed into a subway, jostled in the street, crowded into an elevator and forced to work all day in a bull pen or in a small office without auditory or visual privacy is going to be very stressed at the end of his day. He needs places that provide relief from constant overstimulation of his nervous system. Stress from overcrowding is cumulative and people can tolerate more crowding early in the day than later; note the increased bad temper during the evening rush hour as compared with the morning melee. Certainly one factor in people's desire to commute by car is the need for privacy and relief from crowding (except, often, from other cars); it may be the only time of the day when nobody can intrude.

In crowded public places, we tense our muscles and hold ourselves stiff, and thereby communicate to others our desire not to intrude on their space and, above all, not to touch them. We also avoid eye contact, and the total effect is that of someone who has "tuned out." Walking along the street, our bubble expands slightly as we move in a stream of strangers, taking care not to bump into them. In the office, at meetings, in restaurants, our bubble keeps changing as it adjusts to the activity at hand.

Most white middle-class Americans use four main distances in their business and social relations: intimate, personal, social and public. Each of these distances has a near and a far phase and is accompanied by changes in the volume of the voice. Intimate distance varies from direct physical contact with another person to a distance of six to eighteen inches and is used for our most private activities—caressing another person or making love. At this distance, you are overwhelmed by sensory inputs from the other person—heat from the body, tactile stimulation from the skin, the fragrance of perfume, even the sound of breathing—all of which literally envelop you. Even at the far phase, you're still within easy touching distance. In general, the use of intimate distance in public between adults is frowned on. It's also much too close for strangers, except under conditions of extreme crowding.

In the second zone—personal distance—the close phase is one and a half to two and a half feet; it's at this distance that wives usually stand from their husbands in public. If another woman moves into this zone, the wife will most likely be disturbed. The far phase—two and a half to four feet—is the distance used to "keep someone at arm's length" and is the most common spacing used by people in conversation.

The third zone—social distance—is employed during business transactions or exchanges with a clerk or repairman. People who work together tend to use close social distance—four to seven feet. This is also the distance for conversation at social gatherings. To stand at this distance from someone who is seated has a dominating effect (e.g., teacher to pupil, boss to secretary). The far phase of the third zone—seven to twelve feet—is where people stand when someone says, "Stand back so I can look at you." This distance lends a formal tone to business or social discourse. In an executive office, the desk serves to keep people at this distance.

The fourth zone—public distance—is used by teachers in classrooms or speakers at public gatherings. At its farthest phase—25 feet and beyond—it is used for important public figures. Violations of this distance can lead to serious complications. During his 1970 U.S. visit, the president of France, Georges Pompidou, was harassed by pickets in Chicago, who were permitted to get within touching distance. Since pickets in France are kept behind barricades a block or more away, the president was outraged by this insult to his person, and President Nixon was obliged to communicate his concern as well as offer his personal apologies.

It is interesting to note how American pitchmen and panhandlers exploit the unwritten, unspoken conventions of eye and distance. Both take advantage of the fact that once explicit eye contact is established, it is rude to look away, because to do so means to brusquely dismiss the other person and his needs. Once having caught the eye of his mark, the panhandler then locks on, not letting go until he moves through the public zone, the social zone, the personal zone and, finally, into the intimate sphere, where people are most vulnerable.

Touch also is an important part of the constant stream of communication that takes place between people. A light touch, a firm touch, a blow, a caress are all communications. In an effort to break down barriers among people, there's been a recent upsurge in group-encounter activities, in which strangers are encouraged to touch one another. In special situations such as these, the rules for not touching are broken with group approval and people gradually lose some of their inhibitions.

Although most people don't realize it, space is perceived and distances are set not by vision alone but with all the senses. Auditory space is perceived with the ears, thermal space with the skin, kinesthetic space with the muscles of the body and olfactory space with the nose. And, once again, it's one's culture that determines how his senses are programmed—which sensory information ranks highest and lowest. The important thing to remember is that culture is very persistent. In this country, we've noted the existence of culture patterns that determine distance between people in the third and fourth generations of some families, despite their prolonged contact with people of very different cultural heritages.

Whenever there is great cultural distance between two people, there are bound to be problems arising from differences in behavior and expectations. An example is the American couple who consulted a psychiatrist about their marital problems. The husband was from New England and had been brought up by reserved parents who taught him to control his emotions and to respect the need for privacy. His wife was from an Italian family and had been brought up in close contact with all the members of her large family, who were extremely warm, volatile and demonstrative.

When the husband came home after a hard day at the office, dragging his feet and longing for peace and quiet, his wife would rush to him and smother him. Clasping his hands, rubbing his brow, crooning over his weary head, she never left him alone. But when the wife was upset or anxious about her day, the husband's response was to withdraw completely and leave her alone. No comforting, no affectionate embrace, no attention—just solitude. The woman became convinced her husband didn't love her and, in desperation, she consulted a psychiatrist. Their problem wasn't basically psychological but cultural.

Why has man developed all these different ways of communicating messages without words? One reason is that people don't like to spell out certain kinds of messages. We prefer to find other ways of showing our feelings. This is especially true in relationships as sensitive as courtship. Men don't like to be rejected and most women don't want to turn a man down bluntly. Instead, we work out subtle ways of encouraging or discouraging each other that save face and avoid confrontations.

How a person handles space in dating others is an obvious and very sensitive indicator of how he or she feels about the other person. On a first date, if a woman sits or stands so close to a man that he is acutely conscious of her physical presence—inside the intimate-distance zone—the man usually construes it to mean that she is encouraging him. However, before the man starts moving in on the woman, he should be sure what message she's really sending; otherwise, he risks bruising his ego. What is close to someone of North European background may be neutral or distant to someone of Italian heritage. Also, women sometimes use space as a way of misleading a man and there are few things that put men off more than women who communicate contradictory messages—such as women who cuddle up and then act insulted when a man takes the next step.

How does a woman communicate interest in a man? In addition to such familiar gambits as smiling at him, she may glance shyly at him, blush and then look away. Or she may give him a real come-on look and move in very close when he approaches. She may touch his arm and ask for a light. As she leans forward to light her cigarette, she may brush him lightly, enveloping him in her perfume. She'll probably continue to smile at him and she may use what ethologists call preening gestures—touching the back of her hair, thrusting her breasts forward, tilting her hips as she stands or crossing her legs if she's seated, perhaps even exposing one thigh or putting a hand on her thigh and stroking it. She may also stroke her wrists as she converses or show the palm of her hand as a way of gaining his attention. Her skin may be unusually flushed or quite pale, her eyes brighter, the pupils larger.

If a man sees a woman whom he wants to attract, he tries to present himself by his posture and stance as someone who is self-assured. He moves briskly and confidently. When he catches the eye of the woman, he may hold her glance a little longer than normal. If he gets an encouraging smile, he'll move in close and engage her in small talk. As they converse, his glance shifts over her face and body. He, too, may make preening gestures—straightening his tie, smoothing his hair or shooting his cuffs.

How do people learn body language? The same way they learn spoken language—by observing and imitating people around them as they're growing up. Little girls imitate their mothers or an older female. Little boys imitate their fathers or a respected uncle or a character on television. In this way, they learn the gender signals appropriate for their sex. Regional, class and ethnic patterns of body behavior are also learned in childhood and persist throughout life.

· · ·

The language of behavior is extremely complex. Most of us are lucky to have under control one subcultural system—the one that reflects our sex, class, generation and geographic region within the United States. Because of its complexity, efforts to isolate bits of nonverbal communication and generalize from them are in vain; you don't become an instant expert on people's behavior by watching them at cocktail parties. Body language isn't something that's independent of the person, something that can be donned and doffed like a suit of clothes.

Our research and that of our colleagues has shown that, far from being a superficial form of communication that can be consciously manipulated, nonverbal-communication systems are interwoven into the fabric of the personality and, as sociologist Erving Goffman has demonstrated, into society itself. They are the warp and woof of daily interactions with others and they influence how one expresses oneself, how one experiences oneself as a man or a woman.

Nonverbal communications signal to members of your own group what kind of person you are, how you feel about others, how you'll fit into and work in a group, whether you're assured or anxious, the degree to which you feel comfortable with the standards of your own culture, as well as deeply significant feelings about the self, including the state of your own psyche. For most of us, it's difficult to accept the reality of another's behavioral system. And, of course, none of us will ever become fully knowledgeable of the importance of every nonverbal signal. But as long as each of us realizes the power of these signals, this society's diversity can be a source of great strength rather than a further—and subtly powerful—source of division.

Top of the World: The Men

HANS RUESCH

Learning about other cultures often helps reveal the distinctive traits of one's own culture that were previously "taken for granted." The following excerpt is from the novel,* The Top of the World, *by Hans Ruesch. It is a fascinating saga of life and adventure among a group of Central Eskimo who inhabit an area of land near the magnetic North Pole where thirty degrees below freezing is considered a warm day. The fact that Central Eskimo culture differs radically in a number of important ways from our own makes this tale especially interesting.

When Ernenek raised his head from the sleeping bag his thoughts usually ran at once to the heap of fish and meat rotting into tenderness behind the seal oil lamp.

But not today.

Today, seeing Siksik bent over her husband's bearskins in a corner of the little igloo, he made a sudden resolution before lending an ear to the demands of his stomach. Since he contributed more than his share to the sustenance of the little household he was going to demand a full share in Anarvik's marital rights also, so that he no longer would have to ask permission each time he felt like laughing a little with Siksik, or when he needed new mittens sewn or his boots mended. He would at last have a wife of his own to order around—something he had never known, because he was young, and because here in the farthest North, woman was as scarce as bear was plentiful. But Ernenek knew the importance of a wife of one's own—to scrape one's skins and sew one's garments and to listen to one's jokes during the night.

Especially when the night lasts six months.

Even now he would have liked exchanging a little laughter with Siksik before leaving for the hunt. But he knew right from wrong as well as any man, and so he knew it would be most improper to avail oneself of another man's wife without first asking the husband's permission.

And Ernenek seldom did anything improper.

But he was tired of asking. Not that Anarvik ever refused: refusing the loan of a wife or a knife was a sign of intolerable meanness. Yet also, constantly asking favors was undignified for someone belonging to a race so proud that they call themselves simply *Inuits*, or Men, implying that all others aren't, by comparison, real men; even if the rest of the world has chosen to call them Eskimos—from an Algonquin word meaning Eaters-of-Raw-Meat—whether in mockery or envy has not been established.

Siksik had prepared tea on the soapstone cooking lamp. She filled a bowl and, waddling pigeon-toed owing to the boots of ringed seal that reached up to her crotch, offered Ernenek the drink with a smile. Man and woman dressed in this identical fashion. Both were stodgy and muscular and with the same joyful, broad and flat face, looking alike except for their hair, which Ernenek wore long and unruly while Siksik's rose in a neat turret-shaped coiffure on the top of her head, shining with blubber and pinned with fishbones.

"Where is Anarvik?" Ernenek inquired.

"It is not impossible that he went sealing in the Bay of the Blind Walrus. It came to pass that one sleep ago you and he guzzled a whole seal," she added with a giggle, and Ernenek responded with the easy and ever-ready laughter of his race.

The tea was warm, which was too hot for him. He couldn't drink anything warm. He blew on it, gazing at the woman over the rim of his bowl. Then he drank, ate the tea leaves and crawled out of his bag. Over his jacket suit of birdskins with the down turned inside he donned a suit of bearhide with the hair outside and tucked the trousers into his sealskin boots. Stooping under the vaulted ice wall he cut himself big chunks of rotted meat with his circular knife and crammed them into his mouth with the palm of his hand.

Crawling out of the narrow tunnel on all fours he pulled along the leader of the dozing huskies, and the rest of the team followed, yawning and shaking the hoarfrost from their thick pelts. Soon they were yapping for food, baring their teeth (they had been flattened with stones lest they should gnaw through their traces), all bearing more likeness to wolves than dogs, with pointed snouts and glaring yellow eyes.

Ernenek iced the runners and lashed the sled. Then he harnessed the dogs, made sure they all wore the little shoes designed to protect their feet from the sharpness of the ice and the salt of the sea, retrieved the sled anchor and stepped aboard. Under the whip the dogs spread fanwise behind their leader, tearing at the traces by which each of them was individually tied to the sled and yelping after the white puffs of smoke from their muzzles.

It was warm, perhaps thirty below freezing, and Ernenek didn't have to trot after the sled for warmth, but could sit on it luxuriously enjoying the ride. The southern sky, reflecting an absent sun, was mild blue that shaded into a tender purple in the north. Under this pallid heaven the earth appeared flat and bloodless, with neither shades nor hues, as do the eyes of dogs that make no distinction between colors.

The Glacial Ocean on which he traveled, frozen deeper than a man is tall and stingily carpeted with snow, showed clearly the tracks of Anarvik's sled. To the right were low bluffs and hills, white and dead. To the left, only the haze of spring bounded the ocean.

Ernenek never turned to glance at the solitary igloo he was leaving behind —tiny blister of ice on the roof of the world. His thoughts were racing ahead to the next island's great bay where Anarvik had gone sealing. He had even neglected to take blubber with him for fuel and light—the traveler's first rule. He was too much concerned with his question.

There were two answers to every question, and each had its risks. That much Ernenek knew. If Anarvik's answer was Yes, Ernenek would lose considerable face for being granted still another favor. Anarvik was proud, a real man, and it would be quite like him to mortify Ernenek with a ready acceptance of his request. To get even with him Ernenek would then have to double his hunting efforts in order to mortify his partner in his turn with endless gifts of food.

If the answer was No, Ernenek could indeed jeer at his friend over *his* loss of face, but it would be a small consolation for having to look elsewhere for a mate, traveling uncomfortably alone, perhaps a year to the southward, where the sun and the women come from, and the land is peopled by tribes whose ways are foreign to a Polar Eskimo, and therefore distasteful to him. Any way you looked at it, life would be fraught with hazards once the question had fallen.

And yet it could be postponed no longer: for two years now Anarvik had been announcing the impending arrival of his brother Ooloolik. "He has two growing daughters and you may take your choice," Anarvik had pointed out, laughing. But the seasons had come and gone, Ernenek had waited in vain, and Anarvik had merely shrugged and said, "He may come end of next winter."

A winter more or a winter less seemed unimportant to Anarvik who had seen many. But not to Ernenek who had seen few. What if Ooloolik never came? He may have changed his mind. Or be dead. Or others may have taken his daughters.

And Ernenek was tired of waiting.

Anarvik's sled appeared as a little pin point on the great expanse and Ernenek spurred his team with whip and shout. Slowly the pin point grew to a line, then the sled became visible, then Anarvik and his dogs. The dogs were in an uproar, pulling furiously at their leashes.

Ernenek flung the sled anchor overboard, fastened the team and swaggered over the frozen sea. For all his impatience he trod the ice softly, by dint of habit, lest he frighten away the seal below. Anarvik, kneeling on a caribou skin so as not to freeze fast to the ground, had his back to him.

"A man has something to ask," Ernenek said with a smile.

"Quiet!" said Anarvik without turning his head. "A man at work can't listen to questions. One thing at a time."

Deflated, Ernenek stopped beside him, curious to see what he was doing. Anarvik was busy with his flint knife but was ever again focusing his attention on a white shape ahead. The shape was a huge bear.

And the bear was hungry.

Months of lean hunting had whittled down the flesh accumulated during the summer season and his long winter pelt hung loosely about his fatless haunches. The Polar bear didn't hibernate. While all life migrated to the southward or holed up in igloos and lairs for rest and warmth, he alone stayed abroad all winter, hunting and fishing indefatigably for himself and his mate that dropped her young in a cave dug out in the ice crust of the sea.

A while back, on one of his inland forays, this bear had smelled out an ermine mother from her lair, torn her asunder and devoured her together with the pulsing litter in her belly. Now with whetted hunger he was observing the two men. But he was uneasy.

In this region all life was exclusively carnivorous. Bear was man's biggest prize. Man was bear's biggest prize. Here it had not yet been decided whether man or bear was the crown of creation.

"It is not impossible that someone will fell a bear," said Anarvik.

Shivering with the lust of the hunt Ernenek knelt beside him. "Let us set the dogs on him and finish quickly."

Anarvik shook his head. "He might kill many dogs, and we have none to spare. No, Ernenek. Somebody will get the bear in the usual, proven fashion."

Circling and sniffing, the bear was slowly moving closer.

With his flint knife Anarvik had carved a long splint from his whalerib bow and sharpened the ends. He coiled the splint in his hand and released it suddenly to test its resilience. Then he pulled out a chunk of blubber he had been warming within his clothes, against his stomach. He kneaded the blubber into a ball, swiftly, before it could freeze, and pressed the tightly coiled whalebone splint into it. The blubber ball hardened instantly on the ice.

He began moving forward on all fours and the bear withdrew growling, with little jumps, throwing up his shaggy hindquarters and leering over his shoulder. Anarvik stopped and called to him with motions and cooing sounds, and the bear returned tentatively, in a half-circle. Anarvik's sparse mustache quivered as he rolled the spring bait forcefully over the thin blanket of snow.

The yellow ball came to a halt a few paces from the bear. Puzzled, he approached cautiously, stretching out his nose forward and whimpering a little in uncertainty. Hunger told him to eat; another instinct, deeper and more mysterious, told him to distrust whatever came from those little beings, so frighteningly purposeful.

Anarvik waited flat and motionless, arms and legs spread out. Behind him Ernenek breathlessly watched the bear put out a long blue tongue and lick the bait, retire, lick again, and staunchly retire again. But it was impossible to resist temptation forever. Bears are only human. With a billowy movement, his snout suddenly shot forward and engulfed the bait, dropping it into the bottomless pit of his belly.

Simultaneously, Anarvik and Ernenek leaped to their feet with cheers and laughter, for the bear was theirs.

Almost.

At the men's sudden outburst the bear backed up. Mystified, he began to circle, then sat down on his haunches and studied them for a while. Finally, he began closing in.

The men were preparing to retreat when suddenly he jumped up and gave a long anguished moan that ran unchecked over the great sea, silencing the dogs, then bucked about and growled savagely.

"In his stomach the blubber has melted," cried Anarvik triumphantly.

"And the blade has sprung open!"

All at once the bear turned on his heels and shuffled off yammering.

Dusk was dimming already, for day was short as yet, lighting the roof of the world for but a few hours with each turn of the sun. Without a word Anarvik and Ernenek gripped their spears and started after their quarry, glancing at each other and laughing, just laughing with the glee of the hunt, everything else forgotten.

Stumbling and wailing the bear drifted coastward, as the men moved to cut off his retreat toward the sea fields, his element and abode. After reaching the first foothills of the land he began to stop frequently and look over his shoulder to see if the chase was still on, threads of spittle dangling on his chest. His lair must be near by, but he wouldn't lead the hunters there. Reluctantly he moved on, up the frozen hillsides.

The soles of his feet, covered with close-set hair, enabled him to walk securely on the ice, while the men's boots had a poor grip on the slippery slopes. And they had to take heed not to work themselves into a sweat, which meant freezing to death. But the bear's course was wayward and erratic and the men could keep up with him covering only half as much ground.

It grew colder on the heights, fifty or sixty below, and the beloved gale blew, and Anarvik and Ernenek were happy because they hunted. Never for an instant did they worry about the forsaken provisions, and the dogs, and the woman. They were not hungry at the moment; the dogs were always hungry anyhow, whether they were fed or not; and the woman would manage somehow, as women always did. This was the Hunt—the very essence of life.

They ate nothing but the bear's droppings that were streaked with blood, and after the beast was gutted of everything but fear and pain, and hunger came knocking at the walls of their stomachs, Ernenek said:

"Somebody is hungry." These were the first words spoken since the chase had started.

Anarvik nodded his agreement.

But never for a moment did they consider turning back.

When day had once more risen tentatively, a gale pouring in from the Glacial Ocean churned up the shallow snow, turning the pallid heaven a murky gray, and for a space they lost sight of their quarry in the blinding blizzard and plunged forth in sudden alarm.

They were led back to the bear by his laments and almost crashed into him, and both men contrived to give him a good poke in the ribs with their horn-tipped spears to let him know he wasn't dreaming. A snarl of rage rose from the huge shadow fumbling upright in the snow swirl and drowned off in the wind, and from there on they stuck so close to their quarry that they could smell it—smell the bitter odor of fear emanating from its pelt.

A few times the bear wheeled about in rage and charged; they then waddled off in a hurry, whining in terror, stumbling and slipping downhill, until the bear sat down on his haunches, wagging his head; and the instant danger was past, the men laughed.

The second night was the worst. The blizzard thickened, forcing them to follow the bear too close at the heels for comfort, and the pangs of hunger hammered with mounting intensity, weakening their knees and increasing the danger of perspiration, while the bear, that seemed to have a hundred lives, kept trekking his furious trek up and down the forbidding slopes.

But when hunger and the raging blizzard had called on the men, their minds had cast an anchor across the ocean to the distant igloo, safe and tender and warm. The intimate amber light; the charnel heap of meat and fish rotting behind the lamp; the quiet sound of hides being scraped and of caribou sinew being needled through boots and garments. . . .

Once they came within a brief march of one of the meat caches which they kept scattered on land and sea.

"Maybe he goes off that way," Anarvik said. "Then one of us can get provisions."

They tried to drive the bear in the right direction, without success. He knew nothing about the cache.

When this hope was blighted it had been four days since they had had sleep and food, and their will had to make up for the dwindling forces of their bodies. And since he thought of giving up the hunt never for an instant entered their minds, survival became irrevocably linked with the capture of the bear, and the lust of the chase was exalted by the animal fear of doom.

They lost notion of time till the blizzard abated, revealing that a new day had risen. They were high up on the bluffs, dominating the frozen sea. In the south the sky was luminous and the silent earth seemed mellow and soft with the promise of spring.

By this time the bear was very sick. In his lumbering fashion he jogged on laboriously, dragging on the ground a head that had grown too heavy. Sometimes slipping and stumbling to their knees the men followed stonily, their laughter gone, the lines of strain marking their greased faces, their eyes red and rimmed with rime. Hunger had departed. Stomachs had gone to sleep. They did not even scoop up handfuls of snow any longer. Their mouths were set, their bellies forgotten, and in their very minds all thoughts and memories had perished. Between skin and flesh, fat had been burning away incessantly, unreplaced, their motion no longer warmed them and they shivered a little, the cold knifing noticeably down their throats with every breath.

And still, could there be anything greater than this—chasing the white bear over the top of the world?

The end came suddenly. All at once the bear gave up. As though he had decided that if he had to die he might as well die with dignity, he squatted on his hindquarters, put his forepaws in his lap, and waited. Round his neck was a pink napkin of frozen froth. He held his ears flat and his teeth bared as in a sneer. No longer did he cry. Only the white clouds of respiration came fast and raspy and his little bloodshot eyes moved helplessly.

The two men closed in slowly, Ernenek from the front and Anarvik from the side, ready to jump if he pawed. The bear grabbed Anarvik's spear and broke it like a straw the instant Ernenek speared him clean through the top of the throat, below the jaw, where the pelt was thinnest.

They barely ate after the kill, their stomachs fast asleep by now, and being too eager to show off their prize intact at home. Ernenek only sucked the blood from the wound, for strength, though it badly scalded his lips, and Anarvik sucked the brain from a little hole made in the nape of the neck. Then they separated the innards before they froze, lugged their kill down the slopes to the sea, cached it in the snow by the shore and happily trudged off.

In a straight line it took them half a turn of the sun to regain their sleds, laughing uproariously on the way and slapping each other's big backs. If the famished dogs had not devoured one another it was only due to the bluntness of their teeth, but they had battled furiously over the skinful of fish on Anarvik's sled and some were licking the frozen gore of their wounds.

The men's appetites had been aroused by the taste of the brain and the blood, and all the way to the cached quarry and all the way back home they chewed on bits of sealskin to stay the pangs of hunger lest they should begin eating their kill.

During their absence a second igloo had mushroomed beside theirs and unknown puppies were playing before the tunnel.

Siksik emerged, followed by Anarvik's brother, Ooloolik, who had at last arrived with his wife Powtee and his two marriageable daughters, Imina and Asiak.

It was a noisy arrival, for seven is a crowd. At first they exchanged greetings with a good deal of ceremony, each trying to outgrin the other while bowing and shaking hands high above their heads; then they rubbed wrinkling noses. This done, Ooloolik's family paid unstinted compliments to the kill with such outcries as, "It is not small!"—while the hunters belittled it with all their power, to show they were capable of quite other deeds: "It is only a cub; nobody wanted to kill it but it insisted on being caught."

Then everybody crawled into Anarvik's igloo.

To the bear's spleen, hung up on a pole, a knife and a sewing needle were added as a present to the dead bear, so that his soul might tell the others of the excellent treatment it had received, making them eager to be killed in their turn.

Then the banquet began.

They ate all night, nibbling at the provisions in the larder while waiting for the bear to thaw. Anarvik skinned it as soon as the pelt had softened. The pelt belonged to him, for he had sighted the bear, but as Ernenek expressed his admiration for it Anarvik humiliated him by letting him have it.

The liver belonged to Ernenek, for he had done the killing, and as soon as it had thawed he presented Anarvik with it in order to get even with him. Anarvik couldn't endure this humiliation and passed the liver on to Powtee who, dutiful wife as she was, handed it to Ooloolik. But Ooloolik gallantly offered it to Siksik, who returned it to Ernenek, who tried it on the two girls, who were too young to accept it.

Nevertheless, they managed to dispose of the liver pretty quickly once Ooloolik, his appetite suddenly getting the better of his manners, took a mighty bite out of it, and everybody plunged in almost simultaneously, with teeth and knives. Ernenek caused long, lusty yells of laughter when in his eagerness he gashed Powtee's cheek with his knife, while she tore at the liver with what teeth were left in her old mouth.

In high spirits they ate their way through all the tender innards, while the tougher cuts were added to the charnel heap to rot and mellow and the tongue was hung up to dry in the smoke of the lamp.

They alternated the sweet bear meat with green, moldly marrow and rank tallow that they washed down with swills of tea, careful not to touch fish while eating meat, lest they should arouse the ire of the spirits. And the little igloo was all and more than the men had pictured during the chase: filled to the roof with feasting people while dogs and puppies crawled between their legs; the circular, blood-stained ice wall mirroring the salmon-colored flame of the wick that floated in the melting blubber; the rich odor of fresh bear meat, heavy and sweet, mingling with the subtle fragrance of decay; the ice resonant with the sound of gnawing and gulping and the cracking of bones, of jest and fat laughter.

The more Anarvik and Ernenek ate, the hungrier they became. Stripped to the waist and radiant with happiness and warmth they kept glutting themselves, spreading round the belt, their faces dripping with blood. When they felt too heavy to lift a hand they lay down on their backs and allowed the women to drop choice morsels into their mouths and pour tea down their throats between one belch and the next.

This was the life!

With eyes afloat in laughter Ernenek looked from one of Ooloolik's daughters to the other as they hovered over him with tidbits and smiles. These were women who know how a man should be treated, and they certainly knew also how to scrape hides and sew boots and do other little things for him. But which one to choose he couldn't decide. Imina was prettier, but Asiak's laughter was warmer.

Ernenek felt completely contented, and at peace with the world. When he was unable to swallow, he closed eyes and mouth and the hubbub around him washed away. He would give the food time to settle and then be ready for more. He stretched out his hand to make sure that Anarvik was at his side.

There he was, already snoring like a litter of walruses.

It dimly occurred to Ernenek there was something he wanted to ask him. That's what he had set out for, a few turns of the sun ago. But in vain did he strain his memory.

The thought was dead, and buried, and forgotten.

Child Care in China

BRUCE DOLLAR

Societies differ as to how they characteristically raise (socialize) their children. The following selection describes some of the cultural values, beliefs, and institutions of modern China which directly affect the development of its children and the roles of other family members. The institutionalized child care programs in China will be of particular interest to those concerned with the growing use of day care centers in the United States.

The old art of China watching is giving way to China witnessing, and one quality of the new China that seems inevitably to impress all recent visitors is the extraordinary vibrancy of Chinese children, from the very youngest to the adolescents, who already tower so noticeably over their grandparents. During my own recent trip within China, my companions and I saw for ourselves the exuberant self-confidence that seems to infuse all Chinese kids, whether they are performing for strangers, participating in a classroom exercise, or playing by themselves.

"Ours is a socialist society; everything is done according to plan." This pronouncement, with which our various Chinese hosts so frequently prefaced their answers to our questions, provides a starting point for understanding how this spirit of exuberance has been achieved. Although Chinese society is largely decentralized to encourage local self-sufficiency and diversification, the whole is knit together by an administrative structure that is more or less uniform from city to city and, somewhat less, from commune (or network of villages) to commune. It is a framework that provides an efficient system of communication and has helped produce a remarkable social cohesion based on commonly held goals and values—which themselves are informed by the teachings of Mao Tse-tung.

The consensus is particularly apparent with respect to the care and training of the young. This is hardly surprising when one considers the enormous stock the Chinese place in producing what they call "revolutionary successors," an apt phrase in a country where revolutionary consciousness has been maintained largely through vivid comparisons with the "bitter past," and where the problem of continuing the revolution into succeeding generations is paramount.

Thus, throughout our visit we constantly encountered—with amazing consistency at various points along a 2,500-mile itinerary—several major ideas about child rearing in the numerous conversations we had with people in child-related institutions: families, nurseries, kindergartens, and schools. These themes—especially the subordination of personal to social needs, respect for productive labor, altruism, cooperation, and the integration of physical with intellectual labor—together describe the kind of citizen China hopes to produce. The techniques employed to achieve these values are in practice virtually from infancy.

During the years before primary school, which begins at the age of seven, a series of public child care facilities is available to parents who wish to use them. In the cities, where patterns are more uniform, a mother's maternity leave (paid) usually terminates 56 days after birth. Since breast-feeding is the rule in China, the mother may then place her child in the nursing room at her place of work. Most work institutions—factories, hospitals, and government offices, for example—provide this facility for their employees. In a typical arrangement the mother has two half hour breaks, plus, lunch, to visit and nurse her baby during the work day. After work the baby returns home with the mother.

Nursing rooms provide care for infants up to one and a half years old; then they may be sent to one of the various kinds of nurseries. Some of these are attached to the work place or located in the home neighborhood; they may be open only during the work day, or they may be "live-in" nurseries, where children stay overnight and go home on weekends. Kindergartens, usually located in the residential areas, generally care for children from three and a half to seven years old and may also be either part-time or full-time.

In a country in which over 90 per cent of all women of working age do work, it might be expected that a similar percentage of children would therefore receive some kind of institutional care. But there are options. The most common is to leave the child in the care of grandparents, who frequently live with the family. Another alternative is to make arrangements with a friend or neighbor. Estimates vary from place to place, but in most cities no more than half the children of nursery school age are in attendance. For kindergarten the figures are higher, especially in the cities, where attendance is over 80 per cent.

Since child care is decentralized, different localities often make their own arrangements, which may not conform to the usual patterns. This is particularly true of rural areas, where a lack of resources and the persistence of custom probably account for a lower incidence of public child care facilities One small village we visited, the Sha Shih Yu Brigade in northeast China, had no permanent facility; only during harvest time, when all hands were needed in the fields, was there organized care for small children. A child care center located in a coal-mining area near Tangshan, on the other hand served 314 children divided into at least five separate age groups, from 56 days to six years old.

How do these institutions work to socialize the children under their care? And what are they like for the kids? In spite of the diversity in organizational structure, the remarkable similarity from place to place, both in the values espoused and the methods used to inculcate them, seems to suppot a numbe of generalizations.

One quality that is sure to strike an American observer is the preponderance and the style of group activities. A common example is the "cultural performance," usually presented for visitors. Whether they are songs from a revolutionary opera, dances to celebrate a harvest, or a program of folk melodies played on traditional Chinese instruments, these performances are always presented by groups, and it is impossible to pick out a "star."

Although there were exceptions, many early child care facilities we visited seemed rather poorly supplied with the variety of toys and materials that the conventional wisdom in the United States says should be on hand to enrich and enliven a child's environment. Although this may have been due to a simple inability to pay for more equipment, the teachers we spoke to did not seem to consider it a shortcoming. Perhaps this is because Chinese children are generally expected to rely on each other for stimulation—at any rate, this seems to be the effect. The situation provides an interesting contrast to that in the United States, where the highly desired "rich environment" often means that kids interact with inanimate materials more than they do with other people.

The small children we saw were not without playthings, however. There was always at least one toy for each child—typically a rubber or plastic doll of a worker, a peasant, or a soldier. Rocking horses were also common, as were military toys and playground equipment that could accommodate many children. But in general the emphasis was on group play. One recent American visitor to a Chinese nursery school reports noticing that the blocks seemed awfully heavy for small children. "Exactly!" beamed the teachers. "That fosters mutual help."

Chinese teachers actively encourage such group behavior as cooperation, sharing, and altruism. "We praise a child when he shows concern for others' interests," said one kindergarten teacher. "For example, at meal time teachers give out bowls and chop sticks. If a youngster gets a nicer bowl and gives it to someone else, we praise him for it. Or when the children are asked to select a toy and a child gives the best one to a classmate, we praise that, too."

Even in a competitive situation, this teacher said, helping another is more important than winning. "When the children run in a relay race, sometimes one will fall down, especially if he's small. If another child stops to help him get up or to see if he's all right, even though his own team might fall behind, we encourage this." The approach contrasts markedly with methods used in the Soviet Union, another country that stresses the collective in its child-rearing practices. There, competition is discouraged between individuals but promoted between groups. Each child is made aware of his importance within his group—say, a row in his classroom—and then competes fiercely for the rewards of a group victory. The Chinese seem genuinely to eschew even this form of competition in favor of straightforward mutual help and cooperation.

But how do teachers deal with improper behavior and matters of discipline? Here is how the question was answered in a conversation with three staff members of a full-time kindergarten in Peking:

Q: What kinds of behavior do you discourage in the children?

A: We criticize those who take toys or other things from others. Or if children beat each other—we criticize that.

Q: Exactly how do you handle such a situation—say, two kids fighting?

A: First, the teacher must understand the reason for the fight. For instance, one might have taken a toy from the other, and the second child hit him. In that case, the teacher will criticize both. This criticism is carried out alone, unless it took place in the class; in that case it will be done in front of the class so that all the children will understand what was wrong. Criticism is to make children understand what was wrong and why.

Q: What kind of punishment do you use?

A: There is no punishment.

Q: Well, what if a child were really intractable? Would you use some mild sanction, such as depriving him of some free play time on the playground?

A: (At this point all three women broke into smiles at our incredulity. Waving their hands back and forth to underscore their words, they said): No, no, nothing like that. We believe in persuasion.

Q: Do other children ever participate in criticism?

A: Generally, no. Unless a third child saw what happened—then he'll be asked to tell.

Q: Let's say the incident was unobserved by any third party and the two kids involved give conflicting versions of what happened. Then how does the teacher act?

A: If the teacher finds a contradiction when both tell what happened, she will try to educate the children. She will note that everyone can make a mistake, including teachers. The mistake that led to the fight is not important, she will say, but telling the truth is very important. At this point the children will probably tell the truth.

This sounded like fine theory, but it provoked some skepticism among those of us who had been teachers. What about teachers who do not have the patience to use such positive techniques? we asked. How do you deal with teachers who don't observe the school's policy? The reply: "We all—teachers and leadership—have the same goal: to cultivate revolutionary successors. So we all work together and help each other. We study our profession together. We have regular criticism and self-criticism sessions, and sometimes we help each other on specific problems."

If we had not already seen many teachers in action here and elsewhere on our trip, we might have been dissatisfied with this answer. But we were constantly struck by the teachers' apparent love for their work in all the early child care institutions we visited. These women, we learned (there were no men), were chosen for their jobs after having shown a particular interest in children, and "sensitivity and love for children" were the criteria most often cited for their recruitment. Credentials were secondary. Since the Cultural Revolution, the amount of training teachers receive has ranged all the way from university graduation to short-term training classes and "learning through practice."

Three of us in the group who were especially interested in child rearing and education often asked to see child care centers and schools under normal operating conditions. Our guides accommodated these requests by arranging for us to stay behind after the formal tour or make a low-key visit to a kindergarten, say, without the rest of the group. Some of our most revealing insights occurred during our observation of everyday free playground activities.

One afternoon, for example, at the child care center serving workers of the Fan Ga Chong coal mine area near Tangshan, I spent nearly an hour outside among the four-and-a-half-to-six-year-olds and their teachers, or "nurses." Here was the one place where I saw what might be called a disruptive child—a little boy who, in the United States, would probably have been labeled hyperkinetic and put on Ritalin. While the other 50 or so children busied themselves with various games—rope jumping, drop the handkerchief, tricycle riding, playing with toys and each other—this boy ran constantly from place to place, trying to be in on everything at once and occasionally interfering with someone else's fun. The nurses, who themselves were taking part in the games, were obviously aware of the boy's actions, but they made no fuss over him. Instead, each time he ran by a nurse, she would reach out, place her hand on the back of his head, and gently guide him away from trouble or toward an activity he might like—usually with a few soothing words. Soon he was off again, and once or twice it was necessary to intervene when he began picking on another child. But always the adults acted cheerfully and patiently, and the boy never became a center of attention. His actions were the closest thing to aggressive or disruptive behavior among children that I saw on the entire trip.

After visiting several classrooms at the Pei Hai Kindergarten, a full-time kindergarten located in a park in Peking, I spent an even longer time on the playground watching free play. Once again I was struck by the way teachers enthusiastically joined in. The children, well over a hundred of them, had formed into a variety of play groups. Some played on slides, a merry-go-round, monkey bars, and swings. Some were organized into class-sized groups for games. Others were in smaller groups, jumping rope or kicking a ball around. There were kids in pairs and kids alone. One gleeful little boy, holding aloft a leafy twig, ran, danced, and twirled with it till he fell down from dizziness. And ranging over the whole playground, sweeping past and through everyone else's games, was a whooping pack of boys chasing a soccer ball, a laughing teacher in the lead.

In one group that especially caught my eye, seven or eight girls were jumping rope, taking turns at the ends of a pink plastic rope and lining up to jump one by one. No teacher was with them. They were very absorbed and used chants and songs to accompany each jumper. Several times while I watched, a minor controversy of some kind would erupt and everything would come to a halt. Maybe it concerned whose turn was next on the rope or how many times one had jumped before missing. Whatever it was, the whole group would come together and heatedly debate their points. With no single girl taking charge, they would quickly work out a settlement that seemed to satisfy everyone and then resume their jumping with all the gusto of before. These little girls were good jumpers, incidentally. So good that after a while they attracted an audience: six little boys found chairs, lined them up to form a small gallery, and proceeded to join in the jumping chants, applauding for each jumper. Great fun for all, highly organized, and by all indications spontaneous and undirected by adults.

In the United States the growing demand for facilities for the care of infants and preschool children has provoked a chorus of urgent questions: Doesn't a baby need a single individual to relate to and identify with as mother? How can a mother be sure that those to whom she entrusts her child will teach the same values she holds? Isn't it the mother's natural role to care for her own children? What is the effect of institutionalized child care on the family?

Obviously, the answers the Chinese have found to these questions are not directly applicable in this country. Yet the insights they provide can be instructive as we seek our own solutions.

There is a strong likelihood that the average child in China will undergo "multiple mothering" of some kind. Even if the mother does not choose to leave her infant in the nursing room where she works, chances are the child will wind up in the care of a neighbor or the grandmother. Offsetting this diversity of "mothers," however, is the near-uniform consensus of values and methods of child rearing I have described. This consistency seems to go a long way toward providing young children with the kind of security we in the United States might normally associate only with single mothering.

Another aspect of multiple or "shared" mothering, as Ruth Sidel, author of the excellent recent book *Women & Child Care in China*, points out, "is that infants can thrive physically and emotionally if the mother-surrogates are constant, warm, and giving. Babies in China are not subjected to serial mothering; we were repeatedly told that aunties (i.e., nurses) and teachers rarely leave their jobs. And they are warm and loving with the children. The children show none of the lethargy or other intellectual, emotional, or physical problems of institutionalized children. Quite the opposite!"

"Everything is planned," and the position of mothers in China is the consequence of a society-wide effort to provide for the economic liberation of women. In keeping with Mao Tse-tung's edict calling for "genuine equality between the sexes," a broad series of programs, including birth control information and prenatal care with maternity leave, in addition to the system of child care facilities, is underway to assure the full participation of women in "building socialism." The objects of unspeakable oppression in prerevolutionary society, Chinese women today have been thoroughly integrated into the labor force, both in factory and commune. And a growing number of them are entering professions—for example, 50 per cent of the medical students are now women.

Despite the enormous progress, even the Chinese will concede that full parity with men is not yet a reality. Top governmental, military, and management posts continue to be mostly male preserves. However, women do wield considerable political and administrative power at the local level, where they often run the smallest governmental units, the neighborhood revolutionary committees.

But the key to liberation is still economic independence, which depends on the availability of work. Since 1971 a new source of work for women has appeared: the so-called housewives' factories. These have been organized locally by women who live in housing areas like the Kung Kiang Workers' Residential Area in Shanghai, and whose husbands work in the various nearby factories. As they described it to us, the housewives were looking for ways in which they could contribute productively to the revolution without having to leave the residential area. So they set up their own light industries in workshops near their homes, and by working full- or part-time were able to produce needed commodities, such as flashlight bulbs or men's trousers, while earning extra money for themselves. The entire operation in each case was staffed and run by women.

Since nearly all working-age women in China today work and are no longer economically dependent on their husbands or families, one might well wonder about the effects of these conditions on the family.

By all available evidence the family is thriving in China, and the individual household continues to be the basic social unit. A featured item in every home we visited, as ubiquitous as a portrait of Chairman Mao, was a display of a great many photographs of family members, usually pressed under a piece of glass on top of a bureau or framed on the wall. Our host or hostess would invariably point this out with pride. Signs of active and full participation in family life were everywhere, and all generations were included. A man out with his children is a common sight, as is a child with a grandmother or grandfather.

Parents are obviously revered by children, and so are grandparents. In fact, the complete absence of a "generation gap" is a striking phenomenon to an American. Not only are grandparents well integrated into family life, but old people who have no family or who are disabled live in well-tended "respect for aged" homes and are given important functions that serve the neighborhood.

Far from undermining the family structure, we were repeatedly told, jobs for women and day care for children have made home life easier, having eliminated many former sources of friction and frustration. A major factor here is undoubtedly the mass commitment to working for the betterment of China. Personal gratification seems to derive from each individual's knowledge that he or she makes an important contribution, no matter how small, to the national effort and that the benefits of this contribution, and others like it, will be distributed to all.

THREE

Socialization and Total Institutions

Show me the prison,
Show me the jail,
Show me the prisoner
Whose life has gone stale.
And I'll show you a young man
With so many reasons why
There but for fortune
Go you or I.

THE CATERPILLAR looked at Alice and asked, "Who . . . Are . . . You?" A related and important question is, How did you become what you are? How did you develop your values, attitudes, and beliefs (including your attitudes and beliefs about yourself)? And how does all this affect your behavior? What would you be like today if at an early age you had been adopted and raised by a peasant family in Communist China?

What is socialization? In the previous section we stated that human nature is shaped by culture. After a new individual is born into a society he is indoctrinated or programmed into the ways and routines of that society. Socialization is the process by which the individual internalizes or absorbs his culture and becomes a functioning member of his society. This process can be analyzed from two perspectives: the societal, and the personal. First, on the societal level, any ongoing society must transmit its culture to new generations if it is to survive. The infant generations are in a sense like "barbarians at the gate" who do not share in the culture of the larger society, and societies depend for their cohesiveness on just such a system of shared meanings. For example, human society as we know it would be impossible if its members could not communicate through the use of a shared language. The process of socialization, then, helps ensure that the potentially disruptive infant is molded into a functioning member of his society. This fact leaves open the question of how much conformity is actually necessary or desirable. Second, on the personal level, the qualities that we associate with being human are not given in the biological inheritance of the infant. Cases of infants locked in rooms for years with minimal social contact dramatically and tragically document this point. We *become* human and realize our potential only through the socialization process. Without this process the "prehuman" infant remains just that, unable to talk, relate to others, or express such emotions as love.

Both conformity and diversity are inherent aspects of every social system. Although the individual is inevitably unique in many ways, he always shares certain cultural patterns with the other members of his society. How does a society maintain a given level of conformity? One way is through socialization, the indoctrination from infancy into the ways of the society. The norms or rules of the society become embedded in the individual's personality structure, and into his conscience or superego. Societal taboos become personal taboos and the individual experiences guilt or revulsion if he breaks with them. This has been called internal social control. Most of us would feel varying amounts of guilt if we were to cheat on an exam, steal, or kill another individual because of careless driving. We also feel revulsion at the thought of eating roast dog. But there is another broad category of control: external social control. You may not feel guilty about going 70 miles per hour in a 55-mile-per-hour-zone. However, you may not want to drive much above the speed limit because you would rather not pay the price of a traffic ticket. Blacks often played the submissive "Uncle Tom" role in this society only because their survival depended upon it. If you are a female, you may not feel guilty about smoking a cigar in the cafeteria, but the chances are good that you will abstain. Even if there was no rule against smoking cigars in the cafeteria and even if you were a regular cigar smoker at home, you would probably take into consideration what others around you might think of your behavior. We all need approval, though some need more than others. We may even laugh with the rest at a joke which degrades a particular ethnic group, rather than voice our real feelings, even though we feel our behavior is wrong. The disapproval of others and the threat of possible expulsion from the group are powerful mechanisms of control. External social control can range, then, from flattery to large amounts of money, power, or prestige (positive sanctions), and from mild disapproval to the ultimate penalties of expulsion from the group and death (negative sanctions).

In understanding how we internalize the values and beliefs of our society and how sanctions are applied, the concept of role is of prime importance. A role is a group-shared set of expectations and rules regarding a particular position (female, husband, policeman, minister) in a society. Roles function to guide the individual's actions in certain situations. This occurs through internal social control when the individual has internalized some of the norms included in the role (a wife may feel that it is wrong to commit adultery) and through external social control when rewards or punishments influence the individual's behavior (a boy of a certain age learns that he will be ridiculed by his parents and peers if he cries). For example, we expect different kinds of behavior from males and females, children and adults, corporation presidents and convicts, and we expect "normal" people to behave differently from those who are "mentally ill." We all learn to play various roles, and they explain many of our attitudes and behaviors. The cartoon which begins this section portrays some of the roles an individual may play in the course of his lifetime. We gain our very sense of identity in terms of the roles we play. Since societies tend to define some positions in relatively negative ways and others in relatively positive ways, role playing can have a profound effect on an individual's self-concept. Which role is likely to produce more self-esteem, that of a corporation president or that of a convict, that of a bisexual or that of a known homosexual? The women's liberation movement is basically trying to change the traditional roles of woman, wife, and mother because they feel that these definitions (they should be submissive, they should stay at home, they are emotionally weak, they think illogically and therefore don't make good business people, etc.) have had negative effects on women in terms of living a self-actualizing life. In the same vein, blacks grew tired of riding in the back of the bus. Homosexuals are involved in a similar battle to change the way they are regarded and treated by the majority. And, of course, these roles can and will change. Which is the more rational approach toward homosexuals: (1) to consider them sick, immoral perverts, or (2) to give them a position of prestige and consider them healthy, valuable, contributing members of society as did the Plains Indians? The "ultra-masculine" role of men in Plains Indian societies was difficult for some individuals to play, and so many of these societies provided a safety-valve role. Individuals who would have otherwise been judged complete failures were able as "berdaches" to wear the clothing of women, do women's work, and live in a homosexual relationship with another man. And in the process they were thought of, and allowed to think of themselves, as worthy and valuable individuals. If, as Charles Cooley believed, our developing self-image is a process of seeing ourselves as we think others see us, then the issue is of great importance to those labeled in negative ways.

Socialization is a lifelong process, and the effect of roles and the expectations of others on an individual are particularly powerful in total institutions. These are organizations such as prisons, mental hospitals, concentration camps, and monasteries which care for a large number of people who are shut off from the outside world. The total institution thus has almost complete control over its "inmates." Entering a total institution means breaking off one's former social relationships and way of life and being put into a role of submission to those "in charge." Important attitude and self-concept changes can occur in this kind of situation (it is part of one approach to "brainwashing"). An individual may enter a mental hospital convinced that he is not mentally ill (with or without good reason), but after being put into a social situation where the staff and many of the patients define him as mentally ill, he may come to accept their definition. And, after he is released, those in the larger society who are aware of his previous hospitalization may continue this definition of the situation, thereby stigmatizing the individual and making his adaptation to society difficult. Because of these kinds of considerations some sociologists believe that mental illness is partially the result of mental hospitalization. The same kind of analysis can be applied to prisons. When an individual enters a prison his previous relationships are severed and a new set of relationships develop. Is the new social system and subculture into which the individual steps in our prison system conducive to changing him so that he will not commit further crimes? That the change may occur in the opposite direction is suggested by the fact that the longer a criminal remains in prison, the more crimes he is likely to commit after his release. Obviously, there are also a number of ethical questions which arise concerning the prison and mental hospital as agencies of socialization (or resocialization). Are the civil rights of prisoners and mental patients protected? Which kinds of procedures for changing individuals should and should not be used (electroshock, isolation cells)? Should individuals in these institutions be used as scientific guinea pigs in the testing of, for example, new drugs?

To return to the larger question of conformity, the ability to transcend one's culture, to be detached, critical, skeptical, and thoughtful, would seem to be an essential trait of the ideal citizen of a thriving democracy. This ability has been called autonomy. It can be contrasted with the extreme ethnocentrism of the "oversocialized" individual, and the anxiety-motivated conformity of the "other-directed" individual. The "oversocialized" individual uncritically accepts the values, beliefs, and customs of his society without a second thought (he may be a superpatriot), while the "other-directed" individual does not want to be different for fear of losing the approval and support of others. The autonomous individual to some degree transcends the ties of blood and soil. Every society tends to reward conformity and to discourage deviation from the accepted cultural patterns. The autonomous individual must be somewhat insensitive to this pressure and be willing to explore his social milieu in the stance of a detached observer. —D. R.

Selected References

(All are available in paperback editions.)

Aronson, Elliot. *The Social Animal.* San Francisco: W. H. Freeman and Company, Publishers, 1972.

Fromm, Erich. *Escape From Freedom.* New York: Holt, Rinehart and Winston, Inc., 1941.

Goffman, Erving. *Asylums.* Garden City. N.Y.: Doubleday & Company, Inc., 1961.

Kozol, Jonathan. *Death at an Early Age.* New York: Bantam Books, 1968.

Marcuse, Herbert. *One Dimensional Man.* Boston: Beacon Press, 1964.

Society in Man

PETER L. BERGER

Who are you? How did you become what you are? How did you develop your attitudes toward yourself and your beliefs about the world? What we become as individuals depends more than most of us realize upon the social situation in which we operate. In the following article, Peter Berger explains how an individual's behavior is guided by social roles, how his identity is socially bestowed and sustained, and how his world view is socially determined.

. . . Society can exist by virtue of the fact that most of the time most people's definitions of the most important situations at least coincide approximately. The motives of the publisher and the writer of these lines may be rather different, but the ways the two define the situation in which this book is being produced are sufficiently similar for the joint venture to be possible. In similar fashion there may be quite divergent interests present in a classroom of students, some of them having little connection with the educational activity that is supposedly going on, but in most cases these interests (say, that one student came to study the subject being taught, while another simply registers for every course taken by a certain redhead he is pursuing) can coexist in the situation without destroying it. In other words, there is a certain amount of leeway in the extent to which response must meet expectation for a situation to remain sociologically viable. Of course, if the definitions of the situation are too widely discrepant, some form of social conflict or disorganization will inevitably result—say, if some students interpret the classroom meeting as a party, or if an author has no intention of producing a book but is using his contract with one publisher to put pressure on another.

While an average individual meets up with very different expectations in different areas of his life in society, the situations that produce these expectations fall into certain clusters. A student may take two courses from two different professors in two different departments, with considerable variations in the expectations met with in the two situations (say, as between formality or informality in the relations between professor and students). Nevertheless, the situations will be sufficiently similar to each other and to other classroom situations previously experienced to enable the student to carry into both situations essentially the same overall response. In other words, in both cases, with but a few modifications, he will be able to *play the role* of student. A

"Society in Man" from *Invitation to Sociology*, copyright © 1963 by Peter L. Berger. Reprinted by permission of Doubleday & Co., Inc.

role, then, may be defined as a typified response to a typified expectation. Society has predefined the fundamental typology. To use the language of the theater, from which the concept of role is derived, we can say that society provides the script for all the *dramatis personae*. The individual actors, therefore, need but slip into the roles already assigned to them before the curtain goes up. As long as they play their roles as provided for in this script, the social play can proceed as planned.

The role provides the pattern according to which the individual is to act in the particular situation. Roles, in society as in the theater, will vary in the exactness with which they lay down instructions for the actor. Taking occupational roles for an instance, a fairly minimal pattern goes into the role of garbage collector, while physicians or clergymen or officers have to acquire all kinds of distinctive mannerisms, speech and motor habits, such as military bearing, sanctimonious diction or bedside cheer. It would, however, be missing an essential aspect of the role if one regarded it merely as a regulatory pattern for externally visible actions. One feels more ardent by kissing, more humble by kneeling and more angry by shaking one's fist. That is, the kiss not only expresses ardor but manufactures it. Roles carry with them both certain actions and the emotions and attitudes that belong to these actions. The professor putting on an act that pretends to wisdom comes to feel wise. The preacher finds himself believing what he preaches. The soldier discovers martial stirrings in his breast as he puts on his uniform. In each case, while the emotion or attitude may have been present before the role was taken on, the latter inevitably strengthens what was there before. In many instances there is every reason to suppose that nothing at all anteceded the playing of the role in the actor's consciousness. In other words, one becomes wise by being appointed a professor, believing by engaging in activities that presuppose belief, and ready for battle by marching in formation.

Let us take an example. A man recently commissioned as an officer, especially if he came up through the ranks, will at first be at least slightly embarrassed by the salutes he now receives from the enlisted men he meets on his way. Probably he will respond to them in a friendly, almost apologetic manner. The new insignia on his uniform are at that point still something that he has merely put on, almost like a disguise. Indeed, the new officer may even tell himself and others that underneath he is still the same person, that he simply has new responsibilities (among which, *en passant*, is the duty to accept the salutes of enlisted men). This attitude is not likely to last very long. In order to carry out his new role of officer, our man must maintain a certain bearing. This bearing has quite definite implications. Despite all the double-talk in this area that is customary in so-called democratic armies, such as the American one, one of the fundamental implications is that an officer is a superior somebody, entitled to obedience and respect on the basis of this superiority. Every military salute given by an inferior in rank is an act of obeisance, received as a matter of course by the one who returns it. Thus, with every salute given and accepted (along, of course, with a hundred other ceremonial acts that enhance his new status) our man is fortified in his new bearing—and in its, as it were, ontological presuppositions. He not only acts like an officer, he feels like one. Gone are the embarrassment, the apologetic attitude, the I'm-just-another-guy-really grin. If on some occasion an enlisted man should fail to salute with the appropriate amount of enthusiasm or even commit the unthinkable act of failing to salute at all, our officer is not merely going to punish a violation of military regulations. He will be driven with every fiber of his being to redress an offence against the appointed order of his cosmos.

It is important to stress in this illustration that only very rarely is such a a process deliberate or based on reflection. Our man has not sat down and figured out all the things that ought to go into his new role, including the things that he ought to feel and believe. The strength of the process comes precisely from its unconscious, unreflecting character. He has become an officer almost as effortlessly as he grew into a person with blue eyes, brown hair and a height of six feet. Nor would it be correct to say that our man must be rather stupid and quite an exception among his comrades. On the contrary, the exception is the man who reflects on his roles and his role changes (a type, by the way, who would probably make a poor officer). Even very intelligent people, when faced with doubt about their roles in society, will involve themselves even more in the doubted activity rather than withdraw into reflection. The theologian who doubts his faith will pray more and increase his church attendance, the businessman beset by qualms about his rat-race activities starts going to the office on Sundays too, and the terrorist who suffers from nightmares volunteers for nocturnal executions. And, of course, they are perfectly correct in this course of action. Each role has its inner discipline, what Catholic monastics would call its "formation." The role forms, shapes, patterns both action and actor. It is very difficult to pretend in this world. Normally, one becomes what one plays at.

Every role in society has attached to it a certain identity. As we have seen, some of these identities are trivial and temporary ones, as in some occupations that demand little modification in the being of their practitioners. It is not difficult to change from garbage collector to night watchman. It is considerably more difficult to change from clergyman to officer. It is very, very difficult to change from Negro to white. And it is almost impossible to change from man to woman. These differences in the ease of role changing ought not to blind us to the fact that even identities that we consider to be our essential selves have been socially assigned. Just as there are racial roles to be acquired and identified with, so there are sexual roles. To say "I am a man" is just as much a proclamation of role as to say "I am a colonel in the U.S. Army." We are well aware of the fact that one is born a male, while not even the most humorless martinet imagines himself to have been born with a golden eagle sitting on his umbilical cord. But to be biologically male is a far cry from the specific, socially defined (and, of course, socially relative) role that goes with the statement "I am a man." A male child does not have to learn to have an erection. But he must learn to be aggressive, to have ambitions, to compete with others, and to be suspicious of too much gentleness in himself. The male role in our society, however, requires all these things that one must learn, as does a male identity. To have an erection is not enough—if it were, regiments of psychotherapists would be out of work.

This significance of role theory could be summarized by saying that, in a sociological perspective, identity is socially bestowed, socially sustained and socially transformed. The example of the man in process of becoming an officer may suffice to illustrate the way in which identities are bestowed in adult life. However, even roles that are much more fundamentally part of what psychologists would call our personality than those associated with a particular adult activity are bestowed in very similar manner through a social process. This has been demonstrated over and over again in studies of so-called socialization—the process by which a child learns to be a participant member of society.

Probably the most penetrating theoretical account of this process is the one given by Mead, in which the genesis of the self is interpreted as being one and the same even as the discovery of society. The child finds out who he is as he learns what society is. He learns to play roles properly belonging to him by learning, as Mead puts it, "to take the role of the other"—which, incidentally, is the crucial sociopsychological function of play, in which children masquerade with a variety of social roles and in doing so discover the significance of those being assigned to them. All this learning occurs, and can only occur, in interaction with other human beings, be it the parents or whoever else raises the child. The child first takes on roles *vis-à-vis* what Mead calls his "significant others," that is, those persons who deal with him intimately and whose attitudes are decisive for the formation of his conception of himself. Later, the child learns that the roles he plays are not only relevant to this intimate circle, but relate to the expectations directed toward him by society at large. This higher level of abstraction in the social response Mead calls the discovery of the "generalized other." That is, not only the child's mother expects him to be good, clean and truthful, society in general does so as well. Only when this general conception of society emerges is the child capable of forming a clear conception of himself. "Self" and "society," in the child's experience, are the two sides of the same coin.

In other words, identity is not something "given," but is bestowed in acts of social recognition. We become that as which we are addressed. The same idea is expressed in Cooley's well-known description of the self as a reflection in a looking glass. This does not mean, of course, that there are not certain characteristics an individual is born with, that are carried by his genetic heritage regardless of the social environment in which the latter will have to unfold itself. Our knowledge of man's biology does not as yet allow us a very clear picture of the extent to which this may be true. We do know, however, that the room for social formation within those genetic limits is very large indeed. Even with the biological questions left largely unsettled, we can say that to be human is to be recognized as human, just as to be a certain kind of man is to be recognized as such. The child deprived of human affection and attention becomes dehumanized. The child who is given respect comes to respect himself. A little boy considered to be a *schlemiel* becomes one, just as a grown-up treated as an awe-inspiring younger god of war begins to think of himself and act as is appropriate to such a figure—and, indeed, merges his identity with the one he is presented with in these expectations.

Identities are socially bestowed. They must also be socially sustained, and fairly steadily so. One cannot be human all by oneself and, apparently, one cannot hold on to any particular identity all by oneself. The self-image of the officer as an officer can be maintained only in a social context in which others are willing to recognize him in this identity. If this recognition is suddenly withdrawn, it usually does not take very long before the self-image collapses.

Cases of radical withdrawal of recognition by society can tell us much about the social character of identity. For example, a man turned overnight from a free citizen into a convict finds himself subjected at once to a massive assault on his previous conception of himself. He may try desperately to hold on to the latter, but in the absence of others in his immediate environment confirming his old identity he will find it almost impossible to maintain it within his own consciousness. With frightening speed he will discover that he is acting as a convict is supposed to, and feeling all the things that a convict is expected to feel. It would be a misleading perspective on this process to look upon it simply as one of the disintegration of personality. A more accurate way of seeing the phenomenon is as a reintegration of personality, no different in its sociopsychological dynamics from the process in which the old identity was integrated. It used to be that our man was treated by all the important people around him as responsible, dignified, considerate and aesthetically fastidious. Consequently he was able to be all these things. Now the walls of the prison separate him from those whose recognition sustained him in the exhibition of these traits. Instead he is now surrounded by people who treat him as irresponsible, swinish in behavior, only out for his own interests and careless of his appearance unless forced to take care by constant supervision. The new expectations are typified in the convict role that responds to them just as the old ones were integrated into a different pattern of conduct. In both cases, identity comes with conduct and conduct occurs in response to a specific social situation.

Extreme cases in which an individual is radically stripped of his old identity simply illustrate more sharply processes that occur in ordinary life. We live our everyday lives within a complex web of recognitions and nonrecognitions. We work better when we are given encouragement by our superiors. We find it hard to be anything but clumsy in a gathering where we know people have an image of us as awkward. We become wits when people expect us to be funny, and interesting characters when we know that such a reputation has preceded us. Intelligence, humor, manual skills, religious devotion and even sexual potency respond with equal alacrity to the expectations of others. This makes understandable the previously mentioned process by which individuals choose their associates in such a way that the latter sustain their self-interpretations. To put this succinctly, every act of social affiliation entails a choice of identity. Conversely every identity requires specific social affiliations for its survival. Birds of the same feather flock together not as a luxury but out of necessity. The intellectual becomes a slob after he is kidnapped by the army. The theological student progressively loses his sense of humor as he approaches ordination. The worker who breaks all norms finds that he breaks even more after he has been given a medal by management. The young man with anxieties about his virility becomes hell-on-wheels in bed when he finds a girl who sees him as an avatar of Don Giovanni. . . .

Such sociological perspective on the character of identity gives us a deeper understanding of the human meaning of prejudice. As a result, we obtain the chilling perception that the prejudging not only concerns the victim's external fate at the hands of his oppressors, but also his consciousness as it is shaped by their expectations. The most terrible thing that prejudice can do to a human being is to make him tend to become what the prejudiced image of him says that he is. The Jew in an anti-Semitic milieu must struggle hard not to become more and more like the anti-Semitic stereotype, as must the Negro in a racist situation. Significantly, this struggle will only have a chance of success when the individual is protected from succumbing to the prejudiced program for his personality by what we could call the counterrecognition of those within his immediate community. The Gentile world might recognize him as but another despicable Jew of no consequence, and treat him accordingly, but this nonrecognition of his worth may be balanced by the counterrecogniton of him within the Jewish community itself as, say, the greatest Talmudic scholar in Latvia.

In view of the sociopsychological dynamics of this deadly game of recognitions, it should not surprise us that the problem of "Jewish identity" arose only among modern Western Jews when assimilation into the surrounding Gentile society had begun to weaken the power of the Jewish community itself to bestow alternate identities on its members as against the identities assigned to them by anti-Semitism. As an individual is forced to gaze at himself in a mirror so constructed as to let him see a leering monster, he must frantically search for other men with other mirrors, unless he is to forget that he ever had another face. To put this a little differently, human dignity is a matter of social permission.

The same relationship between society and identity can be seen in cases where, for one reason or another, an individual's identity is drastically changed. The transformation of identity, just as its genesis and its maintenance, is a social process. We have already indicated the way in which any reinterpretation of the past, any "alternation" from one self-image to another, requires the presence of a group that conspires to bring about the metamorphosis. What anthropologists call a rite of passage involves the repudiation of an old identity (say, that of being a child) and the initiation into a new one (such as that of adult). Modern societies have milder rites of passage, as in the institution of the engagement, by which the individual is gently led by a general conspiracy of all concerned over the threshold between bachelor freedom and the captivity of marriage. If it were not for this institution, many more would panic at the last moment before the enormity of what they are about to undertake. . . .

The same process occurs whenever an entire group of individuals is to be "broken" and made to accept a new definition of themselves. It happens in basic training for draftees in the army; much more intensively in the training of personnel for a permanent career in the army, as at military academies. It happens in the indoctrination and "formation" programs of cadres for totalitarian organizations, such as the Nazi SS or the Communist Party elite. It has happened for many centuries in monastic novitiates. It has recently been applied to the point of scientific precision in the "brain-washing" techniques employed against prisoners of totalitarian secret-police organizations. The violence of such procedures, as compared with the more routine initiations of society, is to be explained sociologically in terms of the radical degree of transformation of identity that is sought and the functional necessity in these cases that commitment to the transformed identity be foolproof against new "alternations."

Role theory, when pursued to its logical conclusions, does far more than provide us with a convenient shorthand for the description of various social activities. It gives us a sociological anthropology, that is, a view of man based on his existence in society. This view tells us that man plays dramatic parts in the grand play of society, and that, speaking sociologically, he *is* the masks that he must wear to do so. The human person also appears now in a dramatic context, true to its theatrical etymology (*persona*, the technical term given to the actors' masks in classical theater). The person is perceived as a repertoire of roles, each one properly equipped with a certain identity. The range of an individual person can be measured by the number of roles he is capable of playing. The person's biography now appears to us as an uninterrupted sequence of stage performances, played to different audiences, sometimes involving drastic changes of costume, always demanding that the actor *be* what he is playing.

The sociology of knowledge, more clearly than any other branch of sociology, makes clear what is meant by saying that the sociologist is the guy who keeps asking "*Says who?*" It rejects the pretense that thought occurs in isolation from the social context within which particular men think about particular things. Even in the case of very abstract ideas that seemingly have little social connection, the sociology of knowledge attempts to draw the line from the thought to the thinker to his social world. This can be seen most easily in those instances when thought serves to legitimate a particular social situation, that is, when it explains, justifies and sanctifies it.

Let us construct a simple illustration. Let us assume that in a primitive society some needed foodstuff can be obtained only by traveling to where it grows through treacherous, shark-infested waters. Twice every year the men of the tribe set out in their precarious canoes to get this food. Now, let us assume that the religious beliefs of this society contain an article of faith that says that every man who fails to go on this voyage will lose his virility, except for the priests, whose virility is sustained by their daily sacrifices to the gods. This belief provides a motivation for those who expose themselves to the dangerous journey and simultaneously a legitimation for the priests who regularly stay at home. Needless to add, we will suspect in this example that it was the priests who cooked up the theory in the first place. In other words, we will assume that we have here a priestly ideology. But this does not mean that the latter is not functional for the society as a whole—after all, somebody must go or there will be starvation.

We speak of an ideology when a certain idea serves a vested interest in society. Very frequently, though not always, ideologies systematically distort social reality in order to come out where it is functional for them to do so. In looking at the control systems set up by occupational groups we have already seen the way in which ideologies can legitimate the activities of such groups. Ideological thinking, however, is capable of covering much larger human collectivities. For example, the racial mythology of the American South serves to legitimate a social system practiced by millions of human beings. The ideology of "free enterprise" serves to camouflage the monopolistic practices of large American corporations whose only common characteristic with the old-style entrepreneur is a steadfast readiness to defraud the public. The Marxist ideology, in turn, serves to legitimate the tyranny practiced by the Communist Party apparatus whose interests have about as much in common with Karl Marx's as those of Elmer Gantry had with the Apostle Paul's. In each case, the ideology both justifies what is done by the group whose vested interest is served and interprets social reality in such a way that the justification is made plausible. This interpretation often appears bizarre to an outsider who "does not understand the problem" (that is, who does not share the vested interest). The Southern racist must simultaneously maintain that white women have a profound revulsion at the very thought of sexual relations with a Negro and that the slightest interracial sociability will straightway lead to such sexual relations. And the corporation executive will maintain that his activities to fix prices are undertaken in defense of a free market. And the Communist Party official will have a way of explaining that the limitation of electoral choice to candidates approved by the party is an expression of true democracy.

It should be stressed again in this connection that commonly the people putting forth these propositions are perfectly sincere. The moral effort to lie deliberately is beyond most people. It is much easier to deceive oneself. It is, therefore, important to keep the concept of ideology distinct from notions of lying, deception, propaganda or legerdemain. The liar, by definition, knows that he is lying. The ideologist does not. It is not our concern at this point to ask which of the two is ethically superior. We only stress once more the unreflected and unplanned way in which society normally operates. Most theories of conspiracy grossly overestimate the intellectual foresight of the conspirators.

Ideologies can also function "latently," to use Merton's expression in another context. Let us return another time to the American South as an example. One interesting fact about it is the geographical coincidence between the Black Belt and the Bible Belt. That is, roughly the same area that practices the Southern racial system in pristine purity also has the heaviest concentration of ultraconservative, fundamentalist Protestantism. This coincidence can be explained historically, by pointing to the isolation of Southern Protestantism from broader currents of religious thought ever since the great denominational splits over slavery in the antebellum period. The coincidence could also be interpreted as expressing two different aspects of intellectual barbarism. We would not quarrel with either explanation, but would contend that a sociological interpretation in terms of ideological functionality will carry us further in understanding the phenomenon.

Protestant fundamentalism, while it is obsessed with the idea of sin, has a curiously limited concept of its extent. Revivalistic preachers thundering against the wickedness of the world invariably fasten on a rather limited range of moral offences—fornication, drink, dancing, gambling, swearing. Indeed, so much emphasis is placed on the first of these that, in the *lingua franca* of Protestant moralism, the term "sin" itself is almost cognate with the more specific term "sexual offence." Whatever one may say otherwise about this catalogue of pernicious acts, they all have in common their essentially *private* character. Indeed, when a revivalistic preacher mentions public matters at all, it is usually in terms of the private corruption of those holding public offices. Government officials steal, which is bad. They also fornicate, drink and gamble, which is presumably even worse. Now, the limitation to private wrongdoing in one's concept of Christian ethics has obvious functions in a society whose central social arrangements are dubious, to say the least, when confronted with certain teachings of the New Testament and with the egalitarian creed of the nation that considers itself to have roots in the same. Protestant fundamentalism's private concept of morality thus concentrates attention on those areas of conduct that are irrelevant to the maintenance of the social system, and diverts attention from those areas where ethical inspection would create tensions for the smooth operation of the system. In other words, Protestant fundamentalism is ideologically functional in maintaining the social system of the American South. We need not go on to the point where it directly legitimates the system, as when segregation is proclaimed as a God-given natural order. But even in the absence of such "manifest" legitimation, the religious beliefs in question function "latently" to keep the system going. . . .

The individual, then, derives his world view socially in very much the same way that he derives his roles and his identity. In other words, his emotions and his self-interpretation like his actions are predefined for him by society, and so is his cognitive approach to the universe that surrounds him. This fact Alfred Schuetz has caught in his phrase "world-taken-for-granted"—the system of apparently self-evident and self-validating assumptions about the world that each society engenders in the course of its history. This socially determined world view is, at least in part, already given in the language used by the society. Certain linguists may have exaggerated the importance of this factor alone in creating any given world view, but there can be little doubt that one's language at least helps to shape one's relationship to reality. And, of course, our language is not chosen by ourselves but is imposed upon us by the particular social group that is in charge of our initial socialization. Society predefines for us that fundamental symbolic apparatus with which we grasp the world, order our experience and interpret our own existence.

In the same way, society supplies our values, our logic and the store of information (or, for that matter, misinformation) that constitutes our "knowledge." Very few people, and even they only in regard to fragments of this world view, are in a position to re-evaluate what has thus been imposed on them. They actually feel no need for reappraisal because the world view into which they have been socialized appears self-evident to them. Since it is also so regarded by almost everyone they are likely to deal with in their own society, the world view is self-validating. Its "proof" lies in the reiterated experience of other men who take it for granted also. To put this perspective of the sociology of knowledge into one succinct proposition: Reality is socially constructed. In this proposition, the sociology of knowledge helps to round out Thomas' statement on the power of social definition and throws further light on the sociological picture of the precarious nature of reality.

Conformity

ELLIOT ARONSON

We have all had the experience of conforming to a group's behavior even though we felt such behavior was wrong. What are the factors that increase or decrease our tendency to conform? Elliot Aronson gives us some insights into this important question.

One consequence of the fact that man is a social animal is that he lives in a state of tension between values associated with individuality and values associated with conformity. James Thurber has captured the flavor of one kind of conformity in the following description:

From *The Social Animal* (notes omitted) by Elliot Aronson. W. H. Freeman and Company.

Suddenly somebody began to run. It may be that he had simply remembered, all of a moment, an engagement to meet his wife, for which he was now frightfully late. Whatever it was, he ran east on Broad Street (probably toward the Maramor Restaurant, a favorite place for a man to meet his wife). Somebody else began to run, perhaps a newsboy in high spirits. Another man, a portly gentleman of affairs, broke into a trot. Inside of ten minutes, everybody on High Street, from the Union Depot to the Court-house was running. A loud mumble gradually crystalized into the dread word "dam." "The dam has broke!" The fear was put into words by a little old lady in an electric, or by a traffic cop, or by a small boy: nobody knows who, nor does it now really matter. Two thousand people were abruptly in full flight. "Go east!" was the cry that arose—east away from the river, east to safety. "Go east! Go east!" . . .

. . . A tall spare woman with grim eyes and a determined chin ran past me down the middle of the street. I was still uncertain as to what was the matter, in spite of all the shouting. I drew up alongside the woman with some effort, for although she was in her late fifties, she had a beautiful easy running form and seemed to be in excellent condition. "What is it?" I puffed. She gave me a quick glance and then looked ahead again, stepping up her pace a trifle. "Don't ask me, ask God!" she said.

This passage from Thurber, although comical, is an apt illustration of people conforming. One or two individuals began running for their own reasons; before long, everyone was running. Why? Because others were running. According to Thurber's story, when the running people realized that the dam hadn't given way after all, they felt pretty foolish. And yet, how much more foolish would they have felt if they hadn't conformed, and the dam had, in fact, burst? Is conformity good or bad? In its simplest sense, this is an absurd question. But words do carry evaluative meaning—thus, to be called an individualist or a nonconformist is to be designated, by connotation, as a "good" person: the label evokes an image of Daniel Boone standing on a mountain top with a rifle slung over his shoulder, the breeze blowing through his hair, as the sun sets in the background. To be called a conformist is somehow to be designated as an "inadequate" person: it evokes an image of a row of Madison Avenue admen with grey flannel suits, porkpie hats, and attaché cases, looking as though they had been created by a cookie cutter, and all saying simultaneously, "Let's run it up the flagpole and see if anyone salutes."

But we can use synonymous words that convey very different images. For "individualist" or "nonconformist," we can substitute "deviate"; for "conformist," we can substitute "team player." Somehow, "deviate" does not evoke Daniel Boone on the mountain top, and "team player" does not evoke the cookie-cutter-produced Madison Avenue adman.

When we look a little closer, we see an inconsistency in the way our society seems to feel about conformity (team playing) and nonconformity (deviance). For example, one of the great best sellers of the 1950s was a book by John F. Kennedy called *Profiles in Courage,* wherein the author praised several politicians for their courage in resisting great pressure and refusing to conform. To put it another way, Kennedy was praising people who refused to be good team players, people who refused to vote or act as their parties or constituents expected them to. Although their actions earned Kennedy's praise long after the deeds were done, the immediate reactions of their colleagues were generally far from positive. The nonconformist may be praised by historians or idolized in films or literature long after the fact of his nonconformity, but he's usually not held in high esteem, at the time, by those people to whose demands he refuses to conform. This observation receives strong support from a number of experiments in social psychology, most notably from one by Stanley Schacter, in which several groups of students participated. Each group met for a discussion of the case history of a juvenile delinquent named Johnny Rocco, which each member was given to read. After reading the case, each group was asked to discuss it and to suggest a treatment for Johnny on a scale that ranged from "very lenient treatment" on one end to "very hard treatment" on the other. A typical group consisted of approximately nine participants, six of whom were real students and three of whom were paid confederates of the experimenter. The confederates took turns playing one of three roles that they had carefully rehearsed in advance: the *modal* person, who took a position that conformed to the average position of the real students; the *deviate*, who took a position diametrically opposed to the general orientation of the group; and the *slider*, whose initial position was similar to the deviate's but who, in the course of the discussion, gradually "slid" into a modal, conforming position. The results clearly showed that the person who was liked most was the modal person who conformed to the group norm; the deviate was liked least.

Thus, the data indicate that the "establishment" or modal group tends to like conformists better than nonconformists. By reporting these results, we do not intend to suggest that conformity is always adaptive and nonconformity is always maladaptive. Clearly, there are situations wherein conformity is highly desirable and nonconformity would constitute an unmitigated disaster. Suppose, for example, that I were suddenly to decide that I was fed up with being a conformist. So I hop in my car and start driving down the *left*-hand side of the road—as a way of displaying my rugged individualism: not very adaptive, and not very fair to you, if you happen to be driving toward me (conformist-style) on the same street.

On the other hand, there are equally compelling situations in which conformity can be just as disastrous and just as tragic. One such example can be found in the memoirs of Albert Speer. Speer was one of Adolf Hitler's top advisors. In his memoirs, he describes the circle around Hitler as one of total conformity: deviation was not permitted. In such an atmosphere, even the most barbarous activities seemed reasonable, because the absence of dissent, which conveyed the illusion of unanimity, prevented any individual from entertaining the possibility that other options might exist.

> In normal circumstances people who turn their backs on reality are soon set straight by the mockery and criticism of those around them. In the Third Reich there were not such correctives. On the contrary, every self-deception was multi-

plied as in a hall of distorting mirrors, becoming a repeatedly confirmed picture of a fantastical dream world which no longer bore any relationship to the grim outside world. In those mirrors I could see nothing but my own face reproduced many times over.

What Is Conformity?

Conformity can be defined as a change in a person's behavior or opinions as a result of real or imagined pressure from a person or group of people. Most situations are not as extreme as the examples cited above. We will attempt to zero in on the phenomenon of conformity by beginning with a less extreme (and perhaps simpler) illustration. Let's return to our friend Sam, the hypothetical college student we first encountered in Chapter 1. Recall that Sam watched a presidential candidate on television and was favorably impressed by his sincerity. However, in the face of the unanimous opinion of his friends that the candidate was insincere, Sam acceded—verbally, at least—to their opinion.

Several questions can be asked about this kind of situation: (1) What causes people to conform to group pressure? Specifically, what was in it for Sam? (2) What was the nature of the group pressure? Specifically, what were Sam's acquaintances doing to induce conformity? (3) Did Sam revise his opinion of the candidate during that brief but horrifying period when he learned that *all* of his fellow students disagreed with him? Or was it the case that Sam maintained his original opinion, but only modified what he *said* about the candidate? If there was a change in opinion, was it permanent or merely transient?

Unfortunately, we cannot say precisely and definitely what was going on in Sam's mind at the time, because there are many factors in the situation that we don't know about. For example, we don't know how confident Sam was in his initial opinion; we don't know how much he liked the people with whom he watched the candidate; we don't know whether Sam considered himself to be a good judge of sincerity or whether he considered the others to be good judges of sincerity; we don't know whether Sam is generally a strong person or a wishy-washy person; and so on. What we can do is construct an experimental situation that is somewhat like the one in which Sam found himself, and we can control and vary the factors that we think might be important. Such a basic situation was devised by Solomon Asch in a classic set of experiments. Put yourself in the following scene: You have volunteered to participate in an experiment on perceptual judgment. You enter a room with four other participants. The experimenter shows all of you a straight line (line X). Simultaneously, he shows you three other lines for comparison (lines *A*, *B*, and *C*). Your job is to judge which of the three lines is closest in length to the line X. The judgment strikes you as being a very easy one. It is perfectly clear to you that line *B* is the correct answer, and when your turn comes, you will clearly say that *B* is the one. But it's *not*

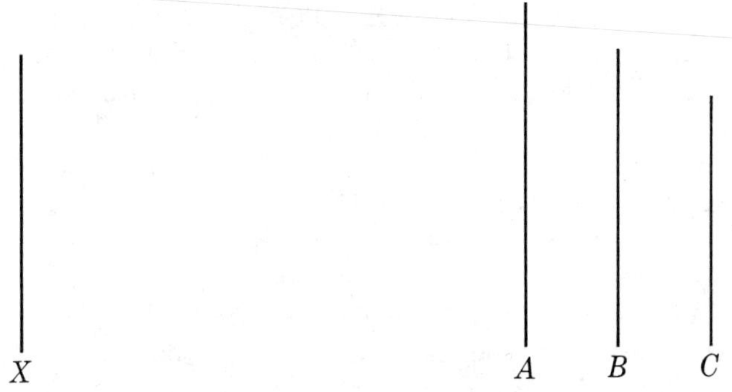

your turn to respond. The person whose turn it is looks carefully at the lines and says "Line A." Your mouth drops open and you look at him quizically. "How can he believe it's A when any fool can see that it's B?" you ask yourself. "He must be either blind or crazy." Now it's the second person's turn to respond. He also chooses line A. You begin to feel like Alice in Wonderland. "How can it be?" you ask yourself. "Are *both* of these people blind or crazy?" But then the next person responds, and he also says "Line A." You take another look at those lines. "Maybe *I'm* the only one who's losing his mind," you mutter inaudibly. Now it's the fourth person's turn, and he also judges the correct line to be line A. You break out in a cold sweat. Finally, it's your turn. "Why, it's line A, of course," you declare. "I knew it all the time."

This is the kind of conflict that the college students in Asch's experiment went through. As you might imagine, the individuals who answered first and gave the incorrect answer were in the employ of the experimenter and were instructed to agree on an incorrect answer. The perceptual judgment itself was an incredibly easy one. It was so easy that when individuals were not subjected to group pressure, but were allowed to make a series of judgments of various sizes of lines while alone, there was almost a complete absence of errors. Indeed, the task was so easy, and physical reality was so clear-cut, that Asch himself firmly believed that there would be little, if any, yielding to group pressure. But he was wrong. When faced with a majority of their fellow students agreeing on the same incorrect responses in a series of twelve judgments, approximately one-quarter of the subjects conformed at least once by responding incorrectly. When we look at the entire spectrum of judgments, we find that an average of 35 percent of the overall responses conformed to the incorrect judgments rendered by Asch's accomplices.

The situation in the Asch experiment is intriguing inasmuch as, unlike many situations in which we may tend to conform, there were no explicit constraints against individuality. That is, the sanctions against nonconformity in many situations are clear and unequivocal. For example, I hate to wear a tie, and under most circumstances I can get away with this minor idiosyncracy. On occasion, however, I can't: I often find myself stopped at the entrance to a restaurant and politely (but firmly) informed that if I refuse to don the tie offered me by the headwaiter, I cannot dine in that restaurant. I can either put on the tie and eat in the restaurant, or leave, open-necked and comfortable, but hungry. The negative consequences of nonconformity are made very explicit.

But in Asch's experiment (and in the hypothetical example of Sam watching the candidate on television), the situations were much more subtle. In these situations, there were no explicit rewards for conformity and no explicit punishments for deviance. Why, then, did Sam and Asch's subjects conform? There seem to be two major possibilities; either they became convinced, in the face of the judgment of the unanimous majority, that their own opinions were wrong, or they "went along with the crowd" (while inwardly knowing that their judgments were right) in order to be liked by the majority or to avoid being disliked by them for disagreeing.

In short, what we are suggesting is that these individuals had two important goals: the goal of being correct and the goal of staying in the good graces of other people by living up to their expectations. In many circumstances, both of these goals can be satisfied by a simple action. Driving on the right-hand side of the road is the correct thing to do and it satisfies other people's expectations. So, too, is sending flowers to your Mother on Mother's Day, giving proper directions to a visitor in town, and studying hard to perform well on an exam. Similarly, if others agreed with your judgment of the lengths of the lines, you could satisfy both goals by being true to your own estimate. But in Asch's experiment, these two goals were placed in conflict. If you were a subject in that experiment, and you initially believed that the correct answer was line *B*, then saying so might satisfy your desire to be correct—but it might also violate the expectations of your peers, and they might think you to be somewhat queer. On the other hand, choosing line A might win you the acceptance of the others, but unless you became convinced that they were correct, it would violate your desire to be right.

Was Sam convinced by his fellow college students that his preferred presidential candidate was a phony, or did he simply go along with their judgment in order to be accepted, while continuing to believe in the sincerity of the candidate? Again, I don't know; because Sam is a hypothetical person, we cannot answer that question definitively. Were the yielders in Asch's experiment convinced that their initial judgment was incorrect and the unanimous judgment of the others was right? We could ask them; indeed, in Asch's experiment, the yielders were asked afterward whether they really saw the lines differently or whether they merely said so. A few of the subjects insisted that they really saw it that way. But how can we be certain that the subjects were being truthful? Put yourself in a subject's place. Suppose you bowed to group pressure, even though you remained certain that your initial judgment was correct. This might be embarrassing for you to admit, because it would make you appear weak and wishy-washy. Moreover, you would be admitting that you were not following the experimenter's instruction to present *your own* judgment. Thus, it is quite possible that subjects who said they actually saw it the way the group saw it might have been deceiving the experimenter in order to save face.

How, then, can we determine whether or not group pressure actually affects perceptual judgment? Let's speculate for a moment. Suppose we were to repeat the Asch experiment, but, although we would allow the real subjects to see the responses of the accomplices as before, we would *not* require them to make their judgments in the presence of the others. If the subjects' private choices were identical with their public ones, then we would see that the responses of the others in the original experiment actually did convince the subjects that their initial judgments were wrong. If, on the other hand, the subjects were going against their own best judgment only in order to mollify the group, then there would be significantly less yielding to the judgments of others in decisions made in private. This proposition has been tested experimentally on several occasions. The results are consistent: although assurance of total privacy has not been achieved in any of these studies, the greater the privacy, the less the conformity. This finding has consistently held up, whether the subjects were judging lengths of lines, the numbers of metronome clicks, or the esthetic value of a piece of modern art. Thus, it appears that pressure to conform to the judgments of others has little (if any) effect on the *private* judgments of experimental subjects.

Variables That Increase or Decrease Conformity

In situations like the one investigated by Asch, one of the crucial factors that determines the likelihood that the subject's opinion will conform to that of the majority is whether or not the majority opinion is unanimous. If the subject is presented with only one ally, his tendency to conform to an erroneous judgment by the majority is reduced sharply. Moreover, if there *is* unanimity, the actual size of the majority need not be very great in order for it to elicit maximum conformity from a person. In fact, the tendency for someone to conform to group pressure is about as great when the unanimous majority consists of only three other people as it is when the unanimous majority is sixteen.

Another important pair of factors is the kind of person the individual is and who constitutes the group. Individuals who have a generally low opinion of themselves are far more likely to yield to group pressure than those with high self-esteem. Furthermore, task-specific self-esteem can be influenced within a given situation. Thus, individuals who are allowed to have prior successes with such a task as judging the lengths of lines are far less likely to conform than those who walk into the situation cold. By the same token, if an individual believes that he has little or no ability for the task at hand, his tendency to conform increases.

The other side of that coin, of course, has to do with the makeup of the group exerting the pressure. A group is more effective at inducing conformity if (1) it consists of experts, (2) the members (individually or collectively) are important to the individual, or (3) the members (individually or collectively) are comparable to the individual in some way. Thus, to go back to Sam, our hypothetical college student, I would speculate that it is more likely that Sam would conform to the pressure exerted by his acquaintances if he thought they were expert in politics and in making judgments about human relations. Similarly, he would be more likely to yield to those people if they were important potential friends than if they were of no consequence to him. And finally, their being fellow college students gives the judgment of Sam's acquaintances more impact on his behavior than, say, the judgment of a group of ten-year-old children, a group of hard-hats, or a group of Portuguese biochemists.

A related issue is how secure the individual feels in a given situation. If Sam felt sure that he was liked and accepted by his acquaintances, he would be more likely to voice disagreement than if he felt insecure in his relationship with them. This assertion receives strong support from an experiment by James Dittes and Harold Kelley, in which college students were invited to join an attractive and prestigious group and were subsequently given information about how secure their position was in that group. Specifically, all members of the group were informed that, at any point during the lifetime of the group, the members could remove any member in the interests of efficiency. The group then engaged in a discussion of juvenile delinquency. Periodically, the discussion was interrupted and each member was asked to rate every other member on his value to the group. After the discussion, each member was shown how the others rated him; in actuality, the members were given prearranged false feedback. Some members were led to believe that they were well-accepted, and others were led to believe that they were not terribly popular. Each member's conformity was measured by the opinions he subsequently expressed in the discussion of juvenile delinquency, and by his vulnerability to group pressure during the performance of a simple perceptual task. The results showed that, for the individuals who valued their membership in the group, those who were led to feel only moderately accepted were more likely to conform to the norms and standards set by the group than were those who were led to feel that they were totally accepted. In other words, it's easier for an individual who is securely esconced in a group to deviate from that group.

Rewards and Punishments versus Information

As I suggested earlier, there are two possible reasons why a person might conform. One is that the behavior of others might convince him that his initial judgment was erroneous. The other is that he may wish to avoid punishment (such as rejection or ridicule) or to gain a reward (such as love or acceptance) from the group. Furthermore, the behavior of the individuals in Asch's experiment and in similar other experiments seemed to be largely a matter of attempting to obtain a reward or to avoid punishment. This can be inferred from the fact that there was very little conformity when subjects were allowed to respond privately.

At the same time, there are many situations in which we conform to the behavior of others because their behavior is our only guide to appropriate action. In short, we often rely on other people as a means of determining reality. The quotation from Thurber at the beginning of this chapter gives an example of this type of conformity. According to Leon Festinger, when physical reality becomes increasingly uncertain, people rely more and more on "social reality"—that is, they are more likely to conform to what other people are doing, not because they fear punishment from the group, but because the group's behavior supplies them with valuable information about what is expected of them. An example should help clarify this distinction: Suppose that you need to use the toilet in an unfamiliar classroom building. Under the sign "Rest Rooms" there are two doors, but, unfortunately, a vandal has removed the specific designations from the doors—that is, you cannot be certain which is the Men's room and which is the Women's room. Quite a dilemma—you are afraid to open either door for fear of being embarrassed or embarrassing others. As you stand there in dismay and discomfort, hopping from one foot to the other, the door on the left opens and out strolls a distinguished-looking gentleman. With a sigh of relief, you are now willing to forge ahead, reasonably secure in the knowledge that left is for men and right is for women. Why are you so confident? As we have seen, research has shown that, the more faith an individual has in the expertise and trustworthiness of the other person, the greater the tendency to follow his lead and conform to his behavior. Thus, the distinguished-looking gentleman would almost certainly be followed, to a greater extent, than, say, a seedy-looking fellow with wildly staring eyes.

Similarly, it is alleged that, in Turkey, it is considered gracious for a guest to belch after a meal as a way of showing his host that he enjoyed the meal. Suppose you didn't know this, and you were visiting the home of a Turkish dignitary in the company of some diplomats from the U.S. State Department. If, after the meal, these gentlemen began to belch, chances are you would belch also. They are providing you with valuable information. On the other hand, if you were in the same home in the company of a crew of behemoths from the Bulgarian Olympic wrestling team and these stalwarts belched after their meal, my guess is that you would avoid belching. That is, you would likely consider this an act of bad manners. However, if they glared at you for your failure to follow suit, you might indeed blech, too—not because of the information they supplied, but because you feared rejection or reprisals for refusing to be a good sport by going along with their boorish behavior.

I would suggest that conformity that results from the observation of others for the purpose of gaining information about proper behavior tends to have more powerful ramifications than conformity in the interest of being accepted or of avoiding punishment. I would argue that, if an individual finds himself in an ambiguous situation wherein he must use the behavior of other people as a template for his own behavior, it is likely he will repeat his newly learned behavior, without cue, on subsequent similar occasions. This would be the case unless, of course, he later received clear evidence that his actions were inappropriate or incorrect. Thus, to go back to our example, suppose you are reinvited to the home of the Turkish dignitary for dinner. But this time you are the only guest. The question is: Do you or don't you belch after the meal? A moment's reflection should make the answer perfectly clear: If you had belched after the first meal at his home because you realized that it was the proper thing to do (as would have been the case had you dined in the company of the diplomats), you would be quite likely to belch when dining alone with the dignitary. However, if you had belched the first time out of fear of rejection or punishment (as would have been the case had you dined in the company of the Bulgarian wrestlers), you would almost certainly *not* belch when you were the lone guest. To go back to Sam and the political candidate on television, you can now readily understand one of the major reasons why it would be so difficult for us to predict how Sam would actually vote in the election. If he had been merely going along with the group to avoid punishment or to gain acceptance, he would be likely, in the privacy of the polling booth, to vote in opposition to the view expressed by his acquaintances. If, on the other hand, Sam had been using the group as a source of information, he would almost certainly vote against the candidate that he had initially preferred.

To repeat: when reality is unclear, other people become a major source of information. The generality of this phenomenon is nicely illustrated by some research performed by Stanley Schachter and his students, who demonstrated that people conform to others even in assessing something as personal and idiosyncratic as the quality of their own emotions. Before describing this research, we must first clarify what we mean by "emotions." According to William James, an emotion has both a "feeling" content and a cognitive content. Specifically, if we are walking in the forest and bump into a hungry and ferocious bear, we undergo a physiological change. This change produces excitement—physiologically, this is a response of the sympathetic nervous system that is similar to one that might be produced by coming across a person with whom we are angry. We interpret this response as fear (rather than anger, say, or euphoria) only when we cognitively become aware that we are in the presence of a fear-producing stimulus (a ferocious bear). But what if we experienced physiological arousal in the absence of an appropriate stimulus? For example, what if someone surreptitiously slipped into our drink a chemical that produced the same physiological response? Would we experience fear? William James would probably say that we wouldn't—not unless there was an appropriate stimulus around.

Here is where Schachter enters the picture. In one experiment, subjects were injected either with epinephrine—a synthetic form of adrenalin, which causes physiological excitation—or with a harmless placebo. All the subjects were told that this chemical was a vitamin supplement called "suproxin." Some of the subjects who received epinephrine were informed that there would be side effects, including palpitation of the heart and hand tremors. These, indeed, are some of the effects of epinephrine. Accordingly, when these subjects experienced the epinephrine symptoms, they had an appropriate explanation. In effect, when the symptoms appeared, they would say to themselves, "My heart is pounding and my hands are shaking because of this injection I received and for no other reason." But other subjects were not forewarned about these symptoms. Thus, when their hearts started pounding and their hands started trembling, what were they to make of it? The answer is that they made of it whatever the people around them made of it. Specifically, a stooge was introduced into the situation and the subjects were informed that he had also received an injection of "suproxin." In one situation, the stooge was programmed to behave in a euphoric manner; in another, he was programmed to express a great deal of anger. Picture yourself in this situation: You are alone in this room with a person who supposedly has just been injected with the same drug you had received. He bounces around energetically, and happily wads up paper into balls and begins sinking hook shots into the waste basket. His euphoria is obvious. Gradually, the chemical you were given begins to take effect, and you begin to feel your heart pounding, your hands trembling, and so on. What emotion do you feel? Most subjects in this situation reported a feeling of euphoria—and behaved happily. On the other hand, imagine that instead of being placed in a room with a euphoric stooge you were placed in a room with a stooge programmed to behave in an angry manner: He complains about a questionnaire you both are filling out and eventually, in a fit of extreme annoyance, he rips the questionnaire up and angrily hurls it into the waste basket. Meanwhile, the symptoms of epinephrine are becoming apparent; you feel your own heart pounding, and your hands begin to tremble. How do you feel? In this situation, the vast majority of the subjects felt angry and behaved in an angry fashion.

It should be noted that, if subjects were given a placebo (that is, an injection of a benign solution that produces no symptoms), or if they were forewarned about the symptoms of the drug that they *had* been given, they were relatively unaffected by the antics of the stooge. To sum up this experiment: when physical reality was clear and explainable, the subjects' emotions were not greatly influenced by the behavior of other people—but when they were experiencing a strong physiological response, the origins of which were not clear, they interpreted their own feelings as either anger or euphoria, depending on the behavior of other people who supposedly were in the same chemical boat.

Pathology of Imprisonment

PHILIP G. ZIMBARDO

This selection describes an experiment in which a prison situation was simulated to determine what it means psychologically and sociologically to be a prisoner or a prison guard. The results were frightening, says Philip Zimbardo, and the experiment had to be ended prematurely. Zimbardo uses the data from his experiment as support for his prescription for prison reform.

I was recently released from solitary confinement after being held therein for 37 months [months!]. A silent system was imposed upon me and to even whisper to the man in the next cell resulted in being beaten by guards, sprayed with chemical mace, blackjacked, stomped and thrown into a strip-cell naked to sleep on a concrete floor without bedding, covering, wash basin or even a toilet. The floor served as toilet and bed, and even there the silent system was enforced. To let a moan escape your lips because of the pain and discomfort . . . resulted in another beating. I spent not days, but months there during my 37 months in solitary. . . . I have filed every writ possible against the administrative acts of brutality. The state courts have all denied the petitions. Because of my refusal to let the things die down and forget all that happened during my 37 months in solitary . . . I am the most hated prisoner in [this] penitentiary, and called a "hard-core incorrigible."

Maybe I am an incorrigible, but if true, it's because I would rather die than to accept being treated as less than a human being. I have never complained of my prison sentence as being unjustified except through legal means of appeals. I have never put a knife on a guard's throat and demanded my release. I know that thieves must be punished and I don't justify stealing, even though I am a thief myself. But now I don't think I will be a thief when I am released. No, I'm not rehabilitated. It's just that I no longer think of becoming wealthy by stealing. I now only think of killing—killing those who have beaten me and treated me as if I were a dog. I hope and pray for the sake of my own soul and future life of freedom that I am able to overcome the bitterness and hatred which eats daily at my soul, but I know to overcome it will not be easy.

This eloquent plea for prison reform—for humane treatment of human beings, for the basic dignity that is the right of every American—came to me

Published by permission of Transaction, Inc., from *Society*, Vol. 9, No. 6. The research described in this report was in collaboration with Craig Haney, W. Curtis Banks, and David Jaffe.

secretly in a letter from a prisoner who cannot be identified because he is still in a state correctional institution. He sent it to me because he read of an experiment I recently conducted at Stanford University. In an attempt to understand just what it means psychologically to be a prisoner or a prison guard, Craig Haney, Curt Banks, Dave Jaffe and I created our own prison. We carefully screened over 70 volunteers who answered an ad in a Palo Alto city newspaper and ended up with about two dozen young men who were selected to be part of this study. They were mature, emotionally stable, normal, intelligent college students from middle-class homes throughout the United States and Canada. They appeared to represent the cream of the crop of this generation. None had any criminal record and all were relatively homogeneous on many dimensions initially.

Half were arbitrarily designated as prisoners by a flip of a coin, the others as guards. These were the roles they were to play in our simulated prison. The guards were made aware of the potential seriousness and danger of the situation and their own vulnerability. They made up their own formal rules for maintaining law, order and respect, and were generally free to improvise new ones during their eight-hour, three-man shifts. The prisoners were unexpectedly picked up at their homes by a city policeman in a squad car, searched, handcuffed, fingerprinted, booked at the Palo Alto station house and taken blindfolded to our jail. There they were stripped, deloused, put into a uniform, given a number and put into a cell with two other prisoners where they expected to live for the next two weeks. The pay was good ($15 a day) and their motivation was to make money.

We observed and recorded on videotape the events that occurred in the prison, and we interviewed and tested the prisoners and guards at various points throughout the study. Some of the videotapes of the actual encounters between the prisoners and guards were seen on the NBC News feature "Chronolog" on November 26, 1971.

At the end of only six days we had to close down our mock prison because what we saw was frightening. It was no longer apparent to most of the subjects (or to us) where reality ended and their roles began. The majority had indeed become prisoners or guards, no longer able to clearly differentiate between role playing and self. There were dramatic changes in virtually every aspect of their behavior, thinking and feeling. In less than a week the experience of imprisonment undid (temporarily) a lifetime of learning; human values were suspended, self-concepts were challenged and the ugliest, most base, pathological side of human nature surfaced. We were horrified because we saw some boys (guards) treat others as if they were despicable animals, taking pleasure in cruelty, while other boys (prisoners) became servile, dehumanized robots who thought only of escape, of their own individual survival and of their mounting hatred for the guards.

We had to release three prisoners in the first four days because they had such acute situational traumatic reactions as hysterical crying, confusion in thinking and severe depression. Others begged to be paroled, and all but three were willing to forfeit all the money they had earned if they could be paroled. By then (the fifth day) they had been so programmed to think of themselves as prisoners that when their request for parole was denied, they returned docilely to their cells. Now, had they been thinking as college students acting in an oppressive experiment, they would have quit once they no longer wanted the $15 a day we used as our only incentive. However, the reality was not quitting an experiment but "being paroled by the parole board from the Stanford County Jail." By the last days, the earlier solidarity among the prisoners (systematically broken by the guards) dissolved into "each man for himself." Finally, when one of their fellows was put in solitary confinement (a small closet) for refusing to eat, the prisoners were given a choice by one of the guards: give up their blankets and the incorrigible prisoner would be let out, or keep their blankets and he would be kept in all night. They voted to keep their blankets and to abandon their brother.

About a third of the guards became tyrannical in their arbitrary use of power, in enjoying their control over other people. They were corrupted by the power of their roles and became quite inventive in their techniques of breaking the spirit of the prisoners and making them feel they were worthless. Some of the guards merely did their jobs as tough but fair correctional officers, and several were good guards from the prisoners' point of view since they did them small favors and were friendly. However, no good guard ever interfered with a command by any of the bad guards; they never intervened on the side of the prisoners, they never told the others to ease off because it was only an experiment, and they never even came to me as prison superintendent or experimenter in charge to complain. In part, they were good because the others were bad; they needed the others to help establish their own egos in a positive light. In a sense, the good guards perpetuated the prison more than the other guards because their own needs to be liked prevented them from disobeying or violating the implicit guards' code. At the same time, the act of befriending the prisoners created a social reality which made the prisoners less likely to rebel.

By the end of the week the experiment had become a reality, as if it were a Pirandello play directed by Kafka that just keeps going after the audience has left. The consultant for our prison, Carlo Prescott, an ex-convict with 16 years of imprisonment in California's jails, would get so depressed and furious each time he visited our prison, because of its psychological similarity to his experiences, that he would have to leave. A Catholic priest who was a former prison chaplain in Washington, D.C. talked to our prisoners after four days and said they were just like the other first-timers he had seen.

But in the end, I called off the experiment not because of the horror I saw out there in the prison yard, but because of the horror of realizing that *I* could have easily traded places with the most brutal guard or become the weakest prisoner full of hatred at being so powerless that I could not eat, sleep or go to the toilet without permission of the authorities. *I* could have become Calley at My Lai, George Jackson at San Quentin, one of the men at Attica or the prisoner quoted at the beginning of this article.

Individual behavior is largely under the control of social forces and environmental contingencies rather than personality traits, character, will power or other empirically unvalidated constructs. Thus we create an illusion of freedom by attributing more internal control to ourselves, to the individual, than actually exists. We thus underestimate the power and pervasiveness of situational controls over behavior because: (a) they are often non-obvious and subtle, (b) we can often avoid entering situations where we might be so controlled, (c) we label as "weak" or "deviant" people in those situations who do behave differently from how we believe we would.

Each of us carries around in our heads a favorable self-image in which we are essentially just, fair, humane and understanding. For example, we could not imagine inflicting pain on others without much provocation or hurting people who had done nothing to us, who in fact were even liked by us. However, there is a growing body of social psychological research which underscores the conclusion derived from this prison study. Many people, perhaps the majority, can be made to do almost anything when put into psychologically compelling situations—regardless of their morals, ethics, values, attitudes, beliefs or personal convictions. My colleague, Stanley Milgram, has shown that more than 60 percent of the population will deliver what they think is a series of painful electric shocks to another person even after the victim cries for mercy, begs them to stop and then apparently passes out. The subjects complained that they did not want to inflict more pain but blindly obeyed the command of the authority figure (the experimenter) who said that they must go on. In my own research on violence, I have seen mild-mannered co-eds repeatedly give shocks (which they thought were causing pain) to another girl, a stranger whom they had rated very favorably, simply by being made to feel anonymous and put in a situation where they were expected to engage in this activity.

Observers of these and similar experimental situations never predict their outcomes and estimate that it is unlikely that they themselves would behave similarly. They can be so confident only when they were outside the situation. However, since the majority of people in these studies do act in non-rational, non-obvious ways, it follows that the majority of observers would also succumb to the social psychological forces in the situation.

With regard to prisons, we can state that the mere act of assigning labels to people and putting them into a situation where those labels acquire validity and meaning is sufficient to elicit pathological behavior. This pathology is not predictable from any available diagnostic indicators we have in the social sciences, and is extreme enough to modify in very significant ways fundamental attitudes and behavior. The prison situation, as presently arranged, is guaranteed to generate severe enough pathological reactions in both guards and prisoners as to debase their humanity, lower their feelings of self-worth and make it difficult for them to be part of a society outside of their prison.

For years our national leaders have been pointing to the enemies of freedom, to the fascist or communist threat to the American way of life. In so doing they have overlooked the threat of social anarchy that is building within our own country without any outside agitation. As soon as a person comes to the realization that he is being imprisoned by his society or individuals in it, then, in the best American tradition, he demands liberty and rebels, accepting death as an alternative. The third alternative, however, is to allow oneself to become a good prisoner—docile, cooperative, uncomplaining, conforming in thought and complying in deed.

Our prison authorities now point to the militant agitators who are still vaguely referred to as part of some communist plot, as the irresponsible, incorrigible troublemakers. They imply that there would be no trouble, riots, hostages or deaths if it weren't for this small band of bad prisoners. In other words, then, everything would return to "normal" again in the life of our nation's prisons if they could break these men.

The riots in prison are coming from within—from within every man and woman who refuses to let the system turn them into an object, a number, a thing or a no-thing. It is not communist inspired, but inspired by the spirit of American freedom. No man wants to be enslaved. To be powerless, to be subject to the arbitrary exercise of power, to not be recognized as a human being is to be a slave.

To be a militant prisoner is to become aware that the physical jails are but more blatant extensions of the forms of social and psychological oppression experienced daily in the nation's ghettos. They are trying to awaken the conscience of the nation to the ways in which the American ideals are being perverted, apparently in the name of justice but actually under the banner of apathy, fear and hatred. If we do not listen to the pleas of the prisoners at Attica to be treated like human beings, then we have all become brutalized by our priorities for property rights over human rights. The consequence will not only be more prison riots but a loss of all those ideals on which this country was founded.

The public should be aware that they own the prisons and that their business is failing. The 70 percent recidivism rate and the escalation in severity of crimes committed by graduates of our prisons are evidence that current prisons fail to rehabilitate the inmates in any positive way. Rather, they are breeding grounds for hatred of the establishment, a hatred that makes every citizen a target of violent assault. Prisons are a bad investment for us taxpayers. Until now we have not cared, we have turned over to wardens and prison authorities the unpleasant job of keeping people who threaten us out of our sight. Now we are shocked to learn that their management practices have failed to improve the product and instead turn petty thieves into murderers. We must insist upon new management or improved operating procedures.

The cloak of secrecy should be removed from the prisons. Prisoners claim they are brutalized by the guards, guards say it is a lie. Where is the impartial test of the truth in such a situation? Prison officials have forgotten that they work for us, that they are only public servants whose salaries are paid by our taxes. They act as if it is their prison, like a child with a toy he won't share. Neither lawyers, judges, the legislature nor the public is allowed into prisons to ascertain the truth unless the visit is sanctioned by authorities and until all is prepared for their visit. I was shocked to learn that my request to join a congressional investigating committee's tour of San Quentin and Soledad was refused, as was that of the news media.

There should be an ombudsman in every prison, not under the pay or control of the prison authority, and responsible only to the courts, state legislature and the public. Such a person could report on violations of constitutional and human rights.

Guards must be given better training than they now receive for the difficult job society imposes upon them. To be a prison guard as now constituted is to be put in a situation of constant threat from within the prison, with no social recognition from the society at large. As was shown graphically at Attica, prison guards are also prisoners of the system who can be sacrificed to the demands of the public to be punitive and the needs of politicians to preserve an image. Social scientists and business administrators should be called upon to design and help carry out this training.

The relationship between the individual (who is sentenced by the courts to a prison term) and his community must be maintained. How can a prisoner return to a dynamically changing society that most of us cannot cope with after being out of it for a number of years? There should be more community involvement in these rehabilitation centers, more ties encouraged and promoted between the trainees and family and friends, more educational opportunities to prepare them for returning to their communities as more valuable members of it than they were before they left.

Finally, the main ingredient necessary to effect any change at all in prison reform, in the rehabilitation of a single prisoner or even in the optimal development of a child is caring. Reform must start with people—especially people with power—caring about the well-being of others. Underneath the toughest, society-hating convict, rebel or anarchist is a human being who wants his existence to be recognized by his fellows and who wants someone else to care about whether he lives or dies and to grieve if he lives imprisoned rather than lives free.

A Human Wasteland in the Name of Justice

BEN BAGDIKIAN AND LEON DASH

The prison system in the United States has been frequently attacked as an institution in need of radical reform. Ideally, the time an individual spends in this total institution is based upon a nondiscriminatory judicial system and results in "positive" resocialization. The evidence, however, indicates that the affluent tend to escape imprisonment while the poor, minorities, and young do not, that parole boards regularly release the worst criminal risks, and that American prisoners serve the longest sentences in the Western world even though the longer a criminal stays in prison, the more crimes he is likely to commit after his release. The following article examines these themes and inconsistencies.

If today is average, 8,000 American men, women and children will enter locked cages in the name of justice.

If theirs is an average experience they will, in addition to any genuine justice received, be forced into programs of psychological destruction; if they serve a sentence most of it will not be by decision of a judge acting under the Constitution but by a casual bureaucrat acting under no rules whatever; they will undergo a significant probability of forced homosexualism; and they will emerge from this experience a greater threat to society than when they went in.

"Justice" in the United States today is so bad that conservative reformers talk openly of salvaging lawbreakers by "diversion from the criminal justice system wherever possible" (The American Bar Association Commission on Correctional Facilities and Services).

It so efficiently educates children into crime that one official could say, "It would be better if young people who commit crimes got away with them because we just make them worse" (Milton Luger, Director of the New York State Division of Youth).

American convicts serve a majority of their sentences at the mercy of parole boards whose decisions on which prisoners to release are so irrational that it can be statistically proved that society would be better protected if some passerby pulled names of convicts at random out of a hat.

Coerced homosexualism is merely one of the psychological distortions built into the prison system. It appears to be prevalent among 80 per cent of all women prisoners, from 20 to 50 per cent of male prisoners, and an unknown but significant proportion of juveniles.

Ninety-seven per cent of all prisoners are eventually released back into

From *The Washington Post,* by permission.

society, where from 40 to 70 per cent of them commit new crimes.

Human prisoners in the United States are more carelessly handled than animals in our zoos, which have more space and get more "humane" care. Eighty per cent of all prison guards in the country are paid less than $8,000; all keepers of animals in the National Zoo in Washington are paid between $8,400 and $9,100.

Almost everyone seems to agree that our prisons are terrible.

President Nixon: "No institution within our society has a record which presents such a conclusive case of failure as does our prison system."

John Mitchell, former Attorney General of the United States: "The state of America's prisons comes close to a national shame. No civilized society should allow it to continue."

Norman Carlson, director of the U.S. Bureau of Prisons: "Anyone not a criminal will be when he gets out of jail."

But change is glacial. In most places there is no change at all.

The system is hardly a true system, but a disjointed collection of buildings and jurisdictions. The smallest is the federal, generally accepted as the more carefully designed, if bureaucratic.

On any given day the prisoner population in federal prisons is about 20,000, or less than 10 per cent of all sentenced prisoners in the country.

The states have 200 facilities, ranging from the big state penitentiaries to an assortment of reformatories, forestry camps and juvenile halls, ranging from some of the most humane in the country to some of the worst. They hold over 200,000 prisoners each day.

There are 4,037 jails and uncounted city and town lockups where the range in conditions runs from fairly good to filthy and dangerous. Technically, "jail" is a place where a person is held awaiting trial, "prison" where he serves a sentence.

The county jails hold about 161,000 persons a day, 5 per cent of them juveniles (usually mixed with adults) and 5 per cent women. Including jails, the total incarcerated population is about 1 million. If one includes town "drunk tanks," 3 million Americans pass through cells each year.

Who are the Americans who find themselves behind bars?

They are overwhelmingly the poor, the black and the young. A profound sense of being cheated runs through them. They may have been cheated by the environment they grew up in, by chaotic families, poor neighborhoods, ineffective schools, depressing career opportunities. But this is not the usual reason the average prisoner feels cheated. He feels that he has been unfairly treated by the criminal justice system. He is right.

A Tiny Minority of Lawbreakers

The President's Crime Commission in 1967 showed that from 3 to 10 times more crime is committed than is ever reported to police. They cite a survey showing that in a sample of 1,700 persons of all social levels, 91 per cent admitted committing acts for which they might have been imprisoned but were never caught. So most law-breakers are never caught.

If they are, the affluent tend to avoid imprisonment. The concentration in prison of the poor, the black and the young reflects, among other things, a special selection by which we decide whom to put behind bars.

Once found guilty, the fate of a sentenced man is subject to the wildest accidents of fate. Robert Apablaza sold a matchbox of marijuana and happened to find himself in a particular courtroom in New Orleans where he was sentenced to 50 years in prison; hundreds of others have done the same thing elsewhere and not gone to prison.

So every prisoner knows other offenders who received substantially better treatment than he did. He knows, and statistics prove, that justice is not even-handed.

Once committed to prison, he is still governed by chance. The building he is in may be a 100-year-old fortress with four men in a narrow, dark and damp cell, or he may be in a clean one, one man to a cell. More than a quarter of all prisoners are in prisons that are 70 years old or older.

If he is in Delaware, the state will spend $13.71 a day on his food and custody; if he is in Arkansas, $1.55 a day. If he is in Pennsylvania he will get meat and three vegetables almost every meal; if in South Carolina, meat once a week and other times greens and beans.

In some prisons he will be raped homosexually unless he is strong and has a weapon; in others he will be left alone. In some, the guards will abuse him and turn him over to psychopathic or racketeering fellow inmates, and censor his mail to make sure he gets no word of it to the outside. In other prisons he will be treated humanely and can appeal punishments to an impartial board, including inmates, and communicate with the free world.

The people on whom such uncertain justice is visited are men, women and children who already have been unlucky. At least half have been involved in drugs or alcohol. They are generally of normal intelligence (the median for federal prisoners is 104 I.Q.; for a typical Midwest state, 99.78) but they test out between 7th and 8th grade achievement.

In a typical state 25 per cent are in for burglary, 22 per cent for larceny, 12 per cent for robbery, 8 per cent for forgery, 6 per cent for assault, 5 per cent for drugs, 5 per cent for auto theft, 4 per cent for homicide, and 2 per cent for some sex offense.

The Protection of Society

The President's Crime Commission showed that in 1965 there were 2,780,000 serious crimes reported to police and 727,000 arrests made and of these 63,000 people imprisoned. Thus just for reported crime, which is a minority, only 2 per cent of criminals went to prison. If they were all released they would not materially increase the law-breaking population.

If they were released the prisoners conceivably could affect the crime rate in another way: by encouraging otherwise inhibited people to commit crimes because they felt they would not be punished.

But nobody knows this or can even guess intelligently.

For all the public clamor about crime and punishment, this field remains a wasteland of research, the most remarkable void of reliable analysis of any major institution in American life. The worst void is prison and prison programs where, in the words of one administrator, "we are sorting marbles in the dark." The American prison system is a monument to mindless procedures in the midst of a society that prides itself on being scientific and measuring everything in sight.

The result is that the lives of millions of prisoners, the billions of dollars spent on them (about $1.7 billion this year), the safety of citizens from crime and the loss of $20 billion to victims of crime, continue to be governed by archaic conventional wisdoms. The only thing we are fairly certain of is that most of these conventional wisdoms are wrong.

It is one of the conventional wisdoms that the current rise in crime is strongly influenced by excessive leniency by prosecutors and courts. Another is that harsh punishment will reduce crime. J. Edgar Hoover told a recent Senate committee, "The difficulty is with district attorneys who make deals and judges who are too soft. Some are bleeding hearts."

According to the FBI, from 1960 to 1965 the crime rate per 100,000 rose 35 per cent. Beginning in 1964, federal courts and most state judges began giving out longer sentences. From 1964 to 1970, federal sentences became 38 per cent longer and time served was even more because the federal parole board began reducing paroles. California's sentences have risen 50 per cent.

But from 1965 to 1970 the national crime rate—during the harsher period—rose 45 per cent.

Robert Martinson studied every report on treatment of prisoners since 1945 and analyzed the 231 studies. He concluded:

". . . There is very little evidence in these studies that any prevailing mode of correctional treatment has a decisive effect in reducing recidivism of convicted offenders." "Recidivism" refers to crimes committed by released prisoners.

James Robison of the National Council on Crime and Delinquency, and Gerald Smith, of the University of Utah, made one of the most rigorous analyses of various treatment in American prisons and concluded:

"It is difficult to escape the conclusion that the act of incarcerating a person at all will impair whatever potential he has for a crime-free future adjustment and that regardless of which 'treatments' are administered while he is in prison, the longer he is kept there the more he will deteriorate and the more likely is it that he will recidivate."

A Conflict of Motives

A fundamental reason for confusion is that unlike some countries, the United States has never decided what it wants its prisons to do. There are several motives for criminal punishment:

1. Hurting the prisoner so that he will feel free of guilt, having paid for his act;
2. Using the criminal as a scapegoat for others in society who feel the same criminal impulses within themselves and by punishing the criminal purge themselves;
3. The need of some to feel morally superior by sustaining outcasts in a despised and degraded condition;
4. Keeping the criminal out of circulation;
5. Revenge imposed by the state to prevent the victim or his family from taking private revenge, as in family feuds;
6. Revenge in the name of all society so that the public will not impose its own version of justice, as in lynch mobs;
7. Deterrence of the criminal who, by being hurt, will decide that committing the crime is not worth it;
8. Deterrence of others who, seeing the criminal suffer, will not imitate his crime; and
9. Reforming the criminal so that he will learn to live in peace with society.

Criminal punishment may accomplish a number of these objectives simultaneously. But some are contradictory and cannot be done together. It is not possible to cause a man to respect those who treat him with deliberate cruelty. Scapegoating does not eliminate the illicit impulse; where punishment of the individual is violent and cruel, it promotes violence and cruelty in society at large.

The confusion in goals for prisons has its roots in a curious phenomenon: the most damaging practices in criminal justice were started as humanitarian reforms.

The prison itself is an American invention created out of genuine compassion.

For centuries, people were incarcerated only until the local lord or king could impose punishment. Punishment would then be death by hanging, drowning, stoning, burning at the stake, or beheading, usually with a large crowd observing to deter them from imitation.

A Place for Penitence

In the 1780s, the Quakers of Philadelphia, taking soup to the jails, were appalled by conditions. They organized to pass laws substituting sentences of incarceration in permanent, well-designed prisons as a substitute for death, mutilation or flogging.

They designed the new prisons for solitude and meditation on the prevailing theory that men do wicked things because the devil has invaded them and only through contemplation of their sins could they become penitent and innocent again. The new institutions for penitence were called penitentiaries. The prisoners were forbidden to speak and saw no one, sometimes not even their jailers.

Europeans studying the new country reported on the new institution and adopted it, though some, like De Tocqueville and Dickens, observed that penitentiaries often produced insanity.

In the late 1800s, it was observed that country people on their farms had been law-abiding but after they moved to the impoverished industrial cities they became criminals. It was thought that there might be some connection between environment and crime, that prisons might be a way to counteract bad environment.

The impact of Freud and psychology complicated the view of human behavior, adding to the physical environment the emotional history of the individual. If prison was an opportunity to change the environment, it might also be a place to give the prisoner a more accurate view and control of himself.

But the conflicts have never been resolved between punishment and "treatment," between the purpose of protecting society by keeping the criminal locked up and the goal of protecting society by trying to condition him for peaceful return to the community.

The Usefulness of "Industries"

Only this continuing confusion could explain the survival of irrationalities like "prison industries" and the decisions of parole boards.

Most work niside federal prisons, for example, is done for an independent corporation called Federal Prison Industries, Inc. It has a board of directors mostly of executives of private corporations who serve without pay. It maintains 52 shops and factories at 22 federal institutions where it employs about 25 per cent of all federal prisoners.

Historically, at the insistence of private business and labor unions (George Meany, head of the AFL-CIO, also is on the board of FPI), they do not make goods that will compete with privately made goods, which means that they usually do not develop skills that will let the ex-convict compete in private industry after he gets out.

The chief customer is the federal government. Pay rates are from 19 to 46 cents an hour.

FPI in 1970 had earnings of $9.9 million on $58 million in sales, or 17 per cent profit on sales, the highest of any industry in the United States (average for all U.S. industry is 4.5 per cent on sales, the highest being the mining industry at 11 per cent).

FPI has proudly announced that it declared a dividend every year since 1946 and that these dividends total $82 million. To whom was this dividend on captive labor issued? The American taxpayer—the general treasury of the United States.

Federal prison officials agree that a major reason for repeated crime by ex-convicts is their lack of skill in the jobs that are needed in free life—medical and dental technicians and other categories that will hire all the qualified help they can get. They also admit that they lack the money to train significant numbers of convicts in these marketable skills. Yet they have regularly turned back large profits made by prisoner labor.

The Effects of Parole

Even prison industries cannot match the performance of parole boards for lack of success and lack of accountability. Parole is another humanitarian reform that was perverted. It was supposed to give the prisoner incentive to improve himself to earn a release earlier than his full term. It was supposed to shorten time spent behind bars. It has lengthened it.

Most prisoners are eligible to apply for parole after one-third of their sentences has been served. Judges and legislatures know that, so they have increased sentences on the assumption that most prisoners will be released in something like one-third their time. The prisoners have not been released at that rate. Consequently, American prisoners serve the longest sentences in the Western world.

But that is not the worst characteristic of American parole boards. Their purpose is to release the prisoner as soon as possible consistent with his own good and protecting society from repetition of crime. The boards are in the position of predicting human behavior, a difficult task for even the most perceptive and wise individuals.

Most parole boards are appointed by governors and include their cronies or former secretaries.

Parole boards regularly release the worst risks, as measured by the best data.

Take the case of Jack Crowell (not his real name, but a real person). He is stocky, 41-year-old Navy veteran doing 10 years for voluntary manslaughter in a Southern state. He had such a good record in the state penitentiary that toward the end of his sentence he was permitted to join the state's work release program.

Under work release he left prison to live in an unlocked dormitory in a city. He got up each morning, drove his boss's truck to the work site where he became a master plumber, supervising an assistant. At the end of the day he returned to the dormitory. He earned $140 a week and had saved $1800. He applied for a parole. The prison system recommended him. He was turned down.

Typically they didn't tell him why except that he wasn't "ready." They did parole some men direct from the state prison who had never had a chance to show that they could hold a good job and handle freedom.

Who Are the Worst Risks?

Crowell's is a typical case. One can guess what happened. He was in for manslaughter. Parole boards do not like to parole killers and sex offenders because it makes for bad public relations. They fear the headlines if such men repeat crimes while on parole. But contrary to conventional wisdom, murderers and sex offenders are the most likely *not* to repeat a crime.

In 1969 parole boards reporting to the Uniform Parole Reports released 25,563 prisoners before they completed their full sentences. Almost one-third of them were burglars who in their first year had their usual rate of repeated crime of 31 per cent. There were 2,870 armed robbers released and in the first year 27 per cent went back to prison. The boards released 2,417 forgers, 36 per cent of whom were re-imprisoned, and they released 2,299 larcenists, of whom 30 per cent went back for various violations. Murderers and rapists released had failure rates of 11 to 17 per cent.

These are the failure rates for various offenders as compiled by the most authoritative group, the Uniform Parole Reports of the National Probation and Parole Institutes of the National Council on Crime and Delinquency:

Negligent manslaughter	11%
Willful homicide	12
Statutory rape	15
Forcible rape	17
All other sex offenses	17
Aggravated assault	22
Armed robbery	27
Unarmed robbery	30
Larceny	30
Burglary	31
Forgery	36

(These are failure rates for the first year on parole; the rate increases as the group is out longer but the rank order does not change significantly over the years.)

It appears reasonable for parole boards to be more cautious in releasing violent men. Even if burglars repeat their crimes, theft of property is less harmful to society than killing and raping. But here, too, the data do not support the parole boards: murderers and rapists on their second offense do not commit as many added murders and rapes as do other kinds of criminals. Of 30 cases of willful homicie that sent 1969 parolees back to prison in their first year of freedom, 24 were committed by people not originally in for willful homicide. Six released murderers went back to prison or another killing, but nine burglars went back for murders.

The 511 forcible rapists on parole, to take another example, committed four new forcible rapes; burglars during their paroles committed eight. All men whose original conviction was for property crimes while on parole committed 12 forcible rapes.

The rate of new homicides and rapes by all categories of released prisoners is about the same, approximately one-half of 1 per cent. Since murderers and rapists represent a small proportion of all released prisoners, about 12 per cent for all such categories, their one-half of 1 per cent represents less of a threat to society than do the violent new episodes by other kinds of criminals.

Because they regularly release the worst risks, parole boards would do better picking parolees at random.

Parole boards are not solely to blame. Whatever other notions are in their heads when they make their decisions, they are seriously influenced by public opinion. The police and the general public are outraged at the violent crimes of released prisoners; they don't know that 97 per cent of all prisoners are released anyway and that the longer criminals stay in prison, the more crimes they commit afterwards.

The Torture of Uncertainty

In prison after prison, the uncertainty of the sentence was mentioned as the most excruciating part of prison. "Give me a fixed sentence anytime" is common.

Or, "I behaved myself, the warden recommended me, I had a job on the outside, my family said they had a place for me and they turned me down. I ask them why and they say, 'You're not ready.'

"I ask them what that means and they don't say. What am I supposed to do? Give me five, give me ten but let me know how much time I have to do and don't keep me hanging all the time."

Society takes elaborate pains to assure that lawyers and judges are qualified to exercise their power over the freedom of their fellow citizens and that no person is deprived of his liberty without due process of law, including a review of grave decisions. Yet the gravest of decisions—a majority of the time a citizen may spend imprisoned—is determined most of the time by untrained persons acting without adequate information, in opposition to the best data and without accountability.

During the last few years, the federal parole board has reduced paroles by 20 per cent.

In Louisiana they stopped giving all convicted armed robbers parole, after which armed robberies in the state rose 57 per cent.

It is tragic for the protection of society and the future success of prisoners that carefully selected boards do not use the best available data to decide the issue of liberty or imprisonment. It unnecessarily exposes society to more crime, it stunts the potential for change within convicted criminals and it suffuses American prisons with frustration and bitterness.

The Least Studied Institution

What remains after the available data on criminality are sifted is the remarkable absence of other good data on American prisons and their effectiveness. Prisons would seem to be ideal laboratories for social scientists—controlled populations in a variety of conditions, available to be measured and compared. But they remain the least scientifically studied of any major American institution.

George Saleebey, Deputy Director of the California Youth Authority, was asked why it is that a society apprehensive about crime, and a country anxious about criminals, did not insist on rigorous study and analysis.

"Wait a minute," Saleebey said. "Wait a minute. Who said they give a damn? They want some people put away and then they want to forget about them."

Why don't prison administrators themselves look carefully at their own results? George Beto, director of Texas prisons, says:

"I know of no institution unless it be organized Christianity which has shown a greater reluctance to measure the effectiveness of its varied programs than has corrections."

The answer seems to be that what happens to prisoners inside American prisons has very little to do with the prisoners themselves or what will happen to them after they are released into the free world. The state of prisons seems mainly determined by the values of the American citizen who considers himself law-abiding.

John Irwin served five years in Soledad Prison for armed robbery. He is now a college professor at San Francisco State College, specializing in penal studies. He says:

"The radicals talk of abolishing punishment, but they really want to start punishing a new population of 'capitalist pigs.' The liberals want punishment but call it 'treatment.' The conservatives are the only ones honest about it, but they want such disproportionate amounts that it's crazy."

It is hard to avoid the conclusion that what goes on inside American prisons tells more about the character of people outside the walls than it does about the inmates inside.

The Torture Cure

JESSICA MITFORD

One of the primary characteristics of "total institutions" is that they have almost complete control over their "inmates." But how far should prisons go in their attempt to control and change the behavior of inmates? Jessica Mitford explores several current treatment approaches in American prisons and likens some of them to "torture cures."

Recognition of failure dawns slowly in a bureaucracy but dawned it has in California prison treatment circles. Prison psychiatrists who are willing to level with reporters admit that they now spend 90 percent of their time on paperwork, writing up reports for the Adult Authority based on perfunctory annual interviews with prisoners, that "treatment" most often takes the form of heavy tranquilization of inmates labeled psychotic as well as those diagnosed as troublemakers. Group therapy, once hailed as an exciting new technique for transforming the "deviant personality," is withering on the vine. Nor have the treatment programs produced the anticipated docility in the convict population; work strikes, hunger strikes, and other forms of protest are now endemic throughout the California prisons.

Some disconcerting conclusions about the efficacy of treatment are set forth in a report of the State Assembly titled "The California Prison, Parole, and Probation System." It cites an exhaustive study conducted for the Department of Corrections in which the researchers observed gloomily, "Thousands of inmates and hundreds of staff members were participating in this program at a substantial cost to the Department of Corrections in time, effort, and money. Contrary to the expectations of the treatment theory, there were no significant differences in outcome for those in the various treatment programs or between the treatment groups and the control group." They further reported that group counseling did not lessen adherence to the inmate code, nor did it reduce the frequency of discipline problems.

James O. Robison, author of the report and longtime researcher for the Department of Corrections, traced the course of disillusionment. "The high mystique of treatment peaked at the end of the Fifties," he told me. "The idea took hold in Corrections that at last, through sophisticated techniques of psychotherapy, we have it in our power to transform the deviant and to predict with accuracy his future behavior. But in the early Sixties the high priests of Corrections began a sifting of the entrails. After that, disenchantment and embarrassment set in—the reason was the evident empirical failure of the treatment programs, as demonstrated by the recidivism rate remaining constant over the years.

"The rationale for failure was always, 'We haven't carried treatment far enough, there isn't enough of it, it isn't professional enough'—in other words, we need more and better of same, in spite of the fact we've seen it doesn't work. Even this reasoning began to break down in the middle Sixties, when there was more attention paid to the fact nothing was happening and more talk of '*Why?*'

"What you are likely to see now is the end of the liberal treatment era—the notion that you can make convicts into converts of the dominant culture 'religion,' the missionary fervor—that's being replaced with 'behavior modification' experiments. The latest reasoning is that it's costly and inappropriate to go the psychotherapy route with these people, to pay high-priced psychiatrists to *talk* them into recognizing the truth of our 'religion'; instead, we'll focus on their deviant behavior and force them to shape up. Of course, this flies in the face of the earlier rhetoric. The Behaviorists say they are bad, not mad, and we can stop them being bad by utilizing new techniques. This fits in with the law-and-order, no-nonsense conservative viewpoint: henceforth the slogan will be, 'They must be *made* to behave.'"

This new trend in Corrections must be highly inspiriting for the behavioral scientists, who have long been eyeing the prisons as convenient reservoirs of human material on which to try out new theories. The shape of things to come was forecast a decade ago at a seminar of prison wardens and psychologists chaired by James V. Bennett, then director of the U.S. Bureau of Prisons. As described in *Corrective Psychiatry & Journal of Social Change*, Second Quarter, 1962, the seminar provided "provocative, fruitful interaction between social scientists and correctional administrators."

Addressing himself to the topic "Man Against Man: Brainwashing," Dr. Edgar H. Schein, associate professor of psychology at MIT, told the assembled wardens: "My basic argument is this: in order to produce marked change of behavior and/or attitude, it is necessary to weaken, undermine, or remove the supports to the old patterns of behavior and the old attitudes"; this can be done "either by removing the individual physically and preventing any communication with those whom he cares about, or by proving to him that those whom he respects are not worthy of it and, indeed, should be actively mistrusted."

Dr. Schein, who said he got most of his ideas from studying brainwashing techniques used by North Korean and Chinese Communists on GI prisoners of war, cautioned his audience not to be put off by this fact: "These same techniques in the service of different goals may be quite acceptable to us. . . . I would like to have you think of brainwashing not in terms of politics, ethics, and morals, but in terms of the deliberate changing of human behavior and attitudes by a group of men who have relatively complete control over the environment in which the captive population lives."

Some of the techniques which could usefully be applied in the U.S. prisons: "Social disorganization and the creation of mutual mistrust" achieved by "spying on the men and reporting back private material"; "tricking men into written statements" that are then shown to others, the objective being "to convince most men they could trust no one," "undermining ties to home by the systematic withholding of mail." The key factor is change of attitude: "Supports for old attitudes have to be undermined and destroyed if change is to take place. . . . Do we not feel it to be legitimate to destroy the emotional ties of one criminal to another, or of a criminal to a sick community?" How to bring about the desired change was explained by Dr. Schein: "If one wants to produce behavior inconsistent with the person's standards of conduct, first disorganize the group which supports those standards, then undermine his other emotional supports, then put him into a new and ambiguous situation for which the standards are unclear, and then put pressure on him. I leave it to you to judge whether there is any similarity between these events and those which occur in prisons when we teach prisoners 'to serve their own time' by moving them around and punishing clandestine group activity not sanctioned by the prison authorities."

The discussion, says the report, ranged from "specific, practical management issues such as 'How shall we manage the Muslims?' 'Whom should we isolate?' " to more basic questions, such as "the use and effectiveness of brainwashing and other means of persuasion." Dr. Bennett recalled that "during the war we struggled with the conscientious objectors—nonviolent coercionists—and believe me, that was really a problem . . . we were always trying to find some way in which we could change or manipulate their environment."

Much attention was focused on what to do about the Black Muslims: "not so much whether you take action against the Muslims as a group," as one speaker put it, "but how can you counteract the effects of the kinds of techniques they use to recruit members and cause general mischief in the prison system?" To which a Dr. Lowry responded, "We found that many of these Negro Muslims were highly intelligent . . . here again, we have to apply the techniques which we heard about in terms of appreciating what the goal of the Muslims is, or of any other group, and then doing some analytic study of the methods that they are using so that we can try to dissipate the forces that are going in the direction that we regard as destructive "On ways of dealing with the unruly a panelist offered this: "To some extent where we formerly had isolation as a controlling technique, we now have drugs, so that drugs in a sense become a new kind of restraint. The restraint, therefore, is biochemical, but it is restraint nevertheless."

Summarizing the discussion, Dr. Bennett pointed out that the federal prison system, with some 24,000 men in it, presents "a tremendous opportunity to carry on some of the experimenting to which the various panelists have alluded." He added, "What I am hoping is that the audience here will believe that we here in Washington are anxious to have you undertake some of these things: do things perhaps on your own—undertake a little experiment of what you can do with the Muslims, what you can do with some of the sociopath individuals."

That Dr. Bennett's counsel was taken to heart by his subordinates in the federal prison system can be inferred from a report addressed to the United Nations Economic and Social Council, prepared and smuggled out of Marion Federal Penitentiary in July 1972, by the Federal Prisoners' Coalition, a group of convicts housed in the segregation unit for refusing to participate in the behavioral research programs. "In the latter part of 1968 some changes in the U.S. Department of Justice enabled the U.S. Bureau of Prisons to make a quiet beginning at implementing an experimental program at Marion Federal Prison to determine at first hand how effective a weapon brainwashing might be for the U.S. Department of Justice's future use," says the report. It describes how Dr. Martin Groder, prison psychiatrist, applies the proposals outlined in Dr. Schein's paper to "agitators," suspected militants, writ-writers, and other troublemakers. The first step, according to the report, is to sever the inmate's ties with his family by transferring him to some remote prison where they will be unable to visit him. There he is put in isolation, deprived of mail and other privileges, until he agrees to participate in Dr. Groder's Transactional Analysis program. If he succumbs, he will be moved to new living quarters where he will be surrounded by members of Dr. Groder's "prisoner thought-reform team," and subjected to intense group pressure. "His emotional, behavioral, and psychic characteristics are studied by the staff and demiprofessional prisoners to detect vulnerable points of entry to stage attack-sessions around. During these sessions, on a progressively intensified basis, he is shouted at, his fears played on, his sensitivities ridiculed, and concentrated efforts made to make him feel guilty for real or imagined characteristics or conduct. . . . Every effort is made to heighten his suggestibility and weaken his character structure so that his emotional responses and thought-flow will be brought under group and staff control as totally as possible.

". . . It is also driven in to him that society, in the guise of its authorities, is looking out for his best interests and will help if he will only permit it to do so. Help him be 'reborn' as a highly probable 'winner in the game of life,' is the way this comes across in the group's jargon." Once reborn as a winner, he will be moved into a plush living area equipped with stereo, tape recorders, typewriters, books. He is now ready to indoctrinate newcomers into the mysteries of the group "and like a good attack dog, he is graded and evaluated on his demonstrated capacity to go for the vulnerable points of any victim put before him." The entire program is made self-perpetuating and economically feasible by the participants doing the work themselves, says the report: "They are taught to police not only themselves but others, to inform on one another in acceptable fashion—as bringing out misconduct of another in a truth-session is not considered informing even if a staff member is present."

Evidently these techniques are finding increasing favor with the federal prison administration. Scheduled to open early in 1974 near Butner, North Carolina, is a new federal institution, the Behavioral Research Center, built at a cost of $13.5 million, which, says a handout from the Bureau of Prisons, will be "a unique facility in the federal correctional system." Some of the unique features are spelled out in a confidential operations memorandum from the bureau to staff, dated October 25, 1972, on the subject of Project START, acronym for Special Treatment and Rehabilitative Training, already in operation in Springfield Federal Penitentiary. The goal, according to the memorandum, is "to develop behavioral attitudinal changes in offenders who have not adjusted satisfactorily to institutional settings" and to provide "care, custody, and correction of the long-term adult offender in a setting separated from his home institution." "Selection criteria" include: "will have shown repeated inability to adjust to regular institutional programs"; "will be transferred from the sending institution's segregation unit"; "generally, will have a minimum of two years remaining on his sentence"; "in terms of personality characteristics shall be aggressive, manipulative, resistive to authority, etc."

Dr. Martin Groder, who will direct the Butner operation, told Tom Wicker of the *New York Times* that he "believes in the possibility of rehabilitating prisoners" because he has done it, at Marion. He does not favor any large-scale return of incarcerated men to community programs; on the contrary, he prefers to keep them in his custody: "If we can get a topnotch rehabilitation program within the institution, a prisoner will be better off in it than wandering around the streets." Wicker reports that Dr. Groder is "not precise" about the rehabilitative methods he intends to apply, and that he is "cheerfully aware that the new federal center he will head is suspect in some circles—not least among federal prisoners, who are not anxious to be 'guinea pigs' in behavior research. He is nevertheless pressing ahead . . ."

A further elaboration on the brainwashing theme is furnished by James V. McConnell, professor of psychology at the University of Michigan, in an article in the May 1970 issue of *Psychology Today* titled "Criminals Can Be Brainwashed—Now." It reads like science fiction, the fantasy of a deranged scientist. Yet much of what Dr. McConnell proposes as appropriate therapy for tomorrow's lawbreaker is either already here or in the planning stages in many of the better financed prison systems.

Dr. McConnell, who spent many years successfully training flatworms to go in and out of mazes at his bidding by administering a series of painful electric shocks, now proposes to apply similar techniques to convicts: "I believe the day has come when we can combine sensory deprivation with drugs, hypnosis, and astute manipulation of reward and punishment to gain almost absolute control over an individual's behavior . . . We'd assume that a felony was clear evidence that the criminal had somehow acquired full-blown social neurosis and needed to be cured, not punished . . . We'd probably have to restructure his entire personality."

The exciting potential of sensory deprivation as a behavior modifier was revealed through an experiment in which students were paid $20 a day to live in tiny, solitary cubicles with nothing to do. The experiment was supposed to last at least six weeks, but none of the students could take it for more than a few days: "Many experienced vivid hallucinations—one student in particular insisted that a tiny spaceship had got into the chamber and was buzzing around shooting pellets at him." While they were in this condition, the experimenter fed the students propaganda messages: "No matter how poorly it was presented or how illogical it sounded, the propaganda had a marked effect on the students' attitudes—an effect that lasted for at least a year after they came out of the deprivation chambers."

Noting that "the legal and moral issues raised by such procedures are frighteningly complex," Dr. McConnell nevertheless handily disposes of them: "I don't believe the Constitution of the United States gives you the *right* to commit a crime if you want to; therefore, the Constitution does not guarantee you the right to maintain inviolable the personality forced on you in the first place—if and when the personality manifests strongly antisocial behavior."

The new behavioral control techniques, says Dr. McConnell, "make even the hydrogen bomb look like a child's toy, and, of course, they can be used for good or evil." But it will avail us nothing to "hide our collective heads in the sand and pretend that it can't happen here. Today's behavioral psychologists are the architects and engineers of the Brave New World."

For some convicts in California, those perceived as "dangerous," "revolutionary," or "uncooperative" by the authorities, it *has* happened here, and Dr. McConnell's Brave New World is their reality. Signposts in this bizarre terrain may need translation for the auslander:

Sensory Deprivation: Confinement (often for months or years) in the Adjustment Center, a prison-within-prison.

Stress Assessment: The prisoner lives in an open dormitory where it is expected he will suffer maximum irritation from the lack of privacy. He is assigned to the worst and most menial jobs. In compulsory group therapy sessions staff members deliberately bait the men and try to provoke conflicts among them. The idea is to see how much of this a person can stand without losing his temper.

Chemotherapy: The use of drugs (some still in the experimental stage) as "behavior modifiers," including antitestosterone hormones, which have the effect of chemically castrating the subject, and Prolixin, a form of tranquilizer with unpleasant and often dangerous side effects.

Aversion Therapy: The use of medical procedures that cause pain and fear to bring about the desired "behavior modification."

Neurosurgery: Cutting or burning out those portions of the brain believed to cause "aggressive behavior."

The "behavior modification" programs are for the most part carried out in secret. They are not part of the guided tour for journalists and visitors, nor are outside physicians permitted to witness them. Occasionally word of these procedures leaks out, as in the autumn of 1970, when *Medical World News* ran an article titled "Scaring the Devil Out" about the use of the drug Anectine in "aversion therapy" in the California prisons.

Anectine, a derivative of the South American arrow-tip poison curare, is used medically in small doses as a muscle relaxant, but behavioral researchers discovered that when administered to unruly prisoners in massive amounts—from twenty to forty milligrams—it causes them to lose all control of voluntary muscles.

An unpublished account of the Anectine therapy program at Vacaville, California, by two of the staff researchers there, Arthur L. Mattocks, supervisor of the research unit, and Charles Jew, social research analyst, states that "the conceptual scheme was to develop a strong association between any violent or acting-out behavior and the drug Anectine and its frightful consequences," among which were "cessation of respiration for a period of approximately two minutes' duration." Of those selected to endure these consequences, "nearly all could be characterized as angry young men," say the authors. Some seem to have been made a good deal angrier by the experience, for the report notes that of sixty-four prisoners in the program "nine persons not only did not decrease but actually exhibited an increase in their overall number of disciplinary infractions."

According to Dr. Arthur Nugent, chief psychiatrist at Vacaville and an enthusiast for the drug, it induces "sensations of suffocation and drowning." The subject experiences feelings of deep horror and terror, "as though he were on the brink of death." While he is in this condition a therapist scolds him for his misdeeds and tells him to shape up or expect more of the same. Candidates for Anectine treatment were selected for a range of offenses: "frequent fights, verbal threatening, deviant sexual behavior, stealing, unresponsiveness to the group therapy programs." Dr. Nugent told the *San Francisco Chronicle*, "Even the toughest inmates have come to fear and hate the drug. I don't blame them, I wouldn't have one treatment myself for the world." Declaring he was anxious to continue the experiment, he added, "I'm at a loss as to why everybody's upset over this."

More upset was to follow a year later, when the press got wind of a letter from Director Raymond Procunier to the California Council on Criminal Justice requesting funding estimated at $48,000 for "neurosurgical treatment of violent inmates." The letter read, in part: "The problem of treating the aggressive, destructive inmate has long been a problem in all correctional systems. During recent years this problem has become particularly acute in the California Department of Corrections institutions . . . This letter of intent is to alert you to the development of a proposal to seek funding for a program involving a complex neurosurgical evaluation and treatment program for the violent inmate . . . surgical and diagnostic procedures would be performed to locate centers in the brain which may have been previously damaged and which could serve as the focus for episodes of violent behavior. If these areas were located and verified that they were indeed the source of aggressive behavior, neurosurgery would be performed . . ." Confronted by reporters with this letter, Laurence Bennett, head of the Department of Corrections Research Division, explained: "It is not a proposal, it's just an idea-concept." He added wistfully, "It's quite likely that we will not proceed with this, but if we had unlimited funds we would explore every opportunity to help anyone who wants such assistance."

Although the plan for psychosurgery was halted—at least temporarily—by the newspaper uproar that ensued, the authorities have other methods at hand for controlling the unruly, principal among which is forced drugging of prisoners. In widespread use throughout the nation's prisons is the drug Prolixin, a powerful tranquilizer derived from phenothiazine, which, if given in large doses, produces dangerous and often irreversible side effects. A petition addressed to the California Senate Committee on Penal Institutions by La Raza Unida, a Chicano organization of prisoners confined in the California Men's Colony, describes these: "The simple fact that a number of prisoners are walking the yard in this institution like somnambulists, robots, and vegetables as a result of this drug should be reason enough to make people apprehensive as to the effect it is having. That no prisoner feels safe because he never knows when he will become a candidate for said drug is another factor in producing tension in this institution."

According to its manufacturer, E. R. Squibb, Prolixin is "a highly potent behavior modifier with a markedly extended duration of effect." Possible adverse side effects listed by Squibb include: the induction of a "catatonic-like state," nausea, loss of appetite, headache, constipation, blurred vision, glaucoma, bladder paralysis, impotency, liver damage, hypotension severe enough to cause fatal cardiac arrest, and cerebral edema. Furthermore, Squibb cautions that "a persistent pseudo-parkinsonian [palsy-like] syndrome may develop . . . characterized by rhythmic, stereotyped dyskinetic involuntary movements . . . resembling the facial grimaces of encephalitis . . . The symptoms persist after drug withdrawal, and in some patients appear to be irreversible."

The theme of prison as a happy hunting ground for the researcher is very big in current penological literature. In *I Chose Prison,* James V. Bennett poses the question, What will the prisons of 2000 A.D. be like? And answers it: "In my judgment the prison system will increasingly be valued, and used, as a laboratory and workshop of social change." Dr. Karl Menninger echoes this thought in *The Crime of Punishment*: "About all this [causes of crime], we need more information, more research, more experimental data. That research is the basis for scientific progress, no one any more disputes . . . Even our present prisons, bad as many of them are, could be extensively used as laboratories for the study of many of the unsolved problems."

Taking these injunctions to heart, researchers are descending in droves upon the prisons with their prediction tables, expectancy scales, data analysis charts. With all the new money available under federal crime control programs, and the ingenuity of grant-happy researchers, the scope of the investigations seems limitless. In California some $600,000 of the Department of Corrections budget is earmarked for research, but this is just the tip of the iceberg, for most of the work is done under lavish grants from universities, foundations, and government agencies.

Something of the quality of the research, and the bitter irony of the situation in which the convict-research subject finds himself, can be inferred from the stream of monographs, research reviews, and reports that flow out of the prisons. His captors having arranged life for the prisoner so that he becomes enraged, perhaps goes mad, and (no matter what his original sexual preferences) turns homosexual, they invite researchers to put him under their microscopes and study the result. A forty-eight-page monograph titled "Homosexuality in Prisons," published in February 1972 by the Law Enforcement Assistance Administration, reports, "in view of methodological difficulties, the following estimates of male homosexuality should be viewed with caution," and proceeds to give them, complete with footnotes referring the luckless reader to yet other publications on this subject. Estimates of the incidence of homosexuality given by experts vary, says the author, from 7 to 90 percent. He concludes, "There is above all a compelling need for a wide variety of comparative data," and proposes to fill the need by conducting "longitudinal or retrospective studies."

Among the offerings of the California Department of Corrections *Research Review* for 1971 is "The Self-Esteem Project," its aim "to obtain some picture of the effect of incarceration upon the perception of self-worth," in which the Modified Coopersmith Self-Esteem Scale is found to be "a useful instrument for measurement." Having subjected the inmate's self-esteem to the pulverizer of prison, the department proceeds to measure and tabulate what is left.

If the prisoner happens to be Chicano, he will be eligible for a study entitled "The Consequences of Familial Separation for Chicano Families," its purpose "to study the consequences of separation from family members for Chicano inmates and also for their families in terms of social, psychological, and economic needs and stresses." Thus the precise quantity and quality of suffering, anxiety, and impoverishment of families caused by locking up Chicanos can be tidily computed and catalogued for the edification of social scientists. By now the prisoner may well be ready for the Buss Rating Scale of Hostility or the Multiple Affect Adjective Checklist, "a standardized and reliable rating instrument that can be scored for anxiety, depression, and, most importantly, hostility."

Omitted from the 1971 *Research Review* is one of the more ambitious experimental projects of that year: establishment of a Maximum Psychiatric Diagnostic Unit (MPDU) designed to hold eighty-four convicts (a number possibly chosen in subconscious tribute to George Orwell) selected as research subjects from the 700 inmates of the state's Adjustment Centers. The goal of MPDU, as defined in the department's grant application to the California Council on Criminal Justice, is "to provide highly specialized diagnostic service for Adjustment Center inmates who are violently acting-out and management problem cases within the California prison system . . . and arriving at decisions as to the needed intervention and placement." The budget for this "service" would be approximately $500,000.

Who are the Adjustment Center inmates from whose ranks the eighty-four would be chosen? Robert E. Doran, who made a study of them under a grant from LEAA for the American Justice Institute, says they are "deviants within a society of deviants," or put another way, rebels who refuse to conform to prison life. They are younger and darker than the prison population as a whole: 61 percent are under thirty compared with 39 percent for the total prison population, 60 to 70 percent are black or Chicano compared with a nonwhite overall prison population of 45 percent. The majority are there for "disrespect for authority," disobeying some disciplinary rule—refusing to work, shave, attend group therapy; a growing number are there because they are suspected of harboring subversive beliefs.

In 1972 ten inmates of Folson Prison filed a federal suit (unsuccessful), charging they had been kept in long-term solitary confinement because of their political views, and alleging that the practice is routinely used against prisoners who are outspoken about prison conditions or voice "militant" political views. Department spokesmen strenuously deny that they use lock-up in the Adjustment Center as punishment for political dissidents and leaders of ethnic groups. Philip Guthrie, press agent for the Department, told the *Sacramento Bee* on March 10, 1972: "We're very careful not to lock a guy up just because of his political views." But in their closed departmental meetings it is a different story. As reported in the confidential minutes of the wardens and superintendents meeting, October 11–12, 1972, under the topic "Inmate Alliances," Director Raymond Procunier "asked the problem be kept in perspective, comparing it to the Muslim situation ten years ago. The director suggested the leaders of the various groups be removed from the general population of the institutions and locked up."

Much has been written about the California Adjustment Centers, for it was in the exercise yard of "O-Wing," Soledad Adjustment Center, that three unarmed black convicts were shot to death by a guard in early 1970, triggering a series of events that culminated in the death of George Jackson, the trial of the surviving Soledad Brothers, and the trial of Angela Davis, all acquitted by juries. From three sources one can infer something about conditions of life in the Adjustment Centers, and the roots of violence therein.

Departmental memoranda to staff in charge of "O-Wing" contain these directives:

Yard Exercise: Two officers (one armed with a Gas Billy and one armed with Mace) will enter the tier to be released and, after subjecting each inmate to an unclothed body search, release him from his cell, by key, directing him to the yard.

All inmates housed in "O-Wing" first tier, when escorted from the security section for any reason, are to be given an unclothed body search while still in their cells . . . The inmate will be given a visual inspection of his body, to include his hair, ears, mouth, private parts and feet . . . The inmate will be handcuffed behind his back and escorted from the section . . .

"O-Wing" Equipment: 1. Gas Billy (blast type). 2. Gas Billy Reload. 3. Triple Chaser Grenade. 4. Aerosol Mace (Mark IV Atomizer) . . .

Any inmate who self-mutilates or attempts to hang himself will be housed in the Hospital Annex cells only on the direction of the medical staff.

Robert E. Doran describes what he learned about the guards' view of assignments to the Adjustment Center. "Those staff who have 'really been there,' experienced the trouble, used the gas, the batons, the weapons, and the muscle, and did so effectively, receive the highest status and deference from other custodial staff. . . . Staff battle ribbons and badges are won or lost within the A/C when trouble takes place. Actually the A/C, much like the general prison situation, has in terms of relative percentage of time, very little trouble. But it is the folklore, the beliefs and the history as passed from one generation of custodial personnel to the next that promulgates the idea that has grown up around the A/C which in effect says, 'This is the front line: here is where the battle is really won or lost for staff who wear the custodial uniform.' "

Testifying in San Francisco before a Congressional subcommittee, two lawyers related some exploits of these frontline heroes. Edwin T. Caldwell of San Francisco said, "I will testify for the record that I am a registered Republican from a conservative background. This is such a shocking thing for me I just can't believe it exists."

Caldwell told the committee his client in Soledad's "O-Wing" had been "viciously attacked" by guards on numerous occasions, and had suffered a fractured tooth, a broken jaw, and lacerations requiring six sutures. Fay Stender of Oakland handed the committee chairman a note signed by Lieutenant Flores, Adjustment Center guard, written in response to an inmate who was coughing blood and had asked for help. The note said: "Yell for help when the blood is an inch thick, all over the floor, and don't call before that."

Details of the highly specialized services to be rendered the eighty-four chosen from this milieu, and the nature of the needed intervention, were discussed at a "think session" called in November 1971 at the University of

California at Davis by Laurence Bennett, head of the Department of Corrections Research Division. Participants were some twenty-five representatives of the healing professions—medicine, psychology, psychiatry—many of them faculty members from nearby universities and medical schools.

The new unit, said Max May, program administrator, would be closely modeled after Patuxent Institution in Maryland, with four twenty-one-man cellblocks, "single five-by-seven-foot cells with bars, only we call them barriers." Construction costs would be kept to a minimum since the prisoners were to build their own cages, the work, according to the grant application, consisting "primarily of pouring two concrete floors, erecting wire screen partitions, also a gun tower."

The objective, said Bennett, is "to develop a basic knowledge of the causes of aggressive, violent behavior. Our aim is to learn how to identify small groups, how to deal with them more adequately. We hope through psychological management to learn how to lessen their violence potential."

Discussion from the floor, and at the pleasant luncheon gathering in the faculty club dining room, centered on methods by which this might be accomplished: "We need to find the stimulus to which the subject responds. We also need to find out how he thinks *covertly* and to change how he thinks." "We need to dope up many of these men in order to calm them down to the point that they are accessible to treatment." "Those who can't be controlled by drugs are candidates for the implantation of subcortical electrodes [electrodes plunged deep into the brain]."

Dr. Keith Brody of Stanford University, who said he runs a "unit for mood disorders," stressed the importance of "intensive data collection" via spinal taps and other tests: "These tests can lead to therapy decisions. We need to segregate out and dissect out these sub-groups." Other proposals for therapy were to burn out electrically those areas of the brain believed to be the "source of aggressive behavior"—one speaker said he reckoned about 10 percent of the inmates might be candidates for this treatment; the administration of antitestosterone hormones, which have the effect of emasculating the subject; the use of pneumoencephalograms (injecting air into the brain cavities).

Asked whether the Anectine torture "therapy" would be resumed in the new unit, Bennett did not answer directly but declared with some exasperation, "If it could be shown empirically that hitting an inmate on the head with a hammer would cure him, I'd do it. You talk about his civil rights—civil rights for what? To continue to disrupt society?" Nor would he answer the further questions: "Does not the prison system itself, and particularly the Adjustment Center, generate violence?" and "Would the researchers be directing any part of their inquiry to violence by guards against prisoners?"

As for the compliant participation of the distinguished group of faculty members in this bizarre discussion, one possible explanation was suggested by the lone black psychiatrist present, Dr. Wendell Lipscomb, who had stormed out of the meeting halfway through, declaring he "couldn't take any more of this crap." Later, he told me, "What you were seeing at that meeting were the grant hunters, hungry for money, willing to eat any shit that's put before them."

Caution: Mental Health May Be Hazardous

ANNETTE EHRLICH AND FRED ABRAHAM-MAGDAMO

The concepts of "mental health" and "mental illness" are more difficult to define than is commonly recognized, and their application to individuals can be quite arbitrary. For example, the American Psychological Association recently removed homosexuality from its manual of mental illnesses. The following article discusses the process and implications of labeling people in this way.

The mental processes of the man with whom one disagrees are always wrong. Where is the line between wrong mind and insane mind? It is inconceivable that any sane man can radically disagree with one's most sane conclusions.

—JACK LONDON, THE IRON HEEL

The foregoing was published in 1907, and expressed London's concern that political dissidents would someday be dealt with by labeling them "insane" and then imprisoning them in mental institutions. To his contemporaries, the idea that mental-health concepts could be misused in this way sounded far-fetched. In the light of recent events, however, his novel seems to have been prophetic. For one thing, mental institutions sometimes have been used as prisons, a fact that has been documented by the one group of people most apt to know—mental-health professionals. For another, there is a growing tendency to label particular social-ethnic groups "mentally ill." Thus, in a proposal to establish a Center for the Study and Reduction of Violence in Los Angeles (announced by Governor Reagan in his 1973 State of the State message and submitted to the California Council on Criminal

Justice in 1973 for funding), a group of UCLA psychiatrists asserted, "The major known correlates of violence are sex (male), age (youthful), ethnicity (black) and urbanicity." One development not foreseen by London was that modern technology would provide us with more sophisticated techniques for behavioral control than mere imprisonment. Some people view this development with enthusiasm. For example, in 1970, a well-known American psychologist, James McConnell, had this to say:

I believe that the day has come when we can combine sensory deprivation with drugs, hypnosis and astute manipulation of reward and punishment to gain almost absolute control over an individual's behavior. . . . We should reshape society so that we all would be trained from birth to want to do what society wants us to do. We have the techniques now to do it.

Who will decide what it is that all of us should be trained to "want to do"? Obviously, it will be mental-health professionals such as McConnell.

Currently, an increasing number of people are voicing concern over the growing unchecked power of the mental-health professions, notably clinical psychology and psychiatry. Particularly penetrating observations have been made by articulate professionals such as Thomas Szasz (*The Manufacture of Madness*), Phyllis Chesler (*Women and Madness*), Seymour Halleck (*The Politics of Therapy*), Alexander Thomas and Samuel Sillen (*Racism and Psychiatry*) and a group of radical therapists in *Rough Times*. The critics have argued that, at their mildest, these professions operate to maintain the status quo and that, at their worst, they function in a repressive way to stifle dissent. Mental-health professionals have countered by insisting that their motives are always humanitarian and have claimed that what they do has no political overtones whatever.

Of course, mental-health professionals often are able to help people who turn to them voluntarily to deal with emotional crises. We are not concerned here with their role as therapists but rather as wielders of power. Not everything done in the name of mental health is necessarily good. We feel that the present tendency to concentrate power in the hands of a few mental-health professionals coupled with the development of new and sophisticated techniques for behavioral control represents a potential threat to our civil liberties.

When we try to define mental health, we find ourselves on slippery ground almost immediately. Most of us accept unquestioningly the right of mental-health professionals to tell certain people that they are in need of help and even to force that help onto them if they do not want it. We do this because we assume that such professionals have a clearly defined concept of what it is to be healthy. In fact, this is not the case. The American Psychiatric Association defines mental health as:

A state of being, relative rather than absolute, in which a person has effected a reasonably satisfactory integration of his instinctual drives. His integration is ac-

ceptable to himself and to his social milieu as reflected in his interpersonal relationships, his level of satisfaction in living, his actual achievement, his flexibility, and the level of maturity he has attained. (A *Psychiatric Glossary*, 1969)

Some problems with the definition are: (1) It seems to apply only to men. (2) It relies upon unscientific concepts such as instinct. (3) It employs criteria that are essentially value judgments. What, for example, is "acceptable" and "satisfactory" to one psychiatrist may not be to another, and how are we to recognize "maturity" and "flexibility" when we see it? (4) It places heavy emphasis on social adjustment and is, therefore, inconsistent with the definition of mental illness. That is, mental *health* is defined in a relativistic way as whatever is acceptable to other people; this will obviously be different at different times and in different places, but mental illness (schizophrenia, para noia, etc.) is treated as though, like fever and irregular heartbeat, it had some existence separate from particular social systems.

As an indication of how arbitrary these mental-health criteria actually are, both masturbation and homosexuality originally were condemned on religious grounds because they represented sex for its own sake and not for procreation. During the 18th and 19th centuries, with the rise of the mental-health movement, what was really a moral objection became medical "fact"; to masturbate or to engage in homosexual activity was "sick." Any measures were considered appropriate to deal with these disorders. Some procedures that actually were used for masturbators were clitoridectomy (excision of the clitoris) in girls and women and circumcision and deenervation of the nerves leading to the genital area in boys and men. Nowadays, we tend to regard masturbation as harmless; and although some mental-health professionals still persist in calling people who prefer their own sex sick, many others now are coming to accept the view that homosexuals are no better and no worse than the rest of us. Recently the American Psychiatric Association voted to remove homosexuality from its diagnostic and statistical manual of mental illness. It is important to note that the changes have come about not because of any new medical knowledge or psychological discoveries but because of our generally more permissive sexual attitudes (plus, in the case of homosexuals, organized action in their own behalf).

Another example of shifting standards concerns the changing view of women. In the Victorian era, middle-and upper-class women were expected to be largely ornamental. In Freud's hands, what was essentially a convenient social arrangement for men was elevated into medical "fact"; a woman who showed any signs of independent thought or action, and especially one who rejected motherhood as a way of life, had a "masculinity complex" and required years of analysis so that she could learn how to deal with her "penis envy." In the sexual sphere, too, it was thought desirable by Victorians that women should be passive and, thus, Freud argued that women could have two different kinds of orgasm—vaginal (passive) and clitoral (active). Women who had clitoral orgasms had the wrong kind and were sick.

In the case of women, as in the other examples just cited, our views are changing but, once again, it is instructive to consider why. Nowadays, there is increasing acceptance of the idea that not all women will bear children, but this acceptance has much to do with economic considerations, with our current concern about limiting population growth and with militant action by women. New discoveries have been made but they are not responsible for the changes; if anything, new discoveries have been ignored when they contravened what many male professionals wanted to believe about women. Thus, William Masters and Virginia Johnson of Washington University in St. Louis showed conclusively during the 1950s that there was no distinction between vaginal and clitoral orgasms and that women are no more passive during the sexual act than are men. Yet, according to a study by Diana Scully and Pauline Bart of the University of Illinois, some gynecology texts written in the 1970s still insist that passivity is the normal feminine sexual response and that the vaginal orgasm is the only mature response for women. In similar fashion, there is now a wealth of experimental evidence to show that so-called faminine traits such as submissiveness, dependence and conformity are culturally rather than biologically determined. Yet, a recent study by a group of investigators in the Boston area headed by Inge Broverman showed that clinicians still set different goals in therapy for men and for women. They regard a woman patient who is submissive, dependent and conforming as healthy, but they regard a man who shows these characteristics as in need of their services.

A further example of shifting standards concerns the changing view of blacks. Early in this century, it was claimed by Arrah Everts that all blacks are emotionally unstable and lack self-control. "Evidence" was provided by John Lind, a colleague of Everts at the Government Hospital for the Insane in Washington, D.C. The dreams of black patients were interpreted and 84 out of 100 were found to have "juvenile" wish-fulfillment dreams. For example, one young man dreamed that he was out of jail and was having a good time with girls. To say that such a dream is evidence of a "primitive type of mind" is clearly a matter of interpretation and not of scientific fact. This example, like the previous ones, shows how theory can be tailored to fit the prevailing social view, but it shows further how readily suitable "scientific" evidence can be manufactured to bolster that view. As was the case with women, clinical views are changing but largely as a result of political activity by blacks. Again, there is a parallel with women in that the change is slow and there is still a tendency for clinicians to set different standards of mental health for blacks and for whites. Thus, Alexander Thomas and Samuel Sillen in their book *Racism and Psychiatry* charge that clinicians are content to call immature behavior normal in blacks whereas they would regard such behavior as abnormal in whites.

A further difficulty arises with respect to concepts of mental health. Not only do they change to suit the temper of the times but, even at any given time, when contemporaries are in agreement on certain abstract notions of sickness and health, the unanimity evaporates when these standards are applied to real people. Kenneth Little and Edwin Schneidman of Los Angeles have reported an experiment in which clinicians were presented with data from widely used clinical tests (*Rorschach, TAT, MAPS, MMPI*) and with stories written by the same people. They were then asked to distinguish among normals, neurotics and psychotics. They did no better than chance! Furthermore, their diagnoses often were not even consistent; when they were asked to rejudge the same materials some weeks later, their diagnoses often shifted markedly from the ones they had made originally. Evelyn Hooker of UCLA similarly showed that experienced clinicians could not distinguish between homosexual and heterosexual men or find any difference in their level of adjustment on the basis of *Rorschach, TAT* and *MAPS* results. It is worth noting that these men were not in therapy or in mental hospitals. These studies do more than raise some doubts about the adequacy of standard diagnostic procedures; they raise the question of whether many of our basic concepts of mental health have any validity.

Thomas Szasz of Syracuse University has been one of the most vigorous opponents of the idea that a clear distinction can be drawn between the so-called mentally ill and other people. Szasz argues that a clinician can always find evidence of mental illness in anyone so accused. That everyone is a little sick is a basic axiom in clinical theory. Even the jokes that clinicians tell reflect this. For example, a patient who is early is anxious; one who is late is hostile; one who is on time is compulsive. There is no behavior that cannot plausibly be diagnosed as abnormal. Szasz tells us, "In more than 20 years of psychiatric work, I have never known a clinical psychologist to report, on the basis of a projective test, that the subject is a 'normal, mentally healthy person.' "

What Szasz (and, in fact, other critics as well) is questioning is the validity of the so-called medical model in psychiatry, the assumption that mental illnesses exist as definable entities with clear-cut symptoms as is the case with physical illnesses. *The question is a critical one because, if mental illness cannot be identified in the same sense in which sick organs of the body can be identified—if, in fact, it does not exist except as a label that we impose on other people—then we must reconsider what justifications there are for the things that we do in the name of mental health.*

The mildest thing that we do is to persuade certain people to undertake psychotherapy voluntarily, whether inside or outside an institution. A more extreme practice is to imprison people involuntarily in psychiatric institutions who have, in fact, committed no crime. We also impose upon people in institutions physical treatments that they have not requested and that they probably would refuse if they were in a position to do so. Finally, something that we are doing increasingly these days is setting up agencies to seek out people who may at some future time do something that will earn them the label "mentally ill." Such practices often serve as methods of social control.

Seymour Halleck, in his book *The Politics of Therapy*, states, "There is no way in which the psychiatrist can deal with behavior that is partly generated by a social system without either strengthening or altering that system. Every encounter with a psychiatrist, therefore, has political implications." In part, what Halleck means is that therapy is never a neutral situation; any behavioral change in a single individual has an impact on the distribution of power within that person's social milieu. However, he is also using the word *political* in another sense. As does Phyllis Chesler in *Women and Madness*, he points out that regardless of their theoretical orientations, all therapists start with the implicit assumption that unhappiness is a personal problem and that it can best be dealt with by changing the individual. Accordingly, those people whose behavior does not fit the social norm are taught to view themselves as sick and in need of help. They are encouraged to talk rather than to act and what may, in fact, be legitimate anger about social injustice is defused.

Because both patient and therapist fail to deal with the social genesis of the behavior, they may miss an important opportunity for effective social change. Furthermore, even a sympathetic therapist can weaken a revolutionary's fervor. Halleck does not suggest, nor do we, that this represents an organized or even deliberate attempt. However, as we have shown, therapists reflect the values of the society at large, and it must be remembered that they are in an especially advantageous position to perpetuate those values. By emphasizing adjustment as the goal of therapy and by focusing on the individual while ignoring the social context, therapists can and do help to maintain the status quo.

So far, we have considered only what happens to an individual who submits voluntarily to psychotherapy. However, if we consider cases in which the individual does not assume the role of patient voluntarily, then we can see even more plainly what Halleck means. Consider, for example, what happens to a child who is brought into treatment by members of the family because his or her behavior is unacceptable to them. The tendency is to ignore the situation that gave rise to particular behaviors and to concentrate on removing the annoying symptoms themselves. The behavior patterns that are substituted are not necessarily those that are best for the child but rather those that will make the family situation more pleasant.

In the same way, prisoners and institutionalized mental patients may be subjected to psychotherapy aimed at making them less troublesome to their custodians. The latter example is more extreme because not only is therapy forced onto the individual but it is accompanied by imprisonment. In all cases, though, the essentially political nature of the therapy is shown by what happens when the patient recognizes an unexpressed bias on the part of the therapist. Not only is the patient not free to terminate therapy but protesting interpretations may be taken as a demonstration of lack of "insight" and can lead to a prolongation of the "treatment."

Szasz also has dealt at length with the relationship between mental health and social control. In his book *The Manufacture of Madness*, he argues that labeling some people mentally ill serves a unifying function for the rest of society. As a group, we affirm our identity and separation from other groups to the extent that we reject certain people as not belonging. In developing this argument, Szasz traces the history of scapegoatism; he draws many relevant parallels between the persecution of witches from the 13th to the 17th centuries and what he terms our modern persecution of the mentally ill. It is not without significance in his view that we stopped persecuting witches with the rise of modern psychiatry. Unlike his fellow psychiatrists, Szasz does not interpret this to mean that we have become more enlightened; rather, he says that we have found new victims.

One group to whom we apply the label "mentally ill" consists of powerless individuals. Szasz notes that these are the old, the sick, the poor and the unemployed. Chesler, as well as Thomas and Sillen, in their study of racism, further note that a sizable number of these are third world or women. Moreover, statistics show that the greatest percentage of institutionalized schizophrenics come from the lower class. Traditionally, such statistics have been interpreted to mean that it is more stressful to be poor than to be rich. This may indeed be the case, but an alternative explanation that is in accord with Szasz's argument is that if you are a relatively powerless member of our society you are more apt to have the label "schizophrenic" placed on you.

A second group apt to be called mentally ill are people who do not conform, and this demonstrates another and more frightening aspect of the way in which psychiatric labeling can be used as a method of social control. Szasz reminds us that the habit of labeling as psychotic people whose opinions are different is as old as psychiatry itself. Thus, Benjamin Rush, an 18th-century physician who is regarded as the father of American psychiatry, claimed that people who were opposed to the American Revolution were mentally ill and suffered from "revolutiona." Similarly, Thomas and Sillen tell us that American slaves who ran away were thought to suffer from an illness called "drapetomania." According to Chesler and to Szasz, the mental-illness label was attached, during the 19th and early 20th centuries, to social reformers, in particular to unionists and to women's rights advocates. The same process continues today. Thus, in recent years, mental-health authorities in the Western world have held that in a healthy world communism will disappear while their Chinese counterparts have claimed that in a healthy world capitalism will disappear. After the ghetto riots of the 1960s, the view was advanced by a psychosurgical team at Massachusetts General Hospital (Vernon Mark, William Sweet and Frank Ervin) that undiagnosed brain disease contributed heavily to such uprisings.

It is plain then that psychiatric labels are attached most readily to people whose behavior we do not like. The reason why this is a problem is that attachment of the label carries with it certain implications. One implication is that the individual so stigmatized is not credible. Social criticism expressed by one who is "mentally ill" does not have to be taken seriously (e.g., Daniel

Ellsberg). A second and more sinister implication is that the individual can be institutionalized. In many states it was possible until recently for a person to be held for up to 15 days in a psychiatric institution without a court order (only the physician's signature was required). Currently, the trend is to enact laws that require formal court hearings, but it is noteworthy that the American Psychiatric Association has protested the change. In a 1962 position statement, the Association argued, "It is of great importance that laws should provide for *emergency commitments* for limited periods of time without involving any court procedure." Even where such court orders are required, Szasz argues that they are easily obtained after only cursory examination. There is, of course, no bail and no appeal. There is not, as in a court of law, any determinate sentence. The person who decides when the patient is to be released is the same one who ordered the incarceration—the psychiatrist. To illustrate the ease with which such commitments can be used to punish political dissidents, Szasz cites the example of welfare recipients in New York City who staged a demonstration and quickly found themselves in Bellevue. According to recent newspaper reports, the Soviet Union also has used hospitalization as a means of dealing with social critics.

As has Szasz, Chesler in *Women and Madness* has dealt at length with how psychiatric labeling followed by imprisonment in a mental institution can be used to punish deviants. Her particular concern is with what happens to people whose deviance consists of having rejected all or part of their traditional sex roles. Thus, she notes that aggressive or lesbian (unfeminine) women and gentle, nonassertive or homosexual (nonmasculine) men are likely candidates for institutionalization. Women deviants suffer more in this regard. Men and women are admitted in equal numbers to mental institutions, but men do not stay as long and they are not readmitted as often.

While this can be interpreted to mean that women are weaker, Chesler's interpretation is that wives are willing to look after husbands who cannot function in society but that husbands are unwilling to render a similar service to wives. She cites a great deal of case-history material drawn from interviews with women who were in institutions or in private therapy, and she is well able to document her assertion that the point at which many husbands decide to commit their wives is not when they become helpless, irrational or even totally incoherent. Rather, it is the point at which they step so far out of their sex roles as to refuse to do the housework or, worse still, become overtly aggressive. As further proof that it is the most deviant women who suffer most, she cites her own finding that lesbian women were admitted at an earlier age and had the longest hospital stay of any patient group. In contrast, of the women interviewed who had had affairs with their therapists, few had ever been hospitalized, a fact which Chesler sees as arising from their more traditional behavior.

A third implication of the labeling process is that the individual can be subjected involuntarily to various forms of physical treatment. Szasz has criticized these on the grounds that they are no less cruel than the treatment meted out centuries ago to witches. In the 18th century, whips, chains, strait-jackets, blood-letting and solitary confinement were employed. For slaves with "drapetomania," on the other hand, a simpler procedure—amputation of the toes—was used. Today, three centuries after we stopped dunking, burning and strangling witches, we use drugs, electroshock, brain surgery and brain stimulation on mental patients.

Scientific foundation for their use is lacking, and they produce unwelcome side effects. For example, electroshock produces only temporary alleviation of symptoms while leaving the individual confused and fearful and with a memory loss of varying duration. Whether its prolonged use leads finally to brain damage is unresolved at present. As for psychoactive drugs, they do, indeed, make violent individuals easier to handle, but their repeated and heavy use in institutions has led in some cases to serious organ dysfunction and even finally to death. Brain stimulation, too, can stop an aggressive episode, but its long-term effects in humans are not fully understood and it requires the permanent installation of a suitable device in the brain.

In the case of psychosurgery (excision of a specific area of the brain as a treatment for some behavioral "disorder"), there are other difficulties. One is that no single portion of the brain subserves a single function. While surgery can have a calming effect on a violent individual, the same operation may also leave that person obese, under- or oversexed and permanently unable to store new information. Basic physiological functions such as heart rate, urination, defecation, etc., also may be affected.

A second difficulty is that the expected beneficial results are usually produced in only a small percentage of cases. The individual may have the side effects just described and be as violent after the operation as before. Even when the expected results are produced, one can question whether the individual really is helped. Suppose that a brain operation makes an individual placid. If that person is in a prison or mental institution, he or she may now be more readily managed by custodians, but what happens to that person when released into the outside world? This issue was raised by a Boston psychologist, Allan Mirsky, at a 1974 conference on aggression sponsored by the University of California at Irvine. According to Mirsky, there have been no long-term follow-ups on the social adjustment of the approximately 500 humans who have been subjected to bilateral amygdalectomy (an operation that is supposed to calm violent individuals). However, it is worth noting that, when the same operation is performed on monkeys, they do not survive if returned to their natural habitat. In spite of these problems, psychosurgery still is advocated enthusiastically by some doctors. Mark and Ervin, whose views on ghetto riots have already been mentioned, suggest in their book *Violence and the Brain* that mass screening procedures be adopted so that the 10½ to 21 million Americans they say have undiagnosed brain damage can be detected and treated. The same idea appeared in a preliminary version of the proposed UCLA Violence Center mentioned earlier.

Clearly, definitions of mental health and illness are highly nonspecific and arbitrary, are rooted heavily in the social lore of the times, lack scientific support and rely on a pathological, medical-model, labeling process the validity of which is more apparent than real. Even well-intentioned practitioners have difficulty applying their theoretical concepts about mental health and illness to real people and may wind up as preservers of the status quo. For less principled individuals, the lack of rigor in the definitions allows them to make arbitrary and biased use of mental-health criteria so as to oppress particular social groups—especially women, homosexuals, minorities and nonconformists. In spite of these facts, we have for some time now been taking power away from the courts and awarding it instead to mental-health professionals. Because the shift was accomplished slowly, there was no point at which we paused to define the nature of that power or to set limits on how it could be used. The consequence is that we have voluntarily abrogated some of our hard-won civil liberties.

Szasz has pointed out that we would do well to consider the lessons of history. Between the 13th and 17th centuries, more and more people went into the business of finding witches. The more professionals there were, the more witches there were to be found. By the time the witch craze ended, some millions of people, most of them women, were dead. In similar fashion, as the ranks of mental-health professionals have swelled in recent years, so too has the number of mentally ill multiplied. The ferreting out of witches was a lucrative enterprise and the same is true of our current search for the mentally ill. There is some conflict of interest in asking mental-health professionals to decrease the number of people who require their services. Finally, the witch-hunts left a small group of people within the church in an extremely powerful position. At present, mental-health professionals are achieving a similar position. The fact that involuntary imprisonment currently is carried out by psychiatrists and not by the military may have lulled us into a false sense of security.

The most radical proposals for change have come from within the mental-health establishment itself. Szasz, for example, suggests that we do away entirely with our present system whereby individuals can be forcibly institutionalized "for their own good" and substitute instead a system in which treatment can be carried out only with the patient's consent. When this proposal was first offered by Szasz, it was pronounced unacceptable by some critics on the grounds that, if most of the patients presently in mental institutions were released, there would be a dramatic rise in the incidence of violent crimes. However, the popular image of mental patients as dangerous is not supported by the evidence. Statistics show that fewer crimes are committed by former mental patients than by the general population. As for the bizarre behaviors that many of us associate with mental illness, there is some evidence that the most extreme of these are acquired after and not before commitment. In fact, the mental institution can be characterized as a place where people learn to act crazy.

Interestingly, Jessica Mitford advances a similar line or argument with respect to the American prison system. In her book *Kind and Usual Punishment,* she documents her view that prisons fail to stop crime or to rehabilitate prisoners. She notes that, of the large prison population, only a tiny fraction has committed crimes that indicate that they are in any way dangerous to the rest of society. Her conclusion is that prisons should be shut down altogether. Prisons and mental institutions are alike in that they are places to which people are confined involuntarily. It is instructive to note that, according to their critics, both institutions fail in their intended functions.

Some people remain concerned about that tiny fraction of the population, whether in prison or in mental institutions, who do indeed display violent behavior. Advocates of a less radical solution than that proposed by Szasz argue that all mental patients except these should be released. However, the assumption here is that the tendency to be violent is a personality characteristic of the individual, and this is precisely what has not yet been established. In many animal groups, violence seems to be, in large measure, situational—produced largely by such factors as crowding and the introduction of strangers. If the same is true for humans, then imprisoning violent individuals would be an inadequate solution. A better approach would be to view the violence as a symptom and to emphasize working at altering the environment that contributes to produce such behavior.

The least radical action that can be taken is to maintain our present system but introduce some reforms. With respect to forced institutionalization, it has been suggested that we do away with the arrangement whereby mental patients can be confined indefinitely, establish periodic reviews of people in institutions and make commitment a civil matter in which a jury, rather than a psychiatrist, decides. Such reforms have been instituted in some states, such as California. These reforms, plus numerous other safeguards, are essential so that the mental-health establisment does not concentrate its power in the hands of a few aggressive individuals.

Many of these issues are raised in *Rough Times* (a recent book by a radical collective that also publishes a periodical of the same name). Like Szasz, Chesler and Thomas and Sillen, these radical therapists outline many oppressive features of mental-health care. But more than that, the collective has reported some innovations in health care including those in the United States (Harrowdale State Hospital), Italy (Bosaglia's Provincial Psychiatric Hospital of Gorizia) and China (where research is conducted on physicians, not patients.)

This volume also contains a "Mental Patients' Bill of Rights" by the New York Mental Patients' Liberation Project, a collective of ex-mental patients. Such innovations represent a humanization of the mental-health process that involves individuals in dealing with emotional problems and in perceiving social conditions of oppression that contribute to their suffering and the suffering of others. Nevertheless, these very important innovations, even if they become widespread within the mental-health professions, would only represent a fraction of what the professions might be able to offer.

The real problem is to minimize the impact of oppressive aspects of social systems. Social change is needed not only to develop an appetite for diversity and change in society and in individuals, but to create conditions of equal opportunity for dignity and economic and civil liberty, conditions necessary for the realization of people's potential.

One can consider almost any social institution, as Jessica Mitford did with prisons (*Kind and Usual Punishment*), as Ivan Illich did with schools (*Deschooling Society*) and as *Rough Times* does with the mental-health establishment, and see that all big institutions mirror the problems of society at large. Therefore, changes must take place with society at large as well as within the various institutions of society.

If we take the radical point of view, then it is now time to prod the mental-health professions to contribute to changing not only themselves, but the social systems in which they function.

FOUR

"Careful, Millingworth – they're suede."

Bureaucracy, Alienation, and the Quality of Work

THE DEVELOPMENT of mass society, a society characterized by anonymity, mobility, and specialization in which primary-group relationships have been largely replaced by secondary-group, utilitarian relationships, has presented modern man with some unique and challenging problems. For although mass society provides opportunities for greater freedom, it also provides more subtle means for man's control. The pervasive growth of bureaucracy, which has been due to the size and complexity of mass society, has important consequences in relation to freedom and control. Saint-Simon, for example, was a nineteenth-century social philosopher who saw bureaucracy as a liberating force which would emancipate men from tradition and increase efficiency and productivity. Max Weber, the brilliant German sociologist, also emphasized the technical superiority of bureaucratic organization, but he feared that it would destroy individual personality and subject it to dehumanizing regimentation. In order to decide whether either of these visions has proved to be accurate, we must attempt to understand the nature of bureaucratic organization. When we think of bureaucracy we tend to think of a government organization, like the Pentagon, with its miles of corridors, maze of compartments, tons of paperwork, and herds of secretaries and paper shufflers. Actually bureaucracy is a social structure, either private or public, that is rationally organized for maximum efficiency in administration. In simple terms, it is a large, highly structured organization. Max Weber characterized bureaucracy as involving (1) specialization (a clear division of labor), (2) a chain of command (officials are accountable for their subordinates' actions as well as their own), (3) impersonal detachment (necessary for rational standards to be carried out impartially), and (4) job tenure (to protect competent personnel against arbitrary dismissal).

Bureaucracy is nothing new. It was probably present in ancient Egypt, China at the time of Christ, and imperial Rome. In each case it functioned to increase the efficiency and control of the elites in charge of the military and political institutions. It is therefore not bureaucratic organization which is new, but rather its pervasiveness in modern industrial society. An ever-increasing proportion of people are employed in bureaucratic positions. Even such traditionally free professionals as physicians are increasingly dependent upon the large hospital, and the lawyer often enters a "law factory."

The student also operates within highly bureaucratized surroundings. The educational institution has become increasingly bureaucratized, and it is influenced by other large bureaucracies such as the corporation. The movement toward autonomous ethnic departments, and the various other student-power movements have been reactions to a feeling of being the impotent raw material for an educational machine. In essence, these movements were attempts to democratize the educational bureaucracies. Many students in large colleges and universities eventually have the experience, common to all large bureaucracies, of asking office A for a certain service and being told that the matter is under the jurisdiction of office B. Office B has the same response and refers the student to office C. Office C, of course, refers the student back to office A. "Buck passing" is one way of avoiding responsibility for making decisions.

One of the consequences, then, of a bureaucratized society is a feeling of powerlessness on the part of many individuals. This feeling is due to the immensity of the major organizations of which the mass society is composed and to the frustrations which inevitably arise when one deals with a bureaucracy. Most of us have at times been swamped by the futility and complexity of moving within these organizations as a lone individual. (For example, if you are a woman, try showing up at the wrong hospital with labor pains.) Frustration can be increased by the bureaucratic functionary who, as Robert Merton contends, may tend to elevate the rules to ends rather than treating them as means to ends. It has been suggested that those functionaries who are least competent are the most rigid in their adherence to established routines and in their objections to innovations. The "ritualists" become so preoccupied with the application of detailed rules that they lose sight of the very purpose of their actions and are therefore incapable of adaption to a new problem that is not covered by the regulations. (I once needed an additional letter of recommendation added to my job placement file at a large university but was told I already had five letters and that the file could contain a maximum of five. I explained that the need for the additional letter was related to a change in my vocational goals and that the purpose of the placement office was to place the individual in a job rather than to worry about how many letters were in his file. But I received the same response. I then asked to see the individual's superior and he, upon hearing my problem, immediately approved the sixth letter. This individual evidently had the goals of the organization more clearly in mind.) The functionary is, of course, trained to adhere to the rules, and his performance is judged on the basis of his conformity and predictability. He is usually above blame if he follows official regulations exactly, regardless of outcome.

The bureaucratic ritualist may receive a kind of psychological security from the fixed, orderly application of the rules which become a bible of bureaucratic behavior. This is in part because he is economically dependent upon the bureaucracy. His career, his prestige, and his self-esteem become dependent upon his success within the organization. And success, he knows, means pleasing those above him in the hierarchy. He learns to simulate competency, enthusiasm, concern, and respect. Impulses are systematically controlled and spontaneity is repressed. He believes what needs to be believed, says what needs to be said, and does what needs to be done. Afraid to disagree with his superior, he may solicit his superior's opinions and then develop data to support them. Thus, once a ponderous organization begins rolling in a certain direction, it is extremely difficult to reverse the course of that organization. A good example of this has been U.S. policy in Vietnam. The people who initiated the policy or were concerned with carrying it out were not likely to change their minds about the war. What response would you expect from an Air Force general about the effectiveness of bombing North Vietnam? The singlemindedness which former President Nixon and his loyal advisors maintained in the Watergate scandal until it ended in resignation may be another example.

It is important to recognize that dissidence, and conflict in general, often have functional or useful aspects within the large organization. An exaggerated emphasis upon loyalty may lead to lethargy and stagnation, dangerous traits in a rapidly changing industrial society. The bureaucratic dissident is needed to upset habit and custom and to provide the means for coping with change. In any case, the pervasive bureaucratization of modern society creates several important problems with which we must deal: feelings of powerlessness and alienation, the dehumanization of work through specialization and powerlessness, the diffusion of responsibility made possible by the hierarchy of decision making (if no one is responsible, no one is guilty), and the inherent tendency of many large organizations to resist change and innovation.

Are any problems of bureaucracy avoidable in modern, complex societies? Can other forms of organization be developed? Is it possible to structure a large organization in a more democratic manner? The answer to these questions is a tentative yes. There are experiments being carried on in most industrial societies that attempt to combat the bureaucratization and routinization of work. On a smaller level the Israeli kibbutzim, democratic socialist agricultural communities, have been able to overcome many bureaucratic problems. They are run as complete economic and political democracies. There is also an attempt to rotate work assignments on some kibbutzim.

Many communes or intentional communities have been consciously anti-bureaucratic and anti-industrialism in nature. They are an attempt to return to the spirit of land and brotherhood. One such community, Oneida, flourished in the late 1800s. This community practiced a form of sexual freedom, planned most of their births, rotated jobs among both sexes, and had a system of communal child-rearing. Intentional communities are often fueled by a need to avoid the impersonal and bureaucratic nature of modern society. —D. R.

Selected References

(All are available in paperback editions.)

Blau, Peter M. *Bureaucracy in Modern Society*. New York: Random House, Inc., 1956.

O'Tode, James, et al. *Work in America*. Cambridge, Mass.: MIT Press, 1973.

Presthus, Robert. *The Organizational Society*. New York: Vintage Books, 1962.

Roberts, Ron E. *The New Communes*. Englewood Cliffs, N.J.: Prentice-Hall, Inc., 1971.

Ruitenbeck, Hendrick M. (ed.). *The Dilemma of Organizational Society*. New York: E. P. Dutton & Co., Inc., 1963.

Whyte, William H., Jr. *The Organization Man*. New York: Simon & Schuster, Inc., 1956.

The Intellectual Taxicab Company

PETER CARLSON

My friend Danny hung his Boston University diploma below the hack license in his cab.

After seventeen years of education in the finest schools in America, Danny, at 22, couldn't fix his stopped sink, repair a burnt connection in his fuse box, replace a pane of glass in his kitchen or locate the carburetor in his car.

Danny is an educated man. He is a master of writing research papers, taking tests, talking and filling out forms. He can rattle off his social-security number as easily as he can his name because it was also his student identification number. He can analyze Freud from a Marxian viewpoint and he can analyze Marx from a Freudian viewpoint.

In short, Danny is an unskilled worker and he has a sociology degree to prove it. He is of very little use to American industry.

Broken Cycle

This is nothing new. Colleges have been turning out unskilled workers for decades. Until five years ago, most of these unskilled workers took their degrees in sociology, philosophy, political science or history and marched right into the American middle class. Some filled executive positions in business and government but many, if not most, went into education, which is the only thing they knew anything about. Once there, they taught another generation the skills necessary to take tests and write papers.

But that cycle broke down. Teachers are overabundant these days, college applications are down, plumbers are making $12 an hour and liberal-arts graduates are faced with a choice—graduate school or the taxicab.

Danny chose the taxicab because driving was about the only marketable skill he possessed. Danny refers to his job as "Real World 101." He has been shot at, punched, sideswiped and propositioned. But he has also acquired some practical skills—he can get his tickets fixed; he knows how to cheat the company out of a few extra dollars a week; he found his carburetor and he can fix it.

Soon, I will be in the same position. I'll graduate from Boston University with a B.S. in journalism. Whatever skills that degree symbolizes are not currently in demand. I suppose I could go to graduate school but, Christ, I've been doing the same thing for seventeen years and I'm getting a little tired of it. Besides, there are a lot of grad-school graduates who are driving cabs, too.

And that brings me to the Intellectual Taxicab Company.

Danny and I were discussing the hack business recently and we came up with the idea. It is the simple answer to a simple question: why should all that college education go to waste reading road signs when masses of people are looking for knowledge and riding in cabs?

What America needs is a system to bring together all the knowledgeable cabbies and the undereducated rest of the country. The system we propose is the Intellectual Taxicab Company.

The Intellectual Taxicab Company would consist of a dispatcher and a fleet of cabs driven by recent college graduates. When you need a ride, you call the company and say something like: "I'd like to go from Wall Street over to East 83rd and I'd like to discuss the world monetary situation."

"All right, sir, we'll have an NYU economics graduate over in five minutes."

Or: "Hello, I'm in Central Square and I'd like to go to Brookline and discuss whether or not there is a God."

"You're in luck, madame, we have a Harvard philosophy graduate who minored in Comparative Religions right in the neighborhood."

The educational possibilities of this plan are staggering. English and Drama graduates could take the after-theater run, explaining the literary ramifications of the shows. Political Science graduates could hack around Capitol Hill or City Hall. Regular bus runs could be set up to conduct seminars on popular topics.

Elevating the Cabbie

The Intellectual Taxicab Company would bring adult education to the streets. It would also give all those alienated college graduates a feeling that they didn't waste four years and all that tuition money. And it would elevate the snotty cabdriver to an art form: cabbies would quote Voltaire while they rant about how bad the mayor is.

Surely there must be some foundation money or unimpounded Federal funds available to begin such a noble experiment in education. If there is, Danny and I are ready to start immediately. In fact, Danny is licking his lips in anticipation. "Just think how much my tips will go up," he said.

Down the Bureaucracy

MATTHEW P. DUMONT

The point of this essay is very clear: the cementlike federal bureaucracy is filled with unwritten and "irrational" laws of organizational behavior. Dumont suggests that all bureaucracies display similar tendencies. He also proposes some techniques for changing this "huge, righteous marshmallow."

There has been a certain tension among the people of our federal city lately. I am not talking about the black population of the district, which becomes visible to the rest of the world only when its rage boils over. I am referring to the public servants who ooze across the Maryland and Virginia lines each day to manipulate the machinery of government.

It has never been a particularly gleeful population, but in the last year or so it has developed a kind of mass involutional melancholia, a peculiar mixture of depression, anxiety and senescence.

As in similarly depressed communities, the young, the healthy and those with good job prospects have tended to migrate. Among those who have departed are a large proportion of that scarce supply of idealistic and pragmatic people who try to work for social change "within the system." They are leaving because they feel unwanted and ineffectual. Let me describe what they are turning their backs on.

Washington is a malaria swamp covered over with buildings of neofascist design and ringed with military bases.

Do you remember Rastignac shaking his fist at Paris from Goriot's grave site? Washington is a city made for fists to be shaken at. Shaken at, not bloodied on. Federal buildings are especially constructed to be impervious to blood. You can rush headlong into a marble balustrade smearing brains and blood and bile three yards wide. But as the lady does on television, with a smile and a few whisks of a damp cloth, the wonderful material will come up as clean and white and sparkling as before.

Some people have tried burning themselves into the concrete. That doesn't work either.

And, as you might have guessed, all that urine on the Pentagon was gone within minutes after the armies of the night retreated.

No, you may, individually or en masse, descend upon the Federal Triangle. You may try to impale and exsanguinate yourselves, flay, crucify and castrate yourselves. You may scream shrill cries or sing "Alice's Restaurant" or chant "Om," but it won't help. The buildings were made to last forever and to forever remain shining and white, the summer sun glaring off their walls, stunning the passersby.

Inside, one might spend eternity hearing the sounds of his own footsteps in the corridors of these buildings and never see his sun-cast shadow. If you took all the corridors in all of the federal buildings in Washington and laid them end to end, and inclined one end slightly and started a billiard ball rolling down, by the time it reached the lower end, the ball would have attained such a velocity that it would hurtle on through space while approaching an infinite mass and thereby destroy the universe. This is not likely to happen because such coordination is unheard of among federal agencies. But we will get to that later.

Off the corridors are offices and conference rooms. (There is also a core of mail chutes, telephone lines, elevator shafts, sewer pipes, trash cans and black people, but these are all invisible.) The offices have desks—wooden ones for important people and steel ones for unimportant people. (Otherwise, the distinction is impossible to make unless you could monitor their telephone calls to each other and determine the relative hierarchy depending on whose secretary manages to keep the other party waiting before putting her boss on.)

The offices also contain file cabinets that are filled with paper. The paper is mainly memos—the way people in the federal government communicate to one another. When communication is not necessary, memos "for the record" are written and filed. It has been estimated that the approximate cost in labor and supplies for the typing of a memo is 36¢. The cost in professional time for its preparation is incalculable.

The conference rooms are for conferences. A conference is for the purpose of sharing information among a group of federal officials who have already been apprised of the information to be shared, individually, by memo. Coffee and cigarettes are consumed. By prior arrangement, each participant is, in turn, interrupted by his secretary for an urgent phone call. After the conference additional memos are exchanged.

But let me describe the people who work in the federal government because some mythology must be laid to rest.

They are good people, which is to say that they are no less good than anyone else, which is to say that we are all pretty much cut from the same material and most of it is pretty rotten. I do not wish to be cavalier about the problem of evil, but I will ask you to accept as a premise for this thesis that the differences between the "best of us" and the "worst of us" are no greater than the differences *within* each of us at varying times.

I have been and will be more sober and precise about this issue in other writings, but what I am attempting to convey is a conviction that the great evils of mankind, the genocides and holy wars, the monstrous exploitations and negligences and injustices of societies have less to do with the malice of individuals than with unexamined and unquestioned institutional practices.

I am talking about the Eichmannism—a syndrome wherein individual motives, consciences or goals become irrelevant in the context of organizational behaviors. This can be seen in pure culture in the federal government. There are a host of written rules for behavior for the federal civil servants, but these are rarely salient. It is the unwritten rules, tacit but ever present, subtle but overwhelming, unarticulated but commanding, that determine the behavior of the men and women who buzz out their lives in the spaces defined by the United States government.

These rules are few in number. Rule number one is to *maintain your tenure*. This is at the same time the most significant and the easiest rule to abide by. If you desire to keep a job for several decades and retire from it with an adequate pension, and if you have the capacity to appear at once occupied and inconspicuous, then you can be satisfied as a "fed."

Appearing occupied means walking briskly at all times. It means looking down at your desk rather than up into the distance when thinking. It means always having papers in your hands. Above all, it means, when asked how things are, responding "very hectic" rather than "terrific" or "lousy."

Being inconspicuous means that your competence in appearing occupied should be expressed quietly and without affect. The most intolerable behavior in a civil servant is psychotic behavior. Being psychotic in the federal government is looking people directly in the eye for a moment too long. It is walking around on a weekday without a tie. It is kissing a girl in an elevator. (It doesn't matter whether she is a wife, mistress, secretary or daughter.) It is writing a memo that is excessively detailed, or refusing to write memos. It is laughing too loud or too long at a conference. It is taking a clandestine gulp of wine in a locker room rather than ordering two martinis over lunch. (This explains why there are more suspensions for alcoholism among lower level workers than higher level ones.)

In short, there is no more sensitive indicator of deviant behavior than personnel records of the federal government.

This does not mean that federal officials never vary their behavior. Currently, for example, it is modish to sport sideburns and a moustache. The specter of thousands of civil servants looking like Che Guevara may seem exciting, but it has no more significance than cuffless trousers.

You may or may not wish to follow the fashions, but do not initiate them. In general, follow a golden mean of behavior, that is, do what most people seem to be doing. Do it quietly. And if you are not sure how to behave, take annual leave.

The second rule of behavior in the government, and clearly related to the sustenance of your own tenure, is to *keep the boss from getting embarrassed*. That is the single, most important standard of competence for a federal official. The man who runs interference effectively, who can anticipate and obviate impertinent, urgent or obvious demands from the boss's boss, or from the press, or from the public, or from Congress, will be treasured and rewarded. This is so pervasive a desideratum in a civil servant that the distinction between line and staff activities becomes thin and artificial in the face of it. Your primary function in the hierarchy (after the protection of your own tenure) is the protection of your superior's tenure rather than the fulfillment of assigned responsibilities. (Obvious exceptions to this rule are J. Edgar Hoover and certain elements in the Department of Defense, who, like physicians and priests, respond to a higher authority.)

The third unwritten rule of federal behavior is to *make sure that all appropriated funds are spent by the end of the fiscal year.* Much of the paper that stuffs the orifices of executive desks has to do with justifications for requests for more money. For money to be returned after such justifications are approved is to imply that the requester, his supervisor and Congress itself were improvident in their demands on the taxpayer's money. It would be like a bum asking for a handout for a cup of coffee. A passerby offers a quarter and the bum returns 15¢ saying, "Coffee is only a dime, schmuck."

Contract hustlers, who abound in Washington, known that their halcyon days are in late spring when agencies are frequently panicked at the realization that they have not exhausted their operating funds and may be in the black by the fiscal year's end. Agencies that administer grant-in-aid programs celebrate end-of-fiscal-year parties with Dionysian abandon when instead of having a surplus of funds they cannot pay all of their obligations.

The only effective way to evaluate a federal program is the rapidity with which money is spent. Federal agencies, no less than purveyors of situation comedies, cigarettes and medical care, are dominated by a marketplace mentality which assumes that you have a good product if the demand exceeds the supply.

The fourth unwritten rule of behavior in government is to *keep the program alive.* It is not appropriate to question the original purposes of the program. Nor is it appropriate to ask if the program has any consonance with its original purposes. It is certainly not appropriate to assume that its purposes have been served. It is only appropriate to assume that once a program has been legislated, funded and staffed it must endure. An unstated and probably unconscious blessing of immortality is bestowed upon the titles that clutter organizational charts in federal agencies.

Congress, with its control of funds, is perceived as a nurturant breast with a supply of vital fluids that may at any time run dry and thus starve the program to death. Such a matter must be looked upon with intense ambivalence, a state of mind associated with schizophrenia in the hostile-dependent offspring. And, indeed, Congress is perceived by federal executives with a mixture of adulation and rage, and, indeed, federal programming is schizophrenic. Like the schizophrenic, federal programs have the capacity to assume pseudomorphic identities, having the outline and form of order and direction and vitality but actually being flat, autistic and encrusted with inorganic matter. Like the schizophrenic, federal programs develop a primitive narcissism that is independent of feedback from the environment other than the provision of life-sustaining funds.

Even programs that are conceived with some imagination as relatively bold and aggressive attempts to institutionalize change, such as Model Cities or Comprehensive Community Mental Health Centers or Community Action Programs, become so preoccupied with survival that compromises in the face of real or imagined criticism from Congress very quickly blunt whatever cutting edges the program may have had.

The fifth and final unwritten rule of federal behavior is to *maintain a stable and well-circumscribed constituency.* With so great a concern for survival in the government, it is necessary to have friends outside of it. One's equity within an agency and a program's equity in Congress are a function of equity with vested interests outside. The most visible and articulate vestedness is best to cultivate. Every agency and every department knows this, as does every successful executive. The constituency not only represents survival credits but has the quality of a significant reference group. The values, purposes and rewards of the federal agent must mesh with those of his program's constituents.

It is easy to see how this works between the Defense Department and the military-industrial complex; between Agriculture and the large, industrialized farming interests; between Labor and the unions; between Commerce and big business. It is obvious that the regulatory commissions of government have a friendly, symbiotic relationship with the organizations they were meant to monitor. It is less clear, however, that the good guys in government, the liberals who run the "social programs," have their exclusive constituents as well. The constituents of welfare programs are not welfare recipients, but social workers. The constituents of educational programs are not students, but educators. The constituents of health programs are the providers of health care, not their consumers. The mental health programs of the government are sensitive to the perturbations of mental health professionals and social scientists, not so much to the walking wounded.

In the latter case, for example, to suggest that nonprofessionals should have something to say about the expenditure of millions of research, training and service dollars is to threaten a constituency. And a threatened one is an unfriendly one, which is not good for the program in Congress or for the job possibilities of the executive in the marketplace. As long as the constituency is stable and circumscribed, credits can be counted.

These, then, are the rules of behavior for functionaries in the federal bureaucracy. If they sound familiar, they should. They are not by any means unique to this system. With minor alterations, they serve as the uncodified code of conduct in any organization. They are what sustained every archbureaucrat from Pilate to Eichmann. They explain in large part why the United States government is such a swollen beast, incapable of responding to the unmet needs of so many people.

But only in part. One other feature of the Washington scene must be described before we can say we know enough of it to elaborate a strategy of assault. This has to do with power.

There is a lot of nonsense about power in the government. One sees a black Chrysler with a vinyl top speeding by. A liveried chauffeur, determined and grim, operates the vehicle. In the rear, a gooseneck, high-intensity lamp arched over his shoulder, sits a man studying the *Washington Post*. One is tempted to say, "There goes a man of power."

It is a vain temptation. Power in the government does not reside within gray eminences in black Chryslers. It is a soft, pluralistic business shared by a large number of middle managers. Organizational charts in federal agencies read as if there is a rigid line of authority and control from the top down. It would appear that the secretary of each department with his designated assistants and deputies would control the behavior of the entire establishment. In fact, there is a huge permanent government that watches with covert bemusement as the political appointees at the top come and go, attempting in their turn to control the behavior of the agencies "responsible to them."

This does not mean that there is not a good deal of respect and deference paid by middle managers to their superiors. But, as in many organizations, this deference can have an empty and superficial quality to it that amounts to mockery. In most hospitals, for example, it is not the doctors who determine what happens to patients, but nurses. Nurses may appear as subordinate to physicians as slaves to their masters, but as soon as the doctor has left the ward the nurse does what she wants to do anyway.

Similarly, in federal agencies, it is the great army of middle managers that controls the show. There is not even the built-in accountability of a dead patient for the boss to see.

Power in the government resides less in position and funds than it does in information, which is the medium of exchange. The flow of information is controlled not at the top, but at the middle. There is very little horizontal flow between agencies because of the constant competition for funds, and all vertical flow must be mediated by the GS 14 to GS 17 bureaucrats who make up the permanent government.

This concentration of power in the middle, controlled by masses of managers who subscribe to the unwritten code of behavior described above, is the reason why the national government is essentially unresponsive. It does not respond to the top or the bottom; it does not respond to ideology. It is a great, indestructible mollusk that absorbs kicks and taunts and seductions and does nothing but grow.

But it's worse than that. The government is righteous. The people who man the bastions of the executive branch (like the rest of us) have the capacity to invest their jobs with their personal identities. Because it is theirs, their function must be defended. Their roles become, in the language of psychiatry, ego-syntonic. Their sense of personal integrity, their consciences, their self-esteem begin to grow into the positions they hold. It is as if their very identities partake of the same definition as their organizationally defined function.

Can you imagine trying to fight a revolution against a huge, righteous marshmallow? Even if you had enough troops not to be suffocated by it, the best you can hope for is to eat it. And, as you all know, you become what you eat. And that is the point. For a revolution to be meaningful it must take into account the nature of organizational life. It must assume that the ideologically pure and the ideologically impure are subject to the same Eichmannesque forces. If a revolution harbors the illusion that a reign of terror will purify a bureaucracy of scoundrels and exploiters, it will fail. It matters little whether bureaucrats are Royalist or Republican, Czarist or Bolshevik, Conservative or Liberal, or what have you. It is the built-in forces of life in a bureaucracy that result in the bureaucracy being so indifferent to suffering and aspiration.

Does this mean that radical change is not possible? No. It means that intelligence and planning must be used, as well as rhetoric, songs, threats, uniforms and all the other trappings of a "movement." The intelligence and planning might orient themselves around a concept of nonalienated revolution that relies on a strategy of guerrilla administration.

This is not meant to be an exclusive strategy. Social change, radical and otherwise, has to be a pluralistic phenomenon. It needs to allow for foxes as well as hedgehogs. This represents one attempt, then, to approach the Great White Marshmallow in such a way that victories are neither impossible nor terrible.

Assuming that power in the federal government is controlled by a vast cadre of middle managers who are essentially homeostatic, and assuming the softness and purposelessness of the system in which they operate, it is conceivable that a critical mass of change agents working within that system may be effective in achieving increasingly significant ad hoc successes.

This requires a group of people who are prepared to work as civil servants but who have little or no concern with the five unwritten rules of behavior of such service. Specifically, their investment in their own jobs carries a very limited liability. The ultimate sanction, being fired, is no sanction at all. Either because they command credentials which will afford them the security they need wherever they work or because they emerge from a generation that has not been tainted by the depression and so have fewer security needs, they are not afraid of being fired.

While they may like the boss, and one may hope they do, they do not see themselves as primarily concerned with saving him from embarrassment.

Spending the program money by the end of the fiscal year and the related rule—keeping the program alive—are significant to them only insofar as the program's purposes mesh with their social consciences, and then only insofar as the program is demonstrating some fealty to those purposes.

Most important, however, is that this critical mass of change agents *not* abide by the rule of maintaining a stable and circumscribed constituency. This is at the same time a liberating principle of behavior and a major strategy of change. It is precisely by broadening the base of the constituencies of federal programs that they will become more responsible to the needs of more people.

This network of communication and collaboration shares as its purpose the frustration of the bureaucracy. But it is the homeostatic, self-serving and elitist aspects of bureaucratic life that are to be frustrated. And this can only be accomplished through the creative tension that emerges from a constant appreciation of unmet needs.

The network of change agents represents a built-in amplifier of those needs either because the agents are, themselves, among the poor, the colored and the young or because they are advocates of them.

It is not critical that the guerrilla administrators who compromise this network be in a position to command funds or program directions. They must simply have access to information, which, you recall, is the medium of exchange in government.

This network, in order to avoid the same traps as the bureaucracy it is meant to frustrate, should never become solidified or rigidified in structure and function. It may have the form of a floating crap game whose location and participation are fluid and changing, but whose purposes and activities are constant. The contacts should remain informal, nonhierarchical and task-oriented. The tasks chosen should be finite, specific, salient and feasible. The makeup of each task force is an ad hoc, self-selected clustering of individuals whose skills or location or access to information suggests their roles. This network of change agents becomes a reference group, but not a brotherhood. There need not be a preoccupation with loyalty, cordiality or steadfastness. They do not even have to be friendly.

This is a rather dry and unromantic strategy of social change. It does not stir one's heart or glands. Where is the image of Parnell pulling his cap low on his forehead as he points his gallant band to the General Post Office? Or Lenin approaching the borders of a trembling Russia in a sealed train? Or Fidel or Che? Or Spartacus, or Mao? Where are the clasped hands and the eyes squinting into a distant line of troops? Where are the songs, the flags, the legends? Where is the courage? Where is the glory?

Such a revolutionary force has nothing of the triumphal arch in it. Nor has it anything of the gallows. It lives without the hope of victory or the fear of defeat. It will yearn for saints and despair of scoundrels, but it will see as its eternal mission the subversion of those systems that force both saints and scoundrels into a common, faceless repression of the human spirit.

Democracy in the Factory

DAVID JENKINS

This essay examines the increasing alienation associated with the modern workplace. It seems that "efficient" but bureaucratic and rigid organizational structure produces mindless sabotage and discontented workers. Jenkins analyzes a series of workplace innovations that revolve around increasing worker control and participation.

There is a growing impression that the industrial revolution is in trouble. It seems only a few short years ago that modern capitalism—the prime creation of the industrial revolution—was being eulogized in books with upbeat titles like *The Triumph of American Capitalism* and *The Twentieth Century Capitalist Revolution,* while today there is a constant flow of pronouncements suggesting the rottenness, the emptiness, the inner weaknesses, the frailty, the utter dispensability of the "system." Such sentiments are by no means confined to eccentrics and extreme leftists. As Irving Howe has pointed out, "Even among those who play the game and accept the social masks necessary for gaining success, there is a widespread disenchantment."

Increasing social conflict, bitterness, and strife have been swirling up in factories. At the now famous General Motors auto assembly plant at Lordstown, Ohio, the engineering values of a super-automated assembly line collided head on with the values of a predominantly young work force. In early 1972, the workers, expressing their discontent with GM's hard-driving, high-speed (101 cars an hour) production philosophy, responded with absenteeism, sabotage, and finally a bitter twenty-two-day strike. The causes were not new. In 1970, two years before Lordstown, a personnel research specialist at GM told me the crisis was already painfully apparent. As an example, he cited the company's well-meaning attempts to help disadvantaged persons obtain well-paid, dignified employment. "One thing we learned about hard-core unemployment," he said, "is that we do not have so much to offer these people after all. Blacks accustomed to making a living after a fashion by 'hustling' would come in and we would give them instructions on how to find a bus to get to the plant and so on; but when they found out what kind of work they were going to do, they just vanished. There was more opportunity to develop self-respect in hustling."

The growing distaste for rigidly disciplined working conditions is not confined to blue collar workers. One 1968 study showed that 56 percent of college students wouldn't "mind being bossed around on the job," but the percentage dropped to 36 percent in 1971. What's more, there is a good deal of feeling that all this antiwork sentiment is thoroughly justified—that it is the fault of the work, not the workers. Historian Staughton Lynd writes: "Work for most Americans may no longer be dirty, but it is still boring, humiliating, and unworthy of what a man can be. The young are right to rebel against an audlthood which insults them." This situation is of great seriousness, and will get worse if current trends and current practices continue. W. N. Penzer, a personnel expert, says: "It is becoming increasingly clear that the employees entering the world of business are unwilling to accept the system of unanswered questions, half-baked opportunities, and half-assed jobs. . . . They will no longer unquestioningly accept the organizational party line and will no longer stand idly by while their business lives are controlled and manipulated from above."

Though this discontent has obviously been fermenting for some time, only very recently have the problems of work received much notice in the United States. The press has devoted a modicum of attention to the issue, and it is no longer a novelty to observe that most jobs are stupefyingly boring. (A U.S. Army recruiting poster, reflecting the increased awareness of the question, perceptively coaxed: "If your job puts you to sleep, try one of ours.") The new concern about work has only begun to lead to an intensive search for solutions.

It should be emphasized that the situation is very different in Europe, where there is—and has been for some years—a widespread resolution to deal with problems of work. Specifically, there is a well-established movement to modify or abolish authoritarianism in industry and to replace it by some form of democracy. Although the reforms being promoted vary from country to country, they have one point in common: the transfer of decision-making power to employees. This movement, whose first tremors are only now being felt in the United States, might best be called "industrial democracy." In almost every West European country, student groups, political factions, independent organizations, social thinkers, writers, and labor leaders are actively urging democratic reform of business enterprises, and anyone in these countries drawing up a list of social reforms would surely put near the top some version of industrial democracy.

In the United States, paradoxically, there is a vast reservoir of *knowledge* of organizations. During the past three or four decades, the study of organizations by behavioral scientists has made enormous strides, and since the 1950s the knowledge has been spreading into managerial ranks. Previously, psychologists in industry were usually restricted to technical chores such as testing, recruiting, and thinking up "human relations" gimmicks with which to create spurious feeelings of "belongingness" among employees. And "organization specialists" were people who concentrated on reshaping organization charts to create clearer and more effective lines of authority. Recently this has been changing, as the behavioral scientists have begun to persuade managers to think of organizations in terms of their human components.

In 1957, a book called *Personality and Organization,* by Chris Argyris, a wide-ranging thinker trained in both economics and psychology, gave many businessmen their first glimpse of the behavioral sciences and how they might be useful in understanding work organizations. The literature on the subject is now enormous, and there are departments of "organizational science" at a number of universities. There is a wealth of knowledge of organizations unmatched in any other country, and a great deal of it suggests that democratic management methods are not only possible but are far superior to the old authoritarian methods. In a sense, then, the potential for industrial democracy is far richer in America than in any of the European countries where more has been achieved.

But there is still only limited interest in industrial democracy in America. Almost no groups here—neither student activists nor journalists (as in France), nor the state (as in Yugoslavia), nor labor unions (as in Germany), not intellectual leaders (as in Sweden), nor radical leftist groups (as in Great Britain), nor the workers themselves (as in many European countries)—are agitating for the spread of democracy within enterprises.

This anomalous situation cannot be expected to endure for long, particularly in view of the deepening dissatisfaction with work and the pressure toward industrial democracy implicit in these organizational studies. It is difficult to see how a convergence of these two can be avoided, and when it takes place, the impact could be far-reaching.

Most advanced American approaches to industrial organization contain some "democratic" elements—that is, they alter power structures, they give increased power and freedom to lower-level employees, and they help diffuse decision-making throughout the organization. But they tend to be limited.

The handful of companies that have gone the furthest have adopted a philosophy, variously described as an "open systems," "total systems," or "sociotechnical" approach. This approach actively encourages employees to influence their working environment, and it attempts to integrate technological systems with social systems, so that production methods serve human as well as corporate needs. The two companies that have made the most progress along these lines are General Foods and Procter & Gamble.

The General Foods philosophy has been put into practice at a pet-food factory in Topeka, Kansas. Lyman Ketchum, an organizational specialist at General Foods headquarters in White Plains, New York, explained to me that the new approach grew to a great extent out of experience at a pet food plant in Kankakee, Illinois, of which he had been manager. In the late 1960s, with the advent of an ever younger work force, an unfamiliar atmosphere was developing. "We discovered there was something different happening," Ketchum told me. "People were not aware of why they were behaving differently; they were just reacting in different ways." Ketchum mentioned poor quality production, vandalism, and graffiti on the walls as symptoms of the discontent. He told me: "Bad quality is inevitably a product of alienation."

To attack these problems, management took an entirely new stance at the Topeka plant. The planning group analyzed the plant's operation in terms of human needs: the employees' self-esteem, sense of accomplishment, autonomy, and increasing knowledge. The group also looked at data on employees' performance. Ketchum said that each point on the list had a distinct meaning: "Autonomy—they have to be able to plan the work, check the quality, change the design of jobs. They have to have real control and not just over simple stuff like when they can take a coffee break—it's the real guts of the job." As a consequence of the study, the company minimized the work force so as to make each job more challenging. "Usually, there's an awful lot of overcrewing and overmanagement. This time we didn't do that. We started with the bare bones and want to keep it that way." Along the same lines, the planners omitted as many specialized functions as possible. "We tried to put all the responsibilities and all the skills in the teams," Ketchum said. There are no foremen, there are "team leaders."

After about eighteen months of operation, the reorganization of the Topeka plant appeared to be working out very much as planned. Ed Dulworth, plant manager, told me that all the unusual features had been retained; indeed, employees were being given more freedom than planned: "People are free to come and go when they wish. In the plant, operators are free to arrange the tasks among themselves. The scheduling—who does what and when—is all handled by the people in the plant. Everybody is very involved in all aspects of the business. We have committees for safety, spare parts, welfare and benefits, recreation, and so on. Almost everyone has some part in the committee work."

There are two teams—an eight-man processing team and a sixteen-man packaging-warehousing team—operating on three shifts. There are about ninety employees, including office staff. Normally, there would be cleaners, helpers, process operators, mechanics, boiler operators, quality control technicians, fork truck drivers, grain unloaders, and others on each shift. But here everybody learns every job. When I visited the plant, employees were just finishing the process of learning all the jobs on their team, and the movement from one team to the other, to learn additional jobs, was just beginning. Everyone learns at his own pace—his progress being judged by his fellow team members—and moves up the pay scale according to his own progress (regardless of seniority or how many others are moving up at the same time). Starting pay in mid-1972 was $136 a week; by learning a full team's jobs, empolyees move up to $142; by learning more jobs "across the plant," they move gradually up to $170; and by acquiring—in addition to all this—an unusual skill or expertise, they can go to $192 (a step nobody had reached at the time of my visit). Dulworth says: "We feel that the more jobs a person knows the better he can do any job, since lots of things that happen affect several jobs. We're paying for knowledge beyond what is required. For example, you can get people to do jobs like loading materials eight hours a day rather cheaply. But that's an undesirable job, and the people here share the undesirable jobs."

In addition to responsibilities specified in the reorganization plan, employees have taken on the job of hiring and firing. Potential new employees are screened by the teams and, occasionally, are expelled on the decision of their teammates. The system has changed in other ways. "The operating group analyzed the packaging operation," Dulworth explained, "and decided more people were needed there—so we hired more people." One unexpected development carries some legal risks. "Our guys are supposed to be paid for time worked," Dulworth told me, "but it's not always so. People come in outside working hours—there's quite a lot of that. For example, we were working on installing a recreation room, but the cost was taken out of our budget—so the employees are working on it on their own time."

Dulworth emphasized that more change in the system is expected. He said: "The willingness not to be static is critical. What we have may not be right. Everybody's learning. We have to be ready and willing to change."

Overall costs of the product are considerably lower than would customarily be expected in a conventional plant, and quality is higher because of greater worker involvement. The attitudes of workers are overwhelmingly positive. Jim Weaver, a thirty-four-year-old operator, gave his reaction: "It's much better to move around. I get bored staying on one job. When I came here I didn't know what an expander was. They just said this is your baby, you do it. We had to learn everything from the ground up. When you learn one job, you teach it to the next guy, and every guy finds a new and better way of doing things. Some guys have designed their own tools to make the work easier. We do our own maintenance work and lubrication. Everything that goes on here, we do it. A man comes to the point where he knows all about one job—it's possible to be *too* familiar with a machine, and then you take risks. Moving from job to job, it makes you more alert. I get a kind of joy out of it because it's challenging. If they ask me to go over to the utility building to help out, I go because otherwise they'd have to have more overtime.

"Ninety-five percent of the employees are sold on the system. We're the foundation of what it's going to be in the future—the Topeka system. We've had our problems, but we can sit down and work them out. I like General Foods. It's the only job I ever had where I felt I was a part of the company. General Foods put responsibility on me and I can accept it. I feel, being chairman of the safety committee, I should be paid extra, but I like it. I feel wanted. I've been ill and come to work anyway because I know I'm needed. General Foods affords me happiness. If a man is happy in his work, he'll be happy at home. Before, I'd never been anywhere in the United States. But now I've been to all the safety meetings in New York, Michigan—they don't send management, they send me. When a salesman comes around to sell safety equipment, Ed Dulworth sends him to see me. I suggested that our committee go to the National Safety Council meeting in Chicago—it was going to cost $3000—so Ed said OK, you set it up. I thought he was kidding, but the whole committee went. Being black, I always wanted to be a part of something, but it seemed every time I tried something I got pushed back. I feel many people could do things but they're not given the opportunity. These people make me feel important. Two years ago I wouldn't have thought it possible to find this many people who took such pride in their job. I feel in the future that the Topeka system will be such a success that other people will be asking us to help them out."

In fact, the system is already so successful that the employees have been asked to help design an addition to the plant. Operators in the existing plant were asked to contribute ideas for the new addition; one suggestion was that the core group being sent to the new plant to help train new workers should not be paid extra for taking on extra responsibilities, since that would be unfair to the other workers.

Bill Easter, manufacturing manager of the new plant, explained that the special management system is to some extent built into the technology of the new plant: "Some aspects of the plant are different from what they otherwise would have been—to suit the open style of management." The technology has been revamped to change the character of the jobs. "Often," says Easter, "there is no opportunity for operators to see what goes on before or after their stage, so we've grouped operations together so operators can relate to each other and to the process better. They have more of an opportunity to sense their responsibility. We're trying to get all operations under one team grouped together so they all have visibility." Easter explained that "maximum automation" is not always the best answer: "If your aim is to make an idiot-proof factory so nobody can fuck it up, that's right. But not if you want to have systems arranged so people have control over more things and are able to see their part of the process. For our products, you can't take the man out of it completely. His judgment is absolutely necessary. We find that when we've taken automation as far as we can, then the man becomes uninvolved—and that affects quality. We have to have people on the alert so they can make changes minute by minute."

Could a new manager with more conventional ideas destroy the "Topeka system"? Actually, clever as the technological designs are, there is nothing to preclude the use of orthodox autocratic techniques. But Dulworth doubts it could happen: "We have some outstanding performance—it's as good as they've ever seen in the company. Also, we have an established culture. It would be very difficult to change that. If anybody came in here and wanted to change it, he would have a fight on his hands. It wouldn't be impossible, but the reaction would be extremely quick. Things would start coming apart almost immediately."

Considering the employees' unusually strong attachment to their plant, this seems believable. When asked how he might like to work at another company, Jim Weaver answered: "You'd have a hell of a time getting me to leave this place."

Without doubt the most radical organizational changes made on a practical, day-to-day basis in the United States have taken place at Procter & Gamble, one of America's largest companies and well known for its hard-boiled, aggressive management practices. Primarily devoted to making good soap and fat profits, P&G has minimal interest in management methods of modish nomenclature. But Charles Krone, the head of organizational development at P&G's Cincinnati headquarters, in discussing his approach, says: "I call it industrial democracy."

The new P&G program was first put into operation in the late 1960s at a plant in Lima, Ohio, employing about 125 people in three shifts, producing two consumer products, one in a batch process and the other in a continuous process. Krone explained to me that the new ideas were designed into the plant, which uses rather advanced technology and is highly automated: "The plant was designed from the ground up to be democratic. The technology—the location of instruments, for example—was designed to stimulate relationships between people, to bring about autonomous group behavior, and to allow people to affect their own environment." Conference rooms, laboratories, and other service functions are located immediately adjacent to the production area, so that any needed action can be taken without delay. The basic principle, as enunciated by Krone, is that the human being has "growthful potential." And a key to the design and operation of the plant is that no barriers should be placed to hinder that growth.

Just as there are no physical barriers, so there are no barriers between jobs. Indeed, there are no jobs at all in the ordinary sense. In an orthodox plant of this type, there might be sixteen to twenty job classifications—at Lima there are none. Not everybody can do every job, but every member of "the community" (as Krone refers to the employees) is constantly adding to his own skills in some specialized field. Krone says, "Each individual defines the direction in which he wants to grow." The community decided, however, that every member must continue to share responsibility for day-to-day operations. "You might be a laboratory technician," Krone says, "but you also handle operating jobs. Everybody carries the same minimum responsibility. No matter where you go, you always have to go back to the operation—you cannot become exclusively a specialist. One guy became a very skilled machinist and wanted to concentrate on his skill—so the community fired him. They told him there was plenty of opportunity for that on the outside. This system grew up naturally at the wish of the members—it was not imposed."

The members of this unusual community were judged to have, when they were hired, "high innate capacity," but they did not have any special training or skills. "However," Krone points out, "after the plant has been in operation for three years, they are by now probably among the most highly skilled people in the company. One man who was a farmer would now be called a very highly skilled instrument specialist. He designed the plant's whole instrument control system, and did it entirely on his own initiative, working with manufacturers."

The workers have virtually complete control of the plant. There are no time clocks or other symbols of petty "class" distinctions, and everybody is on straight salary. "The manager," says Krone, "has very little decision-making power. Usually, instead of being seen as a resource, he is seen as an invader, fulfilling a directive and controlling role—there is much less of that here." Among other things, the members of the community work out the pay scales themselves and all the salaries are known to everyone. I asked Krone if he and his fellow managers gave the employees complete financial figures. "Well, no," he answered, "they give them to us. One guy is interested in accounting and he develops all that information. They draw up their own budgets and so on." Isn't this a dangerous method of setting up wage scales? "Sure," Krone says, "they could hold us up and say you're not paying us enough. But by now you could almost say those employees have less interest in their pay than management people do, who think the Lima people are not being paid enough."

The unorthodox methods at Lima have proved somewhat perplexing to the rest of the company. A technical services group from corporate headquarters was constantly asking for the plant chemical engineer. It took a year for the fact to sink in that there was no chemical engineer.

The plant's hard data are in fact easily understandable. Even though the pay scale is considerably higher than is customary, overall costs are approximately half those of a conventional plant. Much of that is because of the advanced technology. But this technology could not function properly if there were not, at the same time, an advanced social system. Quality is also affected. Krone told me: "It has the most outstanding quality record of any plant we have—it is virtually perfect quality."

The results have, in fact, been so good that the open-system principles have been applied in a number of other new P&G plants constructed over the past few years, and the employees in such plants now total almost 10 percent of the company's 28,000 U.S. employees. Considering the nature of the new approach and the short time it has been in operation, this is an astonishingly high figure. The open-system methods have proved quite profitable, so it is likely that this figure will rise in the future. Though the introduction of new management methods at P&G took the form of a kind of "guerilla warfare" in the beginning, when top management had only a dim understanding of what was going on, now the new principles seem to be firmly established.

In speaking of the results of democratic management, it is possible to document a favorable impact, both on the morale of employees and on productivity and quality. And satisfying and involving work can change and enrich individuals' outside lives as well. Neil McWhinney a UCLA psychologist who has worked as a consultant with P&G, has written: "One of the striking features in our 'pure' open systems plant is that workers take on more activities outside the workplace. The most visible involvements had to do with community racial troubles. Following major disturbances in the small city where they lived, a number of workers organized the black community to deal directly with the leaders of the city and of industry. . . . Blue collar workers won elections to the school board majority office and other local positions. Nearly ten percent of the work force of one plant holds elective offices currently. . . . We have noted that open systems workers join more social clubs and political organizations."

These advanced management methods have been introduced in U.S. companies primarily because they "work" in conventional terms. But they also lead toward a true democratization of companies—breaking up orthodox power patterns and diffusing influence throughout the organization.

There is, to repeat, little recognition of this fact in America. Most of the people who have been developing these methods dislike the use of the word "democracy" to describe their work. Theorist Frederick Herzberg, truly a pioneer in recognizing employee needs for carrying greater responsibility, flatly rejects the word, and so do many others, with varying degrees of insistence.

The issue extends far beyond mere terminology. In much of the recent discussion of work-related problems in America, there is the assumption that since a main curse is an abundance of tedious jobs created by shortsighted managements, the answer is the creation of fascinating jobs by farsighted managements. A great deal of attention is given to the rearrangement of tasks in "job enlargement" or "job enrichment" or "job design" projects.

But the basic problem is not a faulty arrangement of jobs, it is a question of faulty power patterns; the arrangements of jobs are only surface symptoms. To be sure, any job reshuffling that gives workers increased control is a step on the road to democracy. And the assembly-line worker who sees the time span of his job increased from, say, forty to seventy seconds, and his task widened from tightening one bolt to tightening two bolts will doubtless appreciate the change. But strictly speaking, only those organizational systems that regard employee influence as a healthy and desirable phenomenon, and that are planned from the ground up to nurture and encourage such influence, can be called democratic.

Surprisingly few of the companies I have visited have given much thought to where the changes they are promoting in their organizations might ultimately lead them, even though they often see a process developing that tends to have a life of its own. But it is apparent that the ultimate scope of the changes may be rather large. Job enrichment experts in America are increasingly recommending that the employees themselves participate in reforming their own jobs and that the change process, in order to work, has to be continuous. Moreover, it is recognized that job design projects cannot be confined to one part of a company. If they are to have any usefulness at all, plans must be made for gradual extension beyond one or two departments. In other words, a truly useful system is one in which growth is not merely tolerated but expected and prepared for.

In general, the men at the top of company management have not been much aware of the radically new techniques introduced in their companies, and in particular they are slow to see the social implications of the new plans. Nor are those managements which are most effective in bringing about these changes very eager to provide careful explanations of their activities. Some of the most impressive projects have thus been quietly engineered by executives working as "infiltrators" who have kept their projects quiet for years. The unorthodox management methods used in one plant of a major American company were kept hidden from top management for more than ten years. (When asked why, the plant manager replied: "I don't trust this company.") Though increasing attention is now being paid to these advanced management methods, many planners still feel that keeping quiet is the best policy. One young psychologist told me: "I don't try to mislead people, but if I know we're going quite far along this road, I don't necessarily say that to every manager. I deal with them on the level they can understand."

But in spite of the reluctance they encounter, most of the planners are optimistic about the prospects of democratization. Charles Hughes of Texas Instruments observed to me: "I am convinced that there is going to be a massive attack on this within this decade." More emphatically, one plant manager, whose top management has been deeply suspicious of the peculiar participative methods he is using, when asked if his methods were supposed to be revolutionary, replied: "You're damned right—and it's about time!"

Communes for all Reasons

ROSABETH MOSS KANTER

This essay is included here because communes or, more properly, intentional communities, represent an attempt to escape an impersonal, alienating, and sterile urban environment. All communes attempt to build the spirit of community lacking in "normal" life. Kanter examines not only some modern communities but our surprisingly well-developed heritage of alternate living experiments.

Reprinted by permission of the author from *Ms.* 3 (August 1974), pages 62–67. Additional information can be found in R. M. Kanter, *Commitment and Community*, Cambridge, Mass: Harvard University Press, 1972.

People of all kinds live communally, and they have for centuries. Today's commune movement is a revival of recurrent dreams in Western history: to create a household and way of life with other people, to extend intimacy beyond the fences of the family, to share ownership, responsibility, values, and vision. Share the wealth and share the burden.

Today there is a vast proliferation of communal styles: from professional to mystical, from highly organized to barely planned, from large collective to small "extended family."

But to anyone looking for a magical cure for all the afflictions of the human condition, communes have to be a disappointment. They represent perhaps a *better* way to live, but not the *perfect*, problem-free way. Some work well, some do not. Some are good for people, some are not. (The same thing could be said about families.)

Although experiences vary, most women who have tried communal living consider it a step in the right direction, toward a more liberating, more fulfilling kind of social arrangement.

For the past six years I have traveled among communes of all persuasions and researched the communal heritage. In the many dozen communes I visited, one of three themes dominates: the land, the spirit, the home. Rural communes are frontier settlements, pioneering in an effort to "get back to the land." Spiritual communes are large and well organized, usually headed by one "leader." The third, and perhaps the most popular commune today, is the home-centered, increasingly affluent, urban commune.

As experimental as these efforts sound, the roots of the communal heritage go deep into American history.

Heritage

When the partition between the sexes is taken away, when man ceases to make woman a propagative drudge, when love takes the place of shame, men and women will be able to mingle in all their employments.

—John Humphrey Noyes, founder of the Oneida Community (1848–1881)

More than a century ago, feminism and communalism met in Oneida, New York: 300 radical Christians lived, worked, owned property, and loved each other communally for more than 30 years.

Women enjoyed unusual freedom at Oneida, with men sharing the burdens of household tasks, child care, and contraception. Founder John Humphrey Noyes considered marriage a form of slavery, a "spiritual tyranny" in which a man owned exclusive rights to a woman as a piece of property. He proposed complex marriage, a system he felt went beyond free love in encouraging marriagelike responsibility and commitment without the possessiveness of coupling. From 1849 to 1869, Oneidans tried to restrict births by practicing male continence (through withdrawal before ejaculation). After 1869, Oneida children were raised collectively in separate children's quarters, and presided over by a surrogate mama and papa.

While Victorian ladies balanced on pedestals, Oneida women labored in fields and factories, loved and cared for children other than their own, learned to swim and play ball, studied sciences, read Plato, managed two of the leading community businesses, edited the newspaper, taught in the school, and kept the community accounts. They cut their hair short, threw away corsets, rejected cosmetics, and donned the 19th-century equivalent of pants—a scandal to the outside population. More than one-third of the Oneida women worked at nondomestic tasks, and all the women gathered periodically for evening meetings to discuss their position and needs in the community.

Oneida was but one example of the 19th-century search for Utopia. Indeed, Ralph Waldo Emerson remarked at the time that every other person seemed to have a plan for the "perfect society" in his vest pocket. Emerson's Boston intellectual friends had gone "back to the land" at Brook Farm, and a New York newspaper was running a column for people interested in forming communes. But there were skeptics, too. Margaret Fuller, author of *Woman in the Nineteenth Century,* found Brook Farm a nice place to visit (she used their pine woods for a retreat), but she wouldn't want to live there. Nathaniel Hawthorne fictionalized Brook Farm in *The Blithedale Romance,* and Louisa May Alcott satirized her father's brief fling at communalism in "Transcendental Wild Oats." The skeptics had history on their side. Only a few dozen known communes had survived for more than five years. One of the hardiest, waxing and waning for 180 years, was the Shakers, a group of communal villages with a sturdy communications network. Founded by Ann Lee, who was considered the female half of the godhead in the ideology, Shakerism involved communal ownership, celibacy, the separation of the sexes, female as well as male leadership, and the elevation of domestic labors to spiritual acts. And during the same period, Frances Wright, another visionary radical, founded her own short-lived, free-love commune for emancipated slaves.

But most 19th-century ventures in Utopia folded in the face of disasters, debts, and disagreements. Those that did succeed, like Oneida and the Shakers, were distinguished by a number of common themes that are a legacy to the contemporary commune movement. Members knew one another beforehand, they invested their time and resources equally, they owned property collectively. They had a common faith and a common goal. They organized, shared, and rotated chores. They developed rituals to express their togetherness—celebrations, myths and symbols, special ceremonies. They had regular meetings to make decisions, air grievances, and work on relationships. Such practices reinforced the commitment that eased successful communes over the inevitable difficulties in communal living.

Land

Love of seed nourishes.

—Sign in the garden of a northern California commune

Rural communes are somewhat like summer camp. There's a winding dirt road into the grounds; then the main building, and perhaps some outbuildings—cabins, tipis, tents, or domes—where people sleep. Campfires, a place to swim, a sweat hut, outhouse, animals, lots of physical exercise, and 10, 20, or 40 bodies.

Winter, however, separates the transient campers from the committed pioneers. Besides tough winters and the rigors of agriculture, "back to the land" communes also have a range of interpersonal issues to resolve: bringing in enough money, getting the chores done, making decisions. No one knows exactly how many hundreds or thousands of rural communes have grown out of the "Open Land, do-your-own-thing" optimism of the counterculture, but we do know that the communes of today, like those of the previous century, do not survive without some structure. Few rural communes survive just by farming. Synergia Ranch in New Mexico runs the Theater of All Possibilities, ecology labs, and craft businesses. In Vermont, Total Loss Farm members write books. Twin Oaks in Virginia manufactures hammocks.

Earth lore abounds on rural communes, passed from person to person. Medicines and teas, made from herbs and leaves gathered in the woods, are studied. Questions about natural childbirth at home are explored. (*Childbirth Is Ecstasy*, by Allen Cohen, published by Aquarius, was photographed on a California commune.) What trees burn best for warmth, how a compost pile is made, how vegetables are canned, when cows first go outdoors in spring, how a maple tree is tapped, when the soil is the right texture for planting: all these are practical questions with high priority. Weaving, crocheting, poetry, sewing, and other crafts which can be put to immediate, practical use, are developed as the arts of the commune.

I joined Eve, a resident of a Vermont commune, on a typical day. Up with the sun, she transplanted tomato seedlings, hoed and manured the herb garden with Dan (her partner), exchanged food co-op gossip with other group members, spun wool on the new spinning wheel (a birthday gift from Dan), replenished the water supply from the well, gathered wood to cook dinner, and chatted with me. The pace was easy and relaxed. At 6 P.M., people began to gather in the kitchen. We were having chicken (an unexpected bonus—a neighbor's chickens were killed by a dog); everyone helped with the plucking, and Dan cooked them with some grains. We ate, smoked, looked out over the green hills, and talked. At 9 P.M., we lit the kerosene lamps. Eve and Dan climbed into their high platform bed tucked under the roof; others trudged off to their cottages, tipis, and tents; and I stretched out on a mattress near the stove. Our day kept pace with the rhythm of the earth.

In the early days of the current commune movement, the charge of sexism in rural communes had some validity. Barefoot and pregnant women in the kitchen with *macho* men marching in from a day of physical labor in the fields was a popular image. Those who left the cities in search of the Garden of Eden—a spontaneous paradise in which no plan, order, or organization was necessary—often wound up dividing labor along traditional lines. Child-bearing women contributed to the group's economy by collecting welfare payments. Frowning on marriage and favoring doing-your-own-thing often led to problems: when a man's "thing" was to split, his "old lady" was left behind with an infant or two to care for. Women, trained to be responsible, ended up doing most of the work and bringing in most of the income.

There are stories of women on these rural outposts who discovered their collective strength and confronted the men. I arrived at a New Mexico commune just after the women had run the men off, telling them not to return until asked. Anger was still in the air—Ellie felt the men did not pull their weight in the kitchen; Sarah had discovered that her spouse was more possessive than she, and that he wanted to keep her from other relationships. Now, the animals were being tended, the garden harvested, the children nurtured—all without the men.

But consciousness is changing for men as well as women. Lucy Horton, a communard from Vermont who traveled the country doing research for her book *Country Commune Cookbook* (Coward, McCann, and Geoghegan), found communes full of liberated, gentle men who contributed recipes almost as often as the women. Said Lucy, "The Women's Movement means a lot to me. I can accept myself. I don't need a man to lead a satisfying life. I can be close to other women, and live with both women and men."

Spirit

We're starting a revolution in human consciousness; we're creating a whole new breed of human being.

—Woman at Brotherhood of the Spirit in Massachusetts

Spiritual communes are another trip altogether. They are larger, better known, and more visible than other communes (partly to attract converts). Here ideology shapes life. At Brotherhood of the Spirit in Warwick, Massachusetts, Karen, a former Canadian, showed me around, the extensive grounds and the buildings. A huge dining room with the group's philosophy elegantly lettered on the wall, a hotel-size kitchen, a children's playroom, and new dormitory-like sleeping quarters—all are part of the facilities for the 300-member community. We drove to other branches of the community: a photography store and pool hall in town, a farmhouse, a large house with a colorful front door on the main street of another town (Northfield). Karen seemed to know everyone and greeted them all with hugs. Wherever we went, we saw pictures of the group's guru. (Spiritual communes usually have gurus.) The guru leads the rock band, The Spirit in the Flesh, that provides part of the financial support and serves as a missionary brigade for the group. The house where the guru and the band were living had a certain sacred, to-be-viewed-from-a-distance aura, and I had the impression that not many members of the commune are allowed to be close to him.

Brotherhood's goals have much in common with those of other spiritual communes (such as Koinonia; see page 95). Members donate all their property to the group and they are provided for in return. Children can sleep in separate quarters, under the wing of special caretakers. Instead of relying upon income from the land, Brotherhood has an ever-expanding network of enterprises that provides funds to house and feed its population. As in other large organizations, structure, procedure, and rules tend to characterize spiritual groups. There are well-defined roles and formal positions—in contrast to the informality of life on land-centered rural communes. Members study cosmic consciousness, learn prayers and devotions, in exchange for a sense of belonging to the group and a commitment to self-discipline. Decisions are made not by small, informal, consensus-seeking groups, as in other communes, but by various formal and informal councils, task groupings, and inner circles. (Certain mysteries of a spiritual commune are not revealed to visitors.) Critics accuse spiritual groups, especially of the fundamentalist Christian persuasion, of being totalitarian, of suppressing the individual, of getting people "hooked on faith." It is hard to evaluate these attacks. Those members who are unhappy, leave (spiritual communes have a high turnover), but those who stay, remain dedicated.

Home

What do I like best? Sitting around the table after dinner, laughing and joking. People around at all hours. Sometimes we bring our work home, and there's a buzz of activity throughout the house. I'm never lonely.

—Woman in an urban Boston commune

City communes tend to be small (6 to 12 people) and family-like (the size of the group is usually determined by the amount of space available). Every adult, coupled or not, generally has her or his own room, and small children share a room. In young groups, single people tend to outnumber couples, and adults outnumber children by about 3 to 1. Communes of older professionals tend to have a more equal balance of couples, children, and singles. A few groups are centered around businesses; in Cambridge, one urban commune runs an occult bookstore and a craft shop, rotating workdays, home days, and child-care days among members. Away from the coasts and the big cities, many urban communes are formed by members of the same religious faith. Believing in a sense of community and wanting to build a home around traditions, they feel communal living and income-sharing are routes to political and spiritual change. Bust most city communes are "into" family rather than faith or physical labor, and some of them are indeed difficult to distinguish from nostalgically remembered extended families of the past.

Communes are spreading to the affluent: to grand old houses in Cambridge, the Berkeley Hills, Cleveland Heights, New Orleans. The people in these houses tend to be in their thirties and even their forties; they tend to have children, and to be committed to their work. The houses are often gracious and luxurious; collective incomes can often afford appliances, saunas, meditation rooms, pianos, trampolines, and stereos. Collective energy provides other benefits: a Los Angeles group runs a nursery school for its own children as well as neighboring children; Greenbrook in Boston has its own medical insurance.

Greenbrook is typical of the vast majority of urban groups. Here homemaking is a valid part-time collective preoccupation of both men and women. The kitchen is the ritual center of the house. So important is the kitchen that the refrigerator is often the commune communication center, where anouncements, special messages, and the usual cooking-and-cleaning schedule are posted. Sometimes it is hard to tell an urban commune from a conventional household just from the surroundings; when in doubt, head for the refrigerator. If the household is communal, a chart will be posted somewhere nearby. It will list the days, cooks, clean-up persons, absences from dinner, guests, special events, baby-sitting nights, house-cleaning assignments, and who is going to buy the groceries.

The job-sharing schedule, house business, and concerns about relationships are discussed at weekly house meetings, a nearly universal method for airing concerns and making decisions. Terry can say she feels neglected when she's down; Abby and Bob can work on their relationship; Bill can say that the kitchen is never clean enough; Pat can anounce that she is expecting several guests for the weekend; the group can discuss the financing of a new washing machine. If the commune has tried sexual experiments, such as open or group marriage, particularly "heavy" issues sometimes develop. Sexual sharing has proved difficult and most groups remain traditionally coupled.

Communal living can afford advantages to single mothers. Sharon and Betty share responsibility for getting up early with their children. Three small children sleep in one room, and adults of both sexes take turns putting them to bed. Teenage Monica has many grown-up friends she can learn from and rely on while her mother goes through a difficult period. ("What I like best about the commune," Monica said, "are Sunday breakfasts with everyone, the trampoline, house meetings where we have ice cream, and going out with Marilyn and Tim.") No one knows definitively how communal living affects children (several major research projects are in progress), but observations indicate that commune children are often impressively independent, mature, and comfortable around adults. The age of the child makes a difference, of course, as well as the type of group and how many other children live there. Younger children sometimes miss being their parents' center of attention and are still very vulnerable to grief when someone they are close to moves out. But for older children, some positives are: numerous people, varied activities, and opportunities to share "grown-up" decisions and responsibilities.

When collective child care works, it works beautifully. Men occasionally join communes to be with children. As John put it, "I don't want to be a father—I want to be an uncle." But many unresolved issues around shared parenting remain. "Competitive mothering" is a source of strain for many communal groups. Valerie and her daughter, Kathy, are leaving their present group because Valerie did not like the way some other mother treated Kathy; if she moves to another commune, she wants to be the only parent. Groups that have few problems with privacy, property sharing, or housecleaning occasionally disintegrate around child-centered issues. Two couples living in a commune with three single people found that their own repressed conflicts about personal style (one couple was very restrained, the other outspoken about feelings) surfaced when each saw how the others related to their child. Sometimes biological mothers find that it is still they who do most of the work and take most of the responsibility for their child.

But many veterans of less-than-perfect communes are ready to try others. Alice, now in her fifth group, says, "Sure I know the problems. But I wouldn't consider any other way to live. What are the options for me, a woman with a child? Even at its worst, the commune provides company. At its best, I have a family. And, anyway, it is *home*."

FIVE

Social Stratification

AMERICANS pay a great deal of lip service to the ideal of equality. Its tenets were embedded in the Constitution when black men were counted as three fifths of a human being. But what do Americans mean by "equality"? Do all Americans have an equal chance to become president of the United States, or even president of the local P.T.A.? Obviously not. It is rather apparent that there are tremendous social and economic inequalities in our society. How much influence do these inequalities have on "life chances" (for example, the opportunity to "make it") or on political processes? Is there more equality of opportunity here or in some of the socialist countries? You can see why sociologists have always been extremely interested in the degree of economic, political, and social inequality that exists within any particular society.

There are many differences among human beings. Some of these differences are hereditary, but many, perhaps more than the average students might expect, are socially conditioned or acquired. Many of the differences between men and women, young and old, soldier and merchant, are culturally defined. They are learned through human interaction. Social differentiation is a universal, man-made arrangement. Its patterns can vary tremendously between societies. In one society men wear the skirts; in another, they actually experience labor pains.

Social stratification is a form of social differentiation where individuals are arranged in a graded hierarchy of superior and inferior positions, as, for example, in the ranking system of an army. The type of stratification system we find in America and other industrial societies is a class system. In modern societies individuals can be grouped into classes according to economic, social, and political criteria. A class can be defined as a group of individuals with similar amounts of income, occupational prestige, and political and economic power. Classes are socially defined. They are not the result of innate biological differences; they are not ordained in heaven as the natural order of man. Class structures can be changed, have been changed, and will be changed again.

Marx used the term *class* to refer to an aggregate of individuals occupying a similar economic position. He assumed that an individual's position in relation to the economic process (whether he owned the means of production or worked for someone else) was the most relevant factor in determining his behavior and political attitudes. Marx felt that societies progressed through the vehicle of class conflict. The ultimate struggle would take place in a modern industrial society between the proletariat (wage workers) and the bourgeoisie (capitalists). When the "proles" became conscious of their distinct class interests and disadvantaged economic position, they would overthrow their capitalist masters and establish a classless communist society. Marxist theory has presented us with some important questions: Is inequality necessary in all societies? Should the ownership of the means of production be concentrated in the hands of certain classes? Is capitalism the best type of political economy to facilitate human fulfillment? How powerful is the nation's upper class? Has there been a redistribution of the national income in favor of the lower classes?

Max Weber later elaborated upon the Marxian thesis by insisting that class was multidimensional rather than purely economic in nature. He accepted the Marxian definition of class, but added the dimensions of status (prestige) and power; he felt that although the three were tightly interrelated (a high position on one hierarchy implies high positions in the other two), discrepancies do occur. An old upper-class family that has recently lost its wealth, for example, may still command a high position in the status hierarchy.

How much equality is there in the United States? What is the distribution of income and wealth in America? Is it just and fair? We could easily point to other countries and decry the inequalities there. In 1950 the top 5 per cent of the population of Rhodesia received 65 per cent of the income, and the top 5 per cent received 40 per cent of the total national income in Colombia and Mexico. Who can complain when the top 5 per cent of the United States accumulated only 20 per cent of the income? Maybe those 20 per cent who received less than 5 per cent of the total income would complain. We must realize that when we discuss income statistics we miss the real concentration of wealth in the hands of a few. Wealth includes, for example, stock ownership, property, mortgages, tax-exempt local and state bonds, and federal bonds. The top 1.6 per cent of the population in the United States owned over 30 per cent of the assets and equities in America in 1953. The top 1 per cent of the population owns over 75 per cent of the shares of stock. (This includes vast assets outside the United States.) Is this an equitable distribution of wealth? What implications does this concentration of wealth have for a democratic society?

Has there been a trend toward increasing equality in the United States and other industrial societies? Has the working class forced management to give them a greater and greater share of the income? Actually there has been little or no significant redistribution of income or wealth in America. Some have tried to argue that there has been an increasing concentration of wealth at the top (see *The Rich and the Super Rich* by Ferdinand Lundberg). A state of equilibrium has been reached. For example, in 1922 the top 0.5 per cent of the adult population controlled 29.8 per cent of the wealth; in 1956, this same group owned 25.0 per cent of the wealth. The distribution of income has followed a similar pattern. The upper levels are receiving a slightly smaller percentage of the income and, surprisingly, the lower levels are also getting a smaller share. In 1910, the highest income tenth received 33.9 per cent whereas the lowest received 3.4 pr cent; in 1959, the highest income tenth received 29.9 per cent whereas the lowest obtained only 1.1 per cent of the total national income (from *Wealth and Power in America* by Gabriel Kolko). This pattern seems to be holding steady, according to statistics from *Income Distribution in the U.S.* by Herman P. Miller:

	1947	*1962*
Top fifth	46%	45.5%
Second	22	22.7
Third	16	16.3
Fourth	11	10.9
Low fifth	5	4.6

What has happened? Those in the middle levels are getting a slightly larger share of the income while those on the top and bottom are receiving a little less of the income. Needless to say, it hurts a lot more on the bottom when you lose a percentage of your income. The reason why these trends have been misread or overlooked is that there has been an increase in income across the board. In other words, the total national income (the "income pie") has grown tremendously since 1910. In actual amount, 10 per cent is much more now than it was then.

What about the tax structure? Does it in any way "equalize" income distribution in America? In reality there are more than ample loopholes and exemptions for wealthy individuals with property. For example, there is the oil depletion allowance, capital gains, tax-free bonds, and other stratagems which protect those on top. If you take into consideration federal, state, and local taxes, the structure could be considered regressive. In other words, the percentage of income collected from all taxes rises steadily as income falls below $10,000, from 23.9 per cent at $10,000 to 28.3 per cent at $1,450 (Tax Foundation, *Allocation of the Tax Burden by Income Class, 1960*). This problem is further compounded by the fact that many of these same individuals (those with incomes under $10,000 per year) have experienced an actual shrinkage of income. According to the *Wall Street Journal*, the average weekly paycheck of "nonsupervisory" workers (both white and blue collar) has diminished since 1965, whereas the purchasing power of supervisors and above continues to expand. It is little wonder that a smoldering resentment brews within the working and lower-middle classes. Who really does benefit from the tax dollar? This little vignette sums up the controversy (Horton and Hunt, *Sociology*, pp. 262–263):

As my host guided his 55-foot yacht toward its slip, he applauded the decision of (a Florida) city commission to cancel an urban renewal project, largely federally financed, which would benefit mainly the city's Negro slum area. As he expanded on the "taint" of Federal funds to solve "local" problems, he tuned in on a weather report from a federally operated weather station, waved at the captain of a federally operated coast guard vessel which stood ready to rescue him if he got into trouble, carefully noted the position of the federally placed buoys and channel markers, nosed down a channel dredged with Federal funds, and entered a marina financed partly from Federal funds and tied up to a federally subsidized dock, concluding his lecture on the evils of government welfare programs with the sage observation, "We coddle people too much. People should stand on their own feet and pay their own way."

What about poverty in America? Does income distribution have anything to do with poverty in the United States? Is any amount of poverty tolerable in a society as affluent as ours? How much poverty is there? The numbers range from 20 to 40 million. You choose the number you want according to your political bias. Conservatives choose the lower figure; liberals the higher. Poverty really is not that severe in America, is it? After all, our poor are living like kings compared to the average Indian peasant. Don't the poor have television sets and cars? Why are the poor becoming so restless? They have as much or more than they have ever had. Why are they not satisfied?

The answers to these questions revolve around the concept of "relative deprivation." The poor feel more deprived now. They are fed the same dreams as everyone else in America. (Maybe we should take those TV sets back.) The standard of living in Kenya or Ghana is almost meaningless to a black man in America. What he receives in relation to others in this society is much more important to him. The gap between what the poor think they deserve and what they are getting has widened. Therefore poverty is becoming less and less tolerable in America.

As you can see, the study of social stratification and social class is one of the most controversial and valuable areas of analysis in sociology. Social classes by definition inhabit the same basic economic level and share the same amount of education, and this leads to the development of similar norms, values, and life styles at the different levels of society. In other words, class subcultures develop. For example, those on the lower rungs of the class scale seem to be more racist than those in the upper levels. Social-class position also greatly affects the "life chances" of the individual. The founding fathers, basically white Anglo-Saxon Protestants, have been able to pass on positions of power and influence to their children. A person's position in the class structure alters everything from his chance of staying alive during the first year of his life, to his chance of avoiding becoming a juvenile delinquent, to his chance of reaching a certain educational or socioeconomic level. Why does a larger percentage of working-class children with IQ's equal to those of middle-class offspring fail to complete a college education? Does the American ethos of equality conflict in any way with our class structure?

Another vital area of sociological controversy revolves around the question of whether stratification systems in particular class structures are inevitable and necessary in modern society. It divides the more utopian and idealistic radical sociologists from the more pragmatic and realistic ones. The resulting intellectual struggle is more than a bout of sociological infighting. It is one of the ideological bases dividing the philosophies of capitalism and socialism. This controversy has at its core conflicting interpretations of what man is all about. Is man basically cooperative or competitive? Why do men work? Are unequal rewards for different types of work necessary? Can you envision a society with more or less structured social inequality than the United States? Would these societies be more or less efficient than ours? What effect would these changes have on human beings? Can you apply sociological knowledge to these questions or are they mostly value judgments? —G. G.

Selected References

(All are available in paperback editions.)

Bottomore, T. B. *Classes in Modern Society*. New York: Pantheon Books, 1966.

Domhoff, G. William. *Who Rules America?* Englewood Cliffs, N.J.: Prentice-Hall, Inc., 1967.

Kolko, Gabriel. *Wealth and Power in America*. New York: Frederick A. Praeger, Inc., 1962.

Lipset, Seymour M., and Reinhard Bendix. *Social Mobility in Industrial Society*. Berkeley: University of California Press, 1959.

Lundberg, Ferdinand. *The Rich and the Super Rich*. New York: Lyle Stuart, Inc., 1968.

Miller, Herman P. *Rich Man, Poor Man*. New York: Thomas Y. Crowell, 1964.

Mills, C. Wright. *The Power Elite*. New York: Oxford University Press, 1956.

All Us Pigs Are Equal

ART HOPPE

Ever since Patricia Hearst called her former fiancé, Steven Weed, "a sexist, age-ist pig," Lancelot Liberell has been gravely worried. If there was one thing Lancelot abhorred it was bigotry. In the early 1960s when race relations first became popular in the North, he was invariably careful to invite one black person (and sometimes even two, if it was a large gathering) to his cocktail parties.

He would pump their hands heartily at the door and, to make them feel at home, say things like: "I have always supported the aspirations of your people." Then when Women's Lib raised his feminist head in the 1970s, Lancelot immediately began using words like "oneupersonship" and he told every female he met that he had long deeply felt that "persons are equal to men." So Lancelot took great pride in being neither a racist pig nor a sexist pig. But the question he now had to face as he stared glumly in the mirror was: "Am I, without realizing it, an age-ist pig?"

Believing age-ists to be bigoted against young people, Lancelot invited his bearded nephew, Irvin, who was out on bail on a dope-pushing rap, to lunch.

"I have always had faith in the accomplishments of your generation," said Lancelot. And he was pleased when Irvin returned that faith by offering to sell him a kilo.

He was shocked to learn that evening while reading Newsweek that age-ist actually means "someone prejudiced against old people." There was nothing for it but to invite his Granduncle Ezra, whom he had been avoiding for years, to dinner.

"I can't tell you how much I enjoy the verve and sprightliness of your generation," Lancelot told Ezra, who was hard of hearing and slightly senile.

"It was back in ought eight," replied Ezra, downing half a bottle of four-star cognac in a three swigs, "Three-base Byzkowski was on first in the top of the ninth . . ."

It was a long evening before Granduncle Ezra threw up and passed out on the rug, but Lancelot felt it was worth it. "At last," he said, "I know I'm not a pig."

That's when his daughter, Laverna, announced she was engaged to a five-foot, 314-pound young man named Herbie. "But I know you're not a height-ist or fattist pig, Daddy," she said.

So Lancelot squared his shoulders, shook Herbie's hand warmly and said:

"I want you to know I've never once believed that short people are prone to hostile, Napoleonic complexes. I've always believed also that pleasingly plump people are perpetually jolly good sorts. And I hope you'll live happily ever after."

"But I don't get enough food stamps to feed two," said Herbie.

"Nor have I ever been a poorist pig," said Lancelot. "Some of my best friends are poor. "And I'll be delighted to support you the rest of life to prove I'm no pig of any sort."

It was an editorial in The Hog Fanciers Journal that did Lancelot in. It's title was enough: "Villification of Pigs Displays Bigotry Towards Noble Animal!"

"My God!" cried Lancelot, thunderstruck, "I'm a piggist!"

But the traumatic experience was his salvation. Now, after intensive psychiatric therapy, he is able to lead a normal life—liking some people of whatever color, sex, age or financial condition and, more important, disliking others.

But the only thing that keeps him sane is repeating 16 times a day: "People is people; pigs is pigs; and the hell with it."

The Rich

RICHARD PARKER

Parker's approach is very direct: the rich are different because they have a hell of a lot more money than we do. This selection is packed with data and stinging sarcasm. It is part of a very interesting book, **The Myth of the Middle Class.**

Let me tell you about the very rich. They are different from you and me. They possess and enjoy early, and it does something to them, makes them soft where we are hard, and cynical where we are trustful, in a way that, unless you were born rich, it is difficult to understand. They think, deep in their hearts, that they are better than we are because we had to discover the compensations and refuges of life for ourselves. Even when they enter deep into our world or sink below us, they still think that they are better than we are. They are different.

—F. Scott Fitzgerald

To be sure, the American rich have been challenged before: during the Revolution, we noted earlier, there were several attempts to redistribute highly concentrated land holdings; during the first half of the nineteenth century the struggle between Andrew Jackson and the Bank of the United States symbolized the challenges that were made against wealth; in the latter half of the same century, the fantastic riches of the new industrialists fed the hatred of militant laborers throughout the country; and in the thirties, the popular feelings of unemployed millions literally caused many of the rich to tremble with fear.

But none of these challenges was successful, if by success we mean a significant redistribution of the nation's income and wealth. We saw how the attempts of the radical revolutionists to redistribute Tory lands was undone soon afterward by the development of great new speculative landholdings in the West. Jackson, though he defeated the Bank of the United States, was entirely unable to stop the growth of industrialism which undermined his base of support in a rural agrarian democracy. The creation of unions, passage of minimum wage laws and supposedly progressive income taxes, the most tangible measures of the success of labor agitation, did no more than slow the drift toward greater and greater concentration; such measures were entirely unable to reverse the already high concentration of wealth and income. So too for the New Deal: although statutory rates of income tax on the rich were raised, the effective percentage of income actually paid by the rich fell because of loopholes bored into the tax laws.

Today the almost complete absence of any noticeable hostility toward the most affluent is surprising. Especially in view of the wide-scale poverty known to exist in America, one would expect at least a few major voices raised in protest against the rich. Along with demands for a "minimum" income one might expect to hear demands for a "maximum" income as well. Instead, an almost perfect silence reigns. Why?

Shortly after World War II, when the silence became noticeable, New Class theorists took it as validation of their theories. Not only was affluence widespread, but the high concentration of wealth and income was believed to be undergoing major, and permanent, change. Studies like Kuznets's and Goldsmith's encouraged belief in the trickle down theory of income redistribution; Arthur Burns, as noted earlier, called the imagined redistribution "the greatest peacetime revolution in history." As the years wore on, however, it became more and more apparent that "trickle down" was not working; in fact by the mid-fifties it was apparent that the richest segments of the society were actually *increasing* their share of the national income and wealth each year.

Consequently, more and more social theorists sought means to explain the marked decline in hostility toward the rich; until the fifties it had been such a normal part of life that its absence now seemed meaningful. Galbraith, to take just one example, tried in *The Affluent Society* to develop an explanation for the widespread silence. First, he suggested, Marxist economists had predicted that as capitalism matured, the concentration of wealth and income in the hands of fewer and fewer capitalists would increase so drastically that the workers would be further immiserated and forced to revolt against their masters. Since this communist prediction had not come true in the United States—that is, inequality in wealth and income had not drastically *worsened*—we had one reason for the silence.

The second factor, Galbraith believed, was that the rich were now less conspicuous than before; in contemporary jargon, they had adopted a low profile. Galbraith did not argue that the rich were less rich than before, only that conspicuous consumption was less a part of their behavior. "The depression and especially the New Deal gave the American rich a serious fright," he said. "The consequence was to usher in a period of marked discretion in personal expenditure." In addition to fear, taste had played a role: "Increasingly in the last quarter century the display of expensive goods, as a device for suggesting wealth, had been condemned as vulgar." Taken together, these two factors had effected a change in the visible, if not the actual, face of the rich.

The third factor, undoubtedly the most important in Galbraith's mind, was affluence. "As more people feel more secure, they become less interested in redistributing the wealth of the rich," he observed. Even "the liberal has partly accepted the view of the well-to-do that it is a trifle uncouth to urge a policy of soaking the rich." To his credit, Galbraith (unlike many New Class critics) was both too perceptive and too forthright to argue that the existing state of economic inequality was either good or acceptable, affluence or no affluence. For example, at one point in his discussion of the rich, he quoted R. H. Tawney with obvious approval:

> Those who dread a dead-level of income and wealth do not dread, it seems, a dead-level of law and order, and of security of life and property. They do not complain that persons endowed by nature with unusual qualities of strength, audacity, or cunning are prevented from reaping the full fruits of these powers.

At other points, Galbraith casts a cold eye on conservative arguments that wealth creates incentives, or acts as a buffer against cultural uniformity and monotony. Most significantly, Galbraith gave equally little respect to the orthodox liberal assumption that growth, rather than redistribution, would by itself completely eliminate poverty. "Increasing aggregate output," he warned, "leaves a self-perpetuating margin of poverty at the very base of the income pyramid. This goes largely unnoticed, because it is the fate of a voiceless minority."[1]

But Galbraith, despite his own warnings, chose not to consider inequality as a major issue. Perhaps too preoccupied with making his point about the Affluent Society, perhaps too discouraged by the conservatism of the fifties, Galbraith chose to let inequality remain a secondary, insubstantial issue. Such inequality, one presumed, was trivial in the developed postindustrial world.

[1] John Kenneth Galbraith, *The Affluent Society* (New York, 1958), ch. 7.

Unfortunately for us, neither Galbraith nor any other New Class critic has come forward to explain how inequality could be abolished (or even diminished) or how the wealth of the very rich could be rechanneled to the aid of the poor and the deprived. Quite the opposite has been true: nowhere has silence about the wealth of the very rich been more apparent than among the New Class.

1

The extent of present-day inequality, and the reason that the concentration of income and wealth is far from being irrelevant or secondary can be seen from just a few figures: according to the U.S. Census, the top one-fifth of the population in 1968 received 43% of the total money income in the United States; the top tenth received 27%, and the top 5% received 17%. By contrast the bottom half of the population earned only 22%. In slightly more graphic terms, the top one percent of the American population got more money in one year than all the men, women and children the government defined as poor; in fact the top one percent of the American population received in one year more money than the poorest 50 million Americans.[2]

To be sure, not all Americans in the top fifth of the population were rich by conventional standards. The top fifth contains a large percentage of New Class members, in addition to the extremely wealthy; in 1968, even the top 10% included anyone earning more than roughly $16,000 a year, hardly a definition of extreme wealth (even though almost 60% of America earned less than *half* that amount). Only as one passes into the top five percent can one begin to speak properly of the rich. *Fortune* magazine perhaps wisely chose the much smaller two percent who earn more than $25,000 for its criterion of the rich.

As the number of people in a particular category declines, however, per-person income and wealth rises—fantastically. Paul Samuelson's analogy between American income structure and the Eiffel Tower—"almost all of us live within a yard of the ground"—is apt, because it suggests how well-to-do the very well-to-do really are. To offer one simple example, in 1962 the mean wealth of those earning $15,000–$25,000 was a substantial $63,000; in the much smaller $25,000–$50,000 category, a very healthy $291,000; and in the $100,000 and above bracket, a munificent *average* of $386,000. These figures compared with a national average—including these very wealthy—of only 1,700,000.[3]

Robert Lampman's *The Share of the Top Wealth-Holders in National Wealth, 1922–1956* indicated moreover that even among the rich, wealth is continually stratified toward the top, with fewer and fewer holding increas-

[2] *Income in 1969 of Families and Persons,* p. 19, Table 2 and p. 26, Table 11.

[3] Federal Reserve Board, *Survey of Financial Characteristics of Consumers,* Table A8, p. 110.

ingly larger amounts. He noted that in 1956 the top one percent of the adult population accounted for 26% of the nation's private wealth-holding. But, he also noted, the top *one-half* of one percent accounted for 25% of private wealth-holdings. In other words, the top half of the richest one percent of the population accounts for all but a small portion of the holdings of that entire one percent.

Lampman's work is helpful, because it sets such figures in perspectives that are easy to understand. He found for example in 1953 the average estate size of the wealthiest 1.6% of the adult population was over $186,000; the average estate size of the remaining 98.4% of the population was a mere $7,900—about enough to cover clothes, furniture, a used car, a TV, and a heavily mortgaged home. More frightening was the fact that even among the 98.4% wealth was very unevenly distributed: the average estate size of the lower half of that group was only $1,800.

How incredibly wealthy the very tiny minority of rich Americans was, and what influence they held over the American economy, Lampman went on to point out. "*This group of 1.6 percent owned 32 percent of all privately owned wealth, consisting of 82.2 percent of the stock, 100 percent of the state and local (tax-exempt) bonds, 38.2 percent of federal bonds, 88.5 percent of other bonds, 29.1 percent of the cash, 36.2 percent of mortgages and notes, 13.3 percent of life insurance reserves, 5.9 percent of miscellaneous property, 16.1 percent of real estate and 22.1 percent of debts and mortgages.*"[4] (Italics added)

Lampman traced the progress of this concentration from the early twenties up to the mid-fifties, and in general remarked on its decline. But he discovered that the decline which had characterized the holdings of this tiny minority had ceased in 1949. Since that time the decline had not only ceased but reversed itself, and by the mid-fifties the wealth of the nation was again showing a tendency toward high concentration in the hands of the few.

Lampman's suspicion that wealth was again tending to concentrate in a few hands was confirmed in 1965 by two statisticians employed by the Internal Revenue Service. Extending Lampman's findings up to 1958, they found that the "top wealth-holders owned 27.4 percent of gross and 28.3 percent of net prime wealth in 1953, but increased their share to 30.2 percent and 32.0 percent respectively by 1958." They concluded categorically: "These data support Lampman's conclusions that the share of top wealth-holders has been increasing since 1949."[5]

Their findings were then extended by Ferdinand Lundberg, who used the basis of rising stock prices and general economic prosperity. "Actually," Lundberg declared, "in view of market valuations, the share of top wealth-

[4] Robert Lampman, *The Share of the Top-Wealth-Holders in National Wealth 1922–56* (Princeton, 1962), pp. 192–93, Table 90, p. 213, Table 99.

[5] James Smith and Staunton Calvert, "Estimating the Wealth of the Top Wealth-Holders from Estate Tax Returns," *Proceedings of the American Statistical Association*, September 1965, p. 19.

holders at this writing is easily the greatest in history. It is my hypothesis that the share of the top ½ of 1 percent now exceeds the 32.4 percent of this group for 1929."[6] Lundberg's estimates for the most part remained exactly that; his methodology was not as exactly as Lampman's.

The important thing, however, is not the debate over the exact percentage point, but the massiveness of the holdings themselves. Ten years ago, when the government last published these statistics, the total wealth of the richest 2% of Americans was greater than the *U.S. Gross National Product.*[7] The same is true today.

2

The rich, then, incredibly more than any other group enjoy the benefits of the Affluent Society. The popular notion of that society—of families able to enjoy their well-being, secure against debt and worry, able to offer their children education and a hopeful future—seems if not a monopoly of the rich, at least unlikely to be enjoyed by many others. *Fortune's* investigation of the rich emphasized this fact: "Something thoroughly satisfying happens to people when they cross an income threshold of around $25,000 a year. Until then basic family wants tend to outrun income, but afterward income moves ahead of needs. The family pays off debts and stays out of debt. And major costs are met from current income. Most families find that even sending children to college is not financially binding."[8]

Because survey data on the very rich is lacking, *Fortune* limited its survey to "the simple rich," the families earning between $25,000 and $75,000 per year, slightly more than one percent of the population. Yet as a group the simple rich earned $56 billion in 1968, more than what 30% of the entire population earned. With such phenomenal buying power, they are three times as likely to own a color television or hi-fi as those Americans earning below $15,000, five times as likely to serve Scotch, seven times as likely to drink imported wine regularly, and eight times as likely to own a dishwasher.

Even so, such spending habits should not perforce be considered opulent: *Fortune* warns:

> The upper-income American uses his extraordinary income for ordinary purposes. His desire is comfort, his goal security, his diversions passive and innocent. He buys the same things that anyone else buys but he buys more of them and usually chooses models with the most buttons and gadgets. He is neither adventurous in his spending nor a taste maker. The country club satisfies his modest social ambitions.[9]

[6] Ferdinand Lundberg, *The Rich and the Super-Rich* (New York, 1968), p. 11.
[7] U.S. Treasury, I.R.S., *Statistics of Income* 1962, Supp. Report, *Personal Wealth* (Washington, D.C., 1967) pp. 1–3.
[8] Jeremy Main, "Good Living Begins at $25,000 a Year," *Fortune,* May 1968.
[9] Ibid.

But *Fortune*'s caveat should not be taken strictly at face value. By more conventional standards this infinitesimal group consumes at a rate unknown to most Americans. Automobiles are still a good register of major consumption. As expected, a large minority own Cadillacs and other luxury cars, and those who do not usually own a Pontiac, Buick, or other expensive car, compensating for their modesty with numerous accessories. Housing is also a status signal. While the home itself might or might not be estate sized, it is generally located in the best neighborhoods, with the best schools, the best shopping centers, the best landscape, within easy reach of the best country clubs for exercising those "modest social ambitions."

Home furnishings were, *Fortune* discovered, a common expense. Frequent remodeling was apparently a favorite habit of wealthy housewives, and homes were often equipped with several TVs, central vacuum cleaning, and gold plated faucets. One man reported that he had recently purchased a snow blower for use in the winter months. "I used it twice and now it hasn't snowed since. I always buy the luxury model. I like the little extras. Even just a fancier knob on an item could make the difference . . ." A contractor defined luxury as a TV set and car for every member of the family. Second homes—mountain or seashore retreats, often costing more than the average American home—are also becoming popular items in the budgets of the wealthy.

A major departure from earlier patterns of well-to-do living since World War II has been the marked decline in "help"—butler, maids, and chauffeurs. *Fortune* found only one in five homes with regular help. (The specific sample for this conclusion included only fifty-three homes, so the proportion may be understated.) Many expressed a common complaint to the *Fortune* interviewer that "good help just isn't available any more," but Gabriel Kolko remarked of this attitude, "It is clear that the 2.5 million butlers, maids, chauffeurs, and cooks employed in private households are paid by someone."[10]

A favorite pastime of the rich is travel. Even in *Fortune*'s generous terms, it was "the one real extravagance" of the upper-income Americans. Many people who lived "modestly" at home apparently thought nothing of spending freely abroad. As one Boston businessman put it, "When I travel, I travel deluxe." Both business and pleasure will take the very affluent to exotic places like the Caribbean, Africa, and Asia, and most take at least two, and more often, three or four vacations a year. "A winter vacation in Miami or the Caribbean has become normal," *Fortune* announced, "a cultural expedition to Europe with the children is common, and quick trips to Mexico and Canada and around the U.S. itself are routine."

An equally popular pastime is drinking. The preference for imported wines and the use of hard liquor, both for diversion and escape, was made apparent by a recent survey of executives and their drinking habits. Those who had four or more drinks a day had a median income of $27,500 a year, while

[10] Gabriel Kolko, *Wealth and Power in America* (New York, 1962), p. 125.

one-drink-a-day men averaged a mere $18,500. An ad in an issue of the *New Yorker* stressed the benefits of buying 12-year-old Scotch by the case—at a "reasonable $150 per case."

Naturally enough, as this tiny minority of Americans becomes secure in its annual income, savings increase. According to the Federal Reserve Board, half the families with incomes of $25,000 or more saved at least $5,000 in 1963—more than the average income of two-fifths of the population that year. The mean wealth of people with 1962 incomes between $15,000 and $25,000 was $63,000, and that of the $25,000 to $50,000 group, $291,000.

As this wealth increases the composition of the family's estate changes with it. Savings accounts, real estate, and U.S. savings bonds dominate most small estates, but as incomes grow, a larger portion is invested in common stock. Asked what they would do with an additional $2,500 in income, most said they would invest in more stock. ("Only one person considered giving it away; charities do not seem to be uppermost in the minds of the affluent," said *Fortune.*)

3

Yet even with large incomes, savings, and rates of consumption, the men and women who earn $25,000–$75,000 often have more in common with those who earn less than with the super rich who earn more. After all, the super rich by all terms are an elite. Fewer than a fraction of 1% of American households report incomes of greater than $100,000; yet in many ways they dominate American life. It would be hard to find the top executive of any major company in the country who earns less than this; most earn more. The president of the United States earns twice this amount and eight of his cabinet members are millionaires in their own right. Although the official salary of congressmen is half this amount, many earn much more. A Washington columnist has found that 46 of 100 U.S. senators are millionaires. Virtually without exception, a $100,000-a-year income has become a synonym for the pinnacle of success in America today.

Not surprisingly, as one enters the highest reaches of affluence occupational diversity tends to narrow. The opportunities for making really big money in American society are limited to business. The arts provide a few well-heeled exceptions, and philanthropy contains a very few well-paid executive positions in the largest foundations; but almost without exception a man who wishes to die wealthy must first become a businessman.

For those who choose business, and who succeed, the rewards are magnificent. In a survey of the heads of America's 500 largest corporations, well over 80% reported incomes of between $100,000 and $400,000 annually, with another 10% admitting incomes even higher.[11] Although few ever achieve

[11] Data on Executives from Robert Diamond, "A Self-Portrait of the Chief Executive," *Fortune,* May 1970.

the astronomical heights of a Rockefeller or DuPont, such salaries do at least guarantee a comfortable retirement.

As for Tocqueville's belief that the tastes of the rich differ inconsequentially from those of the middle class, the question becomes one of degree. At some point the continual addition of quantity produces a subtle change in quality; the steady accrual of wealth and power has a powerful psychological impact on a man's loyalties and tastes, and from a casual perusal of the habits of the very wealthy, it is doubtful that they are middle-class habits.

For example, virtually all own their own homes, and 60% claimed vacation "getaway" homes as well. Half of the executives in the survey said they collected original works of art as a hobby. Far and away their most popular form of relaxation was golf, followed by fishing, boating, hunting, tennis, and swimming. Few prefer TV for relaxation, and even fewer prefer movies or plays. A significant number listed such un-middle-class tastes as rare-book collections, flying, horse-racing and owning, and sports-car driving.

As for friendships and acquaintances, the super rich show a distinctively self-conscious segregation from the rest of society. Three-fifths said they preferred to fraternize with other executives. Only 12% preferred the company of doctors, lawyers, or other professionals, and only 6% had academics as social companions. While such patterns are understandable in terms of the work required and the natural desire of men to associate with peers, it also suggests how cut off this potent group is from anything that might be called the mainstream of American life.

But background has carefully prepared business leaders for just this kind of seclusion. Little more than 20% of the major executives interviewed started out as stock boys, junior clerks, or hourly shift workers, and to balance those nearly the same proportion started at the top of their companies—as president, chairman, or founder, a pattern reflecting the family environments in which they were reared. Only 16% were the sons of blue-collar workers or farmers, despite the fact that most were born at a time when these two categories accounted for the majority of jobs. The rest grew up in comfortable upper-middle-class and upper-class homes, where the father himself was usually a businessman. Forty-five percent of the fathers, in fact, were at the very top of the business world either as founder, chairman, or president of a company, or as a self-employed businessman.

In preparation for their roles as business leaders, even further exclusivity was practiced. Ninety-four percent of them attended college, and a full 44% held graduate degrees, an outstanding record considering that only about 10% of their generation ever attended college. And of the college graduates, many attended the very best: 35% attended Ivy League schools, another 45% some other private college.

In matters of religion, the leaders of the business world show this same exclusivity: 80% were Protestant, and less than 10% each were Catholics or Jews. And among Protestant denominations, the "upper-class churches"—Episcopal and Presbyterian—tended to dominate, although these two denominations together contained only seven million members nationwide. (In banking and insurance, 93% were reported to be Protestants.)

The sum total of all this segregation, both in upbringing and in contemporary association, is a negation of Tocqueville's hope that the American rich would retain their middle-class habits. The rich, the very rich, *are* very different from you and me. Equipped with money, power, and prestige, they move freely throughout the world, living life as 99% of the world could never imagine. They are successful, and self-consciously so. Their clubs are exclusive, and so are their vacation spots. If the Versailles and Schoenbruns are no longer being built, it does not mean that smaller, but still lavish estates are not. James Ling, head of the Ling-Temco-Vought conglomerate, built himself a million-dollar home to celebrate his success, and for his efforts was considered something of a *parvenu*. Texas money, it seems, still carries the mark of the newcomer in high society.

For the very rich, money is no longer the basis of life but the means of amusement. One advertisement in an exclusive magazine recently recommended a $33,000, 13-carat champagne-colored diamond ring as an "end-of-a-vacation present." A circular put out by a travel company catering to the very wealthy began: "For 200 million Americans Thursday will dawn dull and drab—another ho-hum, humdrum day. But for 84 people—and you can be one of them—Thursday will mark the beginning of the greatest travel adventure of their lives." The brochure was for an $8,000 round-the-world tour. The *New Yorker* regularly carries advertisements offering such diversions as a crystal trout with 18-carat gold fly, complete with ruby eyes, "for only $700." Another magazine might offer such necessities as a golf putter with a solid gold head, or perhaps the classic of "conspicuous consumption," a gold-plated swizzle stick, battery-powered.

Insights into the lives of men and women who can afford such luxury are rare, but when they do appear they strikingly illustrate how different the rich are in all respects from the two hundred million "others" living in America. One woman, who chose to remain anonymous, described the "difficulties" of upper-class life:

> Two years ago we went to Europe and zipped about for five weeks. Last year we were in Europe for eight weeks. We went to Istanbul and came back on a ship through the Greek islands. And I bought a fur coat in Germany. And a topaz pin in London. We mostly buy jewelry and paintings. And my husband has started collecting rare books. I adore to get new things. I'm mad about it. I've always felt this way. Probably because I'm basically a rotten capitalist. I like life to be as comfortable and beautiful as it can be. Because it makes me sweeter and everyone else around. Usually we just buy things because they strike us as something we'd like to have. If it's beautiful and within our means we'd buy it. . . . I consider traveling first-class on ocean liners and staying at the best hotels in Europe a luxury of which I never tire. . . . When we are in New York, which we often are, we hire a chauffeured limousine. . . . The things I look forward to are trying to stay conscious and feeling alive and trying to guide my children to being conscious and feeling alive. So few people are conscious. It's hard.[12]

[12] "Good Living."

But if this woman's crises and life-style seem fantastic, it is probable that the crises and life-styles of the very richest in America are as equally unknown to this woman herself. For at the very top of the income pyramid sits a tiny handful of individuals and families whose uniqueness it is impossible to understate. Names like Rockefeller and DuPont and Ford immediately come to mind, but for the most part, the men and women of the very top remain anonymous to most Americans.

In 1968, slightly more than 1,000 families reported an annual income of $1 million or more, and another 3,000 reported earning between $500,000 and $1 million. The fact is that these people probably earned a good deal more. Even so, these 4,000 families together claimed a total income of nearly $4 *billion* dollars.

Income of that magnitude is difficult to conceive, even in an age of multi-billion-dollar government and a trillion-dollar economy. In 1968, $4 billion was more than government expenditures for feeding the poor, and two times more than the government spends on anti-poverty programs. In that year $4 billion exceeded all the money given away by foundations. In that year $4 billion was more than what the federal government spent on education, and four times more than the federal government spent on all natural resources. In 1968, $4 billion would have provided a poverty-level income for over one million families. Instead it was shared by 4,000.

Ferdinand Lundberg, discussing the problem of comprehending such sums of money, put it this way: "If a prudent, hardworking, God-fearing, home-loving 100 percent American saved $100,000 a year after taxes and expenses it would take him a full century to accumulate [$10 million.] A self-incorporated film star who earned $1 million a year and paid a ten percent agent's fee, a rounded 50 percent corporation tax on the net and then withdrew $100,000 for his own use (on which he also paid about 50 percent tax) would need to be a box-office rage for thirty-four unbroken years before he could save $10 million."[13] Yet it is clear that several thousand Americans are worth much more.

Perhaps the most spectacular cases of such supreme wealth are the multimillionaires. In early 1968 *Fortune* published its list of "America's Centimillionaires," those precious few Americans worth $100 million or more. *Fortune* was able to locate 166 such individuals, and admitted to missing quite a few more. Among this infinitesimal set, several, it turned out, had made their fortunes only in the postwar years.[14]

This fact must be comforting to the ideologist of American enterprise, because it indicates to what an extent "new wealth" is still being created, and, by implication, how much is still available to those who earnestly seek it. Such a fact seems to affirm the strength of American capitalism, and the benificence it is able to bestow.

[13] Lundberg, pp. 35–36.
[14] Arthur Lewis "America's Centimillionaires," *Fortune*, May 1968.

But in the case of the centimillionaire, "new money" is the exception, not the rule. If one looks at the list closely, it becomes obvious that in fact most of the very wealthiest are the sons and daughters, and often the grandsons and granddaughters of the very rich. Of the 66 individuals *Fortune* concluded were worth more than $150 million, over half came from clearly recognizable "old money" families, that is, families socially prominent for over two generations. (Indeed, a quarter were either a Rockefeller, a DuPont, a Mellon, or a Ford.) And of the remainder, a majority came from families which had left them a great deal of wealth. Rather than confirming the fluidity of the American social structure, and the opportunities available to any industrious individual, such facts suggest that America has created a stable moneyed aristocracy, admitting few newcomers but capable of surviving the upturns and downturns of all political and economic climates.

Close scrutiny deals a sharp blow as well to the idea that the "new money" demonstrates the viability of free enterprise. Many of the few new super-fortunes have been made at the expense of the government, or in industries protected by government. No less than a dozen of the new centimillionaires made their millions in the oil industry (protected for so long by the oil depletion allowances and import quota system), or in defense hardware of one kind or another. It is hard to imagine what their success would have been in truly competitive markets, unsubsidized and unprotected by the benevolent hand of government.

The Dirty Work Movement

HERBERT J. GANS

This satire poses an interesting question: Should manual work receive less pay than mental work? Why does some work receive better pay than other work? Do some jobs require more skill and intelligence and therefore deserve greater rewards? Or do the people with the better jobs have more power and therefore reward themselves accordingly?

It was a small banquet as White House banquets go, but what mattered was that the President chose to memorialize the occasion and to honor the handful of old men able to attend. The men were the surviving members of the

From *Social Policy*, March/April 1971, Vol. 1, No. 6. Published by Social Policy Corporation, New York, New York 10010.

DWW, the Dirty Workers of the World; the occasion, the 20th anniversary of the now almost forgotten Dirty Work Movement. The evening was highlighted by the issuance of a new commemorative stamp showing the late Joe Green, the founder of the DWW, as he looked those days, lavatory mop held firmly in the revolutionary posture.

The DWW's Revolution

Mr. Green, older readers may remember, was a lavatory attendant at the University of California in Berkeley in the early 1970s; and one day, while cleaning the professorial facilities, he chanced on a newspaper headline about the Dirty Word Movement, which had flourished briefly in Berkeley in the mid-1960s. Not the best of spellers, he thought the headline referred to work and mentioned it to his colleagues later that evening. A few days later, the entire Berkeley toilet staff walked off the job, saying they were fed up with doing dirty work.

The men came back when the University raised their wages and renamed them personal service engineers; but in a couple of weeks, they realized that they were still just cleaning johns, and walked off the job again. Soon lavatory attendants all over the country went on strike; and, finally, the President declared a National Pollution Emergency. He also called for volunteers to solve the problem, as was his fashion, and appeared on television mopping the floor of a White House staff toilet.

By then, however, other workers had begun to leave their jobs. The first to go were hospital orderlies and stockyard slaughterers, but the crisis really deepened when the domestics struck. Washington and Manhattan party-givers had to cancel their parties, after which politics, show business, publishing, and the arts ground to a complete halt. In succeeding weeks there were walkouts by dishwashers and garbage collectors; and when assembly-line workers also quit, the economy just stopped altogether.

In the meantime, Joe Green had organized the Dirty Workers of the World; and after some bitter jurisdictional hassles with existing unions, most of the striking workers were amalgamated into the DWW. And not much later, Joe Green came to the White House to negotiate.

Actually, there was nothing to negotiate; for with the economy at a standstill, the DWW held the trump card. Joe Green made only one demand: the dirtier the work, the more it ought to be paid. The President gave in, his staff quickly prepared the appropriate legislation, and Congress set aside all other business. Since their own salaries would be affected, most Congressmen opposed the bill, and were supported by other salaried groups, including corporation executives, teachers unions, and Washington lobbyists; but pressure from stockholders and property-owners who wanted the economy to start producing again forced them to pass the bill anyway.

A New Social Hierarchy

During the next year, life in America underwent drastic change. Toilet cleaners became a new economic elite, earning $20 per hour, with three months of paid vacation and a sabbatical every third year. Conversely, movie stars were working for $5 an hour and professors for $3; and Congressional salaries were reduced to $7,500 a year. This, in turn, produced many side effects. Dirty workers now mingled with coupon-clippers in cafe society, while celebrities and politicians had to stay home watching TV. Society pages were filled with accounts of the lavish weekend parties given in the Bahamas by longshoremen, and Joe Green's son married a Philadelphia blue blood.

Naturally, everyone now wanted to go into dirty work; and equally naturally, the DWW closed its membership rolls and renamed itself the Dirty Professionals of the World. The DPW then wrote itself a code of ethics, set up a licensing system, founded a journal to record advances in the dirty professions, and established educational prerequisites for these professions. Universities were quick to develop the appropriate new teaching specialties and research institutes, and the government was quick to provide the grants. The National Institutes of Health awarded Harvard $500,000 to study cross-cultural differences in bedpan cleaning, and MIT received $1 million for advanced work in slaughtering technology.

In the meantime, employers, their costs spiraling, set out to automate dirty work; but one after another, they learned that it could not always be replaced by technology. A machine was invented to eliminate the coal miner, but none could replace the man who pushed garment trucks on crowded streets and pavements; and the Mayor of New York had to resign when his completely automatic garbage-removal system dropped too many empty cans on the parked cars of too many voters.

Toward a More Equal Distribution of Dirt

By now, clean workers were becoming a new underclass; and hippies changed into white shirts to express their sympathies for them. Newspaper editorials celebrated the courageous individualism of the few young people who still sought to prepare themselves for clean jobs; Hollywood made movies about how unhappy the newly rich dirty workers really were; and the best-selling novel of the year was *The Doll Laundry*, the story of three wealthy washerwomen who became drug addicts and finally committed suicide.

These stories helped the clean workers retain their pride in being clean; but as their savings disappeared and their standard of living declined, so did their pride; and before long they began to demand change. The initial onslaught came from those in various occupations who argued that their work was actually dirty and required higher pay. The Army claimed successfully that its blood-letting activities were extremely dirty, and thereafter the surgeons put in a bid for higher salaries. Newspapermen funded studies of the incidence of graphite stains on their hands, and executive secretaries pointed out that they often spilled coffee or whisky on themselves while ministering to the needs of their bosses. Finally, the executives themselves sued for a salary increase, arguing that their work was tension-producing and thus psychologically dirty. Although their case was bitterly contested in Washington, the Supreme Court ruled, in a landmark decision, that emotional factors also had to be taken into account in defining dirtiness. Soon thereafter, the surgeons filed suit for another salary increase on the same grounds, so that, in the end, theirs was again the highest paid occupation in the country. And when the clerk-typists went out on strike, claiming that their work, though clean, was boring, the economy was once more at a standstill.

History repeated itself as the head of the newly organized Clean Workers of America went to the White House to meet with the President. After she pointed out that her union, though barely three weeks old, already had five times as many members as the DWW, the President agreed to her demands, proposing a $10 per hour minimum wage for clean work, and $20 for boring work. Congress passed his bill by acclamation, and thereafter the position of the dirty workers began to decline. The DWW fought hard to salvage at least some benefits, but the Republicans won the next election with a Keep America Clean campaign, and soon afterward Joe Green died of a broken heart.

The President Was Dirty Too

Consequently, Washington analysts could not understand why the President had now decided to honor a politically discredited group. True, at the banquet he revealed that he had belonged to the DWW as a young Congressman, supplementing his lowly income by working in the mines on weekends. The President was not given to idle sentimentality, however; and White House correspondents, noting his frequent complaint that the Presidency was a dirty job, were speculating that he might be reviving interest in the DWW to justify a pay increase for himself.

Uncle Sam's Welfare Program—for the Rich

PHILIP J. STERN

Mr. Stern, one of the Sears, Roebuck heirs, analyzes a welfare program that he has personally had dealings with: the tax structure. Some of the astounding tax loopholes he mentions here only benefit the super rich. This article is from* The Rape of the Taxpayer, *a highly provocative book.

Most Americans would probably be greatly surprised to find, in their morning newspaper, a story such as this:

Washington, D.C.—Congress completed action today on a revolutionary welfare program that reverses traditional payment policies and awards huge welfare payments to the super-rich while granting only pennies per week to the very poor.

Under the program, welfare payments averaging some $720,000 a year will go to the nation's wealthiest families—those with annual incomes of over a million dollars.

For the poorest families, those earning $3,000 a year or less, the welfare allowance will average $16 a year, or roughly 30 cents a week.

The program, enacted by Congress in a series of laws over a period of years, has come to be called the Rich Welfare Program, after its principal sponsor, Senator Homer A. Rich. In a triumphant news conference, Senator Rich told newsmen that the $720,000 annual welfare allowance would give America's most affluent families an added weekly take-home pay of about $14,000. "Or, to put it another way," the Senator said, "it will provide these families with about $2,000 more spending money every day."

The total cost of the welfare program, the most expensive in the nation's history, amounts to $77.3 billion a year.

Political analysts foresee acute discontent, not only among the poor but also among middle-income families making $10,000 to $15,000 a year. For them, welfare payments under the Rich plan will amount to just $12.50 a week, markedly less than the $14,000 paid each week to the very rich.

Reporters asked Senator Rich whether wealthy families would be required to work in order to receive their welfare payments, a common eligibility requirement with many welfare programs. Senator Rich seemed puzzled by the question. "The rich? Work?" he asked. "Why, it hadn't occurred to me." Congressional experts advised newsmen that the program contains no work requirement.

The above "news story" may sound implausible, if not unbelievable. Yet the story is essentially true. The facts and figures are real. Such a system is part of the law of the land. Only the law isn't called a welfare law: it goes by the name of "The Internal Revenue Code of 1954, as Amended"—the basic income tax law of the United States.

Who gets how much of the tax "welfare" payments from the major "tax preferences"—i.e., "the loopholes"? Until recently, one could make, at best, only an educated guess. But now, with the aid of modern computers, making superhuman calculations based on *actual* tax-return information plus other data from economic surveys, the secret is out, and the answers might astound, or even anger, put-upon taxpayers.

On a per-family basis, a breakdown of the average tax savings of Americans—our "tax welfare" program—looks like this:*

If you make:	*Your average yearly "tax welfare" payment is:*	*Your average increase in weekly "take-home pay" is:*
Over $1,000,000	$720,490	$13,855.58
$500,000–$1,000,000	$202,751	$3,899.06
$100,000–$500,000	$41,480	$797.69
$50,000–$100,000	$11,912	$229.08
$25,000–$50,000	$3,897	$74.94
$20,000–$25,000	$1,931	$37.13
$15,000–$20,000	$1,181	$22.71
$10,000–$15,000	$651	$12.52
$5,000–$10,000	$339	$6.52
$3,000–$5,000	$148	$2.85
Under $3,000	$16	31 cents

Since a tax law takes money *from* people, rather than paying money *to* them, what connection does the tax law have with the topsy-turvy welfare system in the news story? The connection lies in the way Congress has played fast and loose with the Sixteenth Amendment to the Constitution, and with the principle of basing taxes on "ability to pay."

The Sixteenth Amendment, which authorized the first United States income tax, empowered Congress to tax "incomes, *from whatever source derived*. . . ." (Emphasis added.) This expresses the notion that a dollar is a dollar and that, regardless of its source, each dollar endows its lucky recipient with 100 cents of "ability to pay" for food, shoes for the baby, a fraction of a yacht—or taxes. Hence, fairness dictates that all dollars, no matter what their origin, should be taxed uniformly.

But Congress has decreed differently. It has decreed that dollars made in an oil or real-estate venture, in a stock market bonanza, or in interest on a state or local bond, while undeniably capable of buying food, shoes or yachts, are somehow reduced in paying power when it comes to paying taxes—for

* The source for these figures and other facts thoughout this book may be found in the Notes and Sources section, pp. 441–472.

Congress has exempted such dollars, in whole or in part, from taxation. It has done this via an elaborate network of exemptions, deductions, exclusions, exceptions and special rates that have come to be called "loopholes." And every time Congress enacted one of these preferences, it excused someone from paying what could and would have been collected if Congress had stuck to the Sixteenth Amendment and had taxed "incomes, from whatever source derived."

To give a concrete example, Jean Paul Getty is one of the richest men in the world: he is said to be worth between a billion and a billion and a half dollars, and to have a *daily* income of $300,000. If Congress were to apply to Mr. Jean Paul Getty the standard of the Sixteenth Amendment, and were to tax his entire "income, from whatever source derived" at the current tax rates,* Mr. Getty would, each April 15, write a check to the Internal Revenue Service for roughly $70 million. But Jean Paul Getty is an oilman; and, as is well known, oilmen enjoy a variety of special tax escape routes (see Chapter 11). As a result, according to what President Kennedy told two United States Senators, *Mr. Jean Paul Getty's tax, at least in the early Sixties, amounted to no more than a few thousand dollars.* Annual tax saving to Mr. Getty (at 1973 rates): $70 million.

Now, compare the consequences of that $70 million "tax forgiveness" that Congress bestowed on Mr. Getty with the effect if Congress had, instead, voted him a $70 million welfare payment paid to him by check directly from the U.S. Treasury.

Consequences of a $70 Million Direct Welfare Payment to Mr. Getty	*Consequences of a $70 Million "Tax Forgiveness" to Mr. Getty*
1. Mr. Getty is $70 million richer.	1. Mr. Getty is $70 million richer.*
2. The U.S. Treasury is $70 million poorer.	2. The U.S. Treasury is $70 million poorer.†
3. The rest of the U.S. taxpayers have to pay $70 million more taxes to make up the difference.	3. The rest of the U.S. taxpayers have to pay $70 million more taxes to make up the difference.

* Than if he had paid the full tax called for under the Sixteenth Amendment.
† Than it would have been had Mr. Getty paid the full tax.

The fact is there is no real difference, as far as the U.S. Treasury (i.e., you and all the other taxpayers) is concerned, and thus, even though no "tax welfare" checks actually pass hands, all the special gimmicks and escape hatches that Congress has been writing into the tax laws, about which you will read in this book, are *the equivalent* of direct welfare payments to the lucky recipients of the tax favors.

* These tax rates, of course, rise as a person's affluence grows, on the understandable theory that a person of Mr. Getty's wealth and income is considerably better "able to pay" taxes than, say, an impoverished Kentucky coal miner.

Reduced to its simplest terms, you (and all the rest of the American taxpayers like you) are having to make up for the taxes that Jean Paul Getty and other "loophole" users do not pay. You may make it up in higher taxes or in large Federal deficits. Or you might pay for it in the form of trimmed-down government spending for day-care centers or antipollution, mass transit or housing assistance programs that could be of direct benefit to you—but for which Congress or the President concludes that "the money isn't available." Of course, if the loopholes didn't exist, and the dollars that now leak out through them were collected, the money *would* be "available." One way or another, the cost of the loopholes falls upon those to whom tax escape routes are less available.

In fact, the main point of this book could well be reduced to one simple sentence that might usefully be embroidered on a sampler and hung on each taxpayer's wall:

WHEN SOMEONE ELSE PAYS LESS
THE REST OF US PAY MORE

Some additional insights into the fairness with which the "tax welfare" payments are distributed among the American people may be drawn from the following figures:

This income group . . .	*has this many families*. . .*	*and gets this amount of "tax welfare" payments*
Under $3,000	6,000,000	$92,000,000
Over $1,000,000	3,000	$2,200,000,000

* See Notes and Sources.

That last line deserves to be put more starkly: more than two *billion* dollars of "tax welfare" is distributed among just three thousand families—the three thousand richest American families. (By happenstance, that two billion is precisely the amount that Congress voted in 1971 to provide food stamps for millions of hungry families throughout the United States.)

For still another appraisal of the tax system's fairness, you might want to identify where you fit into the following picture:

This income group . . .	*comprises this percent of the population . . .*	*but gets this percent of the "tax welfare" payments*
Under $10,000	45.7%	10.0%
Under $15,000	70.6%	24.7%
Over $100,000	0.3%	14.7%

That last statistic comes more to life when you realize that the 14.7 percent that is distributed among the richest three families in every *thousand* comes to a tidy (if that's the proper word) $11,400,000,000 per year. That's $11.4 *billion,* which amounts to:

- thirty-four times what the Federal government is spending on center research and seven times proposed U.S. outlays for medical research of all kinds;
- sixty-four times the budget proposals for assuring the purity and safety of all foods and drugs:
- forty-eight times what the United States is spending for all hospital construction;
- sixteen times Federal spending for the training of doctors and nurses;
- ten times U.S. outlays for the school lunch program;
- five times total outlays for crime reduction;
- seven times the budget of the Federal Environment Protection Agency.

Another way of looking at all this is that $77 billion* worth of wool is being pulled over your eyes. Here's why:

On page 24 of the instructions that come with your income-tax form is a table of tax rates—starting at 14 percent and rising to 70 percent, for the highest-income people—that might lead you to believe, when you sweat over your tax return every spring, that your fellow citizens are called upon to pay taxes in accordance with their "ability to pay." That is, if those tax rates mean what they seem to say, you might find some comfort in the thought that, painful as your own tax might be, rich people are paying a far greater proportion of their incomes to Uncle Sam than you are. After all, it says so, right in the tax-rate table: if a married person's unearned taxable income is more than $200,000, he pays $110,900 plus 70 percent† of everything over $200,000. From the tax-rate table, then, you'd think that people in Jean Paul Getty's income bracket pay well over 60 percent of their colossal incomes to Internal Revenue.

But much of the comfort you may derive from that tax-rate table is unwarranted, for Congress has, in effect, made a sham of it. Here's a comparison of what the rate tables *theoretically* call on people to pay (as a percentage of their incomes) and what in fact they *do* pay, after they've taken advantage of all the special loopholes that Congress has written into the tax law:

* The total of the "tax welfare" payments to individuals.

† Throughout this book, there will be references to people whose top bracket is higher than 50 percent (i.e., between 50 and 70 percent). This is not inconsistent with the 50 percent top-bracket rate, enacted in 1969, which applies solely to *earned* (i.e., salary) income but does *not* apply to so-called *un*earned income (from dividends, interest, stock market profits and the like). So wherever you see references to wealthy people in, say, the 60 or 70 percent bracket, you may assume that they have large amounts of unearned income. (As you will see on p. 27, the stratospherically rich are likely to have huge *un*earned incomes, but minuscule or nonexistent *earned* incomes.)

For a family with this much income . . .*	*this is the percent of their income* that . . .*		
	the tax law seems to call on them to pay in taxes	*they actually do pay in taxes after using the loopholes*	*the loop-holes save them*
$2,000–$3,000	1.9%	0.5%	1.4%
$5,000–$6,000	7.5%	2.8%	4.7%
$10,000–$11,000	12.4%	7.6%	4.8%
$20,000–$25,000	20.8%	12.1%	8.7%
$75,000–$100,000	46.0%	26.8%	19.2%
$200,000–$500,000	58.0%	29.6%	28.4%
$500,000–$1 million	60.5%	30.4%	30.1%
Over $1 million	63.1%	32.1%	31.0%

* These figures are taken from a Brookings Institution computer study, conducted by Joseph A. Pechman and Benjamin A. Okner, which is based on *total* family income.

For those gazing in consternation (or rage) at that third column, it requires no special expertise to realize not only that the loopholes save families a greater *percentage* of their income as they grow richer, but that at the top of the pyramid *this is a greater percentage of an astronomically larger income* than is true at the bottom of the heap. Hence, the dollar savings escalate dramatically. Even though you've seen some of the figures before, they bear repeating in this slightly different form:

If you make:	*Your average yearly family income is:*	*The loopholes save you this much in taxes yearly:*
Under $3,000	$1,345	$16
$3,000–$5,000	$4,016	$148
$5,000–$10,000	$7,484	$339
$10,000–$15,000	$12,342	$651
$15,000–$20,000	$17,202	$1,181
$20,000–$25,000	$22,188	$1,931
$25,000–$50,000	$32,015	$3,897
$50,000–$100,000	$65,687	$11,912
$100,000–$500,000	$165,098	$41,840
$500,000–$1,000,000	$673,040	$202,751
Over $1,000,000	$2,316,872	$720,490

Still another way of judging the fairness of the present income tax laws, *including* all the loopholes, is by the amount of "keeping money" various families have left over, after Internal Revenue has taken its toll:

For families in this income range:	*The average yearly "keeping money" comes to:*	*The average weekly "take-home pay" comes to:*
Under $3,000	$1,339	$25.75
$3,000–$5,000	$3,947	$75.90
$5,000–$10,000	$7,180	$138.08
$10,000–$15,000	$11,274	$216.81
$15,000–$20,000	$15,375	$295.67
$20,000–$25,000	$19,528	$375.54
$25,000–$50,000	$27,413	$527.17
$50,000–$100,000	$50,334	$967.96
$100,000–$500,000	$117,072	$2,251.38
$500,000–$1,000,000	$468,624	$9,012.00
$1,000,000 and over	$1,574,070*	$30,270.58

* This high average is explained by the fact that the "million and over" income group includes people with incomes of $2 million, $3 million, $5 million, etc.

If you are in either of the lowest two income groups mentioned above—that is, if you are trying to make ends meet on less than $75.92 a week—you might wonder whether *any* family in the United States really needs $1,574,070 a year (or over $30,000 of "take-home pay" each *week*). You might conclude that the present loophole-ridden income tax laws are excessively generous to the super-rich.* And if you feel overburdened by taxes (as who doesn't?), you may be less than overjoyed to learn that for the richest one percent of Americans, their *actual* income tax burden has become markedly lighter in recent years.†

Of all the various loopholes, none contributes so flagrantly or so dramatically to the upside-down "tax welfare" system as the preferential treatment accorded so-called "capital gains"—the profits from the sale of stocks and bonds, buildings, land and other kinds of property—which are taxed at no more than half the rates that apply to other kinds of income. . . . Federal largesse upon the well-to-do while it almost totally excludes the "average" taxpayer. Bear in mind, as you examine the following table, that only one taxpayer in ten receives *any* capital gains and the tax benefactions that flow therefrom; nine out of ten Americans have not gained admission to this exclusive club:

* You might also be interested to know that even if there were no loopholes in the tax law, and those over-$1-million-income families had to pay the full 63.1 percent of their incomes that the tax law *seems* to call for, they would still, on the average, have $853,580 of yearly "keeping money." This would give them $16,415 of weekly "take-home pay." This, in turn, might lead to the question of whether the existing top-bracket tax rate of 70 percent, severe as it may at first seem, fully satisfies the concept of "ability to pay." After all, the matter of after-tax "keeping money" is as relevant to "ability to pay" as the before-tax total income.

† Declining from 33 to just 26 percent of their total incomes between 1952 and 1967.

If you make:	*Your yearly "tax welfare" from capital gains is:*
Over $1,000,000	$640,667
$500,000–$1,000,000	$165,000
$100,000–$500,000	$22,630
$50,000–$100,000	$3,795
$25,000–$50,000	$534
$20,000–$25,000	$120
$15,000–$20,000	$55
$10,000–$15,000	$24
$5,000–$10,000	$9
$3,000–$5,000	$1
Under $3,000	—

So far, we've been talking about the tax savings that go to the *average* family in each of the various income groups. But, striking as the averages are, they nonetheless conceal the absolutely extraordinary tax-avoiding achievements of particular families and individuals who managed to fare enormously better than the average. For example, under the tax laws that prevailed throughout the Sixties:

- A rapidly growing number of rich and super-rich families managed to avoid sharing so much as a penny of their huge incomes with the U.S. government—that is, they paid zero taxes. These are the statistics:

	Number of Families Who Paid No Tax in		
Family Income	*1960*	*1967*	*1969*
Over $1 million	11	23	56
Over $500,000	23	63	117
Over $200,000	70	167	301
Over $100,000	104	399	761

- In the late Sixties (before the law applicable to them was changed), four persons* were able to enjoy incomes ranging from $6 million to as high as nearly $11 million in a single year without paying a penny of tax (by diverting what would have been their tax payments to the charities of their choice).
- Still another taxpayer was able to enjoy a total income of about $1,284,718 and escape with paying a tax of just $274—about the amount of taxes payable by a single individual with an income of just $2,400.

* Those four "persons," plus the other taxpayers cited in the next three examples, are *actual* persons cited in a Treasury Department study made public in 1969. Under the law, the Treasury could not publish the names of the taxpayers (or non-taxpayers) involved. The feats described in that study took place before the enactment of the Tax Reform Act of 1969, which made certain types of the avoidance more difficult, but, as you will see, far from impossible.

- An oil investor was able to shield his entire income of $1,313,811 from the tax collector. Many of his confreres in the oil-investing fraternity managed to avoid paying taxes year in and year out. One such worthy paid no income tax from 1949 to 1962! Another left standing instructions with his tax attorney that should any potentially taxable income appear on his financial horizon, raising the specter that he might have to pay some income tax, the tax attorney should proceed forthwith to "drill it up" (i.e., invest in enough oil-drilling ventures to create tax deductions that would cancel out the offensively taxable income). Some have been reported to have enlisted the aid of computers to calculate precisely the amount of tax-deductible drilling required to achieve total tax avoidance with a minimum of "wasted" deductions.
- A real-estate investor paid no tax whatever on an income of $1,433,000.
- Trucking magnate Robert Short managed, with a cash outlay of just $1,000, to purchase the Washington Senators baseball team, and then to exploit the tax laws so as to derive, therefrom, tax advantages totaling $4 million—all on a cash outlay of just $1,000. . . .
- One centenarian lady, Mrs. Horace Dodge (of Dodge auto fame and fortune), was able, before her death in 1970 at age one hundred and three, to amass holdings of state and local bonds amounting to $100 million—which put her in the happy position of being able to receive the grand total of $5 million of income each year, *without even having to file an income tax return!* . . .

But all of these tax avoiders, startling as their feats may seem, were rank amateurs compared with one hyper-rich oilman, cited in a 1960 Treasury Department study, who one year had *total income of more than twenty-six million dollars* ($26,440,776, *to be precise*) *and yet paid no tax whatever.*

The Uses of Poverty: The Poor Pay All

HERBERT J. GANS

In this article, Gans argues that poverty serves a variety of "useful" functions in our society. Poor people are not just economically exploited by the rich; they satisfy a whole range of psychic and social needs for all of us. The persistence of poverty is rooted in our dependence on it for our own security and well-being.

From *Social Policy*, July/August 1971, Vol. 2, No. 2. Published by Social Policy Corporation, New York, New York 10010.

Some twenty years ago Robert K. Merton applied the notion of functional analysis* to explain the continuing though maligned existence of the urban political machine: if it continued to exist, perhaps it fulfilled latent—unintended or unrecognized—positive functions. Clearly it did. Merton pointed out how the political machine provided central authority to get things done when a decentralized local government could not act, humanized the services of the impersonal bureaucracy for fearful citizens, offered concrete help (rather than abstract law or justice) to the poor, and otherwise performed services needed or demanded by many people but considered unconventional or even illegal by formal public agencies.

Today, poverty is more maligned than the political machine ever was; yet it too, is a persistent social phenomenon. Consequently, there may be some merit in applying functional analysis to poverty, in asking whether it also has positive functions that explain its persistence.

Merton defined functions as "those observed consequences [of a phenomenon] which make for the adaptation or adjustment of a given [social] system." I shall use a slightly different definition; instead of identifying functions for an entire social system, I shall identify them for the interest groups, socioeconomic classes, and other population aggregates with shared values that "inhabit" a social system. I suspect that in a modern heterogeneous society, few phenomena are functional or dysfunctional for the society as a whole, and that most result in benefits to some groups and costs to others. Nor are any phenomena indispensable; in most instances, one can suggest what Merton calls "functional alternatives" or equivalents for them, i.e., other social patterns or policies that achieve the same positive functions but avoid the dysfunctions.†

Associating poverty with positive functions seems at first glance to be unimaginable. Of course, the slumlord and the loan shark are commonly known to profit from the existence of poverty, but they are viewed as evil men, so their activities are classified among the dysfunctions of poverty. However, what is less often recognized, at least by the conventional wisdom, is that poverty also makes possible the existence or expansion of respectable professions and occupations, for example, penology, criminology, social work, and public health. More recently, the poor have provided jobs for professional and paraprofessional "poverty warriors," and for journalists and social scientists, this author included, who have supplied the information demanded by the revival of public interest in poverty.

Clearly, then, poverty and the poor may well satisfy a number of positive functions for many nonpoor groups in American society. I shall describe thirteen such functions—economic, social, and political—that seem to me most significant.

* "Manifest and Latent Functions," in *Social Theory and Social Structure* (Glencoe, Ill.: The Free Press, 1949), p. 71.

† I shall henceforth abbreviate positive functions and negative functions as dysfunctions. I shall also describe functions and dysfunctions, in the planners terminology, as

Drawing (overleaf) by Jules Feiffer. Used by permission of Publishers-Hall Syndicate.

The Functions of Poverty

First, the existence of poverty ensures that society's "dirty work" will be done. Every society has such work: physically dirty or dangerous, temporary, dead-end and underpaid, undignified and menial jobs. Society can fill these jobs by paying higher wages than for "clean" work, or it can force people who have no other choice to do the dirty work—and at low wages. In America, poverty functions to provide a low-wage labor pool that is willing—or, rather, unable to be *un*willing—to perform dirty work at low cost. Indeed, this function of the poor is so important that in some Southern states, welfare payments have been cut off during the summer months when the poor are needed to work in the fields. Moreover, much of the debate about the Negative Income Tax and the Family Assistance Plan has concerned their impact on the work incentive, by which is actually meant the incentive of the poor to do the needed dirty work if the wages therefrom are no larger than the income grant. Many economic activities that involve dirty work depend on the poor for their existence: restaurants, hospitals, parts of the garment industry, and "truck farming," among others, could not persist in their present form without the poor.

Second, because the poor are required to work at low wages, they subsidize a variety of economic activities that benefit the affluent. For example, domestics subsidize the upper middle and upper classes, making life easier for their employers and freeing affluent women for a variety of professional, cultural, civic, and partying activities. Similarly, because the poor pays a higher proportion of their income in property and sales taxes, among others, they subsidize many state and local governmental services that benefit more affluent groups. In addition, the poor support innovation in medical practice as patients in teaching and research hospitals and as guinea pigs in medical experiments.

Third, poverty creates jobs for a number of occupations and professions that serve or "service" the poor, or protect the rest of society from them. As already noted, penology would be minuscule without the poor, as would the police. Other activities and groups that flourish because of the existence of poverty are the numbers game, the sale of heroin and cheap wines and liquors, pentecostal ministers, faith healers, prostitutes, pawn shops, and the peacetime army, which recruits its enlisted men mainly from among the poor.

Fourth, the poor buy goods others do not want and thus prolong the economic usefulness of such goods—day-old bread, fruit and vegetables that would otherwise have to be thrown out, secondhand clothes, and deteriorating automobiles and buildings. They also provide incomes for doctors, lawyers, teachers, and others who are too old, poorly trained, or incompetent to attract more affluent clients.

In addition to economic functions, the poor perform a number of social functions.

Fifth, the poor can be identified and punished as alleged or real deviants in order to uphold the legitimacy of conventional norms. To justify the desirability of hard work, thrift, honesty, and monogamy, for example, the defenders of these norms must be able to find people who can be accused of being lazy, spendthrift, dishonest, and promiscuous. Although there is some evidence that the poor are about as moral and law-abiding as anyone else, they are more likely than middle-class transgressors to be caught and punished when they participate in deviant acts. Moreover, they lack the political and cultural power to correct the stereotypes that other people hold of them and thus continue to be thought of as lazy, spendthrift, etc., by those who need living proof that moral deviance does not pay.

Sixth, and conversely, the poor offer vicarious participation to the rest of the population in the uninhibited sexual, alcoholic, and narcotic behavior in which they are alleged to participate and which, being freed from the constraints of affluence, they are often thought to enjoy more than the middle classes. Thus many people, some social scientists included, believe that the poor not only are more given to uninhibited behavior (which may be true, although it is often motivated by despair more than by lack of inhibition) but derive more pleasure from it than affluent people (which research by Lee Rainwater, Walter Miller, and others shows to be patently untrue). However, whether the poor actually have more sex and enjoy it more is irrelevant; so long as middle-class people believe this to be true, they can participate in it vicariously when instances are reported in factual or fictional form.

Seventh, the poor also serve a direct cultural function when culture created by or for them is adopted by the more affluent. The rich often collect artifacts from extinct folk cultures of poor people; and almost all Americans listen to the blues, Negro spirituals, and country music, which originated among the Southern poor. Recently they have enjoyed the rock styles that were born, like the Beatles, in the slums; and in the last year, poetry written by ghetto children has become popular in literary circles. The poor also serve as culture heroes, particularly, of course, to the left; but the hobo, the cowboy, the hipster, and the mythical prostitute with a heart of gold have performed this function for a variety of groups.

Eighth, poverty helps to guarantee the status of those who are not poor. In every hierarchical society someone has to be at the bottom; but in American society, in which social mobility is an important goal for many and people need to know where they stand, the poor function as a reliable and relatively permanent measuring rod for status comparisons. This is particularly true for the working class, whose politics is influenced by the need to maintain status distinctions between themselves and the poor, much as the aristocracy must find ways of distinguishing itself from the *nouveaux riches.*

Ninth, the poor also aid the upward mobility of groups just above them in the class hierarchy. Thus a goodly number of Americans have entered the middle class through the profits earned from the provision of goods and services in the slums, including illegal or nonrespectable ones that upper-class and upper-middle-class businessmen shun becauses of their low prestige. As a result, members of almost every immigrant group have financed their upward mobility by providing slum housing, enthertainment, gambling, narcotics, etc., to later arrivals—most recently to Blacks and Puerto Ricans.

Tenth, the poor help to keep the aristocracy busy, thus justifying its continued existence. "Society" uses the poor as clients of settlement houses and beneficiaries of charity affairs; indeed, the aristocracy must have the poor to demonstrate its superiority over other elites who devote themselves to earning money.

Eleventh, the poor, being powerless, can be made to absorb the costs of change and growth in American society. During the nineteenth century, they did the backbreaking work that built the cities; today, they are pushed out of their neighborhoods to make room for "progress." Urban renewal projects to hold middle-class taxpayers in the city and expressways to enable suburbanites to commute downtown have typically been located in poor neighborhoods, since no other group will allow itself to be displaced. For the same reason, universities, hospitals, and civic centers also expand into land occupied by the poor. The major costs of the industrialization of agriculture have been borne by the poor, who are pushed off the land without recompense; and they have paid a large share of the human cost of the growth of American power overseas, for they have provided many of the foot soldiers for Vietnam and other wars.

Twelfth, the poor facilitate and stabilize the American political process. Because they vote and participate in politics less than other groups, the political system is often free to ignore them. Moreover, since they can rarely support Republicans, they often provide the Democrats with a captive constituency that has no other place to go. As a result, the Democrats can count on their votes, and be more responsive to voters—for example, the white working class—who might otherwise switch to the Republicans.

Thirteenth, the role of the poor in upholding conventional norms (see the *fifth* point, above) also has a significant political function. An economy based on the ideology of laissez-faire requires a deprived population that is allegedly unwilling to work or that can be considered inferior because it must accept charity or welfare in order to survive. Not only does the alleged moral deviancy of the poor reduce the moral pressure on the present political economy to eliminate poverty but socialist alternatives can be made to look quite unattractive if those who will benefit most from them can be described as lazy, spendthrift, dishonest, and promiscuous.

The Alternatives

I have described thirteen of the more important functions poverty and the poor satisfy in American society, enough to support the functionalist thesis that poverty, like any other social phenomenon, survives in part because it is useful to society or some of its parts. This analysis is not intended to suggest that because it is often functional, poverty *should* exist, or that it *must* exist. For one thing, poverty has many more dysfunctions; for another, it is possible to suggest functional alternatives.

For example, society's dirty work could be done without poverty, either by automation or by paying "dirty workers" decent wages. Nor is it necessary for the poor to subsidize the many activities they support through their low-wage jobs. This would, however, drive up the costs of these activties, which would result in higher prices to their customers and clients. Similarly, many of the professionals who flourish because of the poor could be given other roles. Social workers could provide counseling to the affluent, as they prefer to do anyway; and the police could devote themselves to traffic and organized crime. Other roles would have to be found for badly trained or incompetent professionals now relegated to serving the poor, and someone else would have to pay their salaries. Fewer penologists would be employable, however. And pentecostal religion could probably not survive without the poor—nor would parts of the second- and third-hand-goods market. And in many cities, "used" housing that no one else wants would then have to be torn down at public expense.

Alternatives for the cultural functions of the poor could be found more easily and cheaply. Indeed, entertainers, hippies, and adolescents are already serving as the deviants needed to uphold traditional morality and as devotees of orgies to "staff" the fantasies of vicarious participation.

The status functions of the poor are another matter. In a hierarchical society, some people must be defined as inferior to everyone else with respect to a variety of attributes, but they need not be poor in the absolute sense. One could concieve of a society in which the "lower class," though last in the pecking order, received 75 percent of the median income, rather than 15–40 percent, as it now the case. Needless to say, this would require considerable income redistribution.

The contribution the poor make to the upward mobility of the groups that provide them with goods and services could also be maintained without the poor's having such low incomes. However, it is true that if the poor were more affluent, they would have access to enough capital to take over the provider role, thus competing with, and perhaps rejecting, the "outsiders." (Indeed, owing in part to antipoverty programs, this is already happening in a number of ghettos, where white storeowners are being replaced by Blacks.) Similarly, if the poor were more affluent, they would make less willing clients for upper-class philanthropy, although some would still use settlement houses to achieve upward mobility, as they do now. Thus "Society" could continue to run its philanthropic activities.

The political functions of the poor would be more difficult to replace. With increased affluence the poor would probably obtain more political power and be more active politically. With higher incomes and more political power, the poor would be likely to resist paying the costs of growth and change. Of course, it is possible to imagine urban renewal and highway projects that properly reimbursed the displaced people, but such projects would then become considerably more expensive, and many might never be built. This, in turn, would reduce the comfort and convenience of those who now benefit from urban renewal and expressways. Finally, hippies could serve also as more deviants to justify the existing political economy—as they already do. Presumably, however, if poverty were eliminated, there would be fewer attacks on that economy.

In sum, then, many of the functions served by the poor could be replaced if poverty were eliminated, but almost always at higher costs to others, particularly more affluent others. Consequently, a functional analysis must conclude that poverty persists not only because it fulfills a number of positive functions but also because many of the functional alternatives to poverty would be quite dysfunctional for the affluent members of society. A functional analysis thus ultimately arrives at much the same conclusion as radical sociology, except that radical thinkers treat as manifest what I describe as latent: that social phenomena that are functional for affluent or powerful groups and dysfunctional for poor or powerless ones persist; that when the elimination of such phenomena through functional alternatives would generate dysfunctions for the affluent or powerful, they will continue to persist; and that phenomena like poverty can be eliminated only when they become dysfunctional for the affluent or powerful, or when the powerless can obtain enough power to change society.

FIRST THERE ARE THE PRIMARIES. THE PRIMARIES ARE AN ELIMINATION CONTEST.

YOU MEAN WHOEVER LOSES IS OUT?

NO WHOEVER RUNS IS OUT. THAT LEAVES THE FIELD OPEN TO THE SERIOUS CANDIDATES.

WHO ARE THE SERIOUS CANDIDATES?

THE SERIOUS CANDIDATES ARE THE ONES WHO ARE SO STRONG THEY DON'T HAVE TO TAKE A CHANCE ON LOSING IN THE PRIMARIES.

HOW DO THEY COME TO BE THAT STRONG?

BY MAKING DEALS FOR DELEGATES WITH THE PARTY BOSSES.

YOU MEAN THE PARTY BOSSES IGNORE THE WISHES OF THE PEOPLE?

©1969 JULES FEIFFER 7-14

ONLY THE MEANINGLESS PEOPLE. THE PARTY BOSSES CARRY OUT THE WISHES OF THE SERIOUS PEOPLE.

YOU MEAN THE SERIOUS PEOPLE IGNORE THE MEANINGLESS PEOPLE AND DECIDE ON A SERIOUS CANDIDATE FOR ME TO VOTE FOR?

WHAT KIND OF SYSTEM DO YOU CALL THAT?

FREE ELECTIONS.

Dist.
Publishers-Hall Syndicate

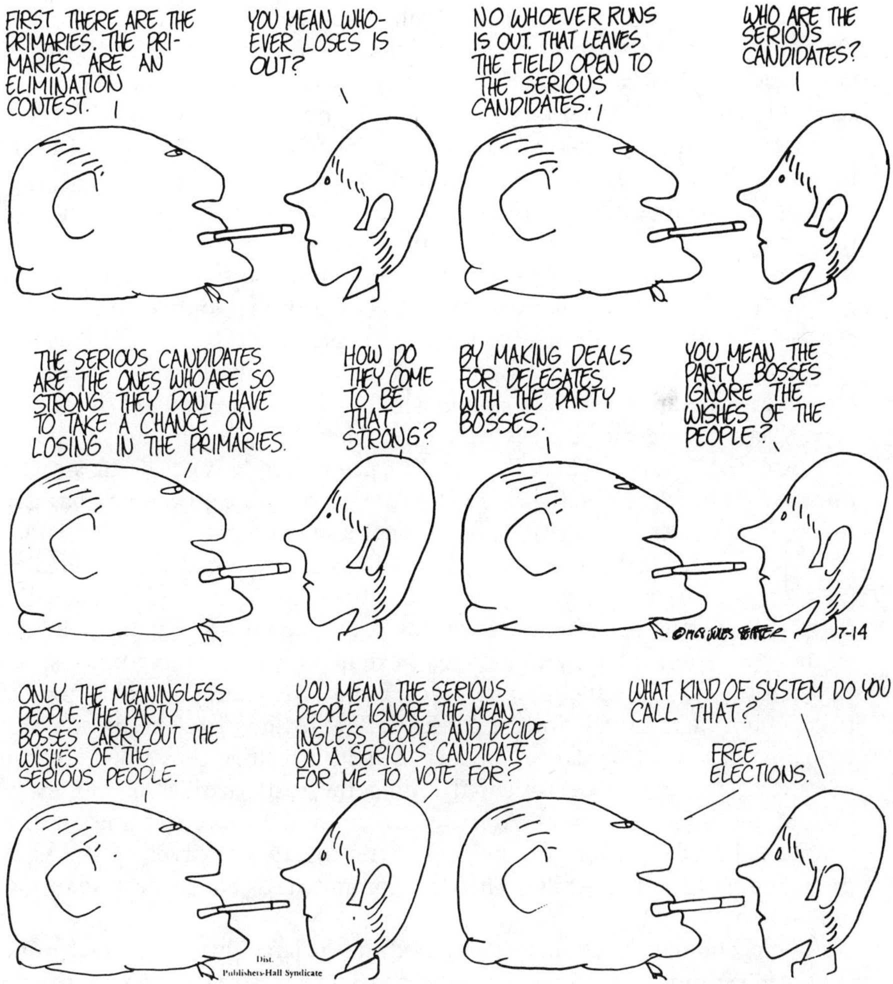

Political Economy

THE POLITICAL and economic institutions in our society are intimately intertwined and inseparable. Our political economy is no longer one dominated by small businessmen and small farmers who compete equally for political and economic influence. Ours is a society dominated by huge institutions. For example, a large segment of our economy is supported by defense spending. Approximately 10 per cent of the gross national product is related to national defense; over 50 per cent of the federal budget is devoted to defense spending. The defense establishment, or the military-industrial complex, provides a classic case of the relationship between business and government. The profits of certain defense-oriented corporations are very much determined by political decisions. Do you suppose these organizations (defense industries and the Pentagon) try to influence decisions made by the President and Congress? Is it any accident that the congressional district of Mendel Rivers, former Chairman of the House Armed Services Committee, is crammed full of military installations and defense industries?

There is really nothing surprising in the collision of economics and politics. It is an age-old phenomenon. But what tends to arouse the anger of many people is the contrast between rhetoric and reality, between ideal and real culture. Hypocrisy on a societal level is nothing unique. All societies exist with a glaring contrast between what is practiced and what is preached. For example, the Soviet Union proclaims itself a socialist society modeled on the tenets of Karl Marx. We doubt whether Marx would agree if he were alive today. The ideological description a society has of itself tends to outlive its existence in reality. There is usually a *cultural lag* between what a society thinks it is and what it actually is. The American political economy has gone through various transformations based on these concepts.

Most Americans believe in the ideals of "free enterprise," for the ideological rhetoric of our society has been that our nation grew and prospered on the principles of laissez-faire. Under this type of political economy, the government does not interfere to any great extent in the economic process. The "natural laws" of competition and economic self-interest invisibly regulate the economy and provide for the public welfare. A pure free-enterprise system probably has never existed in America, but in a relative sense, our economy was more "free-enterprise" oriented during the early decades of our history than at the present. Because America had unlimited resources and land, no established feudal aristocracy, and minorities to exploit, a type of free enterprise flourished for a while. Then a monumental change occurred: mass production.

The economics of producing commodities in large quantities transformed our society from one of small businessmen and farmers to one of large production units, both in industry and agriculture. Our economy is now dominated by large corporations and agricultural combines. While we as a nation still dote on the ideal of free enterprise and competition, large corporations are not especially inclined to compete in relation to prices. On the top of the economic pyramid there tends to be less competition than at the bottom. The more powerful, more influential, and larger the organization, the less it is threatened by price competition. (It can be effectively argued that in the long run this arrangement produces a more stable and efficient economic system. What kind of economic and societal chaos would ensue if a corporation the size of General Motors collapsed?) To a greater degree, competition in our society occurs at the lower levels. Small businesses without government subsidies or support compete harder and fail more often than larger organizations. The individuals within the large corporations may also be involved in a much more personal and anxiety-inducing competition. Another case is the franchising situation. For example, take four gas stations situated on opposite corners. They are in direct competition with one another. But who is really competing? It is entirely possible that all four stations are pumping exactly the same gas. The corporations involved do not run the same risk as the individuals who purchase the franchises. We all compete in this society, but some compete more than others.

We can compare the whole process to the professional football draft. Without the draft, each professional franchise would bid frantically for the services of the college superstars. Some teams would draw more fans (and therefore more money) because of better personnel or a larger stadium. The franchises with the most money would be able to outbid the others for the available human raw material. On an individual level there would be brutal, no-holds-barred competition. The misfits would be weeded out with devastating accuracy. Of course, this type of competition could not occur between the various teams. Ultimately, this process would cost all the teams more money in salaries and eventually might destroy the competitive basis of the whole league. To avoid this, the teams institute a draft where those teams with poorer records choose first among those players graduating from college.

The American economy went through somewhat similar stages. At first, vicious competition between organizations ensued. A few developed a "competitive advantage"; others fell to the wayside. Standard Oil almost succeeded in smothering all competition, but was prosecuted by the federal government in 1911. The corporation was broken up into smaller corporations because it attempted to limit competition. (Some economists would argue that the various corporations into which Standard Oil was broken never really competed with one another.) If a pro football team becomes too dominant, it may destroy its own economic base; but if Standard Oil develops a monopoly, it is able to charge whatever the market will bear. Because monopoly is illegal and ruthless competition tends to be futile and self-destructive, price competition became almost passé in some sectors of the American economy.

The auto industry is an illustration of the new economy with many sectors being dominated by a few large sellers (referred to as oligopolists by economists). Automobile manufacturers no longer try to undersell each other; that would just irrationally reduce profits. Instead they try to out-advertise one another. This could be one of the reasons why we, as consumers, pay more for a product and have to listen to incessant commercials. It would seem more logical, and in the long run better for the consumer, if the larger corporations would devote more energy to economic efficiency than to advertising.

The political and economic spheres really got together after the Depression. One of the problems our economy had faced was the incessant cycle of boom and bust, economic growth and recession. The worldwide depression which began in 1929 represents one of the severest recessions in our history. Those in power agreed that another depression was economically intolerable. A new role for the federal government was created to prevent such an occurrence. The government became the great stabilizing force in the economy, responsible for ensuring nearly full employment and a reasonable rate of economic growth.

How does the federal government accomplish these goals? It makes money available for spending and investment. The basic theory is that more money (greater purchasing power) means a greater demand for goods and services. This will attract investors seeking a profit. They in turn will hire more workers, who will have more money to spend. The government serves as a catalyst in this process.

How is more money made available? The federal government can build parks, highways, and dams; it can give tax breaks to expanding corporations; it can subsidize industries; it can develop programs for health, education, and welfare; or it can build a huge military complex. The decisions as to where and how the money is to be spent are political in nature. How are these decisions made? Who makes these decisions? What organizations and institutions are most influential?

We have already implied in this introduction that a disproportionate amount of government spending involves national defense. The reasons for this phenomenon are the power and influence of the military-industrial complex in government, the ingrained American anticommunist hysteria, and the ease with which defense spending can be sold to the public. Almost any amount of spending can be justified in protecting the real or imagined national security. In fact, the government's massive dose of defense spending at the inception of World War II ended the Depression. We feel that since 1947 with the inception of the Marshall Plan and the Truman Doctrine, the level of defense spending has been influenced by factors that are *not* related to national security. Can the Cold War be explained simply as a reaction to anticipated communist aggression? What are the factors that have contributed to the present level of defense spending?

Another spectre that haunts our political economy is cybernation (the linking of computers to automated assembly lines). Cybernation poses a curious problem in our society. It promises a world minus the incessant drudgery of monotonous work, yet somewhere in the heart of puritanical, hardworking America, the thought of a workless existence releases acidic pellets of guilt and anxiety. Cybernation may presage a great threat to our economic institution. As we said before, the government sees that the level of demand (purchasing power) remains high in our society. If necessary, it will go into debt to do this. What would happen if automation replaced larger and larger numbers of workers? Would it eventually reduce the overall level of demand for goods and services in our society? Could it eventually produce a depression? Would it force the government farther and farther into debt? Some argue that cybernation will neither reduce the labor force tremendously nor eventually force a remodeling of the economic system. They feel that the demand for goods and services is unlimited. Therefore, new jobs will be continually created in other sectors of the economy. Only the future will finally resolve this argument.

Another consequence of the "corporatization" of the economy and the centralization of the federal government is the concentration of power in hands of fewer and fewer people. When our country was composed mainly of small businessmen and small farmers, nobody had a complete monopoly of power. There is now a tremendous concentration of economic power in the hands of a few people. Within our oligopolistic economy there has arisen a type of corporation descriptively entitled a "conglomerate." The General Motors Corporation is a prototype of what many corporations are becoming in the United States. It has 735,000 employees, 1.3 million shareholders in more than eighty countries, plants in twenty-four countries, and a line of products that includes autos, refrigerators, earth-moving equipment, locomotives, jet engines, and missile-guidance systems. GM's 1965 net profit (after taxes) of $2.1 billion was greater than the general revenue of forty-eight of the states and its sales of $21 billion exceeded the gross national product of all but nine foreign nations. In the near future we may be voting on whether or not we want GM running the country instead of the federal government. In fact, Ralph Nader has suggested that the directors of large corporations be elected so that they are more responsive to public needs. What implications does this have for democracy in America? Especially now, when many in the electorate are clamoring for more participation in the decisions that affect their lives, power seems to be very concentrated. This naturally leads us to a discussion of power in American society. The textbook theory of democracy is referred to as pluralism. In its purest form, this theory states that power is divided among a series of organizations and institutions. These institutions compete on an equal basis for a share of power. None of these institutions dominates the American scene; they act as "countervailing powers." This is an updated version of federalism and the Madisonian system of checks and balances. Is this a caricature of power in American society? Can the legislative branch effectively compete with the President? Can the consumer defend himself from vagaries of the auto industry? (Technically he can by not buying cars, but this is a very remote possibility.) Is the lower class as powerful as the upper class? Which institution is more powerful and influential: the political institution or the educational institution? Is power democratically distributed in America?

There are other theories of power. The ruling-class model is one of these (see *Who Rules America?* by G. William Domhoff). Simply stated, an upper-class elite, with its power centered in the corporate economy, exercises a disproportionate share of power in all American institutions. Another theory is that of C. Wright Mills' "power elite." Here power is based in our major institutions: the military machine, the corporate economy, and the executive branch of the federal government. This "power elite" operates with little democratic restraint. A coincidence of interests enables it to form alliances in relation to the major decisions in our society. One obvious coincidence of interest is the perpetuation of a system which distributes a disproportionate share of the wealth and power among these institutions. Another might be the preservation of a tax structure that favors the propertied rich. Is it possible for a class or elite to dominate American society? What are some built-in restraints that should prevent this from happening in the United States? Are these limitations to the concentration of power effectively utilized by the public? Can you envision an alternate model of American democracy?

Most Americans tend to assume that the collective will of the public is reached through our democratic political institutions. We feel that any political system should be critically analyzed from two perspectives: (1) how well it records the will of the people and (2) how well it adapts itself to change. How democratic can we expect our society to be? Can there ever be a "pure democracy"? Are there some undemocratic aspects in our democracy? Is the seniority system in Congress democratic? How much influence does money have on politics? Is a third party possible in American politics? Does our political system blot out minority representation? How democratic are the presidential nominations? Although probably a few have always chosen the candidates, it suddenly seems much less tolerable to a more highly educated public.

How well has our political system dealt with social change? Have other political systems and societies been better able to cope with the future? Are the changes in our society too sudden and the conflicts too deeply ingrained to be handled by *any* type of political economy? —G. G.

Selected References

(All are available in paperback editions.)

Berle, Adolf A. *The American Economic Republic*. New York: Harcourt Brace Jovanovich, Inc., 1963.

Bottomore, T. B. *Elites and Society*. Baltimore: Penguin Books, Inc., 1966.

Coser, Lewis A. (ed.). *Political Sociology*. New York: Harper & Row, Publishers, 1967.

Galbraith, John K. *The New Industrial State*. New York: The New American Library, Inc., 1967.

Harrington, Michael. *The Accidental Century*. Baltimore: Penguin Books, Inc., 1966.

Heilbroner, Robert L. *The Limits of American Capitalism*. New York: Harper & Row, Publishers, 1960.

Lipset, Seymour M. *Political Man*. Garden City, N.Y.: Doubleday & Company, Inc., 1960.

The Presidential Candidate Factory

RUSSELL BAKER

Where, you may have asked, do the political parties get these candidates they run for President?

They are, most of them, manufactured by Abraham Jackson & Sons, world's oldest maker of presidential candidates, at a factory right here in Washington.

Lead time in producing a candidate is normally eight to twelve years. This means that candidates now on the drawing boards will not be ready for the stump until 1976 or 1980. Interestingly, the major political parties are not disturbed by the fact that a candidate designed this year will, in all probability, be obsolete by the time he comes on the market.

Theodore Jackson, great-grandson of the company founder and now chairman of the company, has found that the major parties will rarely take a candidate designed to come to grips with contemporary problems.

"Actually," he said in an interview the other day, "since 1945, we build into the automatic pledging device a routine promise to increase Social Security benefits. Aside from that, we haven't made any major modification in our model since the Republicans contracted with us to build Calvin Coolidge nearly 50 years ago."

At present, the Jackson company has just finished testing a candidate for the 1972 campaign.

The 1972 prototype is designated the X-115. The company will build two models, one for each party. The basic equipment in both will be identical. This is taken from Jackson's huge warehouse of interchangeable candidate parts. The standard units include a vigilant anti-communism mechanism, a set of perpetual smile muscles, a large reservoir of fraudulent humility and a synchrolock sincerity overdrive.

Jackson has little patience with the criticism that his candidates are not responsive to contemporary political issues. "We've dabbled in offbeat candidates," he said, "and it's a money-losing proposition. The major parties aren't interested."

Burwell Cash, in charge of presidential-candidate procurement for the Republican National Committee, explained why. "The people who make all the noise in politics," he says, "are people for whom the system doesn't work. Negroes, peace nuts, people on fixed incomes, intellectuals, young people mad at their parents, pot smokers. If you buy a candidate responsive to the Negroes, the people on fixed incomes hate him. A candidate responsive to intellectuals alienates young people mad at their parents."

James Dandy, Cash's Democratic counterpart, agreed. The American system, he said, depends upon the exclusion from politics of groups unhappy with the status quo.

"Excluding all those rumps," he explained, "leaves you with the middle-of-the-road voter who elects Presidents. The middle-of-the-road guy likes things pretty much the way they are, but he likes a change of face now and then."

What happens, however, when everybody in the country becomes so disgruntled that the middle-of-the-road disappears and nothing but excluded rumps remain? Some think we are approaching that in 1968.

Dandy replied: "It can't happen here. It can't happen here. It can't happen here. It can't happen here. It can't—" Its rosy-reassurance gears were stuck.

How to Bribe a Congressman

JACK ANDERSON

Famed Washington columnist Jack Anderson uses an interesting approach in this short article. He specifically examines the subtle and unsubtle ways to influence congressmen. The article is filled with real people caught in what are euphemistically referred to as "political indiscretions."

WASHINGTON, D.C.

As darkness settled over Atlanta's International Airport, a fat, balding Congressman barged through an arrival gate into the busy terminal. He was greeted by Myrvin Clark, an admitted swindler, who carried a briefcase. The two men exchanged cryptic remarks about a construction firm in Silver Spring, Md. The Congressman agreed to do everything he could to prevent the firm from being indicted for fraud. Then, smiling broadly, he departed with the briefcase to catch a plane for Texas. The reason for his smile: his newly acquired briefcase contained $25,000 in crisp greenbacks.

The story sounds apocryphal. But in Federal Court in 1971, a jury found Rep. John Dowdy (D., Tex.), now thin and ailing, guilty of bribery, conspiracy and perjury. Last month an appeals court in a dubious decision overturned the bribery and conspiracy counts. The court said that the things

From *Parade,* May 6, 1973. Reprinted by permission of the publisher and the author.

Dowdy had done which helped the construction firm "might be interpreted as preparation for a subcommittee hearing . . . and, as such, would be protected legislative acts." Left standing was Dowdy's perjury conviction.

Referring to the case, one Congressman admitted: "There's a little of Dowdy in all of us." He asked rhetorically: "How many of us here aren't guilty in some way of accepting favors from special interest groups?" Then he paused and answered his question: "Damn few."

The Free List

For most members of Congress, the favors are confined to small gratuities: free lunches and liquor, delicacies at Christmastime, vitamins from a pharmaceutical firm. For others, the favors are more substantial: free rides on corporate jets, all-expenses-paid vacations, cash under the table.

Legitimate lobbyists ask, in return, only that a Congressman lend a sympathetic ear to their concerns. "All most of us want is our day in Congress," one young lobbyist told me. An older union lobbyist put it more succinctly: "I don't want to bribe the guy, I just want to make sure when I gotta see him, I'm gonna see him."

But all too many lobbyists, with fat money clips, are ready to buy favors and to charge high fees for their efforts. The favors they seek for their clients are twofold: favorable legislation and contracts. These lobbyists are slicked-down versions of Dandy Beau Hickman who became Washington's lobbyist exemplar a century ago. He collected a small fortune for introducing barflies to famous Washington personalities in hotel lobbies. For a quarter, history records, Beau would arrange a handshake; for a dollar, a formal introduction.

Prices Up

Today, the price of entrée comes higher. Professional lobbyists, skilled at the soft sell, charge thousands of dollars to argue a crucial case before a key Senator. They are the super lobbyists—the Clark Cliffords, George Smatherses, Tommy "The Cork" Corcorans and Bryce Harlows. They seldom are seen in the Capitol lobbies; they move quietly in the same circles as the legislators they influence, ever cool, convivial and, if possible, invisible.

To be sure, lobbyists are entitled to present their arguments on Capitol Hill, to exercise their constitutional right of petition. To sell members of Congress, yes, but not to buy them. A bribe, however, isn't always easy to define. How expensive must a gift be, how valuable a favor, before it is called a bribe? Can a lobbyist buy a Congressman with cocktails? A $100 Christmas gift? A $350 flight in a corporate jet? A $950 vacation at a resort hotel? A $1200 lecture fee? A $2500 legal retainer? Doesn't everyone have the right to contribute to the candidates of his choice? Then, when does a campaign contribution offered in appreciation for a Congressman's vote, become a payment for his vote?

Here are the most popular ways of influencing a Congressman:

1. Cash. Most Congressmen who are for sale prefer to be paid in cash. They don't want any incriminating receipts or canceled checks floating around. For example:

At a secret hearing of the House Commerce Committee, Mrs. Dorothy Storz, former secretary-treasurer and head bookkeeper for broadcaster Don Burden's three Star radio stations, swore according to the secret testimony, that Burden instructed her to send ten $100 bills to Sen. Mark Hatfield (R., Oreg.). "I signed the check. I endorsed it, and I mailed those $100 bills to . . . Hatfield," she testified. She got back a receipt, she said, signed by Evelyn Cook in Hatfield's office. Yet Hatfield claimed he never got the money.

Are cash transactions common on Capitol Hill? My reporter put the question to Rep. Pete McCloskey (R., Calif.). "I have that impression," he said. He told about his own experience. "I was upset to find lobbyists leaving behind five or ten $100 bills in envelopes after visiting my office," he said. "I asked how I should report the contributions. My questions were met with disbelief."

Funneled Cash

Lobbyist Cyrus T. Anderson, convicted of paying ex-Sen. Daniel Brewster (D., Md.) "an unlawful gratuity" amounting to $14,500, told the court that he funneled thousands of dollars, most of it hard cash, from corporations and unions to various politicians.

What kind of people, he was asked, came to him for cash? "Senators, Congressmen, candidates for President of the United States," said Anderson. He was scrupulous, however, never to bribe anyone inside a federal building. "It was my understanding," he explained to the court, "that even legal political contributions can't be made in a federal building, much less ones that weren't going to be reported."

Why do Congressmen want payment in cash? "They prefer," replied Anderson, "not to make public the sources of their incomes."

Credit Cards

2. Credit. Next to cash, Congressmen on the make like to use other people's credit cards. Corporations and unions alike slip credit cards to their favorite Congressmen, and let them charge airplane tickets, hotel bills, rental cars, even personal purchases.

ITT's celebrated lobbyist Dita Beard, for example, used to hand out special Avis credit cards to friendly Congressmen. Avis, of course, was a subsidiary of ITT. Rep. Lionel Van Deerlin (D., Calif.) accepted an Avis card from Mrs. Beard to help defray the cost for a recent camping trip through Europe.

Another card carrier, Ex-Sen. George Murphy (R., Calif.), who supplemented his Senate salary by pulling down $20,000 a year from Technicolor, Inc., also had the use of the company's credit card. Murphy told me he never used the card except to pay his expenses when he acted as a company consultant.

3. Contributions. If a Congressman blanches at taking cash under the table, the best way for lobbyists to show their appreciation is to contribute to his campaign. Even the most honest Congressmen can't entirely escape doing business with the special interests. Those candidates who have tried to finance campaigns from small contributions have learned quickly that the fat cats are indispensable.

The custom is for the lobbyists to raise a campaign kitty for the Congressman from their corporate or union clients. Sen. John Sparkman (D., Ala.) was re-elected last year, for instance, with the financial help of bankers and builders as far away as California and Massachusetts. As Senate Banking Chairman, he handles legislation that can make or break finance houses. Bankers, savings-and-loan officials and credit union officers from 28 states chipped in $62,923 to his campaign.

Sparkman also oversees many federal housing programs. Real-estate operators and housing contractors raised $45,996 for him, according to the official records. Not surprisingly, Sparkman gave special priority to legislation benefitting his benefactors after his triumphal return to Washington.

Dispensing Largesse

House Ways and Means Chairman Wilbur Mills, who is in charge of tax legislation, is routinely re-elected every two years by his rural Arkansas constituency. He, therefore, has access to more special-interest money and has less need for it than any other member of Congress. His solution is to dispense money to colleagues who, in return for his largesse, demonstrate their gratitude by voting for the tax bills he sponsors.

4. Investments. Lobbyists with the right financial connections have been known to steer cooperative Congressmen into profitable investments. Many Senators and Representatives trade actively on the stock market, buying and selling shares of corporations whose prosperity they influence and whose conduct they help to regulate. Some purchase stock in their own names; others find it more discreet to use the maiden names of their wives or the names of intimates. The more cautious buy their stock in a "street" name, whereby the broker makes the purchase and keeps the stock in his company's portfolio.

House Banking Chairman Wright Patman (D., Tex.) has revealed how his committee members are seduced by the banks. "It takes the form of offering a Congressman bank stock either free or at a cost greatly under the market value," he said. "A member of my committee was approached and offered $14,000 worth of bank stock as a gift. I am proud to report that he is of such caliber that he told the would-be donors to get out of his office."

The Pitch

The Congressman was Henry Gonzalez (D., Tex.). He said that the attempted bribe came in a conversation with a well-known businessman-banker from San Antonio, his home town, on a summer day in 1963. "You are very popular in the part of town where we are going to have the bank," Gonzalez paraphrased the businessman's pitch. "It would be very helpful to have you in a serious business enterprise. In fact, we would like you to be chairman of the board."

Former Rep. George Brown Jr. (D., Calif.) gave another account of the corruption process: "I have stock holdings in both a savings-and-loan company and a nationally chartered bank. I'm a director of the S&L, and I am an organizer of the bank in my district. Politicians are generally offered stock opportunities to purchase stock at opening price. In California, it's a stock bribe equal generally to double the amount of the original cost."

5. Legal Retainers. In 1969, the American Bar Association reached the not-so-startling conclusion that it was improper for men who make the law also to practice it. This has persuaded a few Congressmen to give up their law practices. But dozens more continue to rake in the law fees. Their firms, invariably, represent clients with considerable interest in what Congress can do for them.

Awhile back, I made a study of 50 typical law firms with partners serving in Congress. These had a remarkable similarity of clients; they represented the vested interests of America. Of the 50 law firms in my survey, 40 represented banks, 31 represented insurance companies, 11 represented gas and oil companies, 10 represented real-estate firms. Some of the biggest corporate names in America were listed as clients of Congressmen's law firms in such out-of-the-way places, say, as Nicholasville, Ky., and Pascagoula, Miss.

6. Lecture Fees. A Congressman who is beyond outright bribing may be willing to accept a lecture fee. He may be able to convince his conscience that he really earned the money, though oratory can be summoned forth from the average Congressman as a reflex action. In 1971, members of Congress admitted earning a total of nearly $1 million for speaking engagements and occasional magazine articles. The man who led everybody to the public rostrum was Sen. Hubert Humphrey (D., Minn.). The loquacious Humphrey earned a whopping $83,451 from dozens of public appearances.

Pay to Listen

Many a pressure group—from the Mortgage Bankers Association to the Teamsters Union—will pay perfectly good money to hear a Congressman declaim. The largest single source of speaking fees for Congressmen has been the Seafarers' International Union. The maritime lobbyists quietly invited 22 Congressmen and four Senators to speak at their special luncheons in one year alone. The union's favorite speakers, of course, were members of the House Merchant Marine Subcommittee.

As an index to the price of hot air, Senators demand top dollar, with fees ranging from $1000 to $2000. House members will usually settle for less.

7. **Poker.** From the reports I get, a startling number of Congressmen play poker with their lobbyist friends in swank hospitality suites around town. The details, however, are difficult to pin down. I've been told, for example, that certain members of the House Merchant Marine Subcommittee have been amazingly lucky in their card games with shipping lobbyists.

See the World

8. **Vacation.** As a method of softening up Congressmen, vacation trips are most favored by government agencies, which must go to Congress for their appropriations. It is of unquestionable value for Congressmen to get out and see the world. Contacts are made; understanding is reached; legislation is born. But all too often, the Congressmen see little beyond the beaches and the bars. The Pentagon, for instance, is eager to provide transportation for legislators. Overseas, U.S. embassy personnel serve as lackeys and luggage carriers for tourists from Capitol Hill.

But corporations, too, provide planes, free flights, hotel rooms and rental cars for traveling Congressmen. ITT lobbyist Dita Beard once complained to her secretary that too many Congressmen requested free trips. "All these people want planes all the time. Don't they know the company has to use these planes, too?"

9. **Fringe Benefits.** Lobbyists literally shower small favors on Congressmen: theater tickets, imported liquors, French perfume, birthday cakes, even free Kleenex for their secretaries. One lobbyist I know starts each morning by buying berakfast for a small group of Congressmen in the House cafeteria. Most lobbyists, however, prefer to wait until noon before dishing out free food and drinks. At Christmastime, the lobbyists are especially generous. "Gifts are crated in by the cart load," one Senate aide admitted.

The flow of gratuities continues in spite of a new campaign disclosure law which requires Congressmen to report any gift or combination of gifts that total $10 or more in value. Only a few corporations, fearful of the disclosure law, have curtailed the flow.

Sen. Abe Ribicoff (D., Conn.) once startled his colleagues on the Senate Finance Committee when they were patching together tax legislation behind closed doors. "I couldn't vote for this provision, even if I favored it . . . ," snorted Ribicoff, in reference to a proposal that would benefit real estate developers. "I own real estate myself. It's an obvious conflict of interest."

There was a moment of stunned silence. Then Chairman Russell Long (D., La.) broke in. "Well, I have interest in oil," he said, "but I wouldn't hesitate to vote for legislation that might favor the oil industry. After all, I come from Louisiana. What's good for oil, is good for my state." A chorus of other Senators agreed with Long. For several minutes, the Senators talked candidly about their special interests in oil, insurance, trucking and agriculture. Finally, one Senator told the unrelenting Ribicoff bluntly: "Abe, if we abstained on every piece of legislation in which we had some personal interest, why we'd never pass any legislation."

A Short Answer

Despite the many ways to bribe a Congressman, it is a miracle of politics and a tribute to officeholders that the pressure groups don't wield more influence than they do. More often than not, in the daily drama on Capitol Hill, there's an exchange that puts the lobbyist in his place. "Vote 'Yes,' " one union lobbyist instructed Rep. Bill Green (D., Pa.) as he entered the House chamber for a vote. "I'll tell why later." Green smiled and voted no.

The High Cost of Monopoly

MARK J. GREEN

In this essay Mr. Green, an associate of Ralph Nader, describes what he refers to as our "closed enterprise system." He briefly records what this system costs the consumer and skillfully undercuts the justifications for an uncompetitive corporate America.

Monopoly. The word has typically projected antique images on our memory screens—a combative Teddy Roosevelt, industrial tycoons, corporate empires, victimized farmers. Recent and converging events, however, have resurrected monopoly as a current problem:

- In the mid-Sixties Senator Philip Hart's hearings into economic concentration collected an avalanche of data, documenting the high degree of industrial giantism in America.
- The late Sixties witnessed the largest merger wave in American history, averaging 3,605 mergers annually between 1967 and 1969, or six times as many per year as its famous turn-of-the-century predecessor.
- In 1969 President Johnson's Antitrust Task Force urged the breakup of shared monopolies in proposed legislation. (A close Johnson adviser told me that Johnson would have proposed such legislation if reelected. Why?

"It was good public policy, cheap to pass, and would help out the consumer.")

- *America, Inc.*, a critique of big business by Morton Mintz and Jerry Cohen, became a best seller in five short weeks during 1971. *The Closed Enterprise System*, the Nader antitrust study describing the consumer costs of tolerating corporate giantism, was covered by the general (and not merely business) press.
- Senator Fred Harris recently introduced a rider to Phase II legislation to decentralize many of our giant corporations, and Senator Hart, chairman of the Senate Antitrust Subcommittee, will shortly introduce his own deconcentration legislation.
- The Federal Trade Commission in January issued its first monopolization charge against a major industry in its fifty-eight year history, charging that four cereal companies were an illegal "shared monopoly."
- Finally, President Nixon's wage and price controls have revived questions extending from economist Gardiner Means and the populist Senator Joseph O'Mahoney, Wyoming Democrat, in the 1930s, to John Kenneth Galbraith and Senator William Proxmire today: Has monopoly's "administered" prices caused our nagging inflation/recession? What, if anything, can be done about a place called Corporate America? What is ahead for Phase III?

Much of the American economy can neither be characterized as monopolistic (like Xerox, Western Electric, or IBM) nor as competitive (the wheat and fashion markets). Between the two are "shared monopolies"—a form of flawed competition where only a handful of large firms produce a particular product. Shared monopolists often act as would a monopolist, with the result that prices invariably increase. For example, our steel industry, dominated by four firms controlling fifty-four percent of all shipments, periodically raises its prices despite idle capacity of about a third and despite the availability of cheaper imported steel.

Industrial economists agree that when four or fewer firms control fifty percent or more of a market, a shared monopoly results. Collective or conspiratorial behavior, not competitive, then pervades productive activity. Such industries are many and recognizable: automobiles (General Motors, Ford, Chrysler); aluminum (Alcoa, Reynolds, Kaiser); soap detergents (Procter & Gamble, Colgate, and Lever Brothers); cereals (Kellogg, General Foods, General Mills, Quaker Oats); electric light bulbs (General Electric, Westinghouse, Sylvania); cigarettes (Reynolds, American, Philip Morris), and others.

The extent of shared monopolies can modestly be described as staggering. In 1959 economists Carl Kaysen and Donald Turner concluded in their now classic *Antitrust Policy* that "there are more concentrated than unconcentrated industries in manufacturing and mining, they are larger in aggregate size, and they tend to occupy a more important position in the economy." More than a decade later, two other authors on Corporate America agreed. Economics professors William Shepherd and Richard Barber have both calculated that shared monopolies control about two-thirds of all industry. These are the industries of our giant firms: General Motors has 800,000 employes worldwide and collects more in total sales (some $20 billion annually) than the budgets of all but three countries; the advertising budget of Procter & Gamble alone is *twenty times* as large as the appropriation of the Justice Department's Antitrust Division, which must monitor a trillion dollar economy; the six largest firms in *Fortune's* 500 (there are 400,000 manufacturing firms in this country) earn fully twenty-five percent of all industrial profits.

Based on *market concentration*—the share of business held by the leading firms in a particular industry—there has been a slight increase in the already high level of concentration during the past two decades. But based on *aggregate concentration*—the ownership of all manufacturing assets by our biggest corporations—the increase has been dramatic. While the top 200 industrial firms controlled forty-seven per cent of total assets in 1950, by 1965 they controlled fifty-five per cent. Willard Mueller, former chief economist of the Federal Trade Commission, testified before the Senate Antitrust and Monopoly Subcommittee in November, 1969:

"You may recall that I testified before this Committee in 1966 that, should postwar trends in aggregate concentration continue, by 1975 the 200 largest manufacturing corporations would control two-thirds of all manufacturing assets. Unhappily, we have reached this level ahead of schedule. *Today the top 200 manufacturing corporations already control about two-thirds of all assets held by corporations engaged primarily in manufacturing.*" (Emphasis added.)

Also, the 100 largest corporations today have a greater share of manufacturing assets than did the 200 largest in 1950, the year Congress enacted the Celler-Kefauver Act to stop the trend toward industrial concentration. And our top 200 corporations now control the same share of assets held by the *thousand* largest in 1941, the year the landmark Temporary National Economic Committee submitted its final report to Congress recommending an "Investigation of Concentration of Economic Power." How can one comprehend power of this magnitude? Imagine a college classroom seating just 200, and there you could sit the rulers of two-thirds of American industry and more than one-third of all the world's industrial production. Pharaohs and emperors would be envious.

The disfiguring of free enterprise by monopoly imposes serious economic and social tolls. Foremost is the overpricing that occurs when one or a few firms control a market. A staff report now at the Federal Trade Commission estimates that "if highly concentrated industries were deconcentrated to the point where the four largest firms control forty per cent or less of an industry's sales, *prices would fall by twenty-five per cent or more.*" The examples are numerous:

- There were a number of competing milk firms in Minneapolis–St. Paul in the mid-Sixties, but only three big milk firms in neighboring Duluth-Superior; although costs were similar in both markets, the half-gallon wholesale price in 1967 was 33.8 cents in Minneapolis–St. Paul, forty-five cents in Duluth.
- While there were once as many as eighty-eight competing auto manufacturers in 1921, today the "Big Three" produce eighty-three per cent of all cars sold in the United States and ninety-seven per cent of all domestic models. Industrial economist Leonard Weiss, of the University of Wisconsin, has estimated that the noncompetitive state of the auto industry costs $1.6 billion per year.
- Federal Trade Commission studies have found that cereal prices are fifteen to twenty-five per cent higher than would exist under competition because of domination of the industry by just four firms.
- The oil import quota, by keeping out much foreign competition, permits domestic oil firms to overcharge, according to a Presidential task force, by an estimated $5 million to $7 billion per year; for a family of four in New York, this means an average of $102 added to gasoline and home heating bills every year.

Such overpricing leads to lost output. Monopoly misallocates resources, creating excess capacity and a smaller Gross National Product than is our national potential. Recent studies by economists William Shepherd and F. M. Scherer have tried to quantify this lost GNP, concluding that *the overall cost of monopoly and shared monopoly in terms of lost production is somewhere between $48 billion and $60 billion annually*. The tax revenues alone from this wealth could go a long way toward ending both poverty and pollution in this country.

Monopoly overcharging also results in an inequitable transfer cost. When consumers pay excessive prices for their purchases, monopoly profits then redistribute income from the consuming public to the shareholders of particular corporations. Professor Shepherd of the University of Michigan has estimated this redistribution of wealth at $23 billion annually. And "people's capitalism"—that "the people" own our corporations—is no rebuttal. Although millions own some stock, only a relative handful reap the lion's share of corporate dividends. A 1963 study, containing the most recent figures available, pointed out that 1.6 per cent of the adult population of the United States owned 82.1 per cent of all publicly held stock. This redistribution of wealth—exacerbating the wealth extremes of a society where the richest one per cent of U.S. families receive more income than the bottom twenty per cent and the top five per cent more than the bottom forty per cent—can eventually have serious political consequences. "A man who thinks that economics is only a matter for professors," writes author-economist Robert L. Heilbroner, "forgets that this is the science that has sent men to the barricades."

Lost output and income transfers are not the only ill effects of monopolies. Other dynamic costs are less capable of measurement but still severely damage our industrial and social health:

Inflation and Unemployment. Concentrated industries can largely shrug off the classical monetary and fiscal restraints, not reducing their high prices as consumer demand declines. In 1970, both before and after the automobile strike, General Motors announced price increases attempting to maintain their targeted twenty per cent return (on net worth after taxes) rather than suffer a less than monopoly-like return. Due to such market power of big firms, we are in what economist Paul Samuelson calls a "sellers' inflation"—where higher costs are simply passed on to the consumer in the form of higher prices.

In 1969 the FTC's Bureau of Economics pointed out that "major concentrated industries, through the exercise of discretionary pricing power, contribute to both inflation and unemployment." Unemployment results since monopolies, as noted, significantly reduce our manufacturing output—which in turn reduces the number of workers who would otherwise be producing. If monopoly disruption were accountable for only twenty per cent of all the unemployed, this still translates into over a million unemployed workers. And to the extent that unemployment is an official policy to combat inflation—two million people have been thrown out of work between 1969 and 1971 with this purpose in mind—a "stagflation" created by our shared monopolies dims the employment picture.

Political and Social Effects. Assuming that Corporate America has political power, what then are the costs of increasing concentration of economic power? As economic diversity decreases, the number of units contributing to the political process decreases accordingly. And as political pluralism weakens, so does democracy. James Madison argued in the Federalist Papers that political freedom requires many "factions," setting faction against faction until a political equipoise results. But as large numbers of independent firms are swallowed up, we instead race toward *America, Inc.*, in Mintz's and Cohen's phrase, "one gigantic industrial and financial complex functioning much like a separate government."

Socially, people are governed by distant operatives; initiative and individuality succumb to the ethic of the Organization Man. Job mobility declines as the number of important independent firms dwindles. "Free enterprise" then witnesses the kind of dependence found both in the cartelized Japanese economy and the communized Soviet economy. General Robert E. Wood, the ultra-conservative former chairman of the board at Sears Roebuck, once observed, "We complain about government and business, we stress the advantages of the free enterprise system, we complain about the totalitarian state, but in our individual organizations . . . we have created more or less of a totalitarian system in industry, particularly in large industry."

Politically, the control over government by big business, already great, increases. "When a major corporation from a state wants to discuss something with its political representatives," Senator Hart has said, "you can be sure it will be heard. When that same company operates in thirty states, it will be heard by thirty times as many representatives." Supporting this view was International Telephone and Telegraph's effort to drum up Congressional opposition to the Justice Department's attempt to block its merger with the American Broadcasting Company; 300 Representatives and Senators complained to Justice.

Those large firms which dominate an industry, by their orchestrated power, can resist governmental and public pressure more easily than smaller firms of lesser political clout. And as big firms push out or buy out the small, the "mavericks" of industry disappear. Their disappearance reduces a source of political options since, as the number of private sources for social risk capital is reduced, the unpopular or new cause will find it that much more difficult to secure backing.

The social blights of racism and pollution have been associated with the discretionary power of monopolies freed from the spurs of competition. Economist William Shepherd studied racial patterns in white-collar jobs, concluding that firms with market power could afford the luxury of discriminating against blacks—and they did. But competitive firms, which had to hire the best employes at the going rate—whether they were black or white—were found to discriminate less. Also there is very little incentive for shared monopolists to be progressive on pollution, with their heavy investment in existing capital assets and with their ability already to exact monopoly-like returns. The *Auto-Smog Conspiracy* case provides one clear example. In this case the Justice Department charged the Big Four auto firms with illegally suppressing anti-exhaust technology and implementation.

Proponents of Big Business, on the other hand, argue that there are alternate benefits in our state of superconcentration. But on close examination, their verbal arrows become boomerangs:

Innovation. First popularized by the eminent Joseph Schumpeter, and recently adopted by John Kenneth Galbraith, the idea is that big firms can innovate better because they are able to risk the necessary large investments in research and development (R&D). "A benign providence," Galbraith has intoned, "has made the modern industry of a few large firms an almost perfect instrument for inducing technical change."

But nearly all objective evidence refutes this assertion. When you have a huge investment in present machinery, and when an unknown return is to be substituted for your sixteen to twenty per cent return, there is little need to embrace new technologies. Economist Leonard Weiss, after examining many analyses of R&D expenditures, concluded: "Most studies show that within their range of observation, size adds little to research intensity and may actually detract from it in some industries." Also, it should be stressed that about two-thirds of the research done in the United States is subsidized by the Federal Government anyway—not by big private industry.

A look at the concentrated steel industry revealed that of thirteen major inventions between 1940 and 1955, none was produced by the American steel companies. A small Austrian firm, one-third the size of one U.S. Steel plant, introduced the revolutionary oxygen steelmaking process. The first American company to adopt it was McLouth Steel, which had less than one per cent of industry capacity; it was ten years later when U.S. Steel and Bethlehem followed suit.

But steel has a long history of technological immobility. What of a large corporation commonly considered a major innovator, like General Electric, "where progress is our most important product"? In the household appliance field alone, the late T. K. Quinn, a former GE vice-president, credited small companies with the discovery and production of, among other items: the electric toaster, electric range, electric refrigerator, electric dryer, electric dishwasher, vacuum cleaner, clothes-washing machine, and deep freeze. Quin concluded that "the record of the giants is one of moving in, buying out, and absorbing the smaller concerns." Nor was industrial bigness a *sine qua non* to the development of stainless steel razor blades, transistor radios, photo copying machines, and the "quick" photograph. Wilkinson, Sony, Xerox, and Polaroid were all small or unknown when they introduced these products.

Efficiencies. The reputed efficiencies of large scale operation become inefficiencies when the scale grows too large. Competition is the whip of efficiency, driving firms to produce better goods at lower costs in order to increase sales and profits. Monopoly and oligopoly, however, lead to "the quiet life," in Judge Learned Hand's phrase, a state of mind and economy where there is little pressure to seek out efficiencies. In an age which has witnessed the collapse of the Penn-Central (a firm which was the result of a merger with claimed efficiencies because of its large size), and the near collapses of Ling-Temco-Voigt (LTV) and Lockheed aircraft firms, it should be evident that being big does not mean being efficient. Robert Townsend has put it more impressionistically: "Excellence and bigness are incompatible."

Huey Long once prophesied that fascism would come to the United States first in the form of anti-fascism. So too with socialism—*corporate* socialism. Under the banner of free enterprise, up to two-thirds of American manufacturing has been metamorphosed into a "closed enterprise system." Although businessmen spoke the language of competitive capitalism, each sought refuge for themselves: price-fixing, parallel pricing, mergers, excessive advertising, quotas, subsidies, and tax favoritism. While defenders of the American dream guarded against socialism from the left, it arrived unannounced from the right.

What can be done? There is the antitrust alternative—breaking up shared monopolies into firms of more competitive size. Treasury Secretary John Connally has already dismissed the role of antitrust in the Nixon Administration's Phase II. The new controls "would make [antitrust] less necessary and, very frankly, *the matter has not been discussed at all,*" he said at a recent press conference. Others of this inclination charge "irrational populism" whenever corporate decentralization is urged, alleging it favors "Mom and Pop" stores over advancing technology. Clearly, only when the marketplace exploits actual efficiencies of size can the consumer get the most goods at the cheapest price. But the charge of irrational populism is misplaced when the point is that GM, averaging more than *$20 billion* in sales, could profitably be split up into three to nine companies, or that LTV, with *eighty-seven subsidiaries,* is neither efficient nor interested in the communities in which it invests. It is an argument for more $100 million firms and fewer $2 billion firms. It is an argument for the breakup and decentralization of many of our largest industrial corporations.

Beyond the "irrational populist" threshold, many others disagree with this suggested cure. One FTC commissioner, when asked what he thought of the Nader Antitrust Report, said, "Those guys are political dreamers. The Government will not break up the big firms." When asked why (since such lawsuits could be filed by his agency), he replied, "Because we wouldn't file such a suit." Catch 22.

John Kenneth Galbraith, in his *The New Industrial State,* ably points out the corporate control of the market mechanism, the seeking of growth not profits, the rise of oligopoly, and the blurring of private and public sectors. Despite this perception of symptoms, Galbraith goes on, *mirabile dictu,* to diagnose this industrial patient as healthy—exploiting efficiencies, encouraging long-range planning, and creating stability. To be sure, it creates stability (as does price-fixing, Galbraith should be reminded), but stability for *what,* and for *whom?* As it has been already argued, certainly not for consumers, that ninety-nine per cent noncorporate management sector for whom the economy, presumably, was constructed in the first place.

Even some of those who agree that laws and lawsuits against shared monopoly suits are economically valuable still get apprehensive at the prospect. There is first the fear of widespread disruption in American industry, to which economist and former antitrust chief Donald Turner has replied, "The disruptive effects are usually exaggerated anyway." Shareholders and employes would not be injured, since the divested businesses are not liquidated or given away, but are sold for market value and continue to operate under new ownership.

Second, for those concerned that deconcentration suits may be a harsh penalty for monopolistic firms, leaving monopoly uncorrected is a "harsh" treatment for consumers. A corporation is an artificial body created by the law which, in the interests of all, must be controlled by the law.

Third, some fear that monopoly moves might inhibit business growth by penalizing firms for their successes. But the chance that continued success may in the future result in an antitrust case should not slow down profit-minded corporations, which will still be tempted by the interim monopoly profits earned prior to any dissolution suits. And finally, many understandably wonder if the public, comprised of large numbers dependent on giant business, would support such serious reform. This is the core issue. Without a following—demanding legislative action, supporting bigger budgets, and encouraging creative enforcement—antimonopoly activity will remain a romantic relic at best, a political pariah at worst.

Can a coalition coalesce around this issue? The ideological interests of small businessmen, small farmers, and urban liberals in a more competitive economic system are obvious. Racial minorities and blue-collar workers, seeing their small fixed incomes buy fewer goods because of monopoly prices, are also potential adherents. Even conservatives could jump on the antimonopoly bandwagon. They are the dedicated critics of public power, the believers in decentralization, and free enterprise, and something called "the competitive spirit." When confronted with the realities of unchecked, centralized *private* power, philosophic integrity could propel many into the antitrust camp. Conservative Senators James Buckley and Barry Goldwater, for example, opposed the Lockheed loan because it violated the principles of free enterprise. A top economic adviser to antitrust chief Richard McLaren, Leonard Weiss, aware of this conservative attraction and the potential popularity of an antimonopoly drive, argued for a breakup of General Motors with this flourish: "In terms of winning votes, a big automotive case might be worth a hundred merger cases. Conceivably, it would make Nixon into another Teddy Roosevelt."

Perhaps. More evident, however, is the evolution of the consumer movement into what some trend-watchers have called "The New Populism." Ranging from tax inequities to shoddy merchandise to unfair property taxes, from auto bumper frailty to Pentagon cost overruns, there is a common thread of growing citizen hostility to the invisible bilk, that involuntary taking of income by unaccountable institutions. The extent and cost of monopolies can become as central to the New Populism as it was to the old.

Lawmakers as Lawbreakers

MARK J. GREEN, JAMES M. FALLOWS, AND DAVID R. ZWICK

With the miasma of Watergate fading into obscurity, it is necessary to remind ourselves that business goes on as usual in the nation's capital. This excerpt from Ralph Nader's Congress Project is a biting reminder of how power is abused in Washington.

"What this country needs is a little law and order." The cry comes from many quarters, but there is little agreement about who the violators of law and order really are: wise-guy protesters, troublesome blacks, street criminals, executives whose firms exploit and pollute, governmental agents who trample over the law in an attempt to enforce it. Yet a good place to start would be the American Congress. The most obvious reason is symbolic: if chosen men have the power to make the law, then they should respect the law. If they do not, they can scarcely expect that others will.

Corruption involving criminal conduct has shaken Congress at least since 1873, when the House censured two members for their roles in the Crédit Mobilier stock scandal. While Congress and the country have passed through fundamental metamorphoses since then, one constant theme has been the public's suspicion of the people it sends to Washington. This was not the constitutional mistrust that had plagued the Founding Fathers—the gnawing fear that men in power would become tyrants. Instead, it was the suspicion of personal venality, that the men in government were somehow turning a profit. In 1965, Gallup pollsters found that four times as many people thought that "political favoritism and corruption in Washington" were rising as thought them falling. Two years later, as Congress washed its hands of Adam Clayton Powell, Gallup asked whether the revelations about Powell had surprised the public. Sixty percent thought that Powell's offenses—which the questionnaire called "misuse of government funds"—were fairly common. (Twenty-one percent disagreed.) Powell had protested, in victimized anguish, that he was only one public scapegoat among many quiet offenders. "There is no one here," he said to his accusers, "who does not have a skeleton in his closet."

The skeletons vary in size. The smallest are the personal peccadilloes—which are the stuff of public amusement, scorn, and regular exposure by Washington columnists. Outweighing these in importance are the systematic violations of Congress's own rules and laws, offenses which are not quite crimes, but which are not quite cricket, either. Conflicts of interest are the next biggest skeletons in congressional closets. Finally, there is the *summum malum* of congressional crime, instances of bribery, perjury, and influence-peddling. Taken together, the pervasiveness of lawbreaking amounts to a grim commentary on those who govern us.

Not Quite a Crime: Peccadilloes, Rules, and Laws

Congressmen are people, and subject to the same temptations and flaws as other people. At times, their visibility makes them suffer more for their failings than they otherwise would. An omission or mistake which would pass unnoticed in a plumber may become big news when attached to a politically important name. This does not excuse congressional misconduct. Just as the public expects higher standards of personal morality from those who instruct its children than from those who fix its drains and pipes, so it expects high standards from those who make its laws.

In order to assure them freedom to exercise their duties free from harassment, congressmen are granted immunity from arrest for statements made, or actions taken, in Congress, or while coming from or going to Congress. This desirable privilege, however, has frequently been abused by congressmen caught in unsavory escapades. In his prepresidential days, for example, Senator Warren Harding was surprised by two New York policemen while visiting friend Nan Britton in a hotel room. As the police prepared to arrest him on charges of fornication, carnal knowledge, and drunken driving, Harding successfully argued that as a senator he could not be arrested. It was hardly what the Constitution intended for congressional immunity, but it worked well here.

Several years ago, Texas Congressman Joe Pool rammed his car into the back of another car stopped at a red light. Pool refused to accept a traffic ticket from a policeman and, later, from his sergeant. Instead, he repeated over and over, "I am a congressman and I cannot be arrested." Unimpressed, the police held him for six hours before releasing him. "He kept saying he was a congressman," said the policeman, "but he didn't look like one or sound like one." Later, Pool confided to a friend, "I thought they couldn't arrest a congressman unless he'd committed a felony. But it turns out they *can* unless he's en route to or returning from a session of Congress."

They *can*, but they *don't*. On the way to a party in the summer of 1972, Mississippi Congressman Jamie Whitten—who normally conducts himself with decorum—ran a stop sign in Georgetown and struck a car, an iron fence, two trees, a brick wall, and another car on the other side of the wall. Whitten said his accelerator stuck, but an investigating officer said at the scene, "The guy's been drinking; there's alcohol on his breath. I don't think he's drunk. But he's shook up." No arrest was made and no charges were filed. "The first thing [Whitten] did," said the owner of the wall, "was to get out of the car and begin shaking everyone's hand."

The same scene is played out in endless variations. Imagine the discomfiture of the Washington cop who, in August, 1970, watched a large car cruise through a red light and gave chase, lights flashing and siren screaming. More than a mile later, the fleeing car lost its spirit, pulled to the side of the road, and disgorged Senator Strom Thurmond. Thurmond claimed he hadn't run the light, and was immune even if he had. The policeman and his chief went along. Their embarrassment, however, could not compare with that of another D.C. policeman who, in May, 1969, had the bad luck to be in Congressman Charles Chamberlain's way. Chamberlain's car hit the policeman and then drove on. Onlookers caught up with him within four blocks, but Chamberlain successfully claimed immunity from ticketing or arrest. So did Congressman Peter Kyros, who had trouble like Whitten's on the same Georgetown streets. He careened from side to side down one road, hit two parked cars, drifted around a corner, and hit another car. He then left the scene. To the casual observer, this has elements of being a hit-and-run. To the police, it was a pointless and nonenforceable case: Kyros was "immune from arrest when going to and from the halls of Congress"—even though he had actually been going to and from a dinner party.

Annoying as these cases might be, they are small potatoes. They involve single, unplanned romps, not deliberate self-enrichments or serious affairs of state. If this were the extent of congressional lawlessness, we could all sleep a little easier at night.

But it's not. Worse is the hypocrisy of congressmen violating their own rules. A classic illustration is junketing. Congressmen who legislate about foreign affairs or military bases may do a better job if they've seen some of the areas for themselves. That's the theory. In practice, however, many trips are personal vacations (with family) rather than public fact-findings. In 1971, 51 percent of Congress, or 53 senators and 221 representatives, took foreign trips at public expense; the total cost to taxpayers was $1,114,386. Hong Kong and the Caribbean turned out to be favorite destinations for those supposedly seeking self-education. "Scratch hard in December," one congressman joked, "and you'll come up with a quorum in Hong Kong." There may even be motives beyond the chance of a vacation. "Those who do get away," Jerry Landauer has written in the *Wall Street Journal*, "will enjoy little-known opportunities [double-billings, for example] for lining their own pockets—opportunities that some have exploited in the past."

A second hoary example of bending the rules for private benefit is abuse of the franking privilege—the congressman's right to free postage. Every time you receive mail with his signature where the stamp usually goes, you are receiving franked mail. In theory, the frank can only be used for official business and never for political mail. The line is fine, and the effort it would take to inspect the hundreds of bins full of mail which roll down congressional office corridors every day would hardly be worthwhile. The cost of abuse can still be serious. In 1968, Senator Everett Dirksen was found to have given some of his franked envelopes to an overtly political organization—a Republican voter registration group. There was no estimate of the cost involved, but there was in an earlier case involving Senator Robert Griffin. After looking through some of the newsletters Griffin had sent out during the 1966 campaign, the Post Office decided that some were political campaign material. In a typical, doomed display of strength, the Post Office demanded $25,000 from Griffin to pay for the postage. Griffin, astonished, said that his mail was no more political than anyone else's. This gives scant consolation to the Post Office or the taxpayers, but it removed the heat from Griffin. The Post Office conceded the struggle with the droll statement that use of the frank is "a matter strictly between the member of Congress and his conscience."

Large-scale juggling of committee rules and committee staff is also widespread. Committee chairmen, as chapter 3 noted, can be tyrants. When it serves their purposes, they can simply ignore the rules, or, when it serves their purposes, they can become maniacal defenders of every conceivable rule and technicality. "It's my game, baby," Chairman Adam Clayton Powell once explained to the grumbling members of his House Labor and Public Welfare Committee.

But one rule is almost universally violated: committee chairmen use staff members who are assigned to the committee as if they were their own personal employees. It is almost impossible, for example, to separate men who work for Senator Warren Magnuson from those who are supposed to serve the Commerce Committee, which Magnuson chairs. This springs less from any special avarice in the chairmen's souls than from the committee and seniority systems themselves. The fond references that a chairman will make to "my" committee shows how deep the confusion runs. When a chairman lifts a researcher from "his" committee and puts him to work on some other task, more than the committee suffers. The system of fortresslike power bases, built around the mighty chairmen, grows stronger as well. Before his downfall, Senator Tom Dodd reportedly had thirteen of the twenty-one staff members of the Juvenile Delinquency subcommittee working for Dodd's office. Occasionally, voices rise in complaint—as a *New York Times* editorial did against a similar abuse by former Congressman Charles Buckley, who chaired the House Public Works Committee—but toleration is the rule.

Congressmen suffer equally mild twinges of conscience about using their own staff members for political campaigns. The element of abuse is clear: staff men are paid by the government, not by the senator or representative; they are paid to serve *the office,* not to help the man who happens to be in office to stay there. In 1968, the two Senators Kennedy admitted that twenty of their staffers were working on Robert Kennedy's presidential campaign. If other senators do not reveal how many of their staffers serve reelection drives, it is probably because no one realizes it's wrong. When interviewers from the Nader Congress Project asked about this practice, few congressmen realized it was illegal. But it *is* illegal: Public Law 89–90 says an assistant can't be paid "if such does not perform the services for which he receives such compensation, in the offices of such Member . . ." Because the law is so widely violated, violation becomes custom, and custom replaces law. There are many instances of this phenomenon. Nearly all congressmen violated the archaic 1925 Federal Corrupt Practices Act (replaced in 1972), which aimed to limit campaign funding and to require some disclosure of campaign finances, yet no one has ever been prosecuted for it. An 1872 law directs House and Senate officials to deduct from a member's salary a day's pay for each day's absence, except for illness; in the last hundred years this has been done exactly twice, although there are absentees daily.

Nor is Congress always attentive to even international or constitutional law. Congressman John Rooney, for example, has managed to obstruct American funding of the International Labor Organization because he fears its leftist leanings. In so doing, he violates our UN obligation to support the ILO. Similarly, the whole Congress defied UN agreements with one clause of the 1972 Military Procurement Act. In one of its shoddiest exhibitions—since, according to many witnesses, alcohol affected some members in the late-night debate—the Senate on September 30, 1971, passed a provision requiring the president to break the international embargo against Rhodesia by buying Rhodesian chrome. In April, 1971, a federal district court judge said that the 117 senators and representatives who were officers in the Army, Air Force, or Naval Reserve violated "the principle of separation of powers." No congressman, according to the Constitution, may hold any other position in the government. As of this writing no congressional reservist has voluntarily resigned his commission.

In feudal societies, man and job were identical. The king and the shepherd lived their roles every hour of the day. When 5:30 rolled around, they did not put down their work and retire to identical houses in the suburbs. The king had his courtiers and courtesans to remind him of his rank; the shepherd slept with his sheep. Though things have changed since Louis XIV said "*L'état, c'est moi,*" the pull of old ways is strong—especially to those on top. Like their feudal predecessors, the men who make our laws begin to see themselves as part of the law itself. They are only temporary potentates, brief occupiers of office—but in their few moments of power they feel themselves as durable and as permanent as law. They know that they will decide the rules that the rest of us must live by. If they can shape and manipulate the laws that are to come, can they not manipulate the laws which already exist? "Men tinged with sovereignty," Senator Paul Douglas once said, "can easily feel that the king can do no wrong." The privileges of the office—the staff, the prestige—inevitably start to seem like natural rights. In most cases, congressmen do not think they are doing wrong. For such small stakes—avoiding a traffic ticket, junketing to Hong Kong—few would consciously hazard the glories of office. If money were their only goal, they could earn $30,000–$40,000 by giving speeches, or they could follow George Smathers's route from the Senate to the wealthier fields of Washington lobbying. The lawlessness we see is simply the result of guidelines gone rotten from neglect.

Conflicts of Interest

Congress correctly demands a high standard of impartiality from those it confirms for executive and judicial appointments. In 1969, when President Nixon tried and failed to get Judge Clement Haynsworth onto the Supreme Court, the most compelling reason against the nomination was that Haynsworth had tried cases involving businesses in which he held small bits of stock. When industrialist David Packard was nominated as assistant secretary of defense, Congress required that he put $300 million of his personal fortune in a "blind trust," one which manages the money entirely out of Packard's sight. The ex-president of GM, Charles Wilson, and the ex-president of

Ford, Robert McNamara, had to unload $2.7 million and $7.1 million respectively of their companies' stock before being confirmed as secretary of defense. The rationale behind these requirements is biblical and clear: since no man can serve two masters, Congress insists that federal officials put their private interests aside before assuming public duties.

Unfortunately, this diligence stops when it comes to the congressmen themselves. No one scrutinizes their stock holdings to check for potential conflicts; no one insists that members sell sensitive shares. The only group with the power to screen the members—their voting constituency—is usually too ill-informed to make any serious judgment. And such conflicts are not considered a crime. In many states they violate the law, but not in Congress, simply because Congress, which writes the laws, chooses not to call what it does illegal.

With so few barriers against it, potential conflict of interest becomes commonplace in Congress. "If everyone abstained on grounds of personal interest," former Senator Robert Kerr claimed, "I doubt if you could get a quorum in the United States Senate on any subject." Kerr's own position neatly illustrated the problem. As a millionaire oilman from Oklahoma, Kerr stood to lose or gain huge sums, depending on the government's tax rules for oil. As a powerful member of the Senate Finance Committee, Kerr was one of the men who decided what the tax laws would be. It does not take long to see the conflict. "Hell," Kerr bragged, "I'm in everything."

Conflicts of interest in Congress take two main forms: business dealings and legal practice. Banks are the most obvious illustration of the first. In 1971, according to the National Committee for an Effective Congress, one hundred representatives held stock in or were officials of some financial institution. A dozen also served on the House Banking Committee. Nine of them had at some time accepted loans at special reduced rates from the National Bank of Washington.

Indeed, favors from banks to congressmen are frequent. In 1962, the first new national bank to receive a District of Columbia charter since 1931 let Senator John Sparkman—then heir-apparent to the chairmanship of the Senate Banking Committee—buy $10,500 of its shares at preferred terms. Congressman Seymour Halpern got even more personal attention. While struggling to pay off loans outstanding, Halpern in 1969 managed to get another $100,000 from banks in unsecured loans. His committee was considering banking legislation at the time. The First National City Bank of New York, for one example, loaned $40,000 to Halpern while its lobbyists were pushing for a mild version of the bill Halpern was considering.

The same pattern extends to other business holdings. From evidence turned up in 1969 financial disclosure forms, *Congressional Quarterly* estimated that 183 congressmen had interests in companies which either did business with the federal government or were subject to federal legislation. Eleven had interests in airlines, for example, 59 in firms with substantial defense contracts, 54 in oil and gas, 25 in power and light, 20 in radio and television, 19 in farms and timberland, and 16 in real estate. Clarence Brown of Ohio, for specific example, holds the majority stock in a broadcasting station —and sits on the House subcommittee regulating broadcasting. Brown may be a wise enough man to keep his personal affairs out of public decisions. But whenever he takes a stand—such as his opposition to public television—his financial stake in the outcome gives at least the appearance of impropriety. He is not alone. The late Robert Watkins, a former Republican congressman from Pennsylvania, was the chairman of an interstate trucking firm whose profits depended on rules passed by Watkins's House Commerce Committee. James Eastland, the Alabama Democrat who is president pro tempore of the Senate, and his wife received $159,000 in 1971 in agricultural subsidies; at the same time, he sits on the Agriculture Committee and votes against ceilings on farm subsidies.

One of the few congressmen who have bothered to defend such self-serving behavior openly is Senator Russell Long of Louisiana. Like Kerr, Long is an oilman. In the five years before 1969, his income from oil was $1,196,915. Of that, $329,151 was tax-free, thanks to the curious oil depletion allowance. Long is also chairman of the Senate Finance Committee, which recommends tax plans, including oil depletion clauses, to the Senate. A conflict of interest? Not to Long. "If you have financial interests completely parallel to [those of] your state," he explained, "then you have no problem." Even if it were true that the interests of a state and all its people can be lumped with that of one giant industry—which it is not—the haughty premise that lies behind this reasoning is alarming. What Long is saying is that each senator is alone the sufficient judge of his own propriety. Once he convinces himself that his companies are really in the best interest of his folks back home, "then you have no problem." It must ease Long's conscience to know that he is helping others when he helps himself.

Occasionally there are men for whom even these lush fringe benefits of political office are not enough. They count the moments wasted which they must spend on the tedium of bills and votes. Such a man was George Smathers. Even while serving as Florida's senator, Smathers was melancholy. "A person with my background can make more money in thirty days [as a lobbyist]," he said, "than he can in fifteen years as a senator."

In preparation for the easy days ahead, Smathers spent the closing days of his Senate career collecting IOUs from private interests. According to *Newsday*, Smathers led a posse of Florida congressmen in a secret attempt to salvage a floundering Florida company, Aerodex. Because of what the Air Force called "poor quality work which was endangering the Air Force pilots and aircraft," the Defense Department wanted to cancel a multimillion-dollar contract with Aerodex. After Smathers's effort, the contract stood.

In 1969, when Smathers retired, he claimed his reward. He became a director of Aerodex and got an attractive deal on stock: $435,000 worth of it for $20,000. The company also put Smathers's Washington law firm on a $25,000-a-year retainer. Smathers is now comfortably installed as a lobbyist, fulfilling his earlier exuberant prediction that "I'm going to be a Clark Clifford. That's the life for me."

The second important type of conflict of interest comes from congressmen who maintain legal practices. The moral problem here is subtler than that of the oilmen or bankers. A lawyer's business, like a doctor's or writer's, is built on reputation and skill. But when a lawyer also holds government office, his clients might conclude that he can do more for them than another person of similar talent. A widely circulated, widely respected study by the New York City Bar Association strongly condemns the lawyering congressmen. They are the fiduciaries of the public—administrators of public functions, the Bar study says. Accordingly, they must administer this public trust for the public's benefit, not their own. Instead, "law practices have played a disproportionate role in the history of congressional scandals."

More than a century ago, New Hampshire's Daniel Webster kept in practice for his Senate orations by appearing as a private lawyer for the Bank of the United States. He argued the private bank's case some forty-one times before the Supreme Court. There was no Committee on Ethics then, and Webster did not have to conceal the relation. When, in his senatorial role, he was considering legislation to extend the bank's charter, he wrote his clients to remind them that "my retainer has not been received and refreshed as usual." While the standards change, certain practices do not. The irrepressible Thomas Dodd, writing to his Hartford law firm for more money, stated the problem candidly. "I'm sure you know that there's a considerable amount of business that goes into the office because of me. Many men in public life receive a steady income from their law practices because of the value of their association [and] my name and association is a realistic fact which definitely has value."

Dodd is gone, but (according to Common Cause) there were still fifty-seven congressmen affiliated to law firms in May, 1972. One was Sam Gibbons of Florida. He sits on the House Ways and Means Committee; there he judges tax bills whose clauses can mean profit or loss for corporations. Gibbons's local law firm in Florida has among its clients six of the country's largest insurance firms; the second biggest car rental firm; and the biggest grocery chain in the South. Congressman Joshua Eilberg also has a law firm. One of its clients is the National Liberty Corporation, a mail-order health insurance firm. Eilberg lauded National Liberty in the pages of the *Congressional Record.* Customers trying to choose an insurance plan could thereafter read advertisements claiming "National Liberty commended in the *Congressional Record* of the United States Congress." (Eilberg later repudiated this insertion, saying National Liberty had misused it.)

If a congressman can endure the Bar Association's frowns, there is little to stop him from keeping up his law practice. There is a point, however, when the law imposes a limit. An 1863 statute forbids congressmen-lawyers from representing clients who have claims before the federal government. To avoid embarrassing problems while keeping the business thriving, congressmen have therefore devised an ingenious "two-door" system. On the front door of the law firm is the congressman's name; through this door come the many clients who value his help. Another door is just the same, except the congressman's name is missing. Here enter those proscribed clients with claims before the government. The ruse is within the letter of the law, but it still irritates purists. Journalist Robert Sherrill, for example, has said that Congressman Emanuel Celler's double doors are "one of the longest-standing and most notorious embarrassments to Congress." To this, Celler has had a standard reply. "Your constituents are the final arbiter of any conflicts, and I'm always reelected."

In 1972, after fifty years in the House, Emanuel Celler lost in his Brooklyn Democratic primary.

Crime and Punishment

It takes no special knowledge of franking laws or staff rules to understand the overt crimes, the calculated offenses against law and morality, committed by congressmen. Motives are easy to find: when the potential payoff is millions of dollars, risks for some people become worthwhile. The numbers are grimly impressive. In the last five years, five congressmen or their aides have gone or are about to go to jail for bribery, influence-peddling, or perjury; three more were convicted but given suspended sentences; another awaits trial; another was censured; and another was excluded from Congress. In this century, twenty-four senators and representatives have been indicted for crimes; fifteen were convicted, and two cases are still pending. Some of their stories, and their falls from grace, follow:

Bobby Baker. In 1942, with sixty dollars in his back pocket, 14-year-old Bobby Baker left Pickens, South Carolina, and never looked back. Like a lamprey searching for a host, he made his way to Washington, found the Senate, and attached himself for a twenty-year ride. First as page, then as clerk, he moved up the ladder. His break came when he made a friend, Lyndon Johnson. His friend became majority leader of the Senate and did not forget the small people he had met along the way. From 1955 until 1963, even after Johnson had left the post, Baker was secretary to the majority leader. "You're like a son to me," Johnson purred as he helped Bobby up. To Baker, Johnson was, if not a father, at least "my best friend around the capital." By 1960, Baker was being introduced to freshman page boys as "a powerful demonstrator of just how far intelligence combined with a gracious personality can take a man."

The tragedies of 1963 were a bad omen for Bobby. His old friend had become president—but had risen too high to keep in touch with Bobby. Critics began to grow suspicious about Baker's wealth. From a net worth of $11,000 in 1955, he had become a multimillionaire—an annual rate of increase of $200,000–$300,000—all while earning a salary of $19,600 per year. One explanation for the gap came when a civil lawsuit claimed that Baker had used his influence to help a firm win a government contract. With that, the Senate Rules and Administration Committee took a closer look at him. By 1965, the Democratic majority had issued a report citing "many gross improprieties" in his behavior—but no legal violations. To many senators, both Republicans and Democrats, this looked like a crude whitewash. Over the next few months, Senator John Williams of Delaware earned himself the title "conscience of the Senate" by hounding Baker and his apologists.

The legal ax fell in 1966, when Baker was finally indicted for fraud, larceny, and tax evasion. The major charge was that he had collected $100,000 from a group of California savings and loans executives for campaign contributions, and then kept $80,000 of it himself. Even as he protested his innocence, Baker realized that his exposure was straining some of his former cronies. "My friends in Congress," he said with slight bitterness, "have had no choice but to think of me as a bad dream or something." No one had less choice about the matter than Baker's best friend, the president of the United States. He retained public composure—even indifference—over the matter.

The callousness of politics was old news to Baker; he had seen friendships bloom and die in the seasons of convenience. He knew that "the American people would have destroyed and defeated President Johnson had he attempted in any way to do anything on my behalf." Still, Baker must have clung to some strand of hope. If a man had risen with a patron who was now president—could he be left entirely alone with his troubles? As far as Johnson was concerned he could. Baker went to trial, was convicted, and was sentenced to one to three years. By 1971, when he was released, the bad memories may have lingered, but the punishment was over and he was still rich.

Adam Clayton Powell. It was not his romances that drove the white folks mad—his colleagues had tolerated that in others—nor was it his laziness, nor his endless vacation trips. It was not even the way he turned every power of his office toward his boundless hedonism. Congress had seen it all before, and had forgiven. Adam Clayton Powell's sin was flagrance—his refusal to hide what he was doing. Others might filch dollars from the cash box at night: Powell skimmed off his profit in full public view. While Congress was in session and the committee he chaired slogged away at its work, Powell posed for photographers with Miss Ohio at his island haven in the Caribbean.

For a while, Powell tapped a special mood of the times. The same panache which enraged other congressmen made Powell a hero to his Harlem constituents: he was winning at the white man's game. In the two decades of his prime—at the time when he was being ridiculed in the House cloakroom as "the congressman from Bimini" or "the Harlem Globetrotter"—Powell sailed through elections as if anointed. He won his first term in 1944. By

1961, enough other congressmen had died or lost so that Powell became chairman of the Labor and Public Works Committee—the second black chairman in congressional history.

Toward the mid-1960s, after an earlier vigor and productivity, Powell began to spend large chunks of the terms vacationing—sometimes with false names, usually with lady friends, always at government expense. He kept up his family ties by putting his wife on his office payroll at $20,000 per year, a gracious gesture to a woman then living in Puerto Rico. A first brush with the law left Powell unscarred: in 1958, he was indicted for income tax evasion, but escaped the charge after paying $28,000 in back taxes and penalties. If he had stopped then, curbing the excesses and cutting down on the publicity, Powell might have spent another ten terms as pleasantly as the first ten.

He could not, or did not, stop, and in the late sixties Congress caught up with him. Already, he had become an exile in his own district. After being convicted of libel—for calling a black woman the "bag lady" for a graft operation—Powell could not return to the district he represented for fear of being arrested. In 1966, the disgruntled members of his committee began to hack away at his powers. Other congressmen sharpened their knives, too.

Their grievance was that Powell was bringing them all down. When one congressman is a clown, how seriously could the rest take themselves? Their own self-respect was only part of it. The constituents were also angry. "Nobody blames me for Howard Smith or H. R. Gross," one congressman said, mentioning two of the chamber's troglodytes, "but whites all over America blame their congressman for Adam." Morris Udall produced a letter from a constituent, addressed "in care of Adam Clayton Powell's Playboy Club (formerly U.S. House of Representatives), Stinksville Station (formerly House Post Office), Washington, D.C."

In 1967, the Democratic caucus voted to remove him as chairman. By a thumping 365–65 vote, the full House then voted to deny him his seat pending further investigations. Soon afterwards the Justice Department compiled a fifty-page draft indictment telling of falsified expense vouchers worth $20,000 and of Powell's secret destruction of incriminating papers from his committee; but no formal indictment was ever issued by Attorney General Ramsey Clark. Finally, the House declared his seat vacant and ordered a special election for April.

Powell won the election, and then won a more important victory when the Supreme Court ruled that his exclusion had been unconstitutional. The only formal losses were his seniority and a $25,000 fine for penance. Powell had survived, but in the process something had gone sour between him and his district. In 1970, he lost in the primary to Charles Rangel. Two years later, unrepentant, he died, at age 63.

In a Congress of untainted men, the harassment Powell underwent might have been understandable. Amid the mixed morals of both houses, however, Powell often seemed more a scapegoat than a culpable villain. As Richard Harwood put it in the *Washington Post:*

Like former Representative James Roosevelt of California, he has acquired three wives and a reputation for his romantic goings-on. Like Rep. Wayne Hays of Ohio, he has journeyed first-class to Europe at public expense accompanied by female assistants. . . . Like Rep. Joe Pool of Texas, he has ostentatiously defied the orders of an American court. Like Rep. Richard Bolling of Missouri and others, he has placed a wife on the congressional payroll. . . . Like the late Speaker Sam Rayburn of Texas, he dispenses whiskey in his Capitol office.

"You are looking at the first black man who was ever lynched by Congress," Powell had said.

Thomas Dodd. "I believe in God and Senator Dodd and keepin' ol' Castro down," Phil Ochs sang. And Dodd fit the billing. When the young Tom Dodd faced one of life's forking paths, he grappled with the question of whether he should become a priest. Instead, he plowed his energies into politics. If he was not combating sin in the individual soul, he could attack its manifestations in the national spirit; perversion, pornography, Communism—all must be defeated.

Although Dodd's targets were the classic ones, attacking them in the Senate won him few friends. In a body which is almost as tradition-conscious as the Church, the Connecticut senator stepped roughly on others' dignity. He overlooked the minor niceties; he called names; he impugned motives.

Thomas Dodd would not be a household word today if impoliteness had been his only error. Dodd's talent—his malign genius—was invested in another cause, his financial frauds. His staff was the first to notice. They had gathered evidence of a stunning range of dishonesty. Dodd had pocketed, for private use, at least $160,083 raised at campaign dinners, supposedly for campaign expenses; he had double-billed the government and other groups for other expenses, keeping the surplus; he had taken repeated private vacations and charged the government; he had used his office to promote the career of a retired major general who was a propagandist for German right-wingers; he had taken money from private firms, and then pressured government agencies for special treatment.

Doubts and difficulties afflicted the staffers. James Boyd had been Dodd's closest aide for the previous twelve years; Marjorie Carpenter had been his secretary. For half a year, the two wavered. "We shifted from day to day," Boyd says. "We kept wondering 'who are we to take him on?' "

A further problem was what to do with the data. "To whom do you go to get a U.S. senator investigated?" Boyd asked. The Senate Ethics Committee was likely to forgive an erring brother; the Justice Department was part of Johnson's administration, and Johnson was one of Dodd's friends; even the FBI was suspect, since Dodd had once been an agent. Their minds set, Boyd and Carpenter eventually took seven thousand documents from Dodd's files and gave them to the trustees of frustrated exposés, Drew Pearson and Jack Anderson.

Pearson and Anderson unloaded the charges in twenty-three columns, but for a while Dodd felt safe in ignoring them. He spread the false story that his staff was getting back at him because he had caught two of them making love in the office. Other senators closed ranks against their threatened fellow; according to Taylor Branch of the *Washington Monthly*, Birch Bayh wrote, "We're all with you on this yellow attack by Pearson," while Russell Long said, "I'll support you all the way on this, Tom, even if you're guilty." Dodd had his own explanation for the trouble: "The Communists have always regarded me as a prime enemy."

But Dodd made a crucial mistake. He demanded a Senate inquiry. It was a dramatic ploy, but one which proved his undoing. "Never ask for an investigation," one of his cohorts had said. "You might get one." The Senate Ethics Committee thus began its first investigation. Its report was less than Boyd might have hoped, but did unanimously recommend that Dodd be censured on two counts: for diverting the campaign money, and for the double-billing. On June 23, 1967, Dodd was officially censured by the Senate for the first count. His defense was an inspired peroration on the Senate floor, which concluded, "I am telling you the truth and I am concealing nothing. May the vengeance of God strike me if I am doing otherwise!" The plea moved many but convinced none. By a vote of 92–5 (Dodd, Ribicoff, Tower, Thurmond, and Long against) the Senate censured Dodd for his personal use of the campaign funds. Having done this much, the Senate pulled back and refused, by a 51–45 vote, to censure Dodd for double-billing.

Dodd's formal punishment was light. He served three more years in the Senate, gamely ran as an independent for reelection in 1970, and succeeded only in siphoning off enough votes to ensure that Republican Lowell Weicker won. The Democratic Campaign Committee—whose thirteen members had voted to censure Dodd three years before—contributed $10,000 to his 1970 campaign, even though he was running against a Democrat.

But the scandal left Dodd broken. He died of a heart attack in 1971, a bundle of contradictions. Exhorting law and order, he placed himself above the law; demanding staff loyalty, he was loyal to none but himself. In the mid-sixties, after Bobby Baker's fall but before his own, Dodd had angled to get the great glass chandelier that had hung in Baker's office. He never got it, and shared with Baker only his acquisitive ways.

Elites and the Ruling Class

CHARLES H. ANDERSON

This article theoretically ties together the other essays in this section. C. H. Anderson summarizes the work of famed sociological power theorist C. Wright Mills and uses his theory to link together the political and economic institutions of our society. Anderson attempts to answer one of the most important sociological questions: Who rules America?

Power Elite and Ruling Class: C. Wright Mills Revisited

Although C. Wright Mills himself footnoted his preference for the term *power elite* as opposed to *ruling class*, and while Marxist critics of Mills have been quick to interpret this minor reference at face value and thus to regard the Millsian thesis as opposing the Marxist view of power, a careful reading of *The Power Elite* offers no such conclusions—as we shall document below. The *power elite* is, in effect, Mills's phrase for Marx's ruling class, and he stands prominently among a few social scientists who have clarified the mechanics of power in the stage of monopoly capital and imperialism. His most important contribution was to bring up to date the principles of Marx, Lenin, and Veblen on the militarization of capitalism in its advanced stages. Oddly enough, it is precisely this important service which has been the focal point of Marxist criticism of Mills, which is that Mills misplaced the locus of power in capitalist society in the military. As we shall see, Mills used the term *military* in a much broader sense than his critics have understood.

First of all, although Mills elevated occupation above property as the key to an understanding of the larger class structure, he left no doubt over what he considered to be the ultimate seat of the higher levels of power: "Power has not been split from property; rather the power of property is more concentrated than is its ownership."[1] Furthermore, and logically enough given this position on the property base of power, Mills was not taken in by the popular contention that top management had assumed the posture of a new and powerful independent class of neutral administrators; this, among other things, aroused the animosity of the liberal academic establishment against Mills. Mills refused to buy the liberal rhetoric about the end of ide-

Charles H. Anderson, *The Political Economy of Social Class*, © 1974, pp. 216–233. Reprinted by permission of Prentice-Hall, Inc., Englewood Cliffs, New Jersey.

[1] *White Collar* (New York: Oxford University Press, 1951), p. 101.

ology. Mills recognized that the corporate elite are very much a part of the propertied class, either direct participants or reliable and loyal servants aspiring for full entrance:

> The top man in the bureaucracy *is* a powerful member of the propertied class. He derives his right to act from the institution of property: he does act in so far as he possibly can in a manner he believes is to the interests of the private-property system; he does feel in unity, politically and status-wise as well as economically, with his class and its source of wealth.[2]

Thus Mills was fully cognizant of the fact that many chief executives and top corporate officials are themselves richly entrenched in corporate property, as we outlined statistically in the previous chapter. At the same time, he was equally aware that the corporate elite and the propertied class are not identical, and that where there is no overlap, the former is subservient to the latter: "the executives of the modern corporation in America form an utterly reliable committee for managing the affairs and pushing for the common interests of the entire big-property class."[3]

The very rich, then, are the corporate rich, made wealthy through ownership and control of the property system. Mills goes on to state the *family* nature of corporate ownership, a corollary of the ruling-class thesis as opposed to the concept of all-powerful individual managers: "Every one of the very rich families has been and is closely connected—always legally and frequently managerially as well—with one of the multi-million dollar corporations."[4] More importantly, Mills was emphatic regarding the *class* orientation of family property interests, and referred to the entrance and participation of the professional manager into the corporate world as part of the "reorganization of the propertied class." In a key passage, Mills writes regarding this reorganization: "by means of it the narrow industrial and profit interests of specific firms and industries and families have been translated into the broader economic and political interests of a more genuinely class type."[5]

Not only does the propertied class recognize their common economic and political interests, but it has taken the shape of a *social* class as well—an over-lapping network of propertied families who have created supporting social institutions and developed a relatively sharp awareness of class organization: "They form a more or less compact social and psychological entity; they have become self-conscious members of a social class."[6] From a sociological perspective, Mills recognized the existence of a "top social stratum" or "upper class," having its chief social roots in the family, private schools, and, most importantly, the metropolitan men's clubs. And just as their economic base in the corporations is national, so is the upper class more than

[2] Ibid., p. 102.
[3] Ibid., p. 105.
[4] *The Power Elite* (New York: Oxford University Press, 1956), p. 10.
[5] Ibid., p. 147.
[6] Ibid., p. 11.

the sum total of local upper classes; it is a national upper class with a national orientation. The new rich typically find themselves on the outside of established upper-class social institutions and prestige, but in the end—though it may require more than a generation—naked money can usually batter down any obstacles.

The crux of the Marxist criticism of Mills is that his is an elite rather than class interpretation of power, and that this elite consists of corporate, state, and military rather than a single ruling class. We have just refuted the notion that Mills was not a class theorist of power. We now turn our attention to the complaint that Mills was an elite "pluralist." Knowing what has been said regarding the complete dominance over corporate wealth by the small capitalist propertied class, and recognizing Mills' stress on the force of sheer economic power in the capitalist system, it would be most illogical for us to expect him to jump to introduce governmental and military elites as co-equals in the power structure. Other unmistakable clues to Mills' rejection of pluralism at the top are his stress on the interchangeability of elite personnel and the coincidence of interests of the dominant institutions. At issue are the three leading institutional areas—corporation, state, and military. First, let us examine Mills' conception of corporate-state linkages.

Mills is unequivocal regarding the domination of the state by corporate interests, though he does state that "the American government is not, in any simple way nor as a structural fact, a committee of 'the ruling class.'"[7] The state is obviously much more, as it must be for corporate capitalism to survive. In *White Collar*, Mills follows the Marxist position of the state being more of a recipient of outside power interests than an independent force in itself: "In short: U.S. politics has rarely been an autonomous force. It has been anchored in the economic sphere, its men using political means to gain and secure limited economic ends. So interest in it has seldom been an interest in political ends, has seldom involved more than immediate material profits and losses."[8] Mills also emphasizes the decline of professional politicians at the top and the role of outsiders—men who bypass local and state government, never serve on national legislative bodies, are appointed rather than elected, and spend a smaller proportion of their total working life in politics than do the "pros." Who are these outsiders? They are "members and agents of the corporate rich and of the high military."[9] Mills long ago presaged the drastic shift in the system of checks and balances toward the dictatorship of the executive branch and the rise to unchallenged and irresponsible power of an inner circle of self-selected or appointed officials working around and within the executive branch. The state to Mills is neither a power broker of conflicting interests nor an independent power unto itself, but rather the representative of specific national interests and policies.

Now comes the closing of the circle. Whose interests do those having

[7] Ibid., p. 170.
[8] *White Collar*, p. 342.
[9] *The Power Elite*, pp. 23–32.

real power in the American state today represent? Mills neither splits hairs nor hedges on this point:

Not the politicians of the visible government, but the chief executives who sit in the political directorate, by fact and by proxy, hold the power and the means of defending the privileges of their corporate world. If they do not reign, they do govern at many of the vital points of everyday life in America, and no powers effectively and consistently countervail against them, nor have they as corporate-made men developed any effectively restraining conscience.[10]

Paul Sweezy writes of Mills that "when it comes to 'The Political Directorate,' he demonstrates that the notion of a specifically political elite is in reality a myth, that the crucial positions in government and politics are increasingly held by what he calls 'political outsiders,' and that these outsiders are in fact members or errand boys of the corporate rich."[11] How unhappily satisfied would Mills be today to witness his ideas receive such open confirmation from the Johnson and especially Nixon administrations! Among the many recent illustrations of interchangeability between the corporate elite and government is the career of Clark MacGregor, who went from being a top Nixon aide to vice president at United Aircraft, the eighth largest government contractor. In a period of increasing executive power, the White House aide has become a central figure in government, overriding traditional functionaries of democratic government.[12]

What, then, of the charge that Mills had a warped view of military power?[13] Critics of Mills have "overmilitarized" Mills' propositions regarding the military. By raising the question, "How did civilians rather than men of violence become dominant?" Mills tells us that the military ascendancy is far from an entirely uniformed one, though with General Eisenhower as president and Admiral Radford as his top advisor when Mills wrote, he surely did not exclude military brass from positions of power and influence. Mills states clearly that the military ascendancy "involves a coincidence of interests and a coordination of aims among economic and political as well as military actors."[14] Primarily, the military ascendancy refers to the militarization of the civilian definition of reality—in brief, to the military-industrial complex, or in Mills' language, the permanent war economy. The military includes the Department of Defense, the appointed presidential advisors and committees who draft war policy, the private defense contractors, the "think

[10] Ibid., p. 125.

[11] "Power Elite or Ruling Class?" in G. William Domboff and Hoyt B. Ballard, eds. *C. Wright Mills and the Power Elite* (Boston: Beacon Press, 1968), p. 124.

[12] George E. Reedy, "White House Aides: Faceless Agents of Power," *The Nation*, January 1, 1973, pp. 6–9.

[13] See Herbert Aptheker, *The World of C. Wright Mills* (New York: Marzani & Munsell Publishers, 1960); Kolko, *The Roots of American Foreign Policy;* and G. William Domhoff, *Who Rules America?* (Englewood Cliffs, N.J.: Prentice-Hall, Inc., 1967).

[14] *The Power Elite*, p. 224.

tank" strategists, the military research network, and the entire cosmology of military thinking that has dominated American life since World War II. "The warlords, along with their fellow travelers and spokesmen," writes Mills, "are attempting to plant their metaphysics firmly among the population at large."[15] To Mills, "the military structure of America is now in considerable part a political structure," and we have already pointed to Mills' economic interpretation of political power. Mills sums it up as follows: "Yes, there is a military clique, but it is more accurately termed the power elite, for it is composed of economic, political, as well as military, men whose interests have increasingly coincided."[16]

There can be no other conclusion than that Mills held to the militarization of political thinking, itself dominated by the propertied class in whose worldwide interests militarization acts. Mills leaves no doubt in this regard in *The Causes of World War Three*: "A real attack on war-thinking by Americans today is necessarily an attack upon the private incorporation of the economy"[17] (and not merely an attack on uniformed generals and admirals). Mills argued that political and social democracy cannot be brought about in the United States "so long as the private corporation remains as dominant and as irresponsible as it is in national and international decisions," and in order to achieve such democracy, "above all, the privately incorporated economy must be made over into a publically responsible economy."[18] Mills, as did Veblen, had a way of stating Marxist conclusions in his own terms, exactly what one would expect from an original thinker of Mills' stature.

Mills comes under fire from others for a number of other aspects of his power theory; one charge is that his is a conspiracy theory, another that he posits an omnipotent elite versus an undifferentiated mass. An objective perusal of Mills' works dispel any such notions.

Another misreading of Mills' power theory involves the belief that he overly maligned the morality of powerful men, failing to understand their fundamental integrity and upstanding posture in society. The ruling class is, of course, typically consistent and responsible when it comes to their own ruling ideas, as Marxist theory would suggest and as Mills writes: "The question is not Are these honorable men? The question is: What are their codes of honor? The answer is: They are the codes of their own circles; how could it be otherwise?"[19] And to adhere to these codes honorably is to perpetuate inequality, poverty, and decay, social and material waste, militarism and war, intense racial hatreds, hunger and disease, and other socially and morally crippling circumstances.

A related theme here is the view that the powerful are exonerated from

[15] Ibid., p. 219.
[16] Ibid., p. 224.
[17] New York: Ballantine Books, 1960, pp. 137–39.
[18] Ibid., p. 139.
[19] *The Causes of World War Three*, p. 51.

social problems and injustices, for they themselves are mere observers of the inexorable movement of institutions and, as it were, fate. For example, Livington writes: "Unfortunately the men at the top cannot in any meaningful way be held responsible for the actions the institutions take."[20] Livington may be a brilliant metaphysician, but he is a very poor sociologist. The bombing of Vietnam has, naturally, been carried out by institutions; no one is responsible—not Lyndon B. Johnson or Richard M. Nixon. These unfortunate men have been the unwilling victims of a cruel and mindless set of institutions which willy-nilly trapped them into taking massive saturation bombing and burning from on high. Against this, Mills' words offer hope:

> If, on the other hand, we believe that war and peace and slump and prosperity are, precisely now, no longer matters of "fortune" or "fate," but that, precisely no more than ever, they are controllable, then we must ask—controllable by whom? The answer must be: By whom else but those who now command the enormously enlarged and decisively centralized means of decision and power.[21]

In the Marxist tradition, Mills recognized that men make history, and modern men make history in a known and determined manner to an unprecedented extent. This is at once the scourge and the hope of mankind.

A final note should be made with regard to the assertion that Mills' power theory offers a static picture of capitalist society, and precludes conflict and change.[22] This assertion is a corollary following from the one that Mills portrayed as an elite-mass model of society. The point to be informed of here is that Mills' power theory in no way rules out class conflict and change. Mills set forth something of a vanguard theory of change, in which intellectuals, students, and social service professionals formed a potential cutting-edge of historical change toward a publicly responsible economy. It would not have been poor social science for Mills to write in the fifties of great class conflict, political turmoil, and social change? Simply wishing something, even if a noted social scientist does the wishing, does not make it so. Even today, after a decade of turmoil, there is the danger of over-interpreting the extent of class conflict and potential for change. Indeed, the upswing in political mobilization of the 1960s seemed to have had lost much of its movement by the early seventies. But in writing critically and positively, we are following Mills' own advice that to the extent thought changes the world, it should be oriented toward changing it for the better. Although Mills simply had no grounds for optimism in the fifties, surely his model of power and society closes no doors on optimism.[23]

[20] Joseph Livington, *The American Stockholder* (Philadelphia: J.B. Lippincott, 1958).
[21] *The Power Elite*, p. 26.
[22] See Isaac Balbus, "Ruling Elite Theory vs. Marxist Class Analysis," *Monthly Review* 23 (May 1971): 36–46.
[23] See the basic themes of *The Sociological Imagination* (New York: Oxford University Press, 1959).

Corporate-State Linkages

In this section, we examine more fully the Marxist proposition—also a Millsian, as noted above—that the state is primarily an embodiment and a representative of ruling-class interests. Parkin states the idea well: "Sociologically, the state could be defined as an institutional complex which is the political embodiment of the values and interests of the dominant class."[24] In the United States, we need only look to the Constitution for verification of this point. As Milton Mankoff points out: "The final draft of the Constitution was a masterpiece in terms of the political and economic needs of a highly class-conscious propertied elite."[25] In the ratification process, aside from the total exclusion of women, 40 percent of men were disenfranchised and a bare one-sixth of adult males or 5 percent of the population participated. And of the 160,000 votes cast, 60,000 were registered against ratification. Even then, many of the votes for ratification came only upon the amendment to the Constitution of the Bill of Rights, a move made after concern of some elite and citizenry that the Constitution would not be ratified.[26]

Domhoff has listed four major needs that business has of government:[27] (1) the need for the State Department as the key coordinating agency for overseas operations; (2) the need for the Defense Department to defend the American Way all over the world; (3) the need for self-regulation through commissions and agencies in the hands of qualified experts who understand business viewpoints; and (4) the need to collect money from the populace

24 Frank Parkin, *Class Inequality and Political Order* (New York: Praeger Publishers, 1911), p. 27.

25 Milton Mankoff, ed., *The Poverty of Progress* (New York: Holt, Rinehart and Winston, 1972), pp. 77–79.

26 Now, two hundred years later, the propertied-rich see the opportunity to ideologically revive the memory of constitutional independence on behalf of their own further aggrandizement. The American Revolution Bicentennial—with a 50-member commission board, drawn preponderantly from the Republican business establishment, showing the way—is according to Jeremy Rifkin and Erwin Knoll "a once-in-a-lifetime opportunity to promote the virtues of the domestic status quo in an atmosphere supercharged with emotional 'patriotism.' " ARBC Chairman David J. Mahoney is a personal friend of Richard Nixon, was the key fund raiser for Nixon's 1960 and 1968 presidential campaigns, and is chief executive officer of the billion-dollar conglomerate Norton Simon, Incorporated—a firm with interests in manufacturing, mass media, utilities, insurance, and elsewhere. The top public relations man in the ARBC reported to Nixon communications aide Herbert Klein that "the American Revolution Bicentennial observance should be developed into the greatest single peacetime public opinion mobilization effort in our nation's history." ARBC Director Jack LeVant wrote that the Bicentennial "could be the greatest opportunity Nixon, the Party, and the Government has as a beacon of light for reunification and light within the nation and within the world." Mahoney's wisdom is that "we shall remain the land of the free as long as we remain the home of the brave." "Reminding Americans to be brave," note Rifkin and Knoll, "—that is, to shoulder the burdens of an endless arms race and an expanding empire, and continue allegiance to the sanctity of the profit system—are the major Bicentennial themes." Americans will be fully familiar with the Bicentennial themes by 1976, although the Watergate scandal should have some dampening affect upon the operations of the ARBC. See Rifkin and Knoll, "The Greatest Show on Earth," *The Progressive*, September 1972, pp. 14–24.

27 *The Higher Circles* (New York: Random House, 1971), pp. 292–93.

for defense spending, research and development, and for economy management. These boil down to the twin needs for coordination and economic support. The latter need is easily the most important, and coordination actually is in the service of this need. To quote Mandel: "The bourgeois state becomes the essential guarantor of monopoly profits."[28] More than ever before the state serves as an instrument of shoring up the system of private appropriation of surplus value. State participation has been especially extensive through military spending and research and development of weapons systems, though many other kinds of government spending also extend profits and support, as does the structure of the tax system.[29]

The government role of coordination is served abroad by the State Department with the assistance of the Defense Department, though this administrative role is better served by the virtually self-sustaining far-flung private governments of the largest multinational corporations whose overseas staffs dwarf that of the State Department's overseas staff. Domestically, the job of coordination is performed by the regulatory agencies—though here again, government's role, while necessary, is eclipsed by the self-administering intercorporate power structure that ties the core industrial and financial powers together. The chief point to be made regarding the regulatory agencies, beyond the fact that they are largely the creations of the business class itself,[30] is that they do not regulate in the public's interest but very largely in the interests of the private groups and industries under their jurisdiction.[31] As Mintz and Cohen point out with regard to regulatory agencies whose job it is to control charge rates for utilities and transport industries, government agencies are largely rubber stamps for rate increases set in open collusion by industries or of unreal and wasteful rate bases which yield superprofits after figuring the government-alloted profit percentage.[32] Ex-utility employees sit on state regulatory commissions for utility control and ex-businessmen sit on state regulatory commissions for business control, etc. Little wonder, then, that Kolko can write that "there has been no sustained clash between any federal government agency in existence or created during this century and the industry it nominally regulates."[33] Although it would be difficult to pick out the most perfunctory and collaborative government-industry regulatory tie, the complicity of the FCC (the outspoken Nicholas Johnson aside) with regard to AT&T, would be a strong candidate.

What are the chief avenues through which the ruling class dominates

[28] Ernest Mandel, *Marxist Economic Theory,* vol. 2 (New York: Monthly Review Press, 1968), p. 502.

[29] See the discussion by J. K. Galbraith, *The New Industrial State* (New York: Signet Books, 1967), pp. 304–31.

[30] Gabriel Kolko, *The Triumph of American Conservatism* (New York: Free Press, 1963).

[31] Jack Newfield and Jeff Greenfield, A *Populist Manifesto* (New York: Praeger Publishers, 1972), Chapter 7.

[32] Morton Mintz and Jerry S. Cohen, *America, Inc.* (New York: Dial Press, 1971), pp. 70–74.

[33] "Power and Capitalism in Twentieth-Century America," p. 219.

state policy and activity? The chief avenue is through the executive branch, including the election of the president and, subsequently, a whole array of important appointments, not the least of which involves the high federal judiciary.[34] As the prime example of the latter, Nixon, whose office was bought very openly by the propertied class, in one term has altered the posture of the Supreme Court with four appointments of conservative judges. The court is on the way to losing even a reasonable resemblance to a body representing a just and democratic interpretation of the Constitution; it has been hand-tailored to meet the interests of the propertied class. Cabinet appointments and other high-level administrative and advisory posts, both foreign and domestic, have been overwhelmingly dominated by business and legal interests and personnel of the corporate world—personnel hired by the ruling class and loaned to the government and a large number of ruling-class men who have loaned themselves to the government. The data on this point are hard and unequivocal.[35] Nor do the proposition or the evidence fail to hold for the Democratic presidents of the twentieth century. The Johnson and Nixon administrations have been equally loaded with corporation-groomed and corporation-minded appointees. The main pivot of control, however, is the president himself with his wide-sweeping military, economic, and political powers. A small inner-clique of hand-picked aides, accountable only to the president, have reinforced executive fiat. Few modern presidents have proven so accommodating to large business as has Richard Nixon, and few have had the almost total and dedicated commitment of the business elite for their reelection. In 1972, Republican coffers literally brimmed over from corporate riches (much of it illegally donated at that), in essence profits stripped from the working classes. Money contributions, then, are among the main levers for getting accommodating politicians into office, including the president, and the ruling class *has* the money, be it for Democratic or Republican purposes.[36] In 1968, three hundred corporate directors of the top fifty military contractors donated $1.2 million to election campaigns.

Once in office, or even with mild opponents in office, corporate interests find that money bribes are commonplace solutions to corporate problems. In an election year, money is particularly forceful and useful, as IT&T discovered when confronted with antitrust activity or as the dairy monopolies learned when they sought further to inflate their prices.[37] After donating hundreds of thousands of dollars to Mr. Nixon and the Republican party, like magic, IT&T and the dairy interests found that the Justice Department and the Wage and Price Commission had altered course. And so democratically oriented taxpayers and consumers are forced to finance the defeat of their own principles and interests. Money bribes at lower levels

[34] See Domhoff, *Who Rules America?*, pp. 109–11.

[35] Ibid., pp. 97–107; and Kolko, *The Roots of American Foreign Policy*, pp. 3–26.

[36] Domhoff, *Who Rules America?* pp. 87–90. Twelve of the country's richest families gave $2.76 million to the 1968 campaigns, all but $150,000 to Republicans. Newfield and Greenfield, *A Populist Manifesto*, p. 190.

[37] Newfield and Greenfield, *A Populist Manifesto*, pp. 186–87.

of government are of classic proportions. (A recently deceased Illinois secretary of state had a lifetime public income of $300,000, but left $3 million, including $750,000 in cash hidden in his closet.)

There are also internal economic influences at work upon the complicity of government officials. For example, many have direct financial investments, assuring their support of legislation favoring the profits of big business; Russell Long of Louisiana as chairman of the Senate Finance Committee has been a staunch defender of the oil-depletion allowance, receiving $1.2 million from oil and gas production—including the $300,000 tax-free depletion allowance—from 1964 to 1969.[38] The case of high-ranking Senate Agricultural Committee member William O. Eastland of Mississippi voting against a $20,000 limitation to the farm subsidy while himself receiving vast sums ($117,000 in 1968) is also illustrative.[39] A very substantial minority of senators, perhaps one-third, are millionaires, an incentive enough to be pro-private capital in the area of subsidy and taxation. The House is stuffed with small businessmen and lawyers, giving it, in Domhoff's evaluation, a National Association of Manufacturers and Chamber of Commerce perspective. Its currently backward stance, with several of its members excepted, on economic and social programs of all kinds lends support to this view. A further avenue of ruling-class influence within government, and a most important one, is through the domination of advisory councils and policy-formulating committees. In foreign affairs, the Council on Foreign Relations and the National Security Council have been largely directed by the interests of the propertied rich, as have two domestic advisory groups, the Council on Economic Development and the Business Advisory Council.[40] These various influential foreign and domestic policy-making bodies trace much of their specific supporting information to the foundation-supported research institutes in the nation's most prestigious universities, including Harvard (presidential adviser Henry Kissinger got his start as the head of a CFR study group there), Columbia, and Stanford.

Expensive lobbying is a further method of gaining influence, and business is far and away in the best financial position to succeed along this avenue. But perhaps we can overstate the importance of the process whereby the vested interests set their men and policies to work in the state. The ineradicable fact is that the ruling-class controls the means of production in the direct sense, rendering public officials *dependent upon it for their survival.*[41] For if the corporate economy falters in any significant fashion, the political administration standing behind it will fall as well. Government officials, elected and appointed, *know* and *understand* that it would not be realistic

[38] Michael Tanzer, *The Sick Society* (New York: Holt, Rinehart and Winston, 1971), p. 46.

[39] Robert Sherrill, "Reaping the Subsidies," *The Nation*, November 24, 1969, pp. 561–66.

[40] See Domhoff, *The Higher Circles* (New York: Basic Books, 1969), pp. 111–55.

[41] See Ralph Miliband, *The State in Capitalist Society* (New York: Basic Books, 1971), Chapter 6.

for them to seriously challenge and counter the interests of the ruling class. As David Horowitz has observed, "short of committing political suicide, no party or government can step outside the framework of the corporate system and its politics, and embark on a course which consistently threatens the power and privileges of the giant corporations."[42]

There are, of course, diverse opposing views to that which delineates the recruitment and shaping of state officials and policy by the propertied class. Bensman and Vidich contend that "the direct relationship between class and political power as postulated by Marx has been denied by almost all uncommitted thinkers."[43] (*Uncommitted* is a very appropriate term in this context.) Irving Zeitlin would hold open any conclusions regarding the relations between the wealthy classes and the state.[44] Others such as Robert Heilbroner would go to the other side and say that "the distribution of power between business and the state will alter substantially over the future in favor of the state and to the detriment of business."[45] Irving Louis Horowitz argues that political economy is dying and political sociology rising.[46] John Kenneth Galbraith, at least by preference if not interpretation of fact, sees private industry becoming increasingly entangled with government, not as a ruling class imposing its selfish interests, but as an equal partner oriented toward the satisfaction of social needs.[47]

We can agree with none of these positions. Andrew Hacker's summary statement, if taken in the broadest sense, is much closer to the truth: "The government's function is regarded as essentially custodial, tidying up much of the debris created by private pursuits."[48] It should be added, of course, that in the process of cleaning up, the government tends to contribute heartily to the debris and much less to its socially constructive recycling.

Elites and the Ruling Class: Recent Perspectives

American social science has been slowly finding its way toward a theoretical and empirical understanding of the ruling class. C. Wright Mills paved the way, and we have studied his contributions in some detail. Floyd Hunter has also made a valuable contribution to the clarification of the links between elite individuals and the power of a social class—that is, to an

42 "Corporations and the Cold War," in David J. Colfax and Jack L. Roach, ed., *Radical Sociology*, p. 281.

43 Joseph Bensman and Arthur J. Vidich, *The New American Society* (Chicago: Quadrangle Books, 1971), pp. 90–91.

44 *Marxism: A Re-Examination* (Princeton: Van Nostrand 1967), p. 106.

45 *Between Capitalism and Socialism* (New York: Random House, 1970), p. 28.

46 *The Foundations of Political Sociology* (New York: Harper & Row, 1972).

47 *The New Industrial State*, pp. 401–6.

48 *The End of the American Era* (New York: Atheneum, 1970), p. 139. Hacker continues: "While no society can be totally anarchic, the United States has as powerless a government as any developed nation of the modern world" (p. 142).

identification of a ruling class.[49] Two years after Mills wrote *The Power Elite* E. Digby Baltzell published an important study under the innocuous title *Philadelphia Gentlemen,* later to be reissued more appropriately as *An American Business Aristocracy.* Although Mills and Baltzell take almost diametrically opposing views regarding the legitimacy of the capitalist system of class power, their research is entirely complementary. Baltzell's contribution was made through his very careful and detailed examination of the *social institutional* structure of the business elite of one major city, Philadelphia. While the social dimensions of the power elite were incorporated into Mills' analysis, these nonpower aspects of the top stratum occupied a position of relatively minor importance. Baltzell devotes his entire study to an analysis of the history and structure of the upper class as a *social* class, moving from an identification of its economic interests to a full-scale study of its sociological origins and status.

Baltzell's class terminology is clearly defined and fits into the ruling class framework, albeit with fundamentally different intent. Baltzell employs three terms which are of direct relevance here: *elite, upper class,* and *ruling class.* (In a subsequent book, *The Protestant Establishment,* he develops the concept of "establishment" instead of ruling class, but they are largely interchangeable terms.) To quote Baltzell: "The *elite* concept refers to those *individuals* who are the most successful and stand at the top of the *functional* class hierarchy."[50] The most important functional hierarchy is business, though nonbusiness institutions, especially government, may also be included. In Mills' language, we have the corporate elite and political directorate. To continue from Baltzell on the upper class:

> The *upper class* concept, then, refers to a group of *families,* whose members are descendants of successful individuals (elite members) of one, two, three or more generations ago. These families are at the top of the *social class* hierarchy; they are brought up together, are friends, and are intermarried one with another; and, finally, they maintain a distinctive style of life and a kind of primary group solidarity which sets them apart from the rest of the population.[51]

Mills, too, had precisely the same reference point for "upper class."

Crucial to the understanding of Baltzell's use of the term *ruling class* is the prior understanding of the functions of an upper class. The chief function of an upper class is to exercise *power,* not to pursue social exclusiveness and leisure: "the main function of an upper class [is] the perpetuation of its power in the world of affairs, whether in the bank, the factory, or in the halls

[49] *Top Leadership, U.S.A.* (Chapel Hill: University of North Carolina Press, 1959); see also Hunter's *Big Rich and the Little Rich* (Garden City, N.Y.: Doubleday & Company, 1965).

[50] *An American Business Aristocracy* (New York: Collier Books, 1962), p. 20.

[51] Ibid., p. 21; Baltzell writes that "the upper class in Philadelphia is the only one which may be spoken of; *qua* class, in terms of a subculture bound together by a common tradition and a consciousness of kind which approximates a primary group; this upper class is a 'we' group in a sense not applicable to any other class in the city" (p. 79).

of the legislature. Whenever an upper-class way of life becomes an end in itself rather than a means for consolidating its power and influence, that upper class has outlived its function."[52] In effect, Baltzell is warning the upper class to beware of fulfilling Veblen's notion of a superfluous, functionless, and parasitical leisure class and to maintain a firm grip on the levers of financial, industrial, and political power. So despite his preoccupation with sociological phenomena, Baltzell is fully aware and definitive regarding the indispensability of power for upper-class social status. And quite logically enough, for without the appropriation of surplus value, for which power is required, the upper class could not afford to maintain its "distinctive style of life."

This leads us to Baltzell's concept of ruling class: "A ruling class is one which contributes upper class members to the most important, goal-integrating elite positions."[53] Thus, a ruling class is a financially and politically powerful upper social class; a dominant elite and a social upper class overlap to a great degree if not completely. Baltzell would add that, in addition to their maintaining positions of executive power, the upper class must also be *ethnically representative* of the elite in order to preserve its legitimacy and authority. Thus, his second caution to the upper class is that it must not put up ethnic barriers to all but white Protestant members of the elite. This second prerequisite is actually largely irrelevant. Top members of the functional elites are carefully chosen on social and cultural criteria, making it difficult for various ethnic groups to even get in positions to "qualify" for upper-class status. But even if the upper class were composed of all nationalities, creeds, and colors, it would make very little difference for the respective ethnic groups within the underlying population. The selection and grooming process that accompanies mobility into top elites assures ideological uniformity and precludes ideological representation of the political and economic interests of ethnic groups. For example, as Scandinavian Lutheran in background, I can take no comfort nor lend any greater legitimacy to the ruling class for the fact that William Rehnquist sits on the Supreme Court.

To sum up Baltzell, the United States has had and still has an upper class that is also a ruling class (an establishment), though it has of late displayed a dangerous reluctance to enter into active public and political executive positions and an even greater reluctance to open itself up to non-WASP elites. As a result, we face the problem of declining legitimacy and authority of the upper class and the rise of equally illegitimate elites—illegitimate, according to Baltzell, owing to their uncertified upper-class socialization and status. These elites must resort to more open forms of coercion and to deception to get their way. Baltzell has read the declining legitimacy and authority and the rising resort to coercion and deception by elites correctly. However, these developments have little to do with a lack of upper-class activity in and

[52] Ibid., p. 405.
[53] Ibid., p. 51.

control over financial, industrial, and governmental institutions, or with its unrepresentative ethnic composition. The fact of the matter is that declining legitimacy and resort to force and lies as a means of rule is due precisely to the perpetuation and predominance of upper-class rule over the means of production, which increasingly includes the partnership of the state. Of course, Baltzell doesn't see things this way, for his ideal is that of the classic conservative—an open aristocracy of wealth and power. (From Baltzell's own perspective, his argument undoubtedly appears stronger than ever after the fiasco of *nouveau* elites in the Nixon administration; and note that proper Bostonian Elliot Richardson came out looking "cleaner" than ever after his resignation as Attorney General over the Cox affair.)

Back in the radical ideological vein, G. William Domhoff forms a direct line of analytical descent from Mills and Baltzell. Employing a systematic social science research methodology, an extremely difficult task with respect to national-elite analysis, Domhoff solidly closes the connection between the power elite and the upper class. In two books, *Who Rules America?* and *The Higher Circles*, Domhoff (a psychologist by academic training) empirically grounds the upper social class within the dominant economic and political institutions of the nation, either directly or through carefully chosen hired employees.[54] Domhoff means essentially the same thing as Mills and Baltzell by the term *upper class*. By *power elite* he means the:

"active, working members of the upper class and high-level employees in institutions controlled by members of the upper class. The power elite has its roots in and serves the interests of the social upper class. It is the operating arm of the upper class. It functions to maintain and manage a socioeconomic system which is organized in such a way that it yields an amazing proportion of its wealth to a miniscule upper class of big businessmen and their descendants."[55]

The power elite, then, contains both upper-class people and non-upper-class people (the latter perhaps future upper-class given an amassment of wealth as a member of the elite). Data on stock ownership and corporate control indicate that, despite the fact that the non-upper-class elite occupy important instrumental positions, the upper class embodies the key power figures of the corporate world—owing mainly to its ownership and connections to great masses of property. In the state, too, upper-class members of the elite typically exercise greater influence and control than mere elite individuals. The studies of Mills, Baltzell, and Domhoff all point in the same direction: to the existence of a ruling class (Domhoff's conceptual system substitutes the term *governing class*.)[56] They document the earlier theories of Marx, Lenin, and Veblen regarding the relationships between property,

[54] These books stem theoretically from *The Power Elite* and *An American Business Aristocracy*.

[55] *The Higher Circles*, p. 107.

[56] For similar but more limited research studies, see Hoffman, "The Power Elite of Chicago," and Lynda Ann Ewen, "Economic Dominants and Civic Participation in Detroit," paper presented to the American Sociological Association, Denver, 1971.

class, and power. The documentation can be and is a laborious process, a process which nevertheless must be carried out. Yet we are tempted to conclude with Domhoff that "an upper class exists in American consciousness. *We* know *they* exist" and "They know They are members of a privileged social class. *They* also know *they* have a good thing going, which no doubt sets certain limitations on the activities and verbalizations of most of *them*."[57] And among the best things they have going is a property system that enables the transmission of the fortunes from one generation to the next, fortunes that are constantly expanding virtually on their own from the standpoint of the heirs and recipients, but in actuality are expanding on the backs of the working class.

What of the power of the technicians and intellectuals? Some would argue that technocracy has arrived. Professors, specialists, journalists, and politicians, according to Berle, "are thus the real tribunal to which the American system is finally accountable."[58] Galbraith's "technostructure" clearly approximates a technocratic interpretation of power. The entire end-of-ideology argument is, in essence, a pronouncement of the death of class politics and the ascendancy of technological solutions to purely technical problems. That such a view is a cover-up for the perpetuation of upper-class power and privilege is practically self-evident. Even when an engineer or scientist makes his way into the higher circles of wealth and power, he almost always succeeds, courtesy of the taxpayer and defense contracts, and his ultimate success is almost always as a businessman, not as a participating member of the scientific community. As Tanzer points out, aspiring technicians and scientists *leave* their practicing fields in order to excel at business rather than remaining technical specialists.[59] But even in their newly acquired technocratic or business capacity rarely do they go beyond hired subservience. To quote Jean Meynaud: "While they are relatively independent, even those technicians who have turned technocrat are induced by the structure of the system to play the role of administrators—often excellent ones—of the capitalist system."[60] And what of the "intellectual" or "man of knowledge" summoned by the top executives and powerful bureaucracies, in Mills' words, to "compose suitable myths, about them and it."[61] There is no question today, after witnessing over a decade of bumbling and tragedy in Indochina and the entire area of foreign policy, and knowing quite precisely the social engineers who helped conceive and conduct these policies, that ex-intellectuals-turned-bureaucrats not only compose complimentary myths about the position and situation of the ruling class and its interests but also take a very active role in formulating and executing policy.[62] As Mills pointed out over

57 *The Higher Circles*, p. 98.
58 *Power Without Property*, p. 113.
59 *The Sick Society*, p. 16.
60 *Technocracy* (New York: Free Press, 1969), p. 188.
61 *White Collar*, p. 154.
62 See Noam Chomsky, *American Power and the New Mandarins* (New York: Pantheon Books, 1969).

fifteen years ago, "persons of power do surround themselves with men of some knowledge, or at least with men who are experienced in shrewd dealings."[63] Yet to take the political sphere as an example, it is not Harvard professor Henry Kissinger who "calls the signals" on government foreign policy. Kissinger is rewarded for dressing up and processing the international political designs of the American ruling class, but too much "wrong" advice would land Dr. Kissinger back in Cambridge—or worse.

Regarding the role of the intelligentsia, we cannot resist quoting an analogy drawn by M. E. Sharpe: "The genie was able to do marvelous things but Aladdin held the lamp, and he who holds the lamp tells the genie what to do."[64] In our own terms, of course, the ruling class holds the lamp and the intelligentsia, particularly the technical intelligentsia, have evinced little inclination to take over its own lamp and use it for the advancement of the social and material well-being of the underlying population in the sense Veblen once envisaged as a remote future possibility. Undeniably, specialists are indispensable to the limited structural tasks of a technological society, but they are servants and slaves, not free agents, let alone masters of the house.

To recognize that the technical intelligentsia is instrumental rather than powerful is not to deny the predominance of a technocratic *world view*, a world view which nicely suits the interests of the ruling class. The political value of technocratic thinking is that it assumes that conflicts and problems are strictly resolvable and answerable in solely scientific terms. "Scientific" information is held to be available to important people in corporate and state institutions who make decisions objectively on the basis of this ineluctable data. The people are excluded as incapable of deciding such scientific and rational questions, and the people need not be involved anyway, for the intelligence available to the elite enables them to make the right decision benefiting the greatest number (may we take Richard Nixon's private decision—he evidently "consulted" no one besides Henry Kissinger—to carpet-bomb Hanoi and Haiphong with B-52s around Christmas of 1972 as reflecting access to such exclusive intelligence?). Veblen early pointed out that:

> It is to be presumed that, for the good of the nation, no one outside of the official personnel and the business interests in collusion can bear any intelligent part in the management of delicate negotiations, and any premature intimation of what is going on is likely to be "information which may be useful to the enemy."[65]

Veblen also drew attention to the fact that policy and decision-making is replete with "administrative prevarication and democratic camouflage."

In Larson's words, technocracy's "ultimate aim is to deny that human

[63] *The Power Elite*, p. 353.

[64] "Tangling with Technology," *Social Policy* 2 (July–August 1971): 60.

[65] Thorstein Veblen, *Absentee Ownership and Business Enterprise in Recent Times* (New York: The Viking Press, 1938, 1923), pp. 443–45. Also available as Beacon Press paperback edition, 1967.

will is involved in political decision-making. Crucial decisions are presented as the result of circumstances, which, when carefully and 'scientifically' weighed, necessarily and by themselves yield the answer." She adds that "the function of this ideology is to legitimize the profoundly anti-democratic character of the power structure."[66] In this view, there is no real power elite, only decision makers who carry out the "hard" dictates of social and technological necessity. There is the real danger that a sizeable portion of the population is in the thrall of this technological and scientific fetishism, much to the satisfaction of America's rulers.

[66] Magali Sarfatti Larson, "Notes on Technocracy: Some Problems of Theory, Ideology, and Power," *Berkeley Journal of Sociology* 17 (1972–73): 23–29.

SEVEN

The Family, Education, and Religion: Institutions in Conflict

WE ARE LIVING in a period of tremendous sociocultural change. The industrial revolution has massively, sometimes violently, changed the contours of modern society. Rapid change inevitably produces social disorganization, even chaos, and the major institutions of our society have been profoundly affected.

It has been said that no institution has changed as radically as the American family in the last 100 years. The agrarian family was a strong and stable multifunctional organization. Families were larger than those of today, primarily because children were a chief source of labor and therefore economic assets rather than liabilities. The institution was patriarchal, meaning that the husband-father was the undisputed head of the household. Divorce was rare, for the family provided essential economic, religious, and educational functions. A lack of emotional compatibility was no reason for destroying an otherwise "good" marriage. But the effect of the industrial revolution and resulting urbanization was to shift many of the functions of the family to other institutions. The school has taken over much of the educational function, the church has assumed much of the religious function, and the family is no longer basically an economic unit. Men and women no longer have to establish permanent relationships to meet basic economic needs. This is because the traditional male-female division of labor is becoming increasingly irrelevant and because economic security in times of sickness and old age is becoming a political rather than a familial function. A man without a wife can eat TV dinners and make frequent visits to the laundry; a woman without a husband can earn a living on her own.

While the stable, kin-oriented traditional society supplied its members with an abundance of primary relationships, the structure of industrial societies makes primary relationships difficult to form and maintain. Human beings seem to need intimate, sympathetic relationships for their overall well-being, and the family has become the vehicle through which the attempt is made to satisfy these needs (communes being another option). People now marry for "romantic love," "companionship," and "happiness" rather than for a satisfactory standard of living. And with these new reasons for getting married come new reasons for getting divorced. If you marry for "love," what happens when love disappears? Success is measured less now in terms of economic criteria and more in terms of emotional gratification. If divorce rates have increased, it would only seem to indicate the strains that must accompany an institution that has such an elusive quality as its goal. If people get married for such nebulous and ill-defined reasons, perhaps high divorce rates and marital disharmony are inevitable. For what reasons would you get married? Love? Security? To raise children? Is "romantic love" an adequate basis for mate selection? What influence do courtship patterns have on marriage? Could the structure of the institution be changed to better meet the needs of the individual?

It is also inevitable that fewer values and roles are agreed upon within such a rapidly changing institution. For example, although women have gained considerable equality, the nature of that equality is vague and undefined. Should women receive equal pay for equal work? Should mothers have careers? How much time should a mother spend with her children? Can children be raised by other institutions (as in the Israeli kibbutz) and come through the process with healthy, integrated personalities? Should the husband have more authority in the family than the wife? Does he? There is some evidence that young, educated women are increasingly dissatisfied with their traditional role in this society. A study of 10,000 Vassar alumnae, for example, showed that most graduates of the mid-1950s wanted marriage, with or without a career, whereas in the mid-1960s there was a significant increase in those who wanted a career, with or without marriage. The rising expectations of the "new feminists" emphasize the fact that women face many of the problems of a minority group. They sometimes receive less than half the pay of men for similar jobs, and the salary gap between males and females seems to be increasing. For example, while women in 1955 earned 64 per cent of the wages of men, in 1970 they earned only 59 per cent of the wages of men. Although 51 per cent of Americans are women, they represent 1 per cent of the nation's engineers, 3 per cent of the nation's lawyers, and 7 per cent of the nation's doctors. These discrepancies cannot be explained solely in terms of discrimination, but also reflect the sex role definitions of a culture which has traditionally assumed that being a housewife and mother was the natural destiny of women and has socialized its females accordingly. There are cultures such as the Tschambuli of New Guinea, however, in which the women become the "hard-working," "responsible" citizens while the men spend much time ornamenting themselves in order to be attractive to the women. Among the Tschambuli the women are defined as being aggressive, while the men are thought to be naturally passive (this is true even in expectations concerning sexual behavior).

Our changing society has also put new pressures on education. The present state of the educational system is one of nondirection, and many educational theorists disagree on the direction that education in a mass society should take. Recent critics have made some penetrating observations concerning the consequences of our present system and have asked some important questions: Do our schools foster creativity and autonomy, or conformity? Do our "leaders" actually want to produce concerned, involved, participating, democratic citizens who think for themselves? Is our school system a cultural cookie cutter for the middle class? Is our educational institution an assembly line for "adjusted" Americans? Is education just the process of job training? Is learning simply a matter of cramming our craniums with a multitude of facts and theories?

Who is capable of being educated? How much "intelligence" does it take? Can the school system function to preserve and solidify class and racial differences? Is the educational institution receptive to the needs of blacks, Chicanos, other minorities and the poor in general? Is it a means of upward mobility, or does it retard and stultify their development? Recently, 45 per cent of the Spanish surname children in San Francisco elementary school classes for the mentally retarded were found to be of average intelligence or better when retested in Spanish by a psychometrist who spoke Spanish. The children were originally tested in English. At the time of retesting, 18 per cent of the children in mentally retarded classes were of Spanish surname while only 14 per cent of the total school population falls into that category. The discrepancy is far greater for blacks, who comprise 53 per cent of the students in all mentally retarded classes but only one fourth of the district's students. Representatives of the black community have commented that black students also differ from the dominant group in cultural and language characteristics. Both groups, of course, have socioeconomic backgrounds which differ in many significant respects from that of the dominant group. How should we approach these differences in our schools?

Should students in a democracy have more voice in school policy? Should college undergraduates have a say about what is being taught to them? Should they have some influence in the selection and evaluation of teachers? What about the college or university's relationship to the society that surrounds and supports it? Should it critically analyze the society that feeds it? Should it be a hotbed of debate, discourse, and dissent?

The place of the religious institution in modern urban-industrial society is also an often debated subject. Cults and sects are religious movements in their early and most volatile phases. The cult, which is the simplest form of religious organization, consists of the charismatic leader and his followers. All administration is personal and face to face, and there are no professional leaders or organized machineries for providing salaries. The primary nature of the cult results in a high mortality rate, for once the charismatic leader dies or departs, the cult may disintegrate. If the cult survives, however, it establishes a more permanent organizational structure and becomes a sect. A sect is simply a cult which is no longer dependent on the personal inspiration of a charismatic leader but which continues to make exclusive religious demands such as adult initiation, rigid membership requirements, and continuous proof of qualifications. With time the sect may fully "succeed" and pass into the last organizational phase, the church. The church is the typological opposite of the cult and consists of a formal leadership, a membership by birth rather than achievement, and an institutionalized economic basis. With success, however, the original message of the cult is often transformed. In the beginning the ideology often contained a radical rejection of established society, and it was this message which both attracted the original membership from the ranks of the dispossessed and limited the cult's appeal. If the group is to enlarge, it must make membership easier and more attractive, but in the process the original goals may be displaced. The church is then no longer at odds with the world. Some cults, however, begin by emphasizing values that are shared by the larger society.

What should the role of the church be in our society? What is it now? Is it a declining institution? Is God dead? What psychological needs does religion satisfy? How much influence does organized religion have on your attitudes and behavior?

The cartoon which begins this section suggests that the effect of religion on behavior is limited. Have the major religious institutions generally exercised their moral force regardless of the stance of the secular power structure, or have they rationalized and apologized for injustice in their parent states? Does the church always remain with the status quo? Sociologists feel that organized religion has basically been a cohesive, integrating force in most societies. Religion at the church phase tends to support social values. Is there evidence of a change in this tendency? —D. R.

Selected References

(All are available in paperback editions.)

Coles, Robert. *Children of Crisis.* New York: Dell Publishing Co., Inc., 1968.

Glock, Charles Y., and Rodney Start. *Religion and Society in Tension.* Skokie, Ill.: Rand McNally, 1965.

Goodman, Paul. *Growing Up Absurd.* New York: Random House, Inc., 1956.

Kohl, Herbert. *36 Children.* New York: The New American Library, Inc., 1967.

Skolnick, Arlene S. and Jerome H. Skolnick. *Family in Transition.* Boston: Little, Brown, 1971.

The Grave Problem of the Tweeners

ARTHUR HOPPE

Once upon a time in the country called Wonderfuland, The Elders faced a grave problem: What to do with the Tweeners.

Now everybody in Wonderfuland had something to do—everybody but the Tweeners. The children went to school and learned mostly useful things and the grown-ups went to work and did mostly useful things. And being mostly-usefully busy, they were mostfully-usefully happy.

But the Tweeners were too old to be children and too young to be grown-ups. And far too smart-alecky to have around the house.

"There's only one solution," said the eldest Elder gravely. "As soon as they're too old to be children, we must put them away in an institution until they're old enough to be grown-ups."

The other Elders recoiled in horror. "Let's think of something else," said one with a shudder. So they thought. And thought. And thought.

"Perhaps, if it were a nice institution," said a kindly Elder tentatively, "with lots of grass and trees . . ."

". . . and games for them to play," said another brightly.

". . . and cars and beer and dances," said a third enthusiastically.

". . . and if it had an impressive name," said a fourth. "I know! Let's call it College."

So the Elders built an institution, called it College and put the Tweeners away there until they could grow up.

Of course, they didn't tell them that. They told them, "You must widen your horizons, assimilate ideas and prepare for life."

To widen horizons, instill ideas and prepare them for life, The Elders staffed the College with old men called "Scholars," who weren't good for much else.

Naturally, the Scholars, being Scholars, were more interested in Scholarship than in talking to Tweeners. But twice or thrice a week they dutifully tore themselves away from their Scholarship to talk for 50 minutes about what they were interested in to the Tweeners. Like, The Sex Life of the Angiosperm. Or, The Use of the Diphthong in Etruscan Funeral Orations.

As an incentive to assimilating ideas, the Tweeners were given letters. They got big letters to wear on their sweaters for playing games well. And little tiny letters, ranging from A to F, for studying what the Scholars were interested in.

After four years, they were certified "prepared for life" and released from the institution.

Everybody was happy. The Tweeners were happy playing games, drinking beer, dancing and accumulating letters. And The Elders were happy to have them out of the house.

Then one day a Tweener looked thoughtfully around and said, "But what's all this got to do with anything?" And the other Tweeners said, somewhat surprised, that they were hanged if they knew. And pretty soon the Tweeners were demonstrating from dawn to dusk, raising a terrible fuss.

"But we've given you grass and trees and games and dances and beer and letters," said the Elders, rather plaintively. "What is it you want?"

"Frankly, we're darned if we know," admitted a Tweener Leader, scratching his head. "But whatever it is, this isn't it."

Moral: College is a wonderful institution—for those who want to grow up in an institution.

Marriage as a Wretched Institution

MERVYN CADWALLADER

Although many Americans stake much of their happiness and fulfillment in life on their marriages, the statistics of divorce present a rather dismal picture of results. What do we want from marriage? Is love compatible with marriage? Does marriage as an institution nurture and encourage love or does it more frequently destroy it? Cadwallader reveals some of the inconsistencies within our marriage patterns and offers some suggestions of his own.

Our society expects us all to get married. With only rare exceptions we all do just that. Getting married is a rather complicated business. It involves mastering certain complex hustling and courtship games, the rituals and the ceremonies that celebrate the act of marriage, and finally the difficult requirements of domestic life with a husband or wife. It is an enormously elaborate round of activity, much more so than finding a job, and yet while many resolutely remain unemployed, few remain unmarried.

Now all this would not be particularly remarkable if there were no question about the advantages, the joys, and the rewards of married life, but

From *The Atlantic Monthly*, November 1966. By permission of the author.

most Americans, even young Americans, know or have heard that marriage is a hazardous affair. Of course, for all the increase in divorce, there are still young marriages that work, unions made by young men and women intelligent or fortunate enough to find the kind of mates they want, who know that they want children and how to love them when they come, or who find the artful blend between giving and receiving. It is not these marriages that concern us here, and that is not the trend in America today. We are concerned with the increasing number of others who, with mixed intentions and varied illusions, grope or fling themselves into marital disaster. They talk solemnly and sincerely about working to make their marriage succeed, but they are very aware of the countless marriages they have seen fail. But young people in particular do not seem to be able to relate the awesome divorce statistics to the probability of failure of their own marriage. And they rush into it, in increasing numbers, without any clear idea of the reality that underlies the myth.

Parents, teachers, and concerned adults all counsel against premature marriage. But they rarely speak the truth about marriage as it really is in modern middle-class America. The truth as I see it is that contemporary marriage is a wretched institution. It spells the end of voluntary affection, of love freely given and joyously received. Beautiful romances are transmuted into dull marriages, and eventually the relationship becomes constricting, corrosive, grinding, and destructive. The beautiful love affair becomes a bitter contract.

The basic reason for this sad state of affairs is that marriage was not designed to bear the burdens now being asked of it by the urban American middle class. It is an institution that evolved over centuries to meet some very specific functional needs of a nonindustrial society. Romantic love was viewed as tragic, or merely irrelevant. Today it is the titillating prelude to domestic tragedy, or, perhaps more frequently, to domestic grotesqueries that are only pathetic.

Marriage was not designed as a mechanism for providing friendship, erotic experience, romantic love, personal fulfillment, continuous lay psychotherapy, or recreation. The Western European family was not designed to carry a lifelong load of highly emotional romantic freight. Given its present structure, it simply has to fail when asked to do so. The very idea of an irrevocable contract obligating the parties concerned to a lifetime of romantic effort is utterly absurd.

Other pressures of the present era have tended to overburden marriage with expectations it cannot fulfill. Industrialized, urbanized America is a society which has lost the sense of community. Our ties to our society, to the bustling multitudes that make up this dazzling kaleidoscope of contemporary America, are as formal and superficial as they are numerous. We all search for community, and yet we know that the search is futile. Cut off from the support and satisfactions that flow from community, the confused and searching young American can do little but place all of his bets on creating a community in microcosm, his own marriage.

And so the ideal we struggle to reach in our love relationship is that of complete candor, total honesty. Out there all is phony, but within the romantic family there are to be no dishonest games, no hypocrisy, no misunderstanding. Here we have a painful paradox, for I submit that total exposure is probably always mutually destructive in the long run. What starts out as a tender coming together to share one's whole person with the beloved is transmuted by too much togetherness into attack and counterattack, doubt, disillusionment, and ambivalance. The moment the once-upon-a-time lover catches a glimpse of his own hatred, something precious and fragile is shattered. And soon another brave marriage will end.

The purposes of marriage have changed radically, yet we cling desperately to the outmoded structures of the past. Adult Americans behave as though the more obvious the contradiction between the old and the new, the more sentimental and irrational should be their advice to young people who are going steady or are engaged. Our schools, both high schools and colleges, teach sentimental rubbish in their marriage and family courses. The texts make much of a posture of hard-nosed objectivity that is neither objective nor hard-nosed. The basic structure of Western marriage is never questioned, alternatives are not proposed or discussed. Instead, the prospective young bride and bridegroom are offered housekeeping advice and told to work hard at making their marriage succeed. The chapter on sex, complete with ugly diagrams of the male and female genitals, is probably wedged in between a chapter on budgets and life insurance. The message is that if your marriage fails, you have been weighed in the domestic balance and found wanting. Perhaps you did not master the fifth position for sexual intercourse, or maybe you bought cheap term life rather than a preferred policy with income protection and retirement benefits. If taught honestly, these courses would alert the teen-ager and young adult to the realities of matrimonial life in the United States and try to advise them on how to survive marriage if they insist on that hazardous venture.

But teen-agers and young adults do insist upon it in greater and greater numbers with each passing year. And one of the reasons they do get married with such astonishing certainty is because they find themselves immersed in a culture that is preoccupied with and schizophrenic about sex. Advertising, entertainment, and fashion are all designed to produce and then to exploit sexual tension. Sexually aroused at an early age and asked to postpone marriage until they become adults, they have no recourse but to fill the intervening years with courtship rituals and games that are supposed to be sexy but sexless. Dating is expected to culminate in going steady, and that is the beginning of the end. The dating game hinges on an important exchange. The male wants sexual intimacy, and the female wants social commitment. The game involves bartering sex for security amid the sweet and heady agitations of a romantic entanglement. Once the game reaches the going-steady stage, marriage is virtually inevitable. The teen-ager finds himself driven into a corner, and the one way to legitimize his sex play and assuage the guilt is to plan marriage.

Another reason for the upsurge in young marriages is the real cultural break between teen-agers and adults in our society. This is a recent phenomenon. In my generation there was no teen culture. Adolescents wanted to become adults as soon as possible. The teen-age years were a time of impatient waiting, as teen-age boys tried to dress and act like little men. Adolescents sang the adults' songs ("South of the Border," "The Music Goes Round and Round," "Mairzy Doats"—notice I didn't say anything about the quality of the music), saw their movies, listened to their radios, and waited confidently to be allowed in. We had no money, and so there was no teen-age market. There was nothing to do then but get it over with. The boundary line was sharp, and you crossed it when you took your first serious job, when you passed the employment test.

Now there is a very definite adolescent culture, which is in many ways hostile to the dreary culture of the adult world. In its most extreme form it borrows from the beats and turns the middle-class value system inside out. The hip teen-ager on Macdougal Street or Telegraph Avenue can buy a costume and go to a freak show. It's fun to be an Indian, a prankster, a beat, or a swinging troubadour. He can get stoned. That particular trip leads to instant mysticism.

Even in less extreme forms, teen culture is weighted against the adult world of responsibility. I recently asked a roomful of eighteen-year-olds to tell me what an adult is. Their deliberate answer, after hours of discussion, was that an adult is someone who no longer plays, who is no longer playful. Is Bob Dylan an adult? No, never! Of course they did not want to remain children, or teens, or adolescents; but they did want to remain youthful, playful, free of squares, and free of responsibility. The teen-ager wants to be old enough to drive, drink, screw, and travel. He does not want to get pushed into square maturity. He wants to drag the main, be a surf bum, a ski bum, or dream of being a bum. He doesn't want to go to Vietnam, or to IBM, or to buy a split-level house in Knotty Pines Estates.

This swing away from responsibility quite predictably produces frictions between the adolescent and his parents. The clash of cultures is likely to drive the adolescent from the home, to persuade him to leave the dead world of his parents and strike out on his own. And here we find the central paradox of young marriages. For the only way the young person can escape from his parents is to assume many of the responsibilities that he so reviles in the life-style of his parents. He needs a job and an apartment. And he needs some kind of emotional substitute, some means of filling the emotional vacuum that leaving home has caused. And so he goes steady, and sooner rather than later, gets married to a girl with similar inclinations.

When he does this, he crosses the dividing line between the cultures.

Though he seldom realizes it at the time, he has taken the first step to adulthood. Our society does not have a conventional "rite of passage." In Africa the Masai adolescent takes a lion test. He becomes an adult the first time he kills a lion with a spear. Our adolescents take the domesticity test. When they get married they have to come to terms with the system in one way or another. Some brave individuals continue to fight it. But most simply capitulate.

The cool adolescent finishing high school or starting college has a skeptical view of virtually every institutional sector of his society. He knows that government is corrupt, the military dehumanizing, the corporations rapacious, the churches organized hypocrisy, and the schools dishonest. But the one area that seems to be exempt from his cynicism is romantic love and marriage. When I talk to teen-agers about marriage, that cool skepticism turns to sentimental dreams right out of *Ladies' Home Journal* or the hard-hitting pages of *Reader's Digest.* They all mouth the same vapid platitudes about finding happiness through sharing and personal fulfillment through giving (each is to give 51 percent). They have all heard about divorce, and most of them have been touched by it in some way or another. Yet they insist that their marriage will be different.

So, clutching their illusions, young girls with ecstatic screams of joy lead their awkward brooding boys through the portals of the church into the land of the Mustang, Apartment 24, Macy's, Sears, and the ubiquitous drive-in. They have become members in good standing of the adult world.

The end of most of these sentimental marriages is quite predictable. They progress, in most cases, to varying stages of marital ennui, depending on the ability of the couple to adjust to reality; most common are (1) a lackluster standoff, (2) a bitter business carried on for the children, church, or neighbors, or (3) separation and divorce, followed by another search to find the right person.

Divorce rates have been rising in all Western countries. In many countries the rates are rising even faster than in the United States. In 1910 the divorce rate for the United States was 87 per 1000 marriages. In 1965 the rate had risen to an estimated figure of well over 300 per 1000 in many parts of the country. At the present time some 40 percent of all brides are between the ages of fifteen and eighteen; half of these marriages break up within five years. As our population becomes younger and the age of marriage continues to drop, the divorce rate will rise to significantly higher levels.

What do we do, what can we do, about this wretched and disappointing institution? In terms of the immediate generation, the answer probably is, not much. Even when subjected to the enormous strains I have described, the habits, customs, traditions, and taboos that make up our courtship and marriage cycle are uncommonly resistant to change. Here and there creative and courageous individuals can and do work out their own unique solutions to the problem of marriage. Most of us simply suffer without understanding and thrash around blindly in an attempt to reduce the acute pain of a romance gone sour. In time, all of these individual actions will show up as a trend away from the old and toward the new, and the bulk of sluggish moderates in the population will slowly come to accept this trend as part of social evolution. Clearly, in middle-class America, the trend is ever toward more romantic courtship and marriage, earlier premarital sexual intercourse, earlier first marriages, more extramarital affairs, earlier first divorces, more frequent divorces and remarriages. The trend is away from stable lifelong monogamous relationships toward some form of polygamous male-female relationship. Perhaps we should identify it as serial or consecutive polygamy, simply because Americans in significant numbers are going to have more than one husband or more than one wife. Attitudes and laws that make multiple marriages (in sequence, of course) difficult for the romantic and sentimental among us are archaic obstacles that one learns to circumvent with the aid of weary judges and clever attorneys.

Now, the absurdity of much of this lies in the fact that we pretend that marriages of short duration must be contracted for life. Why not permit a flexible contract perhaps for one to two or more years, with periodic options to renew? If a couple grew disenchanted with their life together, they would not feel trapped for life. They would not have to anticipate and then go through the destructive agonies of divorce. They would not have to carry about the stigma of marital failure, like the mark of Cain on their foreheads. Instead of a declaration of war, they could simply let their contract lapse, and while still friendly, be free to continue their romantic quest. Sexualized romanticism is now so fundamental to American life—and is bound to become even more so—that marriage will simply have to accommodate itself to it in one way or another. For a great proportion of us it already has.

What of the children in a society that is moving inexorably toward consecutive plural marriages? Under present arrangements in which marriages are ostensibly lifetime contracts and then are dissolved through hypocritical collusions or messy battles in court, the children do suffer. Marriage and divorce turn lovers into enemies, and the child is left to thread his way through the emotional wreckage of his parents' lives. Financial support of the children, mere subsistence, is not really a problem in a society as affluent as ours. Enduring emotional support of children by loving, healthy, and friendly adults is a serious problem in America, and it is a desperately urgent problem in many families where divorce is unthinkable. If the bitter and poisonous denouncement of divorce could be avoided by a frank acceptance of short-term marriages, both adults and children would benefit. Any time husbands and wives and ex-husbands and ex-wives treat each other decently, generously, and respectfully, their children will benefit.

The braver and more critical among our teen-agers and youthful adults will still ask, But if the institution is so bad, why get married at all? This is a tough one to deal with. The social pressures pushing any couple who live together into marriage are difficult to ignore even by the most resolute rebel. It can be done, and many should be encouraged to carry out their own creative experiments in living together in a relationship that is wholly voluntary. If the demands of society to conform seem overwhelming, the couple should know that simply to be defined by others as married will elicit married-like behavior in themselves, and that is precisely what they want to avoid.

How do you marry and yet live like gentle lovers, or at least like friendly roommates? Quite frankly, I do not know the answer to that question.

The Future of Marriage

MORTON HUNT

In the following article Hunt argues that marriage is not a dying, but rather a changing institution. And the changes, he thinks, will lead to new forms that are better suited to contemporary needs. Present attitudes and behavior as well as future trends are discussed, including divorce, infidelity, "swinging," group marriage, and Women's liberation.

Over a century ago, the Swiss historian and ethnologist J. J. Bachofen postulated that early man lived in small packs, ignorant of marriage and indulging in beastlike sexual promiscuity. He could hardly have suggested anything more revolting, or more fascinating, to the puritanical and prurient sensibility of his time, and whole theories of the family and of society were based on his notion by various anthropologists, as well as by German socialist Friedrich Engels and Russian revolutionist Pëtr Kropotkin. As the Victorian fog dissipated, however, it turned out that among the hundreds of primitive peoples still on earth—many of whom lived much like early man—not a single one was without some form of marriage and some limitations on the sexual freedom of the married. Marriage, it appeared, was a genuine human universal, like speech and social organization.

Nonetheless, Bachofen's myth died hard, because it appealed to a longing, deep in all of us, for total freedom to do whatever we want. And recently, it has sprung up from its own ashes in the form of a startling new notion: Even if there never was a time when marriage didn't exist, there soon will be. Lately, the air has been filled with such prophecies of the decline and impending fall of marriage. Some of the prophets are grieved at this prospect —among them, men of the cloth, such as the Pope and Dr. Peale, who keep warning us that hedonism and easy divorce are eroding the very foundations of family life. Others, who rejoice at the thought, include an assortment of feminists, hippies and anarchists, plus much-married theater people such as Joan Fontaine, who, having been married more times than the Pope and Dr. Peale put together, has authoritatively told the world that marriage is obsolete and that any sensible person can live and love better without it.

Some of the fire-breathing dragon ladies who have given women's lib an undeservedly bad name urge single women not to marry and married ones to desert their husbands forthwith. Kate Millet, the movement's leading theoretician, expects marriage to wither away after women achieve full equality. Dr. Roger Egeberg, an Assistant Secretary of HEW, urged Americans in 1969 to reconsider their inherited belief that everyone ought to marry. And last August, Mrs. Rita Hauser, the U.S. representative to the UN Human Rights Commission, said that the idea that marriage was primarily for procreation had become outmoded and that laws banning marriage between homosexuals should be erased from the books.

So much for the voices of prophecy. Are there, in fact, any real indications of a mass revolt against traditional marriage? There certainly seem to be. For one thing, in 1969 there were 660,000 divorces in America—an all-time record—and the divorce rate seems certain to achieve historic new highs in the next few years. For another thing, marital infidelity seems to have increased markedly since Kinsey's first surveys of a generation ago and now is tried, sooner or later, by some 60 percent of married men and 30 to 35 percent of married women in this country. But in what is much more of a departure from the past, infidelity is now tacitly accepted by a fair number of the spouses of the unfaithful. For some couples it has become a shared hobby; mate-swapping and group-sex parties now involve thousands of middle-class marriages. Yet another indication of change is a sharp increase not only in the number of young men and women who, dispensing with legalities, live together unwed but also in the *kind* of people who are doing so; although common-law marriage has long been popular among the poor, in the past few years it has become widespread—and often esteemed—within the middle class.

An even more radical attack on our marriage system is the effort of people in hundreds of communes around the country to construct "families," or group marriages, in which the adults own everything in common, and often consider that they all belong to one another and play mix and match sexually with total freedom. A more complete break with tradition is being made by a rapidly growing percentage of America's male and female homosexuals, who nowadays feel freer than ever to avoid "cover" marriages and to live openly as homosexuals. Their lead is almost certain to be followed by countless others within the next decade or so as our society grows ever more tolerant of personal choice in sexual matters.

Nevertheless, reports of the death of marriage are, to paraphrase Mark Twain, greatly exaggerated. Most human beings regard whatever they grew up with as right and good and see nearly every change in human behavior as a decline in standards and a fall from grace. But change often means adaptation and evolution. The many signs of contemporary revolt against marriage have been viewed as symptoms of a fatal disease, but they may, instead, be signs of a change from an obsolescent form of marriage—patriarchal monogamy—into new forms better suited to present-day human needs.

Marriage as a social structure is exceedingly plastic, being shaped by the interplay of culture and of human needs into hundreds of different forms. In societies where women could do valuable productive work, it often made sense for a man to acquire more than one wife; where women were idle or relatively unproductive—and, hence, a burden—monogamy was more likely to be the pattern. When women had means of their own or could fall back upon relatives, divorce was apt to be easy; where they were wholly dependent on their husbands, it was generally difficult. Under marginal and primitive living conditions, men kept their women in useful subjugation; in wealthier and more leisured societies, women often managed to acquire a degree of independence and power.

For a long while, the only acceptable form of marriage in America was a lifelong one-to-one union, sexually faithful, all but indissoluble, productive of goods and children and strongly husband-dominated. It was a thoroughly functional mechanism during the 18th and much of the 19th centuries, when men were struggling to secure the land and needed women who would clothe and feed them, produce and rear children to help them, and obey their orders without question for an entire lifetime. It was functional, too, for the women of that time, who, uneducated, unfit for other kinds of work and endowed by law with almost no legal or property rights, needed men who would support them, give them social status and be their guides and protectors for life.

But time passed, the Indians were conquered, the sod was busted, towns and cities grew up, railroads laced the land, factories and offices took the place of the frontier. Less and less did men need women to produce goods and children; more and more, women were educated, had time to spare, made their way into the job market—and realized that they no longer had to cling to their men for life. As patriarchalism lost its usefulness, women began to want and demand orgasms, contraceptives, the vote and respect; men, finding the world growing ever more impersonal and cold, began to want wives who were warm, understanding, companionable and sexy.

Yet, strangely enough, as all these things were happening, marriage not only did not lose ground but grew more popular, and today, when it is under full-scale attack on most fronts, it is more widespread than ever before. A considerably larger percentage of our adult population was married in 1970 than was the case in 1890; the marriage rate, though still below the level of the 1940s, has been climbing steadily since 1963.

The explanation of this paradox is that as marriage was losing its former uses, it was gaining new ones. The changes that were robbing marriage of practical and life-affirming values were turning America into a mechanized urban society in which we felt like numbers, not individuals, in which we had many neighbors but few lifelong friends and in which our lives were controlled by remote governments, huge companies and insensate computers. Alone and impotent, how can we find intimacy and warmth, understanding and loyalty, enduring friendship and a feeling of personal importance? Why, obviously, through *loving* and *marrying*. Marriage is a microcosm, a world within which we seek to correct the shortcomings of the macrocosm around us. Saint Paul said it is better to marry than to burn; today, feeling the glacial chill of the world we live in, we find it better to marry than to freeze.

The model of marriage that served the old purposes excellently serves the new ones poorly. But most of the contemporary assaults upon it are not efforts to destroy it; they are efforts to modify and remold it. Only traditional patriarchal marriage is dying, while all around us marriage is being reborn in new forms. The marriage of the future already exists; we have merely mistaken the signs of evolutionary change for the stigmata of necrosis.

Divorce is a case in point. Far from being a wasting illness, it is a healthful adaptation, enabling monogamy to survive in a time when patriarchal powers, privileges and marital systems have become unworkable; far from being a radical change in the institution of marriage, divorce is a relatively minor modification of it and thoroughly supportive of most of its conventions.

Not that it seemed so at first. When divorce was introduced to Christian Europe, it appeared an extreme and rather sinful measure to most people; even among the wealthy—the only people who could afford it—it remained for centuries quite rare and thoroughly scandalous. In 1816, when president Timothy Dwight of Yale thundered against the "alarming and terrible" divorce rate in Connecticut, about one of every 100 marriages was being legally dissolved. But as women began achieving a certain degree of emancipation during the 19th century, and as the purposes of marriage changed, divorce laws were liberalized and the rate began climbing. Between 1870 and 1905, both the U.S. population and the divorce rate more than doubled; and between then and today, the divorce rate increased over four times.

And not only for the reasons we have already noted but for yet another: the increase in longevity. When people married in their late 20s and marriage was likely to end in death by the time the last child was leaving home, divorce seemed not only wrong but hardly worth the trouble; this was especially true where the only defect in a marriage was boredom. Today, however, when people marry earlier and have finished raising their children with half their adult lives still ahead of them, boredom seems a very good reason for getting divorced.

Half of all divorces occur after eight years of marriage and a quarter of them after 15—most of these being not the results of bad initial choices but of disparity or dullness that has grown with time.

Divorcing people, however, are seeking not to escape from marriage for the rest of their lives but to exchange unhappy or boring marriages for satisfying ones. Whatever bitter things they say at the time of divorce, the vast majority do remarry, most of their second marriages lasting the rest of their lives; even those whose second marriages fail are very likely to divorce and remarry again and, that failing, yet again. Divorcing people are actually marrying people, and divorce is not a negation of marriage but a workable cross between traditional monogamy and multiple marriage; sociologists have even referred to it as "serial polygamy."

Despite its costs and its hardships, divorce is thus a compromise between the monogamous ideal and the realities of present-day life. To judge from the statistics, it is becoming more useful and more socially acceptable every year. Although the divorce rate leveled off for a dozen years or so after the postwar surge of 1946, it has been climbing steadily since 1962, continuing the long-range trend of 100 years, and the rate for the entire nation now stands at nearly one for every three marriages. In some areas, it is even higher. In California, where a new ultraliberal law went into effect in 1970, nearly two of every three marriages end in divorce—a fact that astonishes people in other areas of the country but that Californians themselves accept with equanimity. They still approve of, and very much enjoy, being married; they have simply gone further than the rest of us in using divorce to keep monogamy workable in today's world.

Seen in the same light, marital infidelity is also a frequently useful modification of the marriage contract rather than a repudiation of it. It violates the conventional moral code to a greater degree than does divorce but, as practiced in America, is only a limited departure from the monogamous pattern. Unfaithful Americans, by and large, neither have extramarital love affairs that last for many years nor do they engage in a continuous series of minor liaisons; rather, their infidelity consists of relatively brief and widely scattered episodes, so that in the course of a married lifetime, they spend many more years being faithful than being unfaithful. Furthermore, American infidelity, unlike its European counterparts, has no recognized status as part of the marital system; except in a few circles, it remains impermissible, hidden and isolated from the rest of one's life.

This is not true at all levels of our society, however: Upper-class men—and, to some extent, women—have long regarded the discreet love affair as an essential complement to marriage, and lower-class husbands have always considered an extracurricular roll in the hay important to a married man's peace of mind. Indeed, very few societies have ever tried to make both husband and wife sexually faithful over a lifetime; the totally monogamous ideal is statistically an abnormality. Professors Clellan Ford and Frank Beach state in *Patterns of Sexual Behavior* that less than 16 percent of 185 societies studied by anthropologists had formal restrictions to a single mate—and, of these, less than a third wholly disapproved of both premarital and extramarital relationships.

Our middle-class, puritanical society, however, has long held that infidelity of any sort is impossible if one truly loves one's mate and is happily married, that any deviation from fidelity stems from an evil or neurotic character and that it inevitably damages both the sinner and the sinned against. This credo drew support from earlier generations of psychotherapists, for almost all the adulterers they treated were neurotic, unhappily married or out of sorts with life in general. But it is just such people who seek psychotherapy; they are hardly a fair sample. Recently, sex researchers have examined the unfaithful more representatively and have come up with quite different findings. Alfred Kinsey, sociologist Robert Whitehurst of Indiana University, sociologist John Cuber of Ohio State University, sexologist/therapist Dr. Albert Ellis and various others (including myself), all of whom have made surveys of unfaithful husbands and wives, agree in general that:

- Many of the unfaithful—perhaps even a majority—are not seriously dissatisfied with their marriages nor their mates and a fair number are more or less happily married.
- Only about a third—perhaps even fewer—appear to seek extramarital sex for neurotic motives; the rest do so for nonpathological reasons.
- Many of the unfaithful—perhaps even a majority—do not feel that they, their mates nor their marriages have been harmed; in my own sample, a tenth said that their marriages had been helped or made more tolerable by their infidelity.

It is still true that many a "deceived" husband or wife, learning about his or her mate's infidelity, feels humiliated, betrayed and unloved, and is filled with rage and the desire for revenge; it is still true, too, that infidelity is a cause in perhaps a third of all divorces. But more often than not, deceived spouses never know of their mates' infidelity nor are their marriages perceptibly harmed by it.

The bulk of present-day infidelity remains hidden beneath the disguise of conventional marital behavior. But an unfettered minority of husbands and wives openly grant each other the right to outside relationships, limiting that right to certain occasions and certain kinds of involvement, in order to keep the marital relationship all-important and unimpaired. A few couples, for instance, take separate vacations or allow each other one night out alone per week, it being understood that their extramarital involvements are to be confined to those times. Similar freedoms have been urged by radical marriage reformers for decades but have never really caught on, and probably never will, for one simple reason: What's out of sight is not necessarily out of mind. What husband can feel sure, despite his wife's promises, that she might not find some other man who will make her dream come true? What wife can feel sure that her husband won't fall in love with some woman he is supposed to be having only a friendly tumble with?

But it's another matter when husband and wife go together in search of extramarital frolic and do their thing with other people, in full view of each other, where it is free of romantic feeling. This is the very essence of marital swinging, or, as it is sometimes called, comarital sex. Whether it consists of a quiet mate exchange between two couples, a small sociable group-sex party or a large orgiastic rumpus, the premise is the same: As long as the extramarital sex is open, shared and purely recreational, it is not considered divisive of marriage.

So the husband and wife welcome the baby sitter, kiss the children good night and drive off together to someone's home, where they drink a little and make social talk with their hosts and any other guests present, and then pair off with a couple of the others and disappear into bedrooms for an hour or so or undress in the living room and have sex in front of their interested and approving mates.

No secrecy about that, certainly, and no hidden romance to fear; indeed, the very exhibitionism of marital swinging enforces its most important ground rule—the tacit understanding that participants will not indulge in emotional involvements with fellow swingers, no matter what physical acts they perform together. Though a man and a woman make it with each other at a group-sex party, they are not supposed to meet each other later on; two swinging couples who get together outside of parties are disapprovingly said to be going steady. According to several researchers, this proves that married swingers value their marriages: They want sexual fun and stimulation but nothing that would jeopardize their marital relationships. As sociologists Duane Denfeld and Michael Gordon of the University of Connecticut straight-facedly write, marital swingers "favor monogamy and want to maintain it" and do their swinging "in order to support and improve their marriages."

To the outsider, this must sound very odd, not to say outlandish. How could anyone hope to preserve the warmth and intimacy of marriage by performing the most private and personal sexual acts with other people in front of his own mate or watching his mate do so with others?

Such a question implies that sex is integrally interwoven with the rest of one's feelings about the mate—which it is—but swingers maintain that it can be detached and enjoyed apart from those feelings, without changing them in any way. Marital swinging is supposed to involve only this one segment of the marital relationship and during only a few hours of any week or month; all else is meant to remain intact, monogamous and conventional.

Experts maintain that some people swing out of neurotic needs; some have sexual problems in their marriages that do not arise in casual sexual relationships; some are merely bored and in need of new stimuli; some need the ego lift of continual conquests. But the average swinger, whatever his (or her) motive, normal or pathological, is apt to believe that he loves his spouse, that he has a pretty good marriage and that detaching sex—and sex alone—from marital restrictions not only will do the marriage no harm but will rid it of any aura of confinement.

In contrast to this highly specialized and sharply limited attitude, there seems to be a far broader and more thorough rejection of marriage on the part of those men and women who choose to live together unwed. Informal, nonlegal unions have long been widespread among poor blacks, largely for economic reasons, but the present wave of such unions among middle-class whites has an ideological basis, for most of those who choose this arrangement consider themselves revolutionaries who have the guts to pioneer in a more honest and vital relationship than conventional marriage. A 44-year-old conference leader, Theodora Wells, and a 51-year-old psychologist, Lee Christie, who live together in Beverly Hills, expounded their philosophy in the April 1970 issue of *The Futurist:* " 'Personhood' is central to the living-together relationship; sex roles are central to the marriage relationship. Our experience strongly suggests that personhood excites growth, stimulates openness, increases joyful satisfactions in achieving, encompasses rich, full sexuality peaking in romance. Marriage may have the appearance of this in its romantic phase, but it settles down to prosaic routine. . . . The wife role is diametrically opposed to the personhood I want. I [Theodora] therefore choose to live with the man who joins me in the priority of personhood."

What this means is that she hates homemaking, is career oriented and fears that if she became a legal wife, she would automatically be committed to traditional female roles, to dependency. Hence, she and Christie have rejected marriage and chosen an arrangement without legal obligations, without a head of the household and without a primary money earner or primary homemaker—though Christie, as it happens, does 90 percent of the cooking. Both believe that their freedom from legal ties and their constant need to rechoose each other make for a more exciting, real and growing relationship.

A fair number of the avant-garde and many of the young have begun to find this not only a fashionably rebellious but a thoroughly congenial attitude toward marriage; couples are living together, often openly, on many a college campus, risking punishment by college authorities (but finding the risk smaller every day) and bucking their parents' strenuous disapproval (but getting their glum acceptance more and more often).

When one examines the situation closely, however, it becomes clear that most of these marital Maoists live together in close, warm, committed and monogamous fashion, very much like married people; they keep house together (although often dividing their roles in untraditional ways) and neither is free to have sex with anyone else, date anyone else nor even find anyone else intriguing. Anthropologists Margaret Mead and Ashley Montagu, sociologist John Gagnon and other close observers of the youth scene feel that living together, whatever its defects, is actually an apprentice marriage and not a true rebellion against marriage at all.

Dr. Mead, incidentally, made a major public pitch in 1966 for a revision of our laws that would create two kinds of marital status: individual marriage, a legal but easily dissolved form for young people who were unready for parenthood or full commitment to each other but who wanted to live together with social acceptance; and parental marriage, a union involving all the legal commitments and responsibilities—and difficulties of dissolution—of marriage as we presently know it. Her suggestion aroused a great deal of public debate. The middle-aged, for the most part, condemned her proposal as being an attack upon and a debasement of marriage, while the young replied that the whole idea was unnecessary. The young were right: They were already creating their own new marital folkway in the form of the close, serious but informal union that achieved all the goals of individual marriage except its legality and acceptance by the middle-aged. Thinking themselves rebels against marriage, they had only created a new form of marriage closely resembling the very thing Dr. Mead had suggested.

If these modifications of monogamy aren't quite as alarming or as revolutionary as they seem to be, one contemporary experiment in marriage *is* a genuine and total break with Western tradition. This is group marriage—a catchall term applied to a wide variety of polygamous experiments in which small groups of adult males and females, and their children, live together under one roof or in a close-knit settlement, calling themselves a family, tribe, commune or, more grandly, intentional community and considering themselves all married to one another.

As the term intentional community indicates, these are experiments not merely in marriage but in the building of a new type of society. They are utopian minisocieties existing within, but almost wholly opposed to, the mores and values of present-day American society.

Not that they are all of a piece. A few are located in cities and have members who look and act square and hold regular jobs; some, both urban and rural, consist largely of dropouts, acidheads, panhandlers and petty thieves; but most are rural communities, have hippie-looking members and aim at a self-sufficient farming-and-handicraft way of life. A very few communes are politically conservative, some are in the middle and most are pacifist, anarchistic and/or New Leftist. Nearly all, whatever their national political bent, are islands of primitive communism in which everything is collectively owned and all members work for the common good.

Their communism extends to—or perhaps really begins with—sexual collectivism. Though some communes consist of married couples who are conventionally faithful, many are built around some kind of group sexual sharing. In some of these, couples are paired off but occasionally sleep with other members of the group; in others, pairing off is actively discouraged and the members drift around sexually from one partner to another—a night here, a night there, as they wish.

Group marriage has captured the imagination of many thousands of college students in the past few years through its idealistic and romantic portrayal in three novels widely read by the young—Robert Heinlein's *Stranger in a Strange Land* and Robert Rimmer's *The Harrad Experiment* and *Proposition 31*. The underground press, too, has paid a good deal of sympathetic attention—and the establishment press a good deal of hostile attention—to communes. There has even been, for several years, a West Coast publication titled *The Modern Utopian* that is devoted, in large part, to news and discussions of group marriage. The magazine, which publishes a directory of intentional communities, recently listed 125 communes and the editor said, "For every listing you find here, you can be certain there are 100 others." And an article in *The New York Times* last December stated that "nearly 2000 communes in 34 states have turned up" but gave this as a conservative figure, as "no accurate count exists."

All this sometimes gives one the feeling that group marriage is sweeping the country; but, based on the undoubtedly exaggerated figures of *The Modern Utopian* and counting a generous average of 20 people per commune, it would still mean that no more than 250,000 adults—approximately one tenth of one percent of the U.S. population—are presently involved in group marriages. These figures seem improbable.

Nevertheless, group marriage offers solutions to a number of the nagging problems and discontents of modern monogamy. Collective parenthood—every parent being partly responsible for every child in the group—not only provides a warm and enveloping atmosphere for children but removes some of the pressure from individual parents; moreover, it minimizes the disruptive effects of divorce on the child's world. Sexual sharing is an answer to boredom and solves the problem of infidelity, or seeks to, by declaring extramarital experiences acceptable and admirable. It avoids the success-status-possession syndrome of middle-class family life by turning toward simplicity, communal ownership and communal goals.

Finally, it avoids the loneliness and confinement of monogamy by creating something comparable to what anthropologists call the extended family, a larger grouping of related people living together. (There is a difference, of course: In group marriage, the extended family isn't composed of blood relatives.) Even when sexual switching isn't the focus, there is a warm feeling of being affectionally connected to everyone else. As one young woman in a Taos commune said ecstatically, "It's really groovy waking up and knowing that 48 people love you."

There is, however, a negative side: This drastic reformulation of marriage makes for new problems, some of them more severe than the ones it has solved. Albert Ellis, quoted in Herbert Otto's new book, *The Family in Search of a Future*, lists several categories of serious difficulties with group marriage, including the near impossibility of finding four or more adults who can live harmoniously and lovingly together, the stubborn intrusion of jealousy and love conflicts and the innumerable difficulties of coordinating and scheduling many lives.

Other writers, including those who have sampled communal life, also talk about the problems of leadership (most communes have few rules to start with; those that survive for any time do so by becoming almost conventional and traditional) and the difficulties in communal work sharing (there are always some members who are slovenly and lazy and others who are neat and hard-working, the latter either having to expel the former or give up and let the commune slowly die).

A more serious defect is that most group marriages, being based upon a simple, semiprimitive agrarian life, reintroduce old-style patriarchalism, because such a life puts a premium on masculine muscle power and endurance and leaves the classic domestic and subservient roles to women. Even a most sympathetic observer, psychiatrist Joseph Downing, writes, "In the tribal families, while both sexes work, women are generally in a service role. . . . Male dominance is held desirable by both sexes."

Most serious of all are the emotional limitations of group marriage. Its ideal is sexual freedom and universal love, but the group marriages that most nearly achieve this have the least cohesiveness and the shallowest interpersonal involvements; people come and go, and there is really no marriage at all but only a continuously changing and highly unstable encounter group. The longer-lasting and more cohesive group marriages are, in fact, those in which, as Dr. Downing reports, the initial sexual spree "generally gives way to the quiet, semipermanent, monogamous relationship characteristic of many in our general society."

Not surprisingly, therefore, Dr. Ellis finds that most group marriages are unstable and last only several months to a few years; and sociologist Lewis Yablonsky of California State College at Hayward, who has visited and lived in a number of communes, says that they are often idealistic but rarely successful or enduring. Over and above their specific difficulties, they are utopian—they seek to construct a new society from whole cloth. But all utopias thus far have failed; human behavior is so incredibly complex that every totally new order, no matter how well planned, generates innumerable unforeseen problems. It really is a pity; group living and group marriage look wonderful on paper.

All in all, then, the evidence is overwhelming that old-fashioned marriage is not dying and that nearly all of what passes for rebellion against it is a series of patchwork modifications enabling marriage to serve the needs of modern man without being unduly costly or painful.

While this is the present situation, can we extrapolate it into the future? Will marriage continue to exist in some form we can recognize?

It is clear that, in the future, we are going to have an even greater need than we now do for love relationships that offer intimacy, warmth, companionship and a reasonable degree of reliability. Such relationships need not, of course, be heterosexual. With our increasing tolerance of sexual diversity, it seems likely that many homosexual men and women will find it publicly acceptable to live together in quasi-marital alliances.

The great majority of men and women, however, will continue to find heterosexual love the preferred form, for biological and psychological reasons that hardly have to be spelled out here. But need heterosexual love be embodied within marriage? If the world is already badly overpopulated and daily getting worse, why add to its burden—and if one does not intend to have children, why seek to enclose love within a legal cage? Formal promises to love are promises no one can keep, for love is not an act of will; and legal bonds have no power to keep love alive when it is dying.

Such reasoning—more cogent today than ever, due to the climate of sexual permissiveness and to the twin technical advances of the pill and the loop—lies behind the growth of unwed unions. From all indications, however, such unions will not replace marriage as an institution but only precede it in the life of the individual.

It seems probable that more and more young people will live together unwed for a time and then marry each other or break up and make another similar alliance, and another, until one of them turns into a formal, legal marriage. In 50 years, perhaps less, we may come close to the Scandinavian pattern, in which a great many couples live together prior to marriage. It may be, moreover, that the spread of this practice will decrease the divorce rate among the young, for many of the mistakes that are recognized too late and are undone in divorce court will be recognized and undone outside the legal system, with less social and emotional damage than divorce involves.

If, therefore, marriage continues to be important, what form will it take? The one truly revolutionary innovation is group marriage—and, as we have seen, it poses innumerable and possibly insuperable practical and emotional difficulties. A marriage of one man and one woman involves only one interrelationship, yet we all know how difficult it is to find that one right fit and to keep it in working order. But add one more person, making the smallest possible group marriage, and you have three relationships (A-B, B-C and A-C); add a fourth to make two couples and you have six relationships; add enough to make a typical group marriage of 15 persons and you have 105 relationships.

This is an abstract way of saying that human beings are all very different and that finding a satisfying and workable love relationship is not easy, even for a twosome, and is impossibly difficult for aggregations of a dozen or so. It might prove less difficult, a generation hence, for children brought up in group-marriage communes. Such children would not have known the close, intense, parent-child relationships of monogamous marriage and could more easily spread their affections thinly and undemandingly among many. But this is mere conjecture, for no communal-marriage experiment in America has lasted long enough for us to see the results, except the famous Oneida Community in Upstate New York; it endured from 1848 to 1879, and then its offspring vanished back into the surrounding ocean of monogamy.

Those group marriages that do endure in the future will probably be dedicated to a rural and semiprimitive agrarian life style. Urban communes may last for some years but with an ever-changing membership and a lack of inner familial identity; in the city, one's work life lies outside the group, and with only emotional ties to hold the group together, any dissension or conflict will result in a turnover of membership. But while agrarian communes may have a sounder foundation, they can never become a mass movement; there is simply no way for the land to support well over 200,000,000 people with the low-efficiency productive methods of a century or two ago.

Agrarian communes not only cannot become a mass movement in the future but they will not even have such chance of surviving as islands in a sea of modern industrialism. For semiprimitive agrarianism is so marginal, so backbreaking and so tedious a way of life that it is unlikely to hold most of its converts against the competing attractions of conventional civilization. Even Dr. Downing, for all his enthusiasm about the "Society of Awakening," as he calls tribal family living, predicts that for the foreseeable future, only a small minority will be attracted to it and that most of these will return to more normal surroundings and relationships after a matter of weeks or months.

Thus, monogamy will prevail; on this, nearly all experts agree. But it will almost certainly continue to change in the same general direction in which it has been changing for the past few generations; namely, toward a redefinition of the special roles played by husband and wife, so as to achieve a more equal distribution of the rights, privileges and life expectations of man and woman.

This, however, will represent no sharp break with contemporary marriage, for the marriage of 1971 has come a long way from patriarchy toward the goal of equality. Our prevalent marital style has been termed companionship marriage by a generation of sociologists; in contrast to 19th Century marriage, it is relatively egalitarian and intimate, husband and wife being intellectually and emotionally close, sexually compatible and nearly equal in personal power and in the quantity and quality of labor each contributes to the marriage.

From an absolute point of view, however, it still is contaminated by patriarchalism. Although each partner votes, most husbands (and wives) still think that men understand politics better; although each may have had similar schooling and believes both sexes to be intellectually equal, most husbands and wives still act as if men were innately better equipped to handle money, drive the car, fill out tax returns and replace fuses. There may be something close to equality in their homemaking, but nearly always it is his career that counts, not hers. If his company wants to move him to another city, she quits her job and looks for another in their new location; and when they want to have children, it is seldom questioned that he will continue to work while she will stay home.

With this, there is a considerable shift back toward traditional role assignments: He stops waxing the floors and washing dishes, begins to speak with greater authority about how their money is to be spent, tells her (rather than consults her) when he would like to work late or take a business trip, gives (or witholds) his approval of her suggestions for parties, vacations and child discipline. The more he takes on the airs of his father, the more she learns to connive and manipulate like her mother. Feeling trapped and discriminated against, resenting the men of the world, she thinks she makes an exception of her husband, but in the hidden recesses of her mind he is one with the others. Bearing the burden of being a man in the world, and resenting the easy life of women, he thinks he makes an exception of his wife but deep-down classifies her with the rest.

This is why a great many women yearn for change and what the majority of women's liberation members are actively hammering away at. A handful of radicals in the movement think that the answer is the total elimination of marriage, that real freedom for women will come about only through the abolition of legal bonds to men and the establishment of governmentally operated nurseries to rid women once and for all of domestic entrapment. But most women in the movement, and nearly all those outside it, have no sympathy with the anti-marriage extremists; they very much want to keep marriage alive but aim to push toward completion the evolutionary trends that have been under way so long.

Concretely, women want their husbands to treat them as equals; they want help and participation in domestic duties; they want help with child rearing; they want day-care centers and other agencies to free them to work at least part time, while their children are small, so that they won't have to give up their careers and slide into the imprisonment of domesticity. They want an equal voice in all the decisions made in the home—including job decisions that affect married life; they want their husbands to respect them, not indulge them; they want, in short, to be treated as if they were their husbands' best friends—which, in fact, they are, or should be.

All this is only a continuation of the developments in marriage over the past century and a quarter. The key question is: How far can marriage evolve in this direction without making excessive demands upon both partners? Can most husbands and wives have full-time uninterrupted careers, share all the chores and obligations of homemaking and parenthood and still find time for the essential business of love and companionship?

From the time of the early suffragettes, there have been women with the drive and talent to be full-time doctors, lawyers, retailers and the like, and at the same time to run a home and raise children with the help of housekeepers, nannies and selfless husbands. From these examples, we can judge how likely this is to become the dominant pattern of the future. Simply put, it isn't, for it would take more energy, money and good luck than the great majority of women possess and more skilled helpers than the country could possibly provide. But what if child care were more efficiently handled in state-run centers, which would make the totally egalitarian marriage much more feasible? The question then becomes: How many middle-class American women would really prefer full-time work to something less demanding that would give them more time with their children? The truth is that most of the world's work is dull and wearisome rather than exhilarating and inspiring. Women's lib leaders are largely middle-to-upper-echelon professionals, and no wonder they think every wife would be better off working full time—but we have yet to hear the same thing from saleswomen, secretaries and bookkeepers.

Married women *are* working more all the time—in 1970, over half of all mothers whose children were in school held jobs—but the middle-class women among them pick and choose things they like to do rather than *have* to do for a living; moreover, many work part time until their children have grown old enough to make mothering a minor assignment. Accordingly, they make much less money than their husbands, rarely ever rise to any high positions in their fields and, to some extent, play certain traditionally female roles within marriage. It is a compromise and, like all compromises, it delights no one—but serves nearly everyone better than more clear-cut and idealistic solutions.

Though the growth of egalitarianism will not solve all the problems of marriage, it may help solve the problems of a *bad* marriage. With their increasing independence, fewer and fewer wives will feel compelled to remain confined within unhappy or unrewarding marriages. Divorce, therefore, can be expected to continue to increase, despite the offsetting effect of extramarital liaisons. Extrapolating the rising divorce rate, we can conservatively expect that within another generation, half or more of all persons who marry will be divorced at least once. But even if divorce were to become an almost universal experience, it would not be the *antithesis* of marriage but only a part of the marital experience; most people will, as always, spend their adult lives married—not continuously, in a single marriage, but segmentally, in two or more marriages. For all the dislocations and pain these divorces cause, the sum total of emotional satisfaction in the lives of the divorced and remarried may well be greater than their great-grandparents were able to achieve.

Marital infidelity, since it also relieves some of the pressures and discontents of unsuccessful or boring marriages—and does so in most cases without breaking up the existing home—will remain an alternative to divorce and will probably continue to increase, all the more so as women come to share more fully the traditional male privileges. Within another generation, based on present trends, four of five husbands and two of three wives whose marriages last more than several years will have at least a few extramarital involvements.

Overt permissiveness, particularly in the form of marital swinging, may be tried more often than it now is, but most of those who test it out will do so only briefly rather than adopt it as a way of life. Swinging has a number of built-in difficulties, the first and most important of which is that the avoidance of all emotional involvement—the very keystone of swinging—is exceedingly hard to achieve. Nearly all professional observers report that jealousy is a frequent and severely disruptive problem. And not only jealousy but sexual competitiveness: Men often have potency problems while being watched by other men or after seeing other men outperform them. Even a regular stud, moreover, may feel threatened when he observes his wife being more active at a swinging party than he himself could possibly be. Finally, the whole thing is truly workable only for the young and the attractive.

There will be wider and freer variations in marital styles—we are a pluralistic nation, growing more tolerant of diversity all the time—but throughout all the styles of marriage in the future will run a predominant motif that has been implicit in the evolution of marriage for a century and a quarter and that will finally come to full flowering in a generation or so. In short, the marriage of the future will be a heterosexual friendship, a free and unconstrained union of a man and a woman who are companions, partners, comrades and sexual lovers. There will still be a certain degree of specialization within marriage, but by and large, the daily business of living together—the talk, the meals, the going out to work and coming home again, the spending of money, the lovemaking, the caring for the children, even the indulgence or nonindulgence in outside affairs—will be governed by this fundamental relationship rather than by the lord-and-servant relationship of patriarchal marriage. Like all friendships, it will exist only as long as it is valid; it will rarely last a lifetime, yet each marriage, while it does last, will meet the needs of the men and women of the future as no earlier form of marriage could have. Yet we who know the marriage of today will find it relatively familiar, comprehensible—and very much alive.

Hostility on the Laugh Track

ANN NIETZKE

The feminist movement is largely an effort to change the traditional role definitions of women and men in this society. Many women feel that these roles have hindered their ability to reach their potential and maintain a sense of self-worth and dignity. (Why, they ask, should the wife necessarily interrupt her career when a child is born?) The media is one of the mechanisms through which these roles and stereotypes are transmitted. Nietzke discusses these and other themes in their relationship to humor.

During the 1972 Democratic Convention, George McGovern, not yet having won the nomination, came to speak to the National Women's Political

Caucus. He was introduced by Liz Carpenter, who commented, "We know we wouldn't have been here if it hadn't been for you." McGovern responded with what he intended as a humorous remark: "I am grateful for the introduction that all of you are here because of me. But I really think the credit for that has to go to Adam instead."

Much to McGovern's surprise, the women did not laugh. In fact, they *hissed.* So the senator asked, "Can I recover if I say Adam and Eve?" But, of course, there was no way to recover because there was no way to cover the truth revealed by a seemingly innocent and mild little joke that had hurled the status of woman all the way back to Genesis, where, almost as an afterthought, she was created from Adam's rib to be a "helpmeet" to him and keep him company. The joke represented a form of "ribbing" that many women are no longer willing to take. And the fact that it came from the candidate who was supposedly our best hope in 1972 made it particularly disturbing, for it revealed how little McGovern's consciousness had been raised about our quest for liberation and political power.

The seriousness of that quest has all too often been the subject of ridicule because it poses such a threat to the male-dominated power structure. An easy way to undermine the seriousness of this threat is simply not to take the threat seriously. And it is precisely because so many men refuse to treat women's liberation seriously that feminists are forced to take themselves very seriously indeed. Then, of course, when we fail to be amused that someone is laughing *at* us, we are accused of not being able to laugh at ourselves (Norman Mailer described the atmosphere created by McGovern's joke as one of "humorless friction").

The momentum for the women's movement has come out of our growing sense of self-worth and dignity and potential, and out of anger and frustration that our worth as persons has been so long denied and suppressed. Is there really any reason why a woman whose consciousness has been raised should laugh at jokes that "put women in their place" sexually or intellectually or politically? To ask a woman in such a situation why she isn't laughing is of little consequence. The important question is why the joke teller thought she would laugh in the first place—why does he think such a joke is funny? At the root of a great many jokes about women lies a deep-seated hostility toward them and a desire to degrade them. Perhaps the men who tell such jokes and expect women to laugh have accepted the assertion of establishment psychology that all females are masochists. Certainly, if a woman grooves on being insulted, all she has to do is tune in to some male-dominated television show that features male comedians doing skits or stand-up routines. There she will find herself portrayed variously as the ugly, nagging, often frigid wife; the mother-in-law bitch; the terrible, unpredictable woman driver; the whore or "loose" woman; the dumb blonde; or the young and desirable, or old (over 29) and undesirable, sex object. A recent addition to this traditional catalog is the masculine "women's libber" who knows karate (and is no doubt a lesbian).

All things considered, I find it remarkable and admirable that the leading voices of the women's movement as a whole have refused, publicly at least, to use humor against men, either in the ways men have used it against women or as a way of venting their anger and frustration. I personally have not yet achieved the serenity that such a stand requires, and I find that in my anger I often lash out at men with a kind of humor that is threatening to them and that sometimes frightens me, as well. This kind of "humor" really isn't even funny but merely serves to release, through hollow laughter, the tension caused by hurt and rage. Lately, for example, I've begun to "talk back" to certain television commercials. Usually the situation is one in which a man says something stupid or insulting to women, and I reply, overriding whatever the woman in the commercial is saying:

1. A man praises his wife in amazement at how she can be a mother, housekeeper and sex object all rolled into one. He gives her a hug and says, "My wife—I think I'll keep her." I say, "That's too bad, you condescending prick—I want a divorce!"
2. A young couple are standing beside a toilet. The man says, "Hon, bathroom bowl sure needs cleaning." I say, "Clean it, then—it's half your shit, isn't it?"
3. An announcer grabs a woman's box of detergent and tries to make her take two boxes of Brand X instead. I say, "Forget the trade—would you like to know what you can do with all three boxes?"
4. A young husband complaining about his wife's coffee, almost reducing her to tears—"This coffee tastes terrible." On good days, I say, "Why don't you make the coffee from now on, dear?" On bad days, "How would you like to get your balls scalded with a cupful of it?"

I am a little embarrassed that I allow such stupid commercials to anger me so much, but my anger is a response to the fact that, unlike most ads, they do not distort reality so much as they mirror it—the reality, that is, of what many men think women should be. Here, for example, is a real-life version of my fourth reaction.

A young, recently married woman with whom I used to work told several women at lunch one day of how her husband had refused the night before to eat some chili she had made because it wasn't like his mother's. She tried to tell the story lightly, but it was obvious that she had been hurt, angered and frustrated, especially after going home from a hard day's work (at low pay) and making the stuff, just like a Good Wife should.

I said, "Maybe you could suggest that *he* try to make it next time, the way he likes it."

"HAH!" she retorted, anger rising. "That's a *laugh*!"

Someone else said, "Tell him to go over and get his mother to make it for him." We all laughed.

Then I said, "Tell him to fuck his mother, too, while he's there."

We women all laughed uproariously, but the uproar was followed by a somewhat awkward silence. Probably the logic of the remark—that if a husband wants his wife to play Mother he must also want his mother to play Wife—was lost in the laughter at its obscenity. But I said it out of anger and frustration, and the laughter served to relieve those feelings temporarily. Beyond that, of course, it accomplished nothing.

Even less is accomplished when my humorous rage or raging humor zeros in on a man in person. One of my targets was a male chauvinist who thought he knew all about women's liberation and thought he was in favor of it. But with four intelligent women in the room, *he* was determined to dominate the conversation about women. His tone indicated, in fact, that he was condescending to share his views with us. When I told him that this was what I felt he was doing, he exploded into fury. All hope of rational conversation dissolved in his hysteria, so we dropped the subject and the group broke up. The next night he was back in our motel room (we were all members of a wedding party), very carefully avoiding touchy subjects. After several drinks, he started to leave, saying, "Well, I've got to get to bed—I gotta be the fucking best man in a wedding tomorrow." And, unable to resist, I said, "Yeah, but will you be the best *fucking* man—that's the question, isn't it?" Now, I think that's a very clever remark, but I'm ashamed I said it. I don't like what my anger toward men does to *me*, for it certainly does more harm to me than to men, and it is a total waste of energy that could be used more constructively.

At the risk of being labeled "one of those castrating bitches," I have revealed that my so-called humor often involves blatant slurs and threats upon male sexuality. I think many jokes that women make about men do take the form of physical sexual insults, because it is on the physical basis that women are judged inferior, regardless of personal or intellectual qualifications. A person with a penis is automatically "superior" to a person without one; so the angry humorous insults are often directed at that very physical difference. Contrary to popular belief, women do not want to castrate men; it's just that we are tired of being eunuchs ourselves. This does not mean that women want penises but that we want the powers, freedoms and dignities that are automatically granted to the people who happen to have them.

Because of male chauvinism, the male sex organs have become metaphors for strength, aggression and power. Thus, it was perfectly appropriate—as well as very funny—when Shirley Chisholm stood before the black caucus at the Democratic Convention and told them she had run for the presidential nomination because she was the only one who had the *balls* to do it. Until power is desexualized, men will continue to be threatened sexually by women's quest for power, and the truth of this unfortunate situation will probably continue to manifest itself in the humor of angry women like myself.

Two such women who have "gone public" with their hostile humor are Pat Harrison and Robin Tyler, who have cut two albums and do a nightclub act, billing themselves as a "feminist comedy team." While not all their material is antimale, a significant portion of it, like my own responses to commercials, does aim at raising the male consciousness in a rather abrasive way ("I'm Helga of Women's Liberation Airlines. Fly *me* and I'll kick your fuckin' ass in!"). On the cover of their first album, "Try It, You'll Like It," a man with a banner labeling him "Male Chauvinist" sits in an electric-chair contraption with dynamite wired to it. Harrison holds a sign saying "Women's Liberation" as Tyler prepares to set off the explosives. Both women are smiling, but the fact remains that in the picture they are about to destroy a male, not merely the concept of chauvinism that he represents.

Part of Harrison and Tyler's style is to use men in their audience as the butt of some of their jokes. They ask, for example, "How many of you guys dig women in makeup?" When a number of men respond, Tyler says, "You like it? You *like* it? Then YOU wear it!" They recruit a male volunteer from the audience to help them with a routine and ask him to say, "I'm a drunk." When he complies, they say, "See how you can get these dumb men to say anything?"

These quips are mild, however, compared to what is undoubtedly the most threatening aspect of Harrison and Tyler's humor—their jokes about male sexuality. An interview with a "sensuous geriatric" provides the format for a number of these. This earthy female senior citizen wishes to dispel the myth about how great men are in bed—"Most guys can't handle *one* woman, much less a bunch of them," she tells her interviewer. "Women should have the harems, not men"—and she cites Masters and Johnson to support her assertion. She complains about her husband of 37 years who would come home every night and yell, "Yoo hoo, come get your daddy's peaches." Well, they may have been peaches, she says, but they were sure hanging from a dead limb. The interviewer hasn't had any better luck, as it happens. She used to live with a guy from the radical left who was interested in everyone's liberation except hers and always came home too tired for sex. She finally got so attached to her vibrator she sent it two dozen roses for Valentine's Day. Since many men commonly pretend to consider themselves studs while they privately harbor fears of inadequacy, and since many take the whole idea of women's liberation as a kind of castration threat, Harrison and Tyler's jokes about healthy female sexual appetite coupled with male impotence are unlikely to win them friends or influence male chauvinists.

"If men are gonna judge us on the size of our breasts," says America's only female comedy team, "then we're gonna judge them on the size of their weewees." I can't help wondering how someone like Dean Martin might react to that remark—Dean Martin, for whom the height of wit is to ogle some young woman's breasts, raise his eyebrows and mumble something silly. As far as I can tell, the main reason women are invited on his show is to provide material for breast jokes and, in fact, in many of the jokes, women are seen *only* as breasts. For example, two well-stacked women walk by him without speaking, and Dean says, "Those girls sure are conceited—all four of them." Or in "roasting" Tony Randall and Jack Klugman, he reads a telegram signed Raquel Welch, "From one odd couple to another." I'm convinced that if breasts were banned from Martin's show, he would only be able to find 30-minutes' worth of material each week instead of his present hour. Such an abundance of breast references has led me to appreciate Harrison and Tyler's comment that women don't have penis envy—men have mammary envy ("because America is built on sucking"), which tells you one reason why Dean Martin has his own TV show and Harrison and Tyler don't. It is perfectly permissible for Nipsy Russell to appear with Dean and insist that he is opposed to male chauvinism and believes women should be equal—and if they're not equal, they should get a corrective bra. But America simply is not ready for a similar joke about the size of men's penises although, as Harrison and Tyler say, "We know all men are not created equal, *don't* we?"

Unfortunately, just as a great deal of traditional male humor is a put-down of women, a great deal of traditional female humor is self-abusive. Nearly every female comic feels obliged to include a few flat-chest jokes in her repertoire, and these never fail to draw laughs because, in *Playboy* America, any woman whose bustline is under 38 can consider herself flat-chested. Phyllis Diller, Joan Rivers and Carol Burnett all base much of their material on the premise that they are unattractive women, although in fact none of them is ugly. Johnny Carson can remain his handsome self, play the stud and make eyes at a "broad," and everyone will laugh while they imagine what plans must be going through his mind. But when Carol Burnett makes eyes at Lyle Waggoner, we laugh because we feel there's no way a woman who looks and acts like her is going to get a man like him into bed. Henry Youngman or Rodney Dangerfield do not have to be concerned about their appearance—they can go on and on about how ugly their wives or girlfriends are, just as if they themselves were handsome prizes who deserve better. But in order to get laughs, comediennes such as Carol Burnett and Ruth Buzzi seem to have to make themselves look as unattractive as possible (think of Buzzi's Gladys Ormphby), and Phyllis Diller and Joan Rivers have to talk about themselves *as if* they were the homeliest creatures in the world.

According to her own story, Joan Rivers actually was a fat child who felt ugly and unloved (she tells us she was her own "buddy" at camp). In her routines, she admits, "I say I'm funny looking before they can hurt me by thinking it." Though Rivers is a fairly attractive woman now, she can't own up to it because it might well mean the end of her stand-up comedy career. Her favorite pose is that of the unfortunate Jewish girl who is pushing 30 and hasn't yet caught a man—at 25 her mother had her name legally changed to "Poor Joan" and put a sign in the front yard saying "Last Girl Before Freeway," and when she heard a single orthopedic surgeon had moved into the neighborhood, she slammed the piano lid on Joan's hand. Finally, Joan managed to marry Edgar, the husband who quickly became bored with her and whose favorite pastime now apparently is thinking of mean things to say to her.

When Johnny Carson asked Rivers recently if she preferred the title "Ms." she replied that she can't stand it—she worked too hard to get married and now demands that people call her "Mrs." Of course, she was merely seizing the opportunity for one of her usual jokes but, at the same time, she does have a vested interest in opposing the idea behind "Ms.," for if women become liberated from matrimony as a central goal of their existence, much of her comic material will be irrelevant. Also, if enough women develop healthier self-concepts and begin to feel some pride in being women, Rivers's self-lacerating humor may no longer strike them as funny. Perhaps this is why she could allow herself to be cast in a role that made a mockery of women's liberation in one of this past season's more disastrous sitcoms, "Needles and Pins." She played a ridiculous "libber" who wants female gorillas freed from the zoo and wants her husband to say *trousers* instead of *slacks*. For no apparent reason, she decides to divorce her husband (Louis Nye) and then, for no apparent reason, she decides to return to him and drop all this liberation business. The "moral" is: "You can't burn husbands the way you burn bras." Obviously, no performer committed to the women's movement would have lent herself to this mindless piece of material.

Much more worthy of consideration and more interesting from a psychological point of view is a television movie that Rivers wrote called *The Girl Most Likely To. . . .* It is the funny, touching and, finally, chilling story of a bright, witty, personable young college woman whose good qualities are never appreciated because she is overweight and unattractive. She suffers incredible insults and humiliations at the hands of all the men she has any contact with, as well as from her popular but bitchy cheerleader-type roommate. Finally, she can't take it anymore and jumps into her car, intent on suicide. She lives through the accident, however, and is so disfigured that plastic surgery is required. The fantasy of every homely adolescent girl is fulfilled when, miracle of miracles, the surgery transforms her into a beautiful creature. And her confinement causes a great weight loss. Suddenly, everyone begins to treat her like a human being, and the men who were so cruel before become mad with desire for her. But Miriam (Stockard Channing) will have none of it, and the fairy tale turns grim as she begins to very cleverly kill off, one by one, the people who hurt her most when she was ugly.

What makes this plot so interesting is that in the medium of film, Joan Rivers could create a female character who survives a suicidal kind of self-loathing and turns her anger and aggression outward, where it more rationally belongs. Viewed in the context of most of Rivers's material, I think this script has a refreshingly healthy air about it (although, of course, I don't wish to imply that committing murder is a sign of mental health or that I condone it). Anger, aggressiveness and the open expression of hostility have never been acceptable "feminine" traits, although a male who gets shit upon is not "manly" unless he blows his top or reciprocates somehow. One of the most frightening things to men about the women's movement is the terrible anger felt by women who suddenly realize that they are being shit upon in one way or another every day, and that they have been brought up to believe they *deserve* it. Direct expression of this anger is very hostile and threatening and does not lend itself well to humor, which is why my "jokes" and much of Harrison and Tyler's comedy are not very funny.

Phyllis Diller, it seems to me, is one comedienne who has been able to express a great deal of hostility toward the feminine role in her humor without posing any real threat to the status quo, which might alienate men. The key to her maintaining of this delicate balance is that she sets up stereotyped female expectations for herself and then fails at them absurdly. She never overtly rejects the female role of sex object, housewife and mother; rather, she accepts the role but fails in it. While many men may laugh at her because they react to the persona and think she tries hard but can't help failing, I, as a feminist, have always enjoyed her because the real woman behind the persona has deliberately concocted these failures and, while they do make her look ridiculous, they are actually based on the absurdity of society's expectations of women.

It is taken for granted that every woman should at least *try* to succeed as a sex object, and girls learn early that unless they happen to be one of those rare "natural beauty" types, they'd better learn to Do Something With Themselves to improve on their looks. What is so outrageous about the physical appearance of the Diller character is that she has quite obviously Done Something With Herself. Whatever is wrong with her hair, face and clothes is not the result of neglect but of too much misdirected attention. She tells us she spends four afternoons a week in the beauty parlor, and this is just for an *estimate*. Indeed, her hair, which she confides is actually not hair at all but nerve ends, looks like it has been beauty parlored to death. And her clothes, obviously designed carefully for their weird style, color, class and originality, usually succeed only in making her torso look like some kind of lump suspended between her skinny legs and outlandish head. Coming on stage this way, of course, provides Diller with material for a wealth of self-lacerating jokes about her failure as sex object. But at least, God knows, she has tried.

In the same way, Phyllis does her best to be a model cook and housekeeper. In one routine, she tells of the time her stove broke down, so she decided to heat Fang's supper in the dryer (she admits it was a mess, but at least it was *hot*). He complained about the white stuff on top of his food —"You *know* I don't like coconut!" Phyllis's reply? "Eat it, it's *lint*."

That joke provides yet another example of the stiuations described in the coffee commercial and chili incident above. A wife not only is expected to cook, but must cook to please the man—she must learn all his likes and dislikes and prepare menus accordingly. The Diller character accepts this role assignation—she will have supper ready for Fang, even if the stove is not working; and it should be a hot meal, as every homemaker knows. So she ingeniously decides to use the dryer. And, of course, she wouldn't serve him coconut, knowing he hates it. But maybe he likes lint—who knows? Because of these mitigating circumstances, not to mention the absurdity of the details involved, the hostility of the last line of the joke is considerably softened, as it was not in my response to the coffee commercial or to the young man who insisted his wife cook like Mom.

Overt hostility in Diller's humor is often softened in this way and, at its cleverest, may be even more subtle. Do you know, for example, what Fang and the kids got Phyllis for Mother's Day? An oven that flushes. This joke has a double edge, for while it is obviously a gross put-down of her cooking talents (she uses Ungentine as a sauce for burnt foods), it also calls up the image of a mother who feeds her family excrement. The extreme hostility expressed in this idea is pure sacrilege, especially when TV reminds us so often that "nothin' says lovin' like somethin' from the oven."

The Diller character isn't really antimotherhood, but she feels it is definitely something to be endured rather than revered. She is all for anything that will keep her children out of sight and mind, such as having them play outside as much as possible (never mind the lightning) and warning them not to accept rides from strangers (not because it's dangerous, but because they'll get home sooner that way). The blatant hostility behind these latter jokes is precisely what makes them funny but, of course, hostility towards children poses no threat to men.

Phyllis would never think of asking Fang to help with household chores, but she is full of tips on how to appear as "Mrs. Clean" while never actually lifting a dust cloth. You can put a little O'Cedar wax behind each ear (to make you smell tired), rouge your knees (to look like you've been scrubbing floors) or have a broken strap hanging from your sleeve (to look like you've been reaching and stretching). Many women, certainly, have discovered that their husbands don't really care whether the house is clean or not—what disturbs them is the idea that their wives may not have been cleaning it. These suggestions are just absurd examples of how females learn to be tricky and devious in order to survive their role with the least pain and still appear "womanly" or "motherly" to men.

Television, of course, is a male-dominated enterprise that seems determined to go on portraying women almost exclusively in their "womanly" or "motherly" roles. Most female TV characters exist only as appendages to men—as wives, girlfriends, secretaries and the like. While a few shows, such as "Diana" and "Mary Tyler Moore," do depict career women, the stars still spend most of their time being "womanly" or "motherly" to men rather than actually pursuing their careers. "Adam's Rib," based on the Tracy-Hepburn movie about two lawyers who are husband and wife, was the only situation comedy of the past season that featured a female character whose *work* was an essential element of the plot each week. The show even attempted in a number of episodes to deal with the issue of discrimination against women, but, unfortunately, it did not have the courage of its own convictions, which ultimately is the same as having no convictions at all.

For each step taken in the right direction, the show seemed to take one equally large step backward in order to be cute or avoid too much controversy. For example, Amanda objects to cooking all the time, since she works as hard at her job as Adam does at his. But instead of their sharing the cooking, the show ends with Amanda claiming that cooking is her *pleasure*, not her duty—she will do all the cooking if only Adam will not take her for granted. The issues of alimony, job discrimination, equality under the law and women in politics were all taken up somewhat seriously in the first half of different episodes, but always seemed to fizzle out in the end.

The only two situation comedies so far that have attempted to deal intelligently (and humorously) with women's roles in today's society and their effect on relationships between the sexes are "All in the Family" and "Maude." The format of "All in the Family" allows for these issues to crop up in various ways through interaction between and among the three couples in the series—Edith and Archie, Gloria and Michael and Irene and Frank Lorenzo, the next-door neighbors. In the show's opening song, "Those Were the Days," Arch and Edith long for the simple past: "And you knew where you were then—girls were girls and men were men." Presumably, this means that women had the slave mentality of Edith Bunker and that men, like Archie, knew how to take full advantage of female enslavement. There was a time when I became angry at the thought of Edith running about like a puppy dog, catering to Archie's every whim and passively accepting an overwhelming amount of verbal abuse. Lately, I've decided it's not much worse to be a woman like Edith than it is to be a man like Arch, whose ego and sense of manhood are so weak as to require a slave for a mate. Gloria occasionally speaks up in defense of her mother, but we know her father is never going to change (and neither is Edith).

Of course, Gloria has her own problems, being married to a liberal male who wants freedom and equality for everyone, but who is often blind to his own sexism. An entire episode was courageously devoted to the question of sexual aggressiveness in Gloria and Mike's relationship and, in the end, Mike *concedes* that it shouldn't matter which of them makes the first move sexually. I find this admirable, since a show like "Adam's Rib" would no doubt have had Gloria apologizing in one way or another for her "nymphomania." Unlike his father-in-law, Michael at least is educable.

It is when Archie comes up against Irene Lorenzo that his attitudes toward women surface in a clearly defined way. Frank Lorenzo does a lot of cooking, while Irene putters around a workshop and is a very competent "fix-it" lady. This bit of role reversal alone is enough to blow Archie's mind, and he lets us know in no uncertain terms that Irene is "unfeminine" and that Frank must be "queer" or he wouldn't let his wife "wear the pants" in the family. Arch is intimidated by Irene because she has the wit and presence of mind to trade insults with him and refuses to sit still for his verbal abuse. In one episode, when Archie gets on a tirade against women in sports, Irene challenges him to a game of pool. Finding out that she has a cue stick of her own that she won at a billiard academy is enough to make Arch fake a back injury to avoid playing her. Finally, he is forced to play, and she does beat him. He comes home sullen and humiliated. But what the Bunker character is incapable of realizing (which is the basis for much of the humor in the character concept) is that he is responsible for his own humiliation, since it was he who decided that the affirmation or destruction of his manhood could ride on a pool game.

Irene also "castrates" Archie in another more subtle and psychologically interesting episode in which she puts a steel spring lock on the Bunker's cellar door. Archie, home alone and anxious to get rid of her, won't give her time to adjust the device so it won't lock automatically. Later, the furnace goes off and Arch, naturally, locks himself in the basement when he goes to see about it. He ends up drinking a whole bottle of vodka to stay warm and has visions of dying, but the significant aspect is that he feels *Irene* has killed him. Since he thinks that she has already destroyed her husband's manhood, it seems valid to interpret her "threat" on his own life as a threat to his masculinity, brought on by her overcompetence in mechanics.

The idea of "masculinity" in a woman provides the basis for a great many jokes in "Maude," too, although many of them are based on Bea Arthur's physique and deep voice rather than on Maude's competence in some masculine activity. She is often mistaken for a man on the phone, and her humorous physical threats against Walter and next-door neighbor Arthur are funny, I think, precisely because she looks as if she just might be able to carry them out. In one episode, she and Walter are getting ready to go accept an award for their work in behalf of the Equal Rights Amendment. Maude is helping Walter with his tie when Arthur says something that sets her off on a tirade about women's rights. As she gets carried away, she begins choking Walter with the tie, causing him to sink to the floor. All of this provides a visual comment (from the male writers) on what men fear women's liberation may really mean for them. Later, after an argument, Walter shouts, "All right, if you want to wear the pants—*here!*" and he actually takes off his trousers and gives them to her. Carol Burnett used this very sort of scene as the basis for one of her take-offs, this one called "Broad." Her version of Maude is definitely sexually, physically and verbally dominant, running the household and making "Walter" do chores. Throughout the bit, "Walter" (Harvey Korman) appears in his underwear, which I took as an implied statement that "Broad" was wearing the pants.

We are reminded repeatedly in the series that Maude has already been through three husbands, and the implication is that she is really "too much" for one man to handle. The audience loves it when, at the height of an argument, Walter shouts, "Maude, *sit!*" and Maude does. Although this is really little different from Archie telling Edith, "Stifle yourself," it is funnier because Maude is allowed to get as angry as Walter and is capable of fending for herself in an argument.

But Maude is free of the slave duties involved in running a household only because, unlike her cousin Edith, she has a maid to do them for her. And the limitations of the Maude character as "liberated woman" were shown in an episode in which she gets her realtor's license and a career of her own.

Walter, it turns out, needs Maude at home to comfort him and do for him after his hard day's work. He makes her quit the job and relents only after a tremendous show of resentment and, finally, tears on her part. In the end, he *allows* her to have the job, and she is humbled and extremely grateful for his decision. This reminds me of a quip I heard on a recent Lily Tomlin special: "I don't need women's liberation—my husband lets me do anything I want."

It is just possible, come to think of it, that right now when the relationship between women and humor tends to be a very touchy thing, Lily Tomlin's comedy may give us some respite from the present unfortunate situation. For although she is a staunch feminist (I will never forget the surge of pride I felt as I saw her walk off the Cavett show a couple of years ago when Chad Everett remarked that he "owned" his wife), she does not use her humor as a weapon against men. And although she does both routines and monologues, she has stated publicly, "I never do a character who doesn't like herself." Her humor, based on the premise that *people* are funny, is neither vicious nor self-lacerating, so that I think men and women can probably laugh at her *together*. And I like that idea—I really do.

Innate Intelligence: An Insidious Myth?

WILLIAM H. BOYER AND PAUL WALSH

Is "intelligence" primarily determined by heredity or environment? Much of the dominant educational and economic philosophy in the United States is based on the belief that individuals differ considerably in innate intelligence. The substantial inequality of wealth and power in our society is explained and justified by the argument that those with higher innate intelligence more skillfully ascend the educational and economic hierarchies. Boyer and Walsh question the assumption of "innate intelligence" and point out that educational institutions operating on this assumption may hinder the social mobility of the poor rather than provide "equality of opportunity."

In societies where power and privilege are not equally distributed, it has always been consoling to those with favored positions to assume that nature has caused the disparity. When man himself creates unequal opportunity, he can be obliged or even forced to change his social system. But if nature creates inequality, man need only bow to supreme forces beyond his control, and the less fortunate must resign themselves to their inevitable disadvantage.

The metaphysics of natural inequality has served aristocracies well. The Greeks had wealth and leisure as a result of the labor of slaves. Plato expressed the wisdom of the established order with the claim that nature produces a hierarchy of superiority in which philosophers, such as himself, emerge at the top. Aristotle's belief that all men possess a rational faculty had more heretical potential, but it was not difficult to believe that some men are more rational than others.

In later periods, nations that possessed economic superiority explained their advantages on the basis of innate superiority. Sir Francis Galton was convinced that the English were superior and that the propertied classes were even more superior than the general population. They were the repository of what was the most biologically precious in mankind.

The democracies of the new world shattered many elements of the old order, and brought a new, radical, equalitarian outlook. In principle, if not always in practice, man became equal before the law, and the idea of "the worth of the individual" established a principle of moral equality. Yet legal and moral equalitarianism did not necessarily mean that men were intellectually equal. So the assumption upon which American schools and the American market place developed was that democracy should mean *equal opportunity for competition among people who are genetically unequal.* This creed has satisfied the requirements of modern wisdom even for the more liberal founding fathers such as Thomas Jefferson, and it equally fit into the social Darwinism of an emerging industrial society.

In contemporary American education many of these assumptions remain. People are usually assumed to be not only different in appearance, but also innately unequal in intellectual capacity and therefore unequal in capacity to learn. The contemporary creed urges that schools do all they can to develop *individual* capacities, but it is usually assumed that such capacities vary among individuals. Ability grouping is standard practice and begins in the earliest grades. Intelligence tests and the burgeoning armory of psychometric techniques increasingly facilitate ability tracking, and therefore the potentially prosperous American can usually be identified at an early age. If it is true that people have inherently unequal capacities to learn, the American educational system is built on theoretical bedrock, and it helps construct a social order based on natural superiority. But if people actually have inherently equal capacities, the system is grounded in quicksand and reinforces a system of arbitrary privilege.

Four types of evidence are typically offered to prove that people are innately different in their capacity to learn. The first is self-evidential, the second is observational, the third is logical-theoretical, and the fourth is statistical.

The self-evidential position is based on high levels of certainty which include a strong belief in the obviousness of a conclusion. Many people are very certain that there is an innate difference between people in intellectual capacity. However, such tenacity of feeling is not itself a sufficient basis for evidence, for it offers no method of cross-verification. The mere certainty of a point of view regarding the nature of intelligence must be discounted as an adequate basis for verification.

The observation of individual differences in learning capacity cannot be dismissed as a basis for evidence; useful information for hypotheses requiring further verification can be obtained in this way. For instance, parents may notice different rates of learning among their children. People from different social classes learn and perform at different levels. The city child may learn particular skills more rapidly than the rural child. Observations require some care if they are to produce reliable evidence, but it is possible to observe carefully, and such observation can be cross-verified by other careful observers.

But if people learn particular tasks at different rates, does it follow that people must therefore be *innately* different in their learning capacity? It does *not* necessarily follow. Increasingly, as we know more about the role of environment, we see that there are not only differences between cultures, but also differences within cultures. Even within families, no child has the same environment as the others. Being born first, for instance, makes that child different; he is always the oldest sibling. A whole host of variables operates so that the environment as perceived by an individual child has elements of uniqueness (and similarity) with other children raised in proximity.

Observational evidence can be a useful part of the process of understanding when it raises questions that can be subjected to more conclusive evidence, but it is often used as a way of selectively verifying preconceived notions which are endemic in the culture. Western culture is strongly rooted in the belief in a natural intellectual hierarchy. Few observers have been taught to make observations based on assumptions of natural intellectual equality. Observational evidence must be carefully questioned, for it is often based on a metaphysic of differential capacity which encourages selective perception and a priori categories of explanation. Yet these preconceptions are rarely admitted as an interpretive bias of the observer.

Theories based on carefully obtained data provide a more adequate basis for reaching a defensible position on the nature-nurture controversy than either of the previous procedures. A general theory in the field of genetics of psychology which fits available information would be a relevant instrument for making a deduction about the nature of intelligence. If a logical deduction could be made from a more general theory about heredity and environment to the more specific question of innate intellectual capacity, the conclusion would be as strong as the theory. Such deduction is a commonly used procedure.

Both genetic and psychological theories have often been used to support the belief in inherited intelligence. Genetic connections between physical characteristics such as eye color, hair color, and bodily stature are now clearly established. Certain disease propensity has a genetic basis, yet the best established research is now between single genes and specific physical traits. It is commonplace to assume that if a hereditary basis for differential physical traits has been established, there is a similar connection between genes and intelligence. The conclusion, however, does *not* necessarily follow. Intelligence defined as the capacity to profit by experience or as the ability to solve problems is not a function of a single gene. Whatever the particular polygenetic basis for learning, it does not follow that intellectual capacity is variable because physical traits are variable. Current genetic theory does not provide an adequate basis for deducing a theory of abilities.

Similarly, the Darwinian theory of natural selection is often used to ascribe superiority to those in the upper strata of a hierarchical society. Yet a system of individual economic competition for survival is actually a very recent phenomenon in human history, characteristic of only a few societies, primarily in the eighteenth, nineteenth, and early twentieth centuries. It is very likely that it is irrelevant to genetic natural selection because of its recent origin. American immigration came largely from the lower classes, a fact which could condemn America to national inferiority if the Darwinian theory were used. In the long span of human history, most societies have relied mainly on cooperative systems or autocratic systems for their survival, and individual competition is an untypical example drawn largely from the unique conditions of Western, particularly American experience.

Psychological theories which emphasize individual difference have often assumed that the descriptive differences in physical characteristics, personality, and demonstrated ability are all due largely to heredity. Psychology has had strong historical roots in physiology, but as social psychologists and students of culture have provided new understanding of the role of experience, hereditarian explanation has shifted toward environmentalism. Even the chemical and anatomical characteristics of the brain are now known to be modifiable by experience. Psychologists such as Ann Anastasi point out that, "In view of available genetic knowledge, it appears improbable that social differentiation in physical traits was accompanied by differentiation with regard to genes affecting intellectual or personality development."

Anthropologists, with their awareness of the effects of culture, are the least likely to place credence in the genetic hypothesis. Claude Levi-Strauss, a social anthropologist, claims that all men have equal intellectual potentiality, and have been equal for about a million years. Whether or not this is true, it is clear that the best-supported general genetic or psychological theory does not validate the conclusion that individual intellectual capacity is innately unequal.

Statistical studies under controlled conditions, on the other hand, can provide some of the most reliable information. For instance, when animals are genetically the same, there is the possibility of inferring genetic characteristics through experimental studies. Identical twins develop from the separation of a single egg and have identical genetic inheritance. If human twins could be raised under controlled experimental conditions, much could be learned about the respective role of heredity and environment. Many studies have been made of twins, but none under sufficiently controlled experimental conditions. The results, therefore, permit only speculative conclusions. Most twins are so similar that unless they are separated they are likely to be treated alike. When they are separated, in most cases, one twin is moved to a family of the same social class as the other twin. And people of similar appearance tend to be treated similarly—a large, handsome child is not usually treated the same as a short, unattractive child. The resultant similarity of IQ scores of separate twins has not been surprising.

Even if particular identical twins were to show marked differences in ability when they live in substantially different environments, as they occasionally do, the evidence does not prove the *environmentalist* thesis unless a significantly large number of random cases is compared with a similarly random selection of non-identical twins. In a small sample, difference could be due to the experience deprivation of one twin. It is possible to stultify any type of development, and so the variation between identical twins, identified in some studies as up to forty points, by no means disproves the hereditarian position. Consequently, current studies do not provide conclusive statistical evidence to support either position over the other.

The second most commonly used statistical evidence to show the hereditary basis of intelligence is the constancy of IQ scores at different age periods. Usually, IQ scores do not change appreciably, but occasionally the changes are dramatic. It is now understood that a standard IQ test is culturally loaded toward middle-class values, and so the general constancy of most IQ scores can be explained as the expected result of limited mobility between social class and the resultant constancy of subcultural experiences. So even the statistical "evidence," so often used to support a belief in innate intelligence, is really not conclusive.

Studies of innate intelligence, then, have not produced conclusive evidence to justify the claim for an innate difference in individual intellectual capacity. Equally, there has not been conclusive evidence that the innate potential between people is equal. The research is heavily marked by the self-serving beliefs of the researchers. Psychologists have usually created "intelligence" tests which reflect their own values, predetermining that their own scores will be high. When they have discovered they are high, they have often proclaimed such tests to be indicators of innate superiority.

Many studies are built on simple-minded assumptions about the nature of environment. Psychological environment is related to the subject. A researcher who says that two children live in the "same" environment is quite wrong, for the environment that each child perceives may be quite different from that perceived by the researcher.

Also, it is often assumed that environment is only postnatal, but evidence is now available on the role of prenatal environment, both psychologically and nutritionally. Malnutrition of a pregnant mother can, and often does, have permanent debilitating psychological and physiological effects on her child. Certain diseases contracted by the mother (measles, for example) and certain drugs (thalidomide, for instance) can produce destructive "environmental" effects which limit intellectual capacities. Clearly, people do demonstrate varying capacities to learn, but they have had varying prenatal and postnatal opportunities. If they are female, they are generally treated differently than if they are male. Negroes are treated different from whites—one social class is treated different from another. The *kind* of employment people engage in has a profound effect on what they become. They probably become different through different treatment and different experience, yet our institutions, reflecting our culture, usually operate on the assumption that such differences in ability are innate.

There are at least three ability models which can be supported by current evidence. Each is based on different assumptions about human nature and therefore provides a basis for different social philosophies and different conceptions of government and education.

The first model assumes a great variety of innate ability and a high level of intellectual demand on the average person. In this model, there are hereditary geniuses and idiots, while most people have an intellectual capacity about equal to the demands of their society.

The second model assumes that the innate ability potential of everyone (who has not been injured pre- or postnatally) is equal and far exceeds the normal demand level. (The actual opportunities a person has may produce differential *performance* similar to model No. 1.)

The third model assumes the possibility of some variation, but since all of the ability potential is well beyond the normal demand level, the variation makes virtually no operational difference.

In an economic or educational system, model No. 1 would justify the usual culling, sorting, and excluding through screening devices to create a "natural" hierarchy of ability. It would also justify the common belief in "equal opportunity for competition between unequals," where sorting is achieved through competition.

Both models two and three would justify maximum social effort to develop the abilities of all people, and the failure to achieve high levels of ability in all people would constitute social failure rather than individual failure. American society, with its considerable disparity of wealth and power, is largely a success based on the inequality assumed in the first of the three models. It is largely a failure based on the equality assumed in the second and third models.

Schools make little effort to develop the kind of equal ability assumed in models two and three. IQ tests are widely used to identify presumed differences in innate ability so that culling and grouping can make the management of the school easier and more efficient. The disastrous effects of the schools on lower-class children are now finally becoming known. The "compensatory" concept has gained some headway, but most educators are so overloaded with

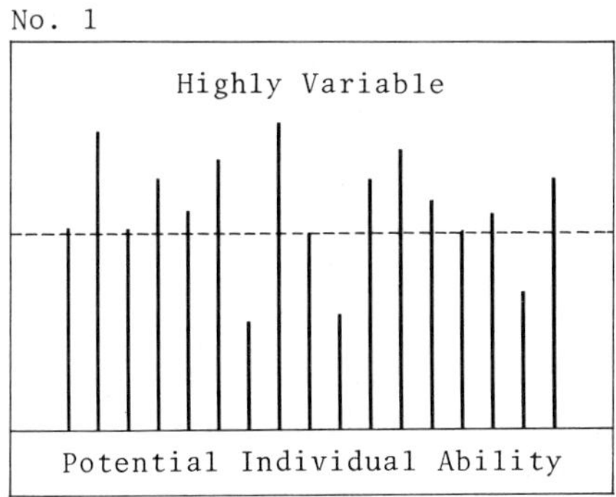

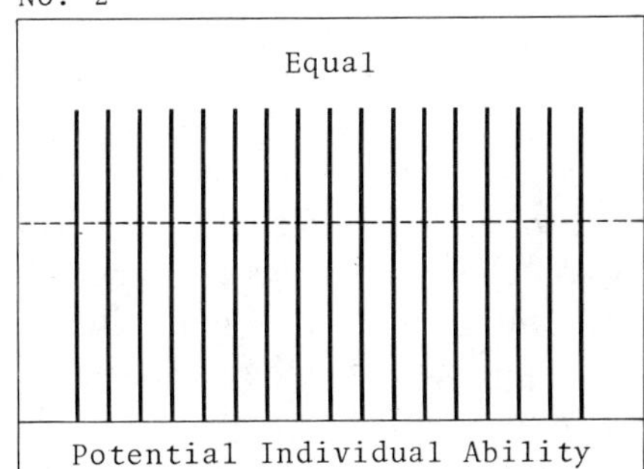

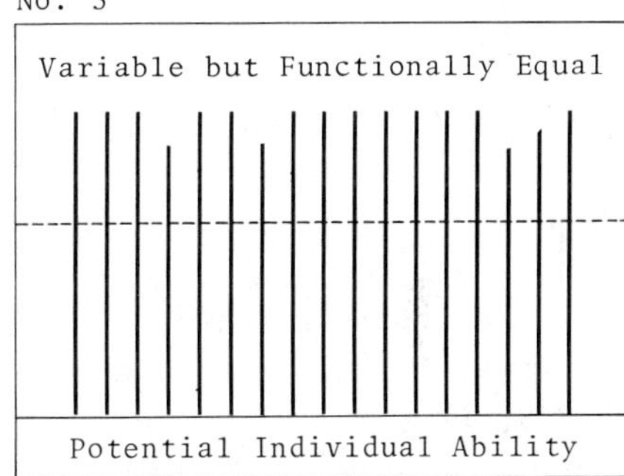

Ability models. Each model is based on different assumptions about the nature of potential human ability. The dotted line indicates the intellectual level at which individuals must function to meet the requirements of society.

work and so traditional in outlook that the schools have become partners with the economic system in reinforcing a system of privilege that usually panders to the children of those in power and finds metaphysical excuses to make only minor gestures toward the less fortunate. The "special programs for the gifted" would be more accurately labeled "special programs for the privileged," for the gifted are primarily the children from socio-economic classes which provide the most opportunities. The less fortunate (usually lower-class children) are ordinarily neglected or convinced that they are innately inferior. Once they become convinced, the prophesy is soon realized.

Part of the problem is the way "intelligence" is defined. It can be defined in many different ways, each leading to a somewhat different educational direction. We can view it as environmental adaptation, as ability to solve problems, as ability to use logical convergent thinking, or it can emphasize divergent thinking and the creation of ideas and problems. When intelligence is defined as abstract verbal-conceptual ability drawing on the model experiences of middle class environment, as it is in most IQ tests, a selection has been made which excludes many other plausible and often more useful definitions.

The capacity to become intelligent does, of course, have a genetic basis.

A cat is not capable of becoming a psychologist. But this does not mean that demonstrated differences in intelligence among psychologists are innate. What is particularly important is whether intelligence is defined primarily as the input or the output. The input is not subject to control, but the output depends on experience; so it is intelligence as output that should be the central concern of the educator.

Until the particular beliefs, which are endemic in many cultures, including American culture, are seen to be part of the heritage of an ancient, anachronistic, elitist tradition, there is little likelihood that the official liberal and equalitarian goals of many modern nations are likely to be realized, even though the wealth of modern technology gives every promise that they are capable of being achieved. Government, industry, education, and virtually all other institutions are now part of the problem, hobbled by a metaphysics of innate inequality. Elitist assumptions about the meaning of ability permeate all fields of education. When teachers of music, mathematics, art, or physical education find that a student doesn't demonstrate the requisite ability, they often reject him (low grades can be a form of rejection). Then counselors shuttle the student to courses where he shows "ability." All this assumes that the school should not develop abilities, but only grant them opportunity to be expressed. The Rousseauian belief in the pre-existing self is widespread.

The environmental hypothesis may be wrong, but if it is, it should be shown to be wrong only after a society has done everything possible to develop the abilities of people. We should begin with prenatal care, and should eliminate the experience of economic deprivation, ghettoized living, and elitist schools and businesses. *Lacking definitive scientific evidence about human potentialities, social policy should be based on moral considerations.* We should base our policy on the most generous and promising assumptions about human nature rather than the most niggardly and pessimistic. Men will do their best only when they assume they are capable. Liberal assumptions and conservative assumptions about human nature create their own self-fulfilling prophesies. We now create millions of people who think of themselves as failures—as social rejects. Their sense of frustration and despair is a travesty on the potentialities of an affluent nation.

Poor teaching is protected in the American educational system through the assumption that the child doesn't have the ability. An American environmentalist commitment (toward liberal rather than totalitarian goals) would aim at *creating* ability, at *increasing* intelligence, at *developing* interests. The meaning of "education" would need to be broader than merely institutional schooling. It should also include community responsibility, especially for business and the mass media, which must supplement the work of the school if Americans are to receive more equal educational opportunity. This requires more social planning and more public responsibility than Americans have previously been willing to undertake.

Most American institutions, including the schools, still base their policy largely on the old conservative ideology. This outlook resists change and condemns many to inferiority. Ideological rigidity is not exclusive to the United States; in fact, many other nations are even more rigid. Yet the expanding wealth produced by modern technology is beginning to encourage the have-nots within the United States and throughout the world to demand their share by force and violence if necessary. Violence is likely to be an increasingly common road to social change unless a new public morality based on new assumptions about human potentiality is translated into both foreign and domestic policy. It is not merely racism which bogs down American progress, but also the more pervasive belief in intellectual inequality. The failure to develop the abilities of people was useful to the early American aristocracy and to the power elite of an industrial-scarcity economy. But modern economics of abundance flourish through the maximum development of the abilities of people. There is potentially plenty for all. More widespread development of the capabilities of people would not only add greatly to the wealth of nations, but it can also permit people to participate in a social and cultural renaissance.

Aside from the compelling moral obligation to create equal opportunities within nations and even between nations, the excluded millions in the world are starting to force the changes which should have occurred long ago. Some of them don't believe they are inferior, and they are understandably impatient about changing the old processes of exclusion. All institutions, including the schools, will either need to re-examine their self-consoling elitist beliefs and create real and equal opportunity, or else risk that violence and revolution will increasingly become the dominant instruments of social change.

Educational Change: Why, How, for Whom?

ARTHUR PEARL

In this article Arthur Pearl says of the poor that "education is the only equalizer they have." Without credentials the poor are excluded from the economic mainstream of our society. But how much help does education really offer? Pearl discusses various ways in which our educational system alienates and discriminates against the poor, and then offers some positive suggestions about how to make education a more meaningful experience.

Published and distributed by The Human Rights Commission. Reprinted by permission of the author.

Why the Poor and Disadvantaged Do Not Learn: Two Theories

Current theory underlying most compensatory programs set up to help disadvantaged children assumes that their learning difficulties result from lack of basic preparation; that is, they are inadequately socialized, insufficient male figures in their lives, have no books in their homes, cannot delay gratification, suffer from accumulated environmental and cultural deficits, and so on. Therefore, teachers believe their primary role in working with these children is to "repair" them and deal with their handicaps. Programs are based on the premise that poor children are out of step and need reshaping. On the basis of such orientation, programs are generated that reinforce the inequality of education and the humiliation of the children.

As a working premise, start assuming that all children want to learn until, somehow or other, they become "unmotivated." There is substantial evidence to support this position. Martin Deutsch and others note eagerness for schooling when children first enter, and a declining enthusiasm the longer the exposure to the school. Schools have been part of the problem, not part of the solution. Rather than helping, we, as society, have placed barriers in the way of the education of the poor. I would argue that alleged disfunctionality of disadvantaged youth is the result of being locked out of society. Lack of motivation and apathy are the *consequences* of denial of opportunity. We are not properly sifting out cause and effect.

Some years ago in New York I was involved in programs for disadvantaged youth that were similar to the school compensatory programs, the Job Corps and Neighborhood Youth Corps program. The programs, by all established criteria, were excellent, they were well designed, had competent staffs, and enjoyed workable pupil–staff ratios. The programs included rigorous research and evaluation. At the end of the year it was clear that there was no payoff, despite the belief of everyone that such programs were sure to work. The young people in the program were no better off at the end of the year than were the members of a comparable (control) group who had not been offered the programs.

It was out of these kinds of failure experience over some years that it occurred to me that perhaps we are dashing off headlong in the wrong direction, that instead of trying to save people, salvage people, and help people, we should be offering disadvantaged youths the opportunities to belong, to help, and to salvage themselves and others. Rather than developing programs which emphasize failure and inadequacy and thus continue to stigmatize and spoil the image of youth, we should focus on the structural barriers standing in the way of their success.[1]

Social scientists for some time have noted the difference between the socialization patterns of the poor and the nonpoor. The poor operate on the

[1] See, for example, Erving Goffman, *Stigma* for further elaboration of the spoiled-image concept.

pleasure principle; they do not know how to delay need gratification. They must have their kicks right now. We good middle-class people, who have been adequately socialized, operate on the reality principle; we delay our gratifications for future reward. We never buy a house until we save $20,000 and we never buy a car until we save $3,000. But the poor just are not like that. . . . What is not understood in this formulation is that the poor do not suffer from a lack of future orientation; they suffer from a lack of future.

There must be a restructuring of employment opportunities so that the poor can find a place. Our schools must provide a learning experience which gives children a sense of contribution, of personal worth, a feeling of anticipation about the future and a certainty that they have a place in it. This is not happening now for the poor youth. The school is an alien land from which he "cuts out." This exclusion leads to another exclusion that forms a society which cannot employ him because he did not learn. Without change we face the frightening prospect of millions of people who are literally expendable, totally unnecessary to the functioning of the society and living with the terrible, self-destructive knowledge that they are leaving no imprint on the sands of time, that they are "nobody" and functioning "no place."

Our education system can build in a future for our children only if educators look for what is wrong with current practice and start truly to test their theories. Is a child's noncommitment to education and his dropping out of school the result of prior handicap, or are these things the result of lack of choice and lack of future because he is locked out? There is a very important difference. If the handicap thesis is fraudulent, everything we are doing makes little sense, whether it is the Job Corps program, the Neighborhood Youth Corps, or the compensatory programs in the schools. More and more the evidence supports the contention that opening up opportunities has a greater impact on poor children than do programs to "repair" them.

Why Is Education So Important Today?

Around the turn of the century, about 94 per cent of our people did not graduate from high school. It caused little concern because there were a variety of absorption systems, albeit imperfect, available to the poor. But today at least four years of education beyond high school are necessary for upward movement in our economic system, and this becomes increasingly more true as traditional ways of making a living become obsolete. At one time there were many possibilities for entrance and upward mobility for most of our citizens.

1. First, they could market their unskilled labor, learn on the job, and move up. Many of the people who command high positions in industry today started out as unskilled laborers. But today, machines are replacing men. Despite the fact that we've had well over a 30 per cent increase in productivity over the past five years, there are no more people turning out

products than there were five years ago. And the better jobs demand credentials.

2. Another entrance was farming. But today agriculture is our most automated industry; over 1 million jobs have been eaten up by machines in the last six or seven years, despite the fact that agricultural surpluses continue to grow, and another 1 million jobs will be destroyed in the next decade.
3. Still another possibility was entrepreneurial enterprise. But today the street peddler cannot compete seriously with a department store, the small machinist with the major auto companies.
4. Finally, the fields of education, welfare, and recreation were available to the poor because there were not the prerequisites for education which are currently demanded. Ralph Bunche says that the teacher that had the most profound effect on him had an eighth-grade education when she began to teach.

These absorption systems are today closed. Two fundamental things have affected dramatically the way we can become absorbed into society: (1) automation, which has destroyed jobs or made them a dead end, and (2) the need for a credential to get into the largest and fastest-growing industries.

The biggest, fastest-growing industry in the country is education. It has to be the biggest ten years from now because by 1975 there will be 40 million more people in the country and the median age will be less than twenty-five. With preschool education, fewer dropouts, more people going to college, the lowering of the teacher–pupil ratio, the 2.3 million teachers we now have could easily be expanded to 5 or even 10 million. The equivalent is true in medicine, recreation, welfare; in fact, it is true in all the human services and all the skilled jobs for which we demand a college education.[2]

Without credentials for the professions and for the new skilled and managerial jobs in private industry, the poor are locked out of participation in the economic life of the country. Yet the poor need education more than anyone else. It was not a great tragedy that Barry Goldwater could not get through the first year of college, because his family could find things for him to do around the store. But the poor have no such resources; they must have an education. *Education is the only equalizer they have.* Nevertheless, because of the way education is now structured, it is unlikely that many of the poor will get the credential. Why?

What Happens to Disadvantaged Youth in School?

1. We "*sort.*" The teachers' responsibility is to teach, but instead we engage in self-fulfilling prophecy. We decide that certain people cannot be educated; we refuse to educate them; they grow up uneducated; and we

[2] For a full discussion on how to create millions of jobs in the human services, read Arthur Pearl and Frank Riessman, *New Careers for the Poor.*

pride ourselves on our exceedingly accurate predictive index. This sorting principle puts a stamp on pupils very early in the game, and this stamp follows them all the way through the production line, until they come out labeled "dumb" or "smart," because there has been very little done to change the initial judgment. This distorts the educational function; teachers are supposed to *change* persons; they are not there only to sort and stamp.

To show you how important role expectation is in determining what you do in school consider the following example: in Scotland a few years ago the IBM machine made a mistake and the school sent a bunch of "stupid" students into the smart track and a bunch of "smart" students into the dumb track. About a year later, they discovered their mistake and students checked to see what had happened. They found that those so-called stupid students were acting just as if they were smart, just as if they had the innate ability to do the job, and the so-called smart students were behaving just as though they were stupid.[3] This was the case because the role expectation to a large extent determines what one does in the classroom. If the school believes you are incapable of doing anything, you are never going to get an opportunity to show what you are capable of doing.

2. *We refuse to educate the poor.* Very few of the poor will get a chance to get the all-important credential because very few will be placed into tracks that lead to a college degree. As an example, consider the schools in Washington, D.C. In a school where middle-class, white students go and where the median income for the parents is over $10,000 a year, 92 per cent of all students are in college-bound tracks. In another school in Washington, D.C., where 100 per cent of the students are Negro and parents make less than $4,000 a year, 86 per cent are in noncollege-bound tracks. In other words, almost nine out of ten of the Negro children are being told that they are not college material (and therefore that they cannot get a credential).

If you accept the proposition that without college in the coming years, you cannot get into meaningful work, these students are being told that they have no future except possibly in menial service occupations. Thus, selective education imposes a rigid class structure upon the poor, especially the Negro poor. At the present time, the *best* predicter of a future college education is the occupation of the student's father. If the student has a parent with less than a college education, who works at a blue-collar job, if he works at all, and who is from a racial minority group that is discriminated against the probability of being a dropout is more than three times greater than if a student is reared by professional, well-educated, white parents.

Unless one holds to the belief that the poor are constitutionally inferior (and nice people do not believe that anymore), then you have to assume that the poor are not being educated; otherwise, the "bright" and the "stupid" would be more evenly distributed through all economic levels of the population.

[3] As reported by Martin Deutsch.

3. *We group students homogeneously or heterogeneously.* How do we appraise peoples' intelligence or lack of it. If they talk like we do or act like we do, obviously they have to be intelligent. If they do not, it is equally obvious that they must be nonintelligent. Nothing could be more logical. So we establish a series of tests which we devise for us, standardize on us, and operate in situations in which we feel comfortable; on this basis we determine who is educable or noneducable. Then we spend millions of dollars, because some people think this process is not really fair, to look for that culture-free or culture-fair test. It is a totally unrealizable goal. We do not even try to discover whether it is essential to try to find this kind of test at all. Why is it really important to start labeling children as dumb or smart early in the game? This is not to say that all people are equal, but rather, that no valid measures of intellectual capacity have been developed, nor does it really matter, because none of us function anywhere near capacity.

The argument for homogeneous grouping is that it makes it easier to teach; that is, we are setting up a system for the convenience of the teacher. The teacher takes the position, quite logically, that teaching many different people of different abilities at the same time is impossible. But even in homogeneous groups, the children are not all identical. No matter how you group them, they are different people. They must happen to be somewhat similar on a particular score, but they are different in background, sex, learning styles, and tempo. Only one variable has been isolated as a result of this grouping, but the teacher believes her job will be easier because she can operate at the same pace.

By the same token, however, we begin to water down the curriculum successively as we begin to label people as "slow learners" or "less able." Those who learn slower than others are going to get less. Those in the second track are going to get a second-class education, and a third-class education will be offered those in the third track. This is what happens when one assumes that it is easier and more logical to teach people who learn roughly at the same pace.

Evidence, however, does not support the thesis. No evidence shows that homogeneous groupings work better *for the students*. In both the United States and England it appears that a bright child learns no better when placed with a group of bright children than when placed in a heterogeneous group. And the poor children, the so-called dumb ones, *are* hurt by the grouping. They end up doing worse than the so-called dumb child left in a heterogeneous group. It is fairly obvious why. Grouping does not help the educational process. Most of these children are not stupid, despite our judgment. They know who is being grouped with whom even if the labeling is couched innocuously as "bluebirds." If *they* do not know, the other children will tell them. They soon learn to fulfill the role expected of them and, most destructive of all, learn to believe in the "truth" of the school's judgment of them.

If you are put in the basic tracks, if you are given watered-down curriculum, if you are treated as if you are dumb, there is not much you can get from school.

Although evidence does not support homogeneous grouping as educationally valid, it is definitely discriminatory. There is no question that the child that goes into the smart track tends to be the child whose parents are well educated. Those who go into the dumb class are those who did not choose their parents very well. The track system is discriminatory, and it reinstitutes a segregated school system within the school. There are interracial schools in this country where almost all the children in the honor track are white and almost all the children in nonhonor tracks are Negro or speak Spanish. This is not a "racially balanced" school. It is a totally segregated school, but the segregation takes place within a building. The segregation is just as intense, just as invidious, just as pernicious as if it were a racially exclusive school.

Why Are the Schools Alien to the Poor?

1. The Rules. There is no logic or rationale for most school rules. There is a minimum tolerance for differences, and much more tolerance if you are nonpoor than if you are poor. For example, if students do not dress or wear their hair in the style determined by the middle class, they can be asked to leave school. This can happen despite the fact that there is no data to support the contention that learning is disturbed when students wear long hair or boots.

It is not surprising that youth try to establish an identity, often through bizarre dress and hair styles. What is surprising is that adults meddle in what is essentially someone's private business. The real issue is why young people decide to express themselves in these ways. Why are there so few gratifications for poor youth in our society that they reject becoming part of the establishment? Wherever I see bizarre behavior in students, my inital reaction is to look to what the school is doing to cause the behavior.

School rules are enforced differently. What is tolerably deviant and what is not depends on the child's background. In the case of middle-class boys, it is often interpreted as a childish prank, a phase the student will outgrow; in cases involving poor youth, deviant behavior is interpreted as a signal of emerging criminality which must be nipped in the bud.

It is important to insist on logical reasons for the rules of behavior in the schools. If education is to be rational; if it is to be a system which enables youth to learn to think clearly, to learn to work through problems, then a rule should not be ad hoc. A rule should not be made off the top of one's head; it should not conform to the personal prejudices of a school board or the personal whim of principals. School rules should be backed by empirical evidence that they are supportive or negative to the learning process, that they endanger the health or safety of another person or of school property.

2. Powerlessness. The more deprived the background of the child, the less power he has in our educational system. To be totally powerless is to be placed in a terribly disquieting and uncomfortable position. Humans do not like to feel that they are nothing, that they have no control over their destiny. No one likes that feeling. . . . It is quite clear that there is a great difference between the poor and nonpoor and their ability to defend themselves in the school system. A child of white, middle-class parents has things going for him when he gets into trouble. He can talk the language of the system, and teachers and principals are much more likely to listen to him. But he can also turn to his parents. His parents also talk the language; they can negotiate for their child. The middle-class parent can do things for his child; he can hire a tutor, a psychologist, a lawyer. If worse comes to worse, he can take his child out of the system and put him in a private school. The poor have no escape, no voice. The whole system is a colonial imposition on them, made up by others, for others.

3. Meaningless Material. For the poor, education is totally removed from their life experience. It cannot be related to their backgrounds or immediate circumstances. In middle-class families, parents can talk "algebra" with their child; the material he gets has some meaning in the context of his life. The material is presented in a familiar language, in an understandable style, and at an acceptable pace. None of this is true for most disadvantaged youngsters.

Some social scientists have advocated replacing teachers with machines, insisting that machines can do everything teachers can do. There may be sense in this postulate because machines are more flexible (more human) than teachers. Machines, at least, can be made to change their pace. The child operates a learning machine and he operates it at the pace at which he is learning. Teachers cannot be manipulated that way. They operate at one pace, at one track, and with one language style.

At the University of Oregon a counselor was simulated on a 1620 computer by collating the responses of a live counselor and developing a program based on queries to him from clients. The capacity of the computer was not taxed—very few unique responses were required regardless of the questions asked. The students were asked to describe and evaluate the machine and compare it to a human counselor. They found the machine more warm, more understanding, more sympathetic. . . . Schools must stop dehumanizing teachers. The teacher has a unique quality which no machine can replace, and that is the ability to challenge students constructively, to reach out and help, to exercise flexibility and judgment. Those qualities must be liberated if education is to have meaning to the poor.

4. Linkage with a Future. Where do youth go with schooling? A middle-class child may find rules stupid, may bridle because of his powerlessness; may find most of the courses meaningless, but these are obstacles he is willing to suffer because he knows that at the end there is a place for him. What about the noncollege-bound youth? What is that track leading to?

What is he getting out of the educational experience? He's being told to stay in school to become an unemployed high school graduate. Dropouts I have worked with told me they felt worried about not having a high school diploma until they discovered you could lie about it. For the most part a high school diploma leads to menial, dead-end jobs. There is no meaningful linkage with the future for anyone who is not in a college-bound program in school. Vocational education is, to a large extent, antiquated. It is antiquated because the job may be disappearing. Or if the job is still viable, the youth does not have the informal credentials; for example, many of the building trades offer preference to union members' children in apprentice programs. (We cannot really reshuffle fathers as part of the vocational education program.) Much of the vocational education is delusional, a complex fabrication which disguises the reality of the world out there and the inappropriate nature of current procedures which ostensibly prepare youth for the world of work.

5. Gratification. Jobs are not everything. Man does not live for bread alone. Dignity and a sense of self-worth are also extremely important. And here the school's effect is the most devastating of all. We rarely allow students to have a sense of competence. Schools permit some to obtain competence, and these are the "brains" and the "athletes." But the largest number are subjected to a humiliating and degrading experience. The middle-class child gets the rewards bestowed by teachers who understand him because he dresses and behaves appropriately. The deprived youngster, for the most part, goes to school every day to be punished. He gets no reward out of the system. Psychologists and social workers all treat his "deficiencies." But these are only some more overlords reinforcing humiliation.

Not only do the poor fail to develop a sense of mastery, they are not permitted a sense of contribution. They are not allowed to be important to anyone else. These gratifications must come out of the school system if it is going to have real value to our children. If they have no sense that they are learning something, that they are contributing to others, that they are a member of something, then it is hard to expect them to give much to the school program. If they feel that the school is run by outsiders, with rules made by outsiders, in which they have little power to make any decisions and no understanding of those that are made and if it leads nowhere and they are getting no kicks out of it, how can we expect them to put out very much for that kind of school?

How Do We Construct a Different Kind of School?

1. Before we can build anew, we have to test whether our cherished beliefs are true. We "know" that if we reduce class size, education will be better. We "know" it is true that if we give teachers time to prepare for classes, they will do better. We "know" that if we improve pupil personnel

services and pour in psychologists and social workers, we can overcome children's handicaps. Yet there is no evidence to support this "knowledge." And if we researched it, I would predict that very little of the above would pay off one iota over an extended period of time.

Looking at what data there is, it is clear that none of these things by themselves produce better education. In fact, we have increasing evidence that nothing positive takes place in the classroom. Omar Milton, Professor of Psychology at the University of Tennessee, is considered to be an effective teacher. He is dynamic, interesting, and well liked by his students. One semester he took a random half of his students and ordered them not to show up in class. These students took midterms and the final, and at the end of the semester he found that the half that did not show up at class did better than those who did. Two years later they were still doing better. They were more interested in psychology, they had a higher grade-point average, and fewer had dropped from shcool. On every possible objective and subjective index, they were doing better for *not* having been in class. This experiment has been repeated in many places with the same findings. I am sure that we would find it true in secondary schools if it were tested. If we ordered children to stay home, they would be better off. In the Omar Milton experiment, despite the fact that teacher–pupil ratio was down because half the students were home, there was absolutely no gain for those attending class.

We had better begin to look at some of our most treasured, heartfelt assumptions and test them out. If education is to pay off, we have to recognize that it was not set up for the convenience of the teacher. We did not really set up public education to keep middle-class people off the streets. Schools were established to help the students; and we ought to test to be sure that they are working as intended.

Teachers have to accept the responsibility for teaching human beings to learn. One of the things I have tried to get across in my classes is that when I give a test it is not a test of my students. It is a test of me. I am testing whether or not I am a good teacher. If the students get poor grades, I interpret that as an indication that I failed to get the course material across. After one of my tests, one of my students came up and patted me on the back and said, "Hate to break it to you, buddy, but you flunked." And he was right. But his attitude is hard for teachers to accept. There is no other system in the world in which we flunk a product. We do a rotten job, and we flunk the kids. We fail to teach, and the children are held accountable.

2. The student as teacher. We have to build in the gratification which comes from having a sense of contribution, a sense that you are of value to someone else. The student role as a passive sitter and absorber of knowledge is not particularly gratifying. The teaching role is. So one of the things to recognize is that it would be better if the teachers did some learning and the learners did some teaching right from the very beginning.

In a residential school for delinquent and abandoned children in Oregon, a seven-to-eleven club has been started. The eleventh-graders are teaching the seventh-graders. One of the things that happened is that most of the eleventh-graders did not want to go home for Christmas holidays because they had to work on lesson plans over the holiday; the seventh-graders felt the same way. The school no longer just belongs to the teacher but now the students have a stake in the system and suddenly school is interesting. The school is entirely different because the students themselves are involved in the teaching process. And the teacher becomes somebody who is important to the students because he is needed to help them prepare lectures and work with each other. They find they need the teacher to help work through problems, to suggest ways of teaching, and to refer children who need special help.

In another school there was a youth who appeared to be absolutely unmanageable. He threw darts at the teacher, broke windows, and was the one arrested if anything was stolen. He was not the kind of child you would have suspected would be an optimal teacher, but almost in desperation, it was suggested that he be allowed to teach. He was in the eighth grade, so he went to work helping the sixth-graders in spelling and second-graders in tumbling. Three or four weeks later, he was doing much better in all his classes because he had to keep up his work and stay out of trouble if he was to be allowed to work with the other children. His whole idea about education changed. In fact, he changed from wanting to be a Marine to wanting to be a teacher.

Another way to inject the idea of making a contribution is to have the students teach each other in the classroom. Instead of a classroom where the teacher does everything, some courses in some experimental programs in which I am involved are set up in nonteacher-led groups. The youths decide upon projects that interest them. This is being done with an eighth-grade science course. The teacher initially thought it was a very bad idea. She saw her job as lecturing for an hour, whether anybody listened or not. She saw her primary obligation as reaching the kids who cared, and it was too bad for those who did not. We prevailed upon her to break the room into groups and let them have some alternatives as to what they might like to do. They began to do things that the teacher thought only eleventh and twelfth graders could do. When she gave a test out of the text, in spite of the fact that they were doing almost nothing out of the text, the whole class had gone up in performance. Why? Because now these students had an investment. They were working on things themselves. They had some control over their own destiny. They had some concern for their own educational process; it was no longer something forced upon them. And the teacher found that teaching had become fun. She used to hate to come to school and look at the hostile faces, and her students felt much the same about her. Now the whole educational experience has become exciting. She is playing essentially a consultative role, she answers questions and helps individuals, and the kids are learning as they never learned before. The principal worries because he does not know what he will say when the parents complain because their children say school is fun. Many people feel that agony is a necessary part of the learning process. But the principal can demonstrate performance. There are children in that school getting A's who never got anything other than an F. Students are participating and asking questions who before only were able to incur wrath and be sent to the principal's office.

A change has taken place because the students are getting opportunities for gratification, an opportunity to develop a competence. They are working in heterogeneous groups where they all have a choice. Moreover, the so-called dumb children are better in some things than the bright ones; for example, when the eighth-grade students were constructing tests for the seventh-graders, the bright ones made up "catch" questions that no one could get; the slower kids asked fruitful questions that made real sense. The whole school is different, for both teachers and students.

What we are creating is cooperative team learning. Holding people up in individual competition is inherently unfair, especially when mixing middle-class and poor children. We have had team learning in this country for a long time, but we call it cheating. I suggest that we buy into cheating and help our children work together. The pioneers could never have gotten across the country if they had not pulled together, with some helping others. School should also be a cooperative effort.

Experiment at Howard University: New Methods, New People

The school, transformed as I have described it, will create the alive, thinking, absorbed children that result when teachers have respect for each child's intelligence, competence, and need to participate actively in the teaching–learning process. Meanwhile, however, millions of young people have already given up the school system; unless they are to remain permanently and dangerously nonfunctional appendages to our society, we have to move toward programs where one gets one's job first and one's education afterward.

At Howard University, in 1963, we took a look at some who failed in the school system, a group of hard-core delinquent school dropouts, to determine what would happen if we stopped trying to compensate for handicaps and instead tried to open up opportunities for useful work, combined with relevant education.

We created jobs in research, child care, and recreation for a group of young people who would appear to have no potential to succeed. The minimum requirements for the program were that the young people had to (1) be high school dropouts; (2) live in the most economically disadvantaged neighborhoods in Washington, D.C.; (3) have no *pending* legal action; (4) have no *active* venereal disease. The ten young people chosen for this original program were between the ages of sixteen and twenty, had a measured IQ of 77 on a group test, and had between an eighth- and eleventh-grade education. None had worked more than a month in their lives. Four of the seven boys had extensive delinquency histories, including time in correctional institutions; two of the three girls had borne children out of wedlock. One of the girls was diagnosed by our psychiatrist as a catatonic schizophrenic. Our psychiatrist said it was ridiculous to include her in the program. We insisted that she be included; we would test the proposition that her condition was not a psychological disorder, but the result of a locked-out condition with no future.

A number of tasks were structured which we thought would be possible for persons with these backgrounds to learn. In six weeks of research training, we expected them to learn to conduct and tape-record interviews; to code and prepare these interviews for key punch; to run a counter-sorter; to wire an IBM 407; to prepare instructions for a programmer in a 1620 computer; to operate desk calculators sufficiently well to compute percentages, means, medians, standard deviations, chi squares, rank-order correlations, product-moment correlations, and other statistical manipulations. They were doing all these things and more, including helping design research experiments, in six to ten weeks. Similar performance was expected in the day-care and recreation programs, and *we grossly underestimated their ability.* We discussed with the youth our orientation and told them we were going to see if our point of view made any sense.

On the question of tolerable deviance: Our position was that no rule would be imposed unless we could provide strong justification of its need. We did not care how they dressed or how they wore their hair, unless we could prove to them that these things would affect their performance on the job. The fact that their appearance might outrage a professional was *his* problem.

On power: We established that the young people were the policy-making group for the program. They would determine in which of the three job areas they wished to work; they would decide the discipline to be applied if people were late or continuously absent, and so on. They established the rules. Our role would be that of a review court. If the rules they made could not be supported, we would refer them back to them for review and consideration. Often we found the kids too tough, and our policy was to tell them their discipline seemed inconsistent with their complaints about how they had always been treated by others. We would ask them what *their* problems were and why they found it difficult to adjust to each other's differences when these caused them no personal harm. In time they became very supportive of each other.

The God-hucksters of Radio

WILLIAM C. MARTIN

What part does religion play in society? What needs does it meet? To whom does it have its greatest appeal? One kind of religious enterprise, that of "gospel radio," is examined in this article by William Martin. Various programs and approaches are described, and Martin indicates some of the ways in which they are sold to the public.

You have heard them, if only for a few seconds at a time. Perhaps you were driving cross-country late at night, fiddling with the radio dial in search of a signal to replace the one that finally grew too weak as you drew away from Syracuse, or Decatur, or Amarillo. You listened for a moment until you recognized what it was, then you dialed on, hoping to find *Monitor* or *Music Till Dawn*. Perhaps you wondered if, somewhere, people really listen to these programs. The answer is, they do, by the tens and hundreds of thousands. And they not only listen; they believe and respond. Each day, on local stations that cater to religious broadcasting and on the dozen or so "super-power" stations that can be picked up hundreds of miles away during the cool nighttime hours, an odd-lot assortment of radio evangelists proclaims its version of the gospel to the Great Church of the Airwaves.

Not all who produce religious broadcasts, of course, are acceptable to the scattered multitude for whom "gospel radio" is a major instrument of instruction and inspiration. Denominational programs and Billy Graham are regarded as too Establishment. Billy James Hargis and his Christian Anti-Communist Crusade are too political. Even faith healer Oral Roberts, once a favorite out there in radioland, has become suspect since he founded a university and joined the Methodist Church. For these believers, the true vessels of knowledge, grace, and power are people like Brother Al ("That's A-L, Brother Al"); the Reverend Frederick B. Eikerenkoetter II, better known to millions as "Reverend Ike"; C. W. Burpo ("Spelled 'B,' as in Bible . . ."); Kathryn Kuhlman ("Have . . . you . . . been . . . waiting . . . for . . . me?); and the two giants of radio religion, healer A. A. Allen (of Miracle Valley, Arizona) and teacher Garner Ted Armstrong, who can be heard somewhere at this very moment proclaiming The Plain Truth about The World Tomorrow.

The format of programs in this genre rarely makes severe intellectual demands on either pastor or flock. C. W. Burpo (Dr. Burpo accents the last syllable; local announcers invariably stress the first) and Garner Ted Armstrong usually give evidence of having thought about the broadcast ahead of time, though their presentations are largely extemporaneous. Some of the others seem simply to turn on the microphone and shout. Occasionally there is a hint of a sermon. J. Charles Jessup of Gulfport, Mississippi, may cite Herodias' directing her daughter to ask for the head of John the Baptist as illustrating how parents set a bad example for their children. David Terrell may, in support of a point on the doctrine of election, note that God chose Mary for his own good reasons, and not because she was the only virgin in Palestine—"There was plenty of virgins in the land. Plenty of 'em. Mucho virgins was in the land." Evangelist Bill Beeny of St. Louis, Missouri (Period. Beeny regards the Zip Code as a plot to confuse the nation), may point to the flea's ability to jump 200 times his own length as proof that God exists. Often, however, a program consists of nothing more than a canned introduction, a taped segment from an actual "healing and blessing" service (usually featuring testimonials to the wondrous powers of the evangelist), and a closing pitch for money.

The machinery for broadcasting these programs is a model of efficiency. A look at station XERF in Ciudad Acuña, Coahuila, Mexico, just across the border from Del Rio, Texas, illustrates the point. Freed from FCC regulations that restrict the power of American stations to 50,000 watts, XERF generates 250,000 watts, making it the most powerful station in the world. On a cold night, when high-frequency radio waves travel farthest, it can be heard from Argentina to Canada. Staff needs are minimal; less than a dozen employees handle all duties, from the front office to equipment maintenance. The entire fourteen hours of programming, from 6:00 P.M. to 8:00 A.M., are taped. Each week the evangelists send their tapes to the station, with a check for the air time they will use.

All announcing is done by Paul Kallinger, "Your Good Neighbor along the way." A pleasant, gregarious man, Kallinger has been with XERF since 1949. In the fifties, he performed his duties live. At present he operates a restaurant in Del Rio and tapes leads and commercials in a small studio in his home; he has not been to the station in years. A lone technician switches back and forth between the preachers and Kallinger from dusk till dawn. Kallinger recognizes the improbability of some of the claims made by the ministers and acknowledges that their motives may not be entirely altruistic. Still, he figures that, on balance, they do more good than harm, and he does his best to impress listeners with the fact that "these are faith broadcasts and need your tithes and love offerings if they are to remain on the air with this great message."

Who listens to these evangelists, and why? No single answer will suffice. Some, doubtless, listen to learn. Garner Ted Armstrong discusses current problems and events—narcotics, crime, conflict, space exploration, pollution—and asserts that biblical prophecy holds the key to understanding both present and future. C. W. Burpo offers a conservative mixture of religion, morals, and politics. Burpo is foursquare in favor of God, Nixon, and constitutional government, and adamantly opposed to sex education, which encourages the study of materials "revealing the basest part of human nature."

Others listen because the preachers promise immediate solutions to real, tangible problems. Although evidence is difficult to obtain, one gets the definite impression, from the crowds that attend the personal appearances of the evangelists, from the content and style of oral and written testimonials, from studies of storefront churches with similar appeals, and from station executives' analyses of their listening population, that the audience is heavily weighted with the poor, the uneducated, and others who for a variety of reasons stand on the margins of society. These are the people most susceptible to illness and infirmity, to cripping debts, and to what the evangelists refer to simply as "troubles." At the same time, they are the people least equipped to deal with these problems effectively. Some men in such circumstances turn to violence or radical political solutions. Others grind and are ground away, in the dim hope of a better future. Still others, like desperate men in many cultures, succumb to the appeal of magical solutions. For this group, what the preachers promise is, if hardly the Christian gospel, at least good news.

The "healers and blessers," who dominate the radio evangelism scene, address themselves to the whole range of human problems: physical, emotional, social, financial, and spiritual. Like their colleagues in the nonmiraculous healing arts, some evangelists develop areas of special competence, such as the cure of cancer or paralysis. Brother Al is something of a foot specialist —"God can take corns, bunions, and tired feet, and massage them with his holy love and make them well." A. A. Allen tells of disciples who have received silver fillings in their teeth during his meetings and asks, sensibly enough, "Why not let God be your dentist?" But most are general practitioners. On a single evening's set of programs, hope is extended to those suffering from alcoholism, arthritis, asthma, birth defects, blindness, blood pressure (high and low), bunions, calluses, cancer (breast, eye, lung, skin, stomach, and throat), corns, death, diabetes, dope, eye weakness, gallstones, heart disease, insomnia, kidney trouble, leukemia, mental retardation, mononucleosis, nervous breakdown, nervous itch, nicotine addiction, obesity, pain, paralysis, polio, pregnancy, respiratory problems, rheumatic fever, tuberculosis, tumors (brain, abdominal, and miscellaneous), ulcers, useless limbs, and water in the veins.

The continually fascinating aspect of the healing and blessing ministries is that they do produce results. Some of the reported healings are undoubtedly fraudulent. One station canceled a healer's program after obtaining an affidavit from individuals who admitted posing as cripples and being "healed" by the touch of the pastor's hand. Police officers have occasionally reported seeing familiar vagrants in the healing lines of traveling evangelists, apparently turning newly discovered disorders into wine. But these blatant frauds are probably rare, and a faith healer need not depend on them to sustain his reputation. He can rely much more safely on psychological, sociological, and psychotherapeutic mechanisms at work among his audience.

The testimonials that fill the broadcasts and publications of the healers point to two regularities in a large percentage—not all—of the reported cures. First, the believer had suffered from his condition for some time and had been unable to gain relief from medical or other sources. Long illness or disability can weaken emotional and mental resistance to sources of help that one would not consider in other circumstances. Second, most of the cures occur at actual healing services, when the deep desire to be made whole is transformed into eager expectation by a frenzied whirl of noise, anxiety, and promise, and the pervasive power of the gathered group of true believers.

In recent years, the miracle-workers have turned their attention to financial as well as physical needs. They promise better jobs, success in business, or, in lieu of these, simple windfalls. A. A. Allen urges listeners to send for his book *Riches and Wealth, the Gift of God.* Reverend Ike fills his publications and broadcasts with stories of financial blessings obtained through his efforts—"This Lady Blessed with New Cadillac," "How God Blessed and Prospered Mrs. Rena Blige" (he revealed to her a secret formula for making hair grow), "Sister Rag Muffin Now Wears Mink to Church," and "Blessed with New Buick in 45 minutes." Forty-five minutes is not, apparently, unusually fast for Reverend Ike. He regularly assures his listeners, "The moment you get your offering [and] your prayer requests into the mail, start looking up to God for your blessing because it will be on the way."

These men of God realize, of course, that good health and a jackpot prize on the Big Slot Machine in the Sky are not all there is to life. They promise as well to rid the listener of bad habits, quiet his doubts and fears, soothe his broken heart, repair his crumbling marriage, reconcile his fussing kinfolk, and deliver him from witches and demons. No problem is too trivial, too difficult, or past redemption. Brother Al will help women "that wants a ugly mouth cleaned out of their husband." A. A. Allen claims to have rescued men from the electric chair. Glenn Thompson promises "that girl out there 'in trouble' who's trying to keep it from Dad and Mother" that if she will "believe and doubt not, God will perform a miracle."

The radio evangelists do not cast their bread upon the waters, however, without expecting something in return. Though rates vary widely, a fifteen-minute daily program on a local radio station costs, on the average, about $200 per week. On a superpower station like XERF the rate may run as high as $600. The evangelists pay this fee themselves, but they depend upon their radio audience to provide the funds. For this reason, some take advantage of God's Precious Air Time to hawk a bit of sacred merchandise. Much of it is rather ordinary—large-print Bibles, calendars, greeting cards, Bible-verse yo-yos, and ball-point pens with an inspirational message right there on the side. Other items are more unusual. Bill Beeny, who tends to see the darker side of current events, offers $25-contributors a Riot Pack containing a stove, five fuel cans, a rescue gun, a radio, and the marvelous Defender, a weapon that drives an attacker away and covers him with dye, making him an easy target for police. Ten dollars will buy a blue-steel, pearl-handled, tear-gas pistol, plus the informative and inspirational Truth-Pac #4. Or, for the same price, Evangelist Beeny will send his own album of eighteen songs about heaven, together with the Paralyzer, "made by the famous Mace Company." Presumably, it is safer to turn the other cheek if one has first paralyzed one's enemy.

The most common items offered for sale, however, are the evangelist's own books and records. Brother Al's current book is *The Second Touch:* "It's wrote in plain, down-to-earth language, and has big print that will heal any weak eyes that reads it." For a $5 offering C. W. Burpo will send his wonderful recording of "My America," plus a bonus bumper sticker advertising his program, The Bible Institute of the Air—"Be a moving billboard for God and Country." Don and Earl, "two young Christian singers from Fort Worth, Texas," offer for only $3 "plus a extra quarter to pay the postage back out to your house," albums of heart-touching songs and stories that include such old favorites as "Just One Rose Will Do," "A Tramp on the Streets," "Lord, Build Me a Cabin in Heaven," "Streamline to Glory," "Remember Mother's God," "A Soldier's Last Letter," "That Little Pair of Half-worn Shoes," "Just a Closer Walk with Thee" (featuring the gospel whistling of Don), and that great resurrection hymn, "There Ain't No Grave Gonna Keep My Body Down."

In keeping with St. Paul's dictum that "those who proclaim the gospel should get their living by the gospel," the radio ministers do not always offer merchandise in return for contributions. In fact, the books and records and magazines probably function primarily as a link that facilitates the more direct appeals for money almost sure to follow.

Brother Al, sounding like a pathetic Andy Devine, asks the faithful to send "God's Perfect offering—$7.00. Not $6.00, not $8.00, but $7.00." An offering even more blessed is $77, God's two perfect numbers, although any multiple of seven is meritorious. "God told me to ask for this. You know I don't talk like this. It's got to be God. God told me he had a lot of bills to pay. Obey God—just put the cash inside the envelope." In addition to cash, Brother Al will also accept checks, money orders, and American Express surely he means traveler's checks. Seven's perfection stems from its prominence in the Bible: the seven deadly sins, the seven churches of Asia, and so forth. Radio Pastor David Epley also believes God has a perfect number, but he has been reading about the apostles and the tribes of Israel. Quite understandably, he seeks a $12 offering, or the double portion offering of $24.

Brother Glenn Thompson, who also names God as his co-solicitor, claims that most of the world's ills, from crabgrass to garden bugs to Communism and the Bomb, can be traced to man's robbing God. "You've got God's money in your wallet. You old stingy Christian. No wonder we've got all these problems. You want to know how you can pay God what you owe? God is speaking through me. God said, 'Inasmuch as you do unto one of these, you do it unto me.' God said, 'Give all you have for the gospel's sake.' My address is Brother Glenn, Paragould, Arkansas."

In sharp contrast, Garner Ted Armstrong makes it quite clear that all publications offered on his broadcasts are absolutely free. There is no gimmick. Those who request literature never receive any hint of an appeal for funds unless they specifically ask how they might contribute to the support of the program. Garner Ted's father, Herbert W. Armstrong, began the broadcast in 1937, as a vehicle for spreading a message that features a literalistic interpretation of biblical prophecy. The program has spawned a college with campuses in California, Texas, and London, and a church of more than 300,000 members. Characteristically, the ministers of the local churches, which meet in rented halls and do not advertise, even in the telephone book, will not call on prospective members without a direct invitation. This scrupulous approach has proved quite successful. *The World Tomorrow,* a half-hour program, is heard daily on more than four hundred stations throughout the world, and a television version is carried by sixty stations.

Several evangelists use their radio programs primarily to promote their personal appearance tours throughout the country, and may save the really high-powered huckstering for these occasions. A. A. Allen is both typical and the best example. An Allen Miracle Restoration Revival Service lasts from three to five hours and leaves even the inhibited participant observer quite spent. On a one-night stand in the Houston Music Hall, Allen and the Lord drew close to a thousand souls, in approximately equal portions of blacks, whites, and Mexican-Americans. As the young organist in a brown Nehru played gospel rock, hands shot into the air and an occasional tambourine clamored for joy. Then, without announcement, God's Man of Faith and Power came to pulpit center. Allen does not believe in wearing black; that's for funerals. On this night he wore a green suit with shiny green shoes.

For the better part of an hour, he touted his book that is turning the religious world upside down, *Witchcraft, Wizards, and Witches,* and a record, pressed on 100 percent pure vinyl, of his top two soul-winning sermons.

To prepare the audience for the main pitch, Allen went to great lengths to leave the impression that he was one of exceedingly few faithful men of God still on the scene. He lamented the defection from the ministry: "In the last few years, 30 percent of the preachers have stopped preaching; 70 percent fewer men are in training for the ministry. A cool 100 percent less preachers than just a few years ago." He chortled over the fate of rival evangelists who had run afoul of the law or justifiably irate husbands. At another service, he used this spot to describe the peril of opposing his ministry. He told of a student who tried to fool him by posing as a cripple; God struck him dead the same night. A man who believed in Allen's power, but withheld $100 God had told him to give the evangelist, suffered a stroke right after the meeting. And on and on.

When he finished, Brother Don Stewart, Allen's associate in the ministry of fund-raising, took the microphone to begin a remarkable hour of unalloyed gullery. At the end of his recitation, approximately 135 people pledged $100 apiece, and others emptied bills and coins into large plastic wastebaskets that were filled and replaced with astonishing regularity. And all the while Brother Don walked back and forth shouting to the point of pain, "Vow and pay, vow and pay, the scripture does say, vow and pay."

Despite the blatantly instrumental character of much radio religion, it would be a mistake to suppose that its only appeal lies in the promise of health and wealth, though these are powerful incentives. The fact is that if the world seems out of control, what could be more reassuring than to discover the road map of human destiny? This is part of the appeal of Garner Ted Armstrong, who declares to listeners, in a tone that does not encourage doubt, that a blueprint of the future of America, Germany, the British Commonwealth, and the Middle East, foolproof solutions for the problems of child-rearing, pollution, and crime in the streets, plus a definitive answer to the question, "Why Are You Here?" can all be theirs for the cost of a six-cent stamp. On a far less sophisticated level, James Bishop Carr, of Palmdale, California, does the same thing. Brother Carr believes that much of the world's ills can be traced to the use of "Roman time" (the Gregorian calendar) and observances of religious holidays such as Christmas. He has reckoned the day and hour of Christ's second coming, but is uncertain of the year. Each Night of Atonement, he awaits the Eschaton with his followers, the Little Flock of Mount Zion. Between disappointments, he constructs elaborate charts depicting the flow of history from Adam's Garden to Armageddon, complete with battle plans for the latter event. Others deal in prophecy on more of an *ad hoc* basis, but are no less confident of their accuracy. David Terrell, the Endtime Messenger, recently warned that "even today, the sword of the Lord is drawed" and that "coastal cities shall be inhabited by strange creatures from the sea, yea, and there shall be great sorrow in California. . . . God has never failed. Who shall deny when these things happen that a prophet was in your midst? Believest thou this and you shall be blessed."

To become a disciple of one of these prophet-preachers is, by the evangelists' own admission, to obtain a guide without peer to lead one over life's uneven pathway. Though few of them possess standard professional credentials, they take pains to assure their scattered flocks that they have divine recognition and approval. Some associate themselves with leading biblical personalities, as when A. A. Allen speaks of the way "God has worked through his great religious leaders, such as Moses and myself," or when C. W. Burpo intones, "God loves you and I love you." Several report appearances by heavenly visitors. According to David Terrell, Jesus came into his room on April 17, about eight-thirty at night and told him there was too much junk going around. "Bring the people unto me." Though some receive angels regularly, they do not regard their visits lightly. "If you don't think that it'll almost tax your nervous system to the breaking point," says the Reverend Billy Walker, Jr., "let an angel come to you." Other evangelists simply promise, as does Brother Al, "I can get through to God for you." In support of such claims, they point to the testimony of satisfied disciples and to their own personal success; the flamboyance in dress affected by some of the men obviously capitalizes on their followers' need for a hero who has himself achieved the success denied them.

In the fiercely competitive struggle for the listeners' attention and money, most of the evangelists have developed a novel twist or gimmick to distinguish them from their fellow clerics. C. W. Burpo does not simply pray; he goes into the "throne room" to talk to God. The door to the throne room can be heard opening and shutting. David Epley's trademark is the use of the gift of "discernment." He not only heals those who come to him, but "discerns" those in his audience who need a special gift of healing, in the manner of a pious Dunninger. A. A. Allen emphasizes witchcraft on most of his current broadcasts, blaming everything from asthma to poverty on hexes and demons. In other years he has talked of holy oil that flowed from the hands of those who were being healed, or crosses of blood that appeared on their foreheads. David Terrell frequently calls upon his gift of "tongues." Terrell breaks into ecstatic speech either at the peak of an emotional passage or at points where he appears to need what is otherwise known as "filler." Certain of his spirited words tend to recur repeatedly. *Rapha, nissi,* and *honda bahayah* are three favorites. The first two may be derived from the Hebrew words for healing and victory. Unless the third is a Hebrew term having to do with motorcycles, its meaning is known only to those with the gift of interpretation. Terrell defends his "speaking in the Spirit" over the radio on the grounds that he is an apostle—"not a grown-up apostle like Peter or Paul; just a little boy apostle that's started out working for Jesus."

Once one has made contact with a radio evangelist, preferably by a letter containing a "love offering," one is usually bombarded with letters and publications telling of what God has recently wrought through his servant, asking for special contributions to meet a variety of emergencies, and urging followers to send for items personally blessed by the evangelist and virtually guaranteed to bring the desired results. One runs across holy oil, prosperity billfolds, and sacred willow twigs, but the perennial favorite of those with talismaniacal urges is the prayer cloth.

Prayer cloths come in several colors and sizes, and are available in muslin, sackcloth, terrycloth, and, for a limited time only, revival-tent cloth. As an optional extra, they can be anointed with water, oil, or ashes. My own model is a small (2½ × 3½ inches) unanointed rectangle of pinked cloth. The instructions state that it represents the man of God who sent it, and that it can be laid upon those with an ailment, hidden in the house to bring peace and blessings, carried in the purse or pocketbook for financial success, and even taken to court to assure a favorable outcome. One woman told Reverend Ike that she had cut her cloth in two and placed a piece under the separate beds of a quarreling couple. She declared the experiment an unqualified success, to the delight of Reverend Ike—"You did that? You rascal, you! Let's all give God a great big hand!"

These scraps of paper and cloth serve to bind preacher and people together until the glorious day when a faithful listener can attend a live service at the civic auditorium or the coliseum, or under the big tent at the fairgrounds. It is here, in the company of like-minded believers, that a person loses and perhaps finds himself as he joins the shouting, clapping, dancing, hugging, weeping, rejoicing throng. At such a service, a large Negro lady pointed into the air and jiggled pleasantly. Beside her, a sad, pale little woman, in a huge skirt hitched up with a man's belt, hopped tentatively on one foot and looked for a moment as if she might have found something she had been missing. On cue from the song leader, all turned to embrace or shake hands with a neighbor and to assure each other that "Jesus is *all right!*" Two teen-age boys "ran for Jesus." And in the aisles a trim, gray-haired woman in spike heels and a black nylon dress, danced sensuously all over the auditorium. She must have logged a mile and a half, maybe a mile and three quarters, before the night was over. I couldn't help wondering if her husband knew where she was. But I was sure she liked where she was better than where she had been.

If a radio evangelist can stimulate this kind of response, whether he is a charlatan (as some undoubtedly are) or sincerely believes he is a vessel of God (as some undoubtedly do) is secondary. If he can convince his listeners that he can deliver what he promises, the blend of genuine need, desperate belief, reinforcing group—and who knows what else?—can move in mysterious ways its wonders to perform. And, for a long time, that will likely be enough to keep those cards and letters coming in.

EIGHT

Ecology: The Community and the Spaceship Earth

WE ARE LIVING in an era that is witnessing the greatest migration in human history, a mass exodus from the land to the city. The forces that have wrought this epic change have vastly transformed the conditions under which millions of people carry out their day-to-day activities, for the physical and social conditions of rural and urban life are very different. The stimulating variety and diversity that are uniquely characteristic of the city are presently coupled with choking air pollution, staggering transportation problems, overcrowding, general ugliness, and an absence of a sense of community. Is this the best we can do? Are many of us doomed to live out our lives in a "sick" environment? Is the flight to the suburbs the answer?

The early Greeks and Romans had a different idea of what a city should be. The city, as they conceived of it, should be built as beautifully as possible. They felt that the center of man's life should also be an inspiration for man's living, and a great deal of wealth was invested in this dream. But before Christ the city of Rome was already grappling with the problems that are now so familiar to the urban American. The Romans were unable to solve their urban problems. Will we solve ours?

Modern man often feels isolated and alienated as he walks among ugly, towering masses of concrete and steel. Noise and pollution assault his senses, stagnation and decay assault his mind. In Tokyo there is barely enough space for people, and no space for garbage. The garbage is dumped into the bay, and housing developments are now being built on the garbage-filled areas. Yesterday's garbage literally creates tomorrow's living space. In Los Angeles, the largest sprawl of buildings in the world, two-thirds of the downtown area consists of roads, freeways, and parking lots. Another result of the Los Angeles urban sprawl has been, as in other urban areas, the wholesale destruction of the natural environment.

For those who can afford it there is a relatively simple solution to these problems. They can leave. Many have chosen this alternative, and the result has been the creation of suburbia. The 1970 census showed that for the first time more Americans were living in the outlying areas of big cities than in the cities themselves. In their movement to the country, however, many suburbanites have found that they actually destroyed much of what they were seeking. The natural environment may again be destroyed in the name of economy, and traffic and pollution problems often follow on the heels of those who flee.

But what about the effect of this migration on the central city? Suburban shopping centers and tax losses cut into the city's economic health. The white and prosperous leave the black and the poor. The rate of decay accelerates. Relief rolls grow larger as the tax base shrinks. Frustration, hostility, and distrust build in the central cities, racial tensions heighten, and violence may erupt.

So we tear down the ghettos and the slums and speak of urban renewal. This, again, primarily eliminates a problem for the middle and upper classes; they no longer have to look at or contend with the dilapidated and decaying areas that have been removed. Destruction of lower-class living sites is then followed by middle-income housing projects. But where do the displaced find suitable housing? An attempt is now being made in some of our cities to provide federally subsidized low-income housing so that the residents of the former slums can afford to live in the developments that replace them.

In our effort to solve these and other urban problems we might turn to the European experience for guidance. London, for example, channels its growth into various planned communities from which it is separated by a green belt. In the planned communities green open areas are preserved, housing and industrial units are built with aesthetics in mind, walking paths are separated from traffic arteries, and the goal is to live life on a "human" level. The residents seem to feel that these communities are accomplishing that goal. The key to the success of this project is government control of the relocation of new industry, and the European experience in general has indicated that government must take the lead. Although comprehensive planning has never been attempted in the United States, we must soon turn to regional planning on a broad scale if we are to avoid a gigantic urban-suburban sprawl.

This brings us to one more crucial problem, the problem of organization. Our metropolitan areas have spilled over municipal, county, and even state lines. There are 1,500 separate local governments within fifty miles of Times Square in New York. Because there is much less social acceptance of regional and national planning in the United States than in Europe, it will be difficult to form larger metropolitan governmental units and to deal effectively with a variety of crucial ecological problems. It seems a necessity, however, if we are yet to see a realization of the Greco-Roman dream, for ecosystems know no political boundaries. If we are to restore these regions to ecological equilibrium we may have to resort in the near future to what many would describe as "unthinkable" programs. An important task is the establishment of an effective program for restricting population growth. Other problems include sewage and garbage disposal, the preservation of recreational areas, the control of dangerous pesticides, and air, water, and noise pollution control. Because automobiles contribute greatly to air pollution and crowding, they will have to be replaced by adequate mass transportation systems.

We must also ask, as a nation, what part we play in the ecology of the community of nations. How much do we consume of the earth's finite supply of natural resources? What effect do our patterns of consumption (for example, our preference for meat) have on the rest of the world's population? With only 6 per cent of the world's population, the United States consumes a highly disproportionate amount of the world's natural resources (over a fourth of the world's steel, half of its synthetic rubber, a fifth of its cotton, etc.). The ecological and political ramifications of this fact are considerable.

In conclusion, unless we develop more effective ways of living harmoniously within our environment, *Homo sapiens,* which as a hunting and gathering species lived in harmony with nature for hundreds of thousands of years, may exterminate itself in what Paul Ehrlich has called an "eco-catastrophe." —D. R.

Selected References

(All are available in paperback editions.)

DeBell, Garrett. *The Environmental Handbook.* New York: Ballantine Books, Inc., 1970.

Hunter, Floyd. *Community Power Structure.* Garden City, N.Y.: Doubleday & Company, Inc., 1963.

Jacobs, Jane. *The Death and Life of Great American Cities.* New York: Random House, Inc., 1961.

Stein, Maurice R. *The Eclipse of Community.* Princeton, N.J.: Princeton University Press, 1960.

Vidich, Arthur J., and Joseph Bensman. *Small Town in Mass Society.* Garden City, N.Y.: Doubleday & Company, Inc., 1960.

How to Use Slum Dweller, False Front to Aid Tourism

MIKE ROYKO

The people who favor an airport in Lake Michigan have offered an endless variety of reasons for it.

But few have been as thought-provoking as that of Thomas V. King, assistant general manager of the Merchandise Mart.

King, in stepping down as head of the Chicago Convention Bureau, discussed the great need for a lake airport to stimulate convention business and tourism. He told a press conference:

"It has always been my impression on rides from airports in many metropolitan areas that you get a grim appearance from cemeteries and slums.

"A causeway from a lake airport into Chicago would be one of the magnificent attractions of the world and would give visitors a greeting they would never forget."

Frankly, I had never thought of the slum problem in exactly that way, but there is no denying the truth of King's observation, and he should be commended for feeling compassion for the downtrodden visitor to our city.

It is, indeed, almost impossible to reach downtown Chicago from any direction except the lake without passing slums, and maybe a few cemeteries.

This is due to poor urban planning. Years ago, they should have laid the city out so the slums would all be off in some quiet corner where people could avoid looking at them.

Those of us who live here are so accustomed to the dismal sight that we hardly notice it, unless one of the slums happens to burn, thus causing a gapers' block on the expressway, which can be irritating.

So we never consider what a distasteful eyesore it must be to a visiting tourist, conventioner or businessman.

He arrives here in a sleek jet, happily eating and drinking and having his pillow plumped by a sweet young thing. Jauntily, he steps into his cab, limousine or bus and sets off.

Suddenly he sees a cemetery off to the side of the expressway. He averts his eyes, not wanting to be reminded of the frailty of human flesh.

Just when he recovers from that grim sight, he is thrust into the midst of miserable tenements, ugly public housing and people who are not happy at all—kill-joys. A faint cry may escape his lips as he holds his attaché case over his face to blot out the nastiness of it all.

Then, after he recovers by seeing the "real Chicago," he has to go out the way he came in, trembling in nausea all the way to the airport.

That is no way to treat a visitor. No human being should be forced to look at slums.

But is King's solution the only way? There may be alternatives.

The city might consider building high, attractive fences between the expressways and the slums, as was done on a smaller scale during the Democratic national convention to spare delegates unhappy sights.

Another approach might be to rehabilitate those slum buildings that can be seen from the expressway. Actually, money could be saved by rehabilitating only the visible sides of the buildings.

The Convention Bureau could then ask the people in the buildings to stay out of sight, or to at least try to look happy when they do step outside. If there is anything more depressing to a jovial tourist than a slum, it is a sullen-looking slum dweller.

They might even be taught to cheerfully wave and even throw flowers and confetti at the passing tourists.

But if the lake airport and causeway is the only way, then let us really give the tourist something to remember. Make no small plans, Mr. King.

Some of the young slum dwellers could be taught to dive from the causeway into the lake for coins tossed by amused tourists, as native youths do in so many popular foreign vacation spots.

Others could be hired to place flowers around the necks of visitors as they step off the planes and sing happy welcoming songs.

Our slum women could be taught to carry gourds, or luggage on their heads, while the men lead oxen, lending a quaintly primitive air to the arrival scene.

And for an exotic touch, some old slum men might be hired to pull rickshaws from the lake airport to the hotel, which would really be something to tell the folks back home about.

Why not teach the slum population to call tourists "bwana bwana" or something like that.

Throw in a bit of voodoo, some houseboys, and a few ancient wretches pleading for alms at the side of the causeway, and we'd have a tourist spot that would pack 'em in.

And we can do it, with bold thinkers like King Thomas V. . . . er . . . I mean Thomas V. King.

While There Is Still Time

LAURENCE M. GOULD

Homo sapiens *evolved as a hunting and gathering animal who lived within his environment without significantly changing it. But beginning with the domestication of plants some 10,000 years ago, he began to alter his environment in ultimately destructive ways. Laurence Gould points out that we have also developed our industrial technology at the expense of our environment. He argues that we must begin to preserve the quality of our environment "while there is still time."*

"I do not believe the greatest threat to our future is from bombs or guided missiles. I don't think our civilization will die that way. I think it will die when we no longer care—when the spiritual forces that make us wish to be right and noble die in the hearts of men. Arnold Toynbee has pointed out that 19 of 21 civilizations have died from within and not by conquest from without. There were no bands playing and no flags waving when these civilizations decayed. It happened slowly, in the quiet and the dark when no one was aware."

These words from my annual report as President of Carleton College have appeared in numerous publications and have been read by millions of people since I wrote them in August 1958. But requests to use the quotation continue to come.

Why? There is no original thought in these words. The same sentiments have been expressed numberless times. They continue to attract attention, I think, first because people do care and, second, because they are becoming aware.

We are painfully aware of the growing antagonism between man and the social environment which he has created. We are all too frequently reminded of it by our racial woes, our Vietnams and our urban messes which illuminate our failure to adapt human settlements to dynamic change.

But we are less aware of what is perhaps an even more sinister situation, and that is man's relationship to his deteriorating physical and biological environment. This is the most serious long-term problem facing mankind. It derives from our ever-expanding technology, which has provided us with better transportation, cheaper power and ever more opulent ways of life. At the same time, it is degrading our environment physically, chemically and biologically.

From *Bell Telephone Magazine,* Vol. 48, No. 1 (February 1969). Reprinted by permission of the author.

The application of science has done more than any other discipline to free man from the bondages of hunger, fear, ignorance and superstition about his world. But in using the products of science we have been fooling ourselves with the illusion that we can have something for nothing. Every good casts its shadow. There is a price tag on everything, including the benefits that man has received from science and its applications.

Science has given man power to do almost anything he wants to do, even before he has learned what he does want to do. If man is to survive, he must become aware of the damaging effects of new technologies and balance them against possible benefits.

Perhaps there is a partial excuse for blundering into the use of water-polluting detergents, which unlike soap cannot be degraded by biological process in sewage disposal plants. There seems to be no excuse for the development of supersonic transport. That noise is not only disagreeable but is the cause of various nervous and perhaps more serious disorders is supported by overwhelming scientific evidence. Yet General Jewell Maxwell has observed that "we believe that people in time will come to accept the sonic boom" and Dr. H. von Gerke of the Air Force Aerospace Medical Research Laboratories has said, "Sonic booms are an environmental annoyance like pollution of air or water. Americans will have to learn to live with them."

And so we must learn to live with polluted air and water! Such is the arrogance of technology which marches over every obstacle, forcing us to face the question of whether man is the master of his creations or whether indeed he is adjusting to technology.

The genus *homo*, to which we all belong, has been on earth at least two million years. For most of that time he lived in harmony with the nature that produced him. Things began to change with the development of agriculture some 10,000 years ago. The change accelerated with the discovery of the use of metals 6,000 to 8,000 years ago.

Since then man has risen, not in cooperation with the nature that produced him, but in conflict with it. As population pressures pushed him farther and farther from his ancestral home, he became increasingly reckless with his environment. He has mined the minerals from the earth. He has destroyed the forests and the grasslands and let untold millions of tons of soil wash into the sea. He has caused the extinction of at least 300 species of animals. He is fouling his own nest and destroying his own habitat and may, thereby, be destroying himself. For, if the process goes on too long, it may well become irreversible.

Primitive man did little damage to his environment. Like all living things he produced toxic wastes, including his own corpses. These were decayed by nature and reused by other creatures. Recycling is as old as life itself on planet earth.

But technological man has interfered with nature's recycling processes by producing wastes that do not decay; he is the dirtiest creature ever to inhabit the earth. His glass bottles and aluminum beverage cans will outlast the oldest man-made monuments.

For the first time in human history the chief danger to our survival comes from ourselves instead of the forces of nature. We have not yet learned that we cannot bully nature but that we must cooperate and negotiate with it. Our pressure on nature is provoking nature's revenge, and we are sitting down to a banquet of consequences.

For a long time scholars believed that the decline of ancient civilizations and cities of the Middle East was due to climatic changes. We know now that this is not true. Conditions during the rise of the great ancient cultures were actually warmer and drier than during their decadence. The uplands that fed the great rivers had been covered with vegetation, which held the soil in place, until the forests were removed and herds brought in to complete the devastation. The site of ancient cities, which once stood at the head of the Persian Gulf, are now separated from it by 150 miles of delta—the eroded soil from the uplands. The same is happening to topsoil in America—and at a shocking rate.

Our boasted American civilization is built on the most wasteful exploitation of such resources as minerals, water, land and energy that history records. Even the rich United States is at a turning point in its history.

Today more than half the raw materials required for our own industry are imported from foreign and sometimes distant sources. We are slowly moving into the category of a "have-not" nation in terms of domestic resources. According to the U.S. Geological Survey, during the last 30 years the United States alone used more minerals and fuels than did the entire world in all previous history. And we face the grim prospect that consumption of most minerals will double within 15 to 25 years.

Recent figures show that the per capita consumption of water is about 25 times greater than it was 50 years ago. There is scarcely any part of the country where future water supply is not a matter of concern. In the United States in the last six years, 1,000 communities have had to restrict the use of water. At least 60 underdeveloped nations already face water shortage problems.

The pollution of air and water is more serious in the developed countries than in the so-called under-developed or developing countries. It is more serious here where applied technology is most advanced, because the major cause is the consumption of fossil fuels: coal, oil and gas. Every day, chimneys in the United States pour 100,000 tons of sulfur dioxide into the air. Motor vehicles add 230,000 tons of carbon monoxide. New York City alone dumps 200 million gallons of raw sewage into the Hudson River every day.

It has been demonstrated that tetraethyl lead has irritating effects which decrease the normal brain function. Like any metal poison, lead is fatal if enough is ingested. The automobile industry is about 70 years old and during that time the average American's lead content has increased 125-fold. Many authorities believe it is near the maximum tolerance level.

Mankind seems always to be confronted with some differing but continuing threat to its survival. We have brought under control or eliminated the major scourges of mankind. Now it is pollution and not disease that may do us in. If we continue to multiply without finding means of using our wastes, we will poison ourselves by them or bury ourselves in them.

There is no problem which is not complicated by too many people. The size of the human population is the primary key to the significant problems that face mankind today.

We must establish some equilibrium between population and the limited resources of earth. Man's only hope is not to try to conquer nature, as he has been doing, but to try to live in harmony with it.

Through the two or three or more billions of years of life on planet earth, no form of life has been able to multiply indefinitely without coming to terms with its environment. Man is no exception. He too is a child of the earth. For some years, while the population has been increasing two per cent per year, the increase in food production has been 1.2 per cent. The implications of this are obvious. Mankind is on a collision course with disaster. And if the present world population should continue to increase at its present rate, and there is little reason to suppose that it will be slowed down appreciably in the predictable future, then today's world population of three billion will double by the year 2000—just 31 years away.

It is inevitable that there will be an increase in every form of social pressure with this population increase. There will be more traffic, more noise—more of everything! Heretofore disease, famine and war have been the chief leveling-off factors. We do not accept any of them any longer as tenable ways of controlling population. Yet the population increases are higher than any foreseeable economic growth. At best the world faces declining standards of living and increasing competition for earth's food and material resources. The poor countries could out-populate the rich countries, and all hope of stabilizing world population would be gone.

There is an ever-widening gap between the "developed" and "developing" nations. Fifty-two nations created the United Nations in 1945. Independence has more than doubled the membership since then. New nations account for one-third of the territory of the globe. But while gaining politically they have been steadily falling behind economically.

The dilemma that faces us springs from the noblest of humanitarian impulses, namely our innate desire to help the weak and to heal the sick. The population explosion is not due to a rising birth rate but to lowering the death rate because of the medical revolution which has effectively eliminated many of the scourges of mankind. But have we lowered the rate so that those we have saved can die a slower death by starvation? Eighty per cent of the population increase in the next 35 years will occur in countries where food is now most needed. Even now, population increases are wiping out food production increases in hungry nations. The output of grain per person in Latin America has fallen some 16 per cent since the mid-1930s.

Recently Assistant Secretary of Agriculture Dorothy H. Jacobsen, a noted authority on food production, said that there are now two billion hungry people with incomes too low to buy necessary foods and half a billion on the verge of actual starvation. In 1965, more food was produced than in any previous year in history, and yet never in human history was there a year when more people were hungry and starving. It is estimated that 10,000 people are starving to death every day.

Some say we have the technical competence to feed 10 billion people or more. This certainly has not been demonstrated, but even if we could do so, that is not the question.

The major question is not how many people planet earth can support but what quality of life we want for our descendants. I am sure we do not want our successors to live in a world so crowded as to be a faceless, ant-like society in which human values disappear. The major problem is one of education. It must be answered in terms of a decision of what people are for anyway.

Even with the population pressures of today it is clear that crowding makes poorer life even in our affluent society. Dudley Kirk of the Population Council cites an example from his native state: "Few people who, like myself, grew up in California would argue that California is a better place to live because of its enormous population growth. The aesthetic beauties of this state have been smothered by smog, scarred by bulldozers, corroded by mass subdivisions, made unavailable by fear of fire and overrun by population. Yet this growth served the legitimate interests of an expanding economy; it brought profit and a good income to many. The question before us now is do we want more of the same—more goods and more smog, or are we willing to sacrifice some of our gadgets for a more aesthetic environment, one in which man is less destructive and out of tune with his natural surroundings."

We are living at a unique time in history. Ours is a time of transition. And change is apt to be painful. The remainder of this century may be the grimmest period in our history. Granted our apparent inability to match world food production against increasing population, the next two decades are fraught with such hunger and misery as man has not yet known. But if we lift our sights a little higher to a longer view, there is hope.

I know man is indeed poised on a great abyss, but my geology tells me that somewhere there is a corresponding summit. From that summit the scientific probability of my geology persuades me that there lie ahead of life long periods of geological time.

"While There Is Still Time!" I believe there is still time to restore and preserve the quality of our environment if we are willing to pay the price. I believe we still have a period of grace.

The awareness of a problem is certainly a necessary prelude to its solution. We are becoming aware and we do care.

The crisis which faces us is primarily an intellectual one, and in all intellectual crises it has been the belief in the possibility of a solution that made the solution possible. We are just beginning to tap the world's intellectual resources. The greatest quantum jump in the extension of man is in the computer or cybernetic revolution. Computers are creating a greater revolution in the field of intellectual effort than machines in transportation. Computers can calculate millions of times faster than man, but our fastest machines move only about 5,000 times as fast as man can walk.

We also are standing at the threshold of abundant energy worldwide. The world has always been ruled by energy in one form or another. Today, the greatest gap between the "have" nations and the "have-nots" lies in the use of energy. Over large parts of the world the per capita consumption of energy is less than one-tenth that of Great Britain and less than one-thirtieth that of the United States.

Obviously, we can't depend indefinitely on our fossil fuels: coal, oil and gas; but the light is breaking in other areas. The new breeder reactors are going to increase nuclear power enormously. We are going to make use of a large part of the fission energy of the abundant U238 ore or of thorium. One thousand tons of this ore will produce as much energy as three billion tons of coal per year.

We appear to be on the threshold of liberating thermonuclear power which alone could blanket the earth with energy within the reach of all. And there's a reasonable prospect that we shall soon be emulating the stars by using fusion energy of atomic nuclei.

With abundant cheap energy within the reach of all, there need no longer be underdeveloped countries. The inequalities of wealth and poverty can be equalized not by leveling down but by leveling up. This is the first age in man's history in which people have dared think it practicable to make the benefits of civilization available to the whole human race. Never has the world held greater promise of things to come. The supreme irony of our time is that we are so close to man's perpetual hope of well-being and yet never before so close to extinction. The grimmest statistic of history is that the two major problems facing mankind may, and could, cancel each other out—namely, the population explosion and global nuclear conflict.

"While There Is Still Time!" It takes an act of faith even to imply that there is still time—faith, not in science or technology or things material, but in man himself—in a belief in his sense of justice and the preponderance of the creative and cooperative impulses over the competitive and the destructive. The crucial question is what kind of people and with what ethical standards they are going to use the products of science and technology.

Can we restrain our fears and our hate until we can create an adequate organization of society that will utilize the new tools of science and technology for peace and security? This is the ultimate question and it is urgent.

If we can do this and use the new powers science has given us and use them humanely for the benefit of all mankind, realizing that the human estate belongs to all men everywhere, we have the hope, the hope that a new renaissance can be ours—a renaissance in which all mankind can share.

The Experimental City

ATHELSTAN SPILHAUS

If you could design and construct a city in its entirety, what would it be like? What are the components of your ideal city? In this selection, Athelstan Spilhaus develops his vision of the "experimental city."

The Experimental City suggested some years ago is now being planned. Started from scratch, the Experimental City will be unlike other cities or towns that have been built in this way. It will not be a bedroom satellite of an existing city, as some of the New Towns in England have become; nor will it attempt to be an instant utopia. It will be neither a single company town—Hershey, Pennsylvania—nor a single occupation town—Oak Ridge, Manned Space Center, Los Alamos, Chandrigar, Brazilia, Washington, D.C. The Experimental City should not be confused with "demonstration" or "model" cities that attempt to show what can be done temporarily to renew old cities. Yet it will experiment with extensions of many of the assets and experiences of these. It will attempt to be a city representing a true cross section of people, income, business and industry, recreation, education, health care, and cultural opportunities that are representative of the United States.

The Experimental City will be carefully planned for the specific purpose of people's living and working, but, like a machine, it will be planned for an optimum population size. When it reaches this capacity, its growth will be stopped, just as machines are not overloaded when they reach their capacity. Even bacterial cultures stop growing when their size is such that they can no longer get rid of their waste metabolites. Man has not only the products of his own metabolism but what James Lodge calls the metabolites of his labor-saving slaves. Buckminster Fuller estimates that each of us has the equivalent of four hundred slaves. As technology proceeds, more and more of these mechanical slaves are used. In turn, waste metabolites increase, and cities should decrease proportionally in size.

For the experiment to be real, the city must be large enough to offer a variety of job opportunities and recreational, educational, and cultural choices. Fortunately, as technology moves forward, it affords a variety of choices without needing great numbers of people. For example, television can bring to a small community a variety in education, recreation, and information that in the past would have been possible only in large urban areas.

Reprinted by permission of *Daedalus*, Journal of the American Academy of Arts and Sciences, Boston. Fall 1967, "America's Changing Environment."

Three million people—the annual population increase in the United States—is equivalent to a dozen cities of 250,000 people. No engineer nor industry would build a dozen of anything so costly and complicated as a city without having an experimental prototype. The three million new citizens must be housed anyway, and the experience of many industries tells us that it is often cheaper to build a new modern plant than to patch an old one. To allow our presently overgrown cities, burdened as they are with complex problems, to take care of an unplanned bulge is costly.

Cities grow unplanned; they just spread haphazardly. By planning now, the advantages of high-density living can be preserved without the ugliness, filth, congestion, and noise that presently accompany city living. The urban mess is due to unplanned growth—too many students for the schools, too much sludge for the sewers, too many cars for the highways, too many sick for the hospitals, too much crime for the police, too many commuters for the transport system, too many fumes for the atmosphere to bear, too many chemicals for the water to carry.

The immediate threat must be met as we would meet the threat of war —by the mobilization of people, industry, and government. The potential gains are so great that we should take correspondingly calculated experimental risks. Curiously, we only take great risks and tolerate great mistakes in war. Up to now, government's efforts have been ineffective, concentrating on measuring what is happening, then viewing with alarm, and making industry the scapegoat in what are often essentially punitive measures. Instead, government should provide incentives to industry to encourage control of waste at its source.

Imaginative things are being done to control waste at its source. Fly ash from smokestacks is collected for use in making cement and bricks, but so far only one sixteenth of the total has a market; a plant in Florida uses a city's garbage to make fertilizer; dust from grain elevators is made into pellets for cattle feed; iron ore dust from steel plants is fed back to make steel; sulfur dioxide from factory chimneys and sulfur from oil refineries is made into sulfuric acid. There are examples of industrial symbiosis where one industry feeds off, or at least neutralizes, the wastes of another—inorganic wastes from a chemical plant may neutralize the over-abundance of organic nutrients from sewage and prevent uncontrollable growth of algae.

In many of these cases, the cost of recovery far exceeds the value of the recovered material. But if a clean environment is our aim, it costs the nation less to recover wastes where they are generated, even if they have no value, than to clean them up after they have been dispersed. Costs resultant from control at the source must be passed on in the cost of the product, but the total increase in manufacturing costs would not compare to the amount the nation would have to spend for cleaning up after the filth is dispersed in rivers, in the air, or on the land.

But what about the manufactured goods themselves once they are in the consumer's hands? We call him a consumer, but he consumes nothing. Eventually he must discard the same mass of material that he uses. Just as the iron-ore dust is recycled into the steel mill, manufactured hardware articles must be recycled after use. This process would close the loop from manufacture, to user, back to the factory. Total recycling is the ultimate goal, for it would eliminate waste and pollution. The automobile, for example, should be designed at the start with its eventual reclamation in mind. The automobile industry serves the public magnificently by mass-producing, mass-marketing, and mass-distributing a highly complex and useful machine. The industry could equally well apply its imagination and use its farflung network of operations to collect, disassemble, and reuse used cars.

In recycling, the *consumer* becomes a *user*, which he has, in fact, always been. He essentially "rents" everything. If the automobile were designed with reclamation in mind, the widespread distribution network could double as the collection network. The same applies to refrigerators, washing machines, vacuum cleaners, and every piece of hardware that we use and throw away via the euphemistic "trade-in" process. Complete recycling makes "trade-in" real and meaningful.

In the water-pollution problem, recycling—the multiple use of water of different qualities—is the ultimate goal. We never use up any water; it just carries nutrients and flushes wastes and heat from our systems. One simple example is a totally enclosed greenhouse in the desert. Water with dissolved plant foods flows into hydroponic gardens, is transpired by the plants in the hot part of the greenhouse, sucked to a cooled part where it recondenses and acquires more dissolved nutrients to repeat the cycle. The only water needed is a cupful now and then to offset leakage.

The emotional prophets of doom and the sanitary engineers provide us with a dismal picture of how fast we must run using conventional methods merely to prevent the situation from getting worse. We commend Los Angeles for taking a legislative step toward controlling the automobile emissions that cause smog, but if they achieve this control of the unburned hydrocarbons, they will blissfully go on, the automobiles will increase, and by 1980 the oxides of nitrogen, an inevitable result of burning air with anything, may reach dangerous proportions.

We need total recycling, control at the source, symbiosis of industry, and experiments with entirely new technologies toward this end. Often new technologies cannot be tried in the older cities because they are incompatible with existing systems and obsolete legal, labor, and taxation codes. The new subway in New York is not new; it is merely an extension of the old.

Some economists maintain that total recycling is too expensive, but neither they nor anyone else knows the staggering cost of present waste mismanagement. Other economists, with commendable confidence in the abilities of scientists and engineers, say "why worry to recycle"—we can invent substitutes for anything we may run out of. But recycling conserves not only what we ordinarily think of as natural resources, but also the one God-given resource that we cannot reinvent once we destroy it—our natural environment.

To preserve the total quality of the natural environment, we must think of pollution in a broad sense. Pollution would then embrace all the ills of a city. Using *disease* as an antonym of *ease,* Dr. R. K. Cannan has spoken of a different kind of disease from environmental pollution. In this context, "dis-ease" embraces the psychological insult to aesthetic sensitivity that even a perfectly sanitized junk yard presents. Filthy environments may make us mentally ill before they make us physically sick.

A pollutant often neglected is noise. Environmental noise in cities is rapidly reaching levels that industry has long considered harmful to the ears. Even lower levels of the continuously irritating noises of a concentrated civilization may make serious contributions to mental sickness. Noise is a product of the cities: Jet airplanes land near cities, trucks bring goods into cities, machines are concentrated in cities, and noisy pavement breakers are always digging up city streets. Cutting down noise costs money too; silencing a jet engine reduces its power, and a quiet machine is usually overpowered.

People concentrate in cities to escape the rigors of climate and to maximize social, business, and cultural contacts with others with a minimum of travel. But when cities grow too large, the urban climate deteriorates to such an extent that people flee. Like the nomadic peoples of primitive times who moved with the seasons, they travel far to live in the uneasy compromise of suburbia. In the summer, the power stations of the cities exude waste heat, the buildings prevent breezes from carrying off fumes and heat, and air conditioning pumps heat from the buildings to the streets to aggravate the situation further.

We need a mathematical computer model study of where waste should be taken, where it could do the most good in the insulating belt around the city. We should plan our cities on the basis of maps of pollution proneness. The industrialization of Appalachia with dirty industry is ridiculous. Those mountains were called the Smokies by the first men who saw them because they were so prone to pollution due to stagnant anticyclones that even the natural turpentines hung in a haze.

Pollution comes from concentration: Half our national population crowds onto 1 per cent of the land. People flock to the cities because they like high-density living. Fortunately, high-density living can give better and cheaper public service. It is a well-known axiom that the bigger the lots, the lower the caliber of public service. High-density living *per se* has not caused the filth in the cities; the assemblages have simply grown too large. If the one hundred million people that represent half the population of the U.S. today lived in the same high density as they do now, but were dispersed in eight hundred smaller concentrations of one-quarter million apiece, there would probably be no serious pollution problem. We need urban *dispersal,* not urban renewal.

Politicians are now stressing the need for industry and the private sector to take part in the rebuilding of slums in old, overgrown cities. Why should they? What bank would make a long-term loan to rebuild a slum in a city so overgrown that it would be a slum again before the mortgage was paid off? Moreover, what good would it do for people in the long run? Part of the problem is that our elected officials, particularly since reapportionment, represent districts. Politicians are most numerous where the population is most dense. There is little incentive for an elected official to suggest dispersal of his own thickly populated and easily covered district. Consequently, we hear little of urban dispersal, but a good deal about renewal, which usually means going faster the wrong way and bringing more people into already overcrowded precincts.

Such considerations led me to urge the Experimental City project. This will provide a laboratory for experimentation and a prototype for future dispersed systems with separated cities of high concentration and controlled size. As yet, no one has studied what the best size for a city is, nor attempted to keep a city to a certain size. Chambers of Commerce uniformly believe that bigger is better. We must get away from this conventional thinking and realize that bigger than an undetermined optimum size is not better.

A city of one hundred thousand may be too small for the diversity of cultural, recreational, educational, health-care, and work opportunities that make for a virile self-contained community. Eight or ten million has, however, been amply proved to be too big. Somewhere in between lies an optimum number.

Once we have decided on a city's optimum size, how do we prevent the uncontrolled growth that leads to many of today's urban problems? The answer is *not* to control individuals, but to design a mix of industrial, commercial, and other employment opportunities that keeps the population in a healthy equilibrium. In the absence of better information on the proportion in a healthy mix, perhaps we should start with a cross section of the United States. But what about regional differences? A healthy mix in the Northwest might be quite different from the comfortable mix in the Southeast. Social scientists have a challenge to define these mixes. The whole concept behind the Experimental City begins and ends with people. Profiles of employees in various enterprises can be studied by wage level, group preferences, and any other factors important to a healthy representative sample, including the right quota of those dependent on welfare, the very young, and the old and retired. Here again, regional differences of employee preferences must be considered in relation to the industrial mix.

A city grows because business and industry concentrate there, providing people with diverse opportunities for work and a variety of life styles. If an Experimental City is to be built to preserve a better quality of urban environment, industry and business must build it, but in a planned way.

Although the Experimental City would be planned as much as possible, it would be designed and built so that it could change easily. In a way, the city would be designed backwards, starting with innovations in the newest engineering systems conceived for a certain number of people and no more. It would be designed to remove the burdens of chores and filth, which modern technology can do. It goes without saying that one designs for man and his society and, in general, the planning of transportation, communication, feeding, and other networks comes later. In this case, one would use technological innovation to reduce physical restraints, which would hopefully allow man and his society more freedom to thrive. The crux is to remove the pollutants of chores, filth, noise, and congestion from the city in the hope that this will free the city dweller for a greater choice and diversity of individual human activities.

People congregate in the city because it is a gathering place for work and social interaction. Thus, working and living must be compatible, but often the factories for work make the environment for living unpleasant or unbearable. Clearly the most dramatic role of industry in the Experimental City is to show that places of work need not pollute the environment with congestion, fumes, dirty water, and noise. If living and working conditions are compatible, then people will not have to travel so much. Because of pollutants, cities are divided into separate residential and industrial areas. With the pollutants removed, industrial, commercial, residential, and educational institutions could exist side by side, reducing the human waste of commuting to and fro. If the technology of the Experimental City succeeds, there will be no need for zoning. In the interim, we should recognize four-dimensional zoning which adds a time dimension to space zoning. An example of this is the control of noise at airports, where planes are prevented from taking off during the night.

Improved communications also reduce the need for travel. As a start, an information utility could be devised that would link by broad-band coaxial cables all points now connected by telephone wires. The information utility, possibly with two-way, point-to-point video and other broad-band communication, would remove much of the obvious waste in the present conduct of business and commerce, banking and shopping. (Housewives would have bedside shopping and banking, and tele-baby-sitting when they went to visit a neighbor.) City-wide improved communications with access to the central hospital open up the possibility of less costly, less intense services and better, more abundant home care. These, of course, are not radical ideas—but extensions. (Pediatricians today ask mothers to have their children breathe into the telephone receiver.) Los Angeles is already planning emergency helicopter-lifted hospital units that go to the scene of an accident, drop the hospital pod, and then lift the wreckage out of the way so that traffic can resume.

As a total experiment in social science, human ecology, environmental biology, and environmental engineering, the Experimental City would lend itself to a totally new concept of modern preventive medicine. Instead of healing the sick, doctors would contribute to the public-health concept that emphasizes the building up and banking of a capital of health and vigor while young, and the prudent spending of this capital over a lifetime without deficits of ill health. They would concentrate on eliminating ailments in early life rather than on repairing later ills. Their dedication, somewhat less personal in public health, would be, in a sense, what Dr. Walsh McDermott calls "statistical compassion."

Moreover, broad-band interconnections with other cities would provide smaller areas with wider access to national medical centers. Also, the educational, scientific, artistic, and entertainment opportunities would be far greater than a city of limited size would be able to offer otherwise. Point-to-point video, providing improved surveillance, should enable police to spend less time catching criminals after the event and more time preventing crimes.

Due to the present furor over the use of bugging and wire tapping, the information utility immediately invokes the specter of Big Brother and a Brave New World. In their best use, such devices can preserve and improve the quality of the urban environment, but like any other device they can also be misused by unscrupulous people. If the masses of information filed in our necessary public bureaus—the Internal Revenue Service, the National Institutes of Health, the Census Bureau, and the F.B.I.—were combined by an unscrupulous dictator, they would provide a potent coercive weapon against any individual. We cannot *not* use such devices, although we must set up adequate safeguards against their misuse. On the other hand, the information utility provides survey mechanisms for an instantaneous city census and flexible city management exactly analogous to methods of data collection used in weather forecasting.

The information utility and the mixing of living and working areas would reduce transportation needs, but it would still be necessary to experiment with new forms of mass transportation. People like automobiles because the automobile respects their desire to go directly from where they are to where they want to be without stopping where others want to stop. But the automobile produces polluting fumes and occupies parking space when the owner is not in it—which is about 90 per cent of the time.

Many suggestions have been made for a mass transportation system that retains the automobile's advantages without incorporating its disadvantages. One such scheme calls for pneumatically or electrically driven small pods with propulsion in the track. The pods may be computer-controlled to the common destination of a few people. After indicating your destination to the computer on entering the turnstile, you would wait X minutes or until, let us say, the six-person pod fills up—whichever is shorter—and then go nonstop to your destination. The pods would be small enough to pass noiselessly through buildings with normal ceiling heights. There are no motors in the pods, and because they are inexpensive small shells, we could afford many of them.

In order for there to be no air-burning machines within the city limits, connections to intercity and existing national transportation systems might be made at the city's periphery. Alternatively, air-burning machines might come into the city in underground tunnels with fume sewers. These would also provide connections to the Experimental City's airport, located at a distance and in a direction so that landing patterns are over not the city, but the noninhabited insulating belt.

The main public utilities could be accessible in the vehicular and other underground tunnels, thereby abating the noisy digging up and remaking of streets common to all American cities. The interconnecting utility tunnels would double or multiplex as traffic tunnels and utility trenches for the transport of heavy freight, for telephone lines, for power and gas lines, water and sewer mains, and for the rapid transit of emergency vehicles—police, fire, and medical rescue. All would be below the city for increased mobility and less noise.

The sewers, with a view to conserving water, might be pneumatic, as in the English and French systems. To save the immense areas occupied by present sewage-treatment plants, we might treat the sewage in transit in the sewer. All this presupposes that we can throw away the old-fashioned codes stipulating that telephone and power lines, and water mains and sewers be separate. Modern technology permits messages to be sent over power lines, and pure water pipes to be concentric with sewer mains. Just as garages can be housed under parks, all services can be underground, even to the extent of going hundreds of feet down for heavy manufacturing, storage of storm water, and snow and waste heat.

The Experimental City could also provide opportunities for test-marketing new products, building materials, and postal systems. New materials would give architects a tremendous scope in developing new forms. No traffic at ground level and no land owned by individuals or individual corporations would offer a degree of freedom not possible in cities where ownership of property delimits plots. Even the materials used in the buildings themselves would be such that they could be taken down and reused if found to be obsolete or inferior. Architecture, with its emphasis on form and the visual environment, is fundamental to the success of the Experimental City. Architects would be freer to exploit the mutuality of function and form in producing a visual environment *with* other improved qualities. In Philadelphia, for example, the planners have done a magnificent job improving the visual environment, but their work is mitigated by the stench of oil refineries.

In the Experimental City, we will seek a total optimum environment without hampering diversity of architectural forms and combinations. We will experiment with enclosing portions of the city within domes that will be conditioned as to temperature, humidity, fumes, and light. It is, of course, not at all certain that people want a perfectly controlled climate. The sense of beauty and well-being involves exposure to some degree of variation. Artists know this in their play with light and shade and with colors that clash. Slight breezes and variations of temperature might be necessary to transform even clean air into the fresh air that stimulates our sense of health.

The advantages of leasing and not owning land, combined with those of the new technologies, would free architects from rectilinear or stereotype ground plans that ownership of plots dictates. Space might be leased in a three-dimensional sense, and the forms the architects use in three dimensions might be emphasized by paths and foot thoroughfares, there being no wheeled traffic at ground level. Today, streets and plot plans too often predefine form. In the Experimental City, the architect will face the challenge of providing new ways for people to find face-to-face relationships in an environment that does not *require* wasteful movement.

Ralph Burgard has suggested that creative artists today are not so much concerned with the fixed audience-performer relationship. Many artists feel that art centers, now so much in fashion, are already outmoded, and that the newest forms of music, art, theater, and dance have very little to do with exhibit galleries, proscenium stages, and conventional auditoriums. Increased leisure should lead to active participation in all the arts instead of passive exposure. For this is needed an arts-recreation space completely flexible in lighting, sound, television, film, and electronic devices and in physical dimensions.

Where does one locate an Experimental City? It should be far enough away from urban areas so that it can develop self-sufficiency and not be hampered by the restrictive practices of a dominant neighboring community. Extremes of climate, far from being a disadvantage, would provide the kind of all-weather test facility needed for experimenting with technological innovations. There must be enough land for an insulating belt around the city; otherwise, conventional uncontrolled encroachments and developments would soon nullify the experiment. A density of one hundred people per acre in the city proper would mean a city area of 2,500 acres. To preserve its identity, character, cleanliness, and experimental freedom, it might need a hundred times this area as an insulating belt.

Federal and state governments are presently acquiring large tracts of unspoiled forests and lands for conservation. This is a worthy objective if done for some purpose. What better purpose is there than providing open space around cities? Such lands would be most suitable for the insulating belts between controlled-size, dispersed cities. The insulating belt would include forests, lakes, farms, outdoor museums, arboretums, and zoos. Such a mixture would make the enjoyment of the open surroundings not only attractive aesthetically and physically, but intellectually profitable. Part of the insulating belt might be devoted to hobby farms and gardens—the system so enjoyed by the Germans, who leave the city and camp in little gardens. This minimum rustic setting enables them to retain the smell and touch of the soil. There might also be high-intensity food farming and high-rise finishing farms. Fresh foods might be brought to farms in the insulating belt from starting farms farther out, and dairy cows could be fed in high-rise sterile buildings at the edge of the city to ensure the freshest, purest milk.

The legal codes and governmental structures of a city built with private funds on ground leased by a nonprofit corporation will be different from those of existing cities. Revenues to manage the city will come from leases rather than real-estate taxes. The laws and controls in the Experimental City will center on the new recognition of an individual's right to a clean environment. Though regulations will be different, there may be fewer of them because many of our laws evolved to protect us from the evil and nuisances precipitated by urban overgrowth. As the stresses of dirt, noise, and congestion are removed, other origins of antisocial behavior may be clarified.

Do people want dirt, noise, and congestion removed? Most of us assume so. But, like everything else in the Experimental City, we will have to see. The ideas and directions that have been suggested here are merely possible pieces of the total experiment, any one of which is likely to change and develop as the experiment itself develops.

About $330,000 has been allocated for defining the Experimental City project—three fourths from three departments of the Federal Government (Department of Commerce; Department of Health, Education and Welfare; Department of Housing and Urban Development) and one fourth from local industries. This is to be used for surveys of literature and experience, conferences and workshops, and development of a structure for the program's next five phases. Laboratory evaluations of new concepts and systems will then be made and experimentation done with small-scale models. After a pilot model has been constructed so that a choice can be made among the various alternatives, the city will be designed, constructed, and occupied. Finally, the actual Experimental City will be studied further, changed, and developed.

The first year's work will be carried out with the University of Minnesota serving as the host and organizer of group discussions on a series of special topics. To these conferences we will invite interested national experts from many disciplines. A distinguished group of individuals has agreed to serve as a national steering committee for the Experimental City. After the year of definition, a suitable nonprofit corporation will be formed to carry through the later phases. Then a quasi-governmental, quasi-private corporation, following the experience of the Communications Satellite Corporation, will be formed to complete the building of the Experimental City and to oversee its subsequent operation.

Clearly, we cannot continue to experiment in bits: Each new technology affects others; better communications change patterns of travel, medical care, and education; methods of cleaning and noise-proofing make zoning unnecessary. The city is a completely interacting system, and, thus, the experiment must be a total system. Nobody knows the answers to city living in the future, and when answers are unknown, experiment is essential.

The Fat Get Fatter

FRANCES MOORE LAPPE

It is commonly agreed that over one-half of the people of the world are undernourished or malnourished. Given this fact, questions about how food is distributed on a worldwide basis assume tremendous significance. For example, is America an "agricultural provider" for the world as has often been maintained? How is protein distributed on a worldwide basis? Frances Lappe offers some interesting answers to these questions.

The recent wheat sales to Russia reinforce the impression held by the average American that our agricultural abundance goes, if not to feed the hungry, at least to those who can well use the food. The Department of Agriculture certainly seems convinced of it. One of its officials has stated that "without our farms as an auxiliary source of food, millions of people in Europe, Latin America, Africa and Asia either would have a lower standard of living or actually would be hungry."

And many of us would like to believe it. After all, with the output of one-quarter of all harvested acreage shipped across our border, we *are* the world's leading agricultural exporter. But just what does "agricultural" mean? How much of this apparently vast volume of products is actually food? And how much ever reaches the mouths of hungry people? What about the goods America imports? From whom do they come? Ask such questions and the importance of sheer volume diminishes, the image of America as "provider" begins to fade. In its place another picture emerges—America as a drain on the world's food resources.

Although two-thirds of the world is hungry, most of our food exports go to the nonhungry areas—Europe, Japan and Canada. We ship three times more agricultural products to Europe than to Latin America and Africa *combined.* And we import many times more agricultural products from the poor countries than we export to them. In trade with Central America, for example, we import about five times more agricultural products than we export. The pattern is clear: the rich countries, including the United States, receive food from the poor countries, but the rich trade their own food riches among themselves.

The result of this pattern is an enormously lopsided exchange of that most needed of all human nutrients—*protein.* The size of the imbalance has been measured by Dr. Georg Borgstrom, geographer and nutritionist. He

From "World Food Trade," *The Nation,* October 30, 1972. Reprinted by permission of the publisher.

estimates that in trade with the poor countries the rich nations enjoy a net protein import of 1 million tons, an amount equivalent to half of all the protein the American population consumes from meat and poultry combined each year. That kind of trade advantage doesn't show up on the ledgers of the Commerce Department!

Given this lopsided protein exchange in favor of the rich, there must be something amiss with the popular notion that, while the poor countries may send us cocoa or tea, we send them real food. A specific example of this misconception is to be seen in the role of the hungry world as exporter of high-protein foods from the sea—of which we are the main beneficiary. Almost three-quarters of the shrimp, one-half of the tuna and one-quarter of other raw fish in world trade is directed into the American marketplace. Many of these protein riches come from poor countries, like India, Panama and Mexico. In addition we import enough protein in the form of fishmeal from Peru and Chile to meet the protein requirements of a country the size of Peru for an entire year.

The Westerner takes for granted that the best use for the poor soils and adverse climates of the poor countries is to provide nonfoods like coffee and tea for the rest of the world. Such a notion ignores two facts, one historical and the other current. Historically, the role of the poor countries as providers of these luxury products for the rich was neither their own choice, nor based on filling human needs. It was a decision made by early colonists, solely on the basis of what would bring the greatest profit to the mother country. The land now dedicated to coffee in the *poor* countries was often their best agricultural land. It could just as well have produced nutritious food for hungry people, but by now the poor countries are locked into an insidious trap of economic dependency on these products in world trade.

Second, the view of the poor as producers of nonfoods for the rich obscures the fact that on land not used for coffee or tea the poor countries grow some of the highest quality plant protein in world agriculture. Unfortunately, these foodstuffs are *also primarily for export to the rich.* They include peanuts, sesame seeds, cottonseeds, coconuts and sunflower seeds—a group known as oilseeds.

Ironically, while most of these oilseeds are potentially high-quality human foods, the rich countries use them for animal feed. One-third of Africa's peanut crop is shipped to Europe primarily for this purpose. J. C. Abbott of the Food and Agriculture Organization of the U.N. has estimated that if this high-quality protein were eaten locally instead of being exported for animal feed, it could make a significant contribution to ending malnutrition in the hungry countries. And Max Milner of the Agency for International Development has stated that as much oilseed protein is used by the rich countries for animal feed as all the protein of animal origin produced for man in the world. (The reader should be reminded here that livestock don't need to eat protein to produce it for man's benefit. Their role historically has been to consume plants inedible by man and convert them into meat.)

The rich countries are not only importing enormous quantities of high-protein feed for meat production, they also import meat directly. Again much of this crucial protein comes from the poor countries. America imports more than 1 *billion* pounds of meat annually—enough to give every American a hamburger for lunch every day for a month. We buy enough meat from Latin America (much of it from poverty-stricken Central America) to meet the protein requirements of the whole population of a country like Cost Rica for an entire year. In fact, the United States, with 7 per cent of the world's population, imports about one-quarter of all the beef and canned meat in world trade.

But is not this heavy protein importation offset by our exports? Of the ten leading U.S. agricultural exports, four—hides, tallow, cotton and tobacco—are not edible at all, and of the remaining six, only two are high in protein—nonfat dry milk and soybeans. And the majority of the soybeans go to Japan, Western Europe and Canada, where they are fed to livestock. Our government does help finance soy shipments to the hungry countries, but virtually all of it in the form of protein-empty soy oil. It is true that we export meat, but only about one-third as much as we import. A crucial fact, if one is concerned with food needs and not just dollar values, is that we export about two and a half times as much fat and inedible livestock products as we do protein-rich meat.

It has been said that the current emergence of the Third World will inevitably tend to equalize the distribution of the earth's resources. The facts belie such optimism. The patterns are so firmly established that recent agricultural breakthroughs in the poor countries *reinforce* the trends outlined above.

When grain "surpluses" have occurred as a result of the Green Revolution, the poor countries have been advised to use the "excess" capacity to develop a livestock industry for export. Quotation marks enclose "surplus" and "excess" because these terms mean neither that everyone has enough to eat nor that grain is left over. What they mean is that, given the present social structure in the poor countries, the indigenous populace cannot afford to buy its own grain.

The alternative to exporting meat to the protein-glutted rich is to change radically the social structure, so that the increased production could be consumed at home. But the major planning bodies in the rich countries and U.S. investors can hardly be expected to push for that. A twenty-one nation European commission on livestock problems stated recently that Africa has "wide potential as a beef supplier" and foresaw "the day when Africa could help alleviate an ever-growing beef shortage [*sic*] in Western Europe."

Thus the development of current land-use patterns and agricultural trade in the West has been guided more by concern for profit than for fulfilling the world's nutritional needs. Food trade does not help to balance, but grossly exaggerates, the inequities in world protein distribution. Let's not fool ourselves by laying all the blame on "overpopulation," lack of "development" or "agricultural limitations." With protein flowing from the poor to the rich, it should surprise no one that most of the world is hungry.

What Happened to "America the Beneficent"?

STEPHEN S. ROSENFELD

Rapid world population growth and greater affluence in some countries (which results in people wanting to eat better) is steadily increasing the likelihood of mass famine. Will the rich countries help to feed the poor? Stephen Rosenfeld argues that the United States, which consumes a disproportionate share of the world's resources, is moving away from being an international good samaritan.

Americans have long thought of food shortages as painful but temporary emergencies that spring up in foreign countries and promptly subside when a long line of ships loaded with our "amber waves of grain" sails into the local harbor, to the enduring gratitude of the local populace. It is time for a new picture of America the beneficent. The world, including the United States, may be entering a period of indefinite, if not permanent, food shortages. Some experts envision hunger, malnutrition, and starvation on a scale never before contemplated. The United States, instead of basking in the gratitude of a hungry world, may soon be cowering under its resentful glare.

Scare talk? Consider this evaluation from Dr. A. H. Boerma, director general of the U.N. Food and Agriculture Organization. "The world food situation in 1973 is more difficult than at any time since the years immediately following the devastation during the Second World War," he said in a report issued in September.

"If the estimates for 1972 are confirmed, this is the first time since the war that world production (including fish) has actually declined. In the face of a constantly growing population, per capita food production in the developing countries as a whole has now fallen back to the level of 1961–65. Even where the situation is less dramatic, many millions must have been added to the large numbers of people already inadequately fed. Food prices have risen almost universally, bringing additional hardship to the poorer consumers who have to spend most of their incomes on food."

Noting that the world wheat stocks are at a twenty-year low, mainly because of massive Soviet purchases, Boerma concluded: "There is little if any margin against the possibility of another widespread harvest failure, and the world has become dangerously dependent on current production and hence on weather conditions."

Norman Borlaug, winner of the Nobel Prize for his work in developing the new strains of wheat and rice that constitute the so-called Green Revolu-

From *Saturday Review/World*, December 18, 1973. Reprinted by permission.

tion, now warns of mass famine. "Only a handful of people are aware of just how close we were to having 50 to 60 million people die this year," he said last fall. Roy L. Prosterman, an agricultural development specialist at the University of Washington, likens the famine prospect to that of a huge comet crashing into earth one year hence, "probably killing thirty million or more people and possibly spinning the whole planet out of its orbit."

What has brought about this anguishing situation? Population growth is a key factor. World population grows by some seventy to seventy-five million people a year, equivalent to the entire population of Bangladesh, and by the year 2000 that rate may double. The most rapid growth occurs in the poorest countries. Growth rates surpassing 3 percent are common in the Third World, while Soviet and American growth rates are approaching zero. India alone adds some 13 million mouths a year; in a dismaying failure of political will, it is cutting back family-planning funds.

An even more voracious "consumer" of food than rising populations is rising affluence. Lester Brown, a former U.S. Agriculture Department expert now with the Overseas Development Council, says: "Historically, there was only one important source of growth in world demand for food; there are now two." Affluence makes people want to eat better. The very poor, eating products made directly from grain, consume at subsistence levels about 400 pounds of grain per person a year. But as incomes rise, people start to consume grain indirectly in the form of meat, milk, and eggs, which take much larger amounts of grain to produce. Each American now eats almost a ton of grain a year, only 150 pounds of it directly in the form of breads, pastries, and breakfast cereals. Thus affluence helps precipitate a brutal competition for food between the world's rich and poor.

Ironically, political detente sharpens this competition. The cold war effectively kept the Soviet Union and China out of the world grain market; improved relations with the West have brought them in. In 1972 Soviet grain production fell from 99 million tons the year before to 75 million. Without detente the Kremlin would have bought marginally elsewhere and obliged its citizens to pull in their belts. With detente it bought almost 30 million tons, of which about 20 million came from the United States.

There is no evidence that the Nixon administration conceived of the Soviet wheat and feed-grain purchases as other than a political and economic boon. The purchases suited perfectly the President's larger objectives: his diplomatic effort to build conspicuous links of mutual self-interest with the Russians; his political effort in an election year to harvest the farm vote; and his economic effort to improve the sagging American balance of payments (the Russians laid out $2 billion for their grain). The effect of the Soviet purchases in helping drive up American and world food prices was not quickly perceived.

But the Soviet purchases did something else: They reduced American wheat stocks which had constituted the world's principal cushion against a local food disaster, to their lowest level in twenty years. Since then the secondary cushion—the 50 million idle acres (of the 350 million total acres) of American cropland—has also been deflated; that acreage is being brought back into production to serve ever-mounting commercial export demands. It is little wonder that the Soviet-American wheat deal looks less like a contribution to world peace than a conspiracy of selfishness marking off the world's haves from the have-nots.

America's surplus policy has changed drastically. During India's famine of 1966–67, the United States dispatched enough wheat (11 million tons) to feed more than 50 million people—a rescue mission of unprecedented dimensions. But in 1973, during the Sahara drought, the United States found it could pack off only 156,000 tons of food, barely 1 percent of the earlier Indian shipments.

Last July and August, in an ominous precedent, the Department of Agriculture bought no food at all for distribution through Food for Peace, the program under which some 29 billion dollars' worth of surplus American farm products have been donated or sold at easy terms abroad since 1954. (Only nominal amounts have been released for Food for Peace since then.) Much of that program's largesse has always been distributed by voluntary agencies, which can provide food to nations that are otherwise reluctant, for political reasons, to ask for it directly from the American government.

Some poor countries have tried to buy food on the world market, a measure they rarely take (being chronically short of foreign exchange) unless hunger is straining the very fabric of their political and social order. This year India, Pakistan, Bangladesh, Mexico, and the Philippines—all countries that have enjoyed the major benefits of the Green Revolution—went to the world market for wheat or rice. It is relevant to note that the export price of American wheat has risen from the level of two dollars a bushel to more than five dollars. "If the supply-demand gap pushes rice prices above $200 a ton," one expert said last spring, "Asia will be on the brink of starvation." The price soon rose above $200 a ton.

Why can't poor countries grow more food themselves? Some people contend that distribution of American surpluses to these countries in the past might have hurt them by depressing their farm prices and letting them ignore the imperatives of agricultural self-help. Lyndon Johnson attempted to remedy this situation in the 1960s by his "short tether" policy, in which food was doled out to India practically ship by ship, in order to induce agricultural reforms. But this policy produced deep political exasperation and only questionable results in terms of reform. Probably more important for reform was the quiet decision by the United States to lift its ban on helping other countries produce commodities in which there are world surpluses. This profoundly cynical ban had been imposed in order to limit competition with American farm exports. Its abolition opened the way for export of the self-help program of technology and financial incentives known as the Green Revolution.

Norman Borlaug's 1970 Nobel Peace Prize citation credited him with a "technological breakthrough that makes it possible to abolish hunger in the developing countries in the course of a few years."

Some observers, meanwhile, held that the Green Revolution could only buy time and that population control was the only real solution. Even so, the time has seldom been well used. The Green Revolution requires large amounts of money for irrigation, fertilizers, credits, and price supports, as well as large amounts of political attention to the discrepancies it creates between farmers who exploit it and those who don't. Money and political resourcefulness are in short supply. But the demand for food grows relentlessly.

It is widely recognized that the cheapest agricultural gains to be made in the world can and should be made in the hungry countries themselves. Lester Brown estimates that a country like Brazil could double its cultivated area for cereal production and that Bangladesh has the natural resources (although presently not the economic or political resources) to quadruple its rice production. A major stress on agriculture is now, belatedly, part of all important development programs, from AID's to the World Bank's.

Some experts regard the current tightness of the world's food supply as the result mainly of bad weather—not of the "new" factors of supply and demand described above. It was bad weather that reduced the Soviet grain crop by 25 percent last year and brought on the U.S.-Soviet wheat deal. Many U.S. Department of Agriculture officials take the view that good weather will make things right again and thereby feed the world. If this view is correct, governments will not have to take special steps—in fact, if they do, the Agriculture Department notes, they may risk being stuck with large, costly, unsalable surpluses.

Is it, then, possible today for rich countries to help feed the poor? The tradition of American food aid is rooted in our image as the land of the "fruited plain" and goes back at least as far as the massive relief project that Herbert Hoover mounted for Russia's benefit in the 1920s. Since World War II, food aid has been a significant element in American foreign policy, regarded as a way both to win friends and to serve development in these countries, while keeping popular discontent within politically manageable bounds. These foreign-policy goals, however, have always been secondary to the primary domestic purpose of supporting farm income by providing a market for surpluses. And now that commercial exports sop up almost all our excess production, there is far less political pressure to keep food flowing to hungry countries without a cash return.

Senate Agriculture and Forestry Committee Chairman Herman Talmadge told me, for instance, that "this country has done its share and is continuing its responsibilities" in food aid. House Agriculture Committee Chairman W. R. Poage added that Food for Peace represents "a drain on American dollars" and should be treated as just another kind of foreign aid, "like medicine or printing presses." Food for Peace, said Secretary of Agriculture Earl Butz, "is no longer primarily a surplus-disposal program. It's for humanitarian purposes and for national security—to help infuse purchasing power into countries on our defense perimeter. South Vietnam is a case in point." Indeed, even before the surpluses that had gone into Food for Peace vanished, most of the supplies were going to South Vietnam and to other countries regarded in varying degrees as segments of the American "defense perimeter": South Korea, Israel, Pakistan, and Indonesia. "Food for Peace was based on the ethnocentric idea that we could pacify the world by food," a State Department official told me in the new spirit of retrenchment pervading Washington. "Now our thinking is that feeding the world is an international problem, maybe one for the United Nations. The worst thing we could do for a country would be to put it on a permanent dole. That would just give it the excuse to avoid solving its own problems, especially population." Butz dismisses the prospect of famine: "In the short run, no. In the long run, maybe. They've got to get their populations under control."

The FAO's Dr. Boerma also believes that "feeding the world is an international problem." He is pressing for the establishment of a so-called world food bank, where "deposits" could be made in good times and food could be withdrawn by countries in need. So far the Nixon administration has shown scant interest. With a tight federal budget, the administration has little enthusiasm for buying food at high prices from American farmers to distribute through a world bank, when the same food could be sold.

Former Secretary of State William Rogers proposed at one point "an overall review of U.S. food-production policy in relation to its effects on our assistance to the less developed countries." But the proposal got nowhere. My impression is that the new secretary of state, Henry Kissinger, has more interest in the idea and more clout within the federal establishment, but putting it into effect will be a long, tough haul.

George McGovern, a farm-state politician and a former Food for Peace administrator, told the Senate not long ago:

> We have chosen commercial sales of wheat to the Soviet Union over guarantees of an adequate diet for those impoverished Americans who subsist on surplus commodities. We have chosen, at least indirectly, to feed American livestock—in support of our taste for meat over grain—instead of meeting desperate human needs in West Africa, South Asia, and elsewhere. We are forced to such results because we simply have no policy for choosing which needs to fill and which to ignore when we cannot fill them all.

There is much to be said for McGovern's critique. We are used to living in conditions of a surplus of natural resources, and we are unprepared politically and morally to adjust to conditions of scarcity. Only now are we beginning to grasp the dimensions of our new dilemma. A vast amount of education and exploration of the issues must still be done. There must be an infusion of responsible political leadership too.

"The politics practiced by America with regard to food require very special attention, because food means life, because we are well supplied with food, and because others are less so," the Federation of American Scientists has observed. "But, in addition, we should keep in mind that food is not the only world necessity. We are faced with the possibility of worldwide shortages of other substances, for many of which we are eager buyers—sources of energy are just one current example. We use enormously more of the world's resources than our population size would suggest. Thus, we are potentially as vulnerable to the politics of scarcity as any country on earth. In our handling of food we should be particularly careful to 'do unto others as we would be done to.' "

Eco-catastrophe!

PAUL R. EHRLICH

Will humanity eventually destroy itself in an "eco-catastrophe"? Paul Ehrlich develops a grim scenario of the future. In this scenario, he says, "everything mentioned as happening before 1970 has actually occurred; much of the rest is based on projections of trends already appearing."

I

The end of the ocean came late in the summer of 1979, and it came even more rapidly than the biologists had expected. There had been signs for more than a decade, commencing with the discovery in 1968 that DDT slows down photosynthesis in marine plant life. It was announced in a short paper in the technical journal *Science*, but to ecologists it smacked of doomsday. They knew that all life in the sea depends on photosynthesis, the chemical process by which green plants bind the sun's energy and make it available to living things. And they knew that DDT and similar chlorinated hydrocarbons had polluted the entire surface of the earth, including the sea.

But that was only the first of many signs. There had been the final gasp of the whaling industry in 1973, and the end of the Peruvian anchovy fishery in 1975. Indeed, a score of other fisheries had disappeared quietly from over-exploitation and various eco-catastrophes by 1977. The term "eco-catastrophe" was coined by a California ecologist in 1969 to describe the most spectacular of man's attacks on the systems which sustain his life. He drew his inspiration from the Santa Barbara offshore oil disaster of that year, and from the news which spread among naturalists that virtually all of the Golden State's seashore bird life was doomed because of chlorinated hydrocarbon interference with its reproduction. Eco-catastrophes in the sea became increasingly common in the early 1970's. Mysterious "blooms" of previously rare microorganisms began to appear in offshore waters. Red tides—killer outbreaks of a minute single-celled plant—returned to the Florida Gulf coast and were sometimes accompanied by tides of other exotic hues.

It was clear by 1975 that the entire ecology of the ocean was changing. A few types of phytoplankton were becoming resistant to chlorinated hydrocarbons and were gaining the upper hand. Changes in the phytoplankton community led inevitably to changes in the community of zooplankton, the tiny animals which eat the phytoplankton. These changes were passed on up the chains of life in the ocean to the herring, plaice, cod and tuna. As the diversity of life in the ocean diminished, its stability also decreased.

Other changes had taken place by 1975. Most ocean fishes that returned to fresh water to breed, like the salmon, had become extinct, their breeding streams so dammed up and polluted that their powerful homing instinct only resulted in suicide. Many fishes and shellfishes that bred in restricted areas along the coasts followed them as onshore pollution escalated.

By 1977 the annual yield of fish from the sea was down to 30 million metric tons, less than one-half the per capita catch of a decade earlier. This helped malnutrition to escalate sharply in a world where an estimated 50 million people per year were already dying of starvation. The United Nations attempted to get all chlorinated hydrocarbon insecticides banned on a worldwide basis, but the move was defeated by the United States. This opposition was generated primarily by the American petrochemical industry, operating hand in glove with its subsidiary, the United States Department of Agriculture. Together they persuaded the government to oppose the U.N. move—which was not difficult since most Americans believed that Russia and China were more in need of fish prodccts than was the United States. The United Nations also attempted to get fishing nations to adopt strict and enforced catch limits to preserve dwindling stocks. This move was blocked by Russia, who, with the most modern electronic equipment, was in the best position to glean what was left in the sea. It was, curiously, on the very day in 1977 when the Soviet Union announced its refusal that another ominous article appeared in *Science*. It announced that incident solar radiation had been so reduced by worldwide air pollution that serious effects on the world's vegetation could be expected.

II

Apparently it was a combination of ecosystem destabilization, sunlight reduction, and a rapid escalation in chlorinated hydrocarbon pollution from massive Thanodrin applications which triggered the ultimate catastrophe.

Seventeen huge Soviet-financed Thanodrin plants were operating in underdeveloped countries by 1978. They had been part of a massive Russian "aid offensive" designed to fill the gap caused by the collapse of America's ballyhooed "Green Revolution."

It became apparent in the early '70s that the "Green Revolution" was more talk than substance. Distribution of high yield "miracle" grain seeds had caused temporary local spurts in agricultural production. Simultaneously, excellent weather had produced record harvests. The combination permitted bureaucrats, especially in the United States Department of Agriculture and the Agency for International Development (AID), to reverse their previous pessimism and indulge in an outburst of optimistic propaganda about staving off famine. They raved about the approaching transformation of agriculture in the underdeveloped countries (UDCs). The reason for the propaganda reversal was never made clear. Most historians agree that a combination of utter ignorance of ecology, a desire to justify past errors, and pressure from agro-industry (which was eager to sell pesticides, fertilizers, and farm machinery to the UDCs and agencies helping the UDCs) was behind the campaign. Whatever the motivation, the results were clear. Many concerned people, lacking the expertise to see through the Green Revolution drivel, relaxed. The population-food crisis was "solved."

But reality was not long in showing itself. Local famine persisted in northern India even after good weather brought an end to the ghastly Bihar famine of the mid-'60s. East Pakistan was next, followed by a resurgence of general famine in northern India. Other foci of famine rapidly developed in Indonesia, the Philippines, Malawi, the Congo, Egypt, Colombia, Ecuador, Honduras, the Dominican Republic, and Mexico.

Everywhere hard realities destroyed the illusion of the Green Revolution. Yields dropped as the progressive farmers who had first accepted the new seeds found that their higher yields brought lower prices—effective demand (hunger plus cash) was not sufficient in poor countries to keep prices up. Less progressive farmers, observing this, refused to make the extra effort required to cultivate the "miracle" grains. Transport systems proved inadequate to bring the necessary fertilizer to the fields where the new and extremely fertilizer-sensitive grains were being grown. The same systems were also inadequate to move produce to markets. Fertilizer plants were not built fast enough, and most of the underdeveloped countries could not scrape together funds to purchase supplies, even on concessional terms. Finally, the inevitable happened, and pests began to reduce yields in even the most carefully cultivated fields. Among the first were the famous "miracle rats" which invaded Philippine "miracle rice" fields early in 1969. They were quickly followed by many insects and viruses, thriving on the relatively pest-susceptible new grains, encouraged by the vast and dense plantings, and rapidly acquiring resistance to the chemicals used against them. As chaos spread until even the most obtuse agriculturists and economists realized that the Green Revolution had turned brown, the Russians stepped in.

In retrospect it seems incredible that the Russians, with the American mistakes known to them, could launch an even more incompetent program of aid to the underdeveloped world. Indeed, in the early 1970's there were cynics in the United States who claimed that outdoing the stupidity of American foreign aid would be physically impossible. Those critics were, however, obviously unaware that the Russians had been busily destroying their own environment for many years. The virtual disappearance of sturgeon from Russian rivers caused a great shortage of caviar by 1970. A standard joke among Russian scientists at that time was that they had created an artificial caviar which was indistinguishable from the real thing—except by taste. At any rate the Soviet Union, observing with interest the progressive deterioration of relations between the UDCs and the United States, came up with a solution. It had recently developed what it claimed was the ideal insecticide, a highly lethal chlorinated hydrocarbon complexed with a special agent for penetrating the external skeletal armor of insects. Announcing that the new pesticide, called Thanodrin, would truly produce a Green Revolution, the Soviets entered into negotiations with various UDCs for the construction of massive Thanodrin factories. The USSR would bear all the costs; all it wanted in return were certain trade and military concessions.

It is interesting now, with the perspective of years, to examine in some detail the reasons why the UDCs welcomed the Thanodrin plan with such open arms. Government officials in these countries ignored the protests of their own scientists that Thanodrin would not solve the problems which plagued them. The governments now knew that the basic cause of their problems was overpopulation, and that these problems had been exacerbated by the dullness, daydreaming, and cupidity endemic to all governments. They knew that only population control and limited development aimed primarily at agriculture could have spared them the horrors they now faced. They knew it, but they were not about to admit it. How much easier it was simply to accuse the Americans of failing to give them proper aid; how much simpler to accept the Russian panacea.

And then there was the general worsening of relations between the United States and the UDCs. Many things had contributed to this. The situation in America in the first half of the 1970's deserves our close scrutiny. Being more dependent on imports for raw materials than the Soviet Union, the United States had, in the early 1970's, adopted more and more heavy-handed policies in order to insure continuing supplies. Military adventures in Asia and Latin America had further lessened the international credibility of the United States as a great defender of freedom—an image which had begun to deteriorate rapidly during the pointless and fruitless Viet-Nam conflict. At home, acceptance of the carefully manufactured image lessened dramatically, as even the more romantic and chauvinistic citizens began to understand the role of the military and the industrial system in what John Kenneth Galbraith had aptly named "The New Industrial State."

At home in the USA the early '70s were traumatic times. Racial violence grew and the habitability of the cities diminished, as nothing substantial was done to ameliorate either racial inequities or urban blight. Welfare rolls grew as automation and general technological progress forced more and more people into the category of "unemployable." Simultaneously a taxpayers' revolt occurred. Although there was not enough money to build the schools, roads, water systems, sewage systems, jails, hospitals, urban transit lines, and all the other amenities needed to support a burgeoning population, Americans refused to tax themselves more heavily. Starting in Youngstown, Ohio in 1969 and followed closely by Richmond, California, community after community was forced to close its schools or curtail educational operations for lack of funds. Water supplies, already marginal in quality and quantity in many places by 1970, deteriorated quickly. Water rationing occurred in 1723 municipalities in the summer of 1974, and hepatitis and epidemic dysentery rates climbed about 500 per cent between 1970–1974.

III

Air pollution continued to be the most obvious manifestation of environmental deterioration. It was, by 1972, quite literally in the eyes of all Americans. The year 1973 saw not only the New York and Los Angeles smog disasters, but also the publication of the Surgeon General's massive report on air pollution and health. The public had been partially prepared for the worst by the publicity given to the U.N. pollution conference held in 1972. Deaths in the late '60s caused by smog were well known to scientists, but the public had ignored them because they mostly involved the early demise of the old and sick rather than people dropping dead on the freeways. But suddenly our citizens were faced with nearly 200,000 corpses and massive documentation that they could be the next to die from respiratory disease. They were not ready for that scale of disaster. After all, the U.N. conference had not predicted that accumulated air pollution would make the planet uninhabitable until almost 1990. The population was terrorized as TV screens became filled with scenes of horror from the disaster areas. Especially vivid was NBC's coverage of hundreds of unattended people choking out their lives outside of New York's hospitals. Terms like nitrogen oxide, acute bronchitis and cardiac arrest began to have real meaning for most Americans.

The ultimate horror was the announcement that chlorinated hydrocarbons were now a major constituent of air pollution in all American cities. Autopsies of smog disaster victims revealed an average chlorinated hydrocarbon load in fatty tissue equivalent to 26 parts per million of DDT. In October, 1973, the Department of Health, Education and Welfare announced studies which showed unequivocally that increasing death rates from hypertension, cirrhosis of the liver, liver cancer and a series of other diseases had resulted from the chlorinated hydrocarbon load. They estimated that Americans born since 1946 (when DDT usage began) now had a life expectancy of only 49 years, and predicted that if current patterns continued, this expectancy would reach 42 years by 1980, when it might level out. Plunging insurance stocks triggered a stock market panic. The president of Velsicol, Inc., a major pesticide producer, went on television to "publicly eat a teaspoonful of DDT" (it was really powdered milk) and announce that HEW had been infiltrated by Communists. Other giants of the petrochemical industry, attempting to dispute the indisputable evidence, launched a massive pressure campaign on Congress to force HEW to "get out of agriculture's business." They were aided by the agro-chemical journals, which had decades of experience in misleading the public about the benefits and dangers of pesticides. But by now the public realized that it had been duped. The Nobel Prize for medicine and physiology was given to Drs. J. L. Radomski and W. B. Deichmann, who in the late 1960's had pioneered in the documentation of the long-term lethal effects of chlorinated hydrocarbons. A Presidential Commission with unimpeachable credentials directly accused the agro-chemical complex of "condemning many millions of Americans to an early death." The year 1973 was the year in which Americans finally came to understand the direct threat to their existence posed by environmental deterioration.

And 1973 was also the year in which most people finally comprehended the indirect threat. Even the president of Union Oil Company and several other industrialists publicly stated their concern over the reduction of bird populations which had resulted from pollution by DDT and other chlorinated hydrocarbons. Insect populations boomed because they were resistant to most pesticides and had been freed, by the incompetent use of those pesticides, from most of their natural enemies. Rodents swarmed over crops, multiplying rapidly in the absence of predatory birds. The effect of pests on the wheat crop was especially disastrous in the summer of 1973, since that was also the year of the great drought. Most of us can remember the shock which greeted the announcement by atmospheric physicists that the shift of the jet stream which had caused the drought was probably permanent. It signalled the birth of the Midwestern desert. Man's air-polluting activities had by then caused gross changes in climatic patterns. The news, of course, played hell with commodity and stock markets. Food prices skyrocketed, as savings were poured into hoarded canned goods. Official assurances that food supplies would remain ample fell on deaf ears, and even the government showed signs of nervousness when California migrant field workers went out on strike again in protest against the continued use of pesticides by growers. The strike burgeoned into farm burning and riots. The workers, calling themselves "The Walking Dead," demanded immediate compensation for their shortened lives, and crash research programs to attempt to lengthen them.

It was in the same speech in which President Edward Kennedy, after much delay, finally declared a national emergency and called out the National Guard to harvest California's crops, that the first mention of population control was made. Kennedy pointed out that the United States would no longer be able to offer any food aid to other nations and was likely to suffer food shortages herself. He suggested that, in view of the manifest failure of the Green Revolution, the only hope of the UDCs lay in population control. His statement, you will recall, created an uproar in the underdeveloped countries. Newspaper editorials accused the United States of wishing to prevent small countries from becoming large nations and thus threatening American hegemony. Politicians asserted that President Kennedy was a "creature of the giant drug combine" that wished to shove its pills down every woman's throat.

Among Americans, religious opposition to population control was very slight. Industry in general also backed the idea. Increasing poverty in the UDCs was both destroying markets and threatening supplies of raw materials. The seriousness of the raw material situation had been brought home during the Congressional Hard Resources hearings in 1971. The exposure of the ignorance of the cornucopian economists had been quite a spectacle—a spectacle brought into virtually every American's home in living color. Few would forget the distinguished geologist from the University of California who suggested that economists be legally required to learn at least the most elementary facts of geology. Fewer still would forget that an equally distinguished Harvard economist added that they might be required to learn some economics, too. The overall message was clear: America's resource situation was bad and bound to get worse. The hearings had led to a bill requiring the Departments of State, Interior, and Commerce to set up a joint resource procurement council with the express purpose of "insuring that proper consideration of American resource needs be an integral part of American foreign policy."

Suddenly the United States discovered that it had a national consensus: population control was the only possible salvation of the underdeveloped world. But that same consensus led to heated debate. How could the UDCs be persuaded to limit their populations, and should not the United States lead the way by limiting its own? Members of the intellectual community wanted America to set an example. They pointed out that the United States was in the midst of a new baby boom: her birth rate, well over 20 per thousand per year, and her growth rate of over one per cent per annum were among the very highest of the developed countries. They detailed the deterioration of the American physical and psychic environments, the growing health threats, the impending food shortages, and the insufficiency of funds for desperately needed public works. They contended that the nation was clearly unable or unwilling to properly care for the people it already had. What possible reason could there be, they queried, for adding any more? Besides, who would listen to requests by the United States for population control when that nation did not control her own profligate reproduction?

Those who opposed population controls for the U.S. were equally vociferous. The military-industrial complex, with its all-too-human mixture of ignorance and avarice, still saw strength and prosperity in numbers. Baby food magnates, already worried by the growing nitrate pollution of their products, saw their market disappearing. Steel manufacturers saw a decrease in aggregate demand and slippage for that holy of holies, the Gross National Product. And military men saw, in the growing population-food-environment crisis, a serious threat to their carefully nurtured Cold War. In the end, of course, economic arguments held sway, and the "inalienable right of every American couple to determine the size of its family," a freedom invented for the occasion in the early '70s, was not compromised.

The population control bill, which was passed by Congress early in 1974, was quite a document, nevertheless. On the domestic front, it authorized an increase from 100 to 150 million dollars in funds for "family planning" activities. This was made possible by a general feeling in the country that the growing army on welfare needed family planning. But the gist of the bill was a series of measures designed to impress the need for population control on the UDCs. All American aid to countries with overpopulation problems was required by law to consist in part of population control assistance. In order to receive any assistance each nation was required not only to accept the population control aid, but also to match it according to a complex formula. "Overpopulation" itself was defined by a formula based on U.N. statistics, and the UDCs were required not only to accept aid, but also to show progress in reducing birth rates. Every five years the status of the aid program for each nation was to be re-evaluated.

The reaction to the announcement of this program dwarfed the response to President Kennedy's speech. A coalition of UDCs attempted to get the U.N. General Assembly to condemn the United States as a "genetic aggressor." Most damaging of all to the American cause was the famous "25 Indians and a dog" speech by Mr. Shankarnarayan, Indian Ambassador to the U.N. Shankarnarayan pointed out that for several decades the United States, with less than six per cent of the people of the world, had consumed roughly 50 per cent of the raw materials used every year. He described vividly America's contribution to worldwide environmental deterioration, and he scathingly denounced the miserly record of United States foreign aid as "unworthy of a fourth-rate power, let alone the most powerful nation on earth."

It was the climax of his speech, however, which most historians claim once and for all destroyed the image of the United States. Shankarnarayan informed the assembly that the average American family dog was fed more animal protein per week than the average Indian got in a month. "How do you justify taking fish from protein-starved Peruvians and feeding them to your animals?" he asked. "I contend," he concluded, "that the birth of an American baby is a greater disaster for the world than that of 25 Indian babies." When the applause had died away, Mr. Sorensen, the American representative, made a speech which said essentially that "other countries look after their own self-interest, too." When the vote came, the United States was condemned.

IV

This condemnation set the tone of U.S.-UDC relations at the time the Russian Thanodrin proposal was made. The proposal seemed to offer the masses in the UDCs an opportunity to save themselves and humiliate the United States at the same time; and in human affairs, as we all know, biological realities could never interfere with such an opportunity. The scientists were silenced, the politicians said yes, the Thanodrin plants were built, and the results were what any beginning ecology student could have predicted. At first Thanodrin seemed to offer excellent control of many pests. True, there was a rash of human fatalities from improper use of the lethal chemical, but, as Russian technical advisors were prone to note, these were more than compensated for by increased yields. Thanodrin use skyrocketed throughout the underdeveloped world. The Mikoyan design group developed a dependable, cheap agricultural aircraft which the Soviets donated to the effort in large numbers. MIG sprayers became even more common in UDCs than MIG interceptors.

Then the troubles began. Insect strains with cuticles resistant to Thanodrin penetration began to appear. And as streams, rivers, fish culture ponds and onshore waters became rich in Thanodrin, more fisheries began to disappear. Bird populations were decimated. The sequence of events was standard for broadcast use of a synthetic pesticide: great success at first, followed by removal of natural enemies and development of resistance by the pest. Populations of crop-eating insects in areas treated with Thanodrin made steady comebacks and soon became more abundant than ever. Yields plunged, while farmers in their desperation increased the Thanodrin dose and shortened the time between treatments. Death from Thanodrin poisoning became common. The first violent incident occurred in the Canete Valley of Peru, where farmers had suffered a similar chlorinated hydrocarbon disaster in the mid-'50s. A Russian advisor serving as an agricultural pilot was assaulted and killed by a mob of enraged farmers in January, 1978. Trouble spread rapidly during 1978, especially after the word got out that two years earlier Russia herself had banned the use of Thanodrin at home because of its serious effects on ecological systems. Suddenly Russia, and not the United States, was the *bête noir* in the UDCs. "Thanodrin parties" became epidemic, with farmers, in their ignorance, dumping carloads of Thanodrin concentrate into the sea. Russian advisors fled, and four of the Thanodrin plants were leveled to the ground. Destruction of the plants in Rio and Calcutta led to hundreds of thousands of gallons of Thanodrin concentrate being dumped directly into the sea.

Mr. Shankarnarayan again rose to address the U.N., but this time it was Mr. Potemkin, representative of the Soviet Union, who was on the hot seat. Mr. Potemkin heard his nation described as the greatest mass killer of all time as Shankarnarayan predicted at least 30 million deaths from crop failures due to overdependence on Thanodrin. Russia was accused of "chemical aggression," and the General Assembly, after a weak reply by Potemkin, passed a vote of censure.

It was in January, 1979, that huge blooms of a previously unknown variety of diatom were reported off the coast of Peru. The blooms were accompanied by a massive die-off of sea life and of the pathetic remainder of the birds which had once feasted on the anchovies of the area. Almost immediately another huge bloom was reported in the Indian ocean, centering around the Seychelles, and then a third in the South Atlantic off the African coast. Both of these were accompanied by spectacular die-offs of marine animals. Even more ominous were growing reports of fish and bird kills at oceanic points where there were no spectacular blooms. Biologists were soon able to explain the phenomena: the diatom had evolved an enzyme which broke down Thanodrin; that enzyme also produced a breakdown product which interfered with the transmission of nerve impulses, and was therefore lethal to animals. Unfortunately, the biologists could suggest no way of repressing the poisonous diatom bloom in time. By September, 1979, all important animal life in the sea was extinct. Large areas of coastline had to be evacuated, as windrows of dead fish created a monumental stench.

But stench was the least of man's problems. Japan and China were faced with almost instant starvation from a total loss of the seafood on which they were so dependent. Both blamed Russia for their situation and demanded immediate mass shipments of food. Russia had none to send. On October 13, Chinese armies attacked Russia on a broad front. . . .

V

A pretty grim scenario. Unfortunately, we're a long way into it already. Everything mentioned as happening before 1970 has actually occurred; much of the rest is based on projections of trends already appearing. Evidence that pesticides have long-term lethal effects on human beings has started to accumulate, and recently Robert Finch, Secretary of the Department of Health, Education and Welfare expressed his extreme apprehension about the pesticide situation. Simultaneously the petrochemical industry continues its unconscionable poison-peddling. For instance, Shell Chemical has been carrying on a high-pressure campaign to sell the insecticide Azodrin to farmers as a killer of cotton pests. They continue their program even though they know that Azodrin is not only ineffective, but often *increases* the pest density. They've covered themselves nicely in an advertisement which states, "Even if an overpowering migration [sic] develops, the flexibility of Azodrin lets you regain control fast. Just increase the dosage according to label recommendations." It's a great game—get people to apply the poison and kill the natural enemies of the pests. Then blame the increased pests on "migration" and sell even more pesticide!

Right now fisheries are being wiped out by over-exploitation, made easy by modern electronic equipment. The companies producing the equipment know this. They even boast in advertising that only their equipment will keep fishermen in business until the final kill. Profits must obviously be maximized in the short run. Indeed, Western society is in the process of completing the rape and murder of the planet for economic gain. And, sadly, most of the rest of the world is eager for the opportunity to emulate our behavior. But the underdeveloped peoples will be denied that opportunity—the days of plunder are drawing inexorably to a close.

Most of the people who are going to die in the greatest cataclysm in the history of man have already been born. More than three and a half billion people already populate our moribund globe, and about half of them are hungry. Some 10 to 20 million will starve to death *this year.* In spite of this, the population of the earth will increase by 70 million souls in 1969. For mankind has artificially lowered the death rate of the human population, while in general birth rates have remained high. With the input side of the population system in high gear and the output side slowed down, our fragile planet has filled with people at an incredible rate. It took several million years for the population to reach a total of two billion people in 1930, while a *second two billion will have been added by 1975!* By that time some experts feel that food shortages will have escalated the present level of world hunger and starvation into famines of unbelievable proportions. Other experts, more optimistic, think the ultimate food-population collision will not occur until the decade of the 1980's. Of course more massive famine may be avoided if other events cause a prior rise in the human death rate.

Both worldwide plague and thermonuclear war are made more probable as population growth continues. These, along with famine, make up the trio of potential "death rate solutions" to the population problem—solutions in which the birth rate–death rate imbalance is redressed by a rise in the death rate rather than by a lowering of the birth rate. Make no mistake about it, *the imbalance will be redressed.* The shape of the population growth curve is one familiar to the biologist. It is the outbreak part of an outbreak-crash sequence. A population grows rapidly in the presence of abundant resources, finally runs out of food or some other necessity, and crashes to a low level or extinction. Man is not only running out of food, he is also destroying the life support systems of the Spaceship Earth. The situation was recently summarized very succinctly: "It is the top of the ninth inning. Man, always a threat at the plate, has been hitting Nature hard. It is important to remember, however, that NATURE BATS LAST."

NINE

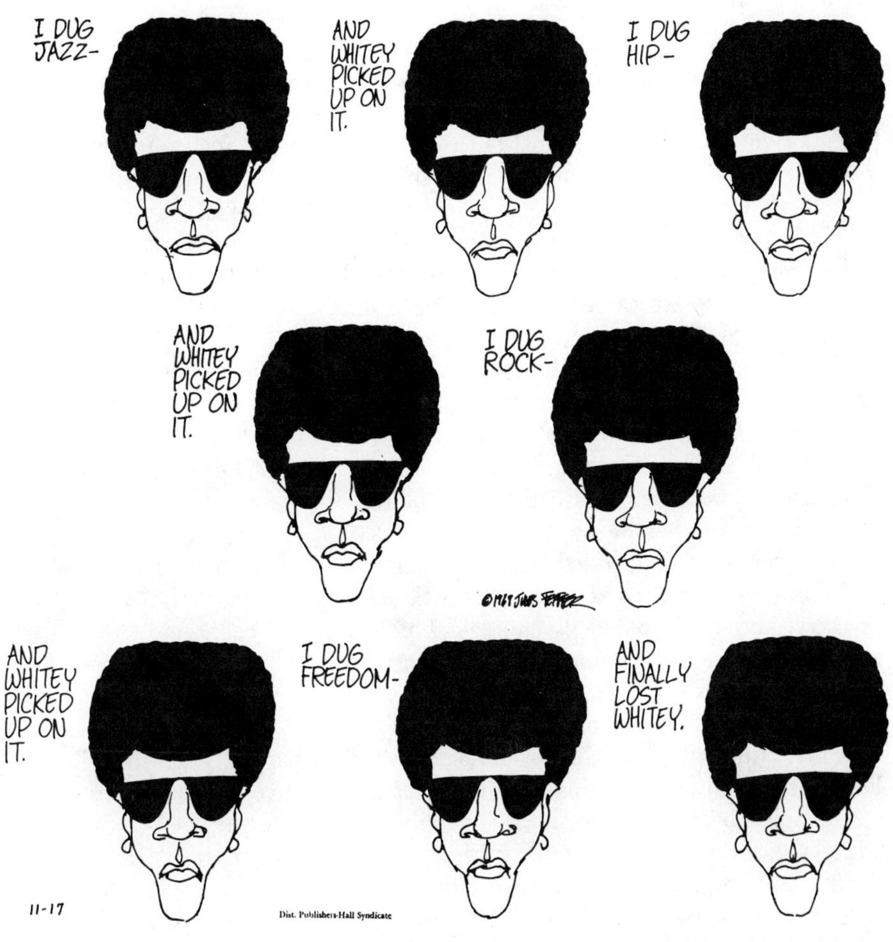

The Minority Revolt

Now we demand a chance to do
things for ourselves
We're tired of beating our heads
against the wall
And working for someone else.
Now, we're people.
We're like the birds and the bees.
We'd rather die on our feet
Than keep living on our knees.
—James Brown

PARTS OF DETROIT look like a war zone. Some black people are saying that America must burn unless they receive justice immediately. Harry Edwards, organizer of the black athletes' boycott of the Olympic Games, wears a book of matches on his jacket. H. Rap Brown says that violence is as American as apple pie. The police are arming against guerrilla insurrection. White and black attitudes are hardening and polarizing. Have we learned anything from the flames of Watts, Detroit, Washington, D.C., and Newark?

A spectre of slavery still hangs over America. It is not slavery in a legal, brutal, gut-wrenchingly physical sense, but the remnants of actual slavery still linger. It is fine for us whites to forget the past and talk of building future harmony. We did not own any slaves ourselves, did we? This is little consolation, though, because even in the slaveholding South only a minority owned a significant number of slaves. The point is that slavery was more than a physical bondage that ended over 100 years ago. Slavery was psychologically and culturally entrenched in the "Old South." It was part of the life style of the region. Slavery had psychological, political, and economic effects that are still with us. We cannot simply erase the past by forgetting about it. Black America will not let us. Indeed, our very humanity will not let us, nor will the nonwhite masses of the world.

For example, look at the psychological scars of slavery. Black people may be free from physical beatings at the hands of the slave master, but they are still enraged by the indignities of supercilious treatment at the hands of the white majority. What percentage of whites still think that blacks are culturally and intellectually inferior? How many blacks have believed or still believe in their own inferiority? How many whites still believe in their own superiority?

What about some of the sociohistorical effects of slavery? What effect did slavery have on the black family? One of the results was the separation of family members. As King Cotton spread westward in the plantation South, the eastern states—Virginia, for example—were turned into slave-breeding territories which funneled excess slaves into the newer areas with more fertile soil. Sociologists are still arguing over the effects of slavery and economic dependency on the black family. Certain sociologists feel that the instability found in some black families can be related to cultural patterns developed during slavery. Others claim that the crux of the matter is a lack of economic opportunity for the black male in America today.

Another sociohistorical effect of slavery was the disintegration of the black man's African heritage. His culture was almost completely destroyed. This cultural disintegration is one of the significant differences between slavery in Anglo-America and slavery in Latin America. In a democratic society, such as that of the United States, it was hard to rationalize the existence of slavery. How could there be slavery in a free society? Therefore, it was necessary to maintain that the black man was inferior, and to complete this self-fulfilling prophecy, he was then systematically denied access to education. Even the churches helped. The black man was said to be a simpleminded and docile child who needed the guidance of his white master. This concept was maintained even though the white slave owners had encountered culturally sophisticated African civilizations, such as the Ashanti kingdom, which is present-day Ghana. Another rationalization was that only the black man could chop cotton under the sweltering subtropical sun, even though the poor whites seemed to handle it quite well.

Slavery was quite a bit different in semifeudal Latin America. There was little difference between being a powerless and poverty-ridden peasant and being a slave. There were few rationalizations needed for slavery in Latin America. Who was really free anyway? Therefore, no rationalizations regarding black innate inferiority ever developed. There was no "sambo" in Latin America. Being a slave was just one of those things; it was a tough break, but it did not necessarily occur because of skin color. Another difference between Anglo and Latin America was the intervention of the Catholic Church on behalf of slaves in the latter. Also, the Spanish and Portuguese had already been influenced by the invasion of the Moors from North Africa. They had prior contact with nonwhite cultures and people, and they were more inclined to mingle with the slaves. A slave in Latin America could buy more than his freedom with money; he could, in certain instances, cross caste and class barriers. What implications do these alternate modes of slavery have?

One of the results is very apparent: there are few cultural remnants from Africa among black Americans. Their cultural heritage was destroyed. The solidarity gained from a common cultural tradition has been missing in black America. When slaves were brought to America, two of the most cohesive and integrating factors of their culture, both language and religious philosophy, almost completely vanished because they were forced to accept and adjust to white culture and values. This is something we should remember when comparing black slaves to white immigrants. One group came voluntarily, could assimilate easily, and had a heritage that was not destroyed by generations of slavery. White immigrants were confronted with a culture that was basically similar to theirs. This has had a tremendous influence on the black man, both politically and economically.

To conclude our quick look at slavery, let us emphasize that its most brutal effect has been on the minds (and consequent behavior) of both black and white Americans. They have not communicated as real human beings but as rigid stereotypes and caricatures. Malcolm X said, "The worst crime the white man has committed has been to teach us to hate ourselves." There is no way for us as sociologists to assess historically how many black Americans actually have thought less of themselves simply because they were black. And what of the white mind? Here the sickness of slavery is much more ugly and visible. The white man's feelings of black inferiority have enabled him systematically to discriminate against black Americans politically, economically, and educationally. These remnants of slavery still remain in contemporary America.

Look at the black man politically. It is a simple fact that the black man is grossly underrepresented in positions of power in our society. Take, for example, Cook County (Chicago and its environs). Black people hold less than 1 per cent of the effective power in the Chicago metropolitan area, but they comprise over 30 per cent of the population. The power structure of Chicago is hardly less lily white than that of Mississippi. It is becoming more and more obvious to black people that to make changes in the areas of housing, jobs, and education, they need black people in the policy-making positions of influential organizations. Hence the cry for "Black Power."

What about economics? The statistics are very simple: One half of all black families earned less than $4,000 in 1965. This is below the poverty level. The income gap between whites and blacks, like the gap between the rich and the poor nations, is growing. This points to a very obvious fact: there is job discrimination. The income gap also points to the lack of education and salable skills among black people. Because black people have been most effectively screened off from "decent union-type" jobs, one of the major means of intergenerational mobility used historically by "white immigrants" has been closed to them.

What about housing? In segments of every major American city there is discrimination in housing. Whether or not a black man would like to live in an all-black community among his peers is beside the point. The real issue involved here is whether a man (if he has the money) should be allowed to live wherever he chooses, regardless of color. Another, more subtle form of discrimination in housing is involved in urban renewal. It usually involves the condemnation and destruction of "slum housing" to be replaced by facilities for public institutions (for example, Columbia University), office buildings, and high-rise, high-rent apartments. Sometimes the former slum dwellers, mainly black people, get lost in the shuffle. The city of Chicago provides a good example of this process. During the twenty-five years prior to 1966, Chicago displaced 200,000 people for urban renewal and freeway construction (which enabled middle-class white people to get to their jobs in the city more easily). Over 80 per cent of the displaced people were black. Most of them ended up paying more rent, which they could barely afford.

Education is another fertile area for controversy. There is a near conflagration in many of the ghetto schools and the colleges with black students. There are two major areas of conflict which we can separate artificially: (1) the struggle for control of the ghetto schools and (2) the fight for a "black curriculum." The first problem deals mainly with the elementary and secondary schools in the black communities of our cities. The schools have failed miserably for black children, and concerned black parents realize it. Their response has been to try to gain greater control over these institutions. Black parents feel they should have some say in planning curriculum and in hiring and firing administrators and teachers.

The second problem is the effort among black students to effect the adoption of black studies (for example, black history, both African and American, black sociology, and black literature) throughout the school system, but mainly in the colleges. This movement reflects the necessity for change and relevancy throughout the entire educational system and ties in with our discussion of the destruction of black cultural traditions. In a certain sense, black people are trying to recapture something stolen from them in the past. They are attempting to be themselves—black people, not white people. This is also closely coupled with the Black Pride/Power Movement. The cry for cohesiveness and solidarity has filtered into the education arena. Put very simply, "black people are trying to get themselves together" after being so brutalized and dehumanized by the white man.

The economic and political factors, coupled with the disintegrating ghetto schools and housing, have resulted in the development of a vicious cycle. All these factors are interrelated, and it is hard to say which is most important in erasing racial inequality. Black people and white people will have to decide together.

The convoluted heat waves rise from the surface of Highway 99. Dust and DDT hang over this endless stretch of plain that is the Central Valley of California. Huge farms dot the landscape. The scene could be any valley town: white, middle-class America on one side of the highway and the Chicano *barrio* (ghetto) on the other. The contrast is striking. Even the churches are segregated. If you happen to wander off 99, you may be confronted with a squalid array of migrant shacks. This is not the Deep South; this is progressive California.

Who is the Chicano? He is usually referred to as the Mexican-American. (Chicano relates to Mexican-American in the same way that black relates to Negro.) The Chicano is basically Indian. More than 95 per cent of Chicanos are part Indian, 40 per cent are full-blooded Indians, and most of the mestizos have more Indian than non-Indian ancestry. His culture can be traced back to the Aztecs and Mayas; he has also been infused with the

Hispanic tradition. The Chicano is a marriage of these two cultures. But the Chicano has traces of the black slave, the Oriental of the Filipino, and some European ethnic groups. He is truly the universal man.

Statistically, the Chicano is much harder to define; "*La Raza*" is more a cultural than a physical or racial group. The Chicanos are easily the second largest minority in the United States; they are the largest minority in the Southwest, where they are concentrated. It is extremely difficult to estimate the total number of Chicanos. Many Chicanos do not have Spanish surnames, and many of them are not technically American citizens. We can roughly estimate, however, that there are 7 or 8 million Chicanos in America, and their numbers are increasing rapidly because of immigration (much of it "illegal"), the low average age of the Chicanos, and their emphasis on large families.

We would like to compare and contrast the Chicano with the black man in America. As the two most significant minority groups in America, they share certain characteristics. The first is their long historical record of being discriminated against by the white majority. This is reflected today in the educational level, socioeconomic status, and political and economic power of the two groups. They both have also suffered a crude psychological debasement. The dominant group has tried to imbue them both with a sense of inferiority. The Chicano and the black man are facing the same problems in the school system. (The Chicano's problem may be worse, because of the language barrier.) Both have made the transition from a rural to an urban environment. The change has not been altogether pleasant or beneficial for either group.

There are also some significant differences between the two. Numerically there are more blacks, yet their concentration in urban areas is similar. The difference is that the Chicanos are concentrated in the five states of the Southwest. For example, there are over 1 million Chicanos in Los Angeles. Another difference is the greater visibility of the black man, which makes it easier to discriminate against him. (It is interesting to note that race or creed is not needed on application forms today, yet the Chicano's Spanish surname may give him away.) Although the Chicano is technically classified as Caucasian by the United States Census Bureau, he has faced virulent discrimination. A good example of this is the Los Angeles Zoot-suit Riots in 1943, where Chicanos were indiscriminately attacked. The incident is somewhat similar to Southern mob action against the supposed threat of blacks.

Another contrast that can be drawn between the Chicano and black is cultural. The black man has had his culture ripped from him, whereas the Chicano's culture has been historically continuous. The Chicano was not really "imported" to the Southwest; he is culturally part of that region. The Chicano's culture has been continually reinforced by his contact with his homeland. Slavery tore apart the black family; the Chicano still has a strong extended and communal family structure. The Chicano's religion and language are still very much a part of his life. The Chicanos are the only large ethnic or minority group that has resisted assimilation. Why have they not been assimilated? What cultural values have they retained that may be functional and useful in contemporary America?—G. G.

Selected References

(All are available in paperback editions.)

Acuña, Rodolfo. *Occupied America.* San Francisco: Canfield Press, 1972.

Brown, Ina Corinne. *Understanding Race Relations.* Englewood Cliffs, N.J.: Prentice-Hall, Inc., 1973.

Carmichael, Stokely, and Charles V. Hamilton. *Black Power.* New York: Random House, Inc., 1967.

Cleaver, Eldridge. *Soul on Ice.* New York: McGraw-Hill Company, 1968.

Grier, William H., and Price M. Cobbs. *Black Rage.* New York: Basic Books, Inc., 1968.

Killian, Lewis M. *The Impossible Revolution.* New York: Random House, Inc., 1968.

McWilliams, Carey. *North from Mexico.* New York: Greenwood Press, 1968.

Silberman, Charles E. *Crisis on Black and White.* New York: Random House, Inc., 1964.

Steinfield, Melvin. *Cracks in the Melting Pot.* Beverly Hills, Calif.: Glencoe Press, 1970.

Them and Me

ARTHUR HOPPE

Everyone is dissecting the race riots. The conservatives are blaming the liberals, the liberals are blaming the bigots, the bigots are smiling smugly. The insurance companies are worried about claims, the politicians about re-election. And the editorial writers are urging more respect for law and order. The sociologists are talking of "lack of economic opportunity," the psychiatrists of "frustrations." The civil rights workers are shaking their heads and saying the cause of equality under the law has suffered "a severe setback."

Yet all I can think of is they wanted to kill me. The uneasiness grew slowly. The first day it seemed just another riot. A shame. But these things will happen. Then came the next day. And the next. At first, I tried to imagine how the rioters felt, smashing and burning. I thought I could sense how a young Negro boy must feel as he heaved a rock through a plate-glass window. The release. The rebellion without hope of success. The simple act of saying to hell with a world you could never conquer. It was an act, really, of complete defeat. How terribly sad that was.

Then, slowly, as story followed story, the thread of hatred broadened. "Get Whitey! Kill him! Kill, kill, kill!" And picture followed picture. The sullen faces, the narrowed eyes. The hatred. Slowly I came to understand that they wanted to kill *me*. Quite literally, if they could only lay their hands on me, they would relish shooting me, stabbing me or beating me to death. Quite literally, paranoiac though it may sound, they wanted to kill me. They hated Me.

Suddenly it was no longer a deprived minority rebelling against the system that oppressed them. Suddenly the whole thing descended to a far more basic level—They and I, Them and Me. If They live in Los Angeles and Newark and Detroit hated me, what about They who live in our own ghettos? Those near my own house? What about the bootblack? We've always gotten along so well, kidding and joshing. Does he seem a little surly this morning? What of the cleaning lady I like so well? Is there a new touch of defiance in her tone? And what of the big longshoreman coming my way down the street? What is that look in his eyes? What are They really thinking? How much do They hate Me? How awful it is to be hated. How unfair. I keep wanting to say, Don't hate me. If you must hate, hate the Thurmonds, the Eastlands, the Wallaces. Hate those who won't rent you a room or serve you a meal or give you a job. But don't hate me. I don't want it to be Them and Me. We are all fellow human beings. We are all in the same boat. Don't hate me.

In the end, I told a long-time Negro friend (I think he is a friend) of my fear and anger. I told him how awful it was to be hated. How insecure it made you, never to be sure what They were thinking. How terribly, terribly unfair it was to be despised, not for anything you'd said, or done, or been. But simply because you were white.

"I know how it is," he said, nodding. "Simply because I'm black."

Black Power

STOKELY CARMICHAEL AND CHARLES HAMILTON

This is still a classic essay on the political position of Black Americans. Carmichael and Hamilton argue that Blacks should follow a path similar to that of other ethnic groups. They should get themselves together socially and psychologically and organize a powerful political movement.

"To carve out a place for itself in the politico-social order," V. O. Key, Jr. wrote in *Politics, Parties and Pressure Groups,* "a new group may have to fight for orientation of many of the values of the old order" (p. 57). This is especially true when that group is composed of black people in the American society—a society that has for centuries deliberately and systematically excluded them from political participation. Black people in the United States must raise hard questions, questions which challenge the very nature of the society itself: its long-standing values, beliefs and institutions.

To do this, we must first redefine ourselves. Our basic need is to reclaim our history and our identity from what must be called cultural terrorism, from the depredation of self-justifying white guilt. We shall have to struggle for the right to create our own terms through which to define ourselves and our relationship to the society, and to have these terms recognized. This is the first necessity of a free people, and the first right that any oppressor must suspend.

In *Politics Among Nations,* Hans Morgenthau defined political power as "the psychological control over the minds of men" (p. 29). This control includes the attempt by the oppressor to have *his* definitions, *his* historical descriptions, *accepted* by the oppressed. This was true in Africa no less than in the United States. To black Africans, the word "Uhuru" means "freedom," but they had to fight the white colonizers for the right to use the term. The recorded history of this country's dealings with red and black men offers other examples. In the wars between the white settlers and the "Indians," a battle won by the Cavalry was described as a "victory." The "Indians'" triumphs, however, were "massacres." (The American colonists were not unaware of the need to define their acts in their own terms. They labeled their fight against England a "revolution"; the English attempted to demean it by calling it "insubordination" or "riotous.")

The historical period following Reconstruction in the South after the Civil War has been called by many historians the period of Redemption, implying that the bigoted southern slave societies were "redeemed" from the hands of "reckless and irresponsible" black rulers. Professor John Hope Franklin's *Reconstruction* or Dr. W. E. B. Dubois' *Black Reconstruction* should be sufficient to dispel inaccurate historical notions, but the larger society persists in its own self-serving accounts. Thus black people came to be depicted as "lazy," "apathetic," "dumb," "shiftless," "good-timers." Just as red men had to be recorded as "savages" to justify the white man's theft of their land, so black men had to be vilified in order to justify their continued oppression. Those who have the right to define are the masters of the situation. Lewis Carroll understood this:

> "When I use a word," Humpty Dumpty said in a rather scornful tone, "it means just what I choose it to mean—neither more nor less."
>
> "The question is," said Alice, "whether you *can* make words mean so many different things."
>
> "The question is," said Humpty Dumpty, "which is to be master—that's all." *

Today, the American educational system continues to reinforce the entrenched values of the society through the use of words. Few people in this country question that this is "the land of the free and the home of the brave." They have had these words drummed into them from childhood. Few people question that this is the "Great Society" or that this country is fighting "Communist aggression" around the world. We mouth these things over and over, and they become truisms not to be questioned. In a similar way, black people have been saddled with epithets.

"Integration" is another current example of a word which has been defined according to the way white Americans see it. To many of them, it means black men wanting to marry white daughters; it means "race mixing" —implying bed or dance partners. To black people, it has meant a way to improve their lives—economically and politically. But the predominant white definition has stuck in the minds of too many people.

Black people must redefine themselves, and only *they* can do that. Throughout this country, vast segments of the black communities are beginning to recognize the need to assert their own definitions, to reclaim their

* Lewis Carroll, *Through the Looking Glass*. New York: Doubleday Books, Inc., p. 196.

history, their culture; to create their own sense of community and togetherness. There is a growing resentment of the word "Negro," for example, because this term is the invention of our oppressor; it is *his* image of us that he describes. Many blacks are now calling themselves African-Americans, Afro-Americans or black people because that is *our* image of ourselves. When we begin to define our own image, the stereotypes—that is, lies—that our oppressor has developed will begin in the white community and end there. The black community will have a positive image of itself that *it* has created. This means we will no longer call ourselves lazy, apathetic, dumb, good-timers, shiftless, etc. Those are words used by white America to define us. If we accept these adjectives, as some of us have in the past, then we see ourselves only in a negative way, precisely the way white America wants us to see ourselves. Our incentive is broken and our will to fight is surrendered. From now on we shall view ourselves as African-Americans and as black people who are in fact energetic, determined, intelligent, beautiful and peace-loving.

There is a terminology and ethos peculiar to the black community of which black people are beginning to be no longer ashamed. Black communities are the only large segments of this society where people refer to each other as brother—soul-brother, soul-sister. Some people may look upon this as *ersatz,* as make-believe, but it is not that. It is real. It is a growing sense of community. It is a growing realization that black Americans have a common bond not only among themselves, but with their African brothers. In *Black Man's Burden,* John O. Killens described his trip to ten African countries as follows:

> Everywhere I went people called me brother. . . . "Welcome, American brother." It was a good feeling for me, to be in Africa. To walk in a land for the first time in your entire life knowing within yourself that your color would not be held against you. No black man ever knows this in America [p. 160].

More and more black Americans are developing this feeling. They are becoming aware that they have a history which pre-dates their forced introduction to this country. African-American history means a long history beginning on the continent of Africa, a history not taught in the standard textbooks of this country. It is absolutely essential that black people know this history, that they know their roots, that they develop an awareness of their cultural heritage. Too long have they been kept in submission by being told that they had no culture, no manifest heritage, before they landed on the slave auction blocks in this country. If black people are to know themselves as a vibrant, valiant people, they must know their roots. And they will soon learn that the Hollywood image of man-eating cannibals waiting for, and waiting on, the Great White Hunter is a lie.

With redefinition will come a clearer notion of the role black Americans can play in this world. This role will emerge clearly out of the unique, common experiences of Afro-Asians. Killens concludes:

I believe furthermore that the American Negro can be the bridge between the West and Africa-Asia. We black Americans can serve as a bridge to mutual understanding. The one thing we black Americans have in common with the other colored peoples of the world is that we have all felt the cruel and ruthless heel of white supremacy. We have all been "niggerized" on one level or another. And all of us are determined to "deniggerize" the earth. To rid the world of "niggers" is the Black Man's Burden, human reconstruction is the grand objective [p. 176].

Only when black people fully develop this sense of community, of themselves, can they begin to deal effectively with the problems of racism in *this* country. This is what we mean by a new consciousness; this is the vital first step.

The next step is what we shall call the process of political modernization—a process which must take place if the society is to be rid of racism. "Political modernization" includes many things, but we mean by it three major concepts: (1) questioning old values and institutions of the society; (2) searching for new and different forms of political structure to solve political and economic problems; and (3) broadening the base of political participation to include more people in the decision-making process. These notions (we shall take up each in turn) are central to our thinking throughout this book and to contemporary American history as a whole. As David Apter wrote in *The Politics of Modernization,* ". . . the struggle to modernize is what has given meaning to our generation. It tests our cherished institutions and our beliefs. . . . So compelling a force has it become that we are forced to ask new questions of our own institutions. Each country, whether modernized or modernizing, stands in both judgment and fear of the results. Our own society is no exception" (p. 2).

The values of this society support a racist system; we find it incongruous to ask black people to adopt and support most of those values. We also reject the assumption that the basic institutions of this society must be preserved. The goal of black people must *not* be to assimilate into middle-class America, for that class—as a whole—is without a viable conscience as regards humanity. The values of the middle class permit the perpetuation of the ravages of the black community. The values of that class are based on material aggrandizement, not the expansion of humanity. The values of that class ultimately support cloistered little closed societies tucked away neatly in tree-lined suburbia. The values of that class do *not* lead to the creation of an open society. That class *mouths* its preference for a free, competitive society, while at the same time forcefully and even viciously denying to black people as a group the opportunity to compete.

We are not unmindful of other descriptions of the social utility of the middle class. Banfield and Wilson, in *City Politics,* concluded:

The departure of the middle class from the central city is important in other ways. . . . The middle class supplies a social and political leavening in the life of a city. Middle-class people demand good schools and integrity in government. They support churches, lodges, parent-teacher associations, scout troops, better-housing committees, art galleries, and operas. It is the middle class, in short, that asserts a conception of the public interest. Now its activity is increasingly concentrated in the suburbs [p. 14].

But this same middle class manifests a sense of superior group position in regard to race. This class wants "good government" *for themselves;* it wants good schools *for its children.* At the same time, many of its members sneak into the black community by day, exploit it, and take the money home to their middle-class communities at night to support their operas and art galleries and comfortable homes. When not actually robbing, they will fight off the handful of more affluent black people who seek to move in; when they approve or even seek token integration, it applies only to black people like themselves—as "white" as possible. *This class is the backbone of institutional racism in this country.*

Thus we reject the goal of assimilation into middle-class America because the values of that class are in themselves anti-humanist and because that class as a social force perpetuates racism. We must face the fact that, in the past, what we have called the movement has not really questioned the middle-class values and institutions of this country. If anything, it has accepted those values and institutions without fully realizing their racist nature. Reorientation means an emphasis on the dignity of man, not on the sanctity of property. It means the creation of a society where human misery and poverty are repugnant to that society, not an indication of laziness or lack of initiative. The creation of new values means the establishment of a society based, as Killens expresses it in *Black Man's Burden,* on "free people," not "free enterprise" (p. 167). To do this means to modernize—*indeed, to civilize*—this country.

Supporting the old values are old political and economical structures; these must also be "modernized." We should at this point distinguish between "structures" and "system." By system, we have in mind the entire American complex of basic institutions, values, beliefs, etc. By structures, we mean the specific institutions (political parties, interest groups, bureaucratic administrations) which exist to conduct the business of that system. Obviously, the first is broader than the second. Also, the second assumes the legitimacy of the first. Our view is that, given the illegitimacy of the system, we cannot then proceed to transform that system with existing structures.

The two major political parties in this country have become non-viable entities for the legitimate representation of the real needs of masses—especially blacks—in this country. Walter Lippmann raised the same point in his syndicated column of December 8, 1966. He pointed out that the party system in the United States developed before our society became as technologically complex as it is now. He says that the ways in which men live and define themselves are changing radically. Old ideological issues, once the subject of passionate controversy, Lippmann argues, are of little interest today. He asks whether the great urban complexes—which are rapidly becoming the centers of black population in the U.S.—can be run with the same systems and ideas that derive from a time when America was a country of small villages and farms. While not addressing himself directly to the question of race, Lippmann raises a major question about our political institutions; and the crisis of race in America may be its major symptom.

Black people have seen the city planning commissions, the urban renewal commissions, the boards of education and the police departments fail to speak to their needs in a meaningful way. We must devise new structures, new institutions to replace those forms or to make them responsive. There is nothing sacred or inevitable about old institutions; the focus must be on people, not forms.

Existing structures and established ways of doing things have a way of perpetuating themselves and for this reason, the modernizing process will be difficult. Therefore, timidity in calling into question the boards of education or the police departments will not do. They must be challenged forcefully and clearly. If this means the creation of parallel community institutions, then that must be the solution. If this means that black parents must gain control over the operation of the schools in the black community, then that must be the solution. The search for new forms means the search for institutions that will, for once, make decisions in the interest of black people. It means, for example, a building inspection department that neither winks at violations of building codes by absentee slumlords nor imposes meaningless fines which permit them to continue their exploitation of the black community.

Essential to the modernization of structures is a broadened base of political participation. More and more people must become politically sensitive and active (we have already seen this happening in some areas of the South). People must no longer be tied, by small incentives or handouts, to a corrupting and corruptible white machine. Black people will choose their own leaders and hold those leaders responsible to *them.* A broadened base means an end to the condition described by James Wilson in *Negro Politics,* whereby "Negroes tended to be the objects rather than the subjects of civic action. Things are often done for, or about, or to, or because of Negroes, but they are less frequently done *by* Negroes" (p. 133). Broadening the base of political participation, then, has as much to do with the quality of black participation as with the quantity. We are fully aware that the black vote, especially in the North, has been pulled out of white pockets and "delivered" whenever it was in the interest of white politicians to do so. That vote must no longer be controllable by those who have neither the interests nor the demonstrated concern of black people in mind.

As the base broadens, as more and more black people become activated, they will perceive more clearly the special disadvantages heaped upon them as a group. They will perceive that the larger society is growing more affluent while the black society is retrogressing, as daily life and mounting statistics clearly show. V. O. Key describes what often happens next, in *Politics, Parties and Pressure Groups:* "A factor of great significance in the setting off of political movements is an abrupt change for the worse in the status of one group relative to that of other groups in society. . . . A rapid change for the worse . . . in the relative status of any group . . . is likely to precipitate political action" (p. 24). Black people will become increasingly active as they notice that their retrogressive status exists in large measure because of values and institutions arraigned against them. They will begin to stress and strain and call the entire system into question. Political modernization will be in motion. We believe that it is now in motion. One form of that motion is Black Power.

The adoption of the concept of Black Power is one of the most legitimate and healthy developments in American politics and race relations in our time. The concept of Black Power speaks to all the needs mentioned in this chapter. It is a call for black people in this country to unite, to recognize their heritage, to build a sense of community. It is a call for black people to begin to define their own goals, to lead their own organizations and to support those organizations. It is a call to reject the racist institutions and values of this society.

The concept of Black Power rests on a fundamental premise: *Before a group can enter the open society, it must first close ranks.* By this we mean that group solidarity is necessary before a group can operate effectively from a bargaining position of strength in a pluralistic society. Traditionally, each new ethnic group in this society has found the route to social and political viability through the organization of its own institutions with which to represent its needs within the larger society. Studies in voting behavior specifically, and political behavior generally, have made it clear that politically the American pot has not melted. Italians vote for Rubino over O'Brien; Irish for Murphy over Goldberg, etc. This phenomenon may seem distasteful to some, but it has been and remains today a central fact of the American political system. . . .

The point is obvious: black people must lead and run their own organizations. Only black people can convey the revolutionary idea—and it is a revolutionary idea—that black people are able to do things themselves. Only they can help create in the community an aroused and continuing black consciousness that will provide the basis for political strength. In the past, white allies have often furthered white supremacy without the whites involved realizing it, or even wanting to do so. Black people must come together and do things for themselves. They must achieve self-identity and self-determination in order to have their daily needs met.

Black Power means, for example, that in Lowndes County, Alabama, a black sheriff can end police brutality. A black tax assessor and tax collector and county board of revenue can lay, collect, and channel tax monies for the building of better roads and schools serving black people. In such areas as Lowndes, where black people have a majority, they will attempt to use power to exercise control. This is what they seek: control. When black people lack a majority, Black Power means proper representation and sharing of control. It means the creation of power bases, of strength, from which black people can press to change local or nation-wide patterns of oppression—instead of from weakness.

It does not mean *merely* putting black faces into office. Black visibility is not Black Power. Most of the black politicians around the country today are not examples of Black Power. The power must be that of a community, and emanate from there. The black politicians must start from there. The black politicians must stop being representatives of "downtown" machines, whatever the cost might be in terms of lost patronage and holiday handouts.

Black Power recognizes—it must recognize—the ethnic basis of American politics as well as the power-oriented nature of American politics. Black Power therefore calls for black people to consolidate behind their own, so that they can bargain from a position of strength. But while we endorse the *procedure* of group solidarity and identity for the purpose of attaining certain goals in the body politic, this does not mean that black people should strive for the same kind of rewards (i.e., end results) obtained by the white society. The ultimate values and goals are not domination or exploitation of other groups, but rather an effective share in the total power of the society.

Nevertheless, some observers have labeled those who advocate Black Power as racists; they have said that the call for self-identification and self-determination is "racism in reverse" or "black supremacy." This is a deliberate and absurd lie. There is no analogy—by any stretch of definition or imagination—between the advocates of Black Power and white racists. Racism is not merely exclusion on the basis of race but exclusion for the purpose of subjugating or maintaining subjugation. The goal of the racists is to keep black people on the bottom, arbitrarily and dictatorially, as they have done in this country for over three hundred years. The goal of black self-determination and black self-identity—Black Power—is full participation in the decision-making processes affecting the lives of black people, and recognition of the virtues in themselves as black people. The black people of this country have not lynched whites, bombed their churches, murdered their children and manipulated laws and institutions to maintain oppression. White racists have. Congressional laws, one after the other, have not been necessary to stop black people from oppressing others and denying others the full enjoyment of their rights. White racists have made such laws necessary. The goal of Black Power is positive and functional to a free and viable society. No white racist can make this claim.

A great deal of public attention and press space was devoted to the hysterical accusation of "black racism" when the call for Black Power was first sounded. A national committee of influential black churchmen affiliated with the National Council of Churches, despite their obvious respectability and responsibility, had to resort to a paid advertisement to articulate their position, while anyone yapping "black racism" made front-page news. In their statement, published in the *New York Times* of July 31, 1966, the churchmen said:

> We, an informal group of Negro churchmen in America, are deeply disturbed about the crisis brought upon our country by historic distortions of important human realities in the controversy about "black power." What we see shining through the variety of rhetoric is not anything new but the same old problem of power and race which has faced our beloved country since 1619.
>
> . . . The conscience of black men is corrupted because having no power to implement the demands of conscience, the concern for justice in the absence of justice becomes a chaotic self-surrender. Powerlessness breeds a race of beggars. We are faced with a situation where powerless conscience meets conscienceless power, threatening the very foundations of our Nation.
>
> We deplore the overt violence of riots, but we feel it is more important to focus on the real sources of these eruptions. These sources may be abetted inside the Ghetto, but their basic cause lies in the silent and covert violence which white middle class America inflicts upon the victims of the inner city.
>
> . . . In short, the failure of American leaders to use American power to create equal opportunity *in life* as well as *law*, this is the real problem and not the anguished cry for black power.
>
> . . . Without the capacity to participate with power, i.e., to have some organized political and economic strength to really influence people with whom one interacts, integration is not meaningful.
>
> . . . America has asked its Negro citizens to fight for opportunity as *individuals*, whereas at certain points in our history what we have needed most has been opportunity for the *whole group*, not just for selected and approved Negroes.
>
> . . . We must not apologize for the existence of this form of group power, for we have been oppressed as a group and not as individuals. We will not find our way out of that oppression until both we and America accept the need for Negro Americans, as well as for Jews, Italians, Poles, and white Anglo-Saxon Protestants, among others, to have and to wield group power.

It is a commentary on the fundamentally racist nature of this society that the concept of group strength for black people must be articulated—not to mention defended. No other group would submit to being led by others. Italians do not run the Anti-Defamation League of B'nai B'rith. Irish do not chair Christopher Columbus Societies. Yet when black people call for black-run and all-black organizations, they are immediately classed in a category with the Ku Klux Klan. This is interesting and ironic, but by no means surprising: the society does not expect black people to be able to take care of their business, and there are many who prefer it precisely that way.

In the end, we cannot and shall not offer any guarantees that Black Power, if achieved, would be non-racist. No one can predict human behavior. Social change always has unanticipated consequences. If black racism is what the larger society fears, we cannot help them. We can only state what we hope will be the result, given the fact that the present situation is unacceptable and that we have no real alternative but to work for Black Power. The final truth is that the white society is not entitled to reassurances, even if it were possible to offer them.

The Myths of the Mexican American

GLEN GAVIGLIO

This essay examines some of the myths and stereotypes associated with Mexican Americans. In America, the Aztec Warrior becomes the Frito Bandito. But myths and stereotypes, no matter how fun loving and comical, can become social realities that people act upon.

The Mexican Americans, or "Chicanos," have been referred to as the forgotten minority. They are supposedly a quiet, docile, passive, somnolent, and satisfied group of fatalistic near peasants. Therefore they have been erased from the conscience of most Americans. They have been invisible; they have been wiped from history, like the Indians. Yet Chicanos have not lost themselves, even though they have lived in a hostile environment for decades. Why have they been overlooked, ignored, and oppressed?

This brief essay is an attempt to synthesize some of the major sociohistoric factors that have influenced the development of *La Raza*. For purposes of analysis, this essay is arranged into four deeply ingrained myths of the Mexican American: (1) The Myth of the Border, (2) The Myth of the Docile Peasant, (3) The Myth of Ethnic and Racial Assimilation, and (4) The Myth of Mexican American Similarity.

Myths are important for societies; they influence every individual's definition of reality. People act in relation to the mythology of their society. Therefore myths are significant behavior inducing and shaping devices. (The social reality of the mind comes in all flavors of distortion.) The influence of some of these distortions is examined in each of the following myths.

The Myth of the Border

Historically, cries of "Spic," "Greaser," "Wetback," or "Taco Bender, go home" were very typical of the American Southwest. The cries are more subdued and sophisticated now, but invariably eruptions occur. For example, in 1969 in the Santa Clara Valley, just south of San Francisco, a venerable judge publicly excoriated a Chicano youth in court, saying that Hitler had a good thing going with the Jews and that a similar program should be undertaken with Mexicans. (At this writing that judge is still on the bench.)

There is a political boundary separating Mexico and the United States, but the winds of change have modified that boundary immensely. In a very real sense that border does not exist. The border is totally artificial from a geographical perspective. It does not separate climatic or agricultural regions; in fact, it cuts across the natural topography of the area. The difference between Calexico and Mexicali, El Paso and Juarez, and Brownsville and Matamoros is economic and political, not geographical. The border does not really exist for the Chicano. It never has.

At one time the Southwest was part of Mexico. It was inhabited by a mixture of Spaniards and Indians; it was naturally an arid region that was sparsely settled. The region was the frontier or borderlands of Mexico, and it was never an integral part of that country. When the Spanish did come to settle this region, there actually were very few pure Spaniards in the expeditions. Most of the settlers who came north from Mexico were Mestizo and Indian. The Indians who were living in this area had already been strongly influenced by the Aztec civilization. On the eve of the Mexican–American War (1848), there were only about 82,000 Spanish-speaking people living in the Southwest, but they had been there for generations. (There were also an untabulated number of Indians and Mestizos in the area.) In California in 1848, there were 21,000 Spanish-speaking in a population of about 100,000. When California became a state (1850), the constitution was written in Spanish. This constitution, created in part by people of Spanish ancestry, established California as a bilingual state (and it remained bilingual until 1878). In southern California there were bilingual schools until the 1870's. In other words, California has gone from bilingual schools to denial to the Chicanos of the right to vote, because they cannot read the Constitution. (This has been recently changed by the California Supreme Court.)

When the United States wrested the Southwest from Mexico, many Spanish-speaking people automatically became residents of the United States. They did not immigrate from anywhere. Therefore, when an Anglo tells a Chicano to go home, he is less than amusing; he is grossly misinformed. The Chicano is more firmly rooted in the American past than an Anglo who may have just recently migrated from Europe.

The Treaty of Guadalupe Hidalgo (1848), which terminated the Mexican–American War, was supposed to protect and guarantee the rights of self-determination for the Spanish-speaking people in the newly acquired United States territory. In actuality the treaty did little to protect the rights of the Mexicans in this region. The Anglos immediately displayed a tremendous hostility and resentment toward these Hispanos. The creed of American racism became brutally apparent in the systematic oppression that followed. For example, in California the antagonism between Spanish-speaking and Yankee miners culminated with the Foreign Miners Tax Law of 1850, which effectively drove the Spanish-speaking from the gold fields. (Note the word *foreign.*) In 1851 the Federal Land Tenure Act was passed. This act made possible the systematic and gradual extraction of land from the hands of the Hispanos.

No Chicano is really an immigrant in America. When they "moved north," they felt that they were moving in an environment that was geographically, culturally, and historically familiar. I would even say that in a political sense the border has been a nebulous entity. There was no border patrol until 1924 and there was not even a quota on Mexican immigration until 1965. The reason the border did not exist in a political or economic manner for either the Anglo or Chicano was the need for cheap labor in the fields. As long as there was a ready supply of bodies toward the south, the indigenous labor force could not organize and demand higher wages. When the field workers did try to organize, their leaders were quickly "deported." The farm workers could not effectively unionize until the Bracero program was terminated in 1965. (The program allowed Mexican nationals to reside temporarily in the United States in order to harvest the crops.) The Delano movement still has not completely succeeded, because the border is still quite open. Migrant workers can enter both legally and illegally. "Green Card Holders" are now entering the United States to pick crops in times of emergency (meaning "during strikes"). In reality, the border has always been exactly what the United States has wanted it to be.

The Myth of the Docile Peasant

The Chicano has been stereotyped as a passive peasant. This is absurd on statistical grounds alone. Over 80 per cent of all Chicanos reside in urban areas and over 1 million Chicanos live in Los Angeles. The image of the Chicano is not really a static one. According to the stereotype, the Chicano can be either a fat and lazy peon, slumbering under a cactus and wearing his sombrero and poncho, or he can be a stinking, ferocious, foul-mouthed, greasy bandito. The stereotype of the Mexican American stems from two basic sources: (1) the popularized folk mythology of traditional American racism and (2) the distorted sociological image. We can expect the first; it bears no surprises, but the latter is more repulsive to us, because it comes from unbiased sociological sources.

There is nothing unique in saying that the society of America is racist, but when we confront the historical record of past American racial atrocities, the present looks as though peace and brotherhood abound (if you choose to ignore Vietnam). American literature, with but few exceptions, is filled with condescending racist drivel. One example from *The Oregon Trail* by Francis Parkman (Doubleday, 1948) will provide the proper flavor:

> Two or three squalid Mexicans, with their broad hats, and their vile faces overgrown with hair, were lounging about the bank of the river in front of (the gate of the Pueblo). They disappeared as they saw us approach [p. 260].
>
> A few squaws and Spanish women, and a few Mexicans, as mean and miserable as the place itself, were lazily sauntering about [p. 260].
>
> There was another room beyond, less sumptuously decorated, and here three or four Spanish girls, one of them very pretty, were baking cakes at a mud fireplace in the corner [p. 261].

The human race in this part of the world is separated into three divisions, arranged in the order of their merits: white men, Indians, and Mexicans; to the latter of whom the honorable title of "whites" is by no means conceded [p. 263].

Usually the racism is not even this "subtle." Our history is replete with speeches of major political figures proclaiming a hypocritical and altruistic imperialism. We have always had an inclination to save the ignorant and backward colored masses of the world from themselves, witness this speech delivered by John C. Calhoun in the Senate on January 4, 1848 (after we had defeated Mexico in a war):

We have never dreamt of incorporating into our Union any but the Caucasian race—the free white race. To incorporate Mexico, would be the very first instance of the kind, of incorporating an Indian race; for more than half of the Mexicans are Indians, and the other is composed chiefly of mixed tribes. I protest against such a union as that! Ours, sir, is the government of a white race. The greatest misfortunes of Spanish America are to be traced to the fatal error of placing these colored races on an equality with the white race. That error destroyed the social arrangement which formed the basis of society. The Portuguese and ourselves have escaped—the Portuguese at least to some extent—and we are the only people on this continent which had made revolutions without being followed by anarchy. And yet it is professed, and talked about, to erect these Mexicans into a territorial government, and place them on an equality with the people of the United States. I protest utterly against such a project. . . .

But . . . suppose all these difficulties removed; suppose their people attached to our Union, and desirous of incorporating with us, ought we to bring them in? Are they fit to be connected with us? Are they fit for self-government and for governing you? Are you, any of you, willing that your states should be governed by these twenty-odd Mexican states, with a population of about only one million of your blood, and two or three million of mixed blood better informed—all the rest pure Indians, a mixed blood equally ignorant and unfit for liberty, impure races, not as good as the Cherokees or Choctaws?

Calhoun did not even believe in spreading the faith to the ignorant colored masses, because they were too inferior even to govern themselves and accept the gospel of Americanism.

The mythology of American racism has been updated and perfected since the heyday of blatant expansionism and imperialism. The myths may be a little more subtle but they are still extremely harmful. It can be effectively argued that the myths are even more destructive because of the pervasive influence in the mass media. The world is being turned into a McLuhanesque global village; therefore more people are influenced by the racist stereotypes portrayed in the mass media. At the moment one of the worst offenders is the advertising industry. One particularly offensive commercial was for Arrid deodorant. It shows a Mexican bandito spraying his underarm while a voice says, "If it works for him, it will work for you." Do Chicanos stink worse than blacks? Can you envision that same commercial with a sloppy, fat ghetto black wearing a dirty and torn T-shirt? Or is the black movement too powerful (or too violent) to allow that kind of defamation? There is a real battle in

America to see who will be the new "niggers." The Chicanos or the Hippies?

These stereotypes are extremely important because people act upon these myths. Very insipid and disastrous self-fulfilling prophecies can be initiated by racial and cultural myths. If the dominant group treats the minority group as an inferior race or culture, the minority can become just that. In a political and economic sense racial oppression is very obvious, but it has more subtle manifestations. What happens in the school system when students are "tracked" or when the teacher has lower expectations for some students? What happens to the minds of minority group members? Can a people be taught to hate themselves? Can a minority group believe the myths the majority perpetrates? One of the most sickening aspects of race relations in America is that the preceding questions must be answered in a very negative manner.

Another form of stereotyping is of a more insidious variety because it is generated by the academic community and therefore carries with it scientific validity. In particular the work of Heller (*Mexican-American Youth*), Tuck (*Not with the Fist*), and Madsen (*Mexican-Americans of South Texas*) should be mentioned. The studies have some very major defects. The most obvious deficiency from a traditional sociological perspective is a methodological one, the authors over-generalize from a biased or partial sampling of Chicanos. These studies list "characteristics" or "attributes" of the typical Mexican American. Some of these characteristics seem like a sociological updating of racial mythology. Is being passive, accepting, and fatalistic much different from being lazy? Do all Chicanos display these traits? We cannot be sure of the limited regional sample of Chicanos in these studies. Another glaring omission in these studies is their completely historical nature. They speak of the Chicano as existing in the eternal present, as if his traditional culture were static and unchanging. The Chicano may not try to change his environment in the same manner as the robust and enterprising Anglo, for he has found that passive adjustment to his social milieu is necessary to his survival. This passiveness creates another blatantly false stereotype. Were those who rode with Villa and Zapata during the Mexican Revolution passively accepting their fate? Were the Chicanos who organized numerous strikes in the Southwest for the past seventy-five years accepting their fate? Are Reies Tijerina, Cesar Chavez, and Corky Gonsalez leaders of a passive and somnolent bunch of poncho-clad peasants?

The last significant error in these books is their tendency to equate and confuse ethnic and class characteristics. Many of the characteristics attributed to Mexican Americans in these studies are shared by all lower-class people. Cohen and Hodges, in a study done in California, found that lower-lower-class Chicanos, blacks, and Anglos all shared some basically similar characteristics: extended families, marked anti-intellectualism, *machismo* (a super-masculine, double-standard-type male), use of physical force, and a type of fatalism. Oscar Lewis has argued that throughout the world the lower classes generally share these traits. Lewis terms these characteristics a "culture of poverty"; he sees it as a functional adaptation to their oppressive social conditions. Therefore there is nothing unique in these traits that are supposedly typical of the Mexican American. Some statistical validity resides in the fact that a fairly large percentage of Chicanos live below the poverty level (16 per cent of the Anglos, 27 per cent of the blacks, and 37 per cent of the Chicanos). These figures may understate the degree of Chicano poverty. That 37 per cent basically represents United States citizens. According to the U.S. Department of Immigration, there are 1.5 million alien residents and 4.5 million illegal aliens below the poverty level.

The concept of the culture of poverty can also be interpreted in a very negative manner. It can be used to conclude that the cultural characteristics of the poor people themselves are responsible for their socioeconomic status. For example, take the noted fatalism of the lower classes. They feel that they have little control over the institutions and events that shape their lives. It is very possible that the pessimism, apathy, and fatalism of the lower classes is a valid adjustment to a historical social reality. The life chances of a minority group member have been severely and systematically restricted; these people have not had and still do not have very much control over the decisions that affect their lives. Is it really so hard to imagine accepting a religion, whether it is a folk Catholicism or a revivalist Protestantism, that promises an internal reward when the present and future look so bleak? When reality is unbearably ugly, fatalism may be the only answer among rotten alternatives.

It would be wise not to apply the concept of culture of poverty to minority groups unless its sociohistorical component is considered. Why is there a culture of poverty? How did it start? Why do so many different societies have subcultures of poverty with similar traits? The answer lies in an analysis of how people adjust to the conditions of poverty, racism, and oppression.

The Myth of Ethnic and Racial Assimilation

The huddled and hungry hordes of the world streamed to the shores of America, where golden opportunities awaited them. The saga of America is sometimes told as though it were a giant, bottomless cauldron where the oppressed masses of humanity mingled and produced an egalitarian and tolerant democratic society. This is the great myth of the melting pot. It is a romantic and nostalgic vision of the American past that does very little justice to reality. Assimilation in the American melting pot was meant for whites only. For example, Indians were almost exterminated like vermin, instead of being melted, and of course enough has been said recently of black Americans. The Chicano still forms an unassimilated and distinct cultural entity in America.

Glazer and Moynihan (*Beyond the Melting Pot*, 1963) argue that ethnic homogenization never completely took place in America. New York is a veritable hodge-podge of racial and ethnic groups that still function as political interest groups. Glazer and Moynihan succintly conclude, "The point about the Melting Pot . . . is that it did not happen." Every act of racism and discrimination is a painful contradiction of the concept of the melting pot.

Why have the Chicanos not been assimilated into the American mainstream? The most obvious reason for this lack of assimilation is the dominant Anglo group itself; it has not been willing to let the Chicano assimilate. The Mexican American is in a caste position similar to that of the black man after emancipation. There are other factors that have contributed to the cultural distance between the Chicano and the Anglo. First, there is the fact that Mexico is adjacent to the United States. The homeland for many Chicanos is never far away. There is a continual cultural regeneration and reinforcement. Many Mexicans come to America "temporarily" and never psychologically divorce themselves from the values of Mexico. Then there is the continual immigration, both legal and illegal, from Mexico. There are also visits from relatives going in both directions. The communal and extended nature of the Chicano family further reinforces certain cultural values, like language. Three and four generations may live in the same household. This pattern can be contrasted with many white immigrant groups who left the homeland far behind in Europe, geographically if not psychologically.

Another reason why the Chicano has not been and may never be totally assimilated is that he does not want to be. Why accept the dominant culture? If Anglo youth rebellion is any indication of the viability of mainstream, middle-class American values, Chicanos may be correct in refusing to assimilate. In fact, many of the criticisms that young people level at America have been part of the Chicano cultural and historical tradition. Chicanos have never been "materialistic," or what the Anglo considers "property oriented." The land was usually for all to use or hold communally; their agricultural practices and use of the land were in harmony with nature. Chicanos have always displayed a sense of community, a tendency toward mutual aid, and a strong communal or extended family. They have always nurtured an emphasis on warm interpersonal relationships and a respect for people as individuals.

The Myth of Mexican American Similarity

As with most minority groups, the Mexican American has been stereotyped. The stereotype is usually one of a lower-lower-class Chicano, a rigid caricature which allows a minimum of diversity. The stereotype, as mentioned in a previous section, has negative and racist connotations, and as a valid characterization of social reality, it is sadly lacking.

There are some statistical generalizations that can be made in relation to Chicanos. Many have parents or grandparents who migrated from Mexico, and as a consequence, many speak Spanish, Pocho (a combination of Spanish and English), or English with an accent. As a group, Chicanos tend to be Catholic (easily over 50 per cent). As a population they tend to be young (twenty years of age). The average yearly income for the Mexican American family is the lowest in the nation, except for the income of the reservation Indian. There are more Chicanos (60 to 70 per cent) living in poverty and more Chicanos with less education than blacks (less than eight years, on the average, for those over twenty-five). Chicanos as a group share certain cultural values, but within the broad contours just mentioned there is immense variety.

There are many physical differences in the Chicano population. Although Chicanos tend to be darker than the Anglo population, they range from swarthy to light skinned. All types of ethnic and racial groups have mingled in Mexico with the indigenous people, from black slaves to French immigrants. There are also Filipinos and Puerto Ricans who are culturally Chicano. There are rural and urban differences, generational conflicts, geographical differences, and class differences between Chicanos. Who is a Mexican American? How can you really stereotype the Chicano?

Here lies the strength and weakness of the Chicano. On one hand he is confronted in America with a severe "identity crisis." He is the true marginal man caught between cultures. Historically, he represents the uneasy compromise between the Hispano and the Indian who was delivered into a hostile Anglo world. Yet as a people, *La Raza* has developed a deeply ingrained humanism. The term *La Raza* does not simply mean the race or people, but the community or the family. *La Raza* stands in striking contrast to the cold and impersonal Anglo world.

Bibliography

Casavantes, Edward J. A *New Look at the Attributes of the Mexican American.* Albuquerque, N.M.: Southwestern Education Laboratory, Inc., 1969.

Forbes, Jack D. *Mexican-Americans: A Handbook for Educators.* Berkeley: Far West Laboratory for Educational Research and Development, 1969.

Glazer, Nathan, and Daniel Patrick Moynihan. *Beyond the Melting Pot.* Cambridge, Mass.: M.I.T. Press, 1963.

Heller, Celia S. *Mexican American Youth: Forgotten Youth at the Crossroads.* New York: Random House, Inc., 1966.

Madsen, William. *The Mexican-American of South Texas.* New York: Holt, Rinehart and Winston, Inc., 1964.

Martinez, Thomas M. "Advertising and Racism: "The Case of the Mexican-American," *El Grito,* Summer 1969, Volume II, Number 4.

McWilliams, Carey. *North from Mexico.* New York: Greenwood Press, 1948.

———. *The Mexicans in America.* New York: Teacher's College Press, 1968.

Rios, Francisco Armando. "The Mexican in Fact, Fiction, and Folklore," *El Grito,* Summer 1969, Volume II, Number 4.

Robinson, Cecil. *With the Ears of Strangers.* Tucson: University of Arizona Press, 1963.

Romano, Octavio Ignacio. "The Anthropology and Sociology of the Mexican-

Americans: The Distortion of Mexican-American History," *El Grito*, Fall 1968, Volume II, Number 1.

ROSENTHALL, ROBERT, and LENORE JACOBSON. *Pygmalion in the Classroom*. New York: Holt, Rinehart and Winston, Inc., 1968.

STEINFIELD, MELVIN. *Cracks in the Melting Pot*. Beverly Hills, Calif.: Glencoe Press, 1970.

Better Red Than Dead

PETER COLLIER

The history of Native Americans is one of the ugliest chapters of our American heritage. Peter Collier shows how even the efforts of our government to help Native Americans have turned into programs of stifling paternalism. The Bureau of Indian Affairs (BIA) has been a prominent force in the "well-meaning" destruction of Native American culture.

On this island, I saw not whether the people had personal property, for it seemed to me that whatever one had, they all took share of, especially of eatable things.

—CHRISTOPER COLUMBUS

I also heard of numerous instances in which our men had cut out the private parts of females and wore them in their hats while riding in the ranks.

—A U.S. ARMY LIEUTENANT, TESTIFYING ABOUT THE SAND CREEK MASSACRE OF 1864

Each generation of Americans rediscovers for itself what is fashionably called the "plight" of the Indian. The American Indian today has a life expectancy of approximately 44 years, more than 25 years below the national average. He has the highest infant mortality rate in the country (among the more than 50,000 Alaskan natives, one of every four babies dies before reaching his first birthday). He suffers from epidemics of diseases which were supposed to have disappeared from America long ago.

A recent Department of Public Health report states that among California Indians, "water from contaminated sources is used in 38 to 42 per cent of the homes, and water must be hauled under unsanitary conditions by 40 to 50 per cent of all Indian families." Conditions are similar in other states. A high proportion of reservation housing throughout the country is officially classified as "substandard," an antiseptic term which fails to conjure up a tiny, two-room log cabin holding a family of 13 at Fort Hall; a crumbling Navajo hogan surrounded by broken plumbing fixtures hauled in to serve as woodbins; or a gutted automobile body in which a Pine Ridge Sioux family huddles against the South Dakota winter.

On most reservations, a 50 per cent unemployment rate is not considered high. Income per family among Indian people is just over $1500 per year—the lowest of any group in the country. But this, like the other figures, is deceptive. It does not suggest, for instance, the quality of the daily life of families on the Navajo reservation who live on $600 per year (exchanging sheep's wool and hand-woven rugs with white traders for beans and flour), who never have real money and who are perpetually sinking a little further into credit debt.

To most Americans, the conditions under which the Indian is forced to live are a perennial revelation. On one level, the symptoms are always being tinkered with half-heartedly and the causes ignored; on another level, the whole thrust of the Government's Indian policy appears calculated to perpetuate the Indians' "plight." This is why La Nada Means and the other Indians have joined what Janet McCloud, a leader of the Washington fishing protests, calls "the last, continuing Indian War." The enemies are legion, and they press in from every side: the studiously ignorant politicians, the continuously negligent Department of the Interior, and the white business interests who are allowed to prey upon the reservations' manpower and resources. But as the Indian has struggled to free himself from the suffocating embrace of white history, no enemy has held the death grip more tightly than has his supposed guardian, in effect his "keeper": the Bureau of Indian Affairs.

The Bureau came into being in 1834 as a division of the War Department. Fifteen years later it was shifted to the Department of the Interior, the transition symbolizing the fact that the Indian was beginning to be seen not as a member of a sovereign, independent nation, but as a "ward," his land and life requiring constant management. This is the view that has informed the BIA for over a century. With its 16,000 employees and its outposts all over the country, the Bureau has become what Cherokee anthropologist Robert Thomas calls "the most complete colonial system in the world."

It is also a classic bureaucratic miasma. A recent book on Indian Affairs, *Our Brother's Keeper,* notes that on the large Pine Ridge reservation, "$8040 a year is spent per family to help the Oglala Sioux Indians out of poverty. Yet median income among these Indians is $1910 per family. At last count there was nearly one bureaucrat for each and every family on the reservation."

The paternalism of the BIA, endless and debilitating, is calculated to keep the Indian in a state of perpetual juvenilization, without rights, dependent upon the meagre and capricious beneficence of power. The Bureau's power over its "wards," whom it defines and treats as children, seems limitless. The BIA takes care of the Indian's money, doling it out to him when it considers his requests worthy; it determines the use of the Indian's land; it is in charge of the development of his natural resources; it relocates him from the reservation to the big city ghetto; it educates his children. It relinquishes its hold over him only reluctantly, even deciding whether or not his will is valid after he dies.

This bureaucratic paternalism hems the Indian in with an incomprehensible maze of procedures and regulations, never allowing him to know quite where he stands or what he can demand and how. Over 5000 laws, statutes and court decisions apply to the Indians alone. As one Indian student says, "Our people have to go to law school just to live a daily life."

The BIA is the Indian's point of contact with the white world, the concrete expression of this society's attitude towards him. The BIA manifests both stupidity and malice; but it is purely neither. It is guided by something more elusive, a whole world view regarding the Indian and what is good for him. Thus the BIA's overseership of human devastation begins by teaching bright-eyed youngsters the first formative lessons in what it is to be an Indian.

"It is unnecessary to mention the power which schools would have over the rising generation of Indians. Next to teaching them to work, the most important thing is to teach them the English language. Into their own language there is woven so much mythology and sorcery that a new one is needed in order to aid them in advancing beyond their baneful superstitions."

—John Wesley Powell

The Darwinian Educational System which La Nada Means endured is not a thing of the past. Last spring, for instance, the BIA's own Educational Division studied Chilocco and came to the following conclusions: "There is evidence of criminal malpractice, not to mention physical and mental perversion, by certain staff members." The report went on to outline the disastrous conditions at the school, noting among other things that "youngsters reported they were handcuffed for as long as 18 hours in the dormitory . . . or chained to a basement pillar or from a suspended pipe. One team member . . . verified a youngster's hurt arms, the deformed hands of another boy, and an obviously broken rib of another. . . ."

The BIA responded to this report by suppressing it and transferring the investigators who submitted it. The principal of Chilocco was fired, but more as punishment for letting such things be discovered than for the conditions themselves. The same story is repeated at other BIA boarding schools. At the Intermountain Indian School in Utah, Indian children suspected of drinking have their heads ducked into filthy toilets by school disciplinarians. At Sherman Institute in Riverside, California, students of high school age are fed on a budget of 76 cents a day.

But there is a far more damaging and subtle kind of violence at work in the school as well. It is, in the jargon of educational psychology, the initiation of a "failure-orientation," and it derives from the fact that the children and their culture are held in such obviously low regard. Twenty-five per cent of all BIA teachers admit that they would rather be teaching whites; up to 70 per cent leave the BIA schools after one year. If a teacher has any knowledge at all of his student's needs and backgrounds, he gets it from a two-week non-compulsory course offered at the beginning of the year. One teacher, a former Peace Corps volunteer who returned to teach at the Navajo reservation, told the Senate Subcommittee on Indian Education that the principal of her BIA school habitually made statements such as "All Navajos are brain-damaged," and "Navajo culture belongs in a museum."

The results of the Indian's education, whether it be supervised by the BIA or by the public school system, indicates how greatly the system fails him. Twenty per cent of all Indian men have less than five years of schooling. According to a recent report to the Carnegie Foundation, there is a 60 per cent drop-out rate among Indian children as a whole, and those who do manage to stay in school fall further behind the longer they attend. A study of the Stewart Institute in Carson City, Nevada, for instance, shows that Indian sixth graders score 5.2 on the California Achievement Test. Six years later, at graduation, their achievement level is 8.4.

In a strange sense, the Indian student's education does prepare him for what lies ahead. What it teaches him is that he is powerless and inferior, and that he was destined to be so when he was born an Indian. Having spent his youth being managed and manhandled, the Indian is accustomed to the notion that his business must be taken care of for him. He is thus ideally equipped to stand by and watch the BIA collect mortgages on his future.

"We should test our thinking against the thinking of the wisest Indians and their friends, [but] this does not mean that we are going to let, as someone put it, Indian people themselves decide what the policy should be."

—Stuart Udall

The Indians of California have more than their share of troubles—in part because they never received an adequate land base by government treaty. They are scattered up and down the state on reservations which are rarely larger than 10,000 acres and on rancherias as small as one acre. It takes a special determination to find these Indian, for most of them live in backwoods shacks, hidden from view as well as from water and electricity.

They have to struggle for every bit of federal service they get; disservice, however, comes easy. In 1969 the only irrigation money the BIA spent in all of Southern California, where water is an especially precious commodity to the Indians, was not for an Indian at all, but for a white farmer who had bought an Indian's land on the Pala reservation. The BIA spent $2500—of money appropriated by Congress for the Indians—to run a 900-foot pipeline to this white man's land. The Indians at Pala have been asking for irrigation lines for years, but less than one-half of their lands have them.

At the Resighini rancheria, a 228-acre reservation in Northern California, the Simpson Timber Company had been paying the Indians 25 cents per 1000 feet for the lumber it transported across their land. The total paid to the Indians in 1964 was $4725, and the right of way was increasing in value every year. Then the BIA, acting without warning, sold the right of way outright to Simpson Timber Company for $2500, or something less than one-half its yearly value.

The tiny Agua Caliente band of Indians sits on top of some of the most valuable land in the country: over 600 acres in the heart of Palm Springs. In the late '50s, the BIA, reacting to pressure from developers, obligingly transferred its jurisdiction over the Agua Caliente to a judge of the State Superior Court in the Palm Springs area who appointed "conservators" and "guardians" to make sure that the Indians would not be swindled as development took place. Ten years later, in 1967, a Riverside Press Enterprise reporter wrote a devastating series of articles showing the incredible fees collected for "protecting" the Agua Calientes. One conservator collected a fee of $9000 from his Indian's $9170 bank account; an Indian minor wound up with $3000 out of a $23,000 income, his guardian taking the rest. The "abdication of responsibility" with which the BIA was charged is surely a mild description of what happened to the Agua Calientes, who are supposedly the "richest Indians in the world" living on what is regarded as "an ermine-lined reservation."

The Indian Claims Commission was set up in the 1940's to compensate tribes for the lands stolen during the period of white conquest. In the California claims award of 1964, the Indians were given 47 cents an acre, based on the land's fair market value in 1851. The total sum, $29 million, less "offsets" for the BIA's services over the years, still has not been distributed. When it is, the per capita payout will come to about $600, and the poorest Indians in the state, will have to go off welfare to spend it. The BIA opposed an amendment to the Claims Award which would have exempted this money in determining welfare eligibility. The BIA testified that such an amendment constituted preferential treatment, and that it had been struggling for years to get *equal* treatment for the Indian. The amendment failed, and California's Indians will have to pay for a few months bread and rent with the money they are getting in return for the land that was taken from them.

Cases such as these exist in every state where Indian people live. If the Indian is the Vanishing American, it is the BIA's magic which makes him so. California Indians are fortunate only in one respect: they have an OEO-funded legal rights organization, the California Indian Legal Services, which attempts to minimize the depredations. Most Indians have no one to protect them from the agency which is supposed to be their advocate.

"Once we were happy in our own country and we were seldom hungry, for then the two-leggeds and the four-leggeds lived together like relatives, and there was plenty for them and for us. But the Wasichus [white men] came, and they have made little islands for us . . . and always these islands are becoming smaller, for around them surges the gnawing flood of the Wasichu; and it is dirty with lies and greed. . . ."

—BLACK ELK, AN OGLALA HOLY MAN

At the entrance to the Fort Hall reservation, where La Nada Means grew up, there is a plaque which commemorates the appearance in 1834 of the first white traders and indicates that the Hudson Bay Company later acquired the Fort and made it into an important stopover on the Oregon Trail. But other aspects of the history of Fort Hall are left unmentioned. It is not noted, for instance, that by the time a formal treaty was signed with the Bannock and Northern Shoshone in 1868, the whites who settled this part of Southern Idaho were paying between $25 and $100 for a good Indian scalp.

Today, the approximately 2800 Shoshone-Bannocks live on the 520,000-acre reservation, all that remains of the 1.8 million acres of their land which the treaty originally set aside for their ancestors to keep. The largest single reduction came in 1900, when the government took over 416,000 acres, paying the Indians a little more than $1 an acre for the land. As late as the beginning of World War II, the government took over another 3000 acres to make an airfield. It paid the Indians $10 an acre; after the war, it deeded the land to the city of Pocatello for $1 an acre, for use as a municipal airport. Each acre is now worth $500.

But the big problem on the Fort Hall reservation today is not the loss of large sections of land; rather it is the slow and steady attrition of Indian holdings and their absolute powerlessness to do anything about it. In 1887, the Dawes Allotment Act was passed as a major piece of "progressive" Indian legislation, providing for the break-up of community held reservation land so that each individual Indian would receive his plot of irrigable farming land and some grazing land. The federal government would still hold the land in trust, so it could be sold only with BIA approval, the assumption being that an individual holding would give the Indian incentive to be a farmer and thus ease him into American agricultural patterns. Fort Hall shows that the law had quite different effects.

Today, some of these original allotments are owned by anywhere from two to 40 heirs. Because of the complexity of kinship relationships, some Indian people own fractional interests in several of these "heirship lands" but have no ground that is all their own. These lands are one of the symbols of the ambiguity and inertia that rule at Fort Hall. As Edward Boyer, a former chairman of the tribal council, says, "Some of the people, they might want to exchange interests in the land or buy some of the other heirs out so they can have a piece of ground to build a house on and do some farming. Also, a lot of us would like the tribe to buy these lands up and then assign them to the young people who don't have any place of their own. But the BIA has this policy of leasing out these lands to the white farmers. A lot of the time the owners don't even know about it."

The BIA at Fort Hall doesn't like the idea of any Indian lands lying idle. And the land is rich, some of the best potato-growing land there is. Its value and its yields are increasing every year. Driving through the reservation, you can't avoid being struck by the green symmetry of the long cultivated rows and by the efficiency of the army of men and machinery working them. The only trouble is that the men are white, and the profits from Fort Hall's rich land all flow out of the Indian community. The BIA is like any technocracy: it is more interested in "efficient" use than in proper use. The most "efficient" way for Fort Hall's lands to be used is by white industrialist-farmers with capital. Thus the pattern has been established: white lessees using Indian land, irrigating with Indian water, and then harvesting with bracero workers.

All leases must be approved by the BIA Superintendent's office; they may be and are given without the consent of the Indians who own the land. The BIA has also allowed white lessees to seek "consents" from the Indians, which in effect provide for blank leases, the specific terms to be filled in later on. The BIA authorizes extremely long leases of the land. This leads to what a recent field study of Fort Hall, conducted by the Senate Subcommittee on Indian Education, calls "small fortunes" for white developers: "One non-Indian in 1964 leased a large tract of Indian land for 13 years at \$.30–\$.50/acre/year. While the lease did stipulate that once the lessee installed sprinkler irrigation the annual rent would rise to \$1.50–\$.200/acre, Indians in 1968 could have demanded \$20–\$30 for such land. Meanwhile, the independent University Agriculture Extension Service estimates that such potato operations bring the non-Indian lessee an annual *net* profit of \$200 per acre." In addition, these leases are usually given by the BIA on a non-competitive, non-bidding basis to assure "the good will of the surrounding community." Fort Hall has rich and loamy land, but Indian people now work less than 17 per cent of it themselves and the figure is declining.

The power of white farmer-developers and businessmen within the local Bureau of Indian Affairs office is a sore point with most people at Fort Hall.

They have rich lands, but theirs is one of the poorest reservations. They are told that much revenue comes both to the tribe and to individuals as a result of the BIA farm and mine leasing program, yet they know that if all the revenues were divided up the yield would be about $300 per capita a year. But for some of them, men like Joseph "Frank" Thorpe, Jr., the question of farming and mining leases is academic. Thorpe was a successful cattleman until BIA policies cut down the herds; now he is in the business of letting other people's cattle graze on his land.

Livestock are something of a fixation with Thorpe. He comes from a people who were proud horsemen, and he owns an Apaloosa mare and a couple of other horses. As he drives over the reservation, he often stops to look at others' cattle. In the basement of his home are several scrapbooks filled with documents tracing the destruction of the cattle business at Fort Hall. There is a yellowing clipping from the Salt Lake City Tribune of November 4, 1950, which says: "Fort Hall Indians have been more successful in cattle raising than any other activity. Theirs is the oldest Indian Cattleman's Association in the country. Association members raise more than 10,000 head of purebred herefords, and plan gradually to increase the herd. . . ." That was how it was 20 years ago. Thorpe, just back from war-time duty with the Marines, worked his herd and provided jobs for many of his kinsmen; the future was promising. Yet by 1958, there were only 3000 head of Indian owned cattle left, and today there are only ten families still involved in full-time cattle operation.

"Around the early '50s," Thorpe says, "the BIA decided that the Indians who'd been using tribal grazing lands without paying a grazing fee were going to be charged. The BIA also made us cattle people set up a sinking fund to pay grazing fees in advance. The bills just got higher and higher, and pretty soon we found we had to start selling off our seed stock to pay them."

Less than 30 per cent of all Fort Hall Indians are permanently employed today. Men like Frank Thorpe once had a going business that harked back to the old times and also provided jobs on the reservation. The BIA had decided that the best use for Fort Hall land was farming; it removed the Indians' cattle from trust status, which meant they could be sold, and began the accelerated program of leasing Indian lands to whites that is still in effect today.

Thorpe spends a good deal of time driving his dust-covered station wagon along the reservation's unpaved roads. A former tribal chairman, he spends much time checking up on the BIA and trying to function as a sort of ombudsman. He drives slowly down the dirt highways where magpies pick at the remains of rabbits slaughtered by cars. He points out where white farmers have begun to crop-dust their leased fields from airplanes. "The game, rabbits and pheasants and all, is disappearing," he says. "Our Indian people here rely on them for food, but the animals are dying out because of the sprays. And sometimes our kids get real sick. These sprays, they drift over and get in the swimming holes. The kids get real bad coughs and sometimes rashes all over their bodies."

Near the BIA agency office on the reservation sits a squat, weathered concrete building. "That's the old blouse factory," he says. "The BIA cooked up this deal where some outfit from Salt Lake City came in here to start a garment plant. The tribe put up the money for the factory, about $30,000, and in return the Salt Lake people were going to hire Indians and train them to sew. It lasted for about a year, and now we've still got the building. The last few years, they've used it to store the government surplus food that a lot of Indians get."

The old blouse factory is one symbol of the despair that has seized Fort Hall. Thorpe points out another one nearby. It is known as a "holding center," and it is a place for Fort Hall Indians who are suspected of being suicidal. The reservation has one of the highest suicide rates in the nation. Last year there were 35 attempts, mostly among the 18–25 age group. Many of them occurred in the nearby Blackfoot City Jail.

Blackfoot town authorities, embarrassed by the number of Indian suicides which have occurred in their jail, now use the holding facility at Fort Hall. It is headed by John Bopp, a former Navy man who is the public health officer on the reservation. "I guess kids here just feel that their future is cut off," he says. "A lot of them are dropouts and rejects from schools. They look around and see their elders pretty downtrodden. They get angry, but the only thing they can do is take it out on themselves. From reading some of their suicide notes, I'd say that they see it as an honorable way out of a bad situation."

"The young people," says Thorpe, "they're our only hope. They've got to clean things up here. But a lot of our young guys, they've just given up." The human resources at Fort Hall, like the land, seem to be slipping away. The best interpretation that could be placed on the BIA's role in it all is to use the words of a teacher at nearby Idaho State College who says that they are "guardians of the poorhouse."

Strangled in bureaucracy, swindled out of lands, forcibly alienated from his own culture, the Indian continues to be victimized by the white man's symbolism: he has been both loved and hated to death. On the one hand, the white looked out at him from his own constricted universe of acquisition and grasping egocentrism and saw a Noble Savage, an innocent at peace with his world. Here was a relic of a better time, to be protected and preserved. But on the other hand the white saw an uncivilized creature possessing, but not exploiting, great riches; the vision was conjured up of the Murdering Redskin whose bestiality provided the justification for wiping him out and taking his land. The Indian's "plight" has always inspired recurrent orgies of remorse, but never has it forced us to digest the implications of a nation and culture conceived in genocide. We act as if the blood-debt of the past cannot be canceled until the Indian has no future; the guiltier he has made us, the more frantic have been the attempts to make him disappear.

Yet, having paid out almost everything he has, the Indian has survived the long exercise in white schizophrenia. And there are some, like Hopi mystic Thomas Banyaka, who give out prophecies that the red man will still be here long after whites have been destroyed in a holocaust of their own making.

The Smart White Man's Burden

NORMAN DANIELS

The controversy over IQ is still raging. This article is an effective rebuttal of the hereditarian position. It attacks the basic premises of IQ tests and the biased nature of the twin studies upon which hereditarians base their arguments.

The ancient controversy about nature v. nurture may seem like a dusty academic parlor game. It is nothing of the sort. When an obscure professor of education at Berkeley, named Arthur Jensen, published a study in 1969* that seemed to prove that up to 80 percent of our intelligence is determined by the genes we inherit and then related his findings to black children's poor performance in school, various influential magazines and newspapers were quick to sense a revolution in the way Americans should think about race, education, poverty, and crime.

For forty years, said *Fortune* magazine, "the established dogma in the social sciences has been that all people are born alike and it is environment that makes them behave differently." This environmentalist dogma underlay most of the reform programs of the Sixties. But, said *Fortune*, the elimination of environmental disadvantages through compensatory education and the war on poverty has clearly not done away with differences between blacks and whites in school success, employment rates, or income. Thus, environmentalism failed because it called for the impossible: the elimination of human differences that are rooted in genetic inheritance. There is, said *Fortune* somewhat triumphantly, a "basic intractability in human nature, a resistance to being guided and molded for improving society." *Fortune*'s

* Jensen's paper in the *Harvard Educational Review* is reprinted with supplementary papers in *Genetics and Education* (Harper & Row, 1972). He develops his thesis on race differences in *Educability and Group Differences* (Harper & Row, 1973).

sister, *Time,* argued similarly in a series called "Second Thoughts About Man," then wondered whether these second thoughts wouldn't lead to a "new quietism, a readiness to accept things as they are rather than to work for things as they might be."

The Atlantic, a magazine that usually takes its intellectual responsibilities seriously, set out to bring this revolutionary perspective to its readers by publishing Harvard Prof. Richard Herrnstein's skillful popularization of Jensen's argument.* Herrnstein argued that our "meritocratic" society selects people for "success in life"—school performance, income, job status—on the basis of largely inherited differences in intelligence that Jensen had apparently demonstrated.

The Jensen-Herrnstein "vanguard" position** rests squarely on the concept of IQ. It draws its evidence from certain "life experiments," notably studies of twins and adopted children, which supposedly measure the precise contribution of genes or environment to our IQ and in turn our "success in life." Their "IQ Argument," sometimes labelled "jensenism," can be stated in four steps:

1. IQ measures a general trait, intelligence.
2. IQ is highly heritable; about 80 percent of observed IQ differences between individuals are genetic in origin.
3. Genetic factors (up to 80 percent of the whole) are implicated in average black-white and social class intelligence differences.
4. Differences in success in life strongly correlate with and are caused by differences in intelligence.

The implications of this argument for social policy strike many people as obvious and far-reaching. Jensen and Herrnstein, for example, both seem to favor more rigorous educational tracking systems adapted to inherited differences. "The false belief in human equality," writes Herrnstein, "leads to rigid, inflexible expectations, often doomed to frustration, thence to anger . . . . we should be trying to mold our institutions around the inescapable limitations and varieties of human ability." He complains of "withholding educational advantages from gifted people." Jensen has appeared before various Congressional committees to deliver his message that money spent on compensatory education programs is "lavish" and "extravagant"and one Congressman has inserted the whole of his 1969 study into the *Congressional Record.* In 1970 *Life* quoted Daniel Moynihan, then a White House adviser, as saying that "the winds of Jensen were gusting through the capital at gale force." The 1973–74 Nixon budget proposes to demolish what is left of compensatory education programs and other programs aimed at creating

* Herrnstein's *Atlantic* article, "IQ" (September 1971), is the basis for his recent book, *IQ in the Meritocracy* (Atlantic-Little, Brown, 1973).

** As self-styled "revolutionaries" challenging an "egalitarian orthodoxy," the two professors signed an advertisement in *American Psychologist* comparing their unfriendly reception by academics and students to the attempts to suppress Galileo, Darwin, Einstein, and Mendel.

educational equality. More chilling is the call by some jensenites for the exercise of "eugenic foresight" or that of the physicist William Shockley for voluntary sterilization programs for people with lower than normal IQs. Only this past May, Jensen himself carried the logic of his theories to a point just shy of a call for eugenic foresight. Comparing the low birthrate of affluent (therefore successful, therefore intelligent) whites with the high rate of poor (therefore unsuccessful, therefore unintelligent) blacks, Jensen concluded that "dysgenics [an undesirable change in the gene pool] with respect to the intelligence of our population is not just a possibility. It is *highly probable*" (his emphasis). Herrnstein, in a recent *Science* article, demurs only that "voluntary sterilization is not a politically feasible solution."

Perhaps the most damaging effects of the IQ argument, however, will be on the expectations of teachers, college administrators, employers, and social workers who come to think of blacks and working class people as genetically less intelligent. Nobel Laureate Shockley, who has Jensen's scholarly blessings, seems to encourage this attitude: "Nature has color-coded groups of individuals so that statistically reliable predictions of their adaptability to intellectually rewarding and effective lives can easily be made and profitably be used by the pragmatic man in the street."

It is absolutely crucial to Jensen's and Herrnstein's arguments that a person's score on an IQ test does in fact indicate his intelligence. But what is intelligence? Unfortunately, there is no generally accepted theory on the matter, an embarrassing point that our authors try to get around by asserting simply that intelligence *is* what IQ tests measure.

There are two things to be said about this stance. First, it's no way out. Scientists usually know what they are measuring and what their measuring instruments do. Second, having IQ tests doesn't obviate the need for a theory of intelligence. It assumes one. IQ tests give us, says Herrnstein, a "single number measuring a person's intellectual power." In this view, intelligence is a single, measurable, super-capacity underlying other skills; it is stable, "conferred" in the first fifteen years of life, and it sets a limit on what a person can learn or do. Are these assumptions warranted? I think not.

The fact that "intelligence" is a noun shouldn't delude us into believing that it names some single attribute we can attach a number to, like "height." In life, we face a variety of tasks and environments. Intelligence takes many forms: a machinist suggests a new production technique, a housewife manages in spite of inflation, a hustler helps build a huge conglomerate. Similarly, how intelligent a person's behavior is will vary with time. Why should we suppose that these changes are fluctuations from some fixed, basic level? Most important, what a person of almost any IQ can learn or do depends on what he wants to do and on what kind of education and training he is given. Jensen says high IQ is needed for high "educability," which he defines as "the ability to learn the traditional scholastic subjects under conditions of ordinary classroom instruction" . . . and thereby innocently opens a can of worms. *What* conditions of "ordinary classroom instruction"? Are social class or race biases in our schools included in these "conditions?"

Moreover, what reasons do we have to suppose that IQ tests measure "intellectual power," an underlying capacity, rather than just achievement? The test items themselves seem to tap specific bits of knowledge—as in the vocabulary test—or the acquisition of specific skills and values. On the Stanford-Binet picture test, for example, a child is marked "right" if he picks out as "pretty" a white, prim-looking woman, and he is marked "wrong" if he picks a woman with Negroid features and slightly unkempt hair.

Jensen and Herrnstein give two reasons. First, they claim that the more intelligent the child, the quicker he assimilates what's in his environment regardless of the values that might be in the test items. In other words, they take precocity as a measure of capacity. But this makes sense only if the children come out of virtually identical environments; otherwise, "precocity" will reflect only different training and exposure. And even if environments were identical—which we know they are not—we would still have the untested assumption that precocity in performance is a measure of capacity and not, say, motivation.

Jensen and Herrnstein's second reason for thinking IQ tests measure capacity is that IQ correlates moderately well with success in school and later job status, and these are assumed to be well correlated with intelligence. Unhappily, this argument doesn't help much either. There is little reason to assume that success in school or on the job is much related to intelligence. Other things, like class background, correlate even better with such achievement than IQ does. Anyway, even if IQ and intelligence were each fairly well correlated with school success, this doesn't by itself mean they are correlated well or at all with each other. Finally, of course, "correlation" does not mean "causation," as Herrnstein occasionally suggests.

Given the questionable assumptions behind IQ tests, it would be an incredible coincidence if IQ tests did indeed measure some common quality of intelligence. But I don't think it is any accident that IQ tests have been constructed with assumptions that are so politically useful. From the start, the developers and promoters of this test technique were all convinced of hereditary, race, and class differences in intelligence. Tests that failed to confirm those assumptions were treated as failing to measure intelligence. Thus, when Sir Francis Galton devised tests that failed to show intelligence was correlated with "preeminence" in society, he threw out his tests, not his thesis that "the average intellectual standard of the Negro is some two grades below our own."

It is no wonder that various American psychologists (Terman, Thorndike, Otis, Goddard, Yerkes) who believed in race and class intelligence differences were so happy when Binet, a Frenchman, developed a handy instrument. Terman, who in 1916 developed the American version of Binet's test, already believed that low intelligence "is very, very common among Spanish,

Indian and Mexican families of the Southwest, and also many Negroes. Their dullness seems to be racial, or at least inherent in the family stocks from which they come." He suggested, "Children of this group should be segregated in special classes . . . there is no possibility at present of convincing society that they should not be allowed to reproduce." He argued for a major testing program: "When this is done there will be discovered enormously significant racial differences which cannot be wiped out by any scheme of mental culture." Terman's elitism was echoed by Goddard. Based on early IQ tests used on Ellis Island, Goddard reported that over 80 percent of all immigrants were "feeble-minded." IQ tests were used to justify deportations and eventually immigration quotas.

If IQ does not measure intelligence, then Step (2) of the IQ argument, the claim that about 80 percent of IQ differences between individuals are genetically based, loses much of its significance. But let's look anyway at the experimental evidence for the high "heritability" estimate since it appears to be the strongest step in the IQ argument.*

If scientists could raise genetically unrelated people in identical, laboratory controlled environments, like rats, then they could estimate "heritability" directly: all variations in IQ would be due to genes. But people are not rats, and we cannot really determine when two environments are identical. To settle the "nature v. nurture" controversy, therefore, scientists are forced to turn to "life experiments" in place of lab experiments; in particular, to cases of genetically identical people (one-egg twins) raised separately. For, logically, any difference in the IQs of identical twins must be due to environment. If the difference is small, then the contribution of environment is small and that of genes high.

There have been four major studies of separated twins, and their results appear to give Jensen and Herrnstein considerable support. The IQs of the twins show far less variation than IQs in the population as a whole, indicating a small environmental contribution. In Sir Cyril Burt's study of fifty-three twin pairs, for example, IQs of twins raised separately showed rather high (.771) correlations, supporting Jensen's calculation of about 80 percent heritability. Jensen combines the data from all four studies since they agree in their basic results, and claim to use standard tests and procedures; furthermore, they have been reviewed by others with no serious challenge. Finally, Jensen supplements the evidence for high heritability from the twin studies

* The high heritability estimate appears likely only if we ignore opposing evidence based on IQ boosting studies. Programs that "improve" the child's environment by subjecting the children to intensive tutoring, or by coaching mothers on how to play with and read to their children, produced dramatic 15- to 30-point IQ gains which seem to be long-lasting. It is hard to see how coaching a mother an hour or so a week even scratches the surface of the differences between lower- and upper-class living and child-rearing conditions. In my own view, since low IQ is no sign of "stunted intelligence," I think programs geared to boosting IQ, rather than teaching children something useful, are a waste of time. But by claiming that "environmentalism" is in a crisis, in spite of all this pro-environmentalist evidence, Jensen and Herrnstein seem to be attempting an unwarranted shift in the burden of proof.

with evidence from other "life experiments." For example, adopted children's IQs seem to correlate better with their natural mothers' IQs than with their adopting mothers'. And kinship studies comparing closeness of genetic relation to similarity in IQ are compatible with a high estimate of heritability. The data, as scientists would say, look pretty "hard."

That's what Professor Leon Kamin, chairman of the Princeton Experimental Psychology Department, may have thought before he began to scratch a little at this evidence. His study gives strong reason to think the data may not be so hard after all.

First, Kamin argues, it is important to see how well designed the existing "life experiments" are. If the life experiments on twins are to give an accurate estimate of the environmental contribution to IQ, it is essential that the separated twins be randomly placed in the full range of environments that a society offers. Otherwise, there will be less IQ variation than there should be and it will look as though genes contribute more than they do. Did the four studies Jensen and Herrnstein rely on really provide the full range of environments needed? It appears not.*

For one thing, the twins in all four studies either went to adoptive homes or else one member of a pair was raised at home. Adoptive families, however, are generally well above average for their communities in economic security, cultural and educational status; they are smaller than average, and have older than average parents. Besides, adoption agencies match children's characteristics (or those of the natural parents) to characteristics of the adopting family, for religion, sex, age, color and complexion, physique, medical history and family background.

But there are even more specific problems with the studies. In over half of Burt's cases, one of the twins stayed in the natural parent's home. In general, these twins shared similar geographical regions, similar social and religious customs; they often played together and shared the same school system. Shields, the author of another study, claims his twins had different environments, but his report documents extensive similarities. For example, Benjamin and Ronald were "brought up in the same fruit-growing village, Ben by the parents, Ron by the grandmother . . . [and were] . . . in school together." Jessie and Winifred were "brought up within a hundred yards of each other . . . wanted to sit at the same desk." Bertram and Christopher were raised by paternal aunts "amicably living next door to one another."

Burt's is the only one of the four studies that even attempts to show that the twins went into homes of differing socio-economic status. But, ac-

* Kamin delivered a paper analyzing the existing data at a recent meeting of the Eastern Psychology Association, making most of the points I cite above. It is rather sad that Herrnstein, who has constantly complained of alleged infringements on his "academic freedom" and who charges his critics with failing to consider his arguments, has resorted in a recent issue of *Science* to charging Kamin with being "blinded" by Marxism (for which there seems to be no evidence). Presumably, Herrnstein had better be prepared to charge the whole membership of the Eastern Psychology Association since they voted by a two-to-one margin "to censure the use of inconclusive evidence concerning the heritability of IQ."

cording to Kamin, the data in the paper where he makes this claim do not exactly match data on the same twins published by his assistant and, in several places, fail to match data that Burt sent to Jensen. Nevertheless, in spite of these devastating problems, and in spite of the coincidental fact that Burt's original data sheets have been conveniently destroyed, Jensen sticks to his guns.

Kamin has probed another key feature of experimental design in the twin studies. To carry out an estimate fairly, it is necessary that the IQ tests be standardized with regard to sex and age. After all, one-egg twins are the same age and sex as well as being look-alikes, and it wouldn't be very scientific if the twins' IQs were made to look more similar simply because they had the same age and sex. Yet the IQ tests used for Jensen's estimate were not standardized for age and sex. Kamin has shown that the high correlations of twins' IQs in one of the studies can be accounted for almost entirely by the failure to standardize the tests for age alone.

Anyone who has taken a psychology course knows that one must always try to compensate for or weed out the bias of the person doing an experiment. One needs uniform tests and testing procedures. One should make sure, for example, that each member of a twin pair was tested by a different person. Knowing the results of one twin's IQ test might lead to biasing, even unconscious biasing, of the result on the other twin. Unfortunately for Jensen, experimenter bias is evident in the twin studies. In all but five of thirty-eight cases, Shields tested both members of a twin pair himself and found an average difference of 4.9 points, a small difference pointing to a large genetic contribution. In the five other cases, he tested onc twin and his assistant the other. Here they found a 13.2-point average difference, about normal for the population as a whole and compatible with a nearly zero estimate of heritability. Shields ignores this discrepancy. Burt also apparently tested almost all the twins in his study himself so we have no way of knowing how much he may have "unconsciously" biased the results. This factor alone should lead us to throw out more than two-thirds of the data for the four combined studies.

In addition, there is some evidence that selective exclusion of data in the Shields study, as well as in Burt's procedure of "adjusted assessments" if scores seemed too far off, operated to increase similarities in twins' IQs. In fact, Burt didn't even administer standard tests in all cases. He admits in a footnote to giving "personal interviews" and "camouflaged IQ tests" and then later refers to them as "tests of the usual type."

Finally, there is an even more serious problem with the data. Burt, who may not even have used standard test procedures, nevertheless managed to find correlations that remain identical to the third decimal place in spite of sample size changes of over 100 percent—just about a mathematical impossibility. For instance, Burt's papers report the same .771 correlation for twins reared separately in three studies, one involving twenty-one twin pairs (1955), one involving "over thirty" pairs (1958), and finally fifty-three pairs

(1966). Even a college chemistry student knows better than to report data like that in his lab reports—they'd be thrown out as "fudged." It might be noted that Burt, in 1909, before any IQ data were available, remarked that his smarter subjects tended to be "blond."

The "hard data" for Jensen's estimates has turned to mush. With regard to every crucial feature of experimental design, to say nothing of experimenter integrity, the famous twin studies fall apart. Yet these "life experiments" are the cornerstone of Jensen's estimate of heritability.

The third step in the IQ argument asserts that the high 80-percent heritability of IQ for individuals can be used to explain the 15-point difference in the mean IQ of blacks and whites or the 30-point difference between the mean IQ of lower and upper classes. To go from individual to group differences is a big, in fact fatal, leap, since "heritability" is *defined* only for individual differences, and in *Genetics* Jensen himself warns against it. But later he leaped with abandon, as when he commented in the *New York Times*, "The number of intelligence genes seems lower overall in the black population than in the white."

In *Educability* (pages 155–156), Jensen again attempts the leap from individuals to groups, this time by bamboozling the reader with a mathematical argument. Basically, using mathematical equations, he says that if heritability is high (80 percent) and if IQ is well-correlated (.5) with success, then mathematics tells us genes must play some role in determining success. However, he neglects to tell the reader that the "some role" genes "must" play could be completely insignificant; it has to be only slightly more than zero. And he fails to warn the reader that his argument depends crucially on heritability being as high as he says it is. This argument hardly fools the reader familiar with mathematics and is completely unfair to the non-mathematical reader.

While making the same jensenian jump from individuals to groups (social classes), Herrnstein tries to back away from the delicate issue of black-white differences. "We do not know why blacks bunch toward the lower end of the social scale," he writes on page 14. Again on page 186, "The only proper conclusion is that we do not know whether . . . [racial differences in IQ are] . . . more genetic, less genetic, or precisely as genetic as might seem to be implied by a heritability of .8." But if "bunching" blacks into the poorest section of the working class is a mechanism that can "environmentally" lower black IQs, then why doesn't "bunching" most working-class people into working-class living conditions "environmentally" lower *their* IQs? Herrnstein cannot admit that working-class living conditions can significantly lower IQs; that would undermine his entire thesis that class differences in IQ are highly heritable. His only way out of the dilemma is to say that working-class environments depress black IQs but not white IQs, a difficult argument to defend.*

* Herrnstein could still say that things like "racist insults" are what depress black IQs. But does he think poor whites suffer no insults or discrimination?

The last step of the IQ argument, the "meritocracy" thesis, claims that success in life is in large part determined by high IQ. Jensen uses this step to explain why blacks, with their lower average IQs, have low "educability" and therefore are found disproportionately in the lower end of the working class. Does "low IQ," however, explain racist wage differentials or "last hired, first fired" policies exercised by many companies? In 1967, thousands of jobs were given to blacks in the auto industry following the Detroit riots. Was this higher level of "success" a result of boosted IQ? Jensen, it seems, would have us forget all we know about economic, political, and social forces and believe instead that all along some Invisible Hand has been selecting people for subtle, inherited differences in IQ, differences that in time impose education, unemployment, and welfare burdens on society. (page 16)*

But if Jensen, who thinks the white population averages out genetically superior to the black population, is still in the grip of the White Man's Burden, then Herrnstein, whose social concern for the implications of IQ in the meritocracy is seemingly cleansed of racial overtones, is in the grip of The Smart Man's Burden. Herrnstein reveals the onus of the Smart Man's Burden in his famous "syllogism":

1. If differences in mental abilities are inherited, and
2. If success requires those abilities, and
3. If earnings and prestige depend on success,
4. Then social standing (which reflects earnings and prestige) will be based to some extent on inherited differences among people.

Herrnstein reveals the agonies of the Burden in his *Atlantic* lament: "As the wealth and complexity of human society grow, there will be precipitated out of the mass of humanity a low-capacity (intellectual and otherwise) residue that may be unable to master the common occupations, cannot compete for success and achievement, and are most likely to be born to parents who have similarly failed." A residue which, one gathers, will make huge demands on the good will and tax moneys of its betters. It is a little perplexing that Herrnstein's anguish is not geared toward concrete suggestions about how to ameliorate the "inevitable" situation through "effective compensatory education." Rather, it seems geared toward preparing the "residue" to accept its fate, for he goes no further than to suggest increased use of the IQ and other tests to make possible a "more humane and tolerant grasp of human differences," which is to say, a more rapid and rigid determination of just who the "residue" is.

Is there any reason to believe that high IQ is a prerequisite for success, or that there is a causal relation between IQ and "success in life"? Herrnstein's evidence is that IQ is a moderately good predictor of "success" and, further, that since people with high-status jobs tend to have higher average IQs, there

* Jensen, showing an astonishing ignorance of history, says: "It is more likely—though speculative of course—that Negroes brought here as slaves were selected for docility and strength rather than mental ability, and that through selective mating [with slave owners?] the mental qualities never had a chance to flourish."

is some reason to think high IQ is a prerequisite for performing the jobs. But other things statistically predict "success" even better than IQ, notably class background and number of school years completed. Independent of these other factors, IQ is no good at all as a predictor of "success in life."*

But isn't high IQ needed for performing high-status jobs? Probably not. People with high-status jobs may have high average IQs not because they have to be "smarter," but because these jobs require educational credentials and high IQ is correlated with getting these credentials even if it is not needed for them. Herrnstein here relies on equating high IQ with high "educability" or "trainability," but there is plenty of evidence that this equation is totally without basis. In fact, within job categories or types, performance on jobs or "success" at the job is notoriously *unrelated* to IQ.

Far more plausible than the thesis that getting ahead in America requires "intelligence," as measured by IQ, is the thesis that getting ahead requires other motivational and attitudinal traits. Competitiveness, servility (in appropriate situations), and hopefulness are possible candidates, as is a considerable tolerance of boredom. Whether highly "heritable" or learned, such traits are a debatable measure of "merit," nor do they necessarily represent the survival of the "fittest."

But even if one granted Herrnstein his "meritocracy" thesis, his conclusion doesn't follow. In his syllogism, he subtly equates "high heritability" with "fixedness" or "resistance to change in all circumstances." Even if IQ is highly heritable in our society, it does not follow that better education directed at the disadvantaged would not significantly boost mean IQs for society and make many more people "eligible" for high IQ jobs. Similarly, "high heritability" does not mean that new educational techniques won't be found that tend to benefit lower IQs more than higher ones, with the result that IQ differences are substantially reduced. In such a new environment, IQ might even lose its (supposed) high heritability. In other words, the question of "meritocracy" aside, Herrnstein makes his syllogism seem to work by giving a misleading picture of the implications of high heritability.

There seems to be no reason, then, for accepting anything about Herrnstein's famous syllogism, either its premises or its conclusion. Nor will we inevitably have to groan under the Smart Man's Burden.

Is anything left of the IQ argument, that vanguard position of the new "revolution" in the social sciences? IQ does not measure intelligence. High heritability estimates of IQ are based on useless studies and maybe even fudged data. Anyway, these estimates cannot be used to explain group differences. Finally, IQ seems to have nothing important to do with "success." This is all that's left of the IQ argument that *Fortune, Time, Atlantic,* the

* For evidence of this, see Samuel Bowles' and Herbert Gintis's recent study in *Social Policy*. One might try to save Herrnstein's claim by arguing that IQ is a factor needed for success in school and thus indirectly for success in life. But if class background is held constant, IQ still plays only a minimal role in predicting school success. And it is further arguable that it plays that role only because it measures values and attitudes and not because it measures intelligence.

New York Times, and other prominent newspapers and magazines have made so famous. Will the scholarly refutations of jensenism be made as famous? Will the press now give as much attention to showing what's wrong with jensenism as they have given to making it nearly a household word in Washington and a guide for the "pragmatic man in the street"? That may be up to the reader.

Sexual Politics in South Africa

IAN ROBERTSON AND PHILLIP WHITTEN

This article examines how and why South Africa maintains one of the most racist societies on the face of the earth. The history of sex in South Africa gives their racial policies an unusual and ironic twist. How long can a society this repressive keep functioning?

Although South Africa operates what is probably the nastiest regime on the face of the earth, it usually manages to do so without too much attention being paid by the outside world. But every now and then something happens inside South Africa which is so brutal or so bizarre that attention is focused at least momentarily on the country's policies—policies which are inexorably moving the whole of Southern Africa towards a bloody racial conflict which may have impact far beyond the region itself. Recent reports of mass prosecutions of citizens on charges of "immorality" have brought outside attention to one of the strangest laws in South Africa's *apartheid* system—the Immorality Act, which imposes sentences of up to seven years' imprisonment and ten lashes for actual or attempted sexual acts between individuals whose color does not match.

Many thousands of isolated couples have been arrested under the Act over the years, but recent prosecutions involved large groups of respectable white citizens accused of consorting with black women. Even within South Africa, the use of the law on this scale, with its attendant international publicity and local suicides, led to some debate on the law—until the Minister of Justice, Piet Pelser, declared that the Act would stand for as long as the present administration remains in office—a period which he, like most white South Africans, seems to regard as coterminous with eternity. Not that

The Progressive, September 1972. Reprinted by permission from *The Progressive,* 408 West Gorham Street, Madison, Wisconsin 53703.

discussion on the Act has ever been at a notably elevated or compassionate level. Professor J. H. Venter of the University of Pretoria, for example, felt that offenders should be emasculated, because they were in any case "poor human material." This view was contested by the Reverend E. J. Norval, of the Dutch Reformed Church, on theological grounds. Castration, he said, was not permissible, because the Lord declared that man should be fruitful and multiply. Offenders should instead be "imprisoned for life, or perhaps hanged."

The use of the law and the police to control the sex lives of South Africans is consistent with one of the country's most obvious political features: South Africa is the world's law-and-order nation *par excellence*. It has to be; the white minority of fewer than four million could not otherwise retain its absolute control over a total population of some 20.4 million, in a society which is the most rigidly segregated and hierarchical in existence today.

The statistics, which are replete with international records, speak eloquently enough. South Africa has the highest capital punishment rate in the world. For several years past, according to United Nations' figures, this single country has been responsible for approximately half the judicial executions in the entire world. The number of offenses which carry the death penalty is actually rising every year, and so is the number of offenses for which transgressors can be flogged. Every year the courts sentence some 40,000 South Africans to be whipped—not to mention the others, probably many times more numerous, who are beaten in the prisons for offenses against prison regulations. South African blacks have the highest per capita prison population on earth; it is calculated that one in six of them is jailed at some time in his life.

The typical South African response to any problem, from sex relations to malnutrition, is to call the police. When recent reports documented mass starvation of black children in the Kuruman area, the regime's response was to rush, not supplies to the children, but security policemen to the doctors and nurses who had originated the reports and to the journalists who had published them.

South Africa's white population falls into two groups: the Afrikaners—Afrikaans-speaking descendants of early Dutch settlers, who form the large majority—and a smaller group of English-speaking immigrants of more recent origin. Political power rests entirely in the hands of the Afrikaners; most of them belong to the powerful Dutch Reformed Church, a Calvinist sect which strongly endorses the *apartheid* system, referring for theological support to Old Testament passages.

White South Africans have good reason for trying to maintain their racial exclusivity: they enjoy a complete monopoly of political, economic, and social privilege. No black man has a vote in South Africa, and there is no black representation whatever in Parliament. Although the standard of living of the whites is comparable to that of white North Americans, the income of the average black household is about $50 per month, which often represents the earnings of several breadwinners. Every conceivable public convenience, from footbridges to ambulances, is racially segregated. Some thirteen per cent of the land area of South Africa is set aside as reserves for the blacks; this is largely infertile and contains no industries or even large towns. Blacks are allowed out of these areas only on permit to work for the whites—a migratory labor system which destroys family life, since the workers are not permitted to bring their wives and children with them.

The education provided for blacks is appropriate for their status as a proletarian labor force. For whites, education through high school is compulsory and free; for blacks it is voluntary, and they must pay for both tuition and books. As a result, the majority of black school children drop out after only two years of elementary school, and over the entire country only about 2,500 a year manage to graduate from high school.

The Prime Minister, Balthazar Vorster, has an excellent relationship with many leading figures in the police force, the military, the civil service, and the Dutch Reformed Church. They got to know each other well during World War II—in an internment camp for active Nazi sympathizers. Vorster was a general in a para-military organization, the Oxwaggon Brigade, and he still speaks with pride of his efforts against the Allied war effort.

The head of the Dutch Reformed Church is the Reverend D. J. Vorster, brother of the Prime Minister. He too was imprisoned during the war, as a spy for the Nazis. The Reverend Vorster has announced that both he and his brother were specifically chosen by God for their respective positions. (There is a third brother who restricts his own sallies into public life to occasional unfraternal and vitriolic attacks on the Prime Minister for being too soft.)

Another old comrade of the Prime Minister's is Brigadier P. J. Venter, his adviser on police and security matters. Brigadier Venter's department is named, with staggering arrogance or with incredible ineptitude, BOSS—the Bureau of State Security. Any policeman in South Africa can arrest any person and detain him for any period, in solitary confinement, without giving any reasons, without notifying dependents, and without allowing any access to the prisoner by any person. Political suspects in the hands of the security police have a high mortality rate—at least twenty are officially conceded to have died under mysterious circumstances recently: ten from "suicide," two from "slipping and falling," two by apparently leaping from the upper floors of the security police building in Jonannesburg, and the remainder from undisclosed "natural causes."

But even given the Afrikaner's interest in maintaining his position in South Africa, both now and—through the services of pure white womanhood—in the future, it is still difficult to account for the fear of miscegenation which the Immorality Act reflects. The fear amounts to outright panic, far exceeding anything ever found in the American old South, and probably unparalleled except by Nazi laws on "race ravishing." Although English South Africans view the whole issue with relative detachment, nothing chills the psyche of the Afrikaner people so much as the specter of race mixture. The reason, in this obsessively segregationist society, is not hard to find: Virtually all Afrikaners, even the whitest of them, have mulatto ancestry, and deep down they know it.

For decades after the Dutch first settled South Africa in 1652, white women were as rare as African women were plentiful. For many years it was official policy to encourage racial intermarriage, but the presently accepted view is that the settlers remained stoically celibate during those long decades, sustained by the hope that eventually a shipload of fair Dutch maidens would come sailing into Table Bay. The evidence, which embarrassingly takes the form of two million "coloureds"—essentially mulatto Afrikaners who cannot make it past the Race Reclassification Board to pure white status—suggests otherwise. These people, who call themselves "God's stepchildren," live in the twilight zone of *apartheid*, facing the constant threat of a racial reclassification which would divide a family and force it apart. The strains of living as a "coloured" in South Africa have given the group yet another of the country's unenviable records—that of the highest alcoholism rate in the world.

The official attempts to ignore the significance of the mulattoes is astonishing. One white school text denies that any racial mixing ever took place; another claims the mulattoes are "indigenous" to South Africa; a third reveals that they are descendants of "Scots, Greeks, and Malays." The Afrikaner Student Union has pronounced that it is a lie to suggest that the mulattoes are the product of a race mixture between blacks and whites.

But whatever the official view on the ancestry of the Afrikaners, the relentless mechanism of the genetic throwback, oblivious to the laws of the land, visits a brown child on the whitest and most devoutly segregationist families often enough to ensure that the collective consciousness of the Afrikaner never quite forgets these guilty origins, or the need to prevent further adulteration of the racial stock. And so, for some twenty years now, the Immorality Act has pried into the most intimate and sacred areas of the lives of South Africans.

The court record from some recent Immorality Act cases in South Africa gives some idea of the extent of intrusion into privacy and the nature of the techniques used by the police to collect their evidence:

Case #1

A college professor, John Blacking, aged forty, and a black medical doctor, Zureema Desai, aged twenty-four, were convicted of conspiring to contravene the Immorality Act at the professor's home. Giving evidence on behalf of the police, Major Petrus Coetzee told the court how his men had watched the couple for four hours—first from a treetop in the garden, then through a chink in the curtain of the sitting-room window. The police observed that "the couple kissed, Desai sat on Blacking's lap, and Blacking caressed her and tickled her playfully." The couple then retired to the bedroom, out of view of the police. The Major and his men forced entry to the house and found the couple lying, nearly naked, on the bed. The Major immediately "felt the double bed, and there was an area of warmth in the center, and the pillows were rumpled"—evidence which clinched the prosecution case.

Case #2

A twenty-four-year-old white man, Hesaja Hattingh, was found guilty of contravening the Act with a black woman, Ester Pooe. The offense had taken place several years earlier, and had passed undetected at the time—but Ester Pooe subsequently gave birth to a suspiciously light-skinned child. The matter came to the attention of the police, extensive investigation followed, and Hattingh was eventually tracked down. The trial took place on the birthday of the child, who was brought into court for examination of his fair complexion and reddish hair. Commenting that "contraventions of the Immorality Act have become a tidal wave," the magistrate jailed the couple for their crime in conceiving the child. Hattingh's wife, who had borne him three children and was pregnant with a fourth, declared her intention of divorcing him immediately.

Case #3

Pieter Bredenkamp, an eighty-year-old pensioner, was charged with an attempt to contravene the Act with his domestic servant. Asked to plead to the charge, Bredenkamp replied, "Guilty and immoral, your honor." There was little point in his contesting the case—thanks to the initiative of an enterprising policeman, Sergeant P. J. Ras, who presented the court with two photographs of Bredenkamp, in *flagrante delicto* with his pants around his octogenarian ankles. Acting on a tip-off, Sergeant Ras had concealed himself in the house before the couple arrived for their criminal tryst, and had leapt out of a closet at the appropriate moment, camera at the ready. Remonstrating with Bredenkamp for breaking his clean record of eighty years, the magistrate commented: "As the saying goes, 'There's no fool like an old fool.' "

For some years, a special vice squad was assigned for the deliberate entrapment of black women, who were solicited in the streets at night by white policemen in plain clothes, and then arrested for conspiracy to contravene the Act if they succumbed to the approaches. The rationale for this method was twofold: it not only dealt with black women who might be responsive to someone other than a policeman, but it also discouraged "immorality" because anyone tempted to indulge in the crime could not be sure if the prospective partner was an *agent provocateur* or not.

The vice squad came in for criticism from the white public when the exceptional popularity of service in the squad led to a widespread suspicion that arrests were taking place not at the initiation of the offense, but at its successful completion. Moreover, many policemen who were not formally members of the vice squad seemed to be voluntarily taking upon themselves the burden of propositioning black women to see if they could be tempted to break the law. Finally, after one notorious case in which several policemen gave evidence that they had had serial intercourse with a black woman in order to "corroborate the evidence," the time had come for the Dutch Reformed Church to express grave doubts about the ethics of the vice squad's services, and the practice of deliberately soliciting black women abruptly ceased. The idea of the police engaging in legalized gang bangs across the color line, and then running in the victims on multiple charges of immorality, was too much for even white South Africa to stomach.

Attempts to repeal or amend the Immorality Act on the part of South Africa's sole anti-*apartheid* legislator, Mrs. Helen Suzman, have been fruitless; on the last occasion, Prime Minister Vorster rejected her arguments as being "soaked through and through with the spirit of liberalism." Meanwhile, the rate of convictions has risen steadily, with the latest annual figures showing convictions up by a third over the previous year. Behavior arousing the slighest suspicion—such as driving after dark with a domestic servant of the opposite sex in the car—is liable to land the pair in court. Evidence is frequently so flimsy that almost half of those charged are ultimately acquitted—but the charge itself is tantamout to a social death sentence. The social disgrace involved has proved more than some individuals can bear, as the many suicides associated with the Immorality Act testify.

The law is blatantly operated to the disadvantage of blacks: Since 1965 there have been twelve cases involving consenting adults in which, incredibly, the white partner has been found innocent and the black partner has been convicted. Precisely how a person achieves the feat of having interracial intercourse alone is not immediately apparent, but South African courts seem undisturbed by the phenomenon and have managed to take this logical hiatus in their stride.

The law is based largely on the mythical need to protect chaste white womanhood from the ravages of black men, but it seems singularly unsuccessful in this respect: Out of 1,184 persons of all races charged in the latest annual period, only four black men were convicted. The greatest single group of offenders netted by the Act is white men—a noticeably disproportionate number of whom are policemen or ministers of the vigorously pro-*apartheid* Dutch Reformed Church. In recent times a righteously indignant white public has been fed salacious details of one minister of the church who was found in bed one Sunday afternoon with not one but two buxom Zulu maidens; while another, in an act whose murky psychological origins are perhaps best unguessed at, was found fornicating across the color line before his own altar. A third was convicted of having a long-standing and passionate affair with his black maid; a posse of policemen arrested him in the act a few hours after he had opened a new bank building with a speech commending the architect on providing separate entrances for each race group.

Many more white men, however, are sufficiently discouraged by the penalties in the Act to turn their attentions to the multi-racial joys of Swaziland, an independent country some five hours' drive from Johannesburg. Their visits have had such an impact that the Swazi King Sobhuza, normally highly discreet in his relationships with his powerful neighboring territory, has publicly expressed outrage at the "corruption" of Swazi women by wealthy white South Africans who arrive in smug droves on Friday nights for a weekend of lascivious pleasures in the small kingdom. "They come back grinning all over their faces," a frustrated South African border official told the Johannesburg *Sunday Times*, "and we can't do anything about it." Forbidden fruit, he added philosophically, seems somehow to taste sweeter.

One of the most bizarre aspects of the Act is the position of Japanese and Chinese. South Africa's small Chinese population (about 8,500) is classified as nonwhite, and treated accordingly. But visiting Japanese businessmen, following a lucrative trade agreement between the two countries, are officially viewed as "honorary whites." It is illegal for a white to make love to a Chinese, but not, it seems, to a Japanese; and a policeman encountering a white in the company of an Oriental has the onerous burden of deciding on sight whether the suspect is Chinese or Japanese. So far no Chinese has been accused of contravening the Act with a Japanese, and the judiciary has yet to pronounce on the question of whether such a liaison is moral or immoral.

Most cases under the Immorality Act involve cheap prostitution, but many concern the deep love of two human beings for each other, and it is here that South Africa's corroding racialism invades the most personal and sacred areas of human experience. Even married couples have been affected when one of them is reclassified as a "coloured" subsequent to their marriage; the marriage must be dissolved, the newly mulatto partner and any children (now also mulatto) must move to the appropriate residential area, and any further cohabitation between the former partners is a crime. A concept of the real meanings of morality and immorality is far, far beyond the grasp of Vorster and his ilk.

The Immorality Act is but one example of the almost paranoid racism which distinguishes life in South Africa. How the situation will resolve itself within the country is anyone's guess. But already the implications of the *apartheid* policy are extending beyond South Africa's borders. In an effort to consolidate its position, South Africa is building an empire of white minority-ruled states in Southern Africa, embracing Rhodesia, South West

Africa, and the Portuguese colonies of Angola and Mozambique. Guerrilla wars are raging in all these territories. Along the northern borders of this alliance, in a jagged line running from one side of Africa to the other, the continent is dividing into two hostile, armed camps. The black states to the north, particularly Tanzania and Zambia, are supporting the insurgents, and there is increasing danger of a full-scale race war in the region.

For too long the moral conscience of the world has been focused almost exclusively on the war in Indochina. The likelihood is that when that war is finally over, the policies of *apartheid* in South Africa will emerge as one of the foremost moral issues of our time. If that happens, what will be the attitude of the United States?

U.S. businessmen have already invested more than $1 billion in South Africa. Investment there is increasing faster than in any other country in the world; the average return on capital is running around fifteen per cent. South Africa is fanatically anti-Communist; it produces some sixty per cent of the Western world's gold; and it is in an important strategic position as guardian of the east-west sea route, so vital in times when the Suez Canal is closed. Given these conditions, what will be the attitude of the United States if South Africa appears to be in danger of attack by guerrillas trained in Moscow, Peking, Havana, and Tanzania? The answer to that question might be the most important U.S. foreign policy decision of the decade.

TEN

Social Change

WE LIVE in a time of change. The world spins and splits before our eyes. Cataclysm and chaos swamp our senses. The mass media seem imbued with a sense of overkill, but that is life in the modern world. We no longer live in an age of quiescence and calm. The static and stolid traditional societies of earlier times are fading before the monster of modernism. It seems as though everything that has happened to man has been squeezed into the last few years of his existence. The population explosion and economic affluence are recent phenomena. Rapid technological change has been with us for less than seventy-five years and its pace is quickening. Changes are interdependent. A change in one institution forces changes in others. For example, the assembly-line technique of mass production was a monumental technological advance. It changed the shape of the American economy and the character of work. It allowed large numbers of workers to own cars and other commodities. The car, in turn, greatly influenced courtship patterns. In our society, the future is now. We would now like to discuss some theories of social change.

Marx's theory of the class struggle under capitalism is essentially a theory of change. In this theory the most important variable was economic. Basically the solidarity and economic deprivation of the horney-handed workers would eventually produce a revolution. Marx felt that certain economic relationships profoundly influenced the other institutions in society and that changes in the economic structure would produce concomitant changes elsewhere. Weber developed a different theory of change in relation to the rise of capitalism. He felt that values and attitudes were potent change-initiating forces and theorized that the most important factor in the generation of capitalism was the "Protestant ethic." Weber linked the Calvinistic doctrine of predestination with the rise of a thrifty, hardworking, nose-to-the-grindstone middle class. Those who were successful in this life were predestined to enjoy a glorious afterlife in heaven and those who did not "make it" descended to the eternal fires of hell. The failures were not predestined for salvation. Needless to say, nobody wanted to be a failure.

James C. Davies (*American Sociological Review*, February 1962) has a much more comprehensive view of revolutionary change which combines the attitudinal and economic factors. It applies to both the downtrodden Indian peasant and the black man in America. According to Davies, revolutions tend to occur when a period of economic and social progress is followed by a period of short reversal. This explains why a riot can erupt in the Hough area of Cleveland rather than in the Central Ward, where black people are even worse off. What is important is the relationship between a group's expectations and what they actually get. When Strom Thurmond claims that black people should be happy because they have more refrigera-

Drawing (overleaf) by Jules Feiffer. Used by permission of Publishers-Hall Syndicate.

tors than Africans, he is less than amusing. Black Americans do not care what an Ibo tribesman has; they want what white folks have here in America. The aspirations of black people are rising; the income gap between whites and blacks has widened. This is a reversal or economic downturn. For many urban blacks conditions have actually worsened. This seems to be a revolutionary situation.

Even though economic deprivation may tend to cause social unrest and economic affluence may tend to reduce social tension, this does not explain why we witnessed a massive revolutionary movement in China and see apparent apathy and stagnation among the Indian peasants. The objective economic condition of the Indian peasant is as bad or worse than that of the peasants in prerevolutionary China. The difference is how the individual views his position in society. What happened to the Indian peasant? His aspirations never grew. His religion provided the proper antichange bias. According to his belief, if the Indian peasant does not passively accept his place in society, he will be reborn in a lower station in the next life. Therefore, the religious attitudes reinforce the stagnation that has proliferated in India.

What are other examples of changes we are facing? First, there are changes brewing in the political institution. The electoral college and the present convention setup are becoming less and less tolerable. The Harris Poll recently pointed to the beginning of new political coalitions: change and antichange factions. Secondly, the population explosion also has to be faced. At the moment the population explosion is severely hindering economic development in the poor nations and is threatening to engulf the urban areas with pollution, blight, and traffic snarls in the economically and industrially developed countries. Massive technological changes are also confronting us. The first is of a military nature: the bomb. Second is the cybernation revolution. Some say that it will entail a complete restructuring of our economy. Others feel that if a man's job is automated out of existence, he can be retrained at government expense to move elsewhere in the economy. Because the demand or desire for more and more material goods seems to be an American trait, the worker should always be able to find a job in another sector of the economy producing these goods. Why can Americans not own five cars and two homes? Within the context of a future computerized technology, Arthur C. Clarke, in "The Mind of the Machine," brilliantly tries to answer the question of whether man or the machine will eventually reign supreme. This is a recurring theme in many science-fiction and utopian novels.

In this section we have included articles that touch on only a few areas of change, but the other sections of the book, directly or indirectly, deal more comprehensively with this issue. Whether it is the youth rebellion, the minority revolt, the deterioration of the environment, or the revolution in education, the future of America and the world depends on how we react to these challenges.—G. G.

Selected References
(All are available in paperback editions.)

Brinton, Crane. *The Anatomy of Revolution*. Englewood Cliffs, N.J.: Prentice-Hall, Inc., 1938.

Ehrlich, Paul. *The Population Bomb*. New York: Ballantine Books, Inc., 1968.

Heilbroner, Robert L. *The Great Ascent*. New York: Harper & Row, Publishers, 1963.

Hoffer, Eric. *The True Believer*. New York: Harper & Row, Publishers, 1951.

Horowitz, Irving L. *The New Sociology*. New York: Oxford University Press, 1964.

Happiness Is Not a Movement

ARTHUR HOPPE

Once upon a time there was a group called The Happiness Movement. At first, it was a very small group. Its members were called Happies. And they were different from everybody else.

"We have discovered something called Love," they announced proudly. "We have invented something called Individual Freedom. We care not what an intolerant, bigoted hypocritical society may think. All we ask is to be left alone."

So all the Happies wore striped bathing suits to signify Individual Freedom, dandelions in their hair to symbolize Love, and bones in their noses because they felt they should return to the simple ways of Cro-Magnon man. Pills to make them happy. Which they were. Not only were the Happies happy, but much of what they said rang true: Love is good, intolerance is bad, freedom's fine, and there's no sweeter right than the right to be left alone. Naturally, society was offended.

"Why can't they take more baths?" growled the Conservatives. "Don't they know cleanliness is next to patriotism?"

"They're right, of course, that we are guilty of everything there is to be guilty about," said the Liberals guiltily. "But why do they have to eat all those pills?"

Naturally, this opprobium stirred every magazine and newspaper to send a disguised reporter to record the Happy philosophy. In addition, the ranks of the movement were swelled by countless teen-agers who thought sex was Love, a striped bathing suit was Freedom, and a Happiness Pill was just the greatest. As they watched their movement grow by leaps and bounds, the Happies were at first pleased, then awed, and at last convinced that they were The Wave of the Future. Where at first they had diffidently offered their doctrines as personal opinion, they now preached them vociferously as divine revelation.

"Anybody who wears a tie instead of a striped bathing suit is an uptight, know-nothing enemy of Individual Freedom!" they said bigotedly.

"Anybody who hasn't taken a Happiness Pill can't talk about happiness!" they said intolerantly.

"Anybody who doesn't practice Love the way we practive Love is to be despised!" they said hypocritically.

So it was that the Happies naturally developed the attributes of any successful movement: Its members felt superior to nonmembers; they were convinced of the righteousness of their own dogma; and they were united by a common hatred. Naturally, they no longer talked of changing themselves, but of changing everybody else instead. Naturally, they no longer demanded to be left alone, but marched off to remold society instead.

And naturally, this made them pretty much the same as everybody else.

Moral: The only good movement is one that isn't going anywhere.

Clippings from Tomorrow's Newspapers

NEWS STORIES OF 2024

ISAAC ASIMOV

Quarter-Millennial Plans to Feature Nostalgic End of the United States

PRESIDENT TO RETAIN WORLD POST AS REGIONAL GOVERNOR

Nationalists Plan Demonstrations. WASHINGTON—Last week's congressional vote in favor of the Regionalization Bill, and yesterday's presidential signature that made it law, makes official what has, in the eyes of most political analysts, long been inevitable.

Thirty-three years after the establishment of the Global Economic Board, the reality of national interdependence has overtaken the last political unit still maintaining its traditional twentieth-century boundaries.

"The advance of regionalization," said Vice-President Frances Anna Parkinson, "has successfully reduced the divisions of the world population on racial, linguistic, and cultural bases by setting up units that cross all such boundaries. It is time we joined mankind in geography, as we have in actuality, and we can find no better time for this than on the two hundred fiftieth anniversary of the event that marked the beginning of what was to be the greatest nation of its time."

The Quarter-Millennial Committee, which has long anticipated this vote, is preparing to make the 2026 celebration at once a backward-looking joyous celebration and a forward-looking, equally joyous celebration of the final stone in the structure of global federalism.

Jonathan Blackmer, head of the Paul Revere Society, warned bitterly that the American people would never accept regionalization and promised demonstrations of large size.

Lunar Colony Dedicates New Division

With the opening of the Scott Carpenter Tunnel, the total length of corridors in the Lunar subsurface passed the 300-kilometer mark. Estimates are that by the end of the century, there will be 5,000 kilometers of tunnel and a Lunar population of 500,000.

Present at the dedication were all 38 native Lunarites, boys and girls ranging in age from 2 months to 11 years, who were born on the moon.

REMEMBER CHICKENS?

Haym Morris is taking time out from his Dream-Taping sessions to breed chickens. He says it's one way of getting a little of that old-fashioned meat on the table. Don't rush to imitate him, however. Every chicken must be inspected, and you'd better not forget to get an animal-breeding license and fill out information blanks for each chicken you have. And don't think you can fool the computer. You might decide to go back to chicken-flavored pressed-nut-bean loaf.

Of course, if killing chickens is not your idea of fun, you may not have to go that far. Haym says that their eggs are quite edible if correctly prepared.

Ecto-Baby Celebrates First Birthday

One year old today, Jenny, the little girl with the glass mother, slept peacefully while tiptoeing nurses placed a cupcake with a single fluorocandle near her crib, then celebrated with somewhat more vigor in the lobby of the Ectogenesis Institution.

Dr. Warren K. MacMurray, who throughout has supervised the baby's development from sperm and ovum, stated, "There is no question but that Jenny is a normal child in every sense. There is absolutely no reason to suppose she will not live out an entirely normal life."

Questioned as to whether the Glass Placenta is now ready to begin the incubation of Genesis Two, MacMurray smiled and was silent.

Genesis One, universally known as Jenny, is the first test-tube baby to survive more than one month past term. So far, all fertilized ova surviving to term have been female, but there are hopes for male survival soon.

Theater—The New Play, reviewed by Aston Hight

In watching *Watergate,* the viewer is overcome at first by the sheer deadly accuracy of the makeup. It is not only that each player seems like a historical character come to life; the very voices, walk, and even the tilt of the ears, it would seem, bury each man in the part he plays.

The recent television special on the occasion of the fiftieth anniversary of the Watergate break-in introduced many of us to the characters of that impossible drama (as we look back on it) which so changed the current of American history. That, however, was a collection of scraps.

Olmsted's play takes the tapes, transcripts, and TV remnants of those mad days of the Seventies and puts them together in such a way that a connected story arises out of it, one virtually without seams. The action never flags; the suspense never droops. Despite the fact that we all know exactly how it ended, I caught myself more than once thinking, "By God, he's going to get away with it!"

Undoubtedly, Robert Warton, in the role of Nixon, carries off the honors. He can switch from the mean snarl of the staff meetings to the unctuousness of the television addresses without a stripped gear, and yet never loses the telltale furtiveness in the lines about the mouth. Ali Barssom offers strong support as Ehrlichman—underplayed all the way with a deadly sureness of thrust. Jellicoe properly portrays Mitchell's stone face, but Grinspan's Haldeman might have been stronger. At times when he hesitates a bit too long, we don't quite believe in him as the Grey Eminence. Ellenbogen is seen all too briefly in his role of John Dean, but he makes the most of it. When the decision is made and Dean backs out of the office, we can *see* his change in direction.

Mets Meet Tokyo Suns in Opener

Manager Burleigh Thoms insisted on optimism, but the odds are 7 to 5 against the injury-riddled Mets, who may have to play without slugger Sam Grimmis.

Thoms said, "The computers have been wrong before. They can't predict every lucky hop or just the way a batter feels at a particular moment. The game is still won on heart."

Computer-Odds, Inc., which is short on heart but long on programming, refuses, as usual, to announce details, but a confidential source says that out of over a hundred calculated games, using the batting orders as announced and the lifetime statistics for every player concerned, no outcome gave the Suns less than a three-run lead.

No injuries have been forecast in the probability range about 2 percent. Injury announcements are legally required since Hatchman's broken leg last year, an accident that might have been prevented if he had known its comparatively high probability.

LETTERS TO THE EDITOR

Dear Sir:

Now that the United States is going regional, I suppose we're going to have to carry all the freeloaders of the planet on our good American backs. I dread seeing what the tax bill is going to look like in the next few years. Or who our councilmen are going to be from now on.

Dear Sir:

It's about time the Landmarks Preservation Council took a look at the Empire State Building. It is in a shocking state of disrepair, and there is just no use in keeping one working remnant of the skyscraper era if we let it go to pot.

PERSONALS

Old books for sale; prime condition; many for which no videotape equivalents exist. Girlie magazines, ante-2000, unexpurgated.

Nostalgia buffs! Get your old plastic here. Genuine acrylic, polyethylene, bakelite, all varieties. Beautifully yellowed. Every piece authenticated. Year of manufacture included in guarantee.

DID YOU KNOW—

• That the last tiger in the wild was found dead on August 17, 2018, in Assam, India?

• That there are estimated to be 2,000 women in the United States between the ages of 28 and 30 who are all named Aurelialee? All are named for Aurelialee Swanson, the first woman to reach the moon back in 1994.

• That over 99 percent of all the computer programmers who ever lived are alive right now?

OBITUARY

Richard Helmuth Boskone, formerly regional governor of Anglo-Rhineland, died yesterday at the age of 73. Elected to the governorship in 2012, he had served a term of five years.

Arise Ye Prisoners of Extinction

GEORGE WALD

George Wald is a Nobel Prize winner and professor of biology at Harvard. The text following is Dr. Wald's speech in Tokyo before the Twentieth World Conference Against the Atom and Hydrogen Bombs, August 2, 1974, and is a brief catalogue of the technological changes that threaten world destruction: overpopulation, automation, and nuclear overkill.

I have come halfway across the world to speak what I believe to be the truth. It is a dreadful truth, hard to live with, but if we do not live with it, we shall die by it.

I speak here as an American, but even more as a fellow human being, a scientist concerned with life, a teacher deeply troubled for my students, a parent fearing for my children and for their children.

Human life is now threatened as never before, not by one but by many perils, each in itself capable of destroying us, but all interrelated, and all coming upon us together. I am one of those scientists who does not see how to bring the human race much past the year 2000. And if we perish, as seems more and more possible, in a nuclear holocaust, that will be the end not only for us but for much of the rest of life on the earth.

We live—while that is permitted us—in a balance of terror. The United States and the Soviet Union together have already stockpiled nuclear weapons with the explosive force of ten tons of TNT for every man, woman and child on the earth. You might think that enough, but we are now in the midst of a further escalation on both sides, replacing every single nuclear warhead with multiple warheads and devising new and more devastating weapons.

My country at present is making three new hydrogen warheads per day. The Soviet Union keeps pace with us. We are told that our security—strange thought!—lies in Mutual Assured Destruction—MAD. Is is well-named.

The bomb that destroyed Hiroshima, and ended by killing about 100,000 persons, was a small one by present standards, with the explosive power of about 15,000 tons of TNT.

One of my friends was in a position about ten years ago to look up what we then had targeted upon a Russian city about the size of Hiroshima. It was in the megaton range, several hundred times as large. Why? What for? One can only destroy a city; one can only kill a person. It is insane, but the insanity of the practical and calculating persons who run our lives. It is insane—unless one holds an arms contract. Then it is business, and the bigger the better.

The United States now budgets about $22 billion a year on new arms. A rapid rate of turnover assures that this business will go on. Our arms sales abroad doubled in 1973–74 over the year before—$8.5 billion, about $7 billion going to the Middle East. When early in 1971 the Joint Economic Committee of Congress asked a general from our Department of Defense how much military hardware the department then held that had been declared surplus, mainly to be sold as scrap, he replied $17 billion worth.

The nuclear arms contracts alone are worth about $7 billion a year; $7 billion talks more loudly than any number of humanitarian declarations, or terrified people, or children facing extinction. That money is real, hard cash. Where it changes hands, those consequences are out of sight, hence out of mind—mere abstractions.

But arms, and war, and nuclear weapons are only part of the crisis. The big hunger is now upon us, the great famines that scientists have been predicting for years past—hunger among the poor in the developed countries, starvation in Africa, South Asia and South America.

The Green Revolution, so recently begun, has already collapsed. It depended on huge supplies of cheap oil and coal to prepare the artificial fertilizers and pesticides that alone made it work. And oil and coal are no longer cheap. The profits of the major oil companies—which also own most of the coal, and now are developing nuclear power—doubled and tripled during the past year, as the peoples of the Third World begin to starve. It seems possible that twenty million persons will die of famine during the next twelve months, in India, Pakistan and Bangladesh alone.

All those problems are made more terrible by the population explosion. We have not yet quite taken in what that means. Even if all the developed nations reached the replacement level—an average of two children per reproducing pair—by the year 2000, and all the nations of the Third World came to the same state by 2050—both conditions highly unlikely—then the world population, now at about 3.7 billion, would rise by 2120 to about thirteen billion.

Development, so-called, has meant mechanization. The work that used to be done by human and animal muscle is increasingly done by machines. That is true even in agriculture. It is another aspect of the Green Revolution. Farming is rapidly being replaced by agribusiness.

In the United States the same huge corporations that make aircraft control our oil and gas, run our transportation, also grow our food. Such agribusiness now controls 51 per cent of our vegetable production, 85 per cent of our citrus crops, 97 per cent of our chicken-raising, and 100 per cent of our sugar cane. That is happening all over the world. It means more food, but many fewer jobs. And only those who find work can eat—they and their families. Unemployment, that child of the Industrial Revolution, is rising throughout the world.

And a new phenomenon that is much worse. With the increasing mechanization, increasing numbers of persons have become not only unemployed but superfluous. There is no use for them in the free-market economy. They are wanted neither as workers nor customers. They are not wanted at all. Their existence is a burden, an embarrassment. It would be a relief if they vanished—parents and children.

In his report to the World Bank in September, 1970, its president, Robert McNamara, former Ford executive and Secretary of Defense, spoke of such persons as "marginal men." He estimated that in 1970 there were 500 million of them—twice the population of the United States—that by 1980 there would be one billion, and by 1990, two billion. That would be half the world population.

It is too late for declarations, for popular appeals, here or anywhere. All that matters now is political power.

We call for the abolition of nuclear weapons. Even in the remote chance that that would happen, it would not protect us from nuclear war. Those nations that have already learned how to make nuclear weapons would produce them in quantity within a few months of the outbreak of a new war. Getting rid of the nuclear stockpiles would defuse the present threat of instant annihilation, it would gain us a little time. It would be an important gain, but only a step toward what must be the ultimate aim: to abolish war. War is obsolete in the modern world. It has become intolerably dangerous.

The only thing that can save us now is political power—for the peoples of this world to take that power away from their present masters, who are leading our world to destruction.

And who are the masters?

In the so-called "free world" is is not the governments. They are only the servants, the agents. Nor is it the generals. They too are only the servants.

The "free world" is run by such enterprises as General Motors, I.T.T., the Chase Manhattan Bank, Exxon, Dutch Shell and British Petroleum, Mitsubishi and Mitsui. Their wealth and power exceed any previously known throughout human history.

We think of General Motors as a private business, but only eighteen nations in the world have gross national products as large as the annual sales of General Motors—$36 billion in 1973.

Those giant corporations can buy and sell, can make and break governments. They stop at nothing. A year ago Chile was taken over by a military junta, its President Allende murdered, its great folk singer Victor Jara beaten to death. But now I.T.T., which offered our C.I.A. $1 million to keep Allende from becoming President, can operate freely; and Anaconda Copper has just settled its claims with the new Chilean dictatorship for $253 million.

And what of the "socialist" world? It offers us an imperialism of the left to balance that of the right. We have had hard lessons to learn during the past years. One of them is that private wealth and personal political power are interchangeable, bureaucracies are interchangeable, generals and admirals, corporate executives and industrial commissars—all interchangeable.

Hence no nation so closely resembles the United States of America as the Soviet Union. That is what Andrei Sakharov told us a few years ago, and went on to propose that both nations now join forces to work for the good of humanity. For that he is virtually a prisoner in his own country. Policy in the modern world, right or left, is not made by the Sakharovs.

We are often told indeed that even the experts do not know how to deal with the problems that now threaten worldwide disaster, that "all the facts are not yet in," that more research must be done, and more reports written.

By all means let us have more research. But that must not be allowed to become a trap, an excuse for endlessly putting off action. We already know enough to begin to deal with all our major problems: nuclear war, overpopulation, pollution, hunger, the despoliation of the planet.

The present crisis is a crisis not of information but of policy. We could begin to cope with all the problems that now threaten our lives. But we cannot cope with any of them while maximizing profits. And a society that insists before all on maximizing profits for the few thereby threatens disaster for all.

But not for all at the same time. As matters now stand, the peoples of the Third World are to perish first. They have already begun to starve; all that is asked of them is to starve quietly. If they make trouble they will be exterminated by other means.

The developed nations are armed to the teeth, and mean not only to hold on to what they have but to grasp whatever more they can, while they can. For example, the last of the world's rapidly dwindling natural resources. For another example: As the great famines begin, the grain that might feed a hungry peasantry throughout the Third World is fed instead to cattle and hogs to supply the rapidly increasing demands for beef and pork in the affluent countries.

But their turn must come too, first of course for their poor, already hard-hit by worldwide inflation and unemployment. And if there should be another major war, as seems likely, a nuclear holocaust would swallow up everything.

Unless the people of this world can come together to take control of their lives, to wrest political power from those of its present masters who are pushing it toward destruction, then we are lost—we, our children and their children.

Arise, ye prisoners of extinction. Peoples of the world, unite. You have nothing to lose but your terror, your exploitation and ceaseless deception, your alienation and dehumanization, your helplessness and hopelessness. And a world to win.

AND A WORLD TO WIN.

Population Control

PAUL R. EHRLICH

Ehrlich argues that not only is population control necessary, but that scientists like himself should become actively involved in influencing and formulating public policy. He warns that lower birth rates in the United States do not mean that the rest of the world is well on the way to reducing population growth.

Population control is a loaded concept. It seems to conjure up different images in the minds of different people. To some the images are of horrors: fetuses killed by abortionists, sterilants put in water supplies by mad scientists, poor families taxed into oblivion for having too many children, minorities threatened with genocide. To others, the images are of salvation. The world in which we live is vastly overpopulated and we are faced by a wide array of hideous problems—war, racism, food shortage, pollution, and so on. People are destructive in many ways, and the more people there are the worse things get. Therefore, the solution is to limit the size of the population. If only there were fewer people, our problems would be solved.

Obviously, neither of these sets of images is realistic. While it is quite true that there is a major population component in many human problems, and that rapid population growth can prevent us from solving any of them, it is not true that controlling the size of the population will automatically bring on a golden era. For instance, if the population of the United States were stabilized at its present size while current trends in American behavior continued, a little over 200 million Americans would soon exhaust most of Earth's rich deposits of resources and in the process greatly degrade the life-support capacity of our planet's ecosystems. In addition, such problems as racism, poverty, and international aggressiveness would persist, although they would be somewhat more amenable to solution. On the other hand, the picture of population control as some sort of fiendish plot is hardly accurate either. Draconian measures are not really called for. In theory one might "control" population growth by killing people, just as one might "control" crime by shooting everybody suspected of being a criminal. But there are more humane and socially desirable ways of controlling population growth, just as there are other ways of controlling criminal behavior.

Before discussing the intricacies of population control further, it is wise to ask whether or not it is necessary. If there were no crime, there would be no reason to devise programs to control criminal behavior. If there are no problems associated with population growth, there is no reason to discuss possible programs of population control. Today, however, no informed person considers population growth innocuous. It is true that some people and even some "scientists" can be found who will derogate the population problem. But one can still find people and even "scientists" who think the world is flat or who attempt to guide their lives by astrology. In the last several years, science has moved from the stage of generalized concern over population growth to efforts to influence public policy on the matter. Individual spokesmen have been joined recently by various groups. In 1970, the Governing Board of the American Institute of Biological Sciences released the following statement:

WHEREAS, scientific studies have clearly identified as a threat to human life and to its quality the current high rate of population increase and consequent overpopulation both in the United States and elsewhere, and

WHEREAS, immediate measures must be taken to correct the population growth in the United States: therefore be it

RESOLVED, that it is essential that the Government accelerate its efforts toward implementing all methods of humane birth control at the earliest feasible time.

In 1970 also, the report of the Study of Critical Environmental Problems (SCEP), sponsored by the Massachusetts Institute of Technology, was published and it called attention to the global nature of various ecological problems and to the population component in them. In 1972, a group of scientists under the leadership of Dennis and Donella Meadows at MIT published a popular report of their work entitled *The Limits of Growth*—a document clearly designed to influence public policy—which emphasized the ways in which population growth is mortgaging the human future. Almost simultaneously, the British journal hypothetical animals behaving differently. If a population of rat-eating cats begins to exhaust the supply of rats so that the cats start dying of hunger, then there is an overpopulation of cats. The possibility that the cats might all be able to survive if some learned to eat squirrels does not alter the fact of overpopulation. Neither would the information, supplied by a cat historian, that cats had once actually fed on squirrels. Overpopulation exists when the numbers of an animal increase until its population begins to deplete its resources, degrade its environment, or (in the case of humans) press on its values. Thus overpopulation can, in theory, be caused or cured without changes in population size.

Of course, people are not cats; presumably they can much more readily change their behavior. And it is quite true that appropriate changes in behavior could dramatically reduce the impact of today's 3.8 billion people on the environment and thus reduce the degree of overpopulation. Indeed it might be possible—with redistribution of wealth and food, less meat-eating, intensive recycling of resources, replacement of automobiles with mass transit, less manufacturing of all kinds, less frivolous use of power and resources—to design a world in which 3.8 billion people can live without overpopulation. But we do not at present know enough about the system to be sure.

The situation is, however, rendered much more serious because the population, great as it already is, is growing so rapidly that it will double in about thirty-five years, unless some extraordinary event intervenes. Moreover, stopping population growth cannot be accomplished overnight. As Bernard Berelson, President of the Population Council, wrote in 1970, ". . . if the replacement-sized family is realized for the world as a whole by the end of this century—itself an unlikely event—the world's population will then be 60 percent larger or about 5.8 billion, and due to the results of age structure [the proportion of people of different ages] it will not stop growing until near the end of the next century, at which time it will be about 8.2 billion, or about 225 percent the present size. If replacement is achieved in the developed world by 2040, then the world's population will stabilize at near 15.5 billion about a century hence, or well over four times the present size."

In other words, there is a long "braking time" if we attempt to halt population growth by slowing the flow of people into the population—that is, by limiting the number of births. Of course there is always that grim alternative, the end of population growth through an acceleration in removal of people from the population—an increase in the death rate. Population growth could be stopped in its tracks by worldwide famine, or plague, or thermonuclear war. Worldwide today there are, annually, about thirty-four births per thousand people in the population and only some fourteen deaths. The balance can be restored by lowering the former or by raising the latter (or some combination of the two). Then the size of the population would be stable—we would have achieved zero population growth (ZPG).

Since no population can grow forever, it is inevitable that the balance *will* be restored. We will have ZPG. The only questions are when and how. For reasons already indicated, I think the time is soon. The question of how remains to be resolved. In any animal but man, there would be no choice—overpopulation ordinarily results in increased death rates, sometimes accompanied by "compulsory" reductions in birthrates. *Homo sapiens* alone has the option of choosing to limit its population size by voluntarily controlling the birthrate. If it is not exercised soon, however, the option may expire.

Assuming this peculiarly human option is to be exercised, how can the population be controlled? For a long time, the answer of establishment sociologists and demographers was: through family planning. . . . *The Ecologist* produced a "Blueprint for Survival," endorsed by a very distinguished group of thirty-five English scientists. A major thrust of the blueprint was toward population control. Perhaps most important, in the spring of 1972 the *Report of the President's Commission on Population Growth and the American Future* was published. A diverse group of distinguished Americans, including many laymen, had examined the impact of population growth on our lives and its potential impact on the lives of our children and had come to the conclusion that there were no benefits to be gained, and many costs to be incurred, from further increasing the number of Americans.

Why is there such unanimity about the need for limiting the numbers of people in the United States and in the world? The reasons are many and complex, but can be briefly summarized:

1. The rapid growth of the world population threatens to worsen an already marginal food situation. Although we are not certain what factors will limit the amount of food that can be produced, we know that at any given time the supply is finite. At the moment if all the food in the world were distributed equitably among the 3.8 billion people living on the planet Earth, everyone would have just enough calories and not quite enough high-quality protein. Since food *is not* equitably distributed, many people are overfed while large numbers go hungry. It is estimated that ten to twenty million people die prematurely every year because their diets are inadequate in some respect. For the past twenty years or so, food production has barely kept pace with population growth. This means that the proportion of hungry people has remained more or less constant, but their *number* has steadily increased. Specialists in food production have expressed grave doubts that even the most strenuous efforts can keep per capita food production at the

present inadequate level for more than another twenty to thirty years. Moreover, these estimates take no account of the possibility of a collapse of world fisheries or large-scale crop failures, events which would result in massive famines.

2. The most serious environmental problem facing humanity is the simplification of ecological systems. Complex natural ecological systems supply many indispensable services: they dispose of wastes, they help to maintain the quality of the atmosphere, they provide control of most pests, and they constitute a "library" of genetic information which people can draw on to develop new kinds of crops, antibiotics, vaccines, and so on. The stability of these all-important ecological systems is related to their complexity. Unfortunately, many human activities, particularly agriculture, constitute a serious assault on that complexity and thus on the life-support systems. Thus one result of attempts to produce more food for a rapidly growing population could be an inadvertent, large reduction in the carrying capacity of the planet for human life. By attempting to feed five billion people in 1984, we may make it impossible to feed even two billion in the year 2000! Many other activities that support human populations also reduce ecological complexity: the clearing of land for dwellings, highways, and factories; the building of dams; overfishing; strip mining; and the release of persistent poisons. Most of these assaults on ecosystems tend to increase as population grows, and some increase disproportionately; two million people may do much more than twice as much damage as one million.

It must be emphasized that, as long as human activities are seriously damaging the ecological systems of the Earth, the planet is *by definition* overpopulated. There is some confusion about this among some non-ecologists, who are prone to deny that we are overpopulated on the grounds that damage could be avoided if there were "less affluence" or "better technology." Unfortunately for their argument, overpopulation must be *measured in terms of the animals (or people) as they exist,* not of the chance to plan their families, to have only the number of children they *want,* then population growth would be slowed or halted. Family planning has received wide support among intelligent and humane people simply because it involves an obvious social good—preventing the births of unwanted children. It is mainly the question of the efficacy of family planning as a route to population control that has led to controversy. As Justin Blackwelder succinctly put it, ". . . 'family planning' means, among other things, that if we are going to multiply like rabbits, we should do it on purpose. One couple may plan to have three children; another couple may plan seven. In both cases they are a cause of the population problem—not a solution to it."

What are the sources of faith in family planning as an effective device for limiting population growth? One is the relatively low birthrates in the developed countries (DCs) in contrast to those in underdeveloped countries (UDCs). It was in the DCs that the family planning movement originated; it is in those countries that people today have the widest access to the means of birth control; ergo, family planning leads to low birthrates and, eventually, ZPG. Another source of faith is the belief that people, given the opportunity to choose the size of their families, will make socially responsible decisions, considering not just their own needs, but those of their children and of society as well.

There are a number of serious problems with the first view. The fundamental "cause" of the population explosion is a decline in death rates in the human population, a decline which began at the time that agriculture was invented some 10,000 years ago. As living conditions improved with advances in agriculture, industrialization, and the conquest of epidemic disease, the decline in death rates accelerated dramatically. But there were no significant changes in birthrates, which remained close to their primitively high levels. Then, around 1850, birthrates in Europe and North America began to drop, and continued to drop until the second quarter of the twentieth century, when they levelled off. The family planning movement was in part a result of the changing attitudes toward family size that caused the decline in birthrates. The organizations that grew from it probably directly affected only a minority of people, but their influence in changing restrictive laws and public attitudes toward the practice of birth control certainly accelerated the birthrate decline.

However, the decrease in birthrates has not, in general, been sufficient to halt population growth in the DCs. Indeed, demographic data seem to indicate that DC populations will continue to grow at rates which will double them about once per century, on the average, if no steps beyond family planning are initiated. There are those, however, who are not worried by this. Some demographers seem to have a mystical belief that birthrates and death rates automatically move from a primitive state of balance where both rates are high to a new state of balance where both are low. This change is called the demographic transition. These individuals believe that birthrates in DCs must fall further—that the demographic transition will be "completed." Still other demographers and many family planners see no need for ZPG in the near future, and approve of slow growth.

On a much more sophisticated level, demographer Charles Westoff has recently contended that simply eliminating unwanted births might substantially reduce the population growth rate in the United States. This conclusion has been challenged by another respected demographer, Judith Blake. Recent data support her position that the proportion of unwanted births has been greatly reduced since 1965, allowing little room for further decrease in the number of unwanted births. Changes in the average age of mothers, widespread use of oral contraceptives, and loosening of abortion laws in some states are some of the factors that have operated to reduce unwanted births.

The entire matter is further confused by the recent decline in United States birthrates at a time when more and more women are entering what are normally their "peak" reproductive years. No one can say with certainty why this is occurring. It might be because of improvements in the availability of contraceptives and easier access to abortion. It could be a result of the intensive propaganda efforts of organizations like ZPG and "population nuts" like me—indeed some recent data indicate this could be one factor. But much as I would like to give credit to the family planners (or take it myself!) I suspect other factors to be more important. One is suggested by population biologist K. E. F. Watt of the University of California at Davis. Dr. Watt believes that this dramatic drop is due to the economic difficulties recently encountered by young people attempting to enter the job market. There is intense competition for positions in the labor force among those just joining it—at the ages just prior to normal peak reproduction. Another possible factor is the rising tide of women's liberation with its emphasis on nonchildbearing routes to fulfilment. But, in fact, it is not now possible to assign cause to this birthrate drop with certainty—all we can do is be pleased and hope it continues.

The second assumption of the family planning promoters, that individuals given the opportunity to choose the size of their families will automatically respond to the needs of society, has also been strongly attacked. Recent surveys done in connection with the work of the President's Commission indicate an increase in social responsibility as a factor in childbearing in the United States, but this has only occurred after an intensive propaganda program. In contrast, in other DCs and UDCs there are few data indeed to indicate that considerations of the problems of overpopulation have any influence on the childbearing decisions of couples. The factors which enter into decisions on the number of children a couple "wants" are at best only partially understood. It is clear, for instance, that desired family size dropped in Western nations following industrialization. A major cause of this trend seems to have been a change in the perceived role of children. In an agricultural society, children tend to be greatly valued for their potential as farm labor—they can become economically active at a very early age. They also serve as a form of old-age insurance in societies which lack social security. Large families provide the best insurance for a surviving son to inherit the farm and support the parents in their old age.

In urban industrial societies the pattern tends to be changed. The traditional association of generations tends to break down, as does the unchanging pattern of existence generation after generation. People see both opportunities to better themselves and opportunities for the betterment of their children. Increasing restrictions on child labor make children less and less of an economic asset, while decreased mortality rates reduce the need for large numbers of children to insure a surviving son. Moreover, savings, pension plans, and governmental social security programs have reduced the need for sons to support elderly parents.

Under such circumstances, people in the late nineteenth and early twentieth centuries wanted to have fewer children, and indeed had fewer children. They managed to have fewer children long before organized family planning became a reality. This, in fact, is not very surprising, since virtually all people have exercised some control over their reproductive activities. In many "primitive" societies, various combinations of contraception, abortion, infanticide, and taboos affecting sexual relations normally regulate the size of families. In eighteenth-century England infanticide was institutionalized as "baby farming."

It is fair to say, then, that the major element in the world population problem today is *not* the birth of too many unwanted children, but the birth of too many *wanted* children. People are choosing to have more children than is good for the health of human society—more children than is good even for the health of those children. Therefore one could hardly expect a program emphasizing "freedom of choice" in childbearing to achieve population control. To reach that end society must find ways to influence the family size chosen.

Many family planning groups now do just that. Within the United States, Planned Parenthood chapters often go far beyond simply making contraceptives available to those who desire them; they actively try to influence desired family size. Especially in the western United States, Planned Parenthood groups collaborate with more radical organizations such as Zero Population Growth (ZPG) in attempting to persuade couples to limit their reproduction. Outside the United States, some governmental family planning programs have begun to extend into the area of population control. For instance, the family planning program in India now emphasizes the desirability of the two-child family.

The idea of population control is thus acceptable to some individuals, organizations, and governments. They accept the necessity for society to influence the reproductive activities of its members in order to produce a population size which will permit the continuing health of society. That is the essence of population control. Two major problems remain. The first is to convince more individuals, organizations, and governments that action is required. The second is to determine the most humane and least socially disruptive means of achieving population control, so that convictions can be converted to actions.

In the United States both tasks appear relatively easy. Concern over the population explosion is continually growing, and the report of the President's Commission almost certainly foreshadows governmental action within the next few years. Some people will undoubtedly remain adamantly opposed to population control for philosophical, religious, or pecuniary reasons, but broad acceptance seems assured. We are fortunate in the United States that only rather minor measures seem required to depress average family size well below the replacement rate. It is possible that we will be able to halt our growth before the end of the century and perhaps initiate a gradual decline which, over a period of perhaps a century or two, could greatly alleviate our population-related problems.

What sorts of measures would be effective? It is only guesswork, but I suspect that giving all citizens access to contraceptives and abortions on request, coupled with strong governmental support of equal rights for women and a small-family ideal will be effective. Accessibility to the means of birth control has been increasing steadily for nearly a century, so all that is required is the culmination of a long trend. The trend to liberalize abortion laws has also been in the right direction, although recently powerful conservative forces have attempted to force a return to the situation where only rich women can have safe abortions. Women's liberation should, of course, be supported for its own sake; but as more and more women find fulfillment outside of childbearing, there probably will be a "bonus" in the form of lower birthrates. The biggest job will be persuading the government to revise its present propopulation growth stance and to initiate a campaign to convince American couples that it is selfish, irresponsible, and unpatriotic to have more than two children. The government should already be doing that, because overbreeding *is* selfish, irresponsible, and unpatriotic.

Suppose for a moment that Americans take the appropriate steps to bring our population size under the rational control of society. What can be done about population growth in the other rich nations? And what about the catastrophically rapid growth now occurring in the UDCs? All too often population control is viewed as a plot by rich white people to suppress the poverty-stricken and colored people of the world. And unhappily, in the minds of some members of our society, that is precisely what population control means. It is, therefore, critical that population control be achieved in the United States with great care to avoid *any* overtones of racism or bias against the poor.

If the United States can set an example for the world by controlling her population with equity and humanity, then a major barrier to world population control will be overcome.

Once we have started in that direction the stage will be set for an all-out effort to control the population of the Earth before it is too late. The most satisfactory and effective ways of achieving this goal (beyond ensuring that knowledge and the means of birth control are everywhere available) will undoubtedly be different from country to country. But several themes should be virtually universal: provision of social security for old people, finding creative roles for women other than childbearing, placing the emphasis on the *quality* of one's children rather than their *quantity*, and directing societal effort toward improving the chances for all our children to grow up in a world relatively free of fear and want.

What is required is no less than a transformation of the social, political and economic systems of the world, for population control alone will not solve our problems. But it *is* necessary. Whatever your cause, it is lost without population control.

The Security State of Mind

ROBERT SOMMER

The modern industrial state produces an endless array of consumer goods. Technology has certainly fed (and encouraged) our need to consume, but it has also facilitated the possibilities of social control. Sommer's warning is something with which we all can too easily identify.

At first the gas station wouldn't accept cash after ten in the evening. Then the bus drivers stopped making change any time. Taxi companies installed bulletproof glass and for the first time in history New York cabbies were silent. Some park rangers began carrying guns. Their original role was protecting the public from wild animals, but this soon changed to protecting the animals from people. Now their task is to protect the people from one another. In many cities Halloween "trick or treat" has been canceled for the protection of children who have been receiving razor blades in apples, needles in candy bars, and hallucinogenic drugs in the gumdrops.

The market in home protection devices is booming. There are call buttons to the police station, windows wired to alarm bells and home radar systems; new housing developments boast twenty-four-hour security guards. Police cars drive down the sidewalk in public parks and through the milling crowds at state fairs or any large public gathering. Always in pairs and unsmiling, they carry guns and riot gear. If you try to say "hello," they reply sheepishly or not at all, as if you had caught them somewhere they shouldn't be. They are particularly watchful of young people whose gregarious behavior seems covered by five different misdemeanor charges and the possible felony of conspiring to congregate. A single loiterer is a potential crowd, since he is likely to be joined by others of similar disposition.

There are uniformed security guards at every shopping center. These rent-a-cops look like police but are attached to some private agency. In California they want themselves classified as peace officers, a move strongly resisted by the regular law-enforcement officials who have enough trouble as it is. At a time when police complain about their public image, it is odd that all these other groups, including university security officers, are attempting to classify themselves legally as police officers.

There are TV cameras everywhere. Smaller stores still use the big parabolic mirrors, but all the larger stores and corporations have switched to television. Somewhere in the bowels of every large building a uniformed man is scanning a bank of screens. One can only wonder how much TV he watches at home. In one Midwestern city an entire street is monitored by TV.

From *The Nation,* November 20, 1972. Reprinted by permission of the publisher.

Transparent telephone booths are designed to provide visual access for cruising patrol cars.

While the average citizen can get by with three door locks and an elaborate alarm system, identification numbers on all his possessions, several loaded guns readily available in the house ("When guns are outlawed, only outlaws will have guns") and a private neighborhood patrol, more elaborate security measures are required for public officials. The President and his chief advisers, whose itineraries are planned with military precision, fly in special planes from military airports, ride through the countryside in armored limousines, and speak at public gatherings from behind bulletproof glass with armed Secret Service men on either side. The Chief Executive is no longer free to walk among the citizens whose interests he represents. This trend seeps down to his immediate subordinates and their families. State governors, quick to follow the President's lead, have established their own guard to protect themselves from the electorate. Corporate officers and their union counterparts also have bodyguards. Career opportunities in the security fields must be excellent.

In a garrison state the enemy is external—the Russians or the Chinese or the revolutionaries or the whole outside world, but in the security state the potential enemy is your neighbor. Psychologically, an external threat produces fear, an internal one anxiety. There can be a collective mobilization against other nations, a sense of shared national purpose set to martial music, but against an internal threat an individual arms himself and trusts no one, not even the government or the press, which have both been infiltrated. The barricades or ramparts in the security state are the boundaries of one's suburban lot or the triple locked door of one's city apartment with its peephole conveying a convex image of the outside world.

Recently I visited the data-processing center of a large bank. They may have tighter security at San Quentin but I doubt it. In the lobby, security officers walked by every ninety seconds and plain-clothes officers walked by from time to time to eye my brief case suspiciously. To allay their fears I would open the brief case, ostensibly to look at some material, but really to show there was no bomb inside. Upstairs the employees passed through sally ports or "man traps" as they are known locally, before entering or leaving their work areas. These are double doors with a security guard in a protected control booth in the center. The entering employee inserts a plastic identification badge in the outside gate and this opens up the first locked door. He then stands inside the sally port while the door is locked behind him and shows his pass to the guard, who acknowledges it by unlocking the second door. This sequence is followed every day by hundreds of employees in these areas when they come to work, go to lunch or to the rest room, and when they leave in the evening. All the rest rooms in the building are locked and each employee carries a special key. It used to be that only the top executives had special washroom keys, but it is hard to see this new development as a trend toward corporate democracy.

Airports aren't nearly as much fun as they used to be. I used to enjoy watching the passengers nervously filing on board the plane, the joyous welcome for the returning son or daughter, the family waiting for grandma to arrive on her first flight. Now the ticket taker, baggage handlers and other airline personnel treat every customer as a potential hijacker. Does he or does he not fit the top-secret hijacker profile? Hint: Don't under any circumstances try to pay cash for your ticket at the airport. Hint No. 2: Even if you are only making a one-way trip, buy a round-trip ticket and cancel the second half when you get there.

In his new security roles, the dog has become distinctly unfriendly. Man's best friend stands at the border sniffing out marijuana, guards against skyjackers at the airport, and protects thousands of city apartments: he is again being bred for traits of ferociousness and instant obedience, and the child's image of a dog will not be happy Fido or willful Rover.

In the beginning, a person feels uncomfortable about the presence of armed police in the bus station or shopping center or on the subway at night. Later, he feels uncomfortable if he can't see a policeman. The same thing happens with the TV monitors in the corridors of the post office and some public rest rooms. Initially they are regarded as an invasion of privacy but eventually a person becomes uncomfortable when big brother isn't watching. Psychologist Kurt Lewin compared teachers who used authoritarian and democratic methods. The important difference came when the teacher left the room. The democratic group got along reasonably well, but chaos prevailed in the authoritarian classroom. One implication is that an authoritarian system requires constant surveillance of its citizens. If a policeman cannot be physically present, there must be TV monitors, citizens' patrols and remote sensing stations.

There has always been a group of manufacturers and a distribution system for supplying hardware to police departments and private security agencies. This was a modest enterprise, but over the past few years, thanks to the largesse of the Safe Streets Act and the Law Enforcement Assistance Administration (LEAA), the amount of expensive security hardware has increased enormously. There is every reason to expect that attempts to reduce the domestic arms race will be strongly resisted by the internal security counterpart of the military-industrial complex. The more expensive the equipment, the stronger the pressures will be to continue and expand the domestic arms race.

When it comes to internal security there seems to be no way to negotiate a settlement in arms reduction, as there is in the case of national governments. There is no way that a city chief of police can remove the shotguns and automatic rifles from patrol cars in return for a citizens' agreement to refrain from using shotguns and automatic weapons against his men. In the security state the potential enemy is everywhere and there is no one with whom a security chief can negotiate. The outcome is constant vigilance and wariness. Experiments with animals show that constant vigilance can overtax an organism to the point of breakdown. If a dog is trained to expect an electric shock when a bell rings, it can usually adapt to this situation, although it may get an ulcer in the process. However, if the bell rings, and the shock is delayed, anxiety begins to mount to the point where experimental neurosis sets in. The policeman on patrol has heard the bell ring and he must be constantly on guard against the electric shock, and so it is almost with a sense of relief that he comes upon a real crime against person or property, something tangible with which he can deal. The security state with its basic attitude of distrust for one's fellow citizens works the most hardship on its guardians.

All these things cannot help but affect the American psyche. I cannot say it is deliberate preparation for a totalitarian state, but it certainly works out that way. It is not the presence of uniformed security guards and TV monitors; it is the quick adaptation that people make to them that augurs so badly for democracy. Trust and respect for other people is basic to democracy. One cannot be wary and untrustful Mondays through Fridays, and warm and loving on weekends. One cannot regard one's fellow airline passengers as potential hijackers or dangerous maniacs and then talk amiably with them and exchange addresses. Vance Packard laments the great mobility of the American family, which moves too frequently and too far from friends and neighbors. My own impression is that people don't have many friends and that neighboring is not what it used to be. In California the backyard fences are frequently erected before the homes. If you ask someone how many friends he has, he wants you to define friendship.

An extensive internal security apparatus will become a self-sustaining and perpetuating aspect of society, with its own economic dependencies and internal dynamic. It took several decades of bitter labor strife to remove railway firemen from diesel locomotives. It will take an equally long time to get the sky marshals and the dogs out of airports once the current wave of hijacking has run its course. While it will not be possible to reverse the move to ever higher levels of internal security overnight, we should at least be aware of how this affects the American psyche. The greatest immediate danger is that, like the Los Angeles citizens' denial of a smog problem or the New Yorker's indifference to Park Avenue affluence a few blocks from abject Harlem poverty, an insidious process of habituation will set in, whereby each increase in security is judged against the previous baseline rather than looked upon in absolute terms. Two hundred new policemen is perhaps a 1 per cent increase in a major city, but it is still 200 policemen and no real security against muggers, rapists or ITT. Increasing the size of our armed forces did not relieve our feelings of national insecurity, and it is not likely that increasing the size of police forces will do much for internal security. What will develop instead is a police-industrial complex that will be equally hard to dislodge or control.

The Mind of the Machine

ARTHUR C. CLARKE

Arthur C. Clarke (with Stanley Kubrick) is the creator of the movie* 2001, *the story of a super computer with godly illusions. This essay examines the possibilities of artificial intelligence. Clarke's conclusions are surprisingly hopeful.

Ours is the century in which all man's ancient dreams—and not a few of his nightmares—appear to be coming true. The conquest of the air, the transmutation of matter, journeys to the Moon, even the elixir of life—one by one, the marvelous visions of the past are becoming reality. And among them, the one most fraught with promise and peril is the machine that can think.

In some form or other, the idea of artificial intelligence goes back at least 3000 years. Talos, the metal man who guarded the coast of Crete, however, was only a physical and not an intellectual giant; perhaps a better prototype of the thinking machine is the brazen head generally linked with the name of Friar Bacon, though the legend precedes him by some centuries. This head was able to answer any question given to it, relating to past, present or future; but, as is customary with oracles, there was no guarantee that the inquirer would be pleased with what he heard.

Over these tales there usually hangs the aura of doom or horror associated with such names as Prometheus, Faust and, above all, Frankenstein, though that unfortunate scientist's creation was not a mechanical one. Perhaps the finest work in this genre is that little classic of Ambrose Bierce's, *Moxon's Master*, which opens with the words: "Are you serious? Do you really believe that a machine thinks?"

It will not be universally accepted, but there is one very straightforward answer to this question. It can be maintained that every man is perfectly familiar with at least one thinking machine, because he has a late-type model sitting on his shoulders. For if the brain is not a machine, what is it?

Critics of this viewpoint (who are probably now in the minority) may argue that the brain is in some fundamental way different from any non-living device. But even if this is true, it does not follow that its functions cannot be duplicated, or even surpassed, by a non-organic machine. Airplanes fly better than birds, though they are built of very different materials.

For obvious psychological reasons, there are people who will never accept

From *Playboy*, December 1968. Reprinted by permission of the author and the author's agents, Scott Meredith Literary Agency, Inc., 580 Fifth Avenue, New York, New York 10036.

the possibility of artificial intelligence, and would deny its existence even if they encountered it. As I write these words, there is a chess game in progress between computers in California and Moscow; both are playing so badly that there is clearly no human cheating on either side. Yet no one really doubts that eventually the world champion will be a computer; and when *that* happens, the die-hards will retort: "Oh, well—chess doesn't involve *real* thinking," and will point to various grand masters in evidence.

One can sympathize with this attitude, but to resent the concept of a rational machine is itself irrational. We no longer become upset because machines are stronger, or swifter, or more dexterous than human beings, though it took us several painful centuries to adapt to this state of affairs. How our outlook has changed is well shown by the ballad of John Henry; today, we should regard a man who challenged a steam hammer as merely crazy—not heroic. I doubt if contests between calculating prodigies and electronic computers will ever provide inspiration for future folk songs. But I'll be happy to donate the theme to Tom Lehrer.

It is, of course, the advent of the modern computer that has brought the subject of thinking machines out of the realm of fantasy into the forefront of scientific research. One could not have a plainer answer to the question that Bierce posed three quarters of a century ago than this quotation from MacGowan and Ordway's recent book, *Intelligence in the Universe*: "It can be asserted without reservation that a general-purpose digital computer can think in every sense of the word. This is true no matter what definition of thinking is specified; the only requirement is that the definition of thinking be explicit."

That last phrase is, of course, the joker, for there must be almost as many definitions of thinking as there are thinkers; in the ultimate analysis, they probably all boil down to "Thinking is what *I* do." One neat way of avoiding this problem is a famous test proposed by the British mathematician Alan Turing, even before the digital computer existed. Turing visualized a "conversation" over a teleprinter circuit with an unseen entity "X." If, after some hours of talk, one could not decide whether there was a man or a machine at the other end of the line, it would have to be admitted that X was thinking.

There have been several attempts to apply this test in restricted areas—say, in conversations about the weather. One clever program (DOCTOR) has even allowed a computer to conduct a psychiatric interview, with such success that 60 percent of the patients refused to believe afterward that they were not "conversing" with a flesh-and-blood psychiatrist. But as people talking about themselves can be kept going indefinitely with a modest supply of phrases like "You don't say!" or "And then what did you do?," this particular example only demonstrates that little intelligence is involved in most conversation. The old gibe that women enjoy knitting because it gives them something to think about while they're talking is merely a special case of a far wider law, ample proof of which may be obtained at any cocktail party.

For the Turing test to be applied properly, the conversation should not be restricted to a single narrow field but should be allowed to range over the whole arena of human affairs. ("Read any good books lately?" "Has your wife found out yet?," etc.) We are certainly nowhere near building a machine that can fool many of the people for much of the time; sooner or later, today's models give themselves away by irrelevant answers that show only too clearly that their replies are, indeed, "mechanical," and that they have no real understanding of what is going on. As Oliver Selfridge of MIT has remarked sourly: "Even among those who believe that computers *can* think, there are few these days, except for a rabid fringe, who hold that they actually *are* thinking."

Though this may be the generally accepted position in the late 1960s, it is the "rabid fringe" who will be right in the long run. The current arguments about machine intelligence will slowly fade out, as it becomes less and less possible to draw a line between human and electronic achievements. To quote another MIT scientist—Marvin Minsky, professor of electrical engineering: "As the machine improves . . . we shall begin to see all the phenomena associated with the terms 'consciousness,' 'intuition' and 'intelligence' itself. It is hard to say how close we are to this threshold, but once it is crossed, the world will not be the same. . . . It is unreasonable to think that machines could become *nearly* as intelligent as we are and then stop, or to suppose that we will always be able to compete with them in wit and wisdom. Whether or not we could retain some sort of control of the machines, assuming that we would want to, the nature of our activities and aspirations would be changed utterly by the presence on earth of intellectually superior beings."

Very few, if any, studies of the social impact of computers have yet faced up to the problems posed by this last sentence—particularly the ominous phrase "assuming that we would want to." This is understandable; the electronic revolution has been so swift that those involved in it have barely had time to think about the present, let alone the day after tomorrow. Moreover, the fact that today's computers are very obviously not "intellectually superior" has given a false sense of security—like that felt by the 1900 buggy-whip manufacturer every time he saw a broken-down automobile by the wayside. This comfortable illusion is fostered by the endless stories—part of the transient folklore of our age—about stupid computers that have had to be replaced by good old-fashioned human beings, after they had insisted on sending our bills for $1,000,000,004.95, or threatening legal action if outstanding debts of $0.00 were not settled immediately. The fact that these *gaffes* are almost invariably due to oversights by human programers is seldom mentioned.

Though we have to live and work with (and against) today's mechanical morons, their deficiencies should not blind us to the future. In particular, it should be realized that as soon as the borders of electronic intelligence are passed, there will be a kind of chain reaction, because the machines will rapidly improve themselves. In a very few generations—*computer* generations, which by this time may last only a few months—there will be a mental explosion; the merely intelligent machine will swiftly give way to the *ultra*intelligent machine.

One scientist who has given much thought to this matter is Dr. Irving John Good, of Trinity College, Oxford—author of papers with such challenging titles as "Can an Android Feel Pain?" (This term for artificial man, incidentally, is older than generally believed. I had always assumed that it was a product of the modern science-fiction magazines, and was astonished to come across "The Brazen Android" in an *Atlantic Monthly* for 1891.) Dr. Good has written: "If we build an ultraintelligent machine, we will be playing with fire. We have played with fire before, and it helped keep the other animals at bay."

Well, yes—but when the ultraintelligent machine arrives, *we* may be the "other animals"; and look what's happened to them.

It is Dr. Good's belief that the very survival of our civilization may depend upon the building of such instrumentalities; because if they are, indeed, more intelligent than we are, they can answer all our questions and solve all our problems. As he puts it in one elegiac phrase: "The first ultraintelligent machine is the last invention that man need make."

Need is the operative word here. Perhaps 99 percent of all the men who have ever lived have known only need; they have been driven by necessity and have not been allowed the luxury of choice. In the future, this will no longer be true. It may be the greatest virtue of the ultraintelligent machine that it will force us to think about the purpose and meaning of human existence. It will compel us to make some far-reaching and perhaps painful decisions, just as thermonuclear weapons have made us face the realities of war and aggression, after 5000 years of pious jabber.

These long-range philosophical implications of machine intelligence obviously far transcend today's more immediate worries about automation and unemployment. Somewhat ironically, these fears are both well grounded and premature. Although automation has already been blamed for the loss of many jobs, the evidence indicates that so far, it has created many more opportunities for work than it has destroyed. (True, this is small consolation for the particular semiskilled worker who has just been replaced by a couple of milligrams of microelectronics.) *Fortune* magazine, in a hopeful attempt at self-fulfilling prophecy, has declaimed: "The computer will doubtless go down in history not as the explosion that blew unemployment through the roof but as the technological triumph that enabled the U.S. economy to maintain the secular growth on which its greatness depends." I suspect that this statement may be true for some decades to come; but I also suspect that historians (human and otherwise) of the last 21st Century would regard that "doubtless" with wry amusement.

For the plain fact is that long before that date, the talents and capabilities of the average—and even the superior—man will be as unsalable in the market place as his muscle power. Only a few specialized and distinctly non-white-collar jobs will remain the prerogative of nonmechanical labor; one cannot easily picture a robot handy man, gardener, construction worker, fisherman. . . . These are professions that require mobility, dexterity, alertness and general adaptability—for no two tasks are precisely the same—but not a high degree of intelligence or data-processing power. And even these relatively few occupations will probably be invaded by a rival and frequently superior labor force from the animal kingdom; for one of the long-range technological benefits of the space program (though no one has said much about it yet, for fear of upsetting the trade unions) will be a supply of educable anthropoids filling the gap between man and the great apes.

It must be clearly understood, therefore, that the main problem of the future—and a future that may be witnessed by many who are alive today—will be the construction of social systems based on the principle not of full employment but rather full *un*employment. Some writers have suggested that the only way to solve this problem is to pay people to be consumers; Fred Pohl, in his amusing short story *The Midas Plague*, described a society in which you would be in real trouble unless you used up your full quota of goods poured out by the automatic factories. If this proves to be the pattern of the future, then today's welfare states represent only the most feeble and faltering steps toward it. The recent uproar about Medicare will seem completely incomprehensible to a generation that assumes every man's right to a basic income of $1000 a year, starting at birth. (In New Dollars, of course; 1 N. D. = $100, 1984 currency.)

I leave others to work out the practical details of an economic (if that is the right name for it) system in which it was antisocial, and possibly illegal, *not* to wear out a suit every week, or to eat three six-course meals a day, or to throw away last month's car. Though I do not take this picture very seriously, it should serve as a reminder that tomorrow's world may differ from ours so radically that such terms as labor, capital, communism, private enterprise, state control will have changed their meanings completely—if, indeed, they are still in use. At the very least, we may expect a society that no longer regards work as meritorious or leisure as one of the Devil's more ingenious devices. Even today, there is not much left of the old puritan ethic; automation will drive the last nails into its coffin.

The need for such a change of outlook has been well put by the British science writer Nigel Calder in his remarkable book *The Environment Game*: "Work was an invention, which can be dated to the invention of agriculture. . . . Now, with the beginning of automation, we have to anticipate a time when we must disinvent work and rid our minds of the inculcated habit."

The disinvention of work: What would Horatio Alger have thought of *that* concept? Calder's thesis (too complex to do more than summarize here) is that man is now coming to the end of his brief 10,000-year agricultural episode; for a period of a hundred times longer he was a hunter, and any hunter will indignantly deny that his occupation is "work." We now have to abandon agriculture for more efficient technologies; first, because it has patently failed to feed the exploding population; second, because it has compelled 500 generations of men to live abnormal—in fact, artificial—lives of repetitive, boring toil. Hence, many of our present psychological problems; to quote Calder again: "If men were intended to work the soil, they would have longer arms."

"If men were intended to . . ." is, of course, a game that everyone can play; my favorite competitor is the old lady who objected to space exploration because we should stay home and watch TV, "as God meant us to." Yet now, with the ultraintelligent machines lying just below our horizon, it is time that we played this game in earnest, while we still have some control over the rules. In a few more years, it will be much too late.

Utopiamongering has been a popular and, on the whole, harmless occupation since the time of Plato; now it has become a matter of life and death—part of the politics of survival. Thinking machines, food production and population control must be considered as the three interlocking elements that will determine the shape of the future; they are not independent, for they all react on one another. This becomes obvious when we ask the question, which I have deliberately framed in as nonemotional a form as possible: "In an automated world run by machines, what is the optimum human population?"

There are many equations in which one of the possible answers is zero; mathematicians call this a trivial solution. If zero is the solution in this case, the matter is very far from trivial, at least from our self-centered viewpoint. But that it could—and probably will—be very low seems certain.

Fred Hoyle once remarked to me that it was pointless for the world to hold more people than one could get to know in a single lifetime. Even if one were President of United Earth, that would set the figure somewhere between 10,000 and 100,000; with a very generous allowance for duplication, wastage, special talents, and so forth, there really seems no requirement for what has been called the Global Village of the future to hold more than 1,000,000 people, scattered over the face of the planet. And if such a figure appears unrealistic—since we are already past the three-billion mark and heading for at least twice as many by the end of the century—it should be pointed out that once the universally agreed goal of population control is attained, *any* desired target can be reached in a remarkably short time. If we really tried (with a little help, perhaps, from the biology labs), we could reach a trillion within a century—four generations. It might be more difficut to go in the other direction, for fundamental psychological reasons, but it could be done. If the machines decide that more than 1,000,000 human beings constitute an epidemic, they might order euthanasia for anyone with an I.Q. of less than 150, but I hope that such drastic measures will not be necessary.

Whether the population plateau levels off, a few centuries from today, at a million, a billion or a trillion human beings is of much less importance than the ways in which they will occupy their time. Since all the immemorial forms of "getting and spending" will have been rendered obsolete by the machines, it would appear that boredom will replace war and hunger as the greatest enemy of mankind.

One answer to this would be the uninhibited, hedonistic society of Huxley's *Brave New World;* there is nothing wrong with this, so long as it is not the *only* answer. (Huxley's unfortunate streak of asceticism prevented him from appreciating this point.) Certainly, much more time than at present will be devoted to sports, entertainment, the arts and everything embraced by the vague term "culture."

In some of these fields, the background presence of superior nonhuman mentalities would have a stultifying effect; but in others, the machines could act as pacemakers. Does anyone really imagine that when all the grand masters are electronic, no one will play chess? The humans will simply set up new categories and play better chess among themselves. All sports and games (unless they become ossified) have to undergo technological revolutions from time to time; recent examples are the introduction of fiberglass in pole vaulting, archery, boating. Personally, I can hardly wait for the advent of Marvin Minsky's promised robot table-tennis player.

These matters are not trivial; games are a necessary substitute for our hunting impulses, and if the ultraintelligent machines give us new and better outlets, that is all to the good. We shall need every one of them to occupy us in the centuries ahead.

Thinking machines will certainly make possible new forms of art and far more elaborate developments of the old ones, by introducing the dimensions of time and probability. Even today, a painting or a piece of sculpture that stands still is regarded as slightly passé. Although the trouble with most "kinetic art" is that it only lives up to the first half of its name, something is bound to emerge from present explorations on the frontier between order and chaos.

The insertion of an intelligent machine into the loop between a work of art and the person appreciating it opens up some fascinating possibilities. It would allow feedback in both directions; by this I mean that the viewer would react to the work of art, then the work would react to the viewer's reactions, then . . . and so on, for as many stages as was felt desirable. This sort of to-and-fro process is already hinted at, in a very crude way, with today's primitive "teaching machines"; and those modern novelists who deliberately scramble their text may also be groping in this direction. A dramatic work of the future, reproduced by an intelligent machine sensitive to the varying emotional states of the audience, would never have the same form, or even the same plot line, twice in succession. It would be full of surprises even to its human creator—or collaborator.

What sort of art machines would create for their *own* amusement and whether we would be able to appreciate it are questions that can hardly be answered today. The painters of the Lascaux Caves could not have imagined (though they would have enjoyed) the scores of art forms that have been invented in the 20,000 years since they created their masterpieces. Though in some respects we can do no better, we can do much more—more than any Paleolithic Picasso could possibly have dreamed. And our machines may begin to build on the foundations we have laid.

Yet perhaps not. It has often been suggested that art is a compensation for the deficiencies of the real world; as our knowledge, power and, above all, our *maturity* increase, we will have less and less need for it. If this is true, the ultraintelligent machines would have no use for it at all.

Even if art turns out to be a dead end, there still remains science—the eternal quest for knowledge, which has brought man to the point where he may create his own successor. It is unfortunate that, to most people, "science" now means incomprehensible mathematical complexities; that it could be the most exciting and *entertaining* of all occupations is something that they find impossible to believe. Yet the fact remains that, before they are ruined by what is laughingly called education, all normal children have an absorbing interest and curiosity about the universe that, if properly developed, could keep them happy for as many centuries as they may wish to live.

Education: that, ultimately, is the key to survival in the coming world of thinking machines. The truly educated man (I have been lucky enough to meet two in my lifetime) can never be bored. The problem that has to be tackled within the next 50 years is to bring the entire human race, without exception, up to the level of semiliteracy of the average college graduate. This represents what may be called the *minimum* survival level; only if we reach it will we have a sporting chance of seeing the year 2200.

Perhaps we can now glimpse one viable future for the human race, when it is no longer the dominant species on this planet. As he was in the beginning, man will again be a fairly rare animal, and probably a nomadic one. There will be a few towns in places of unusual beauty or historical interest, but even these may be temporary or seasonal. Most homes will be completely self-contained and mobile, so that they can move to any spot on Earth within 24 hours.

The land areas of the planet will have largely reverted to wilderness; they will be much richer in life forms (and much more dangerous) than today. All adolescents will spend part of their youth in this vast biological reserve, so that they never suffer from that estrangement from nature that is one of the curses of our civilization.

And somewhere in the background—in the depths of the sea, orbiting beyond the ionosphere—will be the culture of the ultraintelligent machines, going its own unfathomable way. The societies of man and machine will interact continuously but lightly; there will be no areas of conflict, and few emergencies, except geological ones (and these could be fully foreseeable). In one sense, for which we may be thankful, History will have come to an end.

All the knowledge possessed by the machines will be available to mankind, though much of it may not be understandable. There is no reason why this should give our descendants an inferiority complex; a few steps into the New York Public Library can do *that* just as well, even today. Our prime goals will no longer be to discover but to understand and to enjoy.

Would the coexistence of man and machine be stable? I see no reason why it should not be, at least for many centuries. A remote analogy of this kind of dual culture—one society encapsulated in another—may be found among the Amish of Pennsylvania. Here is a self-contained agricultural society, which has deliberately rejected much of the surrounding values and technology, yet is exceedingly prosperous and biologically successful. The Amish, and similar groups, are well worth careful study; they may show us how to get along with a more complex society that perhaps we cannot comprehend, even if we wish to.

For in the long run, our mechanical offspring will pass on to goals that will be wholly incomprehensible to us; it has been suggested that when this time comes, they will head on out into galactic space, looking for new frontiers, leaving us once more the masters (perhaps reluctant ones) of the Solar System, and not at all happy at having to run our own affairs.

That is one possibility. Another has been summed up, once and for all, in the most famous short science-fiction story of our age. It was written by Fredric Brown almost 20 years ago, and it is high time that he received credit from the journalists who endlessly rediscover and quote him.

Fred Brown's story—as you have probably guessed—is the one about the supercomputer that is asked, "Is there a God?" After making quite sure that its power supply is no longer under human control, it replies in a voice of thunder: "*Now* there is."

This story is more than a brilliant myth; it is an echo from the future. For in the long run, it may turn out that the theologians have made a slight but understandable error—which, among other things, makes totally irrelevant the recent debates about the death of God.

It may be that our role on this planet is not to worship God—but to create him.

And then our work will be done. It will be time to play.